DEMOCRACY AND DISCON[T]

Written under the auspices of
the Center of International Studies,
Woodrow Wilson School, Princeton University

DEMOCRACY AND DISCONTENT
INDIA'S GROWING CRISIS OF GOVERNABILITY

ATUL KOHLI
Princeton University

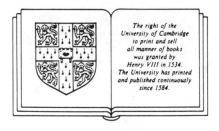

The right of the
University of Cambridge
to print and sell
all manner of books
was granted by
Henry VIII in 1534.
The University has printed
and published continuously
since 1584.

CAMBRIDGE UNIVERSITY PRESS

Cambridge

New York   Port Chester   Melbourne   Sydney

Published by the Press Syndicate of the University of Cambridge
The Pitt Building, Trumpington Street, Cambridge CB2 1RP
40 West 20th Street, New York, NY 10011-4211, USA
10 Stamford Road, Oakleigh, Victoria 3166, Australia

First published 1990
Reprinted 1992

Printed in Canada

Library of Congress Cataloging-in-Publication Data
Kohli, Atul.
Democracy and discontent: India's growing crisis of governability /
Atul Kohli.
p.   cm.
Includes bibliographical references and index.
ISBN 0-521-39161-X (hard). – ISBN 0-521-39692-1 (pbk.)
1. Political stability – India.   2. India – Politics and
government – 1977 –   3. State governments – India.   I. Title.
JQ224.K64   1990
954.05 – dc20   90-37443
                                                              CIP

British Library Cataloguing in Publication Data
Kohli, Atul
Democracy and discontent: India's growing crisis of
governability
1. India (Republic, Politics, history)
I. Title
320.954

ISBN 0-521-39161-X hardback
ISBN 0-521-39692-1 paperback

Contents

Tables and figures

TABLES

FIGURES

Preface and acknowledgments

A crisis of governability is growing in India, and this book is an attempt to explain the roots of the crisis. During the 1950s and 1960s, many scholars and observers were worried about India's political viability. But the nation did not disintegrate into smaller states as some observers had expected, and democracy has survived there as well. The political concern that has been growing since the 1970s involves a different question: Can India's democratic government simultaneously accommodate conflicting interests and promote socioeconomic development? Indian governments that have been elected with large majorities have repeatedly failed to translate popular support into effective policies, and the role of violence in politics has been growing steadily. In late 1989, when this book was nearly finished and about to go to press, the results of a national election raised doubts about the continuing ability of India's politicians to form a stable majority government.

What factors are responsible for this growing crisis of governability in the world's largest democracy? This study analyzes the political changes in India under the two Gandhis, Indira and Rajiv, from the late 1960s to the late 1980s. The materials for the study were gathered mainly through fieldwork in India in 1985 and 1986. The book was substantially written during 1987 and 1988, before the 1989 national elections.

Detailed investigation of local, regional, and national politics leads to the proposition that the roots of India's growing problems of governability are more political than socioeconomic; that is, they are located mainly in India's political structure. A highly interventionist state dealing with a poor economy has become an object of intense political competition. The spread of egalitarian political values and the opportunities provided by democracy have, in turn, helped to transform what was once a heterogeneous social structure into many groups of mobilized activists. Failure of leaders to make timely concessions has only intensified political demands and activity. And finally, the growing weakness of fragmented political parties, which both reflects and exacerbates this process of overpoliticization, has made it difficult for leaders to rule effectively.

A key message of this study is that over the last two decades, India has had too much of the "wrong" kind of democracy and not enough of the "right" kind. A highly interventionist but ineffectual national government and weak political parties are two factors in India's governability crisis that contribute toward making India's democracy the "wrong" type. This suggests that strengthening party organizations and bringing the state's capacities in line with its commitments will remain important prerequisites for better democratic government in India.

This book has been written both for specialists in Indian politics and for anyone interested in the broader problems of democracy in developing countries. Students of Indian politics will find here detailed empirical analyses of local, regional, and national trends. They may agree or disagree with the central theses, namely, that a crisis of governability is growing in India and that the roots of this crisis are political. Those with broader concerns may or may not find the empirical details interesting. What they will find is an analysis of political patterns that have unfolded in a democracy that has been sustained for several decades in a developmental setting. As other low-income countries experiment with democratic institutions, these issues are likely to be of considerable interest. More than in many other developing countries, where experiments with democracy usually have been brief, the political changes in India can help clarify the significance of political parties as agents of stable long-term development: Political parties are one set of institutions that can help resolve the recurring tensions faced by developing democratic countries as they try simultaneously to accommodate conflicting interests and to promote economic development from above.

The support of a number of individuals and institutions has been crucial in the making of this book. John Lewis encouraged the project from the very beginning and then gave it a significant boost by recommending it for funding to the Ford Foundation. Myron Weiner also encouraged the project at its inception by supporting the idea of my revisiting the districts he had studied in detail in the 1960s. Fieldwork in India during 1985 and 1986 would not have been possible without the leave generously granted by Princeton University and the research support provided by the Ford Foundation, New Delhi.

While I was in India, the Center for the Study of Developing Societies (CSDS) provided my intellectual base. A number of issues were clarified in long conversations with Bashiruddin Ahmed, whose kindness and support were indispensable. Others at the CSDS – Rajni Kothari, Dirubhai Sheth, Ramashray Roy, and Ashish Nandy – have always provided a stimulating atmosphere that those who linger over long lunches at the CSDS truly come to appreciate. Outside of Delhi, so many individuals provided help in various parts of India that it would be impractical to list them here. I have acknowledged the roles of these people in specific chapters.

I wrote much of this book during 1987–8. Princeton University provided an additional semester's honorific leave. Donald Stokes, the dean of the Woodrow Wilson School, Princeton University, and Henry Bienen, the director of Princeton's Center for International Studies, facilitated a second semester of leave that, combined with the first, made for a peaceful year of writing in Vermont. The library, the librarians, and members of the Department of Political Science at the University of Vermont proved very helpful. I would especially like to thank Alan Wertheimer for his support and Fritz Gaenslen for interesting lunch conversations during Vermont's cold but beautiful winters.

A number of scholars commented on earlier drafts of this book and helped improve the final product. Those who read the whole manuscript and gave their reactions included Amrita Basu, Henry Bienen, Peter Evans, John Lewis, Joel Migdal, John Waterbury, Myron Weiner, John Wood, and a few anonymous readers. Although they had no hand in the defects remaining in the manuscript, the final product is better for their help. I also had a chance to present the argument of the book at two different seminars. Thanks are due to Richard Sandbrook and Milton Singer for arranging a seminar at the University of Toronto, and to Ashutosh Varshney for arranging a presentation at Harvard University. Comments from the audiences at the two seminars helped me sharpen some points and modify others.

Supriya Roy Chowdhry provided helpful research assistance throughout the project. My special thanks to Edna Lloyd, who cheerfully typed and retyped several drafts of this book. I also want to acknowledge the helpful editorial support and guidance provided by Cambridge University Press, especially by Emily Loose, who worked with this manuscript from the initial review process to the beginning of its production.

Finally, some personal thanks. As always, the love of my parents, brother, and sister has been an important sustaining force. Marie Gottschalk deserves the most special thanks. She was there with encouragement when this book was no more than a gleam in the eye. She then traveled with me to faraway places, sharing rickshaws in the scorching midday heat to visit temples in Madurai and smiling with me at the eggless omelets in Belgaun. She also read parts of the manuscript, helped clarify both the argument and the presentation, and suggested the title for the book, which is dedicated to her for our years of warmth and togetherness.

Princeton, New Jersey
December 1989

PART I

Introduction

1

An overview of the study

Sooner or later all developing countries become difficult to govern, and over the past two decades India has been moving in that direction. This trend contrasts with the situation during the 1950s and 1960s, when India was widely regarded as one of the few stable democracies in the non-Western world.

India is still, of course, a functioning democracy, but increasingly it is not well governed. The evidence of eroding political order is everywhere. Personal rule has replaced party rule at all levels – national, state, and district. Below the rulers, the entrenched civil and police services have been politicized. Various social groups have pressed new and ever more diverse political demands in demonstrations that often have led to violence. The omnipresent but feeble state, in turn, has vacillated; its responses have varied over a wide range: indifference, sporadic concessions, and repression. Such vacillation has fueled further opposition. The ineffectiveness of repression, moreover, has highlighted the breakdown of the civil machinery intended to enforce the law and maintain order. In order to protect themselves, citizens in some parts of the country have begun organizing private armies. The growing political violence has periodically brought the armed forces into India's political arena, whereas the armed forces once were considered apolitical.

The purpose of this study is to describe how and attempt to explain why India has become difficult to govern. Was this outcome inevitable? India had long been considered something of a political exception. Now, to paraphrase one of that nation's leading political analysts, Rajni Kothari, India is fast catching up with the rest of the developing world. What happened? What went wrong? By focusing on the changing conditions of the state and society, as well as on leadership choices, this study attempts to provide answers to the puzzle of why the "world's largest democracy" has become difficult to govern.

INDIA'S PROBLEMS OF GOVERNABILITY

Viewed over a long historical period, the area that is now identified as India was never easy to govern. Precolonial times were marked by recurring conflicts between centralizing monarchs and assertive regional overlords. Colonial rulers laid the basis for centralized power – and thus for a modern state – but the writ of their law never carried far; colonial power seldom penetrated the tradition-bound villages of India. Although the nationalist movement in India during the first half of this century created unity and thus the basis for a new system of authority, it also sowed seeds of divisiveness, leading eventually to the bloodletting that accompanied the creation of Pakistan. Also, the early postindependence period was anything but calm politically. State consolidation often involved armed repression of rebellious groups and forced annexation of political units that were unwilling to join the new republic.

In spite of this turbulent past, the postindependence era raised hopes for a stable, democratic India. That was certainly the vision of the "founding fathers." Under the leadership of Nehru and others, that vision took shape in the form of new political institutions. The new Constitution laid the basis for a British-style parliamentary democracy, arrangements were made to keep the armed forces out of politics, and the diversities of the Indian people were carefully considered in designing the new federal system. The Congress party – the key institutional manifestation of India's newly discovered national unity – reached out into village India to incorporate the previously unmobilized masses, and India's first elections were held. Because elections were held periodically, rural leaders slowly joined the anglicized urban leaders of the Congress party as India's new ruling elite. Dominance by a single party thus provided stability, and it did not appear to be an obstacle to the accommodation of new forces in the polity.

The political arrangements in this early phase were clearly dominated by an educated, nationalist elite. The business class was also politically influential, and the landed and caste elites were slowly brought into the ruling coalition. The new rulers enjoyed widely perceived legitimacy, in part because of the nationalist legacy and in part because the traditional patterns of authority in society, such as the caste structure in the villages, were still largely intact. The dominant political elites, moreover, practiced a reconciliatory approach toward the competing elites, while professing the hope that they would be able to bring the poor and the oppressed masses into the mainstream of India's modernizing political economy. The legitimacy formula that the Congress party had designed was clearly expressed in its proposed strategy for economic development: a marriage between nationalism and democratic socialism. The party's five-year plans accordingly stressed a mixed-economy model of development that sought economic growth, self-sufficiency, and a modicum of wealth redistribution.

These were euphoric times in India, as new beginnings often are. Although many difficult problems confronted the new government, both leaders and followers had considerable confidence in the state's capacity to deal with these problems. The Indian state sought to guide development while standing above the society; it also simultaneously expressed the preferences of important social groups and thus was widely deemed legitimate. Over the past two decades, however, or since about 1967, much has changed. Most important, the state's capacity to govern (i.e., the capacity simultaneously to promote development and to accommodate diverse interests) has declined. Along with this decline, order and authority have been eroding. Since the mid–1960s, the surface manifestation of this process has been widespread activism outside of the established political channels that often has led to violence, a problem compounded by the state's growing incapacity to deal with the pressing problems of law and order, corruption, and poverty. Below the surface lies an important cause of these political problems: disintegration of India's major political institutions, especially the decline of its premier political entity, the Congress party (often referred to simply as Congress).

Today, the Congress party has lost its hegemony over Indian politics. Partly as cause and partly as consequence of its loss of control, Congress has experienced a profound organizational decline. This sprawling party once provided a measure of coherence across this vast and diverse subcontinent. Now, after a number of splits in the party, Congress exists little more than in name. At its apex, the organization has been reduced to Rajiv Gandhi, the heir of India's "first political family," and a few hand-picked supporters. Nothing has dramatized this transformation more sharply than Gandhi's broadside criticism in 1985 of what remained of the Congress party. He blasted the "cliques" that enmesh "the living body of the Congress in their net of avarice," chided their "self-aggrandizement, their corrupt ways, their linkages with vested interests – and their sanctimonious posturings." He went on to complain that "millions of ordinary Congress workers are handicapped, for on their backs ride the brokers of power and influence, who dispense patronage to convert a mass movement into a feudal oligarchy – corruption is not only tolerated – but [is] even regarded as a hallmark of leadership."[1] It is ironic that Rajiv Gandhi's scathing criticism of his own party was delivered in a speech to celebrate the 100th anniversary of its founding.

The institutional decline of the Congress party has not been offset by

---

1 This speech was reported in all major newspapers after it was delivered in Bombay on December 28, 1985. I owe the first two quotations cited earlier to James Manor, "Parties and the Party System," in Atul Kohli, ed., *India's Democracy: An Analysis of Changing State–Society Relations* (Princeton University Press, 1988), p. 92. The long extract is from *Indian Express* (New Delhi), December 29, 1985. It is also worth recalling that during the 1960s, important scholars of the Congress party had attributed much of the "success" of this unique ruling party to its widespread patronage networks or to the crucial role of the "power brokers." See for example, Myron Weiner, *Party Building in a New Nation: The Indian National Congress* (University of Chicago Press, 1967), and Rajni Kothari, *Politics in India* (Boston: Little, Brown, 1970).

the development of an alternative national party. Thus, there is currently a growing organizational vacuum at the core of India's political space. Until recently, India's first political family, the Gandhis, had occupied some of this space, but their hold on power was personalistic, and the perception of their legitimacy did not run deep. There are very few mechanisms still intact for the resolution of power conflicts in contemporary India. For quite some time the Parliament has not functioned as a significant political body that could help resolve conflicts or make policy. Cabinet members had also come to be selected by Indira and Rajiv Gandhi for their personal loyalty, not for their ability or for their control over an independent power base. Unmediated intraelite conflict has further damaged such institutions as the Constitution, the federal system, and the election process. It has also undermined discipline within the bureaucracy, especially among the police forces.

Below the established state elites, the vertical patterns of fealty in India's civil society have been eroding. Members of higher castes and other "big men" have gradually lost their capacity to influence the political behavior of those below them in the socioeconomic hierarchy. As a result, new social groups have entered the political arena and pressed new demands upon the state. Without a dominant party and other conflict-resolving institutions, democratic accommodation of such demands has been difficult. Without established law-and-order institutions, moreover, the agitation and violence that have resulted from these demands have been difficult to control. The result has been a dramatic increase in political violence in India (Figure 1.1). The state has had to increase its reliance on military and paramilitary forces. Thus, the current political situation features an outpouring of diverse new social demands, ad hoc and vacillating responses by the state, and a growing sense that order and authority – and perhaps even democracy – may be disintegrating in India.

It is important to clarify the thrust of this argument at the outset. This study does not claim that India's democracy is about to fall. An analysis of social and political trends alone cannot be used to predict the future of a distressed political regime. As illustrated by the Emergency of 1975–7, during Indira Gandhi's regime, leadership actions can be as much responsible for a breakdown in democracy as can underlying social trends. For a brief moment in 1985, when Rajiv Gandhi became prime minister, his decision to take advantage of his considerable popularity to pursue a more reconciliatory approach similarly demonstrated how important leadership actions can be. India's direction following V. P. Singh's rise to power in late 1989 has yet to be determined. Because leadership actions are both important and difficult to predict, so is the future of this troubled regime.

Two further qualifications should be noted. First, India's political situation in the 1970s and 1980s had some of the elements of both continuity and change that characterized the pre–1967 situation. This study attempts

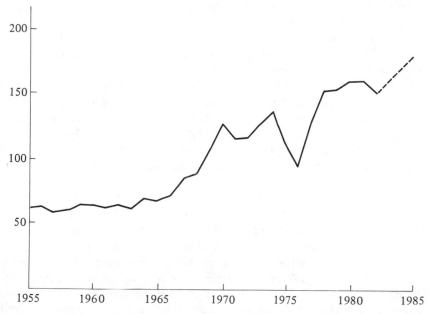

Figure 1.1. Political violence in India, 1955–85 (number of riots per million population). *Source:* Data from 1955 to 1982 are taken from an annual publication: Government of India, Ministry of Home Affairs, *Crime in India.* New Delhi: Government Press. Data for 1983 and 1984 are not available. The 1985 figures are rough estimates provided by government officials. For a discussion of what the government data on "riots" include and why they can be used to gauge public protest and political violence, see Baldev Raj Nayar, *Violence and Crime in India: A Quantitative Study.* Delhi: Macmillan, 1975, p. 17.

to focus on all those changes. Other scholars, by contrast, have emphasized such elements of continuity as the electoral dominance of the Congress party well into the late 1980s, or India's success in avoiding class polarization and the related persistence of the politics of "centrism."[2]

Second, there are some elements of political and social change that tend to strengthen, rather than weaken, India's authority structure. Periodic

2 Myron Weiner, while balancing elements of both continuity and change, seems to emphasize that the 1980 elections "restored" the Congress to its pre-1967 position. See his "Congress Restored: Continuities and Discontinuities in Indian Politics," *Asian Survey,* 22:4(April 1983), pp. 339–55. Lloyd I. and Susanne Hoeber Rudolph similarly balance elements of change and continuity, but emphasize the continued "centrist" nature of Indian politics. See *In Pursuit of Lakshmi: The Political Economy of the Indian State* (University of Chicago Press, 1987), passim, but especially the Conclusion. A good overview of political change in India that is also, on balance, positive about India's achievements is Jyotirindra Dasgupta, "India: Democratic Becoming and Combined Development," in Larry Diamond et al., eds., *Democracy in Developing Countries: Asia* (Boulder, Colo.: Lynne Rienner, 1989), pp. 53–104.

national and state elections, for example, can have significant consequences: The longer a system is in place, the deeper grow its roots.[3] Tenure
strengthens democracy. The national elections in late 1989 again indicated
viability for India's democracy. Political parties on both the left and the
right have come to accept parliamentary democracy. Moreover, India's
macroeconomic performance in the 1980s was quite satisfactory, and such
performance can be an important factor in strengthening the legitimacy of
any government. Thus, it must be acknowledged at the outset that there
are tendencies within Indian politics – some of them elements of continuity
with the past, and some recent changes – that do not fit in with the thrust
of the argument presented here, namely, that India's problems of governability are growing.

A situation of political turmoil can always be viewed in different lights,
much as a cup can be seen as half full, rather than half empty. Though
the focus here is on the problems of India's governability, it is not because
of failure to recognize the strengths and achievements of the "world's
largest democracy."[4] This focus on problem areas stems in part from a
concern about the significant decay seen in India's authority structures over
the past two decades. This focus on problems, moreover, stems from an
analytical judgment that will be supported with evidence throughout this
study: Over time, and on balance, India's problems of governability have
worsened.

Over the past two decades, a legitimate and moderately stable state that
was confident of its ability to lay out India's agenda for socioeconomic
change has evolved into a reactive state. This state is omnipresent, but
feeble; it is highly centralized and interventionist, and yet seems powerless.
It has the responsibility to foster the "life-chances" of its many diverse
social groups, but rather than initiating action, it primarily reacts. Moreover, the state now appears capable neither of dealing with the concerns
of diverse interest groups nor of directing planned development. Its dominant institutions are in disarray, and the search for new legitimacy formulas
goes on.

The purpose of this book is to describe the political situation that has
emerged as the "Congress system" has declined in India.[5] More important,
this study attempts to explain how the political process has been involved

3 This conclusion is supported by the results of various public-opinion polls cited by Bashiruddin Ahmed and Samuel J. Eldersveld, *Citizens and Politics: Mass Political Behavior in
   India* (University of Chicago Press, 1978).
4 Elsewhere, in a broader comparative context, I have highlighted some achievements of
   India's democratic model of development: Atul Kohli, "Democracy and Development,"
   in John Lewis and Valerianna Kallab, eds., *Development Strategies Reconsidered* (Washington, D.C.: Overseas Development Council, 1986), pp. 153–82.
5 To the best of my knowledge, the term "Congress system" was coined by Rajni Kothari:
   "The Congress 'System' in India," *Asian Survey*, 4:12(December 1964), pp. 1161–73.

in the erosion of India's established patterns of authority. Was that erosion of established authority inevitable? The decline of the nationalist legacy, the growing tension between the state's representative and developmental functions, and the pressures from new groups that have emerged as a consequence of political and economic developments must be recognized as factors whose detrimental effects have been difficult to counter. On the other hand, many specific patterns of changes have resulted from deliberate political choices. The task of empirical analysis is to determine how "choices" have interacted with "inevitabilities" to produce this specific political outcome.

THE SCHOLARLY CONTEXT

A study of the erosion of authority in India can benefit both Indian studies and studies of comparative development. Observers of Indian politics have recently devoted considerable attention to India's growing problems of governability.[6] Following the election of a minority national government in late 1989, this concern is likely to increase. India's massive developmental problems demand the state's attention, but no problem in India is likely to be more serious than is disintegration of the major problem-solving institution, namely, an effective democratic state.

This study arises in part from the growing concern with India's eroding authority structures. What this volume offers in terms of novelty is detailed empirical analysis based on fieldwork. It will become clear in due course that the argument developed here differs in important respects from a number of existing theories. Suffice it to note at this point that both the descriptive picture and the analysis that emerge in this empirical study are rather complex; there are no easily identifiable heroes and villains in the story told here.

As far as broader issues are concerned, the analysis presented in comparative political studies over the past 10–15 years usually has focused on the issue of "the state." This useful intellectual development has been aimed at reversing a deep-rooted reductionist tendency within political sociology. Moving away from society-centered explanations, the argument

---

6 The writings here are quite extensive. Many appear in Indian newspapers and weekly magazines and thus are not easily accessible to Western readers. They are even difficult to retrieve within India. An incomplete list of works that are readily available would include the following: Rajni Kothari, *State Against Democracy: In Search of Humane Governance* (Delhi: Ajanta Publications, 1988); W. H. Morris-Jones, "India – More Questions than Answers," *Asian Survey,* 24:8(August 1984), pp. 809–16, Manor, "Party System"; Robert Hardgrave, *India Under Pressure: Prospects for Political Stability* (Boulder, Colo.: Westview Press, 1984); Bashiruddin Ahmed, "Emerging Indian Political System," *The Administrator* (India), 31:1(January–March 1986), pp. 27–42; Rudolph and Rudolph, *In Pursuit of Lakshmi,* chapters 4–6.

has been that state authorities and state structures are significant and autonomous forces that influence both political and socioeconomic changes. This simple but powerful analytical assertion has generated considerable scholarship.[7]

Every intellectual gain, however, poses the danger that issues and approaches that appear not to be in fashion will be ignored. The interest in "the state" poses two such dangers. The first concerns the issues that are likely to be studied: Given the emphasis on the state as a social force, the question of how the state itself evolves may recede into the background. The second danger concerns the causal forces that are likely to be stressed: Social and economic forces are likely to be underemphasized in the new quest to assert the significance of the state.

This study continues to treat the state as a robust social actor. It attempts to develop a state-oriented explanation of the crisis of governability in a developing democratic country, but it also makes a deliberate attempt to correct the distortions often generated by overemphasis on the state. This empirical study is thus aimed at an analysis of the changing nature of the state itself, especially the erosion of the state's capacity to govern. In this limited sense, the concern of this study goes back to the analytical issue of "political instability" raised by Samuel Huntington and others in the 1960s.[8]

The explanation for political instability in the specific case that emerges here, however, varies from those generated by other approaches, both developmental and Marxist. The interaction of state and social forces is emphasized. The primary focus of analysis here is neither "social mobilization," leading up to growing demands by social groups in a "modernizing" society, nor class conflict. Rather, the main concern is with the patterns of politicization that result when the state can influence the life-chances of many social groups and when this state is accessible via dem-

7 The state-oriented literature on developing countries continues to grow. An incomplete list would include the following: Alfred Stepan, *The State and Society: Peru in Comparative Perspective* (Princeton University Press, 1978); Ellen Kay Trimberger, *Revolution from Above: Military Bureaucrats and Development in Japan, Turkey, Egypt, and Peru* (New Brunswick, N.J.: Transactions Books, 1978); Robert H. Bates, *Markets and States in Tropical Africa* (Berkeley: University of California Press, 1982); John Waterbury, *The Egypt of Nasser and Sadat: The Political Economy of Two Regimes* (Princeton University Press, 1983); Nora Hamilton, *The Limits of State Autonomy: Post-Revolutionary Mexico* (Princeton University Press, 1983); Richard Sandbrook (with Judith Barker), *The Politics of Africa's Economic Stagnation* (Cambridge University Press, 1985); Peter Evans, Dietrich Rueschemeyer, and Theda Skocpol, eds., *Bringing the State Back In* (Cambridge University Press, 1985); Atul Kohli, *The State and Poverty in India: The Politics of Reform* (Cambridge University Press, 1987); Vivienne Shue, *The Reach of the State: Sketches of the Chinese Body Politic* (Stanford University Press, 1988); Joel Migdal, *Strong Societies and Weak States* (Princeton University Press, 1989).

8 See Samuel P. Huntington, *Political Order in Changing Societies* (New Haven: Yale University Press, 1968).

ocratic politics. It will become clear in due course that the causal and normative implications of this "statist" focus vary from those of society-centered analyses of political order.

THE STUDY

India's size and diversity pose considerable difficulties for any study attempting to generalize about the polity as a whole. The country has nearly as many people as all of Africa and Latin America combined, and probably as much ethnic diversity as is seen in all of Western Europe. The issue of generalizing over such a range is especially problematic for a study based on fieldwork. Several organizing principles have been adopted so as to make the task manageable.

It was clear from the beginning that any attempt to describe and explain India's growing problems of governability would have to take into account both national and local trends. The building blocks for national trends are provided by local politics, and the actions of the central authorities often are aimed at winning or manipulating the "hearts and minds" of those on the political periphery. Given India's federal structure, moreover, state-level governments often are significant political forces in their own right. Thus, a satisfactory account of India's changing authority patterns must focus simultaneously on the center, the states, and local politics.

The "district" was chosen as the unit appropriate for study of local politics mainly because other scholars had used this research strategy effectively.[9] Five districts were studied in order to tap some of India's regional diversity at the local level. Although the reasons that these districts were chosen will emerge later, there was no real rationalization for analyzing five rather than four or nine districts. Detailed study of more than five districts would have been desirable, but five seemed to be an optimal choice that would be manageable, given a fieldwork team of only one, as well as sufficient to capture important aspects of political diversity.

An important concern of this study is how authority patterns have changed over time, and background data are available because the five districts investigated here were analyzed by Myron Weiner during the early and middle 1960s.[10] The research for this book involved extensive interviews in each district with participants and observers of local politics. This fieldwork was carried out during 1985–6. When these data are compared with those from the earlier benchmark study by Weiner, they should provide insight into how and why India's periphery has become difficult to govern.

9 See for example, Weiner, *Party Building,* and Paul Brass, *Factional Politics in an Indian State: The Congress Party in Uttar Pradesh* (Berkeley: University of California Press, 1965).
10 These are analyzed by Weiner, *Party Building.*

Although the changes over time have led to a governability crisis, the
intensity of the crisis varies from one region of India to another. Why that
occurs is the subject of the second major part of this study. Comparative
analysis of three selected states – Bihar, Gujarat, and West Bengal –
highlights why these changes have led to considerable breakdown of order
in some states but not in others.[11] Bihar and Gujarat were chosen as
examples of states at different levels of development that have experienced
growing political turmoil. The Bihar–Gujarat comparison allows a distinction between different types of breakdowns and helps to delineate some
of the reasons for breakdown, including the significance of "levels of development." The interesting case of West Bengal allows a careful testing
of the argument, because it is one of the few Indian states in which authority
has been restored after a prolonged period of disorder.

Research in these three states has been based on interviews, newspapers,
and published works by other scholars. I have maintained an interest in
West Bengal in part because my earlier work had covered this state, albeit
concerning a different theme.[12] Recent interviews thus provided new information to buttress my prior knowledge of West Bengal. Interest in
Gujarat and Bihar, by contrast, is new for me. I conducted interviews in
both of these states in 1986, and I have consulted the works of other
scholars, both for background material and for some specific interpretations.

The third major concern of this book is how, and with what success,
India's central government (the Center) has dealt with the growing problems of governability. Indira Gandhi's role in the emerging authority crisis
is well known to most scholars of India and is not discussed separately in
great detail,[13] but rather is woven throughout the study. However, the
changing nature of India's central government since Indira Gandhi's death
needs to be investigated. In order to do so, this study analyzes how the
Indian government under Rajiv Gandhi has managed economic policy and
how it has dealt with such troubled political institutions as the Congress
party and Center–state relations with Punjab. This focus on the actions of
leaders provides a microcosm for interpreting power and authority trends
at the national level.

The research on economic policy is based on both interviews and news-

11 A shortcoming of this study is its failure to include detailed, firsthand analysis of the
   political turmoil in Punjab. This is mainly because research access to Punjab was closed
   to me. I have attempted to compensate for this in Chapter 12 by incorporating an analysis
   based on press reports.
12 Kohli, *The State and Poverty.*
13 In addition to the references in footnote 6, see the following: Francine Frankel, *India's
   Political Economy, 1947–77* (Princeton University Press, 1978); Henry Hart, ed., *Indira
   Gandhi's India* (Boulder, Colo.: Westview Press, 1980); Mary C. Carras, *Indira Gandhi:
   In the Crucible of Leadership* (Boston: Beacon Press, 1979).

paper reports. By contrast, the account of how leaders have managed India's political institutions depends more heavily on newspapers. Direct interviews did not reveal much in this area, as senior leaders often were secretive or reluctant to discuss issues concerning the Congress party and the Punjab accord. Newspapers, by contrast, with their established contacts, seemed to carry so much news on these issues that one wonders if there are any political secrets in India.

Data collected on five districts, on three states, and on two crucial sets of policy issues facing the nation constitute the core empirical materials on which this study is based. The three levels of the polity are analyzed with the aim of charting and explaining India's growing problems of governability. Each of the three levels of analysis can help answer one of three interrelated questions: How have authority patterns changed over time? Why do patterns of political turmoil vary across regions? What are the implications of the changed political context for the government's capacity to govern India? The logic of inquiry in each of the three sections is comparative, either over time or across regions and issue areas within India.

THE ARGUMENT

It is tempting to conceptualize the reemergence of political incoherence in India as a continuing aspect of that country's political history. After all, cohesive rule from a Center enjoying widely perceived legitimacy has never been an easy achievement in India. The contemporary turmoil, however, is qualitatively different; it is both more and less intense in some respects than in the past, and therefore both more and less threatening. It is less threatening in the sense that in the current context, the basic existence of India as a viable political unit does not appear to be threatened. Secessionist movements may again arise here and there, and they probably will, but as long as the armed forces are intact, a further division of India is not likely. Political disorder is more threatening now than in the past, however, because political breakdown jeopardizes the predictability on which organized society rests. The rules that govern life, property, and the everyday behavior of common citizens increasingly are not dictated by custom, thus requiring the presence of an effective state and a legal machinery. The state is also deeply involved in the management of economic life, down to the grass roots. The degree to which socioeconomic life once was insulated from national power struggles has been eroded, probably forever.

The qualitative difference between political turmoil today and unstable rule in the past suggests that the political problems of today are, at least in part, the results of the "developmental successes" of the past few decades. India's Congress party was the midwife for the new nation-state. Having performed that crucial role, the party has now withered away. Other institutions came into being during that same time period: a functioning national market, national transportation and communication networks, an emerging but relatively strong indigenous capitalism, and moderately cohesive armed forces. These are the key rudiments of a nation-state that should ensure the existence of India as a viable political unit. Along with these developments, however, came another set of changes: an increased division of labor, the spread of commerce, and diffusion of both national and democratic values. These changes have reduced the isolation of one local community from another. Moreover, because the state has been heavily involved in all of these changes, the growing ineffectiveness of the state is likely to have wide repercussions.

The breakdown of political order in contemporary India puts into question the future capacity of the Indian state to govern. The crucial questions related to the issue of eroding authority are these: How will India be ruled in the future – as a democracy, or by other means? If as a democracy, what type of democracy? Who within the state – which individuals, parties, and socioeconomic groups – will exercise power? And finally, how effective is the state likely to be in solving India's pressing problems? The issue of governability in the contemporary context thus concerns the state's capacity simultaneously to accommodate disparate interests and promote development.

The explanation for India's growing problems of governability developed here stresses multicausality. It is also largely inductive, derived from empirical materials. An analysis that would emphasize one set of variables over others and would allow sharp "differentiation of the intellectual product" simply could not be sustained against the complex empirical findings. A number of related but ultimately independent forces have influenced recent political changes in India.

In order to understand this overall explanation of India's governability crisis, it is important first to summarize the main findings from the three main parts of this study. Political developments in five selected districts are analyzed in Part II, and it is shown that India's political periphery is increasingly difficult to govern. During the 1950s and 1960s, the Congress party had succeeded in penetrating India's countryside by aligning itself with local "bosses." Over the past two decades, however, power struggles in the countryside have increased, sometimes aimed at political goals, and sometimes economic goals. The subjects of contention have been positions of power and status, state-controlled patronage and access to educational institutions, and economic rewards to be derived from land and wages. As a consequence, the traditional authority patterns have been severely challenged.

These power struggles have also been difficult to accommodate within the framework of the Congress party, especially because the party has consistently been weakened from the top during this period. Instead of allowing such conflicts to evolve to some democratic resolution, Indira Gandhi sought to ensure her control over the party by appointing those loyal to her to positions of power. Organizational decline within the Congress party and the many power disputes have both contributed to the erosion of established patterns of local authority. Barring a few exceptions, new institutional patterns of authority have not emerged. The institutional vacuum in the periphery, in turn, helps explain a number of political trends, including coalitional instability and substantial fluctuations in the "political mood" and thus in electoral outcomes, ineffective local government, and the emergence of personal rule, often with ruffians as de facto local leaders.

The erosion of established authority has led to considerable violence in some states. In other states, by contrast, either such breakdown of order has been forestalled or, in rare cases, political authority has been reestablished. Part III of this study undertakes a detailed comparative analysis of three states: Bihar, Gujarat, and West Bengal. Some other states, such as Karnataka, are discussed briefly. All this analysis is aimed at explaining varying regional outcomes.

The situation of total breakdown of order in Bihar, for example, has resulted from corrosion of the authority vested in the social structure and absence of cohesion in political structures. Increasing power struggles in the society and a highly factionalized elite have provided a combustible political mixture that ignites periodically, and in Bihar even the forces of repression are ineffective. Political violence in Gujarat has had a more purposive quality than in Bihar. It results not primarily from a breakdown of social order but from the calculated mobilization strategies employed by competing elites.

In contrast to the situations of these two states, the case of West Bengal demonstrates how the presence of a cohesive party can bring stability even in a highly mobilized political environment: Strong leaders and disciplined ruling parties – forces that can impart a degree of cohesion to state structures – can help moderate the impact of corrosion of authority in the social structure. The emergence of incoherence in both state and social structures, however, is a sure recipe for a breakdown of order.

Part IV of this study shifts attention to developments at the national level. It is at the center of the Indian polity that the significance of the growing authority crisis is seen most clearly. In a state-dominated society, the state has lost its ability to initiate significant economic and political changes. The developmental capacities of India's "soft state" were never all that great to begin with. Under Nehru, however, numerous political and economic policies were initiated and sustained by the federal government. In recent years, by contrast, the major federal policy initiatives either have floundered or have narrowed the support base of the rulers, contributing further to the problems of governability. This conclusion is supported empirically, and the reasons for it are developed later with reference to the attempts by Rajiv Gandhi's government to liberalize the economy and to strengthen some of India's major political institutions.

The irony of India's politicoeconomic situation is tragic: The state is highly centralized and omnipresent, but the leverage of its leaders to initiate meaningful change has diminished. The main reason for this development is that authority has seldom run deep, and the authority structures have in recent years fallen into disrepair. As a result, state authorities have little ability to persuade the people to support government initiatives – to build consensus. Coercion as a strategy of policy implementation is not in the cards, at least not at this time. Thus, major initiatives often face a dead end. It has become a vicious cycle: Weakness in the authority structures makes it difficult to solve precisely those problems whose solutions could strengthen authority. The bulk of political energy is spent fighting one bushfire after another, guided by the central concern of how to hang on to power.

The roots of the decay in the national authority structures are to be found in a dilemma that consistently plagued Indira Gandhi: how to maintain her hold on power while either fending off or accommodating the growing demands of power blocs in the polity. Democratic incorporation of such diverse new demands often would have meant a downward transfer of power. Indira Gandhi perceived – not without some justification – that such moves would weaken the Center and thus both national integrity and the state's capacity to steer economic development. As a consequence, she adopted a recalcitrant stance. Instead of accommodating power challengers, which might not have been easy in any case, she sought to block their access to power by undermining democratic institutions. Cancellations of elections within the Congress party, appointment of loyal but weak chief ministers in the states, and personalization of general elections were all part of this ruling strategy.

The paradox is that the very strategy that enabled Indira Gandhi to hold on to power also undermined the possibility of using that power for constructive ends. Having reduced the significance of important institutions, she found that when she (and, later, her successor, Rajiv Gandhi) needed institutional support to implement desired goals, such support was not available. Personal control over a highly interventionist state has been maintained, but the interventionist arm of that state has gone limp; the trends toward centralization and powerlessness have run in tandem.

This political analysis at the levels of the districts, the states, and the Center is aimed at delineating the forces that have contributed to India's problems of governability. During the first two decades after independence, democratic institutions were introduced into India. With the advantage of hindsight, some have questioned the solidity of those early foundations. The view adopted here is rather that the beginnings of democracy were

well founded and held out considerable promise. Over the past two decades, however, India's institutional capacity to deal with conflict and initiate solutions to pressing problems has declined. The issue now is, What
factors can help explain this "dependent variable," namely, the declining
capacity to govern?

At a proximate level of causation, four interrelated factors can be identified as independent variables in the empirical analysis: the changing role
of the political elite, weak and ineffective political organizations, mobilization of previously passive groups for electoral competition, and growing
conflict between contending social groups, including the conflict between
the haves and the have-nots. How each of these conditions can influence
the problems of governability can now be briefly summarized.

As democratic factionalism and other types of power conflicts have multiplied within India, the leaders often have found their hold on power
fiercely challenged. Many of them, including Indira and Rajiv Gandhi,
characteristically have reacted in ways that have tended to preserve their
power. One important method for preserving power has been populism:
to establish direct contact between the leader and the masses and to undermine those impersonal rules and institutions designed to facilitate orderly challenges. Making direct promises that will affect as large a segment
of the population as possible can enable a leader to mobilize broad electoral
support. The destruction of institutional constraints will leave more matters
to the leader's personal discretion, enabling the leader to promote those
who are loyal, while shunting aside anyone who is a potential challenger
with an independent political base.

This process has undermined the possibility of establishing a system of
impersonal authority based on the procedural rationality of democracy.
As traditional sources of authority have declined and the development of
rational, legal bases of authority has been thwarted, personal rule has come
to prevail. Personalization of power can, of course, be either a cause or a
consequence of weak institutional rule. What is clear in the case of India
over the last two decades is that, on balance, the nation's powerful leaders
– especially Indira and Rajiv Gandhi, but also important regional leaders
like M. G. Ramachandran and N. T. Rama Rao – have worked more to
increase their personal power than to strengthen governmental institutions.
Whether or not V. P. Singh will work to reverse that trend has yet to be
determined.

In addition to the detrimental role of its leaders, India's economic scarcities and heterogeneous social structure have made it difficult to strengthen
political organizations. Whatever the causative factors, which will be discussed in due course, weak political organizations have also contributed
significantly to the growing problems of governability. Weak political parties, for example, have ceased functioning as arenas for accommodation
and resolution of conflict. In a social situation where most traditional modes

of resolving conflicts are eroding and the political system allows, even encourages, association for the pursuit of group interests, which can lead to conflict, an absence of strong political parties leaves a serious authority vacuum. Unresolved conflicts often are fought out on the streets. Ineffectiveness of other institutions, such as the police force, further contributes to growing civil disorder. That is why the Indian state in recent years has increasingly resorted to its last line of defense – the armed forces.

Electoral competition has mobilized many formerly passive socioeconomic groups and brought them into the political arena. On balance, this is a desirable outcome in a democracy. But given the state's limited capacities for redistribution of wealth and the intensity with which electoral support has been courted, these mobilized and dissatisfied groups have further contributed to the growing political turmoil. A major example of this phenomenon is the growing caste conflict between the "backward" and the "forward" castes. Leaders in state after state have utilized "reservations" – the Indian version of affirmative action – as means to gain the electoral support of numerically significant backward castes. Higher castes, feeling that their interests are threatened, have resisted these moves. Once set in motion, however, those who have been mobilized have been difficult to satisfy or control. Conflict has often been the result.

A similar pattern has unfolded as competing elites have sought to mobilize ethnic groups who share language, religion, or race. The groups vary: the Maharashtrians in Belgaum; the Sikhs in Punjab; Hindus versus Moslems in various parts of the country; the Gurkhas in West Bengal. These mobilizations follow identifiable patterns. Leaders manipulate "primordial" attachments so as to gain access to the state. If they are accommodated, the conflict often recedes. Accommodation, however, is not always possible. Moreover, those in positions to make concessions sometimes have not made timely concessions, in order to protect their own political interests. Such recalcitrance has only further encouraged the leaders of ethnic and religious groups to use violence and agitation as means of accomplishing their political goals.

Quite independent of such mobilization aimed at influencing political competition, the general process of economic and social change has shaken people out of their traditional social niches. Changing roles have created a growing awareness of the individual's position in society. Long-established inequalities and beliefs about the legitimacy of these inequalities are thus increasingly under challenge. Members of lower socioeconomic classes have begun associating themselves so as to challenge what they perceive to be unjust domination and exploitation. Privileged groups have also begun to counterorganize. Conflicts along traditional cleavages of caste and community have been around for quite some time, but what is new is the changing character and intensity of such conflicts. In states like Bihar, for example, one barely has to scratch the surface to discover that such group conflicts – often fought out by private armies – increasingly involve economic issues. Traditional conflict is thus evolving into new types of conflicts, and increasingly the theme is class conflict.

These four related variables – the changing role of the political elite, weak political organizations, the mobilization of new groups for electoral reasons, and growing social unrest, including class conflict – direct attention to the interactions between the state and social forces that help explain India's growing problems of governability. These variables are treated here as independent variables only insofar as one is not fully reducible to another. It will be clear to readers that these variables are fairly proximate to the phenomena being explained. Moreover, they "feed into" each other in cause-and-effect relationships. In order to avoid circular reasoning, therefore, one must carefully analyze how, over time, they influence one another and how they affect the dependent variable of interest: India's growing problems of governability.

The overall picture of political change in India that these four variables help delineate is one in which ruling institutions have weakened and power challenges have multiplied. If we "collapse" these four causal variables into broader analytical categories and move one step farther to a "deeper" level of causation, it is eminently clear that in the general explanation developed here, political variables play roles as significant as those of socioeconomic forces, if not more significant. Both the dislocative impact of economic development and growing class conflict have contributed to India's problems of governability. Neither of these socioeconomic variables, however, has been decisive. The forces that also have been significant are best thought of collectively as political forces: the roles of leaders, the impact of weak political institutions, and, most important, mobilization of new groups for purposes of winning power and securing access to the state's resources. None of these political forces is fully reducible to explanation by the underlying socioeconomic conditions. The explanation of the state's declining capacity to govern developed here is thus distinguished from both "developmental" and "Marxist" positions. While taking those positions into account, the explanation proposed here emphasizes the "autonomous" significance of political structures and processes.

Numerous nuances and details of how political variables contribute to problems of governability will emerge in due course. So will the distinctive normative implications of this state–society focus. Suffice it to note at the outset that the additional emphasis on "political causes" of "political change" in a case like that of India should not be surprising. Only a part of this emphasis results from an analytical recasting of the available evidence. For the rest, the empirical materials are simply distinctive. In comparison with earlier historical cases of Western European "modernization," from which both developmental and Marxist arguments originate, the role of the state looms much larger in India's development. Thus, the significance of political forces often can be traced back to this dominant role of the state in socioeconomic change.

In a situation like that of India, the state not only is the agent of political order but also is responsible for socioeconomic development. India's highly interventionist state controls many of the "free-floating" economic resources in a very poor society. Access to the power of the state is bitterly contested, not only for the political ends of exercising power and influencing policy but also as a source of livelihood and rapid upward mobility. The struggle for state power in these circumstances becomes simultaneously a struggle to influence people's life-chances. Thus, the conventional distinctions between the state and the market, or between the public and private spheres of activity, are not clear-cut in the case of India.

Moreover, because the state has been organized as an electoral democracy for nearly four decades, the belief that the state is controllable has spread wide and deep. Competing political elites are willing to utilize any sets of appealing symbols and available means – including violent means – for political mobilization aimed at bolstering their electoral chances. Even before the arrival of democracy, the character of premodern Indian society had been highly fragmented, and an interventionist democratic state has facilitated rapid political mobilization of various castes, classes, and religious and language groups. Add to this the roles of powerful economic actors such as business groups and the landowning peasantry, who depend heavily on state resources and thus wish to block access by others, and a picture emerges of a state that is both centralized and interventionist but that finds it increasingly difficult to accommodate conflicting demands and thus to govern.

One unsettling conclusion of this study is that India's democracy has itself contributed to overpoliticization of the Indian polity. The prescription that follows this argument, however, definitely is not that democracy should be curtailed in India. This study is primarily analytical, aimed at exploring the causes of India's increasing political turmoil. To the extent that it has any clear normative and prescriptive implications, they are, to repeat what I wrote in my preface, fairly general: strengthening party organizations and bringing the state's capacities in line with its commitments are two crucial long-term actions needed for improving the quality of India's democratic government.

THE ORGANIZATION

The study is organized into five parts. The introductory part consists of two chapters. Following this overview, Chapter 2 discusses a number of conceptual and theoretical issues that help orient the empirical materials of this study.

The three major empirical parts that follow constitute the core of the study. The fact that district-level political matters are discussed first represents a judgment that an understanding of trends in the political periphery is necessary for an understanding of politics at higher levels. After the analysis of five districts, the state-level materials are discussed. How the Center copes with the growing authority crisis is the subject of the last empirical part.

An overview of political changes in India is provided in the concluding chapter. What has changed and the how and why of those changes are discussed in summary form. The final chapter also discusses the analytical and normative significance of the Indian materials and of the emphasis on political variables as causal variables for the more general study of problems of governability in developing countries.

2

Some conceptual and theoretical considerations

The purpose of this study is to describe and to explain India's growing crisis of governability. The study's argument is derived primarily from empirical materials. Because any such empirical analysis must begin by defining concepts and specifying the a priori theoretical inclinations, this chapter will define some core concepts of this analysis and outline the state–society orientation that underlies the study. It is argued that many of the explanations commonly offered for "crises of governability" in developing countries, both developmental and Marxist, are too society-centered. In a country in which the state sets the agenda for socioeconomic change and in which extensive state intervention is an integral part of the changing political economy, understanding the nature and role of the state is crucial for the analysis of patterns of political change. This emphasis ought not to lead to an a priori neglect of socioeconomic forces. Rather, it means that both state and societal forces need to be taken into account. Therefore, the theoretical stance that informs this study continually emphasizes the interactions of political and socioeconomic variables.

SOME CONCEPTS DEFINED

The concept of "crisis" used in this study is not intended to imply that a breakdown of political order is imminent. It is, instead, used in its more limited and literal sense. *Webster's Third New International Dictionary* offers several definitions of the term "crisis," among them the following: (1) "the point of time when it is decided whether an affair or course of action shall proceed, be modified, or terminate," (2) "decisive moment," (3) "turning point." The concept of crisis that is used in this study has to do with the situation in which a state's political direction is reaching a crossroads; it does not imply a dramatic feeling of impending disaster. It is chosen to convey to readers a sense that political matters in India are in bad shape, probably are getting worse, and are not likely to go on this way. This does not mean that it is impossible for things to continue as they are; but if they do, the costs will be great. Furthermore, built into the concept of crisis as used here is an assumption that there are things that can be done to avert a final breakdown. "Crisis" thus refers to a deteriorating tendency that if left unchecked will continue to have negative consequences.

The concept of "governability" directs attention to a state's capacity to govern. For the Indian situation, the issue of its growing crisis of governability will refer to three types of problems: (1) the absence of enduring coalitions, (2) policy ineffectiveness, and (3) an incapacity to accommodate political conflict without violence. A government whose power rests on fluctuating coalitions and whose leaders repeatedly fail to fulfill their stated goals and to control politically directed violence will be deemed to be a government with a low capacity to govern.

In a democratic polity, the issue of endurance of coalitions refers mainly to the stability of social support that competing parties may or may not enjoy. A fluctuating social base often implies fluctuating party membership and low levels of identification between parties and supporters. Such parties are also likely to be weak organizationally, without clear and coherent programs. If all or most of the parties in a polity display these characteristics, the governments led by such competing parties probably will be vulnerable to wide swings in public opinion and to populist tendencies. Leaders with considerable personal appeal tend to emerge in such settings. The absence of enduring coalitions thus becomes one good summary indicator of deinstitutionalization in a democratic setting.

The issue of policy effectiveness can be understood in either more or less demanding terms. One conceivably could set up standards whereby some objective definition of a society's problems would be sought and against which the capacity of a government to solve problems would be assessed. Chances are that most governments would come up short in such an exercise. The more modest standard of policy effectiveness adopted here, therefore, is to judge a government's performance on issues that the government itself defines as areas of priority. A government that repeatedly fails to accomplish its stated goals is likely to be a government that does not govern well.

The last and most obvious indicator of increasing problems of governability is the pursuit of political goals by violent means, either by the state or by its citizens. The absence of open violence, especially in nondemocratic settings, does not necessarily indicate a government that governs well, but an increase in politically oriented violence in a more or less open polity nearly always indicates a growing crisis of governability. It indicates that the state does not possess the institutions necessary for peaceful resolution of the society's normal political conflicts.

The issue of governability thus directs attention to both governmental and political traits. Ruling parties without stable social support, a government that cannot meet its own goals, and a polity in which political goals increasingly come to be pursued by violent means are all characteristics of growing problems of governability. A democratic nation that suffers such problems and comes to be characterized by them is likely to be experiencing a crisis of governability.

A third slippery set of concepts that no study of governability can avoid is that of institutions and institutionalization. This study will use the definition of "institutions" developed by Samuel Huntington: organizations and procedures that have come to be accepted by a society and thus have acquired a measure of value and stability.[1] "Institutionalization" then refers to the process whereby organizations and procedures become institutions.

Because the concept of political institutionalization refers to a process whereby political structures and practices take root, it is both essential and fraught with analytical pitfalls for the study of governability. The greatest danger is that problems of political disorder will simply be redefined as problems of institutionalization, in the belief that something has thus been explained. In order to minimize this problem of "explanation by redefinition," I have attempted to follow two principles of analysis throughout this study. First, institutionalization and its opposite, deinstitutionalization, are both descriptions of conditions over time that require explanation, rather than serving as explanations for the problems of governability. Second, institutionalization is not a generalized social process, but a process that applies to specific political organizations and procedures.

SOCIOECONOMIC EXPLANATIONS OF CRISES OF GOVERNABILITY

Political sociologists in both the structural-functional and neo-Marxist traditions have their own relatively well developed explanations for why one should anticipate recurring crises of governability in developing countries. The two explanations even tend to converge at a proximate level of causation. Both tend to view the emergence of disorder (or class conflict) as resulting from the growing disjuncture between the subjective and objective aspects of the social order, that is, the failure of prevailing values (or ideologies) to legitimize the existing division of labor (or the class structure).

This convergence between these two approaches does not hold as one moves deeper into the chain of causation. For many structural-functionalists, the driving forces behind these changes are economic development and its concomitant modernization, whereas for many Marxists the driving force is capitalism. Valuable insights from both of these perspectives have helped orient some of the empirical findings of this study. The two perspectives share a blind spot, however, in their failure to focus

---

1 See Samuel P. Huntington, *Political Order in Changing Societies* (New Haven: Yale University Press, 1968), chapter 1, especially p. 12.

on the analytical consequences of one overwhelming fact: Not only do economic development and capitalism generate destabilizing political consequences in contemporary developing countries, but in most cases the state itself seeks to promote economic development and capitalism.

A popular and well-established line of thinking suggests that the process of industrialization and economic development is inherently unstable. Numerous scholars, ranging from Durkheim, through Parsons and Smelser, to Huntington, have been struck by the fact that the transitional stages between "tradition" and "modernity" often are characterized by anomie, social disorganization, and political decay.[2] The explanation for this state of affairs is believed to involve the corrosive impact of economic development on a society's established beliefs and patterned behaviors. Industrialization differentiates a traditional society. If new patterns of social integration do not keep up with the process of differentiation, social disorganization results. The more politically oriented arguments from this tradition, such as that of Huntington, propose that political decay results from the failure of political institutions to accommodate social groups that are mobilized by a complex set of social forces, especially economic development.

What modernization scholars see as general social disorganization looks like intensified class conflict to scholars in the Marxist tradition. Whereas most Marxists focus on the possibilities of a transformation from capitalism to socialism, when they do focus on transitions from precapitalism to capitalism, they tend to find that process destabilizing. Gramsci thus explained the "crisis of authority" in transitional societies in the following terms: "This means precisely that the great masses have become detached from their traditional ideologies, and no longer believe what they used to believe previously, etc. The crisis consists precisely in the fact that the old is dying and the new cannot be born; in this interregnum a great variety of morbid symptoms appear."[3] Parsons or Smelser could not have said it better. It is small wonder, then, that Gramsci's concept of "hegemony" under cap-

2 For one of many general reviews of the developmental or modernization literature on these themes, see Richard Higgott, *Political Development Theory* (New York: St. Martin's Press, 1983), chapter 2. One of the original formulations that stressed the gap between the forces of "integration" and "differentiation" as the root of developmental instability was by Neil Smelser, "Mechanisms of Change and Adjustments to Changes," in J. Finkle and R. Gable, eds., *Political Development and Social Change* (New York: Wiley, 1971), pp. 27–43; see also Huntington, *Political Order in Changing Societies*, especially chapter 1.

3 See Antonio Gramsci, *Selections from the Prison Notebooks* (New York: International Publishers, 1971), p. 276. A somewhat more recent comparative study that emphasizes the significance of class conflict in the breakdown of traditional social order is that by Eric Wolf, *Peasant Wars of the Twentieth Century* (New York: Harper & Row, 1969), especially the Conclusion. Elements of this insight are also incorporated in the work of Barrington Moore, Jr., *Social Origins of Dictatorship and Democracy: Lord and Peasant in the Making of the Modern World* (Boston: Beacon Press, 1969), especially chapter 9.

italism and the concept of "institutionalization" in modern societies developed by many non-Marxist political sociologists tend to overlap analytically.

A recent and more politically oriented argument originating from this radical tradition traces the roots of authoritarianism to the requirement for increasing industrialization in developing capitalist countries.[4] The argument is that as one moves beyond superficial industrialization, which can occur even under the auspices of open regimes and import-substitution policies, a government's capacity for facilitating economic development is increasingly strained. Sustained industrialization requires a disciplined working class and political stability. It also needs foreign capital and the imposition of austere economic policies. What is especially pressing is the need to shift away from an inward-oriented growth model, which cannot be sustained in the absence of income redistribution, to an export-oriented approach. Such daunting economic tasks can, according to this argument, overwhelm fragile democratic regimes. As if echoing Samuel Huntington, Marxist scholars like O'Donnell have concluded that technocratic and authoritarian regimes, the bureaucratic authoritarian regimes, emerge as a consequence of the requirements of sustaining their capitalist economic development.

Thus, the structural-functional and Marxist explanations for disorder in transitional societies share certain analytical traits. Many of their shared insights will be discussed later in the analysis of the Indian situation. For now, the most important similarity to be noted is that scholarship in both traditions tends to feature transitional stages in which the traditional ideologies fail to legitimize positions of various actors in a hierarchical social structure. Many structural-functionalists predict that the result will be breakdown of social and political order. Marxists, by contrast, see in such transitional stages the decline of traditional dominations, the growing prospect of mobilizing new class consciousness, and thus the possibility of revolutionary change. In spite of these normative differences, there is a striking analytical commonality. The disjuncture between a subjective understanding of the social structure and one's objective position in that social structure tends to create demand overload or class conflict in a polity.

At a proximate level of causation, therefore, one can suggest that there is some consensus in the literature on how best to conceptualize the issue of growing conflict in transitional societies. Its roots are located in the decline of traditional patterns and institutions and in the emergence of new

4 This well-known argument is associated with Guillermo O'Donnell, *Modernization and Bureaucratic Authoritarianism: Studies in South American Politics* (Berkeley: Institute of International Studies, University of California, 1973). For a critical review of O'Donnell's hypothesis, see David Collier, ed., *The New Authoritarianism in Latin America* (Princeton University Press, 1979), especially the chapters by Albert Hirschman, Jose Serra, and Robert Kaufman.

socioeconomic hierarchies and related demands. Because the development of new institutional mechanisms (hegemonic institutions, from the point of view of Marxists) to meet these demands does not always keep up with the pace of change, socioeconomic conflict results, creating recurring problems of governability for those in power. Disjuncture between institutional adaptation and the demands of newly mobilized social groups thus provides a useful way of conceptualizing the roots of growing conflict in transitional societies.

Two qualifications should immediately be added. First, whereas this shared and mostly descriptive formulation of how to conceptualize the issues of growing conflict undergirds this study, the normative positions associated with some structural-functionalists and many Marxists do not. For example, the findings in this study do not lead one to subscribe to the position of "order first, liberty second." There also is no implicit assumption here that with "class justice" the problem of political order vanishes. This study is primarily analytical. Keeping in mind that normative assumptions are nearly impossible to eliminate, an attempt is made here to walk a line between the conservative and radical positions. The findings indicate that the preference is for social democratic outcomes, wherein it may be possible to reconcile issues of order, socioeconomic justice, and democracy.

The second important qualification is more analytical. The focus on the disjuncture between institutions and the demands of newly mobilized groups does not generate a deep or a structural explanation of crises of governability. It leaves unanswered some of the most important analytical questions. How and why are competing political forces mobilized, and under what conditions do political institutions deteriorate or develop? This study rests on the contention that there are no satisfactory general answers to these questions available in the literature and that these questions are best answered with reference to specific empirical materials. In order to develop an empirical explanation, however, the general orientation adopted in this study needs to be clarified a little further.

As one moves further into the causal chain, scholars in the structural-functional and Marxist schools obviously differ as to what basic forces give rise to socioeconomic conflict. From Durkheim, through Parsons, to more recent scholarship, structural-functionalists share the view that societies, defined as cultural units, are inherently consensual and that social order is not a fundamental problem. Thus, breakdown of order often is viewed as a temporary phenomenon that especially afflicts transitional societies. The root causes of this temporary disorder are the forces of economic development, and the accompanying division of labor, that destroy traditional patterns of social solidarity.

For Marxists, by contrast, conflict is endemic to class societies, usually kept under control in the precapitalist stages by some combination of force (e.g., slavery, serfdom, or bonded labor) and religion (the "opium of the masses"). Capitalist development tends both to exacerbate socioeconomic inequalities and to undermine the significance of forced labor and of religion in modern nation-states. As distinct from economic development and the associated decline in traditional patterns of solidarity, therefore, Marxists believe that the basic forces responsible for socioeconomic conflict are the class dynamics released by capitalism.

The decline in traditional values that necessarily accompanies economic development and the sharpening of class inequities and increasing awareness of those inequities are two important sets of forces that may help to explain recurring societal conflict and the related problems of governability in developing countries. These variables will later be seen to be important in the analysis of the Indian situation. A factor that also needs to be noted, however, is the relative neglect of the autonomous significance of political forces in these two theoretical traditions.

The emphasis of both structural-functional and Marxist scholars is on socioeconomic forces. Politics and the state in both schools of thought are dependent variables, determined by the more fundamental social logic.[5] This charge of neglect does not apply fully to such contemporary scholars as Samuel Huntington and Guillermo O'Donnell. Their works not only grow out of these two traditions but also move beyond to consider the independent roles of the state and politics. Taken as two long intellectual traditions, however, structural-functional and Marxist political sociologies, especially their respective explanations for conflict and disorder, tend to emphasize societal considerations over political considerations. In order to redress this a priori imbalance, it is important to draw attention to the significance of political variables.

THE STATE AND POLITICS AS SOURCES OF CONFLICT

The contention that political forces are significant and independent variables that must be considered in analyzing political change can be understood at several different levels of analysis. At the most general level, one must note that political variables are nearly always important in any analysis of a breakdown of order. One can also suggest that at a middle level of generality there are some special political conditions that exist in the countries of the Third World, especially in Third World democracies, that enhance the significance of political variables for understanding recurring

5 I have developed this argument in detail elsewhere: Atul Kohli, *The State and Poverty in India: The Politics of Reform* (Cambridge University Press, 1987), chapter 1, and the "Introduction" to Atul Kohli, ed., *The State and Development in the Third World* (Princeton University Press, 1986), pp. 3–24. Also see Alfred Stepan, *The State and Society: Peru in Comparative Perspective* (Princeton University Press, 1978), pp. 3–45, and Peter Evans et al., eds., *Bringing the State Back In* (Cambridge University Press, 1985), passim.

crises of governability. Finally, there are unique political forces in operation in specific countries. This last set of issues does not concern us for the moment; such issues will be considered in the empirical part of this study.

A number of scholars have suggested that crises of governability, especially breakdowns in democracies, do not result solely, or even primarily, from socioeconomic crises. Rather, the troubles of democracies are political in origin and represent crises of legitimacy.[6] Various regimes, although existing under fairly similar socioeconomic conditions, may be deemed more or less legitimate by the ruled.

A number of purely political variables influence how well a democratic state is governed: the quality of leadership, the leadership choices, the prevailing ideology, the degree of intraelite harmony, and the design of such dominant political institutions as the party system and legislative–executive relations. Demagogic leaders, for example, can easily exacerbate political tensions within a democracy. The presence of widely divergent ideological beliefs or a fragmented political elite can similarly make stable political rule difficult. Most important, democratic values and behaviors take root only over time and only after repeated practice. Thus, even the best-designed democracies are fragile for the short run, and even established democracies can be endangered by an increase in extrasystemic protests or by leaders who do not cherish democratic norms.

The significant role of the state in contemporary developing countries adds an additional set of causal variables. The state in countries like India is not only an agent of political order; it is also responsible for facilitating socioeconomic development. The attempts to establish legitimacy and order in these settings periodically come in conflict with efforts to promote socioeconomic change from above. Whereas the former tend to require that the state accommodate many of the competing demands, effective performance of the developmental function pushes the state to stand above the society in order to act as a rational agent of change. This tension is not irreconcilable. Its continuous presence, however, strains governmental capacities, adding several structural perversions that contribute to recurring crises of governability.

First, as a result of the state's widespread encroachment on the affairs of society, which, on balance, is neither as undesirable nor as easily done away with as some would have it, the distinction between the public realm and the private sector becomes blurred. Thus, the state cannot claim that distributive problems are social and not political problems. Under conditions of competitive politics, moreover, distributive issues, along class,

---

6 The most sustained attention to the political causes of the breakdown of democracies is found in a series of volumes organized by Juan Linz. For a general discussion of this subject, see Juan Linz, *The Breakdown of Democratic Regimes* (Baltimore: Johns Hopkins University Press, 1978).

status, party, or ethnic lines, tend to be rapidly politicized. The resulting demands can strain the government's capacities, both accommodative and developmental. Thus, establishing "hegemony" within the framework of an interventionist democratic state typically tends to overpoliticize the polity; conversely, the absence of democracy makes it difficult to legitimate state power.

Second, a highly interventionist state tends to control a relatively large proportion of a poor society's "free-floating" economic resources. Under these circumstances, individuals and social groups arrive at the view that their everyday struggles for livelihood must be fought not only in the market and in the civil society but also in the state arena. The state and its resources thus become objects of considerable political attention. Again, if the situation is one of competitive politics, access to the state often becomes a matter of bitter contest. Although it is normal in most polities to seek power, both as an end in itself and as a means to influence policy, the added element of intensity seen in low-income, interventionist states stems from the fact that access to state resources is one of the few avenues to rapid upward mobility. Control of the state thus becomes the goal for the competitive energies of many who under different politicoeconomic conditions would pursue other productive tasks.

A highly interventionist state therefore tends to politicize its society more than does a limited state. As the state reaches everywhere, ubiquity characterizes its politics. Of course, in states in which political competition is not allowed, the state's vast presence can be used to stifle political activities. An interventionist democratic state, however, typically encourages considerable politically oriented activism. The pervasiveness and intensity of political activism tend to be even higher in mobilized but low-income settings. This is because alternative outlets for competitive energies in low-income societies tend to be limited.

An interventionist democratic state in a developing country is unusual. Cases of this type have been relatively few, and their political dynamics are not well understood. One thing, however, that should be clear, even on a priori grounds, is that, if sustained, democracy in a low-income setting typically gives rise to an enormous outpouring of political activity. There is no normative suggestion here that this is bad or undesirable. Widespread politicization, however, does put a high premium on a polity's institutional capacity simultaneously to accommodate the resulting demands and to promote socioeconomic development. Well-organized political parties thus become especially crucial. Parties constitute one set of political institutions that can help narrow the gap between the growth in politicized demands and governmental effectiveness. This issue will be discussed in detail later in this study. Suffice it to note at the outset that in the absence of effective mediating institutions like parties, rapid politicization typically exacerbates problems of governability.

Finally, given an interventionist state in a poor economy, those who control state power tend to exercise enormous influence. Because such control often is in the hands of individuals rather than institutions, leaders with personalistic appeal typically are at the helm of the state in low-income developing countries. The personalities and roles of these leaders can have far-reaching consequences for patterns of political change. Whereas this is true in many polities, it takes on added significance in low-income developing countries, where the importance of the leadership is structurally propelled. Whatever may be happening in the social structure in such settings, incompetent and recalcitrant leaders typically tend to exacerbate the problems of governability. Power-hungry leaders, therefore, often are as responsible for weakening democratic institutions as are the demands of newly mobilized social groups.

CONCLUSION

The crises of governability in a developing democratic country can be analyzed either from a modernization or Marxist perspective or from a standpoint that emphasizes the roles of the state and politics in these societies. If the primary goal of such a study were to choose between these alternative theoretical perspectives, selective evidence from the complex Indian case could indeed be found to support either viewpoint. However, when the primary purpose is to unravel an empirical puzzle, as is the case in this study, there is no reason to exclude significant theoretical insight from any quarter on a priori grounds.

A focus on the interactions between state and society provides a synthetic theoretical framework. Social structures undergoing basic transitions typically are afflicted with disorderly processes because of the incapacity of the traditional system of beliefs to legitimize the new socioeconomic hierarchies. Thus, issues of changing values and new patterns of stratification, including the emergence of class conflict, are important for understanding a situation of increasing socioeconomic conflict. The social mobilization that results from these processes of socioeconomic change typically outpaces the institutional capacities for accommodation, thus contributing to crises of governability.

Political variables make additional, autonomous contributions to the emergence of these crises. The issue of governmental legitimacy is only partially a function of socioeconomic conditions. Numerous political conditions also influence whether or not a government will be deemed legitimate. The state's pervasive presence, moreover, tends to enhance the significance of politics and thus of political variables in developing democratic countries. Finally, the quality of the state's leadership is also of enormous significance in either generating or mitigating crises of governability.

The empirical analysis that follows is guided by these fairly general state–society considerations. This study begins with the assumption that political structures and processes enjoy a degree of autonomy from the social structure. Thus, states can influence socioeconomic change, and, moreover, power struggles are not reducible to socioeconomic struggles. Conversely, it would be absurd to underemphasize the significant impact that cultural and class variables have on a society's politics. The task of empirical analysis within a state–society framework must be to assess how and in what proportions these competing variables mix.

PART II

The growing problems of governing the periphery: politics in the districts

Introduction: the districts

Chapters 3–7 analyze political change at India's political periphery, away from the main centers of power. In order to get a sense of how the practice of local politics has changed over time, the five districts analyzed here are the same ones that were investigated in the early 1960s by Myron Weiner in his well-known and insightful book *Party Building in a New Nation: The Indian National Congress.*

The central analytical problem for Weiner was to explain how the Congress party had transformed itself from a nationalist movement into a legitimate and powerful ruling party. Pointing to several factors, Weiner emphasized the adaptive quality of the Congress party. The party had sought to build alliances with the socially powerful rather than fight against them. That had enabled many Congressites to succeed politically, because those whose opinions carried weight and influence in society had joined or were attracted to the Congress party. The implications of this political strategy for Congress's role in facilitating socioeconomic transformation probably were negative. What was clear, however, was that the Congress party had built a relatively legitimate authority structure. That structure used patronage networks anchored by local notables – the landed, the wealthy, the *panchayat* (local government) leaders, the heads of local co-operatives, and the caste elites.

Twenty-five years later the analytical problem has changed. During the early 1960s, Congress was the dominant political force in each of the five districts discussed in the following chapters. Today, political power is vigorously contested in all of these districts. Even in those districts in which Congress can still win elections, Congress is not the same type of political force that it was in the 1960s; the party may hold power, but Congressites do not readily command widespread respect and authority. The authority structure created by the Congress party has disintegrated; the periphery has become difficult to govern. The "Congress system" began to decline as early as the mid-1960s, and it had almost totally vanished by the mid-1980s. The intellectual problem, then, is to determine what has replaced the Congress system at the periphery and how that change has come about.

There is an important caveat concerning the discussion that follows. The district-level findings presented here compose only a part of the larger study. They are discussed mainly to shed light on the more general theme of how and why India's authority patterns have changed. I have omitted most of the background data on the five districts, as well as some of the ethnographic details concerning local groups. Whereas the analysis presented here is self-sufficient for the purposes of this study, readers wanting greater details on district-level politics should consult Weiner's earlier work.

Each of the following five chapters discusses some themes that are unique to the particular district, as well as a set of themes common to all. The unique themes add to our understanding of the diversity of Indian politics. The element of in-depth description in these chapters should give readers a good sense of the texture of local politics. As readers make their way through these detailed empirical materials, however, it will also be important to keep in mind the more general analytical concerns that run through these chapters.

First, there is the issue of the nature of party organization in local politics. The decline of the Congress party as a local organizational entity is documented in each of the following five chapters. Moreover, it is proposed that, with a few exceptions, the other political parties have also failed to generate local-level organizations. We thus have these questions for analysis: Why are the parties organizationally weak? What are the consequences of such weakness for governing the periphery? After discussing these questions with reference to some specific, district-level evidence in the following five chapters, I shall develop more general answers to these questions in the conclusion to this part of the study.

The second general concern running through these five chapters is the changing structure of community power. The declining capacity of the so-called dominant castes, as well as other "big men," to influence the political behavior of the lower strata is documented. The roots of this growing political fragmentation in local politics are traced back to the spread of democratic politics. Many consequences of these changes are also discussed, including the reassertion of ethnic and religious politics.

The changing role of patronage and the use of public resources in local politics is the third common theme in the following chapters. In his earlier study, Myron Weiner found that patronage had been helpful in greasing the Congress machine and thus in helping Congress establish its authority. Some 25 years later, control over the distribution of public resources has become a major source of political contention. It is not surprising, therefore, that the issue of "fairness" regarding who has access to public resources – the issue of corruption – has emerged as one of most significant political issues in contemporary India.

3

Kheda, Gujarat

Situated between the cities of Ahmedabad and Baroda, on the Gulf of Cambay on India's west coast, Kheda, in the state of Gujarat, is a relatively prosperous district. Though predominantly rural, the district has many urban characteristics: a high literacy rate, communities that have electricity, and villages that are connected by all-weather roads. Nearly 40 percent of the land under cultivation in the district is used for such commercial crops as cotton, tobacco, and plants whose seeds yield oils.[1] Several agro-based industries, such as dairy production, are also located in the area.

A significant proportion of the population – more than 60 percent of the landowning population, or 40 percent of the total population of the district – own and operate small pieces of land comprising 0.5–2.0 hectares (1.25–4.94 acres). This distribution of land may give the impression that the district is dominated by smallholder cultivators. Although that is not inaccurate, the picture at each extreme of the wealth spectrum should not be ignored: At the rich end, nearly a quarter of the land is owned in parcels larger than 10 hectares (24.7 acres) by fewer than 2 percent of the population. At the other end, about a quarter of the population own no land, and another quarter own less than 0.5 hectare per household.

The two major caste communities of the district, the Patidars and the Kshatriyas, constitute nearly 60 percent of the total population.[2] The other communities include the high-caste Brahmans (around 5 percent) at one end of the social spectrum and the Moslems (around 9 percent), the scheduled castes and tribes (around 7 percent), and other low castes at the other

I have benefited from discussions with a number of people in Gujarat during the writing of this chapter. Among those who are not always acknowledged directly in the footnotes are Anil Bhatt, Sujata Patel, Pravin Sheth, and Achyut Yagnik.

1 This figure and other demographic and land data cited here are from Government of Gujarat, Bureau of Economics and Statistics, *Handbook of Basic Statistics, Gujarat State, 1977–8* (Gandhinagar: Government Press, 1980).

2 The total population of the district in 1971 was 2.45 million. Because caste figures are not collected by the census, the caste composition of the district is estimated on the basis of rough data provided by local observers in Kheda. The figures for Moslems and for scheduled castes and tribes, however, are from the census and are taken from the source cited in footnote 1.

end. The latter end makes up as much as one-third of the total population. The Patidars constitute about 20 percent of the district's population and are generally well-off. They are mostly landowners, and they control such economically significant local organizations as dairy cooperatives and universities. Although there are both economic and other types of subcommunity differentiations within the Patidars (e.g., those that define group boundaries for marriage), in terms of both social status and economic power they are the dominant local community. Moreover, the sense of solidarity among the Patidars, especially as far as political behavior is concerned, is relatively strong.[3]

The community of Kshatriyas is something of an artifact, because it is more of a political alliance than a traditional caste community. It includes the high-caste Rajputs (about 5 percent of the population) and numerous gradations below them, including the lower-caste Bariyas (about 35 percent of the population), who over the past several decades have been brought together under Rajput leadership for political purposes. The story of the mobilization of the high-caste and low-caste Kshatriyas around the common theme of shared martial traditions has been told many times.[4] Suffice it to note that the Rajputs are mostly large landowners who cherish their direct descent from traditional ruling groups. The Bariyas, are, by contrast, small landowners, sharecroppers, and landless laborers who aspire to upward mobility.[5] The political unity of these economically and socially disparate groups around caste themes has given the Kshatriyas numerical superiority within the district and thus considerable electoral power. That power often is pitted against the strength that the Patidars derive from their economic dominance and traditional high status. Much of the political drama in this district in the 1980s revolved around the conflict between the socioeconomic power of the Patidars and the electoral power of the Kshatriyas.

Three important themes in Myron Weiner's earlier study of this district can be used to examine how Kheda's political patterns have changed over

---

3 In addition to Myron Weiner, *Party Building in a New Nation: The Indian National Congress* (University of Chicago Press, 1967), chapter 4, for a detailed discussion of the Patidars, see the following: David F. Pocock, *Kanbi and Patidar: A Study of the Patidar Community of Gujarat* (Oxford: Clarendon Press, 1972); John R. Wood, "The Political Integration of British and Princely Gujarat," unpublished Ph.D. dissertation, Columbia University, 1972, chapter 9; Anil Bhatt, "Caste and Political Mobilization in a Gujarat District," in R. Kothari, ed., *Caste in Indian Politics* (New Delhi: Orient Longman, 1973), pp. 299–339; Sujata Patel, "The Anand Pattern: A Socio-historical Analysis of Its Origin and Growth," mimeograph, 1986.

4 In addition to Weiner, *Party Building in a New Nation,* chapter 5, for a detailed discussion of the rise of the "Kshatriya Sabha," see Ghanshyam Shah, *Caste Association and Political Process in Gujarat: A Study of the Kshatriya Sabha* (Bombay: Popular Prakashan, 1975).

5 For a discussion of the differentiations within the Kshatriyas and their political ramifications, see A. H. Somjee, "Social Cohesion and Political Clientilism Among the Kshatriyas of Gujarat," *Asian Survey,* 21:9 (September 1981), pp. 1000–10.

the past 25 years. First, Weiner found the local Congress to be a "well organized, highly successful party unit" that was characterized by "dedicated party workers" who showed "comparatively little internal dissension" and exuded a "tone of rationality and modernity."[6] Second, Patidars were the dominant local community, controlling socioeconomic resources and political power. Their position, however, was even then being challenged. The Kshatriyas had begun to chip away at the power monopoly of the Patidars by winning their first set of local elections. What was noteworthy about the political conflict analyzed by Weiner was that it was carried out within established electoral channels: The local party system had adapted itself to and thus accommodated the changing balance of power.[7] Third, the local elite exercised authority over the conduct of local politics. The base of local power was quite narrow, involving Congress leaders and landowning Patidars,[8] and the local elite derived their legitimacy from an association with the nationalist symbols of the Congress party and, more important, by cultivating their image of being problem-solvers within the local community. Although their organization for problem-solving was like machine politics anywhere, the use of public resources at the discretion of the local elite had not yet come to be viewed as corrupt and self-seeking behavior.

Over the past 25 years in Kheda, each of these political characteristics has undergone considerable change. First, although Congress continued to control most elective offices in the late 1980s, the party organization is now in shambles. Second, the nature of political conflict has been transformed. The Patidars are virtually excluded from elective political offices. Local struggles have also come to involve groups lower in the social hierarchy, even below the low-caste Kshatriyas. More important, political control is no longer contested only in the electoral arena; conflict spills over into the streets, often involving physical force and leading to violence. Lastly, the legitimacy of the local-level elite is now widely questioned. They have come to be viewed as self-seeking, corrupt individuals. Kheda's Congressites are no longer considered to be *sevaks* or problem-solvers. Rather, they are men from whom, in the words of a local peasant, "you hide your young daughters."

CHRONOLOGY OF GUJARAT POLITICS

For those not familiar with Gujarat politics, a brief chronology of recent changes may help situate the district-level observations in their broader context. The state of Gujarat was created in 1960, on the basis of linguistic

6 Weiner, *Party Building in a New Nation*, pp. 69, 86.
7 Ibid., chapters 5 and 6, especially p. 113.
8 Ibid., pp. 77–8, 119.

criteria, being split off from the older and larger state of Bombay. For much of the 1960s, Gujarat was ruled by an undivided Congress party. Morarji Desai had been the most important political leader of undivided Bombay. Even after the creation of a separate state, however, followers of Desai continued to rule Gujarat for almost a decade.

The social base of the undivided Congress party in Gujarat, as elsewhere, rested on the elite castes. Brahman and Baniya communities provided the important leaders of the state. The Patidars, a somewhat lower caste, but a landowning community, were also politically significant. They had been mobilized into the nationalist movement by Sardar Vallabbhai Patel. Important Patidar leaders dominated several districts, including Kheda, and vied for state-level leadership. Some of them even sought to displace the Congress party by aligning with the mobilized Kshatriyas under the umbrella of the Swatantra party.

The split in the national Congress party in 1969 had a profound impact on Gujarat politics. Although the details are quite complex and not pertinent to our immediate purpose (see Chapter 9), the main line of political conflict during the 1970s was between the followers of Indira Gandhi and those of Morarji Desai. It would be difficult to identify the social bases of these competing political forces during the 1970s. Clear alliance patterns did not emerge until the late 1970s. In general terms, the elite castes – the Brahmans, Baniyas, and many Patidars – moved closer to Morarji Desai and to the various parties that came to be associated with him – the Congress (O), the Janata Morcha, and eventually the Janata – parties that were formed and re-formed during that period. By contrast, the Kshatriyas and other lower castes started moving closer to Indira Gandhi.

The political patterns that finally emerged around 1980 from that period of confusion continued during much of the 1980s. Indira Gandhi's Congress in Gujarat evolved a successful electoral strategy that brought together the sizable Kshatriya community in alliance with Harijans, Adivasis, and Moslems, yielding the acronym KHAM for that winning electoral strategy. (That strategy and its consequences are discussed in detail in Chapter 9. For now, suffice it to note that Indira Gandhi chose Madhevsinh Solanki to head that newly created popular Congress alliance.) The landowning Patidars, in turn, emerged as the main opposition to Solanki and to Indira's Congress.

Solanki sought to consolidate his new power base by promising "reservations" to various Congress supporters, but especially to the backward castes. As new legislation was passed, the Patidars reacted with a vengeance. The conflict between Solanki's government and the Patidars initiated what became the most violent political period in Gujarat's contemporary history. How the riots over reservation policies slowly turned into communal warfare will be discussed in Chapter 9. For now, it is important to note that the past several years in Gujarat politics have been characterized by considerable turmoil. Moreover, rising communalism is likely to chip away at the KHAM alliance, favoring the emergence of a Hindu voting bloc, and benefiting the opposition parties at the expense of Congress.

PARTY ORGANIZATION

Observers of Kheda politics are unanimous in their view that Congress's local party organization is now defunct. During my stay in the district, I never met a Congressite at the district office. A local journalist observed that "the district Congress office is never open."[9] The area's major newspaper noted that party organization in Kheda was "non-existent" and that "for two years there has been no electricity or phone [in the Congress district office] because there have been no funds to pay the dues."[10] A member of the Legislative Assembly (MLA) in Gujarat pointed out that "the district committee seldom meets."[11] And what is true for Kheda, according to a senior Congress party official, is true for most other districts in Gujarat: District-level party units are "not active."[12]

A rare meeting of the District Congress Committee (DCC), called to discuss the possibility of organizational elections – a proposal floated by Rajiv Gandhi that still had not been implemented by the late 1980s – demonstrated the typical schisms and factions in the local leadership.[13] The local party boss was Ishwarbhai Chavda, a lower-caste Kshatriya from the town of Anand, who derived his power by virtue of being the father-in-law of Madhevsinh Solanki, Indira Gandhi's favorite Gujarati Congressite. Because Solanki had lost power in 1986 as a result of the antireservation riots (he returned to power for a short period in late 1989), Ishwarbhai's local power was then also insecure. In that meeting he questioned the president of the DCC – Gordhanbhai Patel, a Patidar, but by all accounts a politically insignificant man whom Ishwarbhai had pushed into a position of power two years earlier – as to why he was not consulted about the need for the meeting. The DCC president argued that he was merely following New Delhi's directives, directives that posed a potential challenge to the power of the local boss. That meeting also found the leader of another faction, Natwar Singh Solanki, a Rajput and the head of the once-powerful Kshatriya Sabha, quite vocal and at odds with Ishwarbhai. Natwar Singh's

9 Discussion with Shivubhai Dave (a Kheda journalist), Nadiad, March 15, 1986.
10 *Indian Express* (Ahmedabad), February 1, 1984.
11 Interview with Gordhanbhai J. Patel (MLA from Anand, Kheda district), Gandhinagar, March 10, 1986.
12 Interview with Hasmukh Patel [minister of education, government of Gujarat, and secretary, Gujarat Pradesh Committee, Congress (I)], Ahmedabad, March 11, 1986.
13 The details of this meeting were published in *Indian Express* (Ahmedabad), February 23, 1986. The factional struggle that this news report described was corroborated during several local interviews.

protégé, Amarsinhji Vaghela (a minister in the Gujarat cabinet in the late 1980s), found his position strengthened vis-à-vis Madhevsinh Solanki's group, represented by Ishwarbhai. Mrs. Shantiben Makwana, a local scheduled-caste MLA, who was the wife of a member of Parliament in Delhi and who had been at odds with Madhevsinh Solanki because she had not been made a minister in his cabinet, criticized both the Ishwarbhai group and the Natwar Singh group for their anti-Harijan attitude.

Specific personalities aside, the foregoing account makes two things clear: The effectiveness of the Congress party organization in Kheda is minimal, and the local leadership is quite factionalized. This situation contrasts sharply with what Weiner found in the mid-1960s, when the local Congress party had a stable membership, dedicated cadres, little factionalism, a functioning office with files and records, and periodic internal elections.[14] What happened? The question is especially interesting because Congress remains a significant electoral force in Kheda. During the late 1980s, Congress controlled 14 of the 17 Legislative Assembly seats and both of the parliamentary seats from the district (that situation changed in late 1989 and early 1990) and enjoyed nearly 60 percent of the popular vote (Table 3.1).[15]

A simple answer to the question of how that dramatic political change in Congress's local organization came about would point to Indira Gandhi's national political strategy. After Indira split the old Congress in 1969, the organizational infrastructure was inherited not by Indira's Congress but by Congress (O), where the "O" stands for the organizational wing. Indira

14 During an interview, a former Congressite who had observed the infighting during many of these local political changes summed up the nature of the old Congress in a manner that faithfully echoed Myron Weiner's analysis. His summary is worth quoting in full: "The Congress definitely had an organization. Kheda was a model of it. The [party officials were] democratically elected. They met monthly. They took stock of the situation – took in complaints and discussed. Even the AICC [the national organization of Congress] sent a delegation to 'learn from Kheda.' At both the district and the *taluka* level, the party functioned. [A Congressite] was respected in both the *taluka* and in the district. If anyone had a problem at the village level, they would go to the *taluka* [office]. If that did not work, only then it would go up higher. Shankar Lal Purohit [was] Kheda district's organization secretary. He kept the office open. He was paid. District office was always open. If the *taluka* workers came, there was provision for food and shelter at the district office. [A Congressite] was readily identifiable. Congress [workers] tried to help the people." Interview with Satyam Patel [secretary, Gujarat Pradesh Committee, Congress (R)], Ahmedabad, March 17, 1986.

15 For reasons of space, I have not provided details of parliamentary elections in Kheda. Those interested may note that Congress and Swatantra had one seat each in 1967, but Congress (O) won both seats in 1971, and since then Indira's Congress won both seats in 1977, 1980, and 1984 elections. Congress's share of the vote in the 1980 and 1984 elections was 61.4 and 58.2 percent of the total vote, respectively. For details, see V. B. Singh and Shankar Bose, *Elections in India: Data Handbook on Lok Sabha Elections, 1952–80* (New Delhi: Sage Publications, 1984), Tables III.3.1 and III.4.1, and *Times of India* (Ahmedabad), December 29, 1984.

Table 3.1. *Election results for the Legislative Assembly in Kheda district, Gujarat, 1967–85*

Party	Seats won					Votes received (%)				
	1967	1972	1975	1980	1985	1967	1972	1975	1980	1985
Congress[a]	9	13	9	16	14	50.8	50.9	48.8	61.2	63.4
Congress (O)[b]	—	3	6	—	—	—	33.0	29.4	—	—
Swatantra	7	—	—	—	—	47	3.5	—	—	—
Janata[c]	—	—	—	1	3	—	—	—	23.3	30.4
Jan Sangh[d]	—	—	—	—	—	—	—	3.4	—	—
Bhartiya Janata party[e]	—	—	—	—	—	—	—	—	5.3	3.6
Bhartiya Lok Dal[f]	—	—	—	—	—	—	—	3.5	—	—
Others	—	—	2	—	—	2.2	12.6	14.9	10.2	2.6
Total	16	16	17	17	17	100	100	100	100	100

[a]Known as Congress (I) since 1969.
[b]Founded in 1969 and merged into the Janata party in 1977.
[c]Founded in 1977.
[d]Merged into the Janata party in 1977; broke away in 1980; then reformed as the Bhartiya Janata party in 1980.
[e]Founded in 1980.
[f]Founded in 1974.
Source: Compiled from Election Commission of India, *Report on the General Elections to the Legislative Assembly in India, 1970–2*, Volume II (statistical), V. II-C, Part IV, Table 6 on Gujarat (New Delhi: Government of India Press, 1976); Chief Electoral Officer, Gujarat, *Report on the General Elections to the Gujarat Legislative Assembly*, Statistical Review for 1975 and 1980 (Gandhinagar: Government Central Press, 1975, 1980); *Times of India* (Ahmedabad), March 7, 8, and 9, 1985.

Gandhi went on to improve the political standing of herself and the new party primarily by adopting a populist strategy that linked her as a leader directly to the masses. She and her supporters probably did not perceive a need for a strong party organization in that strategy. Accordingly, Indira never rebuilt the party.[16] What one notices at the local level, therefore, is not so much the transformation of the old Congress but rather the emergence of a new Congress that, given its primary concern with winning

16 A number of local leaders suggested this as a reason why the party organization was never rebuilt. Jinabhai Darjee, a veteran Congress (I) leader of Gujarat, for example, suggested that "people were with us. [At that time] we did not need an organization." Interview (original in Hindi; my translation), Ahmedabad, March 10, 1986. Similarly, another former Congress leader had this to say: "After the 1969 split, we won power but lost all distinctiveness. The party was never rebuilt. We hoped Mrs. Gandhi would [rebuild the party, but] her appeal with people was considerable. Maybe she did not need a party – Congress today is merely a crowd. It is a conglomeration." Interview with Satyam Patel (see footnote 14).

electoral power, thought it did not need and thus did not put down any organizational roots.

This focus on national trends, however, obscures numerous local nuances that may explain why Indira Gandhi thought that she did not need an organizational structure, and it also fails to highlight the adverse political consequences of her strategy. More important, an exclusive focus on Indira Gandhi's role ignores the fact that other political leaders also failed to undertake organizational rebuilding, and it overlooks the many local obstacles that existed by the late 1980s to thwart Rajiv Gandhi's attempts to reinvigorate the party.

After the 1971 elections, when Indira Gandhi's national popularity was confirmed, many Kheda politicians switched their allegiance to Indira's new Congress.[17] Those who switched, however, generally were not the established local politicians, the "old guard" of the Patidars who had participated in the nationalist movement. Rather, those joining Indira Gandhi often were the "newcomers" of Kshatriya background. As a veteran Gujarati politician explained, "old Congress was all full. One needed ten to fifteen years of experience before getting promotion in that party. There were many new opportunities in Indiraji's Congress."[18] Many of the aspiring Kshatriyas, therefore, who were both impatient and wary of the Patidar-dominated old Congress, were attracted to Indira Gandhi. Her "pro-poor" and antiestablishment approach was attractive to this new set, but it would not be decisive until it had demonstrated electoral success.

Those who were attracted to the new Congress in Kheda were individuals who felt excluded from the established power structure and wanted power in a hurry. These people had not spent their formative political years participating in a nationalist movement. Rather, they had grown up observing that lucrative careers could be built in a society of scarcity if one had access to the abundant resources of the interventionist state. These were not people who were interested in joining an organization at the bottom and working their way up slowly, while learning the political ropes and contributing to the strength of the organization. Their underlying motivations were quite different. Their view, for which there was some justification, was that the dominant Patidar Congressites were not individuals who were about to share power and privilege with the Kshatriyas. Rather, the Kshatriya upstarts saw the Patidar elite as highly partisan players who were more likely to act for their own benefit and for the benefit of their caste community. Thus, shortcuts to power were sought as a means of simultaneously displacing the dominant groups and gaining access to state

17 Solanki noted that "as the results of the 1971 poll started rolling in, it became clear that Mrs. Gandhi was victorious. At that time many of us decided to join the new Congress." Interview with Madhevsinh Solanki (former chief minister of Gujarat and an MLA from Kheda district), Gandhinagar, March 11, 1986.
18 Interview with Jinabhai Darjee (see footnote 16).

resources, and Indira Gandhi provided a quick opportunity. The slow, laborious task of building a party organization was never carried out.

The Kshatriya background of this emerging political stratum also had political relevance. The mobilization of lower-caste Kshatriyas, who account for a significant portion of this district's population, often proceeded outside of the formal party structure.[19] As a local journalist explained, "before elections, Natwar Singh Solanki [a Kshatriya leader of Rajput background] will hold these meetings in villages. They are like pujas [prayer meetings]. A naked sword will be worshipped. The prowess and unity of Kshatriyas will be stressed. This is how he and other better off Kshatriyas win elections."[20] This suggests that the new Kshatriya elite, seeking to widen their local electoral support, often did so without feeling a need for and without making any contribution to the development of local party organization.

Indira Gandhi's populism attracted the minority communities of Kheda, namely, the Harijans (scheduled castes), Adivasis (scheduled tribes), and Moslems. The local Kshatriyas' growing alignment with Indira's new Congress created a powerful formula for electoral success. In the words of a seasoned Patidar politician who was no friend of Indira Gandhi, the new coalition represented "all those who wanted power and all those who hoped that exploitation will be reduced."[21] Indira Gandhi's popularity rested on the fact that there are many such groups in India. The four hitherto excluded communities of Kheda – Kshatriyas, Harijans, Adivasis, and Moslems – make up some 60 percent of the district's population. Therefore, throughout the 1970s and especially the 1980s, in spite of the several electoral ups and downs during a period of adjustment (Table 3.1), the KHAM alliance of these four communities provided a winning formula for both Indira Gandhi and the local Kshatriya leaders.

It is important to note the uniqueness of the large Kshatriya support that Congress enjoys in Kheda, as well as in Gujarat as a whole. In other districts, where such support does not exist, the electoral liability of weak party organization is more evident. Even in Kheda, however, some of the adverse consequences that flow from a virtual absence of party organization should be noted.

In addition to winning elections, political parties can help socialize new political elites, serve as an arena for bargaining and compromise below the level of the government, and in a state-led developmental experiment of the Indian type, help implement development programs. In highly competitive political situations, however, winning power often becomes the

---

19 See Shah, *Caste Association and Political Process in Gujarat.*
20 Discussion with Shivubhai Dave (see footnote 9).
21 Interview with Babubhai Jasbhai Patel (former chief minister of Gujarat and a native of Kheda district), Gandhinagar, March 8, 1986.

main concern of political parties. The daunting list of what some consider to be appropriate "party functions" may seem to be only "academic" concerns to political participants in such circumstances. Nevertheless, the significance of party organization for consolidating power has become increasingly clear.

For example, as the Patidars unleashed the antireservation movement in the 1980s (as discussed in Chapter 9), the ruling Kshatriya elite, in spite of their large electoral majority, found themselves helpless against a small but powerful minority. Factionalism among the Congress elite, an incapacity to draw up a coherent plan to deal with the Patidar-led agitation, and the inability to mobilize the government's own supporters emerged as significant obstacles to Congress's effort to deal with concerted minority opposition. The lesson Congress should learn is obvious: It is one thing to displace powerful groups from political office by populist mobilization, but in the absence of an effective party organization it is quite another matter to implement policies that will adversely affect these powerful minorities. In a flash of insight rare among Congressites, one veteran Congress politician understood this: "Congress has no organization. With all this [electoral] support, we could not resist the anti-reservation movement."[22]

Efforts to rebuild the Congress party organization now face formidable local obstacles. Internal party elections, for example, would be one important step in reestablishing the local roots and the legitimacy of party officials. Throughout Kheda there is virtual unanimity that such elections either will not take place or will be so manipulated as to be meaningless. The reasons behind these expectations are also clear. Internal elections would threaten all those individuals (like the local boss Ishwarbhai Chavda) who currently hold powerful positions to which they were appointed because of their close association with those higher up in the party structure.

Internal elections would threaten this entire top-down chain of command that was established when local politicians rushed to join the Indira bandwagon in the early 1970s. The mere idea of internal elections now invokes considerable hostility from those in power. One senior Gujarati politician who is in charge of Congress party affairs, and who would have to be responsible for internal elections in Kheda if they were ever to be held, expressed his hostility in the following terms:

Elections do not make too much difference to the functioning of the party. Similar type of people [similar to those who now occupy the offices] would be elected. Each one of us has been elected in any case [as, for example, in the state assembly elections]. Why do we have to be elected again? Congress was never a structure. Theorists like Rajni Kothari do not understand this. Congress was always a movement. Movements do not need elections. Our nominated bodies are all representative bodies. Is it really all that important to have internal elections?[23]

22 Interview with Jinabhai Darjee (see footnote 16).
23 Interview with Hasmukh Patel (see footnote 12).

Clearly, if Rajiv Gandhi ever wanted to rebuild the party and decided to begin by calling for internal party elections, he would have to go over the heads of all such important officials who currently run party affairs at the state and district levels.

What about the state of organizational affairs in the parties and groups other than Congress? One may legitimately wonder what happened to the old Congress organization that Congress (O) inherited. The answer is rather undramatic: Out of power for nearly two decades (except for some periods during 1975–9), Congress (O), which became part of the Janata party, lost the governmental resources necessary for maintaining a patronage network. Because Congress (O) was never organized around an ideology or a program, but rather was based on patronage, it simply withered away without resources. Of course, the Janata party, like Congress (I), still has a rudimentary local structure. Given its association with the wealthy Patidars of Kheda, moreover, it could be revamped if electoral fortunes should ever shift dramatically in its favor. For now, however, the local Janata is no more a party than is Congress (I).

The growing significance of nonparty groups also deserves mention. A sense that the established party machinery and governmental machinery do not serve the interests of the "oppressed" has led to the rise of activists of various sorts. Several groups that organize the *dalits* (scheduled castes) or the tribal groups are active in Kheda,[24] protecting those at the bottom against various forms of local harassment (discussed further in the next section). These groups may also, over time, be able to put pressure on the main parties and the government to take the interests of the dispossessed more seriously. What is important to recognize, however, is that such organizational activity among the minorities can never make up for the absence of parties that can create electoral majorities, control government, and fill a society's core political space.

POWER CONFLICTS

The major political conflict in Kheda still revolves around the Patidars and the Kshatriyas. The shares of the winners and the losers, however, and the mode in which this conflict is carried out, have changed since Weiner studied the district. Other new developments include an increase in overt conflict between the high and low castes, as well as attempts to bridge some old caste cleavages by creating new cleavages, such as that between Hindus and Moslems.

The source of the conflict between the Patidars and the Kshatriyas is not difficult to understand. Whereas the definitions for inclusion among the Patidars and even the Kshatriyas are largely ascriptive, the conflict

24 Discussion with Achyut Yagnik (social activist), Ahmedabad, March 15, 1986.

between these groups is largely concerned with such acquired "achievements" as wealth and power, especially wealth and power derived from the state.

Data on land and wealth distribution in Kheda according to caste are not available. There is, however, widespread agreement among local observers that "the Patels [or the Patidars] are very well off" and that "there are very few poor Patels" in Kheda. The sources of this prosperity are diverse, but ultimately are rooted in land: "Patels in Kheda control considerable amount of land, most of the business, educational institutions, large parts of the bureaucracy and the Amul dairy."[25] A survey of land-ownership by caste for the whole of Gujarat also found that nearly 70 percent of Patidars owned at least six acres of land per household.[26] Because the Patidars of Kheda are generally the Leva Patidars (the highest subcaste within the Patidars), it is fair to assume that their economic situation in Kheda is at least as good as that for Gujarati Patidars as a whole, and probably much better.

In the recent past, the Patidars were virtually uncontested as the dominant caste in Kheda. Weiner noted that Patidars dominated the ruling Congress party during the early 1960s. Local observers often vividly recall that when they were growing up in a Kheda village, also around the 1950s and early 1960s, "no one walked with their head straight in front of the Patidars."[27] Whereas the Patidars have held on to their economic power, their formerly uncontested high social status and especially their control over electoral positions have been fundamentally challenged. This challenge is at the root of much of the local political tension in Kheda.

The Kshatriyas of Kheda have slowly but surely wrested control of elective offices from the Patidars. As Table 3.2 indicates, 19 of the 25 important political offices in Kheda were by the latter half of the 1980s controlled by the Kshatriyas. The Patidars, with all their wealth and with some 20 percent of the district's population, controlled only two of these offices. Furthermore, it is widely recognized in Kheda today that not only the local assembly seats but also the village and *taluk panchayats* (local governments) and quite a few cooperatives have come under Kshatriya control.

Local Patidars deeply resent this political displacement, especially because this new situation seems to them so incommensurate with the wealth they control and the traditional social status they once enjoyed. Kshatriyas, however, given their numbers, see themselves as the legitimate inheritors

25 Quotations from Shivubhai Dave (see footnote 9).
26 The data were collected by The Centre for Social Studies, Surat, under the directorship of Ghanshyam Shah. See Ghanshyam Shah, "Caste Sentiments, Class Formation and Dominance in Gujarat," mimeograph, 1984, p. 31. A revised version of this paper will appear in Francine Frankel and M. S. A. Rao, eds., *Dominance and State Power in Modern India: Decline of a Social Order* (Oxford University Press, 1990).
27 Discussion with Achyut Yagnik (see footnote 24).

Table 3.2. *Caste distribution of the political elite in Kheda district, Gujarat, 1985*

Caste	Offices held[a]		Percentage of total	
Kshatriyas (Rajputs)	3	} 19[b]	12	} 76
Kshatriyas (Bariyas)	16		64	
Patidars	2		8	
Brahmins	1		4	
Moslems	1		4	
Scheduled caste or tribe	1		4	
Others	1		4	
Total	25		100	

[a]Compiled from interviews and based on information concerning 17 members of the Legislative Assembly, 2 members of Parliament, and 6 *panchayat* presidents.
[b]Of the 19 Kshatriya elite, 10 belonged to the Congress party.

of power through the democratic process. This separation between socio-economic power and control over the local political institutions has created a situation that is inherently tension-ridden. The overt conflict that now periodically results as the two sides jockey for further advantage is not surprising. What is interesting and perhaps even somewhat surprising, however, is that some efforts at cooperation are being made by the two communities in order to break their stalemate; on occasion, the hostilities in both communities have turned not against each other but against those at the bottom of the social scale, namely, the scheduled castes.

The low-level conflict that results from the stalemate between the Patidars and the Kshatriyas has become an enduring feature of Kheda's politics. The Patidars complain that "Solanki wanted to humble Patels." That is why, a Patel spokesman argued, "the Patels' crops and cow dung heaps were burnt. They [the Kshatriyas] damaged the tube wells of many Patels by throwing stones in the machine and choking them."[28] These and other similar actions, according to Patels, are attempts to intimidate them and "break their fighting spirit."

The Kshatriya leaders, in turn, point to the frustration they continuously experience because of the limited room they have for maneuvering the government's resources and policies toward their constituents. Realizing these limits, Solanki did not attempt any real socioeconomic reforms, not even reforms resembling what "Urs did in Karnataka."[29] When he did try

28 Interview with Babubhai Jasbhai Patel (see footnote 21).
29 Interview with Madhevsinh Solanki (see footnote 17). For an analysis of Devraj Urs's reforms in Karnataka, see Atul Kohli, *The State and Poverty in India: The Politics of Reform* (Cambridge University Press, 1987), chapter 4.

something minimal, such as increasing the reservations for the lower castes, major agitations resulted throughout Gujarat. Thus, Solanki further commented, "Democratically they [the Patidars] failed to oust me. So they resorted to other methods. But this did not budge us. We are also experienced. We can tackle street violence . . . we have done it before."[30] Thus, although select Kshatriyas have access to the state's resources, it has not been possible to institute public policies that would benefit the Kshatriyas as a community or other low-caste groups of the KHAM alliance. In spite of being in power, Congress's electoral coalition remains fragile and vulnerable. The constraints that social power imposes on state actions have become a real source of frustration for those occupying political offices.

In addition to the hostilities and violence that have marred the Gujarati political scene throughout the 1980s (see Chapter 9) and have attracted considerable public attention, there are other interesting trends. While Ahmedabad was burning as a result of caste conflict, and agitations in the north of Gujarat were intense, the situation in Kheda was relatively calm. One important explanation for this relative quiescence is that the Leva Patidars of Kheda have many family connections overseas. For example, the Patels who own and operate motels in North America and many Patel business families in East Africa have close family ties to Kheda Patels. Thus, young Patels in Kheda often have "foreign horizons." They do not tend to become especially anxious regarding their own educational opportunities when new reservation quotas for the disadvantaged are announced.[31]

Important instances of cooperation between the Patels and the Kshatriyas are also beginning to emerge. Two examples will illustrate the point. First, during the Legislative Assembly elections in 1985, a prominent local Rajput MLA in Kheda, who is now a minister in the Gujarat cabinet, was supplied with jeeps for campaign transportation by the local Patidars. The reason was simple. The Patidars knew that the Kshatriya candidate of the Congress party was likely to win, and they wanted to have working relations with whoever came to occupy the position of power.[32] Second, the powerful Kshatriya boss of Kheda, Ishwarbhai Chavda, chose to support a Patidar, Gordhanbhai Patel, for the position of president of the DCC. The underlying reasoning was that Gordhanbhai Patel was very influential in local educational affairs. Congress Kshatriyas, even though in power, needed

---

30 Interview with Madhevsinh Solanki (see footnote 17).
31 A number of local observers noted this during interviews. Three of these were Babubhai Jasbhai Patel (see footnote 21), Satyem Patel (see footnote 14), and Achyut Yagnik (see footnote 24).
32 Interview with Amarsinhji Vaghela (minister of cooperation, government of Gujarat, and a Congress (I) MLA from Kheda district), Gandhinagar, March 10, 1986.

access to educational institutions to help their students gain admission and their supporters gain teaching positions.[33]

Although other examples of cooperation could be cited, it is difficult to judge the overall extent of such cooperation. My own judgment is that low-level conflict between the two communities continues as the dominant tendency within Kheda, but new trends toward cooperation are beginning to emerge. Both of these tendencies are evident in the following comment expressed by a prominent local Patel: "Patels have found out, being rich, that every dog has its price. So they have decided to pay the price and get things done. These Kshatriyas have no principles. They are poor. So they can be bought."[34] Leaving aside the issue of who is more principled and who "buys" whom, the fact is that in spite of caste distinctions, the political elite and the economic elite of Kheda, though still untrusting, are learning to work together. Were it not for the fact that the power of the political elite rests on the existence of caste and community sentiments, we might well have seen a more rapid erosion of caste-based hostilities, at least among the elite who run the local political economy.

Finally, in this discussion of political conflict within Kheda, the hostility and violence that on occasion have been unleashed against those at the bottom of the socioeconomic hierarchy need attention. The extent of such hostility and conflict is difficult to measure. Nevertheless, the two incidents cited next give a sense of the changing social reality. The first of these incidents occurred in the context of the statewide antireservation agitations led by the Patels against the Solanki government during 1981. The second incident occurred in 1986, but was not part of a wider political struggle.

Example 1. Uttarsanda village, Nadiad *taluka,* Kheda district, February 20, 1981: Patel landowners burned an effigy of Yogendra Makwana (a native Harijan who was a union minister under Rajiv Gandhi). Policemen were present, but left at the behest of the *sarpanch* (village head, and a Patel). That night, a large mob of Patels surrounded the Dalit *basti* (neighborhood). They carried sticks with kerosene-soaked rags tied at one end. The *sarpanch* had released the kerosene quota to caste Hindus only the day before, a few days earlier than scheduled. Sticks were set aflame and thrown at the Dalit huts from all sides. Dalits offered some resistance but were outnumbered. Dalit elders asked their youth to go get help. Nearby dispensary officials did not let the youths use the telephone. Two strong Dalits had to run all the way to the Nadiad town to a Christian missionary, who finally arranged for the police. By the time police arrived, 24 homes had been burned. Later, when police action was taken against those who had started the fire, the Patels imposed an economic boycott on the local Dalits, refusing to employ them, and employed instead migrant tribal labor.[35]

33 Discussion with Shivubhai Dave (see footnote 9).
34 Interview with Satyam Patel (see footnote 14).
35 This information is extracted from an extremely valuable report prepared by one of the

Example 2. Golana village, Cambay *taluka,* Kheda district, January 30, 1986: Conflict broke out over a three-acre piece of land that a local Vankar (member of a scheduled caste) had been allotted by the government for a housing site. The piece of land was near the Rajput *mohalla* (living quarters), and the Rajputs wanted to use the land for threshing purposes. The Vankars, under the guidance of a social worker from Ahmedabad, decided to put a hut on the land in order to secure their hold. The Rajputs tried to get a stay order on the land allotment from the courts, but failed. Following this, about 200 Rajputs surrounded a group of Vankars, including the landowner. As the Vankars ran for their lives, the Rajputs chased them, "broke open houses and shot" the landowner. "Not content with having killed him, they shot at him again and again in the head, face and into his anus." Following that, four more Harijans associated with the conflict were murdered. "It was commonly believed" that the Rajputs "master-minded the attack and SRP [police] men were told not to provide protection to the Vankars."[36]

As one attempts to understand the social dynamics behind these events, what is notable is that the specifics of these events are not unique. Local interviews and reports by other observers reveal that such acts of upper-caste violence against the lower castes are increasing and tend to have certain characteristics in common. For example, the analyst studying the antireservation agitation described in Example 1 concluded that the reservation issue was not the main cause behind caste violence. Rather, the violence was "a manifestation of the caste and class contradictions that have been building up in Gujarat."[37] Similarly, the reporter studying Golana (Example 2) concluded quite independently that the "ghastly murders" represented broader issues: a "climax of several factors like caste rivalry, ego clashes and police apathy."[38] These general underlying factors will be examined briefly.

First, the violence involves groups that for a long time had interacted with each other around fairly set patterns. As those patterns have begun changing because of commercialization and democratization, the results have been profoundly destabilizing. The perpetrators of violence often are the upper castes, Patels and Rajputs in the examples cited earlier, who enjoy high status and own land. The victims often are those who work for the upper castes and have been in positions of subservience, Dalits or Harijans in both the foregoing examples.

Second, the specific issues around which conflict erupts often involve

many civil-rights groups that have become active in India over the past decade. See Committee for the Protection of Democratic Rights, *The Gujarat Agitation and Reservations* (Bombay: Super Book House, 1981), pp. 17–19.

36 Reported in *Indian Express* (Ahmedabad), January 31, 1986. The direct quotations are all from the newspaper report.
37 Committee for the Protection of Democratic Rights, *The Gujarat Agitation,* p. 34.
38 *Indian Express* (Ahmedabad), January 31, 1986.

both concrete resources, such as land, and violations of established social patterns in which hitherto subservient groups dare to challenge established dominance. Consider Example 2 discussed earlier. In and around this area, for a series of historical reasons, including the "Harijan uplift" programs of Gandhi, the Vankars have experienced upward mobility. This has emboldened the Vankars vis-à-vis the upper castes. The upper castes, in turn, resent this social challenge. That was clearly evident in a statement by a Rajput leader in Kheda shortly after the incident: "What else could be the fate of the Harijans if they defy the village *panchayat* bosses?"[39] The implication was clear: If those who have been at the bottom of the social hierarchy for centuries, emboldened now because of changing economic and political conditions, dare question the authority of their social superiors, they must expect to invoke the wrath of the socially powerful.

This last point directs attention to the third common element in the growing conflict, namely, the relative incapacity of the state and its agents to halt the violence of the upper castes against the lower castes. The local political elite have close links to the members of the upper castes in the villages, either because they are of the same caste or because their positions of power have led to some established social relationship. What the police do or refrain from doing is easily influenced by the local political elite. Whenever intercaste violence breaks out, the political elite, such as a local MLA, often come to the defense of the upper-caste perpetrators simply by neutralizing the police. The same results can follow for other reasons: because the police inspectors are of the same caste as those who unleash the violence, because the police are paid off, or simply because the police are concentrated in urban areas and are not readily available to deal with village conflicts.

These common elements in caste violence point to a frightening possibility: As the socioeconomic positions of the lower castes improve, are they likely to be victimized even more harshly by those whose dominance and privileges they challenge? Caste hostilities in Kheda still have not reached the levels seen in other states in India, such as Bihar (see Chapter 8). Nevertheless, the relatively low but increasing levels of social hostilities seen in this part of the country are beginning to threaten the patterns of electoral alliances.

For example, the low-level hostility and the potential for open violence by the Rajputs against the scheduled castes fundamentally threatens the KHAM alliance. Both Harijans and the lower-caste Kshatriyas have become wary of the Kshatriya leadership, especially because that leadership failed to mobilize any support to resist the antireservation movement. Rajiv Gandhi's abandonment of the antipoverty emphasis has also made the

---

39 The statement was made by Natwar Singh Solanki and was reported in the *Indian Express* (Ahmedabad), February 23, 1986.

lower strata wary of the new Congress. Similarly though violence against Moslems still is rare in Kheda, reports of such violence in Ahmedabad are not rare. Local observers suggest that Moslems are becoming alienated from Congress. Whether or not that is true, what is clear is that opportunities for new patterns of mobilization have opened up. As conflict among groups grows, electoral coalitions are far from stable; the local political situation, in the words of a seasoned observer, has become "very fluid."[40]

AUTHORITY OF THE LOCAL ELITE

The typical member of the local political elite that Weiner encountered in Kheda in the early 1960s was a landowning Patidar Congressite. Although the Rajput challengers were very much part of the political scene, it was the Patidar leadership that had, since independence, enjoyed the status of an established local elite.

Two aspects of this Patidar leadership in the past are important for an analysis of the changes in authority patterns. First, the Patidars were genuine local leaders; they were not imposed on Kheda by national or state authorities. Second, an important basis for this local leadership was that the traditional high positions of the Patidars in local communities were largely undisputed. The roles of the political elite and the social elites still had not been sharply differentiated. As a result, the high standing of the Patidars in the civil society gave them considerable legitimacy even in the political arena. The local leadership, though narrow and elitist, was genuinely representative of the local community, because the community itself was very hierarchical. Thus, the basis for authority and civility in local politics was provided by one not-so-democratic trait – narrow, elite domination, in part derived from ascriptive characteristics – and one quite democratic trait – genuine grass-roots leadership, respected in and representative of the local community in regional and national affairs.

The conditions that gave rise to that pattern of local authority have changed. Nationalism has declined, and with it the perception of legitimacy that comes from association with nationalist symbols. That was inevitable. The cohesive, corporate quality of the traditional hierarchical society has also declined. That was clearly evident in the foregoing discussion of the increasing power conflicts within Kheda. Whereas the rates and the patterns of these changes may have been different, it probably was also inevitable that the traditional social cohesion would gradually erode. What was not inevitable, however, was that an alternative basis of local authority would not emerge, and that requires discussion.

The genuine grass-roots leadership that Weiner found in the decades following independence cannot be found in Kheda today, certainly not

40 Interview with Jinabhai Darjee (see footnote 16).

within the framework of the main parties. A leader like Madhevsinh Solanki was able to grow in stature largely because of his close association with Mrs. Gandhi and with his father-in-law, Ishwarbhai Chavda, who is now the tacit Congress boss within Kheda. Chavda's chosen men now occupy key positions in district politics and as district representatives in state politics. As Solanki's local power declined between 1986 and 1989, other Congressites from the district, such as Amarsinhji Vaghela, favored by the new leadership in the state capital, had become prominent. It is clear that political prominence has increasingly become a function of association with those higher up, rather than a result of building an independent local power base. The result is that those who occupy political offices do not readily command respect; there is a growing authority vacuum at the local level.

It would be wrong to assign to Indira Gandhi the entire blame for the growing tendency for local politics to operate in this top-down manner. Although Indira's role was clearly important, the local situation also contributed. Because of the severity of the power conflict between the Kshatriyas and the Patidars within Kheda, and the growing conflicts between the upper and lower castes, there are no longer any simple consensual ways of resolving such conflicts. It is difficult to imagine anything like a return to the old, seemingly consensual Congress party. Those who yearn for the old days would do well to ponder the highly elitist nature of that old consensus, civility, and authority. It is the increasing democratization of traditional hierarchies that has contributed to erosion of the old system. Of course, a centralizing leader seeking to thwart the development of new institutions was not the only possible outcome, or even a necessary outcome. But a political situation of severe power conflict does not easily lend itself to the building of bottom-up organizations that rely on negotiation and compromise for decision making. In such situations, winning elections by manipulating the sentiments of caste and religion, and by generating a direct leadership following, is by far the easiest political strategy for gaining and holding power.

To move away from these general considerations, a more specific discussion of those who occupy political offices in contemporary Kheda will further clarify some of the problems of local-level authority. Two broad categories can encompass most individuals who now occupy political offices. I interviewed or gathered information on 25 members of the local elite in Kheda (Table 3.2). Of these, 16 were of lower-caste Kshatriya background, and another 3 were from groups that were also relatively low in the social hierarchy; only 6 of these local officeholders came from traditional high-caste backgrounds, such as Brahman, Patidar, or Rajput.

Clearly, the authority of those who occupy political office in Kheda can no longer be derived by virtue of high position in the traditional socioeconomic hierarchy. What has further weakened the prospects for legitimizing politicians' hold on power through nontraditional means is that the rationality and legality of democratic norms have been severely undermined by both regional and national leaders. For example, interviews revealed widespread agreement in Kheda that most of those who had been elected would not have been elected if they had not had close associations with the leadership. Whether or not that is true, where issues of authority and legitimacy are concerned, perceptions are important. The basis of these perceptions was twofold. First, the issue of who "got a ticket" (received Congress's approval) to run for election was not decided by local authorities. Many of those interviewed believed that "Solanki's list was accepted by the Congress high command."[41] For the politically active citizenry, that confirmed that so long as Solanki remained in favor in New Delhi, the way to get into office was to ingratiate oneself with Solanki.

Even more important was a second perception. Most observers and participants that I interviewed, including those in office, believed that a large number of those elected in 1985 would not have been elected without the "Rajiv wave."[42] This suggests that those who occupy office are perceived as being there not because they have an independent political base and thus democratic legitimacy but because of a series of procedures that might well be considered manipulative or illegitimate from the standpoint of democratic norms. Anyone who could get a Congress ticket, according to popular perception, could be elected to office in the 1980s.

Looking at the group of elected officials, more specific patterns were evident. Among the 17 members of the Gujarat Legislative Assembly from Kheda, three pathways to political office were followed. The first and smallest group of four MLAs consisted of the "protected" candidates who, for legal or informal reasons of "affirmative action," had to be given tickets. These consisted of the Harijan, Moslem, and women candidates.

The second and largest group of some seven or eight MLAs consisted of candidates for whom the pathway to office can best be described as neotraditional. At least five of these MLAs got tickets because they were related to or enjoyed caste-based affinities to Kheda's local political boss, Ishwarbhai Chavda. Another two or three in this group came from traditional political families. The latter generally enjoyed a greater perception of legitimacy than did those foisted on the community because of their links to the local leadership. What this whole group shared, nevertheless, was that they reached positions of power primarily because of their ascriptive traits, whether derived from family or caste. An important impli-

---

41 Both Congress and opposition politicians agreed with this conclusion with reference to the 1985 Legislative Assembly elections. This quotation is from an interview with Babubhai Jasbhai Patel (see footnote 21). Jinabhai Darjee (see footnote 16), however, also agreed.
42 I asked Amarsinhji Vaghela (the only MLA from Kheda who is now a minister in the Gujarat cabinet) how many Kheda MLAs would have won without the "Rajiv wave." His answer: "very few." Interview with Vaghela (see footnote 32).

cation follows: Although this discussion focuses on what has changed in the political process, many of the old ways remain, and family and caste relations still dominate local politics.

The third group of five MLAs represents an emerging trend that gravely threatens the prospect of building democratic authority. This new type of local politician is the ruffian. In order to understand their growing significance, one must understand what it takes to get into political office these days. As one local political veteran described it, in addition to riding the right national political wave,

you have to collect money. You must make promises to moneyed people that you will do things for them once elected. You have to meet with caste leaders – [to] get their support. You have to have a network of bad characters supporting you. They disrupt meetings of opposition candidates and protect you. You then have to have influence with polling officers. This does not always work – but people try. This is mainly so when my people bring forward voters, their legitimacy will not be questioned. [Influence with polling officers] also helps when votes are being counted. [*Goondas* and criminals] are very important [in winning elections]. Every politician needs a network of them. They wield influence. Even in Kheda there is a lot of this – though not as much as in Ahmedabad. These bad elements intimidate voters. They can also mobilize force. They are very important.[43]

Within Kheda, this ruffian element, though still a minority, nevertheless represents the most important emerging trend. One local leader, Amarsinhji Vaghela, can be seen as representative. A number of observers suggested – though such allegations seldom can be confirmed – that Vaghela made his political career patronizing bootleggers, smugglers, and thugs. He has changed political alliances as often as necessary and is reported to charge a certain sum of money from young men, and sexual favors from young women, in return for his help in securing government jobs. His type may be a minority, but he is the only MLA from Kheda who is now also a minister in the Gujarat cabinet. This type of leader is best understood as the product of an authority vacuum, within which those who can muster force and money will readily gain political influence.

According to local observers, with the emergence of leaders like Vaghela as Kheda's important politicians, the "Sanjay culture"[44] has finally arrived in a district that Weiner had found to be a model of organizational rationality and modernity. Although this is not yet the dominant way to positions of power, it is an important new tendency. It is not too surprising, therefore, that the authority of the local elite is increasingly being questioned. In the words of a local Congress leader, "people do not think of

43 Interview with Babubhai Jasbhai Patel (see footnote 21).
44 The term "Sanjay culture" in India generally refers to the growing tendency in politics toward the inclusion of ruffians, criminals, and thugs. The name given to this trend derives from Sanjay Gandhi, Indira Gandhi's son, who died in the early 1980s, and who inducted many of these "bad elements" into positions of leadership.

a [Congressite] as a *sevak* [helper] anymore; they rather think of him as a selfish crook."[45]

CONCLUSION

A survey of politics in Gujarat's Kheda district highlights a number of trends: Political conflicts among local groups have intensified; the stability of electoral coalitions has declined; the legitimacy of those occupying political offices has come to be widely questioned; political conflicts often lead to violence. None of these trends suggests that political order in this district has collapsed; such a conclusion would be inaccurate. Political offices in Kheda are won by elections, and control of most local political offices goes to the members of whichever community casts the most votes.

These factors impart some degree of democratic authority to the way political affairs are still conducted in Kheda, and yet this discussion documents how the political picture has changed quite remarkably over the past 25 years. Both the authority of local leaders and the efficacy of such local authority structures as the dominant party and the police continue to decline.

What complicates any analysis of this type of political change is an issue discussed in Chapter 2, namely, that the growing problems of governability can be both causes and consequences of certain political trends. For example, growing conflict among social groups can undermine the functioning of consensual political parties. At the same time, however, weakness of institutions like political parties makes it difficult to resolve social conflict peacefully, thus further contributing to the conflict. Similarly, weak parties make it more likely that the functions of political recruitment and socialization will not be performed adequately and that crooks and ruffians may gain political office. Conversely, it is also clear that as more ruffians and corrupt individuals join a party, the weaker the party will be as a coherent organization. Mutually reinforcing relationships of this sort make neat causal analysis difficult and tautological explanations likely. Careful observations over time, however, can help delineate some causal variables that are more important than others for explaining the decline of local authority structures.

To sum up, the decline of the Congress party organization in Kheda was in part a consequence of a national trend, namely, the split in the party in 1969 and the subsequent adoption of a populist political strategy by Indira Gandhi. Local conditions, however, also contributed. The old Congress in Kheda was dominated by the Patidars. The Kshatriya challengers were not accommodated within the old organization. Indira Gandhi offered these challengers a chance to win power outside the old party organization.

45 Interview with Jinabhai Darjee (see footnote 16).

Moreover, the fact that Kshatriya electoral support could be readily generated through *pujas* and other neotraditional modes of political mobilization further reduced the need to expend effort in building a political organization. The organizational decline in this district had several causes: the political choices made by national leaders, growing local power conflict that could not be accommodated within the old dominant organization, and unique local conditions that made organizational activity somewhat peripheral to the central political goal of winning elections and controlling political offices.

The growing conflict within the district is mainly political in nature, though struggles over socioeconomic resources are contributing factors. The conflict between the Patidars and the Kshatriyas, for example, is essentially political, the prize being control over state offices and state resources. The Kshatriyas were mobilized primarily to win elections. Once they came to control political offices, their alienation from the Patidars was complete. As the Kshatriyas have sought to use state power to improve their socioeconomic status, increasing their educational opportunities and obtaining jobs via reservations, the conflict between these communities has intensified and often has led to violence.

The other major line of conflict within the district is between the higher and lower castes, who on occasion have engaged in brutal violence. The sources of disagreement are partly economic, such as ownership of land, but there is also the challenge to the authority of the upper castes posed by the desire of the low castes for upward mobility. The refusal of the state to intervene in such conflicts has helped create a situation in which the socially powerful are free to unleash their vengeance on the weak in the villages without any external force to obstruct them. The deeper, "independent" causes of these growing conflicts within the district are the increasing democratic struggles for power, strife over issues of status and economic resources, the failure of state institutions to provide a systematic arena for bargaining, and failure of the state to control the violence of the socially powerful against the weak.

Finally, the declining perception of the legitimacy of those who occupy political offices in Kheda is both a cause and a consequence of the general organizational decline. The symbols of nationalism that once imparted some degree of legitimacy to an earlier generation of local political elite in this area have now totally lost their political efficacy. Given the social origins of the new elite, they have no traditional high social status on which to build. Democratic legitimacy has not yet replaced the legitimacy formerly derived from social traditions and nationalism, partly because of the time it takes for democracy to become established. Also, the procedures of democracy have been flagrantly violated, often by those in office. As power is associated more and more with the leaders higher up, few among the local elite command respect and authority within the community. Into this vacuum have rushed the new Indian politicians, who can readily mobilize money and force through illegal means. The political spaces left open by the decline of established authority are being filled by those who can create localized de facto "ministates," or local centers of power. The emergence of such power centers has further contributed to the decline of authority. The fluidity of the political situation, in turn, leaves open the possibility of various new forms of mobilization by demagoguery.

The underlying causes of the decline in the authority of the elite and the efficacy of local authority structures include some conditions that are unique to Kheda. Other factors, however, are of a more general nature; these will be discussed later in the analyses of other districts. Such general factors include the role of the political elite who put considerations of winning elections above any other purposive political action, the weakening of local political institutions, and, most important, the growing struggle over access to the state's power and resources among contending social groups.

4

Guntur, Andhra Pradesh

Guntur district, in the state of Andhra Pradesh, is in the delta on the southeast coast of India where the Krishna River empties into the Bay of Bengal.[1] Although Guntur is relatively prosperous by Andhra standards, Andhra's per capita income is somewhat below India's national average. It is a densely populated rural district, with about two-thirds of its cultivated area used for food crops. As is not surprising for a delta, paddy rice is the most significant food crop of the area. Cotton is now the leading nonfood commercial crop, followed by oil-seed crops and tobacco. Two aspects of land ownership in the district are noteworthy: First, Guntur, like much of Andhra, has a high percentage (more than 60 percent) of landless laborers among its rural working population.[2] According to census data, Andhra is the only state in India in which the number of landless laborers exceeds the number of landowning cultivators. Second, there are few large landowners in the district. More than 75 percent of the land is owned in plots of 1–10 hectares (2.5–24.7 acres).

Kammas and Reddis are the two most important landowning agricultural

In addition to the interviews cited throughout this chapter, I learned about Guntur politics from a number of individuals in Hyderabad and Guntur who, for one reason or another, are not always quoted directly. These included K. C. Alexander, N. Inniah, P. A. V. Prasad, M. V. Rama Murty, Madhev Rao, Narsingh Rao, Balwanth Reddy, and K. R. Sastry.

1 The Guntur district analyzed here is not identical with the one analyzed by Myron Weiner in *Party Building in a New Nation: The Indian National Congress* (University of Chicago Press, 1967), part III. Administrative changes in the 1970s created a new district – Prakasam – south of Guntur. This new district includes the Ongole *taluk* and parts of the Baptla and Narasaraopet *taluks* that were formerly part of Guntur. Those changes reduced the size of the old Guntur district, resulting in some reduction in population and a reapportionment of 4 of the 25 assembly seats. Those administrative changes, however, were not so significant as to make comparison between the old and the new Guntur difficult. The new Guntur district retains the core of the old Guntur district.

2 The total population of the district in 1981 was 3.4 million. The rural working population was approximately 1 million. The demographic and land data cited here are taken from Government of Andhra Pradesh, Bureau of Economics and Statistics, *Statistical Abstract 1981* (Hyderabad: Government Secretariat Press, 1983).

castes in the area.[3] Exactly how many Kammas and Reddis are in Guntur is not known. On the basis of the 1931 census and estimates provided by local observers, the following figures can be suggested: Kammas are about 18–20 percent of the local population. As the largest landowning group, they come closest to being the district's dominant caste. The Reddis, who also are important in local economic and political life, constitute about 9–10 percent. The Brahmans are no more than 5 percent. Many castes that are considered to be backward combine to constitute as much as 40 percent of the district's population. It is important to note that as far as the *jati* subdivisions are concerned, the so-called backward classes are extremely heterogeneous, comprising as many as 25 castes. The scheduled castes and tribes, concerning whom more data are available from the census, compose less than 15 percent of the population, as do the Moslems and Christians individually. The scheduled castes and tribes, some Moslems, and many from the backward classes are generally landless laborers.

When Myron Weiner analyzed the politics in Guntur in the 1960s, the Congress party was the dominant political force in the district, as well as in Andhra as a whole.[4] Unlike in the Kheda district, Weiner did not find the Congress party organization in Guntur to be well developed. Multicaste factions, involving both Kamma and Reddi leadership, contested for power and privilege within the Congress party. Instead of debilitating the party, however, that factionalism had a positive consequence. It prompted competing leaders to broaden their power base and incorporate more of the excluded groups. What further strengthened Congress's local position in the early 1960s was the recent introduction of local rural government: *panchayat raj*. *Panchayats* had brought new public resources into the district. That enhanced Congress's capacity as the ruling party to dispense patronage. Along with that growing control over local resources, Congress's capacity to absorb various competing factions increased. Thus, the factional struggles and patronage dispensation that were the core characteristics of the Guntur Congress helped Weiner to explain Congress's dominant political position in Guntur.

Twenty-five years later, Congress is no longer the most important political force in the district or in Andhra as a whole. Although Congress remains a major political force in Guntur, both the district and the state were until recently controlled by a regional party (1983–9), the Telugu Desam (TDP), led by a well-known Andhra movie actor turned politician, N. T. Rama Rao (hereafter, NTR). Kammas and Reddis are still the

3 In addition to Weiner, *Party Building in a New Nation*, chapters 7 and 8, for background information on the Kammas and the Reddis, see Selig Harrison, *India: The Most Dangerous Decades* (Princeton University Press, 1960), pp. 204–45, and Carolyn M. Elliot, "Caste and Faction Among the Dominant Castes: The Reddys and Kammas of Andhra," in Rajni Kothari, ed., *Caste in Indian Politics* (New Delhi: Orient Longman, 1970).
4 Weiner, *Party Building in a New Nation*, part III.

principal groups from which Guntur's political elite have arisen. However, the backward classes have also emerged as a significant political force. Even the electoral support of the scheduled castes and tribes can no longer be taken for granted by competing political parties. As competition between rival parties has intensified, and as power struggles within the civil society have come to involve previously unmobilized groups, two important new political trends are appearing: First, local governments, the *panchayats,* have become objects of intense competition; the struggle over patronage has transformed local institutions so as to serve the interests of the new ruling party. Second, below the more noticeable and publicized interparty rivalries there is emerging in Guntur the same set of political issues observed in Kheda, namely, the use of force to settle political disagreements.

The political changes over 25 years in this part of India suggest three important issues for analysis: (1) How and why did the Congress party lose its one-party dominance, and how does one explain the rise of a competitive regional party under the leadership of a movie actor? (2) What is the changing nature of the power conflict in Guntur, among social groups as well as among competing parties? (3) What will be the consequences of these power conflicts for both the local governments and the authority of those in power? It should be noted that the first of these issues, the relative decline of Congress and the rise of NTR, can be understood only with reference to Andhra politics as a whole. Because Andhra politics are not discussed elsewhere in this volume, the next section provides an overview of political change in Andhra.

THE CHANGING CONTEXT OF ANDHRA POLITICS

When Congress was routed from power by the Janata party in 1977, nationally as well as in most northern Indian states, Andhra remained one of the few Congress strongholds. Within six years, however, after more than three decades of uninterrupted rule, Congress was thrown out of power in Andhra in 1983 by a new regional party. The TDP, led by NTR, ruled Andhra for more than six years. Andhra was one of the few Indian states that was not swept up by the "Rajiv wave" in 1984 and 1985. NTR's party lost power in late 1989, and a competitive two-party system of sorts seems likely to endure. The process underlying this significant political change from Congress rule to the emergence of NTR and back to Congress need not be analyzed in great detail here.[5] Only a broad outline of what happened is necessary for the analysis of district politics that follows.

5 My own somewhat more detailed interpretation of this political change is available: Atul Kohli, "The NTR Phenomenon in Andhra Pradesh: Political Change in a South Indian State," *Asian Survey* (October 1988), pp. 991–1002. Other detailed discussions of Andhra

Most observers of Andhra politics suggest a familiar story: Congress's decline within Andhra was caused by repeated central intervention. Between 1978 and 1983, for example, Indira Gandhi installed four different chief ministers in Andhra. None of these men had any significant independent political base. They were appointed simply because they had proved their loyalty to Indira or to Sanjay Gandhi. Two of them had even lost their Legislative Assembly seats in elections and were brought back into positions of power from the political wilderness. In the words of a seasoned Andhra politician, the reason such candidates were appointed was because they were "weak men" who were not likely to pose any threat to the continuation of Indira Gandhi's power position within Andhra. He explained: "When you put a weak man in, how long is he going to last? The first impression is, who is this man? Why should he be above us? . . . An elected person has a different feeling about his position than an appointed man. An elected man is liked by his people. Appointed man does not have confidence."[6] The weakness of these appointed chief ministers, without an independent political base, encouraged rebellion from other power contenders. Indira Gandhi and her advisers chose to meet such power challenges by replacing their first appointees with other weak leaders, hoping that the new appointees could muster enough support to govern, but would not become so powerful as to attempt to dictate terms to New Delhi.

As each of these imposed chief ministers failed, Andhra sank deeper into political instability. The chief ministries, the cabinet, and other important positions changed hands almost every year. What was worse, each time a new administration was installed, those who had been left out of the choice positions began conspiring immediately for another change in leadership. It also became quite clear to the citizenry that most of the

politics are available: V. Hanumantha Rao, *Party Politics in Andhra Pradesh, 1956–83* (Hyderabad: ABA Publications, 1983); N. Innaiah, *Saffron Star over Andhra Pradesh* (Hyderabad: Book Links Corporation, 1984); Ratna Naidu, "Symbolic Imagery Used by the Telugu Desam in Andhra Elections (1983)," in George Mathew, ed., *Shift in Indian Politics: 1983 Elections in Andhra Pradesh and Karnataka* (New Delhi: Concept Publishing, 1984), pp. 129–38; G. Ram Reddy, "Andhra Pradesh: The Citadel of Congress," in Iqbal Narain, ed., *State Politics in India* (Meerut: Meenakshi Prakashan, 1976), pp. 1–29; G. Ram Reddy, "Politics of Accommodation: The Case of Andhra Pradesh," mimeograph, a revised version of which will be published in Francine Frankel and M. S. A. Rao, eds., *Dominance and State Power in Modern India: Decline of a Social Order* (Oxford University Press, 1990); M. Shatrugna, "Emergence of Regional Parties in India: Case of Telugu Desam," in Mathew, ed., *Shift in Indian Politics*, pp. 95–103; G. Srinivas, M. Shatrugna, and G. Naravana, "Social Background of Telugu Desam Legislators," in Mathew, ed., *Shift in Indian Politics*, pp. 104–27; F. D. Vakil, "Congress Party in Andhra Pradesh: A Review," in Mathew, ed., *Shift in Indian Politics*, pp. 61–93.
6 Interview with Brahmananda Reddy, former Congress chief minister of Andhra Pradesh (1963–71), Hyderabad, March 22, 1986.

important political decisions concerning the state were increasingly being made not in Hyderabad but in New Delhi. These two tendencies – the incapacity of Congress leaders to form a working government and the growing dependence of regional Congress leaders on New Delhi – undermined Congress's legitimacy within Andhra. Observer after observer recounted that the early 1980s in Andhra had been characterized by a growing "power vacuum" or "authority vacuum."[7] It was into that vacuum, apparently, that NTR stepped from the movie screen.

Although this emphasis on Indira Gandhi's relentless intervention as a cause of the decline of Congress in Andhra points analytical attention in the right direction, some important qualifications are needed. First, it should be noted that the worst of this intervention began in 1978, but by that time Congress had already lost a significant amount of popular support in Andhra.[8] The fact that the Janata party won as many as 60 seats in Andhra in 1978 must be attributed to the same national pattern that brought Janata to power elsewhere in the country in 1977.

There is a second and more important qualification. Although it is clear that Indira Gandhi imposed weak chief ministers on Andhra, it is not clear that a different national leader could have behaved very differently. The logic of the overall political situation, both nationally and within Andhra, was such that weak appointed leaders, rather than elected leaders, were the order of the day. Congressites in Andhra, as elsewhere, had won elections in the 1970s not because of their individual popularity but because they were riding on Indira Gandhi's coattails. If the power of the state-level elite derived from Indira Gandhi, it is difficult to imagine how leaders with an independent political base could have emerged within the Andhra Congress to form a state government. Such leaders simply did not exist. These dependent political elite, in turn, knew that the way to rise to power in such a system was either to be personally close to national leaders or to prove their nuisance value by, for instance, organizing agitation, so that national leaders would be forced to co-opt them. Andhra leaders tried both those strategies, and Indira Gandhi, in turn, characteristically played musical chairs, choosing chief ministers from among a handful of relatively weak and dependent state leaders. A national leader of greater political vision might have foreseen that such an arrangement was likely to lead to political suicide. Caught in a system that she had helped create, Indira

7 Although I heard this phrase in numerous interviews, it is important to point out that Congress leaders themselves noted this development: Interviews with A. Madan Mohan, former president of the Andhra Pradesh State Congress (I) Committee, Hyderabad, March 19, 1986; V. B. Raju, former president of the Andhra Pradesh State Congress (I) Committee, Hyderabad, March 20, 1986; and Brahmananda Reddy (see footnote 6).
8 For example, Congress's share of the popular vote in Legislative Assembly elections declined from 52.3 percent in 1972 to 39.2 percent in 1978. See Kohli, "The NTR Phenomenon," Table 1, p. 993.

Gandhi could not have found strong chief ministers who could have exercised genuine state-level authority without changing the whole political system.

Whereas in 1986 many political observers of Andhra were quick to suggest that "she should have left Andhra alone" and "such authority would have emerged," it is important to recall the rampant factional struggles within the Andhra Congress prior to 1978. Andhra had experienced major political agitations in 1966 (over the location of a steel plant), in 1968–9 (the movement for a separate Telengana state), and in 1973 (a movement for a separate state made up of the coastal Andhra districts). All those disturbances involved large-scale political protests that led to violence, riots, and deaths and eventually the fall of the existing governments and the imposition of presidential rule.[9]

An analyst looking for reasons behind those disturbances concluded that "factionalism within the ruling party [Congress] played an important role."[10] Factional leaders who were part of the ruling party but who did not occupy positions of power had sought out volatile issues to mobilize supporters, with the aim of weakening or even dislodging those in power. This suggests that Congress in Andhra did not have its political house in order even prior to Indira's interventions. As a matter of fact, one might argue that such political instability at the state level invited central intervention. That argument would be an exaggeration, because Indira tended to intervene, with varying degrees of success, in both more and less stable states. But the point does help to put Indira Gandhi's role in perspective.

Lastly, among the causes of Congress's decline in Andhra during the late 1970s and early 1980s were the changing political sympathies of the state's important socioeconomic groups. As long as Congress was in power, for example, the Reddis, who constitute about 10–12 percent of the state's population and are spread throughout the state, always had the upper hand. Writing in the 1970s, a leading analyst of Andhra politics concluded that the Reddis had a "pre-dominance over all other dominant castes in Andhra Pradesh."[11] The Kammas, by contrast, are concentrated in the delta districts, including Guntur, and constitute about 5 percent of the state's pop-

---

9 For a description of the events involved in these agitations, see Hanumantha Rao, *Party Politics in Andhra,* pp. 245–78.
10 See Ram Reddy, "Politics of Accommodation," p. 32.
11 Ram Reddy, "Andhra Pradesh," p. 4. The author summarized on the same page the main reasons that the Reddis were Andhra's dominant social group well into the 1970s: "Their higher proportion in terms of their numbers among the peasant proprietor caste in Andhra Pradesh; their traditional power in many *taluks* and villages and glorious antecedent of local rule in many parts of Andhra Desa; their political initiatives and involvement in the Congress and the Communist politics during the last four decades; the availability of better caste leadership from the village, *taluk,* district to the state level; and, above all, their firm base in agricultural wealth."

ulation. Although they have never been ignored by Congress,[12] the Kammas have always resented the fact that the state's politics have been dominated by the Reddis.

Two factors that were at work throughout the 1970s changed the nature of these caste rivalries and the castes' relative power positions. First, the Kammas proved to be more enterprising than the Reddis. They utilized their land wealth to bankroll expansion into numerous commercial activities, such as rice milling, sugar production, tobacco processing, hotels, newspapers, and, of course, the film industry.[13] That changing economic base strengthened the power potential of the Kammas. Although some of that new economic power found expression in the increased number of ministerial positions to which they were appointed, Kammas continued to resent the failure of Indira Gandhi to appoint a Kamma chief minister in Andhra. That would have been very difficult for Indira, because the Reddis were well entrenched in the Andhra Congress. Of the nine Andhra chief ministers before NTR, six had been Reddis, and none had been a Kamma. The increasing disjuncture between their economic power and their failure to capture the highest political offices, with all the symbolic and real gains that would have involved, alienated the Kammas. As a result, they aligned their financial and political support behind NTR, himself a Kamma, who was well connected with other wealthy Kammas in the movie, hotel, and newspaper industries.[14]

Throughout the 1970s, in addition to losing the financial and electoral support of one of the two most important social groups in Andhra, Congress lost significant electoral support among the backward classes. The numerous castes, as many as 20, that constitute Andhra's backward classes account for nearly half of the state's population. The Harijans make up an additional 15 percent. It is obvious that the electoral game can be won only by securing the support of some of these economically insignificant but numerically critical groups.

During the 1950s and early 1960s, the backward classes and the scheduled castes did not compose an independent political force. Faction leaders from

12 Thus, for example, data presented by Ram Reddy in "Politics of Accommodation," Table 13, document that between 1957 and 1983 there were always about 40 Kamma and 75 Reddi MLAs in the Congress-dominated Andhra Legislative Assembly. That 2 : 1 ratio was a fair reflection of the populations of these two groups in Andhra. The caste analysis of the Congress cabinets presented in the same essay (Table 14) outlines a somewhat different picture. All through the 1960s, Reddi ministers outnumbered Kammas by about 3 : 1. During the 1970s, however, Kamma ministers were never fewer than half of the Reddi ministers.

13 Many of those interviewed pointed out the changing position of the Kammas. The most detailed information on this issue was provided to me by V. B. Raju (see footnote 7). More systematic data collected by G. Ram Reddy also substantiate this point; see his Table 10 in "Politics of Accommodation."

14 From interviews with V. B. Raju and A. Madan Mohan (see footnote 7).

dominant castes often succeeded in mobilizing the dependent members of the lower castes for electoral purposes. Analysts of Indian politics have noted that the control of dominant castes over the political life of the villages began declining during the 1960s, and Indira Gandhi's populism was aimed at halting the decline in Congress's electoral fortunes associated with such structural changes in the rural society.[15] It is not surprising that a public-opinion survey of political attitudes in Andhra, conducted by the Osmania University of Hyderabad, found that both the backward classes and the scheduled castes were attracted to Indira Gandhi after the 1969 split in Congress, mainly because of her promises of *garibi hatao* (alleviate poverty). During the 1970s, however, while the scheduled castes largely continued their support for the Congress party, many of Andhra's backward classes were alienated. The same survey group found that by the early 1980s there had been a significant decline in Congress's electoral support among the backward classes.[16]

Observers and participants in Andhra politics have repeatedly suggested in interviews that an important reason that Congress lost the support of the backward classes was Congress's preferential policies toward the Harijans. Brahmananda Reddy noted that whenever he went to the villages, members of the backward classes, pointing to the reservations and other such pro-Harijan policies as the granting of land for house sites, would inquire: "Why should the Congress be so enamored with Harijans? They are poor, but so are we."[17]

Additionally, it is important to note that Andhra's backward classes remain extremely heterogeneous. This is unlike the case of Kheda in Gujarat discussed earlier, where the backward groups tend to act as a relatively cohesive political force. It was possible in Gujarat to mobilize the Kshatriyas as a group around symbolic appeals of caste traditions and by offering symbolic rewards in the form of visible positions to a select few members of the caste. The electoral support of the Kshatriyas proved crucial for Congress in Gujarat. However, given the heterogeneity of Andhra's backward classes, and their lower levels of political mobilization, that option was not readily available to the Andhra Congress. Thus, the Andhra Con-

---

15 See, for example, Rajni Kothari, "The Crisis of the Moderate State and the Decline of Democracy," in P. Lyon and J. Manor, eds., *Transfer and Transformation: Political Institutions in the New Commonwealth* (Leicester, U.K.: Leicester University Press, 1983), pp. 29–46.
16 Reported in Vakil, "Congress Party in Andhra Pradesh," especially p. 68.
17 Interview with Brahmananda Reddy (see footnote 5). Another articulate Congressite had this to add: "Between 1971–80, Harijans and BCs [backward castes] tended to support the Congress. Congress was, therefore, invincible. But slowly, BCs developed jealousy vis-à-vis Harijans. This had some objective basis. SCs [scheduled castes or Harijans] have constitutional protections. She [Indira] also gave tickets and representations to the SCs. This got many BCs upset." Interview with Anjeneya Sharma [former MLA (1972–83), Congress (I); trade-union worker], Guntur, March 24, 1986.

gress has remained an alliance between the Reddis and the scheduled castes. As long as Congress also had the support of the backward classes, it could win elections. As some of the backward classes moved away from Congress, however, Congress's electoral hold on Andhra became precarious.

By the early 1980s, Congress had lost considerable support among "younger age groups – educated urban voters, middle income groups and backward classes."[18] Rampant factionalism within the Andhra Congress and Indira Gandhi's intervention probably delegitimized Congress in the eyes of the urban and the more active rural voters. Alienation of many of the middle-income and well-off Kammas, as well as the backward castes, was discussed earlier. As Congress went into decline, both organizationally and in terms of popular support, there was no other organized political force available in Andhra to fill the growing political void. Because politics abhors a power vacuum, sooner or later some force was bound to occupy that space. As it happened, a well-known movie actor turned politician moved into the center of the political stage.

NTR was well known in Andhra prior to his entry into politics. He had appeared in more than 100 Telugu movies, often portraying gods from Hindu mythology who saved the poor, the weak, and the dispossessed from all that is wicked. His prepolitical popularity among illiterate rural folk, especially women, was considerable.[19] He skillfully combined that popularity with several other themes to put together a motley winning coalition.

NTR emphasized regional themes of Telugu nationalism, highlighted Congress's corrupt political culture, and stressed how repeated interventions from Delhi had destroyed the Telugu people's capacity for and pride in self-government. Those themes probably appealed to many among Andhra's urban middle class. As far as other groups were concerned, NTR promised special new government programs to help women and to provide better educational facilities and jobs for youth. Reservations designed to improve job and educational opportunities for the backward classes provided another major plank for his platform. Plans to sell subsidized rice and to provide free lunches for all schoolchildren were announced, with the aim of cutting into Congress's support among the poor, especially the scheduled castes. Equally as important as the substance of these campaign promises were the political symbols that were used and the idiom in which the message was delivered. Clad in saffron robes, the traditional garb of India's holy men, and riding around in a convertible automobile transformed to look like a chariot, NTR appeared to emulate a figure from the *Mahabharata,* reincarnated to protect the dispossessed from worldly evils.

18 From a public-opinion survey reported in Vakil, "Congress Party in Andhra Pradesh," p. 68.
19 For background information on NTR, see Innaiah, *Saffron Star over Andhra.*

An analyst studying this phenomenon concluded that part of the explanation for NTR's success during the 1980s was that all his populist promises were made not as aspects of socialism, in the tradition of the Congress party, but "through home-grown imageries and idioms available in the backyard of the nation."[20]

Those who have analyzed the social backgrounds of the TDP legislators of Andhra have noted the following: (1) The TDP was not dominated by the Kammas, but through it the Kammas improved their political position compared with what it had been under the rule of Congress. (2) The backward classes were well represented within the TDP. (3) Many of the TDP legislators were well educated, with professional backgrounds (e.g., doctors) but with little political experience.[21] Although the electoral significance of those changes in composition was considerable, it is equally important to note that the backgrounds of the legislators probably had little or no impact on the quality of government under NTR. Decision making within the TDP was highly centralized; the legislators played no significant political role. A local political observer noted that "in our kind of politics it really does not matter whether they [the legislators] do anything or not."[22] Attempts to build the TDP into an organized party did not amount to much, and the TDP remained a one-man show.[23] Thus, the central theme at the TDP's organizational forums was hero worship, the hero, of course, being NTR.[24]

As can easily happen in a government dominated by a single individual, NTR's decisions often were impulsive and arbitrary. For example, in early 1985 he dismissed all village officials, claiming that they represented "feudal

---

20 See Naidu, "Symbolic Imagery Used by the Telugu Desam," p. 135. This article also provides a good general discussion of the themes emphasized by NTR in his electoral campaign. One important point made in that article, as well as in several interviews that I conducted, was that the NTR phenomenon should not be viewed as something similar to the situation in Tamil Nadu. Tamil and Telugu nationalisms are quite different from each other. Telugu is closer to Sanskrit. The religious imagery invoked by NTR is common to much of Hindu India. Moreover, Andhra does not have the strong anti-Brahman tradition nor the intense anti-Hindi attitude found in Tamil Nadu. Thus, Telugu nationalism is relatively tame in comparison with the early Tamil nationalism.
21 See Srinivas et al., "Social Background."
22 See Innaiah, *Saffron Star over Andhra,* p. 105.
23 "Telugu Desam . . . was created by Mr. Rama Rao and everything rallies around him. He is the beginning and the end of it. Even during the elections, the party set up some candidates who were political light-weights but the people voted for them just because of Mr. Rama Rao. . . . The selection of candidates was made by Rama Rao in consultation with few others. The central office of the party was located at Ramakrishna studios [NTR's movie studio] till recently. . . . The district coordinators were nominated by Rama Rao. Membership was enrolled in all villages but elections were not conducted within the party" (Ibid., p. 87).
24 This was noted in what was otherwise a favorable review of NTR. See *Indian Express* (Hyderabad), October 16, 1985.

culture." Observers pointed out that the real reason for the dismissals was that most of those officials had preexisting links with the Congress party.[25] A court decision forced NTR to reinstate many of the dismissed officials.[26] Similarly, free midday meals for children were distributed for about a year. However, as the government learned the economic realities that underlie the aphorism that "there is no free lunch," NTR abruptly discontinued the program in 1985. Subsidized rice schemes, an idea that had been received favorably, were also initiated and terminated several times. Following the same pattern, abolition of all tuition fees was announced but not implemented. It was loudly proclaimed that Telugu would be made the official language of Andhra, but very little was done to implement that announcement. Additionally, NTR's government had more than the usual share of problems with bureaucracy. Several senior bureaucrats, who did not want to be identified, noted that the "morale of the civil service" under NTR was very low, and a lot of that had to do with NTR's "heavy-handedness" and "arbitrariness."

In spite of running a one-man, partyless, relatively arbitrary government, NTR succeeded in winning several elections. Most observers attributed that to several variables, the relative weights of which are difficult to assess: (1) NTR's continued personal appeal, especially to rural illiterates, (2) the visibility of some of his populist programs, (3) the establishment of elaborate patronage networks, and (4) the relative organizational mess within Congress, the main opposition party, a disorganization that continues today. Most of these reasons for NTR's electoral success are similar to those that explain Congress's successes elsewhere under Indira Gandhi. A summary observation by a former Andhra politician seems only a slight oversimplification: "Rama Rao only sophisticated Indira Gandhi's populism."[27]

The TDP under NTR does not appear capable of systematically rebuilding authority in Andhra; certainly it offers little more promise than the present Congress. The authority vacuum, as noted earlier, emerged as Congress's organization and electoral popularity declined. NTR stepped into that political void, but filled it only to the extent of winning a few rounds of elections. It should be noted in this context that NTR failed to capture many of the urban municipalities, including two of the largest, Hyderabad and Vijayawada, in the local-government elections held in 1986 and 1987.[28] As it turned out, that was a sign of things to come, leading up to NTR's loss in 1989.

25 See, for example, *Economic and Political Weekly*, March 9, 1985, pp. 393–5.
26 *Indian Express* (Hyderabad), February 13, 1986.
27 Interview with V. B. Raju (see footnote 7).
28 For the results of Hyderabad municipal elections, which were won by the Moslem-dominated Majlis, see *Indian Express* (Hyderabad), March 3, 1986. The 1987 elections for local government in which the TDP (though victorious overall) lost quite a few urban

The absence of a party, a coherent program, and second and third layers of significant leadership prevented the TDP from laying down a well-organized political base. Without NTR, the TDP probably would not even survive. Even with NTR, the TDP hardly offered Andhra good government. When authority runs so shallow as to reside mostly in a single leader, the quality of government is likely to remain a function of the leadership quality. In the case of NTR, arbitrary decisions were clear indicators of poor government. Failure to design and implement policies that would have addressed the pressing problems of the day was another indicator. The evidence on this is available elsewhere.[29] A third important manifestation was the failure to find peaceful methods to resolve the society's conflicts. Increasing political violence, in addition to highlighting the nature and intensity of socioeconomic conflict, always indicates a government that does not govern well. It is important, therefore, to conclude this discussion of Andhra by noting the pervasiveness of the violence that has come to characterize the conduct of political affairs in the state.

It would be incorrect to describe Andhra as a state that at any time in the recent past has been free of political violence. Part of what is now the state of Andhra, the Telengana region, was the scene of a major communist uprising in the late 1940s and early 1950s. Armed forces were used to crush that insurrection as well as to annex the Moslem princely state of Hyderabad into the Indian republic. Although the decade of 1956–66 was relatively calm, between 1966 and 1980 Andhra suffered the three major disturbances discussed earlier. Those disturbances occurred during a period when Indira Gandhi was at the height of her power in New Delhi and the Congress party was undergoing considerable deinstitutionalization. Each of those disturbances was instigated by Congress leaders and ended when the implicit or explicit goals of the leaders, namely, a share of power in the government, were met. During the 1975–7 Emergency, moreover, many Naxalite leaders were killed in Andhra in "encounters" with the police.

In the past, violence tended to follow one of two patterns: (1) The political activities of a revolutionary elite would be met with state repres-

---

municipalities, including Vijayawada, are discussed in *Economic and Political Weekly*, April 4, 1987, pp. 582–5.

29 For lack of space, I have not discussed many of NTR's policy failures. One analyst, surveying the areas in which the TDP made campaign promises, but accomplished nothing and did not even initiate any programs in the first few years in power, cited the following: an administration free of corruption, support to peasants and small farmers, minimum wages for both urban and agricultural laborers, drinking water to all the villages, protection from natural calamities, rural electrification, job-oriented education, speedy industrialization, streamlining of policy administration, family planning, an end to unemployment among youth, increased autonomy for the judiciary, electoral reforms, rationalization of taxation, construction of houses for the poor, and protection for tree tappers, fishermen, rickshaw pullers, and weavers. See Innaiah, *Saffron Star over Andhra*, pp. 111–19.

sion. (2) Failure to accommodate Congress faction leaders would lead to agitation and violence, with the faction leaders eventually being absorbed into the power structure. The contemporary violence springs from similar disputes over socioeconomic resources and access to state power. What has changed, however, is the pervasiveness of the violence. In the past, the violent incidences were goal-specific and time-bound and appeared as exceptions rather than the rule. A leading analyst of Andhra politics writing in the 1970s could easily note without many qualifications that since 1956, and well into the 1960s, Andhra "presented a picture of stable political order."[30] Today, one could not make a similar statement about Andhra without many qualifications.

A police report on law-and-order problems in Andhra in 1984, for example, presented the following picture of one year in the political life of Andhra:

- Elections to the eighth Lok Sabha involved 445 incidents of "law and order" problems, including riots, assaults, arson, cases of bomb throwing and 10 murders.
- There were 167 political clashes during 1984, including 19 murders. These involved the Congress-I, Telugu Desam, CPI and the CPM as either aggressors or victims.
- 115 communal incidents took place, leading up to 63 deaths and 584 injuries.
- Violence involving "extremists" led to 44 murders and 383 other incidents of snatching of weapons, amputation of limbs and attacks on liquor shops.
- Dismissal of N. T. Rama Rao Ministry by New Delhi led to numerous agitations. This resulted in dislocation of road and rail communications, attacks on Government offices and banks, and destruction of public and private property in mob violence. Police opened fire on 16 occasions, resulting in the death of 26 persons and 31 injuries. 48 policemen were also injured. Eventually the army had to be called in to restore law and order.[31]

What the police report glosses over is that a different type of violence has been growing: violence inflicted on the lower classes and their "extremist" leaders. For example, over the past few years, five districts in Telengana have "been progressively brought under a virtual state of siege with ever-growing development of the Central Reserve Police Force and armed police camps." This is a result of growing conflict involving "the region's landlords and arrack and tendu leaf contractors who have found their age-old exactions challenged by organizations of peasants and agricultural laborers."[32]

In other parts of the state a different pattern has emerged. For example, in Chitoor district on the southern coast, some Harijans had acquired groves of tamarind trees from the government as an incentive for sterili-

30 See Ram Reddy, "Andhra Pradesh," p. 1.
31 Government of Andhra Pradesh, statement on demand No. XIII, made by Vasanta Nageswara Rao, minister of home and legislative affairs, *Police Administration, 1985–86* (Hyderabad: Government Secretariat Press, 1985), pp. 1–5.
32 *Economic and Political Weekly,* February 2, 1985, p. 174.

zation. For various reasons, tamarind has recently become a lucrative product. Local landlords began questioning the ownership of tamarind trees by
Harijans, claiming they were public property. Landlords organized against
the Harijans and hired *goondas,* who beat up a group of Harijans to set
an example. The police failed to provide any protection for the Harijans.
When a civil-rights group went to investigate the incident, they found the
landlords very angry over the fact that the Harijans had become "well-to-
do" and "uppity." The landlords were allowed to consolidate their hold
over the groves of tamarind trees.[33]

Killings of radicals who attempt to organize the peasants, tribes, and
landless laborers have also become quite common. In mid–1985, for example, a survey by the Andhra Pradesh Civil Liberties Committee reported
the killing of 33 activists over the first 20 weeks of the year. Each of those
killings of "extremists" or "Naxalites" was done by the police: 17 during
"encounters," 12 while in police custody, and 4 in various situations in
which police were firing guns. The report noted that 24 people had similarly
been killed in 1984.[34] Many more examples of such incidents could be cited.
The pervasiveness of such violence is best illustrated by a typical newspaper
headline: "Andhra Pradesh: In a state of terror." The story accompanying
that headline concluded that

encounter deaths, police camps, deaths in police custody, attacks on civil rights
activists, followed by the attempt to introduce two repressive bills – one giving the
police greater powers and the other curbing the press – these are part of an extensive, often violent, campaign to suppress any kind of opposition to the government in Andhra Pradesh.[35]

The reporter could have added that the "campaign" was a part of an
attempt to protect the interests of the powerful in society.

The patterns of violence in Andhra help clarify the underlying causes.
Most such incidents involve local issues, and the incidents follow one of
two patterns. The first pattern involves violence against the lower castes,
or against those who seek to organize them, inflicted either by the socially
powerful or by agents of the state. It results from failure of the government's "output" institutions, that is, failure by policy-making bodies and
by the police. Ineffectiveness in these institutions leads to failure to implement even mildly redistributive policies that would reduce the conflict
over scarce resources and failure to protect the poor, lower castes against
the wrath of the upper castes. The second pattern is seen when a contest
for political power is conducted via agitations, which can lead to riots,
destruction of property, and murder. This pattern represents failure of
"input" institutions, that is, institutions like parties and the party system,

33 Ibid., May 4, 1985, pp. 784–6.
34 Ibid., June 22, 1985, pp. 784–6.
35 *Indian Express* (Hyderabad), October 9, 1986.

which should serve to mediate opposing views and provide less-than-violent outlets for the society's normal power conflicts. Taken together, the two patterns reveal the poorly functioning political institutions in this part of the country and the inability of the state to impose its authority.

CONTENDING SOCIAL GROUPS IN GUNTUR

As mentioned earlier, Kammas compose the most important socioeconomic group in Guntur. The Reddis attempt to compete with the Kammas for dominance, but there are nearly twice as many Kammas (20 percent) as Reddis in the district, and the Kammas may own as much as three-quarters of the fertile land,[36] thus giving the Kammas considerable power. The Reddis, however, are the most important caste group in the state of Andhra. They were the most influential group within the Congress party and thus in Andhra politics throughout the 1960s and the 1970s. As a result, the Reddis of Guntur enjoyed a degree of access to state power that they would not have had if the Kammas had been able to translate their district-level numerical and economic superiority into proportionate political power. That disjuncture set up an important line of cleavage and conflict within Guntur that in 1983 was "resolved," if temporarily, in favor of the Kammas with the emergence of the TDP as Andhra's ruling party.

The conflict between the Kammas and the Reddis in this part of India is old and enduring. Local residents say that it dates back to the Middle Ages. In more recent times, some analysts have suggested that the intensity of this conflict may have been behind the role that the Kammas played in the 1950s as the leaders of the local communist parties pitched against the Reddi-dominated Congress.[37] Other analysts, such as Myron Weiner and G. Ram Reddy, have argued that politics in the delta districts of Andhra is more complex than simply the struggle between the Kammas and the Reddis.[38] Such scholarly qualifications notwithstanding, the emergence of NTR was widely discussed in Guntur in 1986 in terms of a defeat for the Reddis and the emergence of a "Kamma *raj.*"

On balance, politics in Guntur in the late 1980s featured divisions along caste and party lines, with most of the Kammas aligned with NTR, and the Reddis, though hesitant and divided in defeat, continuing to hope that Congress would make a comeback. This broad picture requires several qualifications. Nevertheless, if one investigates the social backgrounds of the respective party elites, who votes for which party, and the subjective

36 See Harrison, *India,* p. 207. Harrison notes that this is not a firm figure, but rather a local estimate. My interviews in Guntur also suggested that Kammas own the "majority" of the land, though I could not come up with an estimated figure.
37 Ibid., pp. 204–45.
38 Weiner, *Party Building in a New Nation,* part III; Ram Reddy, "Politics of Accommodation."

Table 4.1. *Caste backgrounds of the political elite of Guntur district,*
Andhra Pradesh, 1986

Caste	MLAs (elected in 1985)	Presidents of *panchayat samithis* (elected prior to 1983)
Kamma	12	8
Reddi (and Kapu)	1	8
Backward castes	4	0
Moslems	1	0
Scheduled castes and tribes	1	5
Total	19	21

Source: Compiled from local interviews.

opinions about those who are in and out of power, then the conclusion emerges that the two dominant castes of Guntur are divided largely along party lines. Moreover, I do not believe that this analysis contradicts Weiner's emphasis on multicaste factions within Congress as the dominant characteristic of Guntur politics. When Weiner studied the district, Congress was the only game in town,[39] and these two dominant castes jockeyed for power within the dominant party. The current situation is more akin to that of the 1950s, when Selig Harrison investigated the area's local politics, and two parties, Congress and the Communist party, were viable competitors.[40] Congress's major competitor now, of course, is not the communists, but the TDP. As two-party competition has reemerged, so have some aspects of the long-established community cleavages.

The data in Tables 4.1 and 4.2 help unravel the nature of the caste and party linkages in Guntur. The presidents of *panchayat samithis* (Table 4.1) were all elected prior to 1983 and thus prior to the rise of NTR. By contrast, the members of the Legislative Assembly (MLAs) (Table 4.1) were all elected in 1985 when NTR's party was returned to power. The contrast between the caste compositions of Guntur's elite in the two time periods is revealing.

Under NTR, the Kammas were by far the most significant group among the district's new political elite (Tables 4.1 and 4.2), followed by the backward castes, as discussed later. The Reddis clearly were not favored politically by NTR. The local elite under Congress (Table 4.1), by contrast, had been more representative of both the Kammas and the Reddis. The pre–1983 data seem consistent with Congress's situation as described by Weiner. However, it is important to note that even under Congress, ele-

39 Weiner, *Party Building in a New Nation,* part III.
40 Harrison, *India,* pp. 204–45.

Table 4.2. *Caste and party affiliations of the political elite of Guntur district, Andhra Pradesh, 1986*

Group	Kamma	Reddi	Backward castes	Scheduled castes, tribes, and Moslems
MLAs (elected in 1985)				
Congress party	2	0	1	1
TDP	8	1	3	1
Communists	2	0	0	0
Presidents of panchayat samithis (elected prior to 1983)[a]				
Congress party	3	7	0	3
TDP	3	0	0	1
Communists	2	1	0	1

[a] As *panchayat samithi* elections were not openly contested along party lines until recently, this table represents informal affiliations of *panchayat samithi* presidents with various political parties. Also, because these individuals were all elected prior to the emergence of the TDP in 1983, the affiliations of some presidents to the TDP represent either a subsequent switch from another party or interim elections to replace a specific president for one reason or another.
Source: Compiled from local interviews.

ments of caste and party alignments were present. It is clear, for example, from Table 4.1 that under Congress, the backward castes were totally neglected, whereas the scheduled castes did rather well. Of the eight Kamma local leaders prior to 1983, only three were with Congress (Table 4.2). The other five Kamma elites either were with the communist parties or later joined the TDP. By contrast, as long as Congress was dominant, Reddis clearly were the largest single group within the party (Table 4.2).

Makineni Peda Ratnaiah (MPR) was typical of the new Kamma TDP MLAs from Guntur in 1986; he was a doctor who had never before been active in politics. When asked why he entered politics and why he joined the TDP, he answered as follows:

I was disgusted with the Congress culture. Anti-social elements [toughs and hoodlums] are in the highest positions.... For example, take Guntur municipal corporation. All the anti-social elements are in it. A family lady cannot even go to many of the polling booths. Indira Gandhi is responsible for this. She never allowed a chief minister to continue. She encouraged corruption. [When asked why she allows corruption, she would answer] it is everywhere in the world. Is that the way for a prime minister to talk? ... NTR is an actor. That helps [in winning elections]. He is also a principled man. He does not smoke or drink.

When asked to describe his constituency and who voted for him, MPR noted the following facts that were both typical and revealing: His constituency was Kamma-dominated, numerically and in terms of socioeconomic influence. In spite of the fact that another Kamma candidate was his opponent, the majority of the Kammas voted for him because he represented NTR's party. In addition, the backward castes generally voted for him, but "Harijans and Reddis tended to vote Congress." To the question why the Kammas voted for him, he suggested that it was mainly because of the "strong anti-Congress feelings in my constituency." Furthermore, as to why the Harijans did not vote for him, he proposed that it was because "they are exploited by the agriculturalists. Kammas are the agriculturalists here. [The scheduled castes] voted against them. They used to vote communist earlier. But now they vote Congress."[41]

Several important themes seen in that interview were repeated in other interviews. First, many of the Kamma elite, especially the new middle class, have felt alienated from Congress in recent years. That may in part have been a function of having been excluded from Congress's spoils system, but it probably also reflected some genuine disillusionment with what many consider to be the "Congress culture." Second, these Kamma elite joined the NTR bandwagon because they saw in it an opportunity to win political office and enjoy the perks that come with office. In that sense, NTR's party was no different from Congress. Third, the TDP's electoral support in Guntur came mainly from the Kammas and the backward castes. Although a detailed survey might not support these conclusions, if we can assume that those who ran for office understood their constituencies, then we must consider their views persuasive, and members of the local elite repeatedly suggested that NTR's main support came from the Kammas and the backwards, and that Congress was supported primarily by the Reddis and the scheduled castes.[42]

A number of variables involved in determining local political perceptions help explain this division of the two dominant castes along party lines. Solidarity with the members of one's own caste is, of course, prepolitical and an integral aspect of rural social structure. When the lore of an age-old rivalry is transmitted across generations, as it still is among especially rural Kammas and Reddis, that contributes to the perpetuation of cohesive political behavior. Even among the more educated, such sentiments run deep. For example, the hostels in Guntur's universities are divided along caste lines. Although there is considerable interaction across caste lines in a setting such as a university, local observers still report that the youth of each caste tend to "live and move together." It is not surprising that such sentiments of caste cohesiveness and division between different castes,

41 From an interview with MPR (a TDP MLA from Guntur), Guntur, March 27, 1986.
42 I interviewed in some detail 8 of the 40 individuals who could be considered members of the "local elite." Local leaders from both Congress and the TDP tended to agree with this broad picture of caste and party affiliations. The two local communist leaders, however, disagreed; they argued that both the Kammas and the Reddis had voted against them because they were communists. This issue will be discussed again later.

formed when young, continue well into adult life and carry over into political behavior. Because the political structure allows these caste divisions to be expressed through different parties that hold out the realistic possibility of capturing state power, it is not surprising that the competing dominant castes have become allied with the two rival parties.

The political factor that did the most to harden this caste cleavage within Guntur was that until NTR, Andhra had never had a Kamma chief minister, and given their local predominance, that had been a major annoyance to Guntur's Kammas: "Kammas have always felt that they did not enjoy the power they deserve. They never had the chief ministership."[43] What further exacerbated the frustrations of Guntur's Kammas was that a Guntur Reddi, Brahmananda Reddy, had been Andhra's chief minister from 1963 to 1971 and subsequently remained an important political figure. That had given local Reddis greater access to state resources, as compared with the Kammas, as well as the self-assurance that comes from being in power: "Prior to the rise of the TDP, [Reddis] felt that they were in power. Kammas felt they were set aside. Brahmananda Reddy's family was very powerful [in Guntur and in state politics]. As long as they remained [powerful], psychologically the [Reddis] felt that they were in power."[44] Thus, the sense of elation among the Kammas in the aftermath of NTR's victory is understandable. Throughout Guntur, I heard comments in 1986 from the Kamma elite suggesting in one form or another that "finally, it is our opportunity."

Lest the case for caste alignments along party lines be overstated, some important qualifications should be noted. Both the Reddis and the Kammas have some important factions and divisions within their communities that, on occasion, take on political significance. The Reddis of Guntur, for example, were divided during the Congress split in the late 1960s. Some joined the Sanjiva Reddy faction, and thus Congress (O) and later Janata, but the majority stayed on with the Brahmananda Reddy faction and thus Congress (I). Over time, however, as it became clear that Janata was not likely to be a significant force within Andhra and that Congress (I) not only was electorally the most popular but also was dominated by Reddis, many of the Reddis who had joined the Janata slowly returned to the Congress party. With Congress out of power between 1983 and 1989, the loyalty of some of the Reddi elite once again came into question. They wanted to establish a working relationship with the TDP government, but not completely abandon Congress, just in case it should return to power, as it did in 1989.

43 Comment made by P. A. V. Prasad, a Guntur correspondent of *Eenadu*, the largest Telugu daily in Andhra, which played a key role in NTR's electoral success. The comment was made during a discussion in Guntur, March 16, 1986.
44 Interview with V. D. R. Manohar, block development officer, Tenali *taluk*, Guntur, March 27, 1986.

The divisions within Guntur's Kammas have been of a different sort. For example, the Kammas who are prominent in tobacco and cotton production often need to deal with the government in New Delhi to secure overseas export contracts. Therefore, some Kammas have had long-established relationships with the Congress party. These Kammas found themselves in a difficult situation during the NTR reign in Andhra. Their solution was to pay money to both parties.[45] Besides such rational divisions within the community, there are, as one might expect, significant factions involving personality conflicts. The political significance of such factions, however, is reduced under the conditions of two-party conflict: "While cleavages often involve two powerful Kammas, when fighting against outsiders, they act together."[46]

The Kammas and the Reddis, of course, are not the only significant social groups in Guntur, but as landowning groups that are relatively high in the ritual hierarchy of caste, they are the two most important groups. The two other numerically significant groups are the backward castes and the scheduled castes. What has changed since Weiner studied this district is that the members of higher castes within the villages can no longer easily influence the political behavior of the lower castes. Indira Gandhi sought the electoral support of the Harijans by appealing to them directly and offering the Harijan elite electoral positions (Tables 4.1 and 4.2), in addition to rewarding them through specific policies, such as land for house sites. Although such measures established a relationship between Congress and the Harijans that is still relatively intact, several caveats should be noted.

First, the Harijans in this area have long been politically active. Well into the 1960s, the communist parties were receiving as much as 20 percent of the popular vote in Guntur (Table 4.3). The decline of the local communists is discussed in a later section, but here it can be noted that because of the contradiction of the Kammas as both the leaders of the communist movement and the main landowners in the area, a viable left alternative could not be sustained in Guntur. Indira's Congress was the main beneficiary of that situation. Her left-leaning populism attracted the Harijans. The political significance of this point is that Congress's continuing failure to implement antipoverty policies may once again alienate the relatively politicized local Harijans from Congress. Indira Gandhi's well-established image as a pro-poor leader postponed that possibility, but during Rajiv Gandhi's tenure, the future of this relationship was in doubt. As a local Congressite tersely noted, "our main support is with the Harijans. With this

---

45 Information from a local journalist (see footnote 43).
46 This point was explained to me by a fellow academic, K. R. Sastry, at the National Institute of Rural Development, just outside of Hyderabad.

man [Rajiv] behaving like a chairman of an American oil company, what is the future of Congress?"[47]

The backward castes of Guntur are extremely heterogeneous. Some are small farmers. Many are toddy tappers, washermen, and weavers. Many are landless laborers. There is even a handful who are quite wealthy. Moreover, they are not organized, nor are they likely to be mobilized around simple themes of caste solidarity. Their numerical significance – as much as half of the district's population – and their heterogeneity are likely to add significantly to the electoral volatility in Guntur in the future. Thus far, the backward castes have tended to behave politically as a group, but it can be argued that for a number of reasons, that may not continue.

First, the term "backward castes" denotes a residual category that is not an integral part of the social structure. It is a category defined by those in power and imposed on the social structure. This politically created "unity" could easily come undone. Second, the backward castes of Guntur ceased to support Congress when they felt that it was excessively favoring the Harijans. Thus, their support for NTR is based in part on their negative sentiment toward Congress, and NTR's failure to deliver could readily change that. NTR has, of course, tried to solidify the relationship by offering new reservation policies to the backwards, but those policies have run into legal problems. Thus, the future political behavior of the backward castes of Guntur will be of considerable electoral significance, but difficult to anticipate.

Regardless of the electoral swings in the future, and they are of secondary consequence for this study, what does this discussion tell us about the modal form that politicized social conflict takes in this part of India? Factional maneuvering involving patron–client links, cleavages around castes, and class conflict are some of the major forms that politicization of social conflict can take. The discussion thus far suggests that many of the district's political issues revolve around alignments between castes and parties. The interactions between castes and parties are now mutual: Whereas the existing caste cleavages shape the decisions of political parties, the natures of the parties and the party system itself mold caste political behavior. This primary focus on caste, however, should not detract attention from the somewhat secondary but significant roles that the issues of class conflict and factionalism play in Guntur politics.

For example, the overall framework of politics in Guntur has some elements of class politics that are so obvious that they can easily recede into the background. The Kammas and the Reddis are the area's landowners, and the Harijans and many of the backwards work on land owned

47 Interview with Anjeneya Sharma (see footnote 17).

by others. The Kammas and the Reddis compete for power, and those who do not own property are not serious contenders for power. A second factor related to this is that whereas the Kammas are clearly a caste, their changing political significance has recently been influenced by changes in their economic activities. As the Kammas have proved to be more enterprising and industrious than the Reddis, the newfound wealth of the Kammas has sought political expression.

Although the relative levels of material wealth of social groups are important factors in explaining their access to political power, challenges to the powerful along class lines are rare in contemporary Guntur. Class conflict definitely is not one of the main forms of local sociopolitical conflict. The poor are found among the Harijans as well as the various backward castes. There are caste divisions involving conflict over relative status as well as mutual competition for the state's resources. Nevertheless, the dominant groups are quick to perceive, and to thwart, any potential threat that may develop along class lines. A few examples will demonstrate this last point.

First, when Indira Gandhi turned somewhat to the left in the early 1970s, and, correspondingly, Narasimha Rao, the Congress (I) chief minister in Andhra at that time, attempted mild land reforms, "the landed gentry of the Circars [a set of coastal districts, including Guntur] who were against the introduction of land reforms . . . found an excuse to start an agitation for a separate Andhra state."[48] That episode is still prominent in the state's political memory. Thus, it is not surprising that one of the earliest political promises made by NTR was that he was against all land reforms. Second, local communist leaders who belong to the reformist communist parties (the CPI and the CPM) have often noted that whenever a viable communist party candidate runs for office, the Kammas and the Reddis band together to vote for one opposition candidate.[49] Lastly, there is the evidence noted earlier of the state repression meted out in the form of "encounter" killings of "extremists" (anyone attempting radical mobilization of the poor).

48 See Hanumantha Rao, *Party Politics in Andhra Pradesh,* p. 262. G. Ram Reddy also concluded that in addition to factionalism within Congress as a cause, "the attempts to weaken the dominant castes . . . gave rise to a major agitation." See Ram Reddy, "Politics of Accommodation," p. 32. Also see Mohit Sen, "Showdown in Andhra," *Economic and Political Weekly,* December 23, 1972, pp. 2487–9.

49 Interviews with the following: Popuri Brahmanandan (president of a *panchayat samithi* and a member of the CPI), Guntur, March 24, 1986; Mande Pitchaiah (president of a *panchayat samithi* and a former MLA from the CPM), Guntur, March 24, 1986; Kolla Venkaiah (former communist leader), Padanandipur village, Guntur, March 28, 1986. This political situation obviously represents a considerable change since the 1950s, when the struggle between the Kammas and the Reddis was expressed in the party struggle between the communists and Congress. This issue is discussed again later.

Table 4.3. *Election results in Guntur district, Andhra Pradesh, 1967–85, Legislative Assembly*

Party	Seats won					Vote received (%)				
	1967	1972	1978	1983	1985	1967	1972	1978	1983	1985
Congress	19	11	12	0	5	49.1	48.6	41.8	31.1	43.8
TDP[a]	—	—	—	18	12	—	—	—	58.5	43.9
CPI[b]	—	2	—	—	1	8.1	7.2	3.4	1.4	2.9
CPM[c]	—	—	1	—	1	12.4	1.7	5.9	2.5	3.1
Swatantra	3	1	—	—	—	12.7	7.3	—	—	—
Jan Sangh[d]	—	—	—	—	—	2.0	1.3	—	1.1	—
Bhartiya Lok Dal[e]	—	—	—	—	—	—	—	—	0.3	—
Janata[f]	—	—	4	—	—	—	—	29.0	—	—
Others	2[g]	4[h]	2	1	—	15.7	33.9[h]	19.9	5.1	6.3
Total	24	18	19	19	19	100	100	100	100	100

[a]Founded 1983.
[b]Communist Party of India.
[c]Communist Party of India, Marxist.
[d]Jan Sangh merged into the Janata party in 1977 and was re-formed as the Bhartiya Janata party in 1980.
[e]Founded in 1974.
[f]Founded in 1977.
[g]Won by independents.
[h]Seats and votes secured mainly by independents.
Source: Compiled from a series of reports: Government of Andhra Pradesh, General Administration (Elections) Department, Volume II (statistics), *Report on General Elections* (fourth, fifth, sixth, and seventh), Government Central Press, Hyderabad, published in the years 1967, 1972, 1979, and 1983. The data for 1985 elections were compiled from the *Indian Express* (Hyderabad), March 7, 1985.

POLITICAL PARTIES IN GUNTUR

Electoral data from Guntur (Table 4.3) reveal that since 1983, Congress and the TDP have been the two main contenders for local power. The TDP dominated in 1986 in the sense that it controlled the majority of the Legislative Assembly seats. However, in terms of electoral popularity, Congress and the TDP were running neck and neck. During the 1987 local-government elections, Guntur was one of the few districts in Andhra in which Congress won the race to head the district-level government (chairman of the *zila parishad*).[50]

Although both Congress and the TDP enjoy considerable electoral support within Guntur, as organized parties they are virtually nonexistent.

50 The results of that election are discussed in the *Economic and Political Weekly*, April 4, 1987, pp. 582–5.

Neither of the parties has a stable membership, elected officers, or a working district office. Thus, the parties have little independent presence or autonomous significance beyond their electoral victories. Because electoral success has depended mainly on leadership appeal (national leadership in the case of Congress, and regional leadership for TDP), the two dominant parties have played minor roles within the district in terms of organized political forces.

The causes and consequences of this organizational vacuum require discussion. When Weiner studied this district, the local Congress party was already quite faction-ridden. In spite of that, Congress as a party had its identity and functions. Now, however, there remain only squabbling individuals, with a vague sense of identity as Congressites, who have little independent political following. Old established Congressites like Brahmananda Reddy are still around, but have moved away from Guntur, living, for the most part, in Hyderabad.

As discussed previously, the causes of Congress's organizational decline here, as elsewhere, are partly regional and partly national. The organizational decline has had important political consequences. Local Congressites have lost much of their authority in district affairs, partly because traditional authority in the social structure has been eroding. Merely being a prominent Reddi is no longer sufficient to ensure that a Guntur Congressite will be respected and trusted in the political circles of Guntur. An additional factor is that the rational and legal bases of authority have been undermined.

A Congressite noted that "natural leadership emerges from struggle and competition . . . from a struggle within the political marketplace."[51] As this marketplace has been destroyed, the process of acquiring power by appointments has further exacerbated the squabbling within the faction-ridden Congress. As soon as an individual is appointed or given a ticket, all other power contenders are quick to question, often publicly, the legitimacy of that decision. The reasons for selection frequently include (1) personal links to those higher up, (2) possession of wealth, or (3) use of strong-arm tactics.[52] None of these reasons can promote the perception of legitimacy that is earned by the individual who comes to power by working at the grass roots and building sufficient local popularity to win, fairly and squarely, in the game of political competition. The squabbling Congressites, lacking any independent political following, have earned their poor

---

51 Interview with V. B. Raju (see footnote 7).
52 A report just prior to the 1985 Legislative Assembly elections noted that "factionalism" within Congress was "totally rampant." Congressites, moreover, publicly accused their party bosses of giving election tickets to "sycophants," to weak candidates, and to those having "links with the underworld," as well as to those "who have been openly involved in corruption scandals." See *Economic and Political Weekly,* February 23, 1985, pp. 302–3.

public image in local politics. Referring to the politics of an earlier generation, an old Congressite in Guntur noted that at one time, "the ordinary man used to respect the [Congressite] as a savior of the country."[53] The image of a Congress political worker today, noted another Guntur Congressite, has become "that of a crook."[54]

Local Congressites are not optimistic about the prospects for rebuilding the Congress party locally. Most of those interviewed suggested that internal party elections, which Rajiv had announced and postponed several times, either would not be held or would be "bogus." One Congressite, who did not wish to be cited specifically on this point, outlined the reasons that any party elections are likely to be bogus:

> The lists of who is or who is not a party member are virtually nonexistent. Since these individuals want to remain in power, they are likely to enroll bogus members by paying for them out of their own pockets. These are also the same officers who, as party bosses, will conduct the party elections. Since even the government machinery cannot hold fair elections, how will a private body?

The same general point that emerged in the discussion of the Kheda district applies here: Party elections are not likely to be held, because they would threaten the power of all those appointed individuals who currently hold party offices. Fair elections to party positions might well uproot the entire appointed structure of the Congress party from bottom to top.

Lastly, it is worth noting that being out of power brings out the worst in the Congress party. When Congress is in power, Congressites may squabble, but it is squabbling with a purpose – to divide up the perks of power. By contrast, when out of power, local party units seem to lose all sense of purpose and political initiative. When asked about the future strategy of Congress to recapture power and reestablish itself in this part of the country, a senior Congressite commented as follows:

> There is no point in discussing the future strategy. No one is discussing this. Executive committee is all splintered. They are all self-seekers. Basically, only the high command [first in Hyderabad and then in New Delhi] can take this decision [i.e., the decision on future strategies]. They have to call us [the senior local leaders], one by one. After discussing, the high command has to pinpoint authority. Only after this, if and when the dirt is removed [from the party] will new and younger elements be attracted to the Congress.[55]

Thus, the main strategy of Congressites in the periphery seems to be to hope that "electoral waves" will continue to be generated by the national leaders and that the national leaders will somehow appoint local leaders who can reestablish Congress's authority.

---

53 Interview with Meduri Nageswararao, former president of the District Congress (I) Committee, Guntur, March 25, 1986.
54 Interview with V. B. Raju (see footnote 7).
55 Interview with A. Madan Mohan (see footnote 7).

Likewise, the authority of those representing the TDP within Guntur had not been firmly established by 1986. The political careers of the 12 TDP legislators in Guntur fell into two broad categories.[56] Nearly half of them had had no political experience before they ran for office and won. The other half had repeatedly, and unsuccessfully, tried to win election on the tickets of different non-Congress (I) parties. Several of these individuals had followed the pattern of starting with the Swatantra party, moving to Congress (O), then to the Janata party, on to the Lok Dal, and finally ending up with the TDP. Those two patterns of ascent had created an impression in Guntur that the TDP legislators either were politically in-experienced or were opportunists who would have joined any party to win election.

That the MLAs followed those career patterns tended to weaken local authority, but did not preclude the possibility that the TDP might establish a genuine local base in Guntur. The MLAs were generally well educated, and many of them were perceived to be honest. Moreover, as local bosses in control of patronage, they could have extended and deepened their support. However, as early as 1986 there were several indications that the TDP was not likely to establish an enduring local base. First, as a study of the TDP legislators tersely concluded, their "clean records" really reflected only their "political inexperience."[57] Second, and more important, the TDP's control over the dispensation of local resources for building patronage networks was far from uncontested, for Congress remained a significant force in the local government. The third and most important indication was the insignificance of the TDP as an organized party.

NTR, like Congress leaders, had not allowed elections within his party. It seems to be endemic to the logic of these parties that are totally depen-dent on "charismatic" leaders for their electoral success that a party or-ganization can only be a constraint on the personal discretion of such leaders. The result, however, was that there were no systematic mecha-nisms for resolving internal disputes within the TDP in Guntur. The word of NTR or of his hand-picked lieutenants, who thus far had been only his family members, was what resolved most disagreements. As long as all power and authority were vested in NTR, a functioning consensus was easily achievable. Without NTR, however, it is difficult to imagine that the TDP would be much of a force within Guntur. The MLAs depended on NTR for their positions, and the party did not have much of an existence independent of its MLAs. The party office in Guntur was seldom open. An MLA from the TDP readily conceded that the district party organi-zation was "not up to the mark."[58]

---

56 This discussion is based on interviews with Guntur MLAs and on information gathered from knowledgeable political observers, especially a discussion with N. Innaiah in Hy-derabad on March 22, 1986.
57 Srinivas et al., "Social Background," p. 127.
58 Interview with MPR (see footnote 41).

A third issue that needs to be discussed here is the decline in the electoral success of the two communist parties (Table 4.3). During the 1950s and the 1960s, the communists had been electorally quite strong in Guntur.[59] As late as 1967, the two communist parties had together received more than 20 percent of the popular vote. The electoral decline of the communists is explained in part by the fact that the pool from which communist leaders in this part of India were recruited had begun to shrink. Much of the earlier leadership had come from the better-educated Kamma elite of Guntur, who resented the Brahman and the Reddi domination of the Congress party.[60] The success of those leaders had been dependent, at least in part, on the fact that they had been able to mobilize a decent following among other Kammas. Kammas, however, are mainly a landowning community. Eventually the realization of the contradiction of a landowning community supporting communists because of caste resentments forced a reassessment, and the reactions took several forms.

First, the reassessment led to a significant decline in radicalism among important segments of the leadership. That moderation on the part of the elite led to a sharp alienation of the more radical minority. It is this militant minority that for the past 15–20 years has generated considerable "extremist" activity in parts of Guntur and other neighboring districts. Brutal police repression has slowly but surely chipped away at the ranks of these extremists. Thus, the ranks of the militant minorities have been dwindling. As a result, the new postindependence generation of Kamma leaders have sought outlets other than communism to give their community a political expression.

Erosion of the base of communist support among the masses in Guntur, in turn, was related to the elitist nature of the earlier leadership. The ability of Kamma communist leaders to mobilize considerable mass support during the 1950s and the 1960s was much like the ability of the dominant castes in other parts of India to mobilize support among those dependent on them. As that traditional caste authority declined, the need to mobilize electoral support around promises of new social programs increased. While the Kamma communist leaders were downplaying their radicalism so as not to lose the support of other Kamma elite, Congress, in its rhetoric at least, moved further to the left. Thus, Indira Gandhi cut sharply into the support that the local communists enjoyed prior to 1967 among the rural poor.[61]

The sectarian conflict among the communist parties was another reason for their decline. Not only did the split that produced the CPI and the

59 See Harrison, *India,* pp. 204–45, and Weiner, *Party Building in a New Nation,* chapter 8.
60 See Harrison, *India,* pp. 204–45.
61 This is supported by the results of a survey showing that the backward castes and the scheduled castes in Andhra moved closer to the Congress party in the post–1969 period. See Vakil, "Congress Party in Andhra Pradesh," p. 66.

CPM hurt the local communists by dividing the former party straight down the middle, but many extreme factions also emerged. In the post–1967 period, a veteran communist leader in Guntur noted that "ideological questions and struggles took most of our time . . . mass struggles slowed down." As the fine points of the "correct" party line were fought out with an intensity that only the committed can understand, "divisions within the movement sapped the energy" of the local communists in Guntur.[62]

THE STRUGGLE OVER LOCAL GOVERNMENT

When the party of NTR won the 1983 Legislative Assembly elections in Andhra, he must have known that the victory was due primarily to his personal appeal. That victory did not mean that he had gained control over the political affairs of Andhra. In order to strengthen his hold on power, therefore, NTR began pursuing several strategies, including an attempt to dislodge Congress's control over the rural *panchayats*. That attempt unleashed a massive power struggle for the control of local governments. When Weiner studied this area, the introduction of *panchayats* had added new resources for patronage and thus had broadened Congress's support base. Local governments still dispense considerable amounts of developmental resources, and the increasing power struggle between the parties naturally involves the competition to control that patronage. The question of which party will get credit for dispensing governmental resources has now become and is likely to remain one of the most hotly contested political issues in Andhra, as in other states.

The *panchayats* in Guntur, as in all of Andhra, were dormant throughout the 1970s. No *panchayat* elections were held during that period. The roots of that decline go back to Brahmananda Reddy's chief ministry in Andhra (1963–71). In order to consolidate his hold on feuding and factionalized *panchayats,* Reddy downgraded the powers of elected *panchayat* officials in relation to those of the administrators. Local administrators could readily be influenced through Reddy's bureaucratic hierarchy. The prolonged period of dormancy, however, sapped the vitality of the rural *panchayats*. A review of local governments conducted by a committee set up at the behest of the Congress government in Andhra in the late 1970s concluded that "administratively crippled, financially anaemic and caught in cobwebs of confusing procedures, they [the *panchayats*] have been emaciated beyond recognition. They are devoid of any practical utility and meaning to the masses of the rural people for whose sake they were constituted."[63] Even

62 Interview with Kolla Venkaiah (see footnote 49).
63 Government of Andhra Pradesh, Panchayat Raj Department, *Report of the State Committee on Panchayat Raj Institutions* (Hyderabad: Government Secretariat Press, 1981), p. 24.

before the emergence of NTR in 1983, therefore, Guntur's *panchayats* were hardly models of effective local government.

The Congress-controlled state government held *panchayat* elections in 1981. Many Congressites of the Reddi caste (see Tables 4.1 and 4.2) gained control over local governments in Guntur. When the TDP won the 1983 Legislative Assembly elections, NTR found these and other vestiges of Congress party power deeply entrenched at the district level and below. Congress's continuing control over local governments must have been perceived by NTR not only as a major obstacle to his diversion of patronage to his own supporters but also as a significant long-term threat to the establishment of a sustainable electoral base designed around new patronage networks. Instead of sharing power with those rightfully elected, therefore, NTR adopted several legally questionable strategies to undermine Congress's local hold on power.

First, as noted earlier, NTR dismissed all village-level officials, arguing that those officials, who had inherited their positions and who tended to side with the landlords, were a part of the "feudal" structure. Within Guntur, however, no one appears to have been taken in by that "progressive" rhetoric. Most observers would have agreed with the Guntur official who suggested that the real reason for dismissing the village officials was that "the village officials were generally [Congress (I)] supporters."[64] As noted earlier, the dismissals later were declared unconstitutional by the courts.

Second, in order to reduce the powers of the Congress-controlled *zila parishad* (district government), NTR created a parallel governmental structure, the District Planning Board (DPB). The DPB in Guntur in 1986 was staffed by Guntur's MLAs, who were mainly from the TDP. Having created that parallel structure, NTR's government then transferred programs involving significant financial outlays away from the *zila parishad* to the DPB.[65] The constitutionality of that action was never tested in the courts. The abrogation of democratic norms, however, that those actions represented can be highlighted by suggesting a parallel from a higher level of government. It would be as if Rajiv Gandhi were to set up an organization parallel to NTR's government, staff it with Congress legislators, and then channel the funds allotted for all national-government programs to Andhra through that new organization.

Lastly, NTR decided to abolish altogether the *samithi,* or the block level of the *panchayat,* and replace each of them with about four lower-level *mandal panchayats.* The rationale again was the "need for decentraliza-

---

64 Interview with K. Raju (joint district collector in Guntur), Guntur, March 26, 1986. For details on the dismissal of village officers, see "Abolition of Village Officers," *Economic and Political Weekly,* March 9, 1985, pp. 393–4.

65 This information is based on several interviews in Guntur, especially with H. Chengappa (District collector in Guntur), Guntur, March 25, 1986.

tion," but most observers agreed that the real reason was to weaken, if not to destroy, the established support networks that had been built up by the Congress. In Guntur, at least, that strategy did not work well. *Panchayat* elections in 1988 reconfirmed Congress's continuing popularity in local politics. The *zila parishad,* as well as a majority of the *mandals,* again came under Congress's control. What is also noteworthy is that those local elections in Guntur were accompanied by considerable physical violence.[66] The intense power contest between the two parties is thus finding expression in the constitutional electoral arena and in the streets. Congress has returned to power in the state as this book goes to press. Intensified conflict over the control of local governmental resources seems likely to continue.

It is important to keep in mind NTR's legally questionable strategies. Otherwise, incidents like Indira Gandhi's dismissal of NTR's government in 1983 might give one the incorrect impression that only Congress uses illegal means to fight its political battles. As illustrated by the example of NTR, when it comes to winning and securing power, many of India's ruling parties other than Congress violate democratic and constitutional niceties.

The intense power struggle between the parties has impaired the daily functioning of local governments. First, the abolition of village officers eliminated what often was the government's only link to the villages. Although much was wrong with that old system, it is not at all clear that the system of officials instituted by NTR was superior to the old one. Meanwhile, district officials complained that with the village officials gone, "village level information was not forthcoming."[67] Second, implementation of programs was slowed down. For example, carrying out a government program often begins with identifying those who are to benefit from the program. But in Guntur, parallel political organizations, one dominated by Congressites and the other by TDP legislators, were competing to ensure that their respective supporters would benefit from government programs. Local officials noted that the power contest had at times been so intense that programs had ground to a halt.[68]

Lastly, the vitriolic interparty conflict had damaged the morale of the nonelected officials – the local bureaucrats. That problem was especially severe in Guntur, where Congress dominated the district government. However, decisions that would affect the careers of local bureaucrats were being made by the state government, which from 1983 to 1989 was controlled by the TDP. A senior *panchayat* official, who did not wish to be identified, poignantly described the situation as follows:

66 For discussion, see "Andhra Pradesh," *Economic and Political Weekly,* April 4, 1987, pp. 582–5.
67 Interview with K. Raju (see footnote 64).
68 Interview with H. Chengappa (see footnote 65). This general point was also made by several *samithi* presidents with reference to either the housing schemes or the national rural employment program.

To do your job well, you have to say no to unreasonable demands. As a BDO [Block Development Officer], however, if you say no to the [*zila parishad* president] or an MLA, he will never be happy. He will complain that you are corrupt, drunkard, womanizer or nepotistic. Ministers [who often are well known to the MLAs] will insult the BDO in public. So BDOs learn to get on. Same with police officers and Collectors. Whoever does not oblige [the ruling party] gets numerous complaints sent up to the minister. You don't want to get on the wrong side of the elected man.... And yet, there is no code of conduct for an elected man.... The morale [among bureaucrats] is really low. Morale is low from the top to the bottom.

As the TDP strove to consolidate its power in Guntur, the insecurity and uncertainty of local government officials increased.

CONCLUSION

I have sought in this chapter to analyze the political drama that unfolded in one district when Congress went into an electoral and organizational decline and a regional party came to power. When Weiner analyzed the same district in the 1960s, factionalism and patronage networks surrounding the local government not only were the core characteristics of the local Congress but also helped explain Congress's local dominance. Over the past 25 years, however, the political scene in Guntur, like that in Kheda, as discussed earlier, has come to be characterized by a growing authority vacuum. A popular film actor stepped into that vacuum for a while to create a regional alternative to a disintegrating Congress. Unfortunately, NTR's government did not prove to be an agent of institutional redevelopment. The problems of building authority and providing good government in this region continue.

The authority vacuum that grew under the rule of Congress in Andhra, and therefore also in Guntur, was due in part to changes in the social structure and in part to the strategies adopted by the political elite to secure power. In Guntur today, it is clear that the superior social positioning of the members of the so-called dominant castes no longer commands the respect and authority that would enable them to influence the political behavior of those beneath them. Whether or not that was true in the past, it is certainly true now that a member of the Reddi elite of Guntur cannot expect to easily convince the members of the backward and scheduled castes in the villages to vote for him simply because of his higher caste status. Backward and scheduled castes have emerged as significant political forces in their own right. As this has happened, the old, seemingly consensual pattern of politics that revolved around dominant caste leaders and their dependent followers has unraveled, probably forever. The political behaviors of various social groups are more unpredictable now than they were in the 1950s or even the 1960s; the stability of electoral coalitions has vanished. The fact that the backward castes constitute nearly half of Guntur's population and are divided into more than 20 *jatis* further adds to the heterogeneity and unpredictability of the political behaviors of local social groups.

It would be difficult for any party to build stable social alliances and a coherent organization in this increasingly heterogeneous local political society. In any case, Indira Gandhi and her Congress followers in Andhra never tried. The Congress party within Andhra and within Guntur was highly factionalized. Indira's populist strategy seemed to fit the short-term need to win elections in an uncertain political environment. Over time, however, that strategy had sharply negative political consequences for Congress in Guntur. As far as electoral issues are concerned, the option for Congress to forge an alliance of the backwards and the Harijans, as in Kheda, was not available in Guntur. In addition to the alienation between the backwards and the Harijans, the heterogeneity of the backward castes and the continued domination of Congress by the local Reddis contributed to Congress's failure to incorporate the numerically significant backward castes. That, along with the significant political role played by Guntur's Kammas, made it difficult for Congress to sustain power in Guntur.

Beyond the electoral issues, Indira's repeated imposition of weak, controllable chief ministers on Andhra wreaked havoc with the state's politics. Between 1978 and 1983, there were four chief ministers, two of whom had lost in the Legislative Assembly elections. Factionalism and squabbling within the Congress ranks reached new highs. Government came to a virtual halt. There was increasing resentment in Andhra regarding the repeated interventions from Delhi. Into that deepening authority vacuum stepped NTR.

Within Guntur, it was clear that the TDP was mainly an alliance of the Kammas and the backward castes. It was also clear that the local TDP was not much of a political party. Its party organization was virtually non-existent; the creation of a significant second tier of leadership below NTR was not encouraged; there was no coherent party program. The prospects that the TDP, dominated by a single popular leader, would put down strong institutional roots were not good. Although NTR temporarily filled the electoral space left open by the decline of Congress, that was not enough to guarantee authoritative government, and that government proved to be short-lived. The ineffectiveness of NTR's government was manifest in the kinds of outcomes that often characterize governments without deep and systematic authority: arbitrary decisions; failure to diagnose problems and implement even modest solutions to some of the pressing societal problems; and most important, the growing role of force and violence in resolving political conflicts.

5

Belgaun, Karnataka

Belgaun district nestles in the northwestern corner of Karnataka, bordering mainly on Maharashtra but also touching Goa at Belgaun's southwestern corner. Like Kheda and Guntur, Belgaun is primarily a rural district, although it is less densely populated than Kheda or Guntur.[1] Belgaun also is not as prosperous a district as Kheda or even Guntur. Were it not for the bustling trading city of Belgaun, the district's per capita income would be much lower.

Several aspects of the patterns of landownership in this district are noteworthy.[2] The percentage of landless laborers in Belgaun is considerably lower than that in Guntur, about the same as that in Kheda, and close to the national average. Among the landowning population, the number of midsize holders is noteworthy. More than 60 percent of the landholdings are between 1 and 10 hectares (2.5–24.7 acres) each, accounting for nearly 70 percent of the cultivated land. Nearly a third of the landholdings are of less than 1 hectare each, accounting for barely 5 percent of the land. These smallholdings probably are all owner-operated by now, because tenancy decreased sharply in Karnataka after the tenancy reforms implemented under Devraj Urs in the second half of the 1970s.[3] At the top end of the landowning spectrum, there are quite a few large landholdings in Belgaun: More than 25 percent of the land is in holdings of more than 10 hectares (24.7 acres) each, but this land is operated by nearly 5 percent of the landowning population, suggesting that ownership may be less concentrated than in Kheda. Overall, these patterns suggest that the rural profile of Belgaun is somewhat more egalitarian than that of Kheda and

---

1 The total population of the district in 1978 was 2.7 million, and the population density was 181 per square kilometer. This and other demographic data cited here are taken from Government of Karnataka, Planning Department, *Draft Five Year Plan, 1978–83* (Bangalore: Government Press, 1983), p. 151.

2 The land data are from Government of Karnataka, State Agriculture Census Commissioner, *Agricultural Census, 1976–77* (Bangalore: Government Press, 1978).

3 See Atul Kohli, *The State and Poverty in India: The Politics of Reform* (Cambridge University Press, 1987), chapter 4.

that this district has a smaller pool of the totally wretched at the bottom of the social scale than does Guntur.

There is a major linguistic divide within the district's population. About 20 percent of the local population trace their roots to neighboring Maharashtra and speak Marathi; the rest of the population speak Kannada. The Marathas, with their distinctive martial traditions, are the main community among the Marathi-speaking population (the Marathis) and are concentrated in the areas near the Maharashtra border. The town of Belgaun has a slight plurality of Marathi speakers and is dominated by the Marathi elite. The issue of whether or not the areas with Marathi pluralities, especially the town of Belgaun, should be transferred from Karnataka to Maharashtra continues to be one of the central political issues in this district.

Among the Kannada-speaking population, the Lingayats are the dominant community. Followers of Siva for several centuries, the Lingayats are more accurately described as a religious community, rather than a caste community. There are significant caste and income differentials within the Lingayats, who constitute nearly a quarter of the district's population. Most of the area's large landowners are Lingayats. These upper-caste, landowning Lingayat elite dominate the Kannada community. At the other end of the social spectrum, the scheduled castes, tribes, and Moslems generally constitute the lower strata and make up another 20 percent of the district's population. The groups in the middle make up the rest of the population – nearly 35 percent. These are mainly the numerous "backward castes," including the numerically significant Kurbu and Reddi castes.

Myron Weiner analyzed two main themes with reference to Belgaun. First, Weiner found that there was considerable political conflict between the Marathi-speaking and Kannada-speaking peoples, especially over the status of the town of Belgaun. The conflict was marked by intensity and passion, involving repeated agitations. The reasons underlying the conflict were complex. They were partly economic, because the town of Belgaun was of considerable economic significance, and because the Marathis were worried about their educational and job prospects in a Kannada-speaking state. The reasons were partly linguistic and cultural, because the two communities tended to follow different traditions. They were partly political, in the sense that neither the government of Maharashtra nor that of Karnataka could let go of Belgaun without incurring the wrath of their respective citizens.

The second major theme discussed by Weiner was the nature of the Congress party in Belgaun. Although Congress had not succeeded in co-opting or diffusing the Marathi–Kannadiga conflict, it had established itself as a dominant and effective local political force. Congress had built its considerable electoral support mainly by aligning itself with the prominent and influential local Lingayats. Although in terms of organization the district office and even some of the *taluka* offices functioned, local Congressites were not effective in handling such modern political tasks as maintaining party records, recruiting and enrolling party members, and holding meetings to discuss issues. Nevertheless, Weiner found Congressites quite adept at such neotraditional roles as expediting solutions to local problems requiring public resources, arbitrating local conflicts, and getting involved in philanthropic work. In summary, Weiner found Congressites to possess "a high capacity to create and sustain" a working political organization.[4]

Over the past 25 years there have been changes in these two issue areas: the Marathi–Kannadiga conflict and party politics in Belgaun. To anticipate the discussion, I argue here that the Marathi–Kannadiga conflict continues. The Maratha elite have lost some of their popular support because, for the most part, the Marathi community has lost hope that the status quo can be changed. Given the right political stimulus from national or state leaders, however, the local elite still can exploit the nuisance value of the linguistic conflict for political advantage. Thus, the Marathi–Kannadiga conflict provides a useful paradigm for many ethnic conflicts in India that for the most part simmer, but occasionally explode.

As for party politics, Congress's unchallenged dominance has been replaced by a competitive situation involving rival elites affiliated with the Congress and Janata parties. Neither of the parties has much organizational presence within the district. In spite of that organizational vacuum, however, confrontation leading to violence over caste, class, and political issues still is not the dominant characteristic of local politics. That is due in part to the fact that some of the political energy is dissipated in the linguistic conflict. More important, however, are these factors: The landowning castes have regained political power in the region; the backward castes have not been mobilized here to the same extent seen in, say, Kheda; and for much of the 1970s and 1980s the state of Karnataka was ruled by moderately competent chief ministers.

AN OVERVIEW OF KARNATAKA POLITICS

Before discussing the specifics of district politics, a brief overview of Karnataka politics may be useful.[5] Throughout the 1950s and the 1960s, po-

---

4 Myron Weiner, *Party Building in a New Nation: The Indian National Congress* (University of Chicago Press, 1967), p. 300.

5 Good general accounts of politics in Karnataka are readily available: James Manor, *Political Change in an Indian state, Mysore, 1915–55,* Australian National University Monographs on South Asia, No. 2 (Columbia: South Asia Books, 1978); James Manor, "Structural Changes in Karnataka Politics," *Economic and Political Weekly,* 12:44(1977), pp. 1865–9; B. B. Patil-Okaly, "Karnataka: Politics of One Party Dominance," in Iqbal Narain, ed., *State Politics in India* (Meerut: Meenakshi Prakashan, 1976); R. K. Hebsur, "Karnataka," *Seminar,* 278(August 1978), pp. 21–6.

litical matters in Karnataka (then Mysore) were dominated by the Congress party in alliance with the two non-Brahman dominant castes of the state: the Vokkaligas and the Lingayats. The Vokkaligas, Karnataka's equivalent of northern Jats, ruled the state until about 1956. After the reorganization of the state, when new districts of Kannada speakers from the former Bombay and Hyderabad regions were added, the Lingayats gained numerical significance. Since then, the political scene in Karnataka has been characterized by the jockeying for power between these two groups, with the Lingayats somewhat enjoying the upper hand.

The first major change in state politics came with Devraj Urs's ascent to the chief ministership in the early 1970s. Riding the coattails of a popular and populist Indira Gandhi, Urs sought to create a broader ruling coalition. To an important degree, he succeeded. Although Urs did not totally exclude the dominant castes, especially the Vokkaligas, he incorporated representatives of the backward and scheduled castes into positions of power and into patronage networks. In that process, however, Urs alienated important segments of the formerly powerful groups, especially some of the Lingayats. Those alienated groups stayed with the old Congress – Congress (O) – which eventually merged into the Janata party. The Janata party, in turn, ruled Karnataka from 1983 to 1989, eventually yieding to Congress (I) in late 1989.

The period between the decline of Devraj Urs's power in 1979 and the emergence of the Janata party in 1983 proved to be chaotic and politically quite significant. Urs's power declined as he split from Indira Gandhi and sought to build his own regional party, the Kranti Dal. Over the short run, that new party failed to capture the state's political imagination. Because Devraj Urs died in 1983, the long-term prospects of that party became moot. Meanwhile, Indira Gandhi installed a grossly incompetent Congress (I) chief minister in Karnataka in 1980: Gundu Rao, a crony of Sanjay Gandhi. As in the case of imposed and incompetent chief ministers in Andhra Pradesh, Gundu Rao pushed Karnataka's government to the brink of collapse. The delegitimization engendered by that experiment contributed significantly to the defeat of the Congress party. Fortunately for Karnataka, that interlude was brief. The Janata party won election in 1983.

The Janata party, which represented a narrow spectrum of old ruling groups, entered the 1983 elections in alliance with Devraj Urs's Kranti-Ranga, the latter supposedly standing for a broad-based coalition. The alliance of those two quite dissimilar parties was facilitated by their mutual hostility toward Congress (I) and Gundu Rao, as well as by electoral opportunism. The immediate result was that the parties and their social bases became totally confused. Once victorious, the Janata party was fortunate to find another competent leader in Ramakrishna Hegde. Hegde ruled the state with moderate effectiveness for nearly four years. He also led the Janata party to its second electoral victory in 1985. Hegde was so popular in 1985 and 1986 that the *New York Times* ran a feature on him, openly speculating that he might be a national challenger to Rajiv Gandhi. However, Hegde's government was soon bogged down in the recurring problem of accommodating rival factions, as well as in the familiar charges and countercharges of corruption. Factionalism within the Janata party eventually created a serious rift, helping Congress (I) to regain power. What is significant for our purposes is that Karnataka's dominant groups, the Vokkaligas and the Lingayats, regained some of their lost political prominence during the Janata phase, especially under Hegde. The political situation in the second half of the 1980s was, of course, not identical with that of the 1950s and 1960s, when the power of dominant castes went unchallenged. The backward castes and other groups cannot be totally ignored anymore. Thus, the ruling group is broader now than it was in the 1950s and 1960s. It is, however, definitely narrower than under Devraj Urs. The dominant castes of Karnataka regained considerable access to governmental power and resources during the Janata phase.

THE MARATHI–KANNADIGA CONFLICT OVER BELGAUN

Political conflict along linguistic lines continues to be an important factor in local politics in Belgaun. The roots of this conflict are located in the reorganization of the Indian states around linguistic lines during the 1950s. As the Kannada-speaking districts of Bombay were transferred to Karnataka, small pockets of Marathis also ended up in Karnataka. They came to be led by an organization called the Maharashtra Ekikaram Samiti (MES). The MES has argued the case of Marathis for nearly four decades. Its case for transferring certain Marathi-dominated areas of Belgaun (mainly the town of Belgaun) to Maharashtra rests partly on the linguistic principle and the related issue of ethnic solidarity on which the states are organized and partly on the argument that Marathis are discriminated against in both education and jobs, especially government jobs, in a state controlled by the Kannadigas.

When Weiner studied this district, he noted that because the linguistic reorganization of the states had been led by a Congress-dominated national government, those opposed to certain boundary decisions, such as the MES, found themselves from the beginning opposed to Congress at the local level. The national government's decision to award the town of Belgaun to Karnataka, Weiner also noted, was mainly a matter of political compromise, with some Kannada-speaking districts of old Hyderabad being given to Andhra Pradesh in exchange for Belgaun being given to Karnataka. By contrast, the case that local Kannadigas made for holding on to Belgaun was mainly historical. Belgaun town had always been an integral part of a district that was primarily Kannada-speaking. In sum, the MES's argument on linguistic grounds, the argument of Kannadigas on historical precedent, and the national decision based on political considerations all combined to set up the basic matrix within which the conflict has evolved.

Weiner found that the conflict over the town of Belgaun resembled the conflict over Trieste, Italy, insofar as it was marked by a passion that bordered on "irrational hysteria." The MES pressed its demand via demonstrations, agitations, fasting until death, and speeches that were argued as if fundamental issues of human rights and international border disputes were involved. In the mid–1980s, after two and a half decades, the hysterical quality of the conflict had subsided. The passions at the community level clearly had been lowered.

An analysis of this political change requires some background information. In 1966, when national elections were approaching, Indira Gandhi found herself under pressure from Maharashtra to show some movement toward resolving this conflict. As a result, she established a one-man commission, the Mahajan Commission; it was agreed to by both parties in the conflict and was to make recommendations for a solution. The timing of the commission's establishment and the release of its report is revealing: The commission was established just a few months before the February 1967 national elections, and its report was released after the elections. The establishment of the commission was claimed to be something of a victory by the Congress government in Maharashtra, and it helped the party electorally. The MES in Belgaun eventually opposed the commission, probably because it suspected that the transfer of Belgaun to Maharashtra, which was the crucial issue, was not likely to be recommended.[6] Because that suspicion was widely shared, the Congress government of Karnataka felt it had little to fear; the status quo was not likely to change. Indeed, the final report recommended that the town of Belgaun remain a part of the state of Karnataka.

By the time the report came out in 1967, the national elections were over, and Congress governments were in power in Bombay, Bangalore, and New Delhi. Maharashtra did not accept the nonbinding recommendations of the Mahajan Commission, but it did not pursue its opposition with any vigor. The electoral considerations that had led to the renewed demands were already receding into the background. Karnataka argued that either the Mahajan Commission report should be accepted fully or the status quo should be maintained. Because the Mahajan Commission report was not acceptable to Maharashtra, the status quo continued de facto. Having barely eked out a national majority, Indira Gandhi had many national problems to worry about that were more pressing than the conflict

---

6 This point is made, for example, in an openly partisan account that favors the cause of the Maharashtrians: Vasant R. Bhandare, *Maharashtra–Karnataka Border Dispute: Politics of Manipulation* (Bombay: Kirti Prakashan, 1985), part V.

over Belgaun. A low level of diffuse hostility was a situation with which all the main actors in the conflict could live.

Local actors with their own political purposes sought to rekindle the issue periodically. The Shiv Sena of Bombay, for example, a "sons of the soil" local party that argues for all sorts of "Maharashtrian causes,"[7] chose to mobilize the Maharashtrians of Bombay in 1969 to demand "justice" for Marathis south of the border. The agitations and rioting that resulted took numerous lives and strengthened Shiv Sena's position in Bombay. In the early 1970s, the MES in Belgaun also periodically organized protests. In contrast to the Shiv Sena, however, the MES protests were relatively peaceful. That was in part because the MES is not a militant party, but beyond that the MES has a big political stake in prolonging the low levels of hostility. The MES really does not want a resolution of the problem and thus does not push for it with any great vigor. A resolution of the problem would take away the MES's raison d'être, as well as the modest political support that MES leaders enjoy in the electoral arena.

The two-year "national emergency" (the Emergency of 1975–7) proclaimed by Indira Gandhi and the rule of the Janata party (1977–80) that followed the Emergency confirmed for the local actors in Belgaun that neither of the major national parties was interested in reopening the issue of revising state boundaries. On the contrary, any new discussion of what was considered nationally to be a settled issue could rekindle numerous other minor state claims. Thus, the delegations periodically sent by the Marathis returned empty-handed from Delhi. Those delegations prompted just enough local interest in the issue to keep the MES in business.

For the 1980s, Table 5.1 documents that the MES remained a significant local force, but it also lost two of its five Legislative Assembly seats between 1978 and 1985. Its electoral decline was not limited to the loss of seats, but also was reflected in lost votes. (See Table 5.3.) What factors can help explain both the continuity and the change in the MES's political position?

The MES is not a political party. It is a single-issue organization seeking the transfer of Marathi-dominated areas of Belgaun to neighboring Maharashtra. There is no formal membership, and there are no elective offices within the MES. Yet, locally the MES is quite powerful. That strength is based on solidarity and dependencies within a well-knit ethnic community. Community leaders also serve as organizational leaders, helping decide the overall political program and the choice of individuals to represent the MES in elections. The center of the organization, to the extent that there is a center, is a newspaper called the *Tarun Bharat*. Supporters and non-

---

7 For an excellent account of the Shiv Sena, see Mary F. Katzenstein, *Ethnicity and Equality: The Shiv Sena Party and Preferential Policies in Bombay* (Ithaca, N.Y.: Cornell University Press, 1979).

Table 5.1. *Caste and community backgrounds of MLAs, Belgaun district, Karnataka, 1978 and 1985*

Caste or community background	Political affiliation			
	Congress	Janata	MES	Total
1978				
Lingayats	4	1	0	5
Marathis	2	0	5	7
Others[a]	5	1	0	6
Total	11	2	5	18
1985				
Lingayats[b]	1	6	0	7
Marathis	1	0	3	4
Others[c]	0	6	0	6
Total	2	12	3	17

[a]Includes two scheduled caste and tribe members, one Jain, one Kurbu, one Reddi, and one Moslem.
[b]One independent Lingayat MLA is not included in this matrix.
[c]Includes three scheduled caste and tribe members, one Jain, one Kurbu, and one Reddi.
Source: Compiled from local interviews.

partisan observers of the MES agree that this newspaper is indeed the center of activity and communication within the Marathi community.[8] Nonpartisan observers are also quick to point out that *Tarun Bharat* is "financed by Shiv Sena and the government of Maharashtra."[9] It is important to emphasize the single-issue nature of the organization. As a Marathi community leader pointed out, "people within the MES have different political views but come together on the unification issue."[10]

The main reason for the MES's ability to mobilize a fair amount of support from Belgaun's Marathi community is, of course, ethnic solidarity. That was so when Weiner studied the district, and it remains so. Over the past two decades, however, certain important changes have occurred that highlight what can happen to the politics of ethnicity over time.

The leaders of the MES now have a vested interest in continuing the ethnic-based political conflict. Local observers treat the current leadership with a considerable degree of cynicism. A local journalist's perception of the contrast between the first-generation MES leadership and the current

8 Interviews with Subhash Ramchandra Jadhav (vice-president of the MES and former mayor of Belgaun), Belgaun, April 26, 1986, and Raghevendra A. Joshi (editor, *Nadoja*), Belgaun, April 23, 1986.
9 Interview with Raghevendra Joshi (see footnote 8).
10 Interview with P. G. Jambawalikar (Marathi community leader), Belgaun, April 22, 1986.

leadership is revealing: "They [the first-generation leaders] were sincere men. But after that, in this new generation, selfish motives dominate. . . . Now, the issue is kept alive by the MES. Their existence depends on the continuity of this issue. If this issue is allowed to die, MES will stop being significant."[11] Consider the words of another local observer: "Electoral positions provide enviable positions. Marathis want these positions. Marathi votes go to Marathis. . . . Marathi MLAs will actually lose their position and relevance if Belgaun is given to Maharashtra. . . . No one really wants this outcome."[12] The analytical significance of those observations is not that ethnicity is not a natural cleavage around which political conflict precipitates, but rather that, over time, leaders of ethnic groups can develop an interest in instigating ethnic conflict for the sake of political benefit.

In addition to using the appeal of ethnic solidarity (i.e., all Marathis should be part of Maharashtra), MES leaders have been helped in maintaining their support by two other factors. First, a large majority of the Marathis in Belgaun, especially in Belgaun town, belong to one caste: the Maratha caste. Moreover, many of these people originally came from neighboring areas in Maharashtra: "90 percent of the Marathis coming here [to the town of Belgaun] came from one district [of Maharashtra], the Sitaru district. [Once a few came], they attracted many more from their district to provide services and support. Hence their population grew very rapidly, especially between 1925–50."[13] The ties of caste and place of origin have therefore reinforced the leader–follower ties within the Marathi community.

Beyond these historical considerations, there is a contemporary factor at work. In the words of a member of the Marathi elite, "the majority of Marathis in Belgaun work for Marathi businessmen."[14] Because access to employment is based on ethnic criteria, ethnicity cuts across political cleavages that might develop around employer–employee relations. Relations of economic dependence have reinforced "primordial" loyalties, helping perpetuate the ethnic-bloc character of Marathi political behavior in Belgaun.

Not all the Marathis support the MES because of traditional bonds and relations of economic dependence. This is especially true for one numerically significant category: educated urban youth. To attract their support, the MES emphasizes issues of educational opportunities and jobs in the context of ethnic relations.[15] Up to grade 10, for example, Marathi children can go to schools where Marathi is spoken. Beyond that, Marathi students

11 Interview with Raghevendra Joshi (see footnote 8).
12 Interview with Bheemasen Torgal (editor, *Samatal*), Belgaun, April 23, 1986.
13 Interview with D. N. Joshi (resident editor, *Samatal*), Belgaun, April 23, 1986.
14 Interview with Subhash Jadhav (see footnote 8).
15 Interview with Kiran Thakur (editor, *Tarun Bharat*), Belgaun, April 22, 1986.

Table 5.2. *Community backgrounds and political affiliations of the elected members of the Municipal Corporation, city of Belgaun, 1984*

Community background	Political affiliation			
	Janata	MES	Others[a]	Total
Marathis	1	28	4	33
Kannadigas	5	0	6	11
Moslems	4	0	3	7
Total	10	28	13	51

[a]Includes 10 independent members, as well as one each affiliated with the Communist Party of India, Congress (I), and the Bhartiya Janata party.
Source: Compiled from local interviews. Mr. Subhash Ramchandra Jadhav, former mayor of Belgaun (1984–5), helped identify the community backgrounds and the political affiliations of the members of the Municipal Corporation.

must choose between schools conducted in English or Kannada.[16] This naturally gives the Kannadiga youth some advantage over the Marathis. Moreover, many of the institutions of higher education, such as medical and engineering colleges, are controlled by the Lingayats.[17] Kannadigas and especially Lingayats are generally favored in government jobs, both because of language and because Lingayats are politically powerful in Bangalore. These issues of state-controlled education and employment opportunities are bitterly fought, especially because of the considerable economic scarcity. The MES benefits politically from this contentiousness; they argue that the reason for their limited opportunities is that they, as Marathis, are stuck in a Kannadiga-dominated state.

These issues of community bonds and political and economic opportunities reinforce one another, thus helping to explain why the MES continues to enjoy the electoral support of many Marathis in Belgaun and hold local assembly seats. Table 5.2 shows that such support is especially significant in the town of Belgaun. The Municipal Corporation of Belgaun continues to be controlled by MES-supported Marathi candidates. In a political landscape in which there are few enduring patterns, the permanence of ethnicity as a political variable is noteworthy. Democratic control over the town of Belgaun is a powerful symbol of the MES's political efficacy; it is a fact to which MES supporters always point when making their case.

Although the continuing support that the MES enjoys is a significant

16 Information from an interview with S. N. Powar (member of the Marathi community of Belgaun involved in educational affairs), Belgaun, April 22, 1986.
17 Information from a discussion with Mr. Sardesai, a prominent Lingayat of Belgaun, who boasted that once his family had been the second largest landowners in old Mysore, trailing only the Maharaja of Mysore, Belgaun, April 24, 1986.

aspect of the local political scene, it is important to emphasize that its support is not as solid as the MES would like others to believe, and more important, it has declined over time. The control that the MES maintains over the Belgaun Municipal Corporation is due as much to the divisions among the opposition as to the support that the MES enjoys. For example, even in the 28 of the 51 wards of Belgaun town where MES councillors won municipal elections, their votes added up to only 40 percent of the total. The vote secured by the MES in the town as a whole (i.e., in the 51 wards) was not much more than one-third of the total vote.[18] The reason that the opposition's challenge is not effective is fairly simple. Consider these words of a Kannadiga supporter:

In Belgaun there are 42% Marathis and 40% Kannadigas. We should be able to win here but we do not. The Marathis are very cohesive. Ours is a divided house. First, we are divided between Kannadigas and Urda speakers. Then, within Kannadigas, there are Christians and Hindus. Within Hindus, there are Brahmins, Lingayats, Jains etc. . . . And then there is always the division between the Congress and Janata.[19]

Divisions within its opposition give the MES its advantage. If some political catalyst should narrow the divisions within the non-Marathis of Belgaun, the MES's electoral position could be fundamentally threatened.

One large contextual variable that has contributed to the decline in MES support is that none of the major state or national parties supports the issue of the transfer of Belgaun. A local journalist suggested that "the crux of the problem [for the MES] is that the issue is closed in both Bombay and Bangalore."[20] Because of that realization, the people have begun to accept the status quo. One can speculate, even without public-opinion data, that after three decades of controversy, and with the prospect of change growing dim, some decline in the MES's support was to be expected.

Two other factors have contributed to the decline in the MES's popular support. First, though one would not guess it from the tone of the political rhetoric, the fact is that local community relations between the Marathi-speaking and Kannada-speaking peoples are quite amicable. Religious differences between the two communities are minor, and there is a long-established local tradition of allowing marriage between similar castes, despite linguistic differences. During interviews, representatives of both communities agreed that, at the community level, there are no problems between the Marathis and the Kannadigas.[21] Even some of the MES leaders

18 Figures calculated from unpublished data made available by the Belgaun Municipal Corporation.
19 Interview with Raghevendra Joshi (see footnote 8).
20 Interview with Bheemasen Torgal (see footnote 12).
21 Interviews with Subhash Jadhav (see footnote 8) and Bheemasen Torgal (see footnote 12).

are married to women whose first language is Kannada.[22] Moreover, there are intricate economic links between the two communities, and over time those links have grown stronger. The two communities continue to work and easily mix together.

As shown by the case of the Sikhs and the Hindus in Punjab, good community relations are no guarantee against political divisiveness. Many factors can be manipulated so as to set one community against another. At present, however, the MES's charges of atrocities against Marathis simply have not fired the local political imagination.

The other factor that hurts the MES politically is the growing differentiation within the Marathi community. The leaders of the MES generally are from well-off, urban families. For example, consider these seven individuals who played important roles in deciding who would run for office with the MES's support:

Bapu Sahib Mahagoenkar: a long time MES activist who heads a transport company in Belgaun; Kiran Thakur: The son of one of the founders of MES and the editor of MES's main vehicle of community influence, the Marathi daily, *Tarun Bharat;* Subhash Jadhav: a former mayor of Belgaun who is a merchant involved with fertilizers; Maloji Rao Ashtekar: also a former mayor of Belgaun who heads a Marathi school; Jagdish Sarada: a former deputy mayor of Belgaun who is in the business of cloth manufacturing; Dr. Indirabhi Khade: former president of Belgaun municipality who heads MES's women's wing and is a practicing doctor; and G.M. Bhatkhande: also a former president of Belgaun municipality who is in the book selling business.[23]

All of these individuals share a prosperous, urban background rooted in either business or the professions, as well as a history of political activity and involvement with the MES.

By contrast, the followers of the MES generally are from the backward castes of Marathas and are either relatively poor urban workers or peasants in the countryside. Although this is not unusual in much of Indian politics, some local observers believe that this rift is becoming politically significant. In the words of one, "many Marathis are realizing that the poor agitate, but the better-off Marathas benefit."[24] If true, this suggests that the erosion of the MES's political support can be attributed to growing class divisions within an ethnic community. Again, however, without public-opinion data that hypothesis cannot be confirmed or refuted. On balance, and on the basis of numerous local conversations, that hypothesis seems not terribly persuasive. Although class divisions may be of some significance, ethnic solidarity remains the chief political characteristic of Belgaun's Marathi community.

More than class divisions, the kind of differentiation that has begun to

22 See, for example, a report on Belgaun conflict in *India Today,* June 30, 1986, p. 35.
23 Information from P. G. Jambawalikar (see footnote 10).
24 Interview with Bheemasen Torgal (see footnote 12).

hurt the MES politically is the growing factionalism among the Marathi elite. As noted earlier, the MES leaders are divided on most political issues, except for the issue of unity with Maharashtra. Even within this limited unity, however, there are now many divisions, concerning not strategy or tactics but, rather, the issue of who should get tickets for elections. A local journalist explained:

There are divisions within the MES now. Kiran Thakur group is the ruling group. B. B. Sainik [a former MLA] leads the dissenting group. Sainik was not given a ticket. His group broke away and fielded a dissenting candidate in the last election. Ultimately the candidate withdrew, but only under pressure from Maharashtra.[25]

Factionalism of this sort has been exploited by the major parties that operate in the area, especially by Congress. As early as 1978, Urs had started giving Congress (I) tickets to some Marathis. As Table 5.1 shows, two of Belgaun's Congress (I) MLAs in 1978 had Marathi backgrounds. One can be sure that these and other non-MES Marathi elite have begun to attract some Marathi votes, thus cutting into the MES's electoral base.

Two constituencies that the MES once controlled, but that have withdrawn their support in recent years, highlight the diverse factors at work in explaining the MES's shrinking base:

Nippani constituency. This constituency is nearly 80 percent Marathi-speaking. It was a natural stronghold of the MES in the past. However, the MES lost the last two elections here. Both times, a Marathi candidate won on a Congress (I) ticket. The main reason for this is factionalism within the Marathi community. Devraj Urs first exploited this rift. Because the fight is between competing faction leaders for political office, there is no easy way for the MES to resolve such a zero-sum situation.

Bagawadi constituency. The Marathi-speaking population is significant here, but is not dominant. About a quarter of the population are Marathis. In the past, the MES won this constituency due to a solid block of Marathi votes. Because the Kannada speakers were divided, they could not put up a cohesive opposition. Before the last elections in 1985, however, the Janata party organized discussions that led to some preelection arrangements. A field of 11 opposition candidates was reduced to 3. The result was that the MES lost to Janata.[26]

These examples clearly suggest that the growing differentiation within the Marathi community and the narrowing of differences among the opposition have contributed to the erosion of the MES's local electoral base.

Finally, a flare-up of that conflict in 1985–6 requires brief attention. The climax of these tensions was a week-long agitation in June 1986 that involved rioting mobs, sabotage of water pipelines, attempts to damage a

25 Interview with Raghevendra Joshi (see footnote 8).
26 Information gathered from local interviews.

major local dam, the derailing of a train, and police shootings that killed seven people and injured many more. What happened? The question is especially important because the good community relations between the Marathis and the Kannadigas, on the one hand, and the decline in the MES's support, on the other, could easily have led an observer in 1985 to believe that the proposal to transfer Belgaun was a dying issue, if not already dead.

One common thread links all the factors that rekindled that local linguistic conflict: the compulsions of electoral competition. First, a major stimulus for renewal of the conflict came from Hegde's decision to make Kannada Karnataka's official language. The reason Hegde adopted such a policy had to do with his need to bolster Janata's political position against that of Congress by capitalizing on whatever regional nationalism existed in Karnataka. That the implementation of the decision would not alter the status quo in Belgaun was made clear when Hegde assured Marathi leaders that Kannada would not be made compulsory in primary education in the border areas.[27] Moreover, Janata and the MES had a tacit electoral arrangement in 1985; the two organizations were hardly warring political forces. And yet, Hegde's statewide decision offered the MES a mobilization issue that was too tempting to pass up, especially in view of the MES's sagging political fortunes.

Two other factors encouraged the MES to renew its agitations. First, the MES's leaders appear to have received the message in 1986 that Rajiv Gandhi was interested in reopening and "resolving" the Belgaun border dispute, "once the Punjab problem had been settled."[28] Because the problem had been considered settled in New Delhi prior to the accession of Rajiv Gandhi, one wonders if the fact that Janata was in power in Karnataka at that time was part of the new political calculation; a gain for the MES could mean a gain for Congress at the expense of Janata.

A second fact further stimulated the renewal of agitations. Local leaders read a message in the national political situation in the second half of the 1980s: If one wanted the attention of national leaders, one had to provoke local violence. As one leader of the MES noted, prior to the revival of violence in mid–1986, "we have met Rajiv twice. But we have not heard much about it since. It seems that he was interested in solving the problem. However, these days it seems violence has become the way to attract attention towards a problem."[29] This statement by a MES leader reveals several important aspects of the political situation in the 1980s: tremendous concentration of power in a national leader, failure of the institutionalized patterns of political communication (upward and downward), Rajiv's subtle

27 See *India Today,* June 30, 1986, p. 34.
28 Ibid., p. 35.
29 Interview with Kiran Thakur (see footnote 15).

indication that the issue might still be alive, and the perception by local leaders that one had to resort to violence to pursue political goals.

What finally tilted the brewing conflict into open violence was that some Maharashtrian political groups attempted to join the argument. Any political leader in Maharashtra who championed the cause of Marathis south of the border tended to gain politically. Thus, it was not surprising that both Sharad Pawar (a powerful Maharashtrian leader who over the years has been in and out of power and in and out of the Congress party) and the Shiv Sena took up the issue. Details of the specific events aside,[30] the entry into Belgaun of Sharad Pawar and his *satyagrahis* (literally, "truth fighters," but read "toughs"), as well as the mobs of Shiv Sena, provoked a confrontation between the agitators and the police. As the conflict broadened, Marathis in the bordering districts who sympathized with the Maharashtrian leaders also got involved. Finally, the police went on a rampage after a police constable was set on fire by the rioting mobs.

Hegde, Rajiv Gandhi, leaders from Maharashtra, and the MES all contributed to the renewal of Belgaun's ethnic conflict. The riots resulted in considerable damage to life and property. Who was to blame? The answer is not easy. When so many actors are partially responsible for a situation, then in an important sense none of them is really responsible. The structure of the situation itself is important. The existing prepolitical ethnic cleavages are, of course, at the heart of the matter. A focus on such cleavages alone, however, will not get one far analytically. Those cleavages were there when Weiner studied this conflict. The conflict in the 1960s was spirited, probably more so than at present, and yet the outcome of the conflict was not violence. Moreover, there is ample evidence in Belgaun today that the violent conflict does not involve the two ethnic communities directly. On the contrary, the two communities in whose names the conflict is fought mix and live together amicably. Thus, ethnic cleavages may provide the necessary context of social structure in which the conflict precipitates, but their existence alone is hardly sufficient for understanding how ethnic conflict evolves. For that, one must focus on how and why ethnic conflict is politically manufactured.

From the center to the periphery, in India today the state controls and thus provides ample "free-floating" resources. Access to those resources is gained primarily by winning elections. As any rapidly growing political stratum seeks electoral positions, economic scarcity and the free-floating resources that can be had from the state create a situation in which competition for political positions is fierce. All preexisting cleavages in society around which political mobilization is possible become a fair game for competing politicians. Linguistic, religious, and ethnic divisions clearly offer attractive opportunities for political mobilization.

30 For details, see *India Today*, June 30, 1986, pp. 34–5.

The situation in Belgaun is a small but significant example of this larger evolving reality. The MES has developed a strong vested interest in keeping ethnic disputes alive to ensure its own political survival. Left alone, the issue probably would have dwindled in significance. Both Hegde and Rajiv Gandhi, however, fueled the conflict for their own narrow electoral goals. That encouraged the MES. Finally, political leaders from Maharashtra, also seeking to make political gains, precipitated the open conflict.

PARTY POLITICS IN BELGAUN

The other major issue in Belgaun politics that deserves attention is the changing nature of party politics in this district. Table 5.3 shows that between 1978 and 1985, Congress's deterioration was more noticeable in regard to the number of legislative seats it controlled from Belgaun than in regard to its popular support. Even in the 1985 elections, when Congress's fortunes declined precipitously in terms of its number of legislative seats, it still received more votes than any other party in the district. That disjuncture reflected both the vagaries of a first-past-the-post electoral system and the fact that locally the Janata party had entered into a tacit electoral arrangement with the MES (under "Others" in Table 5.3). Thus, Congress's electoral comeback in late 1989 is not surprising in view of the fact that from 1987 onward, Janata became deeply factionalized and eventually participated in elections as two parties, rather than as a single party.

I conducted fieldwork in Belgaun during 1985 and 1986. Congress was a significant force within Belgaun at that time, though not as dominant as it had been in the 1960s or the 1970s. Local-government elections in early 1987 further confirmed that trend: Congress remained a significant force in Belgaun, but came in second behind the winner – the Janata party.[31] The emergence of a competitive two-party system of sorts, consequent to the relative decline of Congress, requires discussion.

Prior to the emergence of Devraj Urs, the local Congress had been dominated by the Lingayat elite. There are significant *jati* subdivisions within the Lingayats: Jangamarus are priests, Banajigars are merchants, and Goudarus are landowning agriculturalists. There are also numerous "backward" and poor Lingayats who work the land or provide services to the more prosperous Lingayats. These *jatis* often are endogamous. For some political purposes, therefore, the *jati* subdivisions within the Lingayats override communal unity. For other purposes, however, especially when political struggles involve Lingayats versus non-Lingayats, the Lingayat elite still find the appeal to the communal bond a successful mobilizational tool.

The Lingayat domination of the Belgaun Congress was challenged by

31 See *Economic and Political Weekly,* February 14, 1987, pp. 262–4.

Table 5.3. *Election results in Belgaun district, Karnataka, 1967–85,*
Legislative Assembly

Party	Seats won					Vote received (%)				
	1967	1972	1978	1983	1985	1967	1972	1978	1983	1985
Congress[a]	14	12	10	8	2	59.1	51.2	38.8	43.3	41.3
Janata[b]	—	—	2	5	12	—	—	28.2	30.5	38.7
Congress (O)[c]	—	3	—	—	—	—	30.0	—	—	—
Lok Dal[d]	—	—	—	—	—	—	—	—	0.2	—
Jan Sangh[e]	—	—	—	—	—	0.9	1.6	—	1.7	—
Swatantra	—	—	—	—	—	0.9	0.2	—	—	—
CPI[f]	—	—	—	—	—	—	1.7	—	—	—
Others[g]	4	3	6	5	4	39.1	15.3	33.0	24.3	20.0
Total	18	18	18	18	18	100	100	100	100	100

[a]Known as Congress (I) since 1969.
[b]Founded in 1977.
[c]Founded in 1969, and merged into the Janata in 1977.
[d]Founded in 1974.
[e]Merged into the Janata in 1977, it broke away in 1980, and then was formed again
as the Bhartiya Janata party in 1980.
[f]Communist Party of India.
[g]The sizable numbers of seats and votes grouped in this category generally reflect
the seats and votes captured by the MES. Because the MES is not formally a
political party, its candidates ran as independents.
Source: Compiled from reports of the government of Karnataka, chief electoral
officer and special secretary to the government, *Election Statistics of General Elec-*
tions to Legislative Assembly (1952–77, 1978, and 1983) (Bangalore: Government
Press). The results for 1985 elections were compiled from unpublished data available in the office of the chief electoral officer, Bangalore.

the rise of Urs as Karnataka's leader. In the aftermath of Congress's 1969
split, Urs emerged as Indira Gandhi's main man in Karnataka. Having
risen to power primarily as a result of Indira's popularity, Urs sought to
undermine the old ruling coalition and to form one that would be broader
and distinctly his own, an endeavor that has been evaluated in some detail
elsewhere.[32] It is sufficient to note here that Urs excluded some, but by

32 See Kohli, *The State and Poverty in India,* chapter 4. The thrust of my argument was that
Devaj Urs had some significant, but limited, successes in reordering power and resource
distribution within Karnataka. For another evaluation that quite independently arrives at
a similar conclusion, see V. K. Natraj and Lalitha Natraj, "Backward Classes, Minorities
and the Karnataka Elections," in George Mathew, ed., *Shift in Indian Politics: 1983*
Elections in Karnataka and Andhra Pradesh (New Delhi: Concept Publishing, 1984),
pp. 35–60. There are much more favorable assessments of Urs that tend to suggest that
the nature of the changes initiated by Urs was fundamental: James Manor, "Pragmatic
Progressives in Regional Politics: The Case of Devraj Urs," *Economic and Political Weekly*

no means all, of the Lingayats from his new ruling coalition. In Belgaun, a politician pointed out that in the 1978 elections, "6 of the 18 Congress (I) tickets were given to Lingayats."[33] In addition, Urs sought to incorporate many from the backward and scheduled castes into his ruling coalition. Table 5.1 illustrates the broad nature of Urs's coalition in Belgaun. Of the 11 Congress MLAs from Belgaun in 1978, 4 were Lingayats, 2 were Marathis, and 5 were from less-than-privileged groups.

Urs undertook several other actions to solidify his broad-based alliance. He set aside reservations in government jobs and educational institutions for the "backward classes."[34] When naming individuals to appointive positions in the government, Urs gave preference to members of castes other than the dominant ones. As a local journalist in Belgaun noted, "where government could nominate members, there the worst heat was on the Lingayats."[35] During that time period, moreover, "there was a dramatic proliferation of caste associations and revival of those dormant or moribund, rallies and conferences of backward classes."[36] Limited land reforms and a number of populist programs, such as house sites for the poor, also contributed to Urs's image as a "man of the people."[37]

How successful was Urs's attempt to build a new broad-based coalition? Urs's electoral defeat after his split from Indira Gandhi in the early 1980s cast serious doubt on the depth of his new coalition. Because he died shortly thereafter, the strength of his independent political base within Karnataka was never tested. In retrospect, Urs's achievements appear to have been less remarkable than his supporters claimed. During the Urs period in Karnataka, a challenge to the power of the dominant castes was mounted, and the backward classes experienced some rise in status, and some of that may have been caused by Devraj Urs. It is important to remember, however, that such challenges were emerging in state after state during that period in India. There was nothing particularly remarkable about Urs or Karnataka in that respect. The real test of effective leadership in that context was not the challenge to the dominant castes, but the durability of an alternative coalition. Judged against that criterion, the record of Urs and of his successors has not been impressive.

In the aftermath of the Congress split in the late 1960s and the early 1970s, important segments of the Lingayats in Belgaun maintained their

(annual number, 1980), pp. 201–13; M. N. Srinivas and M. N. Panini, "Politics and Society in Karnataka," *Economic and Political Weekly,* 19:2(1984), pp. 69–75.

33 Interview with Inamdar (a Janata party MLA from Belgaun and the minister of state for health, government of Karnataka), Bangalore, April 12, 1986.

34 See any of the sources cited in footnote 32.

35 Interview with Bheemasen Torgal (see footnote 12).

36 See Natraj and Natraj, "Backward Classes, Minorities and the Karnataka Elections," p. 50.

37 For differing evaluations of this role of Urs, see the sources cited in footnote 32.

loyalty to the old Congress – Congress (O). After Congress (O) was merged into the Janata party, the local Janata and its predecessor, the Lingayat-dominated Congress (O), became virtually indistinguishable within Belgaun. As in Kheda, but not Guntur, Congress (I) in Belgaun was in a position to create a new coalition. Urs attempted to incorporate some segments of the district's dominant caste, the Lingayats, but focused his efforts mainly on the backward and scheduled castes. For much of the 1970s, therefore, the old Congress and the Janata within Belgaun were dominated by the Lingayats, whereas Urs's winning coalition consisted of some Lingayats, backward castes, and other minorities.

James Manor has ably demonstrated that the former modest degree of clarity between parties and their respective social bases was obliterated during the Gundu Rao period.[38] In the early 1980s, the vote of the backward and scheduled castes seems to have been split by Devraj Urs's regional party allied with the Janata party against Congress (I), then led by Gundu Rao. In 1983, the Janata party was the clear beneficiary of that electoral confusion. Dominated by the Lingayats in Belgaun and by the Vokkaligas and the Lingayats in Karnataka as a whole, Janata still was able to attract the support of some of the backward and scheduled castes, thanks to an association with Urs. The incompetence of Gundu Rao must also have hurt Congress, though probably more in the urban areas, where such issues are discussed with considerable frequency and intensity.

One aspect of Congress's fluctuating electoral fortune in Belgaun was its changing social base. It is evident that the hold of the old dominant groups was disturbed, but not broken, by Devraj Urs. The broad-based coalition he put together as Indira Gandhi's key man in Karnataka served Congress (I) well during the 1970s. That could have become a long-term formula for Congress's electoral success; however, it did not. Urs split with Indira and formed his own party, creating a relatively fluid political situation. When Urs joined Janata in an electoral arrangement, he brought some of his support to Janata. Over the short run, Janata benefited. As discussed later, Janata under Hegde made some quick policy moves in the hope of consolidating that initial, nearly accidental gain. However, factionalism within the Janata leadership undermined that possibility.

If the picture of Congress's changing social base is somewhat confusing, the other aspect of its decline, the organizational decline, was a fairly straightforward matter. After the 1969 split, Congress (O) took over the old organization, and Congress (I) under Urs, Gundu Rao, and others never put down any organizational roots. A veteran Congressite in Belgaun

---

38 See James Manor, "Blurring the lines between parties and social bases: Gundu Rao and the Emergence of a Janata Government in Karnataka," in John Wood, ed., *State Politics in Contemporary India: Crisis or Continuity?* (Boulder: Westview Press, 1984), pp. 139–68.

noted that "since 1969, there has never been any organization."[39] A local journalist concurred: "Congress' organization is as bad now as it was under Urs."[40]

The president of the Congress District Committee in 1986 was a local merchant who owned a timber shop. Because he was often busy with his business, the running of the Congress district office supposedly was in the hands of some clerks. The district office was seldom open. The Congress (I) member of Lok Sabha (Parliament) from Belgaun noted that the local party office was unimpressive and that "the old records were not intact."[41] Another Congressite suggested that because Congress was not in power in the late 1980s, "finances were a real problem,"[42] and thus it was difficult to maintain the party organization. By 1986, Congress's local presence (much in contrast to what Weiner had found) extended no further than those Congressites holding office. Because those elected officials often were away at the state capital or national capital, the local party had little significance.

The causes of that organizational decline in Belgaun are somewhat similar to those noted for Kheda and Guntur: the split in the old Congress, and Indira's subsequent populist electoral strategy. In addition, one may legitimately ask why a leader like Urs, who was in power for nearly a decade and who appeared fairly secure, would not make any effort to reinvigorate the party.

Urs was a relatively small cog in a political machine in which power derived mainly from allegiance to the national leader, Indira Gandhi. Had Urs encouraged the rebuilding of the district units and the lower levels of the party, he might well have given rise to a local elite with genuine local power, and that would have threatened Urs, because his own power was derived mainly from an association with Indira Gandhi. Thus, Urs's failure to develop a local party structure is best understood as an extension of the logic that cautioned Indira Gandhi not to encourage party development elsewhere. The personal loyalty of subordinates is a more valuable political commodity in a top-down system than would be the development of party institutions that might constrain the leader's discretion and power.

As to the impact of Congress's organizational decline, given that elections have come to be won mainly on the basis of leadership appeal, there probably have been few short-term electoral consequences. This general point is supported by the fact that the organization of the ruling Janata

39 Interview with Abdul Gaffar Mujawar (a Moslem Congress leader and a former member of the Karnataka Legislative Council), Belgaun, April 27, 1986 (the interview was in Urdu; my own translation).
40 Interview with Bheemasen Torgal (see footnote 12).
41 Interview with S. B. Sidnal [Congress (I) member of Parliament from Belgaun], Belgaun, April 25, 1986.
42 Interview with Abdul Gaffar Mujawar (see footnote 39).

party is also defunct. The impact of organizational decline must instead be analyzed by focusing on factors other than electoral considerations. The following observation by a local political observer in Belgaun captures some of the complex issues concerning the consequences of organizational decline:

Congress organization is wiped out. Only when these MPs [members of Parliament] come [from New Delhi to Belgaun], their houses become the centers of activity. Recently, there was a state-wide agitation by the Congress [against the Janata rule, over issues of corruption]. But nothing happened in Belgaun. One hundred people gave a petition. That is all. Sankranand is a minister. He is always in Delhi. Sidnal is also a MP. The DCC [District Congress Committee] does not work with him. He is also not connected with grassroots. These people win elections only because of Indira or Rajiv. Poor people simply stamp for Indiraji. So these people win elections but have no grassroots contact. People who do fieldwork are not at all rewarded. These MPs do not do any village level travelling.[43]

Two important issues raised in that observation merit discussion. First, one clear consequence of an organizational decline is inability to mobilize support for any political activity other than elections. Congress's attempt to mobilize opposition to the ruling Janata party in 1986 was a fiasco. When protest marches were scheduled by state leaders throughout Karnataka, nothing happened in Belgaun. There were no local leaders with local support to undertake such mobilization. There was no activity even at the party office on the day of the marches. A short while later, state leaders were called to New Delhi to explain that fiasco, suggesting that the results had been much the same in other parts of the state.[44] Clearly, whether in or out of power, Congress leaders cannot count on a party structure to perform such tasks as enrolling and socializing new members, grooming new leaders, representing local interests in the larger political organization, imposing a degree of working unity on squabbling factions, and helping implement programs and policies.

The second issue is both related to and independent of the issue of organizational decline: the rampant factionalism within Belgaun's Congress. As mentioned earlier, the two main leaders of Belgaun's Congress were Sidnal and Sankranand, both of whom as MPs spent most of their time in New Delhi. They headed the rival factions, which tended to get especially worked up over the issue of who from Belgaun would get a Congress (I) ticket. Sidnal was a rich Lingayat who belonged to the "Gundu Rao group" and thus was considered locally to be a "Sanjay man." Sankranand, by contrast, was an old-timer, a prominent local Harijan who had been an MP since 1962 and was a national cabinet minister in 1986.

Sankranand's higher standing in Delhi revealed his closeness to Congress's national leadership and, by the same token, his superior capacity

43 Interview with Raghevendra Joshi (see footnote 8).
44 See, for example, *Deccan Herald,* April 25, 1986.

vis-à-vis Sidnal to influence political matters that concerned Belgaun. Sidnal, in turn, had wealth and higher caste status with which to construct a local power base. During the 1985 Legislative Assembly elections, therefore, Sankranand and Sidnal fought bitterly over whose favorites would get election tickets. At stake was a future power base for one of the two individuals in that top-down political system. Sankranand won because of his closeness to the national leadership, but it proved a Pyrrhic victory. Sidnal sought to undermine Sankranand's candidates in many constituencies. As the Congress leaders fought with each other, Janata benefited. Clearly, a weak political organization and factional strife can be devastating electoral burdens.

What about the Janata party? When Janata first won the Karnataka Legislative Assembly elections in 1983, Hegde was not the party leader. He emerged as the leader over the following months. When Hegde led the party into the 1985 elections, Janata's electoral support in Belgaun increased by a phenomenal 8 percentage points (see Table 5.3). Among the numerous factors that helped Janata, local observers suggested that in Belgaun, "Hegde's role was considerable; his image helped a lot."[45]

When discussing Janata's social base within Belgaun, the significant role of a strong leader bringing unity to facilitate electoral victory must be kept in mind. One analyzes the issue of a party's social base with the assumption that some mutual interests or ties of ideology bring together various parties and social groups. When leadership itself becomes an important factor in an election, however, it becomes more difficult to determine which other factors will attract specific groups to a party. This is especially important in view of the fact that factionalized leadership eventually contributed significantly to Janata's demise in late 1989. With this qualification in mind, the nature of the district-level Janata party can now be analyzed.

As far as party organization is concerned, Janata in Belgaun was not much more of a party than was the local Congress. The Janata party in Belgaun was the old Congress. As a local Janata leader noted, "we took over the entire Congress (O), including records, building and party structure. . . . Congress (O) is Janata in Belgaun."[46] That might be taken to suggest that Janata inherited a fairly robust organizational setup, but such was not the case. By the time Janata became an active and significant local force in 1983, the old Congress had been dormant for nearly 15 years. A local journalist explained how, over those years, the old Congress had atrophied: "Janata party inherited Congress (O). But Congress (O) was mainly people of older generation. Younger people joined Congress (I). Congress (O) remained dormant for a long time. [As a result, it] atrophied.

---

45 Interview with Inamdar (see footnote 33).
46 Ibid. (see footnote 33).

When Janata was formed, there was hardly any new energy in the party."[47] To that one may add that parties based primarily on patronage, like the old Congress, do not do well when they are out of office; they need patronage resources to maintain a network of supporters. Out of power for nearly 15 years, the old Congress simply withered away and thus did not have any real organization to pass on to the new Janata.

One important indicator of organizational effectiveness is the role of the local party organization in the distribution of tickets for elections. A well-knit organization will have available a pool of local party representatives from which to nominate candidates on the basis of their work for the party and their grass-roots support. Moreover, an effective organization can devise impersonal selection criteria that will satisfy or at least appease those seeking the nomination of the party. The Janata party in Belgaun had no such organization. Tickets for elections were given primarily on personal grounds. One local leader, who got a ticket and had no complaint whatsoever toward the party, noted with some pride that election tickets for Belgaun in 1985 were decided "here in Bangalore. . . . Mr. Hegde played a crucial role . . . he knows virtually every elected member personally."[48] In *panchayat* elections in early 1987, the leader-dominant and personalized nature of the Janata party was further evident. Tickets were given mainly to "spouses, sons, daughters, sisters and brothers . . . and other relatives" of those already in power.[49]

After coming to power in 1983, Janata did not do much to strengthen the atrophied party structure it had inherited. Well into 1986, when I conducted fieldwork, the party offices were located in the back of a hotel and had a sleepy quality. The real activity revolved around the homes of a few significant and contending local leaders, who were personally close to Hegde and thus were in positions to influence the flow of governmental powers and resources. Surveying the situation in 1987, another observer arrived at a similar conclusion: "The party even now has a loose organization and its incompatible leadership structure emanating mainly from discrete caste and pre-existing political backgrounds . . . is an important source of its organizational weakness."[50]

Three competing leaders headed the contending factions within the Belgaun Janata. The tacit head of the local Janata was a man named Potdar. Like Hegde, he was a Brahman. Potdar's power derived primarily from his personal links with Hegde. When Janata had been out of power before 1983, Potdar, being a wealthy local man, used to host Hegde and other Janata leaders when they were visiting Belgaun. On his own, Potdar still

47 Interview with Raghevendra Joshi (see footnote 8).
48 Interview with Inamdar (see footnote 33).
49 *Economic and Political Weekly,* January 24, 1987, p. 122.
50 Ibid., February 14, 1987, p. 263.

was not popular in local political circles. He was born to a Kannada-speaking family, but having gone to school in Maharashtra, he used Marathi as his first language. In a linguistically divided district, that was a major political liability. Potdar's personal political weakness was illustrated by the fact that he never won an election; he ran twice and lost both times.

The second important Janata leader was V. L. Patil. A member of a backward caste, the Kurbu, he represents the "Sanjay culture" within Belgaun. A local journalist described him as follows:

> V. L. Patil has his stronghold in the northern talukas. He maintains a gang of *goondas* [ruffians]. It is the northern [i.e., north Indian] political culture. Whoever is against him is eliminated. There have been many political murders in Raibagh taluka. The Congress (I) opposition candidate to Patil had to carry guns and police protection. Even Sankranand [the Congress (I) federal cabinet minister discussed earlier] was attacked twice during campaign in Raibagh. That is V. L. Patil's stronghold. He first won as an independent; he then won as a Congress (I) candidate and now he has won on a Janata ticket.[51]

Clearly, though this ruffian genre of politician is somewhat of an exception in this area, Belgaun is not totally free of it.

The third local leader, Inamdar, belonged to an old political Lingayat family. His political history was more typical than those of the other two leaders. His wealthy father had been a local leader in the undivided Congress. After the 1969 split, he stayed with Congress (O) and won several Legislative Assembly elections. Inamdar had been elected from his father's old constituency on a Janata ticket. As the heir of a wealthy and influential political family, Inamdar had inherited considerable electoral support. His appointment as minister of state in Hegde's cabinet in Bangalore should be understood not so much as a result of his political skills but as an acknowledgment of the collective power of the Belgaun Lingayats.

These three local Janata leaders in the late 1980s had little in common except that they all held positions in the ruling party and the government. Bickering among the three leaders was common, but it was kept within certain limits, largely because of some counterbalances in the different political resources they possessed: No one wanted to cross Potdar because he was close to Hegde. Patil was considered to be a dangerous man; most local leaders liked to establish a working relationship with him. Inamdar represented the Lingayats, the dominant community in Belgaun. Hegde's overpowering position within the Janata party at the time also helped put the brakes on politically damaging factionalism. Once Hegde's position was undermined by national-level machinations within the Janata party, local factionalism came out in the open, with damaging political consequences.

---

51 Interview with Raghevendra Joshi (see footnote 8).

There were three components to Janata's local support base in the late 1980s. First, many of the old established Lingayat families who had stayed on with Congress (O) after the 1969 split in the undivided Congress had by the 1980s become significant powers within the Janata party. Table 5.1 documents that half of the 12 Janata MLAs from Belgaun in 1985 were Lingayats. Although that was not a dramatic increase over the Congress period – in 1978, 4 of the 11 Congress (I) MLAs had been Lingayats – it did mean that Lingayats could control the affairs of the local ruling party. That small but significant increase in the power of the Lingayats had important perceptual consequences. Whereas under the rule of Urs the Lingayats had felt that they were slowly being squeezed out of their old dominant positions, in 1986 there was a strong sense within the district that the members of the old dominant caste were returning to power.[52]

This focus on Lingayats as a group is not meant to give the impression that the group is homogeneous and cohesive. As suggested earlier, there are many caste and income differentials within this religious community. Some of these are politically consequential. For example, an educational organization in the city of Belgaun that plays a crucial role in controlling admissions to institutions of higher education is controlled by Lingayats sympathetic to Congress (I). There are other political divisions among the Lingayats that can be traced back to the Urs period, when Urs carefully co-opted some Lingayats into Congress (I), while alienating many others, probably the majority. On balance, therefore, the majority of the Lingayats stayed with the old Congress and supported the Janata party in the 1980s. Quite a few others, who had at first joined Congress (I), were attempting to appear more sympathetic to the Janata party as they recognized its growing strength. Because the Lingayats constitute as much as 30 percent of the district's population, significant support from Lingayats provided one crucial leg on which the Belgaun Janata stood.

The second component of Janata's electoral support came from elements within the backward and scheduled castes. The nature of that support made for a fairly confusing local picture; patterns were difficult to discern. In most constituencies within Belgaun, one got a sense that both the backward and scheduled castes were divided between the Janata and Congress. As discussed earlier, part of that trend can be traced back to Urs's switch from Indira's Congress to a tacit alliance with Janata. Additionally, Hegde had carefully pursued populist programs, attempting to create an image of continuity following Devraj Urs.[53] That was not easy for Hegde, especially because the dominant castes regained the upper hand in the Janata government he headed in Bangalore. However, confusion surrounding the

52 This sense was clear in interviews with both Janata and Congress (I) supporters.
53 See, for example, the discussion in *Economic and Political Weekly*, January 24, 1987, pp. 122–3.

parties' identities and their social bases, on the one hand, and populist programs, on the other, gave Janata some support from the heterogeneous backward castes and scheduled castes in Belgaun.

What had held together that motley coalition of dominant castes and subordinate castes was a third factor, namely, a competent and popular regional leader, Hegde. Whereas in Andhra, NTR may have been as popular as Hegde was in the mid–1980s, Hegde all along had the image of being much more competent than NTR. That image of competence was the result of his tendency to follow through on political proclamations, his attempt to run a government free of corruption, his attempt to balance the needs of various contending groups, and his articulate, serious, and seemingly responsible political demeanor. Those factors appealed to the urban middle class, especially to the intelligentsia. Because the intelligentsia played an important social role in helping to legitimize or delegitimize leaders, Hegde's popularity had soared, at least between 1983 and 1986.

Such factors as leadership popularity and competence do not readily lend themselves to easy sociological generalization. One must be content with observing that Karnataka was fortunate to have had Hegde as its leader between 1983 and 1987. Over the short run, he helped mold a coalition that was difficult to hold together. He also created a moderately effective government, especially in comparison with other Indian states.

Finally, in this discussion of parties and government in Belgaun, a few comments are in order concerning the role of political violence in this district. As previously discussed, linguistic differences are important sources of political conflict in Belgaun. Their impact can be seen especially in the government of the town of Belgaun. The low but significant level of discord between the Marathi-dominated municipal corporation and the Kannadiga elite, especially those in Bangalore, has become institutionalized. It is important to note, however, that the level of that discord often is limited to harsh words and loud rhetoric. The overt violence discussed earlier was widely perceived to be an exception to normal politics.[54] More significant, an important factor in the violence was the involvement of forces from outside of Karnataka, namely, the Shiv Sena, and Sharad Pawar and his gang of toughs from Bombay.

Similarly, in the rural areas of the district, many local observers described the phenomenon of ruffians-as-politicians as an import into Belgaun of "north Indian political culture." As a general statement, that observation is incorrect, both because violence in politics is prevalent in such south Indian states as Andhra Pradesh and because the roots of the phenomenon are more structural than cultural. Nevertheless, the significance of identifying the nexus among *goondas,* politicians, and the police as a "north Indian import" is that it still is not considered to be a "normal" charac-

54 See, for example, the discussion in *India Today,* June 30, 1986, pp. 34–5.

teristic of local politics. Therefore, the observation of a local journalist that local politics generally are free of *goonda gardi* (strong-arm tactics used by toughs and ruffians) was echoed by many others, in considerable contrast to the common use of such tactics in many other parts of India.[55]

The local-government elections in 1987 were keenly contested. The race between Congress and Janata was fairly close, and the voter turnout was as high as 70 percent. In spite of that high rate of participation, observers described the elections as "fairly peaceful."[56] Moreover, throughout Belgaun one seldom heard of incidents resembling the caste wars that have become the norm in states like Bihar.

The fragmentary evidence that is available leads one to conclude that as far as the issue of governability is concerned, Belgaun presents a picture more of continuity than of change since Weiner's study in the 1960s. The reason that the problems of governability in Belgaun are not more pressing has more to do with its patterns of political mobilization (or their absence) than with the relative efficacy of its political institutions. As documented earlier, the competing parties in this area are organizationally quite weak. Therefore, the fact that the political process is not marked by violence cannot be attributed to the effectiveness of their political structures. The political process is relatively peaceful here mainly because there is much less discord in society in general. The local political institutions are not more effective here than in other parts of India; rather, they simply have to deal with less political "noise" from the social structure.

A question naturally follows: What explains the relative quiescence in the local social structure? To simplify a complex answer, the local patterns of domination exhibit more continuity with the past in Belgaun than in the two districts discussed previously. There are several aspects of this structural continuity.

First, Lingayats were the dominant group, socially as well as politically, when Weiner studied this district. Two decades later, the situation is similar. Lingayats not only remain the dominant social community but also have regained the political power that was beginning to slip away from them in the 1970s.[57] Unlike the Patidars of Kheda, for example, who were partly responsible for making Gujarat virtually ungovernable after political power was snatched away from them by the backward Kshatriyas, the dominant community of Belgaun has not lost its hold over state power. One cannot know what would have happened if the trend initiated by Devraj Urs (i.e., exclusion of the dominant castes from political power) had continued. However, to the extent that there is a lesson to be found

---

55 The observation was made by Raghevendra Joshi (see footnote 8).
56 *Economic and Political Weekly*, February 14, 1987, p. 262.
57 In addition to the district-level data presented earlier, one may note the fact that after the 1985 elections, 75 percent of the Janata MLAs in Bangalore were either Lingayats or Vokkaligas. See *Times of India*, March 11, 1986.

in the contrast between the relatively peaceful Gujarat of the 1960s and the violent Gujarat of the 1980s, one is attracted to the following conclusion: Because the Lingayats, the dominant caste in Belgaun, were able to regain political power in the 1980s, there was no reason for them to pressure the government by encouraging political violence and agitation.

The reason the Lingayats in Belgaun regained political power had to do with a second structural trait: the tremendous heterogeneity of the backward castes. Those most likely to have challenged the power of the Lingayats in the 1980s were the backward castes. Again, in contrast to the situation in Kheda, but similar to that in Guntur, the backward castes in Belgaun do not act as a political bloc. There are numerous *jati* subdivisions within the backward community. Moreover, there is no local tradition of mobilizing the numerous backward castes into a cohesive political force. It is possible to imagine that had Urs-type rule continued for another decade, the local backward castes might well have become more active politically. The actual events, however, moved political change in the opposite direction. The heterogeneity of the social structure was reinforced by the political splintering that followed Urs's break with Indira Gandhi and his alliance with Janata.[58] The continuing political fragmentation of the backward castes within Belgaun has made it difficult for them to mount an effective challenge to the power of the dominant community.

Finally, it is also important to note the relative passiveness of the scheduled castes in this district. In the case of Kheda, we noticed the activism of the scheduled castes, who had improved their socioeconomic positions thanks to the Gandhian legacy. That led to violent reprisals against some of them by the dominant castes. The patterns in Guntur were somewhat different. There, Harijans were mobilized by local communists. In both of those cases, the scheduled castes emerged as an active political force that could not easily be ignored. By contrast, the situation of these castes in Belgaun seems to exhibit more continuity with the past.

Whereas the state leaders feel the need to make populist claims here as elsewhere in India, suggesting that the support of the Harijans cannot be taken for granted even in Karnataka, in Belgaun the local Harijans present a picture of relative acquiescence.[59] This is probably a result of a number

58 Two other observers have arrived at similar conclusions. Referring to the period after the emergence of the Janata party, Natraj and Natraj note that the "post-election developments have shown the basic weakness of the backward classes and minorities, namely, their relative lack of self-confidence and their inability to stick together." See Natraj and Natraj, "Backward Classes, Minorities and the Karnataka Elections."

59 James Manor generalizes this to all of Karnataka's agrarian relations: "[Karnataka] has experienced very little turbulence in agrarian relations at any point in the twentieth century." See James Manor, "Karnataka: Caste, Class, Dominance and Politics in a Cohesive Society," mimeograph, 1983, p. 10. A doctoral thesis currently being written by Rita Jalali at the Department of Sociology, Stanford University, may cast doubt on this picture of the relative acquiescence of Karnataka's Harijans.

6

Calcutta, West Bengal

Calcutta, the capital of British India until 1912, and then the "neglected city" of both British and independent India, is now the seat of government for communist-ruled West Bengal. The poverty and degradation in everyday life in Calcutta are legendary.[1] Instead of dwelling on all that is grotesque, miserable, and dramatic, however, I begin this discussion with some demographic facts that are essential to the political analysis. The area now under the Calcutta Municipal Corporation, the city government, has about 4 million inhabitants.[2] With some 32,000 living in every square kilometer (nearly 85,000 per square mile), Calcutta has three times the population density of New York City. The extent of poverty in this congested city is evident in the fact that as many as 40 percent of the households do not have a single family member with a regular job.[3] Most of the jobless poor live in some two hundred *bustees,* urban slums made up of collections of huts that often lack running water, sewerage, and electricity. A significant minority are homeless and sleep on the streets. Although the exact numbers of *bustee* dwellers and homeless are not known, city officials estimate that about 30 percent of the city's population, some 1.5 million persons, live in *bustees,* and 500,000 to 600,000 live in the streets.[4]

There are four other demographic facts that have political significance. First, the growth in the city's population has slowed down. Calcutta simply

I should like to acknowledge the helpful comments of Sajal Basu during the writing of this chapter.

1 For an excellent general introduction to Calcutta as a city, see Geoffrey Moorhouse, *Calcutta: The City Revealed* (New York: Penguin Books, 1984).
2 The demographic data cited here are taken from Government of West Bengal, Bureau of Applied Economics and Statistics, *Statistical Handbook, 1982* (Calcutta: Sree Saraswaty Press, 1983).
3 This figure is more accurate for urban West Bengal as a whole. See Pranab Bardhan, "Poverty and Employment Characteristics of Urban Households in West Bengal," *Economic and Political Weekly,* August 29, 1987, pp. 1496–502. Because Calcutta is a very significant part of urban West Bengal, I have assumed that the figure for Calcutta is not likely to be all that different. The figure should nevertheless be treated as an estimate.
4 Interview with R. K. Prasanna, municipal commissioner, Calcutta Municipal Corporation, Calcutta, May 2, 1986.

does not attract migrants the way it once did.[5] Second, Calcutta has a very high rate of literacy – nearly 70 percent – and because there is a high percentage of unemployment among the educated, this suggests that many of the city's poor may well be literate. This is an important point, because poverty and unemployment among a literate population can be politically explosive. The third demographic fact is that Calcutta is by no means an exclusively Bengali city. On the contrary, only 60 percent of Calcutta's people are Bengali. Hindi and Urdu are the two other most commonly spoken languages in Calcutta, highlighting the significance of Calcutta's appeal to migrants in the past. In addition to some half a million refugees who moved into the Calcutta area after the creation of East Pakistan (now Bangladesh), nearly a third of the city's people trace their origins to the neighboring states of Bihar and Orissa, the more distant state of Uttar Pradesh, and even states in south India. Finally, it is important to keep in mind that unlike Punjab, Calcutta did not experience a significant out-migration of Moslems at the time of independence. As a result, today nearly 15 percent of the city's population is Moslem.

The basic demographics of Calcutta indicate why this city has been politically volatile for quite some time. Because of severe overcrowding, extremes of poverty, high rates of unemployment among educated youth, great ethnic diversity, and the presence of a large homeless population, one wonders how political order in such a setting can ever be achieved. It is much easier to expect breakdown and chaos here than to expect a functioning and effective local government.

Myron Weiner's earlier investigation sought to explain how Congress managed to rule this city.[6] Weiner emphasized the nature of the Congress party as an organization and the electoral behavior of those residing in Calcutta. Though Congress provided relatively ineffective city government, it was quite popular. Congress competed with local communists, but was generally more successful. Sectarian conflict among the communists kept them in a state of severe disunity. By contrast, even though factionalized, Congress was much more cohesive, largely because of the role played by the Bengali "Tammany boss," Atulya Ghosh. Ghosh ran an effective machine, providing public contracts to Calcutta businessmen, who made con-

5 In the early 1960s, for example, the old city's population was a little under 3 million; in the early 1980s, it is only a little over 3 million. Most observers agree that migration into old Calcutta from outside of Bengal has virtually come to a halt. An important indicator of this is the reduction in the proportion of single males in the city. According to the 1951 census, there were 1,754 men per thousand women in Calcutta. Although Calcutta is still very much a male city, according to the 1981 census there are now some 1,400 men per thousand women in the city. This probably indicates that fewer men without families are migrating into Calcutta, and some of those who arrived earlier have stayed and acquired families.

6 Myron Weiner, *Party Building in a New Nation: The Indian National Congress* (University of Chicago Press, 1967), part 5.

tributions to the city's Congress party that were in turn channeled into services to the better-off influential people in the city and into resources to build party support in the countryside. Congress's electoral support was mainly among minority groups: non-Bengali migrants from Uttar Pradesh, Bihar, and Orissa, Moslems, members of the scheduled castes, and shop-keepers and industrialists, many of whom, especially Marwaris, were also non-Bengalis. Conversely, the settled Bengali residents of Calcutta often did not support Congress; some simply had become apolitical, but quite a few threw their influence behind one of the competing communist parties.

That was the general political picture in the early 1960s. Over the past 25 years there have been some remarkable aspects of political continuity, especially the preservation of Congress's significant electoral base among the non-Bengali population of Calcutta. For the most part, however, the political scene in Calcutta has changed quite dramatically. Calcutta's moderate stability that Weiner documented in the early 1960s gave way to total breakdown and chaos during the decade of 1967–77. How Congress's organizational decline and the internecine fighting among the communists contributed to that decade of chaos is one important theme to be analyzed.

Since 1977, a modicum of order has been restored in Calcutta under the rule of the Communist Party of India, Marxist (CPM). Between 1977 and 1985 the city of Calcutta was ruled directly by the CPM-dominated West Bengal government. Elections to the Calcutta Municipal Corporation (CMC) were held only in 1985, after a lapse of some 15 years. The CPM won those elections, but with a paper-thin majority. In spite of its organizational decline, therefore, Congress remains a potent electoral force within Calcutta.

The political changes over the past 25 years have nearly reversed the political situation for Congress and the communists. Both sets of actors remain electorally significant in Calcutta today, just as they were when Weiner analyzed the city's politics. Congress, however, is now organizationally in total shambles. The communists, by contrast, have emerged as a relatively cohesive political force. They have also, at least for now, defeated Congress in the city elections. A decade of rule under the communists has restored some political order to this chaotic city. How that political change came about and the significance it has had are the main topics in the following discussion.

AN OVERVIEW OF WEST BENGAL POLITICS[7]

Prior to independence, Bengal was one of the few areas in India where Congress did not share power in the British-dominated state legislature.

7 I have written extensively on politics in West Bengal elsewhere. See, for example, Atul Kohli, *The State and Poverty in India: The Politics of Reform* (Cambridge University Press,

Other parties dominated by Moslems, who were a majority in undivided Bengal, had formed the state government. After independence and the partition and the Moslem League's departure to Pakistan, there was a serious power vacuum in West Bengal. The Congress party, as the country's most powerful political force, moved into that vacuum. Over time, Congress boss Atulya Ghosh carved out a fairly effective machine that enabled the party to build here, as elsewhere, an elaborate patronage network. The network originated in Calcutta and spread outward into the countryside. Nehru's friend B. C. Roy presided over Ghosh's machine for nearly a decade. He was replaced by another dominant personality, P. C. Sen, under whom an already corrupt Congress became deeply factionalized and eventually lost power in 1967.

Throughout the years of Congress dominance, numerous left-of-center parties, including the two communist parties – the CPM and the Communist Party of India (CPI) – provided significant opposition to Congress. Because of numerous divisions within the leftists, however, that opposition was not very effective. Around the mid-1960s, there were certain important developments that helped the left politically, but hurt Congress. The most significant developments were the two drought years of 1964 and 1965. Because of shortages of food and rising prices, the left had a heyday mobilizing against the government. Corruption within the Congress government did not help. A factional disagreement within Congress, involving Atulya Ghosh and Ajoy Mukerjee, developed into a major open struggle, with Mukerjee leaving to form his own party, the Bangla Congress.

As a result of those developments, Congress failed to secure a majority of seats in the 1967 elections. Instead, the state government was formed by the United Front (UF), a coalition of 14 different parties, mostly of the left, that was headed by Ajoy Mukerjee. Within the coalition, the most significant force was the CPM, led by Jyoti Basu. That motley coalition did not help the already chaotic political situation. On the contrary, it presided over a deteriorating situation that went from bad to worse.

The left forces within the government ordered the police not to interfere in class struggles. As the power of the state was deliberately thwarted, the pent-up frustrations of the people led to chaos. It was under those conditions of increasing disorder that Delhi dismissed the UF government in late 1967 and established presidential rule. Even though the restoration of order was welcomed, intervention from Delhi is never politically popular in West Bengal. Thus, when elections were called again in early 1969,

1987), chapter 3, for West Bengal under the CPM. For a more detailed historical discussion, see Atul Kohli, "From Elite Activism to Democratic Consolidation: Political Change in West Bengal," in Francine Frankel and M. S. A. Rao, eds., *Dominance and State Power in Modern India: Decline of a Social Order,* 2 vols. (Oxford University Press, 1989–90), volume 2.

Congress further lost political support, and the major partners of the UF gained electorally. Again, the UF formed a government similar to that in its first reign, and again chaos resulted. *Gheraoes,* forced redistribution of land, internecine fighting among political parties, riots, and political murders once again became the order of the day, and presidential rule was reimposed in 1970.

It was India's 1971 war with Pakistan, over the creation of Bangladesh, that finally transformed the political situation. The war had two important consequences. First, Indira Gandhi's popularity soared after the defeat of Pakistan, and Congress in West Bengal benefited. Second, Indira Gandhi took advantage of the situation when West Bengal was under presidential rule. The war had concentrated the armed forces in West Bengal. During that period, Indira saw to it that many of the Naxalites – the armed revolutionaries – were jailed and eliminated. With the extreme left thus reduced in significance and Indira's popularity soaring, the massive 1972 Congress victory in West Bengal may well have seemed for the moment like a restoration of "politics as usual."

The next major event in West Bengal politics obviously was the Emergency, which was to have far-reaching consequences. Congress ruled West Bengal from 1972 to 1977. In the 1977 elections, however, Congress was trounced, and the CPM emerged as the single most important political force in West Bengal. Underlying that victory were several important factors. The CPM benefited from the same anti-Emergency and anti-Congress sentiment that brought Janata to power nationally. Additionally, the CPI, under Soviet instructions, had supported Indira Gandhi during the Emergency. That severely delegitimized the CPI within West Bengal. With the "extreme left" eliminated by Indira Gandhi, and the "revisionist left" delegitimized, the CPM, which already had a considerable power base within West Bengal, finally emerged as the single most important voice of the Bengali left.

The CPM, with Jyoti Basu as the chief minister, has ruled West Bengal with relative success since 1977. This success is manifest first and foremost in repeated electoral victories. Underlying this popularity is a fairly effective "social-democratic" ruling strategy. The CPM has finally eschewed "revolutionary mobilization." They have instead concentrated on consolidating their positions in the villages by providing piecemeal reforms. The CPM is hoping that such reformism may improve the conditions of the middle and lower peasantry without alienating the rich ones. Additionally, the CPM-dominated Left Front government has sought to attract business and investment by discouraging *gheraoes* and labor militancy. More generally, the reform-oriented communists have utilized the party's good organization to offer West Bengal some relief from the chaos and corruption of the past.

THE CHANGING PARTY SYSTEM IN CALCUTTA

The story of the transformation of Calcutta's Congress party begins in the mid–1960s. It was the two drought years, 1964 and 1965, that produced a turning point in the political fortunes of Congress everywhere in India, but especially in Calcutta. Congress had already been weakened within West Bengal by the deaths of Nehru and B. C. Roy. With the many left parties mobilizing, "the worsening economic situation, mounting unemployment, and deepening food crisis" created "a storm of incessant unrest in Calcutta."[8]

The left's political strategy was to keep up the pressure on the Congress state government by organizing demonstrations and encouraging militancy. Congress, instead of coming together under conditions of adversity, responded in a suicidal manner. Mounting difficulties had already weakened the hold of Atulya Ghosh and his pro-Delhi faction within the West Bengal Congress. The more regionally oriented groups led by Ajoy Mukerjee began challenging Ghosh's leadership. Open factional struggles, mutual charges of corruption, and economic malaise contributed to the growing opposition to Congress. One observer noted that "the last years of Congress rule over Calcutta and surrounding district had become so unpopular that P. C. Sen and his ministers were unable to address public meetings or move anywhere without very large police escorts."[9]

Although the UF emerged victorious from the 1967 state elections, Congress in Calcutta still won 12 of the 23 assembly seats and 44 percent of the popular vote (Table 6.1). With the one exception of 1977, Congress always attracted more than 35 percent of the popular vote in Calcutta (Tables 6.1 and 6.2).[10] It is also important to remember that having won the 1965 CMC elections, Congress still was in control of the Calcutta city government in 1967 when the UF came to power in West Bengal. A power struggle between the UF-controlled state government and the Congress-controlled city government began almost immediately.[11] Given their overlapping jurisdictions, the scope for such a struggle was limitless. For example, soon after coming to power, the UF state government ordered a reduction of taxes in all of Calcutta's *bustees*.[12] Clever political ploys such

8 See Sajal Basu, *Politics of Violence: A Case Study of West Bengal* (Calcutta: Minerva Associates, 1982), p. 70.
9 See Moorhouse, *Calcutta*, p. 314.
10 That was also true in the elections to the three Lok Sabha seats in Calcutta. Congress's shares of the vote in 1967, 1971, 1980, and 1985 were 39.0, 35.3, 41.7, and 58.9 percent, respectively. The share of the vote in the exceptional year of 1977 was 25.0 percent.
11 For a detailed study of the experience of the two United Front governments in West Bengal, see Shankar Ghosh, *The Disinherited State: A Study of West Bengal, 1967–70* (Bombay: Orient Longman, 1971).
12 See Moorhouse, *Calcutta*, p. 319.

Table 6.1. *Results of Legislative Assembly elections, Calcutta district, West Bengal, 1967–85*

Party	Seats won					Vote received (%)				
	1967	1972	1977	1982	1987	1967	1972	1977	1982	1987
Congress[a]	12	20	—	10	13	44.0	57.7	25.0	43.3	n.a.[g]
CPM	4	—	13[d]	10[d]	9[f]	25.7	25.7	31.6[d]	36.9[d]	
CPI	4	3	—	—	—	8.5	9.0	1.7	1.2[d]	
Forward Bloc	—	—	2[d]	1[d]	—	4.4	3.8	6.0[d]	5.4[d]	
Janata[b]	—	—	5	—	—	—	—	27.9	1.4	
Jan Sangh[c]	—	—	—	—	—	5.8	—	—	1.7	
Others	3	—	2[e]	1[e]	—	11.6	3.8	7.8	10.1	
Total	23	23	22	22		100	100	100	100	

[a]Known as Congress (I) since 1969.
[b]Founded in 1977.
[c]Merged into Janata in 1977; broke away and re-formed as the Bhartiya Janata party in 1980.
[d]Members of a multiparty alliance known as the Left Front.
[e]These seats were won by another member of the Left Front: the Revolutionary Socialist Party.
[f]These 9 seats were won by the CPM-dominated Left Front, not by the CPM alone. The figures are from *Economic and Political Weekly*, April 18, 1987, p. 693.
[g]These figures were not readily available at the time of writing.
Source: Compiled from reports of the chief electoral officer, government of West Bengal.

Table 6.2. *Results of elections to the Calcutta Municipal Corporation, 1985*

Party[a]	Seats won		Votes received (%)
	Number	Percentage	
Congress	67	47.5	43.8
CPM[b]	49 ⎫	34.8 ⎫	31.6 ⎫
CPI[b]	7 ⎬ 71	5.0 ⎬ 50.4	3.9 ⎬ 41.5
Other Left Front members	15 ⎭	10.6 ⎭	6.0 ⎭
Others	3	2.1	14.7
Total	141	100	100

[a]For details on when parties were formed or re-formed, see Table 6.1.
[b]Member of the Left Front.
Source: Compiled from unpublished data made available by the Calcutta Municipal Corporation.

as that were aimed at boosting the UF's popularity among the urban poor and simultaneously short-circuiting the resource base, and thus the patronage network, of the Congress-controlled CMC.

Following a somewhat similar pattern, the UF government ordered the police not to "interfere" in labor–management strife.[13] Within a few months of that order, the industrial scene in Calcutta became totally chaotic. Within the first few months of UF rule, there were nearly 1,000 *gheraoes* recorded within and around Calcutta.[14] Explaining why such a situation was being encouraged to develop, the UF labor minister, Subodh Banerjee, noted that "I have allowed a duel between the employees and employers in West Bengal, and the police have been taken out of the picture so that the strength of each other may be known."[15] The UF, as a result, may have improved its political standing with labor, but industrial production plummeted, and capital flew to other parts of India. It would take the Bengali left nearly two decades to learn and admit the long-term socioeconomic cost of such short-term political victories.

Meanwhile, the militant situation was exacerbated after the emergence of the Naxalites as a political force (see Chapter 10). Within Calcutta, the Naxalites unleashed urban terror as part of what they conceived to be a revolutionary strategy.[16] Students and "lumpen elements" were organized in a fairly decentralized model of terrorist cells and used primitive weapons to kill "class enemies." The enemies often were members of other political parties (especially the CPM), university professors, informers, and, of course, members of the police.[17] One measure of the chaos that existed in Calcutta in 1970 and 1971 is that even under presidential rule, there could be as many as 60 political murders committed in a day.[18]

Politics became a dangerous profession. Many of the Congress old-timers simply faded from the scene. Those who entered politics in that atmosphere generally were people with an outlook that would allow them to continue to function amid urban terrorism. With the advantage of hindsight, it is

13 For details and documentation, see C. R. Irani, *Bengal: The Communist Challenge* (Bombay: Lalvani Publishing House, 1968), part 4.

14 Figures from Government of West Bengal, *Labour in West Bengal* (Calcutta: Director of Information, Government of West Bengal, 1972).

15 Cited in Moorhouse, *Calcutta,* p. 324; also see Irani, *Bengal,* appendix 6.

16 For an excellent study of the activities of Naxalites in Calcutta, see Biplab Dasgupta, *The Naxalite Movement* (Bombay: Allied Publishers, 1975), chapter 4.

17 For a detailed study of student politics in Calcutta at that time, see Sugata Dasgupta, Ronen Bhattacharjee, and Surendra Singh, *The Great Gherao of 1969: A Case Study of Campus Violence and Protest Methods* (Bombay: Orient Longman, 1974). Like many other studies, it concludes that a major cause of the student-led demonstrations and violence was conflict among the student groups controlled by the different political parties. The conflict between the CPM and CPML student groups was especially significant (p. 145).

18 See Dasgupta, *Naxalite,* p. 109.

evident that Congress adopted a threefold strategy to deal with the changing political situation.

First, Congress encouraged the vicious fighting among the leftist elements, even supporting the Naxalites who were willing to attack the CPI or the CPM.[19] Second, Congress increasingly incorporated into the party many individuals whom Bengalis like to call *mastans,* or whom north Indians call *goondas* (ruffians, hoodlums, and toughs). The political utility of *mastans* in an atmosphere of rioting and murder hardly requires explanation. Their activities are vividly captured in one of numerous reports provided by local observers:

Kasba [an area near Baligunj in the southeast of Calcutta] has been famous since mid–1960 for its concentration of mastans. A group of mastans ran a boxing club here whose main source of income was black marketing in local cinema houses and theft from railway wagons. When factionalism developed within the club over issues of appropriate shares of the booty, the rival groups sought out support of politicians and police. That is how a number of them joined the Congress. Some of these mastans are now local leaders of the Congress in Kasba.[20]

Although one hears many such reports from all parts of Calcutta, the point to be noted is more general. Local toughs were attracted to Congress because the Congress leaders could secure police protection for them. Conversely, the political leaders increasingly needed these toughs as allies to cope with the growing militancy and violence in political life. As these toughs were incorporated within Congress, it was likely that some of them would actually become future party leaders.

The third important development within Calcutta's Congress was the growing importance of the party's youth wing, the Chatra Parishad. Most of the old established Congress leadership of the independence generation had already passed from the scene. The remnants of the old guard were deeply factionalized and quite dispirited by their losses in elections. Those leaders also were quite incapable of generating an effective response to the growing militancy in city politics. With the UF in power, Congress's main political goal was to halt the growing influence of the left among factory laborers, white-collar unions, universities, and neighborhood clubs. In all of those areas, the "vigor of the youth" proved to be much more helpful than the actions of the factionalized old guard.

A detailed case study of the 1969 *gheraoes* at Calcutta University documented the growing significance of the Parishad.[21] The Calcutta Parishad leader, presumably supported by the national Chatra Parishad, had gone to Kerala to learn how Congress's youth movement in that state had coped

19 See Basu, *Politics of Violence,* p. 167, and Dasgupta et al., *The Great Gherao,* p. 72.
20 Paraphrased from Sajal Basu, *West Bengal: The Violent Years* (Calcutta: Prachi Publications, 1979), pp. 94–5. Basu provides numerous similar examples (pp. 94–7).
21 This discussion is based on Dasgupta et al., *The Great Gherao* (especially pp. 70–9).

with the growing significance of the communists. The lessons led to a new orientation: "The Parishad had now decided to take on a fighting role."[22] That militancy was expressed in numerous forms: disrupting the political initiatives of the youth groups of the CPM and the CPI; initiating demonstrations and *gheraoes* against the local centers of the UF's power.

The authors of the study mentioned earlier, who seemed to be favorably disposed to the new developments within Congress, described the political change as follows: "The interview with the Parishad boys was a revealing experience. At a time when Congress lay dormant and strife-torn, the Parishad had shown a rare sign of courage and strength. They were not in the least demoralized [by the UF rule] but had virtually demonstrated that they had already developed a new image of radicalism."[23] Ignoring the endorsement implicit here, what is clear is the newfound activism of Congress's youth wing. Thus, when Congress won the 1972 elections in Calcutta despite widespread charges of repression of the left and vote rigging,[24] the Parishad supposedly played a very important role. Supporters and opponents of Congress seemed to agree on that point. Welcoming that outcome, the previously mentioned study summarized the results of the 1972 elections: "The overwhelming victory that the new Congress has achieved in West Bengal [is] thanks to the contribution of the Chatra Parishad."[25] Another author, less sanguine about the prospect of a Congress under the influence of the new militant youth, observed tersely that by 1972 the takeover of the local Congress by the Chatra Parishad was complete.[26]

Between 1967 and 1972, therefore, the Congress party of Calcutta had been radically transformed. The old guard was replaced by a youthful and militant new leadership. The introduction of *mastans* in various neighborhoods had altered the character of local Congress units. Those new cadres had undergone little political socialization within the party ranks. They were also quite accustomed to the use of violence to achieve their ends. Moreover, there was the growing role of the Chatra Parishad, whose members had not climbed through the party ranks, but were pushed into positions of leadership because there was a vacuum at the top, and because they could mobilize force to meet the political challenges of the day.

One of the consequences of that change was increasing dissension within the Congress party. Squabbling over positions and patronage had always been a characteristic of Congress. In the past, however, that had led only to factional infighting. Because of the new cast of characters in the old fight over positions and patronage, there was a rapidly developing tendency to resort to violence, including political murders. Although data on such

22 Ibid., p. 72.
23 Ibid., p. 78.
24 See Basu, *West Bengal,* pp. 77–83.
25 Dasgupta et al., *The Great Gherao,* p. 79.
26 Dasgupta, *Naxalite,* pp. 110–11.

incidents are not readily available, one local scholar, a Gandhian socialist who supported neither the CPM nor Congress, suggested that between 1972 and 1975, clashes within the Congress party led to 102 murders of Congressites. Trying to explain that development, his line of argument fits closely with what I have been suggesting:

Political dependence on the rowdy cadres has precipitated a situation of *Mastanocracy* [I presume the author means rule of *mastans*] as the mastans have taken shelter under the different fighting groups of the ruling party, the police stand helpless before their violent activities. The mastan elements have become the main actors in the chessboard of in-group political fighting.[27]

Clearly, the attempt to reinvigorate the party with young blood led to some rather grotesque political outcomes, even before the Emergency and the rise of Sanjay Gandhi. Bengalis often take pride in the fact that "what happens in Bengal today, happens in India tomorrow." There seems little reason for pride in the fact that the early emergence of the *goonda*-politician-police nexus in Calcutta politics foreshadowed similar developments in other parts of India.

The contemporary Congress party of Calcutta revolves around the activities of three factions headed by Priya Ranjan Das Munshi, Subrato Mukerjee, and Somen Mitra. Das Munshi was the most significant of these three local leaders in the mid–1980s, Rajiv Gandhi having appointed him head of Congress's state committee.[28] Das Munshi first emerged on the Bengali political scene during 1967–71 as a leader of Calcutta's youth movement. His prominence resulted from the fact that he had demonstrated considerable prowess in mobilizing against the Naxalites. Later he was elevated to head not only the Bengal youth movement but also the All India Youth Congress. In 1971 he won a Lok Sabha seat from Calcutta. During the late 1970s, however, his relations with Congress deteriorated. He quit Congress (I) and joined another party, Congress (S), where the "S" stands for Sharad Pawar. But once again, in 1983, when it became clear that there was little political future in a small party, he rejoined Congress (I). Why he was Rajiv's choice to head the West Bengal Congress is not clear. What is clear is that Das Munshi's upward political climb was due largely to Delhi and was bitterly resented by his fellow Congressites.

Subrato Mukerjee also gained his critical political socialization within the Youth Congress.[29] In his own words,

27 Basu, *Politics of Violence*, pp. 159, 161.
28 The brief discussion that follows is in part based on an interview with Priyaraj Das Munshi, president, West Bengal Pradesh Congress (I) Committee, Calcutta, May 3, 1986. Some of the information is also derived from S. N. M. Abdi, "At Loggerheads," *Illustrated Weekly of India*, April 27, 1986, pp. 20–3.
29 The following account is based on an interview with Subrato Mukerjee (former home minister of West Bengal, 1972–7, and current head of Congress's trade-union movement in West Bengal), Calcutta, May 3, 1986.

I played an important role in Youth Congress since 1969. There was no Congress party left. All fell apart under the struggle with the left forces. Chatra Parishad became *de facto* Congress. The left terrorism created tremendous disillusionment. We confronted this . . . Das Munshi and myself. There was tremendous violence throughout the state.

When Congress won the state elections in 1972, Mukerjee became the minister of state (home) and managed that portfolio for a little more than two years. Between then and the end of the Emergency years (1975–7), massive state repression was unleashed against the left. Mukerjee was in charge of the police and of enforcing law and order during some of that period. One can be sure, therefore, that Subrato Mukerjee has quite a few skeletons in his political closet. His political fortunes have waxed and waned since then, depending mainly on the state of his relations with New Delhi. He was in charge of the 1980 elections, but lost favor after a major electoral defeat. He also headed the West Bengal branch of the Indian National Trade Union Congress (INTUC) in the later 1980s, a role that often put him in confrontation with the leftist forces competing for influence within the trade-union movement.

Somen Mitra, the third important leader in Calcutta in the mid–1980s, was widely regarded as a Sanjay man, meaning that he owed his rise in politics to his personal relationship with Sanjay Gandhi. Because Sanjay Gandhi's cronies generally were of the toughs-as-politicians genre, Mitra was seen as part of the Sanjay culture. Therefore, it was not surprising that until early 1986 he was the head of the West Bengal Youth Congress. However, Mitra's political fortunes began declining following Rajiv Gandhi's rise to power in the mid–1980s.

These specific individuals and their personalities are important for our study of the Congress party only in terms of what they tell us about the nature of the leadership of the local party. Two characteristics stand out. First, local Congress leaders are leaders only because they are appointed from Delhi. As will be seen later, the authority of these externally imposed local leaders seldom is accepted within the local party structure, and they periodically face strong challenges. Second, the current leaders of the Calcutta Congress had their political origins in the "decade of chaos." Most of them are quite adept at using force to achieve their political goals. These political habits are not easy to change, as will be discussed later.

Calcutta's Congress party is at present deeply factionalized and totally without any organization. One observer of the West Bengal Congress noted that even judging by Congress's traditional record of "indiscipline and impropriety," the local party was characterized by an "alarming degree of indiscipline."[30] A discussion of some specific issues will help illustrate this point.

30 See Abdi, "At Loggerheads," p. 20.

Das Munshi was appointed to be head of the West Bengal state Congress party in September 1985. On assuming that position, he said that many of the districts "and most of the blocks have no functional committees, which I feel is one of the basic weaknesses of the party. So I have to organize the party, identify the issues affecting the people, and also, as much as possible, keep the ranks free from factional feuds."[31] Das Munshi, unfortunately, had little independent authority to undertake a task that was nearly as complex as founding a totally new party. That was clearly evident in his response to the question how he would tackle the first problem he faced: naming the party's officers. His response: "I will consult the Prime Minister."[32]

It quickly became evident that neither Delhi's authority nor Das Munshi's authority ran deep in the West Bengal Congress party. As Das Munshi appointed the presidents of the district committees in January 1986, a virtual revolt broke out all over the state. The intensity of the dissatisfaction is well captured in the following description by a journalist:

Violence erupted in several districts when the new DCC-Is [the district committees of Congress (I)] met. . . . At Burdwan, DCC-I member Dhiraj Sain was stabbed and 15 others injured as rival factions clashed on March 23; on March 29 disgruntled Congress-I leaders and workers from north 24 Parganas held a demonstration outside the PCC-I [the state or Pradesh Congress (I) committee] office in Calcutta; on March 16 South Calcutta DCC-I president Bidhu Bhushan Ghosh and four others were injured during fist-fighting and brick-batting between rival groups; on March 9 several persons were severely injured in the north 24 Parganas DCC-I meeting; on March 20 the north Calcutta DCC-I president Dr. Kiran Choudhri resigned after he was subjected to "unprintable abuses" by Congress-I.[33]

The appointment of a new president of the Calcutta-based West Bengal Youth Congress led to a similar outrage:

The Youth Congress-I president, Prodyut Guha's car was stopped by his own party men. The windscreen and windows were smashed, Guha was dragged out and stripped, made to take a dip in the municipal drain and his hair was clipped. His wife Ranjana witnessed the scene. He went home in his underpants after he gave an undertaking in writing that he would not participate in politics again.[34]

So much for Rajiv's efforts to rebuild a disciplined Congress party in West Bengal and in Calcutta.

Many of these general issues of the changing nature of the Congress party were vividly brought out in an interview with a president of a Congress (I) district committee in southern Calcutta.[35] That specific president was

31 Quoted in *The Telegraph*, September 29, 1985.
32 Ibid.
33 See Abdi, "At Loggerheads," p. 20.
34 Ibid.
35 Interview with B. B. Ghosh, president of the South Calcutta District Congress (I) Committee, Calcutta, May 3, 1986.

somewhat unusual in that he was a Congress old-timer who had witnessed many of the changes firsthand. He had been actively involved in the same district committee for some 25 years. As the dean of the faculty of engineering at Calcutta University, he also represented the old *bhadralok* politicians, a fast-vanishing breed within the Calcutta Congress. When asked how he would describe the changing nature of local leadership and organization, he said:

As long as Atulya Ghosh was around, Congress was fairly well organized. There were many devoted workers. There was idealism . . . idealism to work for the country. This traditional Congress stayed intact till the late sixties. After that . . . the left started getting united and factionalism hurt us a lot. The new people who joined were very different . . . they joined to make a living. As Kripalani has said, "politics is now a paying profession." These new entrants are working for themselves. . . . These leaders had nothing before, no traditions, no sense of responsibility for the people. So when the question of sharing the booty comes up, naturally there is struggle [within the party].

Asked how people like that got into positions of power, he responded:

These people occupy positions because of their storm troopers. At the time of organizational elections or organizational struggle, they can bring forward antisocial elements. Educated people are not suited for the times. These people make money through anti-social activities. They then fly to Delhi every week. Delhi leaders think they must be important. [This is how they get their appointments.]

Even if one ignores the self-serving element in those responses, they broadly support the argument being developed here. This can now be summarized in a more analytical fashion.

From its beginnings as a modestly well organized machine in the 1950s and 1960s, the Congress party of Calcutta has been fundamentally transformed. It is now characterized not simply by deep factionalism (that often has typified Congress at other places at times) but by something much more disruptive: factionalism that is openly fought out on the streets. Underlying that change were several causal variables. First, in Calcutta, as elsewhere, there was the national role of Indira Gandhi. Her termination of internal party elections removed the one possible mechanism for peaceful resolution of intraparty clashes and any hope of rebuilding local authority. Second, the decade of chaos in Calcutta politics allowed the emergence of a leadership that did not hesitate to use violent means to pursue their political goals. Third, given Calcutta's general conditions of congested poverty and deprivation, there existed within Calcutta a significant criminal underworld, whose members were variously labeled *mastans, goondas,* antisocial elements, rowdies, or toughs. Over time, many of those elements came to be incorporated into the Congress party. The widespread availability of those "lumpen elements" and their political incorporation changed Congress's fairly routine factional struggles into unusually violent confrontations.

Besides Congress, the other major political force in Calcutta is the left.

From competing and feuding factions in the 1960s and early 1970s, the left has emerged as a relatively unified force under the CPM's dominance. A number of factors help explain this development. Government repression and its own failure to move beyond terrorism have reduced the political significance of the extreme left. As discussed earlier, the Soviet-supported CPI has, over time, lost much of its electoral base. This decline dates back to the Emergency period, when the CPI's support of Indira Gandhi cost it dearly in terms of popular support in Calcutta; note, for example, the CPI's decline in popular vote between 1972 and 1977 (Table 6.1). With both the extreme left and the revisionist left in decline, the CPM has emerged as the single most important left party in Calcutta.

The nature and extent of the CPM's electoral support within Calcutta will be discussed later. What ought to be noted first are some characteristics of the CPM as a party. I have discussed the leadership, the organization, the changing ideology, and the social base of the CPM's cadres in detail elsewhere,[36] and some of that material is further discussed in Chapter 10. For now, we should note some features of the CPM that help fill out the changing picture of Calcutta politics.

On the organizational dimension, the contemporary CPM provides a sharp contrast to Congress. This is not surprising. The party is organized on the principle of "democratic centralism" and has disciplined cadres. The sectarian conflict and ideological infighting of the past have declined. Organizational cohesion allows the CPM to set clear priorities, minimize factionalism, and facilitate the pursuit of party goals as public policies. What the CPM calls democratic centralism is rightly anathema to most democrats, and the related characteristics of the CPM leave much to be desired from a liberal standpoint. And yet, it is precisely those organizational traits that have enabled the CPM to bring some much-needed order and calm to Calcutta's political chaos.

The CPM has, over the years, moved from a revolutionary ideology to a reformist ideology. Underlying that shift were several important factors: (1) the lessons learned during the chaos that resulted from the pursuit of militant strategies under the UF government, (2) the need to broaden the party's electoral base, and (3) the need to attract investment and facilitate growth in a largely private economy. From the standpoint of Calcutta politics, the most significant impact of that deradicalization has been to decrease labor militancy.

The CPM's local leaders generally are upper-caste, educated Bengali men in their sixties who have been party members for several decades. That pattern holds for such state leaders as Jyoti Basu and Binoy Chowdhry as well as for Calcutta's mayor, Kamal Basu, and deputy mayor, Mani Sanyal. Kamal Basu, for example, was born to a lawyer family prominent

36 See the sources cited in footnote 7.

in the nationalist movement.[37] A lawyer himself, he joined the Communist party during his student days at Calcutta University in 1942–3. Since then he has been an active member of the party, first the undivided CPI and then the CPM, serving as a member of the national Parliament, traveling to the East Bloc countries, and participating on various committees, including a committee that supervised the construction of a large sports stadium in Calcutta.

Similarly, the deputy mayor, Mani Sanyal, who belongs to the CPI, comes from a family of high standing.[38] He was politically active in the independence movement and was a member of the old Congress party. He joined the Communist party in 1950. Since then he has been a banker for nearly 20 years. (The existence of communist bankers makes perfect sense in some cities of the world, such as Calcutta and Bologna, where communists have long accommodated themselves to capitalism.) He also served as an elected member of both the CMC and the West Bengal Legislative Assembly and was actively involved in such civic projects as the construction of a second bridge over the Hoogly River.

These brief profiles of two of Calcutta's leftist leaders provide interesting and sharp contrasts to those of the previously discussed Congress leaders. The leftist leaders are older and generally have experienced much longer periods of political socialization within their parties. They also had held many responsible positions prior to their emergence as city leaders. Whatever the merits of new blood and new energy, there is little doubt that these leftist leaders are better prepared to run a city like Calcutta than are the Congress leaders, whose political education was gained while mobilizing local toughs to enhance their personal political standing.

Finally, it should be noted that most of the CPM's Calcutta cadres come from what the party would describe as the petite bourgeoisie. Although crucial elements of the CPM's electoral strength are found among industrial laborers and refugees and in the *bustees,* its cadres within the city generally are drawn from among white-collar workers, segments of the educated Bengali middle class, and, of course, university students and professors.[39] This definitely gives the CPM more of a middle-class character, rather than a lower-class character. This is as true of rural West Bengal as it is of cities like Calcutta.[40]

To summarize and conclude this section, Calcutta's party system in the

37 This brief account is based on an interview with Kamal Basu, mayor of Calcutta, Calcutta, April 30, 1986.
38 Based on an interview with Mani Sanyal, deputy mayor of Calcutta, Calcutta, May 2, 1986.
39 See, for example, Bhabani Sengupta, *CPI-M: Promises, Prospects, Problems* (New Delhi: Young Asia Publications, 1979), chapters 3 and 5.
40 For documentation of the middle-class and lower-middle-class character of the CPM in rural West Bengal, see Kohli, *The State and Poverty in India,* chapter 4.

early 1960s was characterized by a modestly cohesive and dominant Congress party and numerous feuding and factionalized leftist parties. Some 25 years later, the situation is nearly reversed. The CPM has emerged as the cohesive, dominant party. Congress's organization, by contrast, is in shambles.

HOW CALCUTTA VOTES

In spite of the profound changes in Calcutta's parties in terms of leadership, organization, and ideology, there has been amazing continuity in electoral patterns within the city. If one thinks of the left within Calcutta not in terms of a specific party but as a combination of the CPM, CPI, and the Forward Bloc, then Table 6.1 reveals a remarkable fact: The combined vote of these parties since 1967 has hovered around 40 percent. Table 6.2 supports that finding with data on elections to the city government, the CMC. The Congress vote within Calcutta has experienced wider fluctuations, though mainly in unusual elections. The normal vote for Congress is about 45 percent of the total (see the figures for the 1967 and 1982 elections in Table 6.1, and the figures for city elections in Table 6.2). The sharp rise in Congress's vote in 1972 was due to the post-Bangladesh euphoria and to considerable electoral rigging. Similarly, the sharp drop in Congress's vote in 1977 was due to the post-Emergency lull in Congress's popularity. Congress's losses in 1977, it may be noted, were picked up not by the left parties but by other centrist candidates running under the Janata label.

Congress's core electoral support continues to come from the non-Bengali, Hindu population of Calcutta.[41] During the 1985 city elections, for example, Congress won seats in 67 of the 141 city wards (Table 6.2). Most of those wards are concentrated in the old, congested part of Calcutta. Although data on the ward-by-ward distribution of linguistic groups are not readily available, there are data on the male and female populations in all the wards. Because migrants from outside of Bengal often come without families, it is fair to assume that the male-concentrated wards are wards where many of the non-Bengalis live. Following this assumption, it is immediately clear that Congress tends to win in the wards with male-

41 Members of the CPM, Congressites, and local journalists all agreed that the non-Bengali population of Calcutta tends to vote for Congress. Subrato Mukerjee, for example, a prominent Congress leader in Calcutta, noted in an interview that "our major support is in Bado Bazar and in central Calcutta; that is where most Hindi speaking people live" (see footnote 29). A local CPM leader concurred independently: "Non-Bengalis generally vote Congress." Interview with Ashish De, member of the Calcutta District Committee of the CPM, Calcutta, May 3, 1986. Analyzing the most recent Legislative Assembly elections of 1987, a journalist also concluded that "within Calcutta, non-Bengalis tended to vote against the CPM." See *Economic and Political Weekly*, April 18, 1987, p. 693.

concentrated populations. For example, Congress won all of the 20 wards in central Calcutta (wards 36–55). The male-to-female ratio for those wards was 2 : 1. That contrasts with the 3 : 2 ratio for the rest of Calcutta.

How does one explain this proclivity of non-Bengalis to vote for Congress? Weiner explained this tendency, which was already evident in the early 1960s, primarily in terms of the non-Bengalis as migrants and the type of stability-seeking political behavior that one might expect from a migrant population.[42] The consistency of this pattern ever since suggests that additional factors are at work.

Congress used to be a powerful political force in India's Hindi heartland, and in a certain important but qualified way, that continues to be true. The migrant Hindi speakers probably already had a favorable disposition toward Congress when they migrated. More important, communism is quite an alien ideology for most Hindi speakers, especially those coming from Uttar Pradesh. The disposition of the migrants toward Congress likely was strengthened when they settled in an alien culture with seemingly alien political ideas. The recent tendency of the CPM to mobilize along anti-Delhi and pro-Bengali regional themes must have reinforced those existing divisions, creating an ethnic political divide beneath what looks like a class-oriented political issue.

By contrast, the CPM's core supporters are the *bustee* dwellers and those who trace their origins to the refugees from East Bengal (now Bangladesh). Together these groups may constitute as much as half of Calcutta's population. There is wide agreement that the former refugees from East Bengal tend to vote for the CPM.[43] Electoral data from specific constituencies tend to support the popular impression. For example, many of the refugees settled in the Jadavpur area of outer Calcutta. That area was recently incorporated under the jurisdiction of the CMC, mainly because its residents support the CPM.

The reasons for that political alignment have to do with the fact that those refugees have always blamed Congress for the partition that resulted in their displacement. Furthermore, unlike the situation in Punjab, there was no comparable out-migration of Moslems from West Bengal. Thus, land and property were not as easily available for exchange in West Bengal as in Punjab. The refugees have tended to blame their resulting poor socioeconomic conditions on Congress. The identification of the Congress

---

42 Weiner, *Party Building in a New Nation,* especially pp. 366–7.
43 One Congressite, B. B. Ghosh, had the following observation: "Atulya Ghosh was West Bengali. Refugees were from East Bengal. Refugees were not treated well [by the Congress and] by Atulya Ghosh. So refugees have always supported the left parties" (see footnote 35). The summary analysis by Calcutta's communist deputy mayor regarding who generally supports the left within Calcutta is consistent with this view: "Basti people voted for the left front; so did refugees and the Moslems." Interview with Kamal Basu (see footnote 37).

party under Atulya Ghosh as a West Bengali organization, allied with Delhi, only further alienated the East Bengali refugees. Support for the communists originated in those divisions. Of late, however, the communists have further consolidated their political position by undertaking programs that have benefited the refugee population. In the outlying rural areas of Calcutta, where some of the refugees live, these programs are the same as those pursued in the rest of rural West Bengal, and the efficacy of that CPM agrarian strategy has been documented elsewhere.[44]

Given their large numbers, the support of the *bustee* dwellers for the CPM is crucial. Because the *bustees* are spread all over Calcutta, it is difficult to correlate them with specific wards for purposes of data analysis. Thus, one must depend on reports by knowledgeable observers. Numerous local observers suggested that the CPM's support in the *bustees* is quite strong. An analysis of the 1985 city elections concluded that "the majority of the 'bustee' people . . . vote in favor of the Left Front."[45] One strong indicator of that trend was the attention that the CPM-controlled city government devoted to reforms within the *bustees*. For example, unlike the previous Congress governments, the CPM legalized the existence of the *bustees*. That reduced the prospect of mass evictions from these slum settlements. Having recognized the legal existence of *bustees,* the government also initiated new programs to introduce sewerage, running water, and electricity into these areas.[46] Whatever the success of those schemes in the long run, over the short run they indicate the CPM's political priorities, which is one reason for the view of local observers that the CPM enjoys political support in the *bustees*.

Calcutta's socioeconomic groups, whose electoral support is divided between the CPM and Congress and is even somewhat fluid, include organized labor, Moslems, and the Bengali middle class. Data to support any observations on the political behaviors of these groups are not readily available.

The head of the Congress-supported trade unions (INTUC) in Calcutta suggested that the "Communist-controlled unions are in majority in Calcutta." Although membership figures are not reliable, the estimated breakdowns provided by that Congress leader were not disputed by the CPM: "White collar workers are generally with the CPM; factory workers are split, maybe even half and half." He further suggested that the membership figures for INTUC had grown from "3 lakhs to 7 lakhs over the last decade."[47] Although the CPM disputes that figure, it is clear that the CPM

44 See Kohli, *The State and Poverty in India,* chapter 4.
45 See *Economic and Political Weekly,* July 20, 1985, p. 1216.
46 Based on interviews with Kamal Basu (see footnote 37), Leena Chakravarty, chief executive officer, Calcutta Metropolitan Development Authority, March 22, 1988, and A. P. Deb, secretary for local government and urban development, February 22, 1988.
47 Interview with Subrato Mukerjee (see footnote 29); 1 lakh = 100,000.

has lost some support, especially among factory laborers, as a result of the CPM's new emphasis on discouraging labor militancy and strikes.

It would be difficult to demonstrate a simple correlation between membership in a given party-controlled labor union and a decision to vote for that party. During the 1984 national elections, it was reported that the non-Bengali laborers organized by the CPM had joined the "Rajiv wave" and voted for Congress. Following the 1987 elections, however, the same observer noted that the CPM had regained their support.[48] Clearly, class and ethnic issues intermingle in complex ways. What the patterns of unionization do suggest, however, is that the *babu,* or white-collar, unions and a significant proportion of the factory workers support the leftists. A significant minority of the organized working class, however, especially the non-Bengali working class, tend to vote Congress.

The voting behavior of Moslems has also become much more fluid than in the past. Traditionally, as Weiner noted, Moslems used to vote for Congress.[49] That was a result of a widely held belief that Congress was a secular party and would protect the Moslems. Over time, that situation has changed. The communist deputy mayor of Calcutta has bluntly claimed that Calcutta's Moslems now vote for the Left Front. The data suggest that his claim is somewhat exaggerated. For example, one can take the 10 city wards in Calcutta in which Congress and the CPM each ran a Moslem candidate to be an indicator of the wards where the Moslems are concentrated. The Left Front won 6 of those 10 wards, giving credence to the claim that many Moslems now indeed vote for the left. Conversely, the vote counts in those 10 city wards for the CPM and Congress were nearly equal. Congress enjoyed a slight plurality, suggesting that the Moslem vote may well be quite divided.[50]

What explains this change from the past? Congress's tendency in recent years to harp on pro-Hindu and communal themes immediately comes to mind as one possible explanation. In addition, it is important to remember that the CPM is one of the few national parties that has scrupulously avoided entering into collusive electoral arrangements with the Hindu-chauvinist Bhartiya Janata party (the former Jan Sangh). Within West Bengal, unlike many other states, the past decade under CPM rule has been relatively free of communal (i.e., Hindu versus Moslem) conflict. It is quite possible, therefore, that many Moslems in

48 See, for example, *Economic and Political Weekly,* April 18, 1987, p. 694.
49 Weiner, *Party Building in a New Nation,* p. 357.
50 For anyone wanting to follow up on this analysis, the 10 wards I identified as probably having high Moslem concentrations were wards 39, 54, 62, 61, 75, 134, and 137–40. Judging from the names of those contesting elections, four more wards (61, 64, 77, and 78) would appear to be Moslem-dominated. These were not included either because the main contest did not involve Congress versus the Left Front or because one of the main contestants was not a Moslem. Three of these four wards were also won by the Left Front.

Calcutta now think of the CPM as more secular than Congress and less likely to utilize anti-Moslem communal themes for electoral mobilization.

Finally, in recent years the CPM has lost some electoral support among the Bengali middle class. A leader of the Left Front noted that "the middle classes are against us."[51] An analysis of the 1985 city elections in Calcutta further concluded that "not only the upper middle class, but a section of the middle class continues to stay away from the Left Front."[52] It is difficult to confirm that conclusion on the basis of constituency data because of the mixed nature of most constituencies. In broad terms, however, the better-off Bengali middle class generally is concentrated in areas other than central Calcutta. In the south Calcutta district, for example, there are 8 assembly constituencies and 35 city wards. Although the population is mixed, many of the Bengali *bhadralok* live in these areas. The electoral results there were quite mixed. Congress won 5 assembly seats and 16 city wards; the Left Front won 3 assembly seats and 19 city wards. What those mixed results suggest is that the Bengali middle-class vote is quite divided. Considering the past antipathy of that group toward Congress, those results represent a significant political change.

Most observers explained that shift primarily as a negative vote against the CPM, rather than a positive vote for Congress. The president of Congress's district committee in south Calcutta suggested that the party's good performance in recent elections in his area reflected "mainly a negative vote – dissatisfaction with the CPM in the city is quite rampant." He went on to point out that "when Communists were not in power, the Bengali intelligentsia supported them; now, not so."[53]

Underlying that shift appear to be two important considerations. First, the CPM, as part of its overall ruling strategy in West Bengal, has concentrated on rural areas at the expense of urban areas, especially Calcutta. An important consequence of that choice has been the neglect of those city services that affect many middle-class urban residents, leading to some loss of support for the Left Front. Second, there was a more diffuse, cultural reason that often came up in interviews, partly in jest, that captured an important aspect of Calcutta's political reality: "We Bengalis," noted several observers, "are simply anti-establishment." The implication was that many among the middle classes were against Congress when Congress was in power. Subsequently, the reality of the CPM's former revolutionaries turned reformists involved in the mundane tasks of solving some problems, but leaving many others untouched, may well have disillusioned the more romantic among Calcutta's lively political strata.

---

51 Interview with Mani Sanyal (see footnote 38).
52 See *Economic and Political Weekly*, July 20, 1985, p. 1216.
53 Interview with B. B. Ghosh (see footnote 35).

ON THE QUALITY OF LOCAL GOVERNMENT

The decade between 1967 and 1977 was a time of political chaos and ineffective government in Calcutta. Since the CPM came to dominate local political affairs in 1977, there have been some important changes, but there also remain important continuities with the past. The CPM, like many other rulers of Calcutta before it, has not paid much attention to solving the city's pressing socioeconomic problems. However, the CPM has restored political order to the city.

Between 1967 and 1977, Calcutta had an elected city government for the first five years and was ruled administratively by the West Bengal government in the last five years. During the first five years, Calcutta had three governmental changes – from a Congress government to a UF government, and then to presidential rule by fiat. In the second five years, the city was run by the Congress state government until 1975, and then, of course, during the Emergency, Calcutta existed without any real elected government.

To further confuse the situation produced by these frequent governmental changes, there are many overlapping jurisdictions in the city. The West Bengal government controls certain issue areas, including the important area of law and order. The city government is basically in charge of developmental functions such as traffic control and provision of drinking water, electricity, and sewerage facilities. The national government also has important power levers in the city via developmental grants and its control over the Indian Administrative Services (IAS). Under the conditions of presidential rule and under the Emergency, given the presence of the army, the significance of the national government increased. The frequent governmental changes and the overlapping jurisdictions are important factors to keep in mind as we attempt to analyze the responsibility for the decade of chaos.

There were four basic components to the chaos and violence that gripped Calcutta between 1967 and 1977: (1) labor strife, (2) student conflict, including urban terrorism unleashed by the Naxalites, (3) the role of the *mastans* and *goondas,* and (4) state repression. Of course, many contextual variables, such as population congestion, poverty, and massive unemployment among educated youth, contributed to the malaise. The fact is, however, that although those socioeconomic conditions have not changed, the chaos has subsided. What has changed since 1977 is an underlying political condition. Numerous feuding political parties, competing for shares of state power, have been replaced by a moderately cohesive and popular party in control of government. In order to make a convincing analytical case for the significance of disordered political organizations in explaining the descent into chaos, it is first important to trace the political origins of the disorder.

Two of the worst years of labor strife in Calcutta and in other urban areas of West Bengal were 1967 and 1969. Whereas *gheraoes* averaged fewer than 100 per year before 1967 and after 1969, there were 811 and 517 *gheraoes* in 1967 and 1969, respectively.[54] Those were the two years when the motley coalition of 14 left-leaning parties formed the UF government. As noted earlier, the *gheraoes* in 1967 and 1969 were encouraged by labor ministers, who belonged to the Socialist Unity Center and the CPM, respectively, when they, with the approval of their parties, ordered the police to stay out of all labor–management conflicts. With state power thus neutralized, labor militancy was unleashed. Much of labor had been organized by those same left parties that muzzled the police.

One could take that growth in labor militancy as an instance that would support a Marxist analytical claim, namely, that the capitalist state functions in the interest of capital, and with the power of the state out of the way, the natural and deep-rooted class conflict came out into the open. Clearly there is a grain of truth in that insight, but what is more important to point out is that removing the factor of state power from the labor–management equation, whether under capitalism or under socialism, leads to a totally artificial situation. Such a situation can exist only under conditions of breakdown and anarchy, or under special circumstances, as in the previously cited case of a militant left in control of the state in a capitalist economy. The critical question that must be answered, therefore, is why the leaders who were in control of the state apparatus in West Bengal during that time period sought to keep the power of the state out of labor–management conflicts.

The CPM's political behavior must be understood as a function of two variables: confused ideology and the short-term need to broaden electoral support. The CPM at that stage still had not clarified what it means to strive for power by winning elections in a democratic capitalist setup. A realistic analysis of those constraints did not emerge within the CPM until the late 1970s. In the late 1960s, the CPM still thought it was pursuing revolutionary goals through the parliamentary route. Having won the elections and gained power in a coalition government, some CPM leaders advocated seizing that opportunity to mobilize labor, to raise class consciousness, and generally to demonstrate the power of labor.[55] Although that line of action may have enhanced the CPM's credibility as a Marxist revolutionary party, no one within the CPM in the 1960s seems to have understood that unbridled labor strife, flight of capital, and declining productivity would have disastrous implications for governability.

In addition, it is important to reiterate that the CPM at that stage was

54 Government of West Bengal, *Labour in West Bengal.*
55 See, for example, the speeches of the CPM labor minister reproduced in the appendix to Irani, *Bengal.*

a minority party in a coalition government. There were enormous pressures on the CPM to expand its own power base within the coalition, as well as against its opposition, the Congress party. Allowing organized labor to go on a rampage against the employers was a means of extracting better wages and other improvements for labor. It was bound to enhance the CPM's popularity with labor, and as the election results that led to the creation of the second UF government in 1969 indicated, indeed it did. The CPM at that time, however, simply was not capable of understanding the detrimental effects of such a strategy on the overall political and economic situation, and thus the long-term prospects for building broad political support.

Like the unbridled labor militancy, the urban terrorism unleashed by a segment of Calcutta's youth was aimed at settling accounts left over from prior political battles. The Naxalites, for example, were convinced that armed struggle was the only way to achieve their revolutionary goals.[56] That ideological belief led to some grotesque actions. Because "class enemies" were to be eliminated, all who opposed their revolutionary strategy could become victims of "revolutionary anger." Within Calcutta, that attitude quickly led to reckless urban terrorism. Members of the UF government, especially those representing the CPM, became favorite targets, because as "revisionists in power" they were likely to "confuse the masses" and thus were even more dangerous than the real "reactionary forces." Scores of CPM members and other "class enemies" were murdered each year during that period by the Naxalites. Their violence, in turn, led to more violence as the spirit of revenge set in, and political murders and retribution spiraled into a vicious cycle.

Congress and the "lumpen elements," sometimes in alliance and sometimes separately, made their own crucial contributions to that growing turmoil. As noted earlier, Congress had already organized many of its own militant youth to counter the rising militancy from the left. Desperate to offset the strength of its most dangerous political enemy, the UF, Congress often found itself and the Naxalites fighting the same enemy. Congress's youth wing had adopted its own aggressive political strategies, further adding to the growing numbers of *gheraoes,* riots, assaults, and, of course, political murders.

Whenever a community's social and political fiber begins breaking down in this manner, the criminal elements in the society are never far away. That was especially true in Calcutta in the late 1960s, when these lumpen groups were in abundance, many of them already well connected to political parties. Encouraged by the political parties to help fight the interparty conflicts, as well as to settle their own scores in the atmosphere of breakdown, the *goondas* and *mastans* eagerly joined the carnage.

56 See Dasgupta, *Naxalite,* passim, but especially chapter 4.

Finally, of course, the state's repression took a heavy toll. First under the presidential rule of 1971–2, then under the Congress state government of 1972–5, and finally under the conditions of the national Emergency, the Congress-controlled state resorted to severe repression against West Bengal in general, and Calcutta in particular. Amnesty International reported that some 25,000 left activists had been rounded up and jailed during that period.[57] Amnesty International did not estimate how many had been killed. A similar source, however, noted that between 1970 and 1972, 600 CPM members and 320 Naxalites had been murdered in prisons.[58] The reason that the role of the Congress-dominated state fits the argument being developed here is that its behavior was dictated by partisan politics rather than by public interest. Those picked up and jailed for crimes generally were members of the CPM and CPML, whereas Congress's own criminals and *mastans* were busy climbing the ladder of the Calcutta party hierarchy.

The following figures, collected by the office of the West Bengal home minister between 1969 and 1971, give an indication of the scale of the chaos in Calcutta:

In a period of these two to three years, there were recorded 415 political disturbances, 199 deaths by police firing, 139 deaths of political cadres in inter-party clashes, 331 attacks on schools and colleges, 451 inter-party clashes, 1771 political murders, and the arrest of 7462 people without trial.[59]

A vivid description of how all that happened was provided by a scholar who lived through the events. It is important to quote him at length:

Not only political workers were murdered; policemen, teachers and general people were stabbed, chosen cadres and young boys were forcefully taken out from their homes or from public places and instantly killed in open daylight. "Hit and run" tactics of the Naxalites, "see and fire" of the police and its resistance groups, military *combing* in disturbed areas for days together, bomb fighting between gangsters or party-gangster joint squads, all these created an atmosphere of unchained terror. The state machinery was completely within the grip of the gangsters and armed action squads of parties. Fringe areas of North and Central Calcutta, and refugee populated, congested areas of the suburb became inaccessible to any outsider. . . . The main actors of [this] organized violence were state organs, political parties and anti-social gangsters.[60]

Clearly, there is a strong case for both the factual issue, namely, that the decade of 1967–77 was a time of chaos in Calcutta, and the analytical issue,

57 See Marcus Franda, "Rural Development, Bengali Marxist Style," American Universities Field Staff Reports, Asia, 15, 1978, p. 4.
58 The figures were reported by a local human-rights organization; the Association for the Protection of Democratic Rights, and cited in Basu, *Politics of Violence*, p. 155.
59 Reported in Basu, *The Politics of Violence*, p. 92.
60 Ibid., pp. 91, 93.

Table 6.3. *Labor strife in West Bengal, 1969–86*

Years	Number of strikes per year	Number of men in strikes per year	Number of man-days lost per year
1969–76	306	321,122	5,550,000
1980	78	68,411	1,485,399
1981	43	16,952	620,110
1982	29	8,114	309,292
1983	39	12,014	563,946
1984	49	286,460	21,596,573
1985	39	13,527	197,215
1986	30	23,130	273,864

Source: The annual figures for the period 1969–76 are calculated from data of the Government of West Bengal, *Left Front Government in West Bengal: Eight Years* (Calcutta: Department of Information and Cultural Affairs, 1985), p. 183; the annual figures for 1980–6 are taken from *Economic and Political Weekly*, July 25, 1987, p. 1228.

namely, that the feuding political parties, in or out of power, contributed significantly to the chaos.

The contrasting political situation that has emerged since 1977 lends further credence to this argument. As noted earlier, the Left Front re-emerged in 1977. There were two crucial differences between that renewed significance of the left in the late 1970s and the situation that had existed a decade earlier. First, in the 1970s the CPM emerged as the dominant party on the left. Having won a clear electoral majority, the CPM's primary political concern was not how to expand its power base over the short run but rather how to consolidate its gains over the long run. Related to that was a second crucial difference. During the 1970s the CPM had done a lot of soul searching, trying to understand the lessons to be learned from the UF experiment, and devising a new party line suited to its "parliamentary communist" role. What emerged from that ideological rethinking was a party that was considerably more reformist than it had been in the 1960s.

Its new reformist orientation and the political necessity of taking a long-term view regarding how to maintain its power had a profound impact on the CPM's behavior as the party in office. We are concerned here only with the consequence of such changes for the governing of Calcutta. Table 6.3 shows the dramatic decline in labor strife in the 1980s, especially as compared with the 1969–76 period. Although the data are for West Bengal as a whole, Calcutta is the most important urban center in West Bengal. The reduced incidence of labor strife is clearly seen in these figures. The year 1984 was somewhat of an exception because of a prolonged three-month strike in all the jute mills of West Bengal.

Underlying this sharp decline in labor strife are the changed political needs of the CPM. Labor peace is now considered essential to enhance the CPM's image as a party that can govern well. The image of disciplined labor is also essential for attracting new investment. The CPM's new reformist ideology is much more consistent with this new approach than with the old approach of the UF period, when labor mobilization against capital was deemed to be a revolutionary virtue. Changed political circumstances and new patterns of rule have succeeded in taming Calcutta's labor turbulence of the 1967–77 period.

In addition to the reduction in labor strife, Naxalite-led urban terrorism has declined sharply. The CPM cannot take all the credit for that change. An important factor was the brutal repression visited on the Naxalites by the Congress government between 1972 and 1977. Many Naxalite leaders were eliminated from the political scene, being jailed or even killed. The Naxalites' terrorist tactics had alienated many who at one time had sympathized with the idealistic, revolutionary aspirations of that new generation. This is, of course, not to suggest that the Naxalites have been completely eliminated from the political scene. Significant pockets of Naxalite influence remain in some Calcutta institutions, such as the Presidency College. There have, however, been dramatic changes: The Naxalites no longer operate on their former large scale, and they are not using terrorist tactics.

Several factors help explain this decline in urban terrorism. Repression of one cohort of leaders has already been mentioned. In the aftermath, the Naxalites split up into many factions, unsure about how to pursue revolutionary goals within the framework of a fairly powerful state. The fact that a leftist party is already in power also reduces the scope for broadening their revolutionary political base. The CPM's organizational expansion has reduced the political spaces within which the Naxalites can operate. Thus, for example, Naxalite groups now find it quite difficult to extend their influence into Calcutta University, where the CPM's organization is relatively strong and where the party now controls not only the student union and many student activities but also the hiring and firing of various university employees.

The CPM's organizational cohesion has made no small contribution to the emergence of a degree of political order in Calcutta. Unlike Congress, the CPM does not fight out its internal factional struggles in the streets. As discussed earlier, such intraparty warfare continues to characterize Congress. Clashes among rival Congressites, quite a few of whom have their own groups of *goonda* supporters, remain important sources of urban conflict in Calcutta. The CPM cadres, by contrast, are widely acclaimed to be disciplined. This does not mean that they do not harbor power ambitions, or that they have any less hatred for those who defeat them in power struggles, or that they are in any way morally superior. A strong party organization, however, puts severe limits on the means by which internal power struggles can be conducted. A crucial consequence is that rival leaders do not mobilize street gangs and neighborhood forces to test their strengths. Thus, the decline in urban violence under the CPM is not surprising.

There is widespread agreement among diverse observers concerning the relative political stability that the CPM has brought to Calcutta and to West Bengal as a whole. The left-leaning *Economic and Political Weekly,* which often is very critical of the CPM in West Bengal for not being radical enough, concluded its 10-year review of CPM rule as follows: "In fact, there has been no report of any communal riot or caste conflict in West Bengal during the last ten years. [The] Left Front can really take pride in ... the political stability it has ensured."[61] Two much more conservative observers, who were quite severe in their overall assessment of the CPM's performance, conceded that in spite of the numerous difficulties, and in contrast to the growing violence in many other parts of India, Calcutta under the CPM "has remained relatively calm." Attempting to explain that outcome, the analysis of those observers was fairly close to the argument proposed here: "With the help of its superior political organization based on mass support, [the CPM] has largely succeeded in absorbing [various problems]. This is no mean achievement. It is doubtful if any other party or government would have been able to do this."[62] Finally, one may note the editorial comment made by the *New York Times:*

West Bengal's Left Front Government is currently playing a constructive role as gadfly to the country's inertia-bound Congress party. . . . Local industrialists have made their peace with Mr. Basu. They argue that the communists out of power are trouble. In power, they have become realists, adept at persuading fractionized unions to honor their agreements. . . . West Bengal's communists clobber their me-too opponents at the polls because they are smarter, better organized and less corrupt.[63]

That chorus of support for the CPM's performance, coming from across a political spectrum, indicates that on the issue of civil order, the differences between the left and the right are narrow. But more important, it indicates that the CPM's contributions in this area are undeniable.

In contrast to that achievement, the Left Front's record in finding solutions to Calcutta's massive socioeconomic problems is much less impressive. Calcutta was governed directly by the West Bengal state between 1977 and 1985. The important consequence of that direct rule was that the developmental policies in Calcutta reflected the CPM's overall political strategy in West Bengal. As discussed elsewhere,[64] since 1977 the CPM

61 July 25, 1987, p. 1231.
62 See *The Telegraph,* June 28, 1983.
63 "India's Practical Communists," *New York Times,* April 16, 1987.
64 See Kohli, "From Elite Activism to Democratic Consolidation."

has chosen to concentrate its political resources and the government's economic resources in the countryside. Although several important reasons underlie that ordering of priorities, the most obvious and most important is that elections are won or lost in the countryside. Because the CPM's hold on power has depended on concentrating its resources in the villages, Calcutta has been ignored.

After coming to power in 1977, the Left Front government's failure to hold CMC elections must be attributed to fear of losing the city to Congress or to a combination of Congress and other nonleftist parties. As Table 6.1 shows, the combined vote of Congress and the Janata party in Calcutta in 1977 was over 50 percent. Because the CPM had decided against any major new developmental activities in Calcutta, the prospect of winning city elections in Calcutta must have appeared remote. As a result, the CPM simply did not call an election during its first eight years in power.

During that time, however, the CPM was developing a plan to gain democratic control over the CMC. The CPM simply brought new areas under the control of Calcutta's municipal government. Whereas the old CMC had controlled some 100 wards, 41 more wards around the periphery of the city were included under the municipal government. Those new areas included the Jadavpur unit, where former refugees, who supported the CPM, were concentrated. More generally, the peripheral areas had a rural quality. Because many of the CPM's developmental programs were aimed at helping rural areas, those newly added peripheral areas were among the beneficiaries. The CPM calculated that the expansion of the city to include those new areas might enable it to win the CMC elections.

The CPM's calculations were right. When city elections were finally held in 1985, the CPM, in alliance with other leftist parties, eked out a thin majority (Table 6.2), just enough to form the city government. It is clear that without expanding the city, the CPM could not have won that CMC election. It should be noted further that the structure of Calcutta's city government was revised. The city government is now headed by a powerful mayor who has status similar to that of a cabinet minister in the state government. The mayor, like a chief minister, appoints a council that is the city's equivalent of a cabinet. Of the 12 members, 8 currently belong to the CPM, and the other 4 belong to the other Left Front partners. This council meets once a week and is the city's ruling body. The city, furthermore, is now divided into 15 boroughs. Nine of these are controlled by the Left Front; the other six are under Congress control. Because borough councils are responsible for numerous everyday services, such as road maintenance and street lighting, the funds at their disposal are crucial in building political support for the future.

In spite of a fairly narrow electoral base within Calcutta, the CPM, through those organizational changes, brought a fair amount of the city under its control. As to how that newly acquired power would be used, the mayor suggested that the first priority was "to stabilize the existing services . . . water, sewerage and transportation." The thrust of his comments, not surprisingly, was that there were not enough resources to undertake new projects, that "we will meet Rajiv Gandhi for new resources."[65]

There are several reasons why the CPM-dominated CMC is not likely to undertake major developmental initiatives in Calcutta. First, the CPM's attitude that the city's problems cannot even be tackled unless more resources are made available from New Delhi is hardly conducive to finding a long-term solution. Second, Calcutta's industrialists have never made a significant contribution to the life and resources of the city. That is due partly to the non-Bengali character of a fair amount of the investment in Bengal, as well as to the political uncertainty that reigns in this highly mobilized city. In spite of the CPM's improved relations with industry, it is not likely that the city's Marwaris will be sponsoring campaigns to fill the potholes, to buy new buses, or to provide shelter for the homeless.

CONCLUSION

The foregoing analysis of political change in Calcutta has focused on three themes: (1) the changes in the local party system, (2) Calcutta's voting patterns, and (3) the consequences of both for governing Calcutta. The main points developed with reference to these themes, as well as the overall argument, can now be summarized.

The local party system has undergone considerable change over the past 25 years. The Congress party has experienced a profound organizational decline. The CPM, by contrast, has emerged as a relatively cohesive, dominant party. Congress's organizational decline was caused by certain tendencies in both national and local politics. In Calcutta, as elsewhere, Indira Gandhi's neglect of party organization and her repeated imposition of inept leaders took their toll. What made the situation much more complicated in Calcutta, however, was the increase in political chaos after 1967. Congress's organizational decline contributed to the chaotic political situation, but the political chaos also hastened Congress's decline. One important result was that the new leadership roles in Congress were assumed by men who had learned how to survive amidst militancy, riots, interparty and intraparty clashes, and urban terrorism. A related consequence for Congress was the incorporation of numerous thugs and toughs within the party's fold. As the formal party structure declined and leadership passed into the hands of a new generation of "Sanjay culture" leaders, the Calcutta Con-

---

65 Interview with Kamal Basu (see footnote 37). The mayor repeated in another interview on February 3, 1988, that "the CMC has been unable to initiate any significant policies in the last few years mainly for lack of funds."

gress came to be characterized by endless internal squabbling, poor leadership, and intraparty clashes that often resulted in violence.

In contrast, the CPM has been helped by its own actions and by circumstances. The CPM has always paid much more attention to organizational matters, and, over time, those efforts have brought results. In spite of the numerous weaknesses and antidemocratic tendencies within the party, the CPM's leadership in Calcutta is considerably superior to that of Congress, and it has a core of disciplined cadres throughout the city. The shift to a reformist ideology has made the CPM a much more realistic alternative to Congress than in the past. Finally, the CPM has been helped by circumstances. Its rival parties on the left have lost their significance. The Naxalites never established a firm popular base, and much of its leadership was eliminated by the state's repression. The CPI also lost some of its credibility in the aftermath of the Emergency.

These contrasting patterns of organizational changes have not had a significant impact on electoral patterns within Calcutta. Congress continues to enjoy the support of most non-Bengalis in Calcutta. Similarly, the CPM draws its core electoral support from the former refugees and the *bustee* dwellers. The continuity in these electoral patterns since the mid–1960s is noteworthy. The major change in electoral patterns has occurred in the voting behavior of Calcutta's Moslems and the Bengali middle class. Both are now divided between the two parties. The Moslems have moved toward the CPM, hoping to relieve their sense of communal vulnerability. The Bengali middle class, by contrast, has moved away from the CPM. Some have simply become apathetic, and others may have found the CPM's neglect of Calcutta sufficient reason to vote for Congress.

With the CPM's rise to power in West Bengal and in Calcutta, the chaos of 1967–77 subsided. The CPM, however, has not given high priority to an attack on Calcutta's numerous problems. The failure to tackle Calcutta's socioeconomic problems head-on is a result of numerous factors, including the CPM's decision to concentrate its efforts in the politically significant countryside. The restoration of order in Calcutta, by contrast, illustrates the importance of a well-organized party for running a government in a highly mobilized political environment. The CPM has become reformist, and it has filled the political vacuum that formed during the decade of chaos, 1967–77. Thus, it is not surprising that the city of *gheraoes,* Naxalite terrorism, and daily political murders has become a place where Sikhs and Moslems feel relatively safe, where urban terrorism has declined, and where labor strife has subsided.

7

Madurai, Tamil Nadu

Madurai is an ancient temple town in south India. With a population just under 1 million, it is, after Madras, the second largest city in Tamil Nadu.[1] Despite its size, Madurai is more like a sprawling premodern town than a modern industrial city. Except for a towering temple, it has few tall buildings. Paved roads run into dirt paths, and the city bazaars are reminiscent of an upscale, bustling village market rather than an urban shopping area such as one sees in Bombay, Calcutta, or even Madras. Less than a third of the working population, or less than 10 percent of the city's total population, is employed in manufacturing.[2] That reveals the modest industrial base on which the city rests. The majority of the people are involved in the premodern service sector. Madurai is best thought of as an urban center that is halfway between a village and a metropolitan city.

Madurai's population has grown fairly rapidly over the past few decades. That has been part of a general statewide trend that has made Tamil Nadu one of the most urbanized states in India. One major result of that urbanization has been that many slum settlements have developed throughout Madurai. About 30,000 families, or one-sixth of the city's population, now live in some 100 slums.[3]

Moving up the social hierarchy, for political analysis the remaining population can be divided along both community and occupational lines. The two main ethnic communities of the city are the Saurashtras and the Thev-

1 Madurai city is coterminous with the administrative and political unit of the Madurai Municipal Corporation. The city corporation was until recently divided into 65 wards. Each ward elects a member to the city corporation. The city encompasses about three and a half Legislative Assembly constituencies. These are Madurai-west, Madurai-central, and Madurai-east. The administrative unit of Madurai district is much larger than Madurai city. For political purposes, however, all the parties treat Madurai city as a district. All the parties, therefore, have separate district committees for the city, which they generally call the Madurai (urban) committee, and for the rural hinterland, which they call the Madurai (rural) committee. My analysis here is concerned with the administrative unit of Madurai city and thus the political unit of Madurai (urban) district.
2 Demographic data for Madurai are conveniently available in Madurai Municipal Corporation, *Madurai Master Plan* (Madurai: Madurai Planning Authority, 1981).
3 Ibid., pp. 66–7, 161–4.

ars. The Saurashtras trace their origin to western India, whence they migrated south in the Middle Ages, fleeing Moslem invaders. They have maintained their original language and customs. They tend to marry within their community, and most of them continue to work in various modern branches of their traditional trades: weaving and textiles. By local estimates, the Saurashtras constitute about 20 percent of the city's population. There may be as many Thevars in Madurai as Saurashtras. The Thevars are a group of south-Indian lower castes who once followed martial occupations. Within Madurai, most of them now tend to be employed in blue-collar jobs. Together, the Saurashtras and the Thevars may account for as much as half of Madurai's population.

The other significant socioeconomic groups are the middle classes, the bazaar merchants, and the students. Although no firm figures are available, local observers estimate that 10 percent of the city's population may belong to households headed by professionals, business executives, and white-collar government workers. As will be discussed later, these middle-class groups tend to have distinct political preferences and thus are politically quite significant. The same must be said of the bazaar merchants, who are concentrated in the heart of the city, around the main temple. Their political behavior is also distinctive and will be analyzed in due course.

The last important demographic fact that ought to be mentioned at the outset is the youthfulness of the city's population. Nearly 60 percent of the city's people are under the age of 25.[4] The 15–24-year age group accounts for about one-third of the under–25 group, which suggests that the pool of college students and other non-college-attending youths available for political recruitment is quite large. The youth in general, and students in particular, have played important roles in Madurai's politics.

Myron Weiner, in his study of Madurai politics, analyzed the political roles of the social groups within the city and the nature of the local Congress party.[5] The Congress party was the most significant electoral force within the city in the early 1960s. Some of the local groups had clear political preferences. The Saurashtras tended to support Congress, and the Thevars generally were sympathetic to a local party, the Forward Bloc. The political preferences of other ethnic and occupational groups were not as clear and as easily identifiable. The local Congress party was not well organized. What facilitated its modest degree of cohesiveness and its electoral success were the repeated interventions of the state Congress, especially its leader Kamraj, in the political affairs of the district. Although such intervention from popular state leaders enabled Congress to win city elections for seats in the Legislative Assembly, Congress was not able to control the city government

4 Ibid., pp. 24–5.
5 Myron Weiner, *Party Building in a New Nation: The Indian National Congress* (University of Chicago Press, 1967), part VI.

itself. The attachments of local groups to Congress were not strong, and the city government did not generate enough resources to run an effective machine. In the absence of both ideological and patronage links, the local Congress, though electorally dominant, remained a weak political force in terms of the durability of its coalitions and organizational capacities.

Over the 25 years since Weiner's study, the political scene changed dramatically. Although the Congress party retains some national-level following within Tamil Nadu, it is no longer a major actor in state politics or in Madurai. Whereas Congress retains a small local significance, the major political competitors in the city are the two Tamil nationalist parties: the Dravida Munnetra Kazhagam (DMK) and its offshoot, the ADMK (where "A" stands for the founding leader of the undivided DMK, Annadurai). The Communist Party of India, Marxist (CPM) also retains some significance. As these four parties have competed for influence, the patterns of group behavior have become extremely heterogeneous. All the Saurashtras do not support Congress anymore, and the identification of the Thevars with the Forward Bloc has diminished significantly. Thus, communitywide party identification has become even weaker than in the 1960s. In terms of party organization, whereas the DMK and the CPM exhibit fair degrees of organization, at least in the cities, the ADMK and Congress (I) operate virtually without any organization.

As one views these political changes over the past 25 years, certain themes stand out: The first is the electoral decline of the Congress party. Second, as a number of parties compete for support among a population that does not exhibit strong group-centered political preferences, local authority has become extremely diffuse. Third, the Madurai political scene has lost some of its locally distinctive features, such as the former preference of the Thevars for the Forward Bloc. What has replaced the importance of local factors in city politics is the growing significance of statewide trends and state politics.

THE CHANGING CONTEXT OF TAMIL NADU POLITICS

Prior to an analysis of political change in Madurai, some familiarity with the changing nature of Tamil Nadu politics is essential.[6] The most dramatic

---

6 My account of changing Tamil Nadu politics builds mainly on two excellent studies: Margurite Ross Barnett, *The Politics of Cultural Nationalism in South India* (Princeton, N.J.: Princeton University Press, 1976); David Washbrook, "Tamil Nationalism, Dravidianism and Non-Brahminism," mimeograph, 1983, a revised version of which appears in Francine Frankel and M. S. A. Rao, eds., *Dominance and State Power in Modern India: Decline of a Social Order*, 2 vols. (Oxford University Press, 1989–90), volume 1. The historical literature on Madras is excellent; for references, see the essay by Washbrook. Of the other relevant literature covering more specific issues and/or more recent periods, the following good accounts are noteworthy: Pandav Nayak, "Tamil Nadu: Politics of Pragmatism," in

change in Tamil Nadu politics came in 1967 when the DMK, a regional nationalist party with a populist posture, defeated the Congress party and established a new state government. Since then, Congress has never returned to power. The undivided DMK under the leadership of its founder, Annadurai, ruled Tamil Nadu until his death in 1969. Annadurai was replaced by Karunanidhi as the DMK's leader, the latter being reelected to power in 1971 with an increased majority. Karunanidhi ruled until 1976. However, he presided over a DMK that increasingly lost its radicalism, in terms of both regional nationalist demands and the pursuit of socioeconomic reforms.

In 1972 there was another major turning point: The DMK split, and M. G. Ramachandran (MGR), the famous Tamil movie actor, formed his own party, the ADMK. The factional conflict between Karunanidhi and MGR dominated the next several years, with MGR finally emerging victorious in the 1977 elections. Following that, MGR ruled Tamil Nadu without interruption for a decade. His death in 1988 left Tamil Nadu with a legacy of poor and arbitrary government, deep factionalism, and a considerable power vacuum. The DMK was returned to power in Tamil Nadu in early 1989. However, the victory of the ADMK and Congress (I) alliance in the late–1989 national elections indicated that the DMK's popular base may be crumbling. The analysis in this chapter carries the political story of this southern area to the end of MGR's rule in 1987.

Three issues that emerge from this brief chronology require explanation: (1) the decline of Congress and the emergence of the DMK in 1967, (2) the subsequent split in the DMK and the emergence of MGR, and (3) the nature of MGR's rule within Tamil Nadu. During this discussion, it is important to keep in mind that Tamil Nadu, in 1967, was the first Indian state in which a regional nationalist party won election and formed a government. Because it was the first instance of such a development, the DMK's emergence was regarded at that time as quite remarkable. Since then, however, many similar parties and governments have emerged in the non-Hindi states of India. In retrospect, the case of the DMK appears much less dramatic than it seemed in 1967.

The story of the decline of Congress and the concomitant rise of the DMK in Tamil Nadu has been told many times. Leaving aside the numerous subtle issues that still provoke controversy among the region's specialists, the basic outline of how those changes occurred is relatively straightforward. It is important to keep in mind three aspects of Tamil Nadu's social structure: (1) Unlike those in the Hindi heartland, the Brahmans in Tamil

Iqbal Narain, ed., *State Politics in India* (Merrut: Meenakshi Prakashan, 1966), pp. 404–36; Robert Hardgrave, "Politics and the Film in Tamil Nadu: The Stars and the DMK," *Asian Survey,* March 1973, pp. 288–305; Duncan Forrester, "Factions and Film Stars: Tamil Nadu Politics Since 1971," *Asian Survey,* March 1976, pp. 283–96.

Nadu have always been a small minority – less than 5 percent of the population. (2) Unlike the other south Indian states of Karnataka and Andhra Pradesh, Tamil Nadu did not have any statewide non-Brahman dominant castes. (3) Tamil Nadu experienced early urbanization; as many as 30 percent of Tamils were living in the cities even prior to independence. These contextual variables help explain some of the long-term developments that made it difficult for Congress to build an enduring political base in Tamil Nadu and left open the political space for development of a regional party.

The Congress party in this part of India, as elsewhere, built its preindependence base on the Brahmans. That the Brahmans were few in number and that the non-Brahman castes were already active in city life provided the necessary conditions for the early rise of an anti-Brahman movement. The first institutional manifestation of that movement was the Justice party, which was led by the elite of the non-Brahman castes and sided with the British against both Brahmans and Congress in the hope of securing concessions in government jobs and in education. The Justice party eventually was delegitimized both because of its elitist nature and because of the rising tide of nationalism. That had significant consequences, especially because Congress became identified as a Brahman party in a region where Brahmans had not been able to establish cultural and political hegemony. The early development of a cleavage between the Brahman and anti-Brahman forces opened up the political space for later anti-Congress developments.

The link between Congress and the Brahmans became the target of Tamil nationalists in the postindependence period. The Congress party in Madras could not easily break out of that mold. In contrast to the situation in Karnataka, for example, there were no dominant non-Brahman castes such as the Lingayats or the Vokkaligas that could provide a natural alternative political base. The continued Congress-Brahman alliance enabled the regional nationalists to mobilize against caste domination and domination by north Indians simultaneously. Hammering on the theme of the distinctiveness of the Tamil tradition, and linking that with an opposition to northern Hindi rule and its "lackeys" (the southern Brahmans), the leaders of the Dravidian movement found a ready audience among the numerous backward castes that were already concentrated in the cities. To simplify a complex picture, Tamil nationalism and a petit bourgeois base among the urban backward castes provided the core support for a regional nationalist party: the DMK.[7]

There has never been a good account of how the urban-based DMK broadened its support in the villages. Attributing that success to Tamil nationalism is not quite satisfactory. That would leave out the crucial issues of who within the villages supported the DMK and why they were attracted

7 For details, see Barnett, *Cultural Nationalism,* passim, but especially parts II and III.

to the DMK in the second half of the 1960s, when the DMK finally emerged victorious. Scattered insights, however, can be pulled together to get a sense of how that political change may have come about. First, throughout India the power of Congress's rural "vote banks" had diminished by the 1960s, and Tamil Nadu was no exception. The middle and lower peasants were increasingly available for new political commitments. Where Tamil Nadu was an exception was in the ready availability of an alternative to Congress. The DMK was already a powerful political force in the cities of Madras by the mid–1960s. Several important factors helped link that urban movement to the villages.

Students played a crucial role in the DMK's anti-Hindi agitations of the 1960s. Many of them had active rural links because of family connections. As cultural leaders of sorts in the villages, it is fair to assume, the students returning from the cities to the villages must have played a significant role in the transmission of new political values.[8] The early radical rhetoric of the DMK, a commitment to the common people, probably also appealed to all those who had not benefited from two decades of Congress rule. David Washbrook has argued that small peasants provided crucial support for the DMK in the villages.[9] Other analysts have found evidence to indicate that many of the scheduled castes voted for the DMK in 1967.[10] It is clear, therefore, that the DMK's rural support, like its urban support, was not based on elite groups. Rather, it was based on the middle and lower groups, who shared an antipathy toward the Brahman and non-Brahman landowning elite in the countryside.

That alliance of the have-nots was made possible not only by the themes of nationalism and populism but also because of the effectiveness of the medium used to transmit the political message: Tamil movies.[11] All of the DMK's leaders – Annadurai, Karunanidhi, and MGR – had been involved in the movie industry in one capacity or another. From the very beginning, therefore, movies were used to popularize such themes as the injustices of the caste system, the glories of Tamil history, and the social need for the Robin Hood type of hero who would deliver the poor, the weak, and the dispossessed from the clutches of the rich and the wicked.

What finally helped translate those long-term processes at work for the DMK into an electoral victory in 1967 were two short-term circumstances. First, there were the language riots of 1965. As New Delhi attempted to institute Hindi as India's national language, agitations and riots led by the

---

8 Another analyst, discussing the successful electoral strategies adopted by the DMK in 1967, suggested that "one of these was to bring students of peasant families under its influence." See Nayak, "Tamil Nadu," p. 413.
9 Washbrook, "Tamil Nationalism," p. 3.
10 See Forrester, "Factions and Film Stars," p. 291.
11 For a good discussion, see Hardgrave, "Politics and the Film in Tamil Nadu," and Forrester, "Factions and Film Stars."

DMK, and widely supported by students, broke out in the major cities of Madras. The poor handling of those riots by the Congress state government cost Congress dearly in the 1967 elections. Additionally, the two consecutive droughts and the related poor economic situation in the mid–1960s led to food shortages and increasing food prices. Both language and economic issues fed right into the DMK's overall political posture of opposition to the Center (the national government) and support for the common people. Thus, both long-term structural processes and short-term fortuitous circumstances helped the DMK mobilize new groups into politics and finally displace Congress in 1967.

The rise and consolidation of power by the DMK had a profound impact on Tamil Nadu's politics. The highest leadership posts in the state slipped out of the hands of Brahmans and went to the well-educated elite of the non-Brahman castes. The intermediate and local leadership more accurately reflected the real power base of the DMK: the backward castes. Unlike the leaders of the Congress party of the 1960s, the first-generation leaders of the DMK often were passionately motivated by concerns of cultural nationalism. Thus, the Congress political style was replaced and, over the short run, reinvigorated by regional nationalism. So widespread was the appeal of the DMK that Congress was forced to deemphasize its Brahman associations. Moreover, all parties experienced increases in pro-Tamil and anti-Hindi sentiments, and a shared belief in more power for the states came to be held across party lines.[12]

As the DMK settled down to rule, the predictable happened. Over time, the DMK lost much of its anti-Center militancy, as well as its commitment to socioeconomic reforms. The reasons for that deradicalization in Tamil Nadu were the same as elsewhere. Once the DMK achieved its major goal of securing power, realpolitik concerns took over, and the mobilizing ideologies slowly lost their relevance for guiding governmental actions. Nationally, Indira Gandhi had split the Congress party. Within Tamil Nadu, much of the old Congress remained loyal to Kamraj. That meant that Indira Gandhi had almost no independent political base within Tamil Nadu and had to search for political allies in that part of the country. Conversely, as a regional party in power, the DMK knew that good relations with an assertive New Delhi under Indira would greatly facilitate the task of ruling Tamil Nadu. Furthermore, the DMK and Indira Gandhi had in Kamraj a powerful common enemy. Those circumstances pushed Indira's Congress and the DMK closer together politically and in 1971 led to an electoral alliance between the two parties. Over the years there have been quite a few fluctuations in the alliance of Congress (I) with various factions of the DMK. Nevertheless, ever since, some sort of political arrangement has

---

12 This information on the nature of the leadership and the followers of the DMK is derived from Barnett, *Cultural Nationalism,* chapters 7 and 8.

been maintained between New Delhi and one of the two DMKs, including the successful alliance of Congress (I) with the ADMK for the late–1989 Lok Sabha elections. Thus, 1971 marks the beginning of the end of the deeply hostile attitude of the DMK toward the Center.

Within Tamil Nadu, the DMK, from the beginning, was not a radical party in the class sense of the word. It was an anti-Brahman party, but its leadership often was drawn from other landowning castes. The Brahmans, though a small minority, were deeply entrenched in the upper reaches of the social structure – in education, in industry, and especially in government administration. As a cultural nationalist party, the DMK was not about to mount an attack on that hierarchical social structure. In order to expand its power base, the DMK declined to take significant action on any of its radical electoral promises, such as land reform, an attack on the caste system, or an attempt to alter the traditional exploitative practice of dowry marriage. Over the short run, that deradicalization enabled the DMK to attract the support of many elite groups.[13] It was not surprising that in 1971 the DMK was returned to power with an enlarged and consolidated majority.

Over a longer time period, however, deradicalization was not without political costs. Because the DMK decided to rule without making waves, several developments followed. The need to maintain a working relationship with the Center led the DMK to downplay its anti-Hindi stance. There is evidence to indicate that that decision alienated many of the students, who at one time had formed the backbone of the DMK's urban political base.[14] The softening of its anti-Brahman attitudes and its failure to follow through on an any meaningful redistributive policies cost the DMK support among the urban slum dwellers and the rural scheduled castes.[15] More important were the developments at the top – the growing factionalism among its leaders. The most significant of those rifts led to the emergence of MGR as a leader in his own right.

MGR was an extremely popular Tamil movie actor. He had carefully cultivated his image as a Good Samaritan. He played the hero in many Tamil movies, in which he would end up saving women, the poor, and the oppressed from various evil elements of society. Even in the 1970s there probably were few villages in Tamil Nadu where gaudy posters depicting MGR as a movie hero could not be found. In 1986 such posters were everywhere. The DMK, especially its founding leader Annadurai, exploited MGR's popularity from the beginning. His image as a hero of the common folk fit well into the DMK's populist orientation, and he often appeared beside Annadurai during political campaigns. Karunanidhi con-

13 See Washbrook, "Tamil Nationalism," passim.
14 See Forrester, "Factions and Film Stars."
15 See Barnett, *Cultural Nationalism,* chapters 9 and 10; Forrester, "Factions and Film Stars."

tinued that practice for a few years. As a result, MGR's popularity as a movie hero was gradually transferred to MGR as a political leader. Slowly but surely he came to be widely perceived as a man of the people both on and off the screen.

MGR no doubt was aware of the DMK's dependence on his personal popularity. Because MGR felt that he was not receiving his political due in terms of position and power, he slowly began putting pressure on Karunanidhi. The factional rift between the two grew throughout 1971 and 1972, until Karunanidhi finally expelled MGR from the DMK. Given his enormous personal popularity, that expulsion only generated further sympathy for MGR and added to his popularity.

MGR founded his own party, the ADMK, where the "A" was to denote that MGR's DMK was closer to the ideals of the founding leader (Annadurai) than was Karunanidhi's DMK. MGR's new party differed little from the DMK in its overall policy orientation. The crucial differences lay elsewhere. MGR vigorously courted the favor of Indira Gandhi, even flying to New Delhi in 1975 to congratulate her and to express his personal support for the Emergency. Indira Gandhi returned that favor in 1976 by dismissing the DMK government, proclaiming presidential rule in Tamil Nadu, and thus paving the way for MGR's electoral triumph in 1977. Within Tamil Nadu, MGR did not attempt to build any party organization. His movie fan clubs became the main vehicle for electoral mobilization. The head of his fan-club associations, R. M. Veerapam, emerged as one of his main political lieutenants, and his favorite leading lady and mistress, Jayalalitha, eventually came to be groomed as a possible heir apparent.

There has not yet been an adequate scholarly study of Tamil Nadu under MGR. Scattered evidence, however, leaves little doubt that Tamil Nadu was governed poorly during 1977–87, the decade of MGR's rule. The popular movie actor and his entourage ruled the state as a personal fiefdom and brought it near economic and administrative collapse. During those years, Tamil Nadu fell from its rank as the third most industrialized state in India to 13th position.[16] The links between the ruling strategy and economic decline are relatively clear. In order to consolidate his popularity among the low-income, illiterate population, MGR pursued numerous populist schemes, the most popular of which was free lunch for the state's school-age children. As the costs of those populist schemes mounted, nearly two-thirds of the state's budget came to be devoted to consumption expenditures.[17] The resulting short-term gains in popularity entailed unconscionable long-term economic costs. Public expenditures to support investment declined. Cities like Madras became less attractive for invest-

16 See *India Today,* January 15, 1986, p. 12.
17 Ibid., p. 12.

ment. Some of the existing capital moved out, and new investment slowed down.

Whereas the undivided DMK had had a reputation for being only moderately dishonest, corruption flourished under MGR. Specific examples of that in Madurai will be discussed later. More generally, the following is only one of many journalistic accounts that could be quoted:

The MGR administration has the dubious distinction of being one of the most corrupt in the state's recent political history. Unless several palms are greased, no expectant mother gets proper attention, let alone admission to a maternity ward, in any of the government-run hospitals. To get a birth certificate one must go through the local functionary of the ADMK, who has his own demands. At the gate of the central jail in Madras, application forms for visitors, priced at 50 paise each, are openly sold for a rupee. Even the dead are not spared. Entry into public cremation grounds is regulated by unauthorized entry fees ranging upwards of Rs. 100 per body.[18]

The pervasiveness of the corruption made a mockery of one of MGR's proudest claims, namely, that his was a cleaner government than that under the undivided DMK.

Another major indicator of ineffective government under MGR was the arbitrariness of decisions. Interview after interview with senior civil servants in Madras revealed a deeply dispirited bureaucracy. Centralization of power under MGR was complete. All important papers had to be signed by MGR personally. That was difficult under the best of circumstances. During the last several years of his rule, when MGR's health and mental functions were severely impaired, that centralization took a heavy toll on state administration. Objections by civil servants only got them transferred to positions in the boondocks. The results of such centralization of power in a popular but mentally impaired leader are well captured in the following:

It can only happen in Tamil Nadu: objections are raised to the nomination of an actress to the legislative council and the chief minister [MGR] decides to do away with the council itself! If that sounds preposterous even for the mercurial M. G. Ramachandran, it needs to be remembered that earlier last month, the government decided to abolish horse-racing because MGR could not stomach racing magnate M. A. M. Ramaswamy's hold over the Guindy race course. . . . MGR has proved again that when it comes to springing ludicrous surprises there is nobody to beat him.[19]

The comedy of such arbitrariness in government was surpassed only by the tragedy of its consequences for the running of the government.

MGR did not allow the development of a second tier of leadership. Those who knew him closely described him as a "suspicious man" who

18 *Probe India,* April 1986, p. 60.
19 *India Today,* June 15, 1986, p. 72.

"will not let any one grow."[20] Below MGR, therefore, there was a real power vacuum within the ADMK. Many thoughtful observers of Tamil Nadu politics suggested, even before MGR's death, that "ADMK will disappear after MGR."[21]

The major factions within the ADMK were controlled by MGR's long-term associates from the movie industry. One faction was headed by R. M. Veerapam, the former manager of MGR's movie studios. Because his popularity was not great, Veerapam backed MGR's wife, Janaki Rama-chandran, as the person most likely to inherit MGR's political position. The other faction was headed by MGR's frequent companion, Jayalalitha. A well-known movie actress of very light skin color, Jayalalitha was enor-mously popular in color-conscious Tamil Nadu. If she persists in her pursuit of power, she may well be able to translate her personal popularity into political capital. In any case, the bitter feud between Janaki and Jayalalitha that followed the death of MGR was more like a medieval court intrigue than a political succession in a democracy. Failure to resolve that feud laid the groundwork for imposition of presidential rule in January 1988.

MGR's personalistic, arbitrary, corrupt, and factionalized government began to cost him electoral support in his last days. For example, even in the local-government elections held in 1986, the DMK won many more seats than did the ADMK, or even the ADMK-Congress alliance.[22] When the ADMK and Congress (I) failed to reach an electoral arrangement for the 1989 state elections, that opened the door for the DMK's electoral comeback. To what extent the ADMK's loss of electoral support between 1985 and early 1989 was caused by MGR's failing health and eventual death, as distinct from the ineffectiveness of his government, is difficult to estimate. Chances are that both factors were significant, with the absence of MGR from the podium being the more important, because it was MGR's personal appeal that turned out the numerically significant votes of the illiterate village folk.

The ADMK under MGR had moved far from the fairly militant anti-Hindi and anti-Brahman posture of the DMK in the 1960s. Note, for example, that MGR himself was not of Tamil origin; he was of Malyali background. His wife and his "leading lady" were both Brahmans. Nothing illustrated the political change in Tamil Nadu more dramatically than the two Brahman women feuding over the leadership of a party that claimed to represent Annadurai's anti-Brahman goals. MGR's continued electoral alliance with Congress similarly revealed the dilution of the anti-Hindi,

20 Interview with K. Manoharam (former finance minister under MGR, 1977–9; now deputy general secretary of the DMK), Madras, March 28, 1986.
21 This specific comment was made by Cho S. Ramaswamy (editor of *Thuglak*), Madras, March 30, 1986, and was echoed by Mohan Ram (assistant editor of *Hindu*), during a discussion in Madras, March 30, 1986.
22 See *Probe India,* April 1986, pp. 59–60.

antinorthern attitude. That dilution was also evident in the fact that Congress has redeveloped an electoral base within Tamil Nadu. None of this suggests that Tamil nationalism is not still a significant theme or that it cannot be reignited by the DMK or by another leader. If that does happen, however, it will have to be politically manufactured. For now, Tamil nationalism has receded as the dominant theme in Tamil Nadu politics.

The last issue that deserves attention poses more of an analytical problem. Political change in Tamil Nadu has been characterized by a pattern of deinstitutionalization similar to that seen in many other parts of India. An interesting point, however, is that Congress has been a relatively insignificant force in this state for nearly two decades. Congress lost its hold over Tamil Nadu even before Indira Gandhi split the old Congress. Therefore, deinstitutionalization in Tamil Nadu cannot be attributed to the organizational decline of the Congress party or to Indira Gandhi's actions. On the contrary, the factors that contributed to the emergence of personal and arbitrary rule in Tamil Nadu were more general factors that were at work in other parts of India as well, and they are worth repeating.

The DMK's displacement of Congress from power in 1967 was facilitated by an alliance of the backward and the lower castes, mobilized around themes of regional nationalism and populism. That victory revealed the growing incapacity of the social elite, the Brahmans and other landowning elite castes, to ensure political compliance from those beneath them in the social hierarchy. Furthermore, the emotional impact of regional nationalism and populist promises made it possible for the DMK to offer a little something for everyone, but only over the short run.

Its failure to follow through on nationalist and populist policies began costing the DMK valuable electoral support in the early 1970s. The DMK's dilemma at that time had a more general significance. The DMK was working under tight constraints: (1) It was a regional party, ruling a state within a federal unit. (2) Within Tamil Nadu, the Brahmans were firmly entrenched at the top of the social structure. (3) The economy was dominated by property-owning groups. Therefore, the DMK could pursue its antinorthern, anti-Brahman, pro-poor policies only within fairly narrow limits. The more scrupulously the DMK observed those limits, the more support it lost. In such difficult political situations, where no party can satisfy everyone, and where stable, issue-oriented electoral alliances are difficult to establish, leaders with personal popularity have greater impact. A leader's personal following can create a power center and authority even when ruling coalitions are difficult to establish around ideological or rational-interest criteria.

When a leader with great personal popularity ascends to power, what happens will depend heavily on the nature and the quality of the leader. More often than not, however, following the logic that leaders hunger for power, powerful leaders tend to surround themselves with people who are loyal (i.e., people who are not likely to challenge for power). Because these loyal followers do not command any independent legitimacy, typically they are resented by virtually everyone. Thus, a faction-ridden second tier of leadership often is characteristic of governments dominated by leaders who owe their power primarily to a personal following. Because institutionalized rules and norms tend to put limits on personal discretion, thus detracting from the power of the leader, the other characteristic response of powerful leaders is to inhibit the development of institutional rule. Only exceptional leaders resist the temptations of power. Those few recruit their lieutenants on criteria other than loyalty and initiate the development of institutions that can put rules above individuals. MGR and Indira Gandhi were not of such fiber; the policies of MGR in Tamil Nadu, and those of Indira Gandhi elsewhere in India, seem to have been part of a pattern that obviously was not determined, but definitely was influenced, by the broader political situation.

THE MAIN PARTIES OF MADURAI

After the undivided Congress lost power in Tamil Nadu in 1967, Kamraj sought to rebuild the party there, and over the short run he succeeded. As a Congress (I) leader reminisced:

Come 1967, when Congress was defeated, then it suddenly became clear to Congress that there was a need for organization. DMK by now was well organized. So Kamraj started building the party. He toured all the districts. He talked with workers in detail and started assessing the party strength. He immediately corrected the position. By the 1969 split, the party was much stronger and with Kamraj. That is why, after the split, Mrs. Gandhi could not make a dent into Tamil Nadu. Congress here stood for Kamraj.[23]

Local leaders in Madurai concurred with that understanding of Kamraj's role and success in the post–1967 period: "During Kamraj's time, organization was strong in our district. There were local committees everywhere. There was also internal party democracy."[24] The electoral results shown in Table 7.1 are consistent with that analysis. Following the split in Congress in 1969, Kamraj's Congress, or Congress (O), virtually eliminated Congress (I) as an electoral force in the 1971 elections in Madurai.

As long as Kamraj was alive, Indira's Congress could make no inroads in Madurai. That was primarily because the local head of Congress at that time was a "Kamraj man." Party organization under Kamraj generally meant not a formal party structure but rather having a loyal individual in

23 Interview with Tindivanan K. Ramamurthi [Congress (I) member of the Rajya Sabha], Madras, March 29, 1986.
24 Interview with Nedumaran [former Congress (I) secretary for the state committee of Tamil Nadu], Madurai, April 6, 1986.

Table 7.1. *Results of Legislative Assembly elections in Madurai, Tamil Nadu, 1967–84*

Party	Seats won					Vote received (%)				
	1967	1971	1977	1980	1984	1967	1971	1977	1980	1984
Congress[a]	—	—	1	—	1	32.3	—	19.3	12.4	15.9
ADMK[b]	—	—	2	1	1	—	—	28.5	22.9	34.0
DMK	1	2	—	—	1	18.3	27.8	26.2	27.1	18.6
CPM	2	—	—	1	—	41.3	10.9	—	14.8	14.2
CPI	—	1	—	—	—	4.2	19.3	5.6	—	—
Congress (O)[c]	—	—	—	—	—	—	40.1	—	—	—
Jan Sangh[d]	—	—	—	—	—	3.7	1.7	—	0.5	—
Janata[e]	—	—	—	—	—	—	—	19.3	3.1	—
Others[f]	—	—	—	1	—	0.2	0.2	1.1	19.2	17.3
Total	3	3	3	3	3	100	100	100	100	100

[a] Known as Congress (I) since 1969.
[b] Founded in mid-1970s.
[c] Founded in 1969, Congress (O) was also known in Tamil Nadu and other parts of south India as Congress (Nijilingappa) or as the Kamraj-controlled Congress. Congress (O) merged into Janata in 1977.
[d] Merged into Janata in 1977; re-created as the Bhartiya Janata party in 1980.
[e] Founded in 1977.
[f] Includes, since 1980, the votes secured by a new local party, Congress (Kamraj).
Source: Compiled from the following reports: Government of Tamil Nadu, Chief Electoral Officer, General Election Results, *Tamil Nadu Assembly, 1952–71* (Madras: Director of Stationery and Printing, 1971); *Results of General Elections to Tamil Nadu Legislative Assembly: 1977, 1980 and 1984* (Madras: Tansi Press, 1985).

a position of power. The significance of that personal loyalty was illustrated by the fact that after Kamraj's death in 1976, Congress (O) lost much of its identity as a party; a fairly significant portion of Kamraj's party merged into Indira's Congress. Those who did not join Congress (I) also tended not to join the DMK. Rather, they first joined Janata, and later remained more or less uncommitted. Those broad trends are evident in Table 7.1.

Congress (I) within Madurai evolved according to a pattern similar to that seen elsewhere. In the words of a former local Congress leader, "Mrs. Gandhi installed a system of appointment. A system thus evolved whereby to get to be a leader, you have to run to Delhi. Local leaders have no say. Very often local leaders and masses have no contact." As to the consequences of that system of appointments for the local Congress, the same leader explained it in the following terms:

After Kamraj's death . . . local Congressmen, who were mostly former members of the Congress (O), wanted to elect one Mr. Ambalam as the chairman of the District Committee. Delhi did not want him. Mrs. Chandrashekhar, who had never been part of the Congress (O) but was closer to Cong (I) [had influence in Delhi]. She wanted her own henchman. She nominated one Mr. Raju. [Delhi appointed him.] Local workers did not accept him. He became a dummy president. In 1977 Congress was a disaster here. . . . Fighting [within the party] was a common knowledge. Each group [faction] issued their own press statements. That hurt the party's image.[25]

The poor performance of Congress (I) in the 1977 elections in Madurai (Table 7.1), though not due solely to those local developments, tended to support that analysis of the changing nature of the local party.

Congress (I) continues to be a relatively weak and factionalized force in Madurai, although Congress (I) in Madurai attracts more electoral support than in many other parts of Tamil Nadu. This has to do with the loyalty of some of the Saurashtras to Congress, as discussed later. For now, it is important to note how the top-down system of leadership operates in practice.

I asked the president of a district committee of Congress (I) how he got his position. Various aspects of his response are revealing:

I ran for elections in 1971 but lost. Since then I have not run for elections. I replaced Mr. Ratnam [as the appointed head of the District Committee] in 1983. He was replaced because there was a change at the state level. Mr. Palayandi was appointed the State President of the Congress (I). I was his man. So I was nominated. New state President cannot function without his own men.

I asked why a state president needs his "own men" in the districts. "If I [in the districts] do not like him [the state president], he will not be invited to Madurai. I can organize against him. I can generally make his life miserable in this district. Politics is not like bureaucracy. We strive for power . . . hence groupism." I asked how he became the state president's man.

Palayandi is a Moopanar man [Moopanar was one of the six national general secretaries of Congress (I) in New Delhi in 1986; he was originally from Tamil Nadu]. So am I. That is why I am with Palayandi. . . . I was formerly in an anti-Moopanar group. After Nedumaran [a local faction leader] was expelled from Congress (I), I stayed on with the Congress. I contacted Moopanar. Since then we have been very close. . . . Social contact with each other is very important. We have to have his confidence. I visit Moopanar whenever he comes. Even loose talk can spoil confidence. Contact and confidence – these are the keys [to become someone's man]. Invitation to marriages and to parties, these all establish contact and confidence.[26]

There are important insights concerning the nature of the local Congress party implicit in those responses, and they can be readily formalized in an analytical framework.

Power within Madurai's Congress is derived not primarily from one's local influence and popularity but rather from one's personal relationships

25 Interview with Nedumaran (see footnote 24).
26 Interview with M. K. Rama Krishnan (president, District Congress Committee), Madurai, April 15, 1986. The original interview was in Hindi. The translations are my own.

with those nearer the top of the party hierarchy. Thus, the attention of local leaders is concentrated mainly on those above them, rather than on their constituencies. Only the leaders at the very top owe their power to electoral popularity. Below them, however, from Moopanar in New Delhi to the president of the Congress (I) District Committee in Madurai, there stretches a chain of top-down command that links individuals on the basis of personal loyalty. Those higher up in the party need individuals below them to perform such minimal political tasks as making arrangements for visits by dignitaries. Mobilization and organization around a party platform are not tasks that local leaders at the periphery are called on to perform. Elections are won or lost by the Congress party's national leaders campaigning on national themes. The leadership capacities of the local leaders and their popularity among local groups are neither valued nor deemed essential within the contemporary Congress party.

This top-down power structure of loyal minions creates a workable arrangement for national leaders as long as they can muster majorities, either because of favorable circumstances, such as appropriate electoral alliances, or by creating electoral gimmicks. What it does at the political periphery, however, is create a serious authority vacuum. Congress's local leaders are not really local leaders in the sense of being popular and influential.

Congress was not a highly effective local party in Madurai even in the early 1960s when Weiner studied this district. The loyalty of Congressites to Congress was weak, and factional conflicts were repeatedly resolved by Kamraj's intervention from Madras. Political changes over the past 25 years have moved the local Congress even further down the road of organizational ineffectiveness. Two of those changes are worth repeating. First, note the changing nature and degree of centralization. Whereas local conflicts in the 1960s were settled by Kamraj, a popular regional leader, the chain of command in 1986 originated with Moopanar, who was appointed to his position in New Delhi primarily because he had Rajiv's favor. Power has come to be centralized in New Delhi, rather than in Madras, and in the hands of an appointee rather than a popular Tamil leader. The second change is that local leaders are even less firmly rooted in the local scene than they were in the early 1960s. In the past, leaders who headed competing factions had some local roots. In 1986, the Congress leader in Madurai was a man who had never won an election and owed his position primarily to those above him.

Two broad sets of consequences flow from these changes in the nature of the local Congress party. First, given the centralization of power in New Delhi, Congress cannot simultaneously be a regional party and a local party. Because regional nationalism remains a force within both Tamil Nadu politics and Madurai politics, Congress's incapacity to deal with this regional challenge on regional issues should be immediately evident. Second, considering the fact that local Congress leaders are not really popular or influential, Congress's prospects for broadening its electoral base within Madurai will remain either a function of the local popularity of national leaders or a function of the popularity of a Tamil leader who reaches an electoral arrangement of convenience with Congress.

In contrast to Congress (I), the DMK in Madurai is a more complete political party. The urban party has a stable membership, active party workers, and a diffuse but identifiable ideology, and internal party elections are held. This organizational presence helps sustain a relatively stable political base, but it does not easily translate into electoral majorities. Because the focus of what follows is mainly urban Madurai, a qualification is necessary: The emphasis on organizational presence does not easily generalize to rural areas, where all of India's elections are really won or lost.

Pon. Muthuramlingam, S. S. Themmaralu, T. Krittinan, and C. Kaverimaniam are four of the more prominent local leaders of the DMK. Muthuramlingam is one of three MLAs (the only DMK MLA) who represent Madurai in Madras.[27] He belongs to the Thevar caste. He joined the DMK in 1956–7 as a student when he was attracted to the party because of its language commitment. After remaining active for several years within the party, including a stint in prison for participating in anti-Hindi agitation sponsored by the DMK in 1965, he graduated to become an active party worker. Subsequently he served between 1970 and 1975 as chairman of a local *panchayat* and as a district secretary of the party. During 1975, when the DMK opposed the Emergency announced by Indira Gandhi, he, along with many other DMK leaders, was imprisoned. He ran in three elections unsuccessfully, including one directly against MGR in 1980. He finally won a seat in the Legislative Assembly in 1984.

Themmaralu and Krittinan are, respectively, the organization secretary and the district secretary of the local DMK.[28] Both have been active in the party for more than two decades. They share the DMK's deeply felt opposition to the caste system and its commitment to issues of Tamil language, culture, and civilization. Their organizational tasks include recruiting party members in the 100 divisions into which the DMK has divided Madurai for political purposes. Both of these leaders have emphasized that they work for the party out of commitment and that neither they nor other party officers have access to "a salary, phones or cars."

Kaverimaniam is a former member of the Legislative Assembly (1971–6) and the former district secretary of the DMK (1979–84) in Madurai city.[29] He joined the party in 1959. He participated actively in the antiin-

---

27 This account is based on an interview with Pon. Muthuramlingam (a DMK MLA from Madurai), Madurai, April 14, 1986.
28 Based on an interview with these two men in Madurai, April 16, 1986.
29 Based on an interview with him in Madurai, April 15, 1986.

flation agitations organized by Annadurai in Madurai in 1961–2, as well as in the anti-Hindi agitations of 1965. The DMK rose to power in Madurai on those waves of agitation. Kaverimaniam was thus an integral part of the rising DMK. Having served in various capacities, both within the party and in the Legislative Assembly, he finally lost his party position in internal party elections in 1984. He described his victorious opponent, Mr. Dowood, a local Moslem leader of the DMK, as "a very good, experienced party member." Kaverimaniam continues to be a prominent member of the local DMK.

All these local leaders share certain traits. They all joined the DMK because they were attracted to its commitment to Tamil cultural nationalism. None of them are Brahmans. They have all experienced prolonged periods of political socialization within the party hierarchy. Moreover, they have respect for their party and actively undertake party-sponsored activities. Elections within the party are a regular feature. Defeated in internal elections, Kaverimaniam praised his victorious party colleague and continued to work for the party. Such simple demonstrations of political civility and loyalty are lacking in many other Indian parties, especially in the contemporary Congress (I).

The DMK's ideological orientation is difficult to ascertain. It is better thought of as a set of value attachments rather than a full-blown ideology. When interviewed, local leaders emphasized that they remained faithful to the goals of Annadurai. When pressed as to what those goals mean today, they generally pointed to their opposition to the caste system and their commitment to a pro-Tamil, and therefore anti-Hindi, orientation. The leaders also often described themselves as socialists. When pushed as to how they were different from, say, the CPM, the following was a typical response: "We are socialist but we believe in non-violence. We are not only a political party. We are also a cultural organization. We concentrate on issues of language, culture and civilization. The Communist parties are not interested in this."[30] Thus, the DMK is best thought of as a party that continues to stand for issues of Tamil nationalism, with a populist tinge.

The party boasts of some 50,000 enrolled members in the city of Madurai. Although independent confirmation of that figure is not possible, thoughtful nonpartisan observers generally agreed that the DMK is relatively well organized: "DMK's organization is a legacy of Annadurai. Karunanidhi also takes interest. They are very systematic and the best organized [of the noncommunist parties in Tamil Nadu]. Their internal elections are genuinely contested. That is why the party has survived in spite of electoral losses."[31] Or, in the words of a prominent journalist, "the DMK is better

---

30 Interview with S. S. Themmaralu (organization secretary of Madurai DMK), Madurai, April 16, 1986.
31 Interview with Cho Ramaswamy (see footnote 21).

organized. They have units, cadres and regular members. They believe in a vague ideology. . . . They will probably swallow large chunks of the ADMK whenever it divides and is defeated.''[32] Given that organizational base, the DMK undertakes periodic political activities even when it is out of power. For example, in Madurai in mid–1986, the party leaders were busy organizing agitations around the issue of repression of Tamils in Sri Lanka. In addition, the party organizes frequent dramatic presentations with political themes and periodically invites public speakers. It also maintains reading rooms within the city and organizes celebrations for such occasions as the birthdays of its founding leaders.

In spite of having good leaders, organization, and an active party membership, the DMK in the recent past has not proved to be the most popular political party in Madurai. The reasons for that are discussed later, but they generally have to do with the DMK's deradicalization in the early 1970s, an uncertain rural base, and the subsequent rise of MGR. MGR capitalized on similar themes of regional nationalism, and he added to that his tremendous personal popularity as a movie hero and a Good Samaritan, all of which appealed to the rural majorities. MGR's triumph, however, failed to dislodge the DMK from its place as a major political competitor in Madurai (Table 7.1). By 1986, when MGR's health was poor, the DMK swept the local elections throughout Tamil Nadu, suggesting a potential electoral comeback in the next elections. Madurai was one of the three cities in Tamil Nadu in which MGR did not allow elections to the municipal corporations. That prohibition was an indication of MGR's fear of the DMK's electoral strength. Following MGR's death, the DMK seems destined to become the major political force in Madurai.

Besides Congress and the DMK, MGR's party, the ADMK, is the third major political force in Madurai. In terms of votes received, the ADMK was the most popular party when the last state elections were held in 1985 (Table 7.1). As discussed later, however, the ADMK benefited in that election from its electoral alliance with Congress (I). Prior to 1985, as Table 7.1 also makes clear, the ADMK's electoral strength in Madurai was about the same as that of the DMK. Now that MGR is gone, the ADMK's electoral fortunes will depend on Jayalalitha's continuing capacity to attract personal support.

The ADMK in Madurai in 1986 was virtually indistinguishable from the name and image of MGR. City streets were dominated by larger-than-life-size posters of MGR, clad in his Tamil *lungi* and wearing the dark sunglasses that became his political trademark. Gaudy posters, garlanded pictures, loud music from MGR's old films, and tapes of MGR's voice on loudspeakers were encountered throughout the city. Propaganda of that type

32 Interview with Mohan Ram (see footnote 21).

was clearly the backbone of MGR's personal popularity, especially among the illiterate folk.

Those who made the propaganda operation possible were not really members of a political party. MGR had a lot of people working for him, but not as integral parts of a well-knit party. Those who headed the propaganda organizations generally were former members of MGR's film clubs. Others who joined had mixed motivations. There were students who were genuine admirers of MGR, both as a movie star and as a populist leader. There were opportunists who hoped to gain access to governmental resources by getting close to the center of power. There were workers who were placed on the payrolls of the public bureaucracy directly under MGR's control.

The state-level factions within the ADMK had their counterparts within Madurai. Most local observers, for example, could point out the individuals who belonged to the Veerapam group or the Jayalalitha group. None of those local ADMK representatives, however, had an independent political base. Anyone who did tended to stay on with the DMK when MGR split from it in 1972. Other leaders, like K. Manoharam, now a prominent state-level leader of the DMK, joined MGR for a while, but switched back to the DMK after realizing that "MGR will not let any one grow under him."[33]

LOCAL GROUPS AND THEIR POLITICAL BEHAVIOR

Political authority in Madurai is very diffuse. One aspect of that diffuse authority structure is that many parties are competing for electoral support. The other issue that needs to be discussed concerns the individuals and groups who support these parties.

The Saurashtras in Madurai are immigrants from western India and constitute between 20 and 30 percent of the city's population. In spite of the fact that they have lived in this part of India for several centuries, they have maintained their linguistic identity and generally have preserved the endogamous nature of their community. When Weiner studied Madurai in the early 1960s, he found that the Saurastras generally supported the Congress party. That link derived in part from the fact that the Saurashtras identified with Congress leaders from western India, such as Gandhi, but it was reinforced by the economic subsidies provided by the Congress government for textile manufacturing, the industry in which most of the Saurashtras worked.

Whereas the majority of the Saurashtras in Madurai still support Congress, a significant minority do not. A local Congress leader estimated that about 60 percent of the Saurashtras still support Congress; nearly 30 per-

33 Interview with K. Manoharam (see footnote 20).

cent, he suggested, are now organized by the CPM, and the remaining 10 percent may be committed to one of the two Dravidian parties.[34] Although those figures may or may not be accurate, that general impression was not disputed by any of the numerous local political observers or participants that I interviewed. For example, a local leader of the Saurashtra community, a city leader of the DMK, and an independent politician all confirmed that pattern of political differentiation within the Saurashtra community.[35]

It is important to note the special sense in which a majority of the Saurashtras still support Congress. That support does not mean that the Saurashtras necessarily vote for the Congress party in every election. Congress is no longer a powerful political force within Tamil Nadu, certainly not in local elections. Congress, therefore, repeatedly enters into electoral arrangements with one of the two Dravidian parties, especially the ADMK. Thus, the Saurashtras of Madurai who support Congress tend to vote for the party with which Congress establishes an electoral alliance.

The Saurashtras of Madurai are concentrated in the eastern part of the city, or in the areas that correspond to the Madurai-east Legislative Assembly constituency. During the last Legislative Assembly elections in 1984, Congress (I) and the ADMK reached an electoral arrangement whereby Congress (I) did not run a candidate in Madurai-east, and the ADMK did not run one in Madurai-central. The ADMK won the Madurai-east seat with 51 percent of the vote, suggesting that local Saurashtras, who tend to support Congress, well understood the electoral arrangements and thus supported the ADMK. The CPM candidate provided the main opposition to the ADMK in Madurai-east. The fact that he won nearly 44 percent of the vote tends to support the view that a significant minority of the Saurashtras are now sympathetic to the local communists.

The results of the last set of elections to the Municipal Corporation of Madurai, held in 1978, also tend to support this overall picture. The Madurai-east Legislative Assembly constituency has 17 city wards within its boundaries. During the 1978 city elections, the ADMK, Congress (I), and the CPM won elections in 6, 5, and 4 of those wards, respectively.[36] Although one should not try to deduce too much from such data, they do suggest two things: (1) When the ADMK and Congress (I) compete for support in Saurashtra-dominated areas, the ADMK does not do badly, indicating that some Saurashtras may well prefer the ADMK. (2) The CPM indeed enjoys some support among the Saurashtras.

The explanation of these trends is relatively straightforward. Economic

---

34 Interview with M. K. Rama Krishnan (see footnote 26).
35 Interviews with K. L. N. Krishnan (president, Saurashtra College, Madurai), Madurai, April 16, 1986, C. Kaverimaniam (see footnote 29), and Nedumaran (see footnote 24).
36 Based on unpublished data made available by the Municipal Corporation of Madurai.

differences among the Saurashtras provide the necessary but not sufficient precondition for the inroads made into the community by the CPM. During an interview, a Saurashtra community leader explained their internal economic differentiations: About 2–3 percent of the heads of households are rich industrialists who own textile mills, engineering industries, and pump-manufacturing plants. Some 20–30 percent can be considered middle class in terms of income and generally are traders, shopkeepers, or professionals. The heads of another third of the households are employed as hand-loom weavers and mill workers. The rest are petty traders and vendors. He went on to point out that the "Communists are very strong" among the hand-loom weavers and the mill workers.[37] Most local observers agreed with that description of the nature of the CPM's support within the Saurashtra community.

The CPM has organized the mill workers and the weavers around a fairly classic set of class themes, such as higher wages and better working conditions. However, if such economic considerations provided a sufficient explanation for the CPM's organizational success, the whole city would be seething with class conflict. It is not. This internal economic differentiation within an ethnic community recalls a contrasting political situation that we encountered earlier in the chapter on Belgaun, namely, the situation of the economically differentiated but politically unified Marathi community. An absence of significant political issues that would unite an ethnic community and the presence of an established radical leadership are additional factors that help explain why some Saurashtras in Madurai vote communist. The latter point is especially important. The fact that some communist leaders are themselves Saurashtras probably is of considerable political significance.

Two other factors help explain why some Saurashtras may have shifted their support from Congress to one of the Dravidian parties. First, there is the obvious weakness of Congress (I) as a viable political alternative in Tamil Nadu. In the words of a community leader, "Until the Congress was the ruling party in Tamil Nadu, we supported the Congress exclusively. Once the DMK came into power, the seniors [the older people] remained loyal to the Congress. But with the weakness of the Congress in Tamil Nadu many started deviating. Some joined the DMK. Others joined the ADMK." A closely related issue is that of generational change. The same community leader continued: "There is a real generation gap. Congress party has now not been around for 20–30 years. My son grew up in a hostel and college. He has different ideas. I can not expect him to believe in Congress. So he joins other parties."[38] Whereas in our discussion of Belgaun and Calcutta we saw that the ethnic coin was a coin that did not

37 Interview with M. K. Rama Krishnan (see footnote 26).
38 Ibid.

readily melt, it has proved to be less resistant in Madurai. The open-ended analytical implication is one to which scholars of the politics of ethnicity have long been attracted, namely, that the degree to which ethnicity will be politicized is likely to be a function of the broader political situation.[39]

Thevars are the second most significant community in Madurai. In the recent past they have tended to revere their own leaders and to support a militant party, the Forward Bloc. Today, however, the Forward Bloc has virtually vanished from the Tamil Nadu political scene. The electoral support of the Thevars is now divided between the DMK and the ADMK. This behavior is consistent with their earlier anti-Congress orientation and with the fact that they are Tamil speakers. Within the scope of the two DMKs, however, there is no consistent pattern or discernible reason why some Thevars support the DMK, whereas others support the ADMK. The majority of the Thevars are working-class people. They are employed as mill workers, contract laborers, and masons. Although there are poor and rich Thevars, economic differences are less sharp in this community than among the Saurashtras. Many of the Thevars are concentrated in the Madurai-west Legislative Assembly constituency. Voting behavior within this constituency gives some indication of the political behavior of Thevars.

The DMK and the ADMK have been the major political competitors in this constituency over the past decade. The CPM does not enter the contest, because of arrangements with the DMK. Similarly, Congress does not enter the fray, because of an alliance with the ADMK. The ADMK won this constituency by a large majority in both 1977 and 1980. During the city elections of 1978, the ADMK won elections in 13 of the 17 wards located within this constituency. In 1980, Madurai-west was considered to be so solidly for the ADMK that MGR chose it as his place to run. In 1984, however, the DMK beat a lesser candidate representing the ADMK. Most local observers suggested that whereas the Thevars had formerly supported the ADMK, many of them switched their allegiance to the DMK in the early 1980s. The reason for that switch in party preference often was cast in terms of MGR's poor health and ineffectiveness. Seasoned local observers suggested that the Thevars, mostly of the working class, were a politically shrewd group, certainly more so than the illiterate slum dwellers. They were not taken in so much by MGR the movie idol as by his promise of concrete rewards under his populist leadership. They were also aware of MGR's increasing ineffectiveness. Because the programmatic distinction between the DMK and the ADMK was not all that great to begin with,

39 See, for example, Nelson Kasfir, "Explaining Ethnic Political Participation," in Atul Kohli, ed., *The State and Development in the Third World* (Princeton University Press, 1986), pp. 88–111.

the switch from the ADMK to the DMK by some of the Thevars was readily understandable.

Dividing up the city population on the basis of occupational criteria can facilitate an analysis of the political behaviors of some of the other groups in Madurai. First, there are those who generally do not have adequate employment and live in the city's slums: nearly 150,000 people, including non-voting-age children and teenagers. These slums are concentrated around the railway tracks and the river that run through the city. One can readily identify the city wards in which the slums are concentrated.[40] The results of the 1978 city elections suggest that the votes of the slum dwellers were divided between the ADMK and the CPM. Some slums had been well organized by the CPM. Conversations with slum dwellers indicated that they found the CPM's platform appealing not so much because of promises of radical change as because of its organized program to resist evictions from the slums. A reduction of their vulnerability, rather than promises of efficacious action, was what linked the urban marginals to the reform-oriented CPM. MGR's support in the slums, by contrast, was based in part on his movie-idol status and in part on some success with populist schemes, such as free lunch for children.

Moving up the social hierarchy, a significant minority of the working class has never been organized. Several knowledgeable individuals noted that members of this group often voted for MGR.[41] The reasoning was that unorganized workers tended to be "less politically sophisticated" and thus were more likely to be taken in by the mere "promises" and "charms" of a movie idol turned leader.

As far as the organized working class is concerned, the patterns of unionization are extremely heterogeneous. A single factory can have five or six unions competing for support. The big change since the early 1960s, when Weiner studied Madurai, is that union alignments are now less along caste lines and more along party lines. A number of observers concurred in that observation,[42] which is generally consistent with a related observation, namely, that caste plays a decreasing role in elections in Madurai.

Two important implications of union fragmentation must be noted. First, the working class is so divided along party lines that any precipitation of conflict along class lines does not seem likely, at least in the short run.

40 The commissioner of the Municipal Corporation of Madurai, M. Devraj, helped identify these wards in an interview in Madurai, April 17, 1986.
41 Muthuramlingam, who won the Madurai-west constituency in 1984, suggested that he had failed in his constituency to secure the votes of the unorganized workers. Interview (see footnote 27).
42 This point was made specifically in three different interviews with individuals of very different political persuasions. The interviews were with Nedumaran (see footnote 24), Pon. Muthuramligam (see footnote 27), and M. K. Rama Krishnan (see footnote 26).

Politics in the districts

The second point is that the impact of union fragmentation on electoral behavior is not clear. The members of both the DMK and the CPM suggested that union membership influences electoral behavior, but Congress's union organizers disagreed. These differences probably indicate that workers belonging to the more militant and better-organized unions, such as that of the CPM, tend to vote for the parties that have organized them. By contrast, those belonging to the Congress-organized unions, which tend to be more cooperative toward management, probably make independent political judgments at the time of voting.

The political preferences of the middle-income groups are also divided. The educated professionals tend to support the DMK. There are two important pieces of evidence that support this claim. Most of these better-off, educated people in Madurai live north of the river, in the northern part of the city, and the DMK consistently does rather well in elections in these areas. In addition, the local DMK leaders, who freely admitted their failure to attract the support of the slum dwellers and the unorganized working class, were consistent in their claim that "the educated middle class is with us."[43] Independent local observers agreed.[44] Themes of cultural nationalism have long provided a bond between the better-educated Tamils and the DMK. During the 1970s, some of that support was lost to MGR. As MGR's rule declined in effectiveness, however, those educated, middle-income groups were among the first to switch their allegiance back to the old DMK.

The other significant subgroup within the middle-income group comprises the traders and bazaar merchants. Many of these are concentrated in the middle of the town, around the Madurai Temple. Congress (I) and its offshoot, Congress (Kamraj), generally compete for support in this Madurai-central constituency, indicating that the bazaar merchants are not as attracted to the Dravidian parties as is the rest of the population. Part of the reason for this, as already explained, is that some of the bazaar merchants are Saurashtras. Congress's influence in the central town also owes something to the concentration of the temple-related Brahmans around the temple. Finally, themes of commerce, rather than of linguistic and cultural nationalism, have always been central in molding the political preferences of the traders. The DMK, with its emphasis on Tamil pride, and a concern for the "small man," has never had much to offer the commercially minded, middle-income groups of Madurai.

Finally, in this discussion of the political behaviors of various socioeconomic groups, some reference should be made to the changing role of students. Students have always provided the backbone in the DMK move-

---

43 That claim was repeated in numerous interviews, including those with Pon. Muthuramlingam (see footnote 27) and S. S. Themmaralu (see footnote 30).
44 Interview with Nedumaran (see footnote 24).

ment. They were the main participants in the anti-Hindi agitations of the mid-1960s that eventually brought the DMK to power in 1967. Once in power, however, the DMK compromised its stand on anti-Hindi issues, costing it important support among students.[45] The matinee idol, MGR, picked up some of that support because he had a fairly large following among the student-age population. After his expulsion from the undivided DMK in 1972, many of the young in Madurai switched their loyalties to MGR:

All the MLAs and the office bearers stayed with the DMK. The official organ of the party stayed with us [the DMK]. But unfortunately, there were a large number of MGR supporters. They were generally below 30. They raised a really strong protest against MGR's expulsion. There were no agitations. But there were numerous complaints. Students obstructed MLAs in their cars. They tried to occupy the party branch offices. Much of this was not guided – it was a spontaneous outburst. People have blind faith in MGR.[46]

There is now evidence to indicate that the DMK won back some of that student support from MGR, the main reason being that MGR cooperated with New Delhi's actions against Tamils in Sri Lanka. The DMK mobilized numerous demonstrations against the government's anti-Tamil policies in Sri Lanka.[47]

To recapitulate the main points of the discussion thus far, the competing parties compose a kind of multiparty system in Madurai, and the social bases of the various parties are fairly heterogeneous. When one compares this contemporary picture of politics in Madurai with what Weiner found in the early 1960s, the overall impression is increasing political fragmentation and diffusion of authority. Even in early 1960s, Madurai had not presented a picture of cohesive authority and a well-functioning government. Over the past 25 years, political change in Madurai has moved further in the direction of political fragmentation. The Congress party lost its dominance to the DMK, but survived as a minority party. The ADMK replaced the DMK as the dominant party, but the DMK also survived as a minority party. Following MGR's death, the ADMK under Jayalalitha will face an uphill battle, probably also facing the future as a minority party. The fragmentation at the party level is matched at the societal level by a weakening of group political commitments. Today, neither the Thevars nor the Saurashtras act as a cohesive political community. Neither caste nor class can provide a ready basis for aggregation of political interests in contemporary Madurai. Given this fragmentation at both the party level and the community level, the intriguing question concerns what will happen to authority and local government in such a setting.

45 For documentation, see Barnett, *Cultural Nationalism,* chapters 9, 10, and 11.
46 From an interview with C. Kaverimaniam (see footnote 29).
47 Interview with Nedumaran (see footnote 24).

Table 7.2. *Results of elections for the Madurai Municipal Corporation, 1978*

Party[a]	Seats won		Vote received (%)
	Number	Percentage	
Congress (I)	9	13.8	21.9
ADMK	37	57.0	27.9
DMK	6	9.2	20.5
CPM	8	12.3	5.7
CPI	4	6.2	2.9
Others	1	1.5	21.1
Total	65	100	100

[a]For details on when the parties were formed or re-formed, see the footnotes to Table 7.1.
Source: Compiled from unpublished data provided by the Municipal Corporation of Madurai.

THE CITY GOVERNMENT OF MADURAI

During the past two decades, Madurai has only twice had an elected city government, first in 1968 and then in 1978. For 12 of the past 20 years, Madurai has been run administratively, that is, directly from the state capital, Madras. The repeated failure to call city elections must be attributed to fear of electoral loss. The DMK did not allow city elections between 1972 and 1977. Then, after 1982, MGR continued to run Madurai and other cities, including Madras, administratively. Thus, the short answer to the question of what happens to government in a highly fragmented political society is fairly simple: It ends up being run by fiat.

The Madurai city government graduated from being a municipality to a municipal corporation in 1971. Until recently, the city was divided into 65 wards. (The results of the 1978 city elections have been discussed and are summarized in Table 7.2.) Recently the city was reorganized into 100 wards. Elections in those 100 wards were expected, but MGR's widespread defeat in municipalities and *panchayats* in early 1986 led to their indefinite postponement.[48] Therefore, the city is run by an officer of the Indian Administrative Services, who takes his orders directly from Madras, often directly from the office of the chief minister.

The Madurai Municipal Corporation (MMC) employs a staff of some 7,000 people. The annual expenditure of the MMC in 1985 was nearly 2

48 See, for example, the report on this issue in *Indian Express* (Madras edition), April 17, 1986.

million rupees.[49] When the city government is elected, the employment and expenditure decisions are made by select committees, and control over those decisions is highly valued. This is where opportunities exist for building a machine, for broadening political support, and for personal gain. Under conditions of a majority government, these committees generally consist of members of the majority party. When the prospects of winning a clear majority appear slim, however, leaders in Madras fear losing control over patronage resources to the opposition. That is why they prefer to have the city run by administrators, by appointed committees, and by an appointed mayor. It is much easier to control these appointed individuals than to try to influence elected politicians from opposition parties.

The government offered by the MMC under the direct control of MGR was widely regarded as corrupt and ineffective. It is impossible to get accurate data on corruption, but some examples will help support this contention. Without elected councilors, the formal authority to make decisions now rests with the appointed officers. The appointed officers, however, are continually pressured by other elected representatives seeking to have their own preferences taken into account. The city commissioner explained that "these days the MLAs, the MPs and the MLCs all approach us. There are other channels of political influence. Ministers from Madras make requests. We try to accommodate most of the reasonable demands."[50] These demands can concern numerous issues, including appointments to jobs controlled by the MMC. Those who are in a position to influence employment decisions can receive significant cash payoffs from those who finally get employment. As a well-informed local observer noted:

There are no secrets [about this in Madurai]. To get a job of a teacher [through the MMC], you have to pay 7 to 10 thousand rupees. The going rate for a clerk's job is 5000 rupees. Who can secure help has nothing to do with party affiliation. Nothing happens without money. If you are rich, you can get your work done [through the MMC].[51]

Such examples of corruption are legion. Almost everyone I interviewed agreed that nothing moves at the MMC without payment. Even the commissioner himself admitted that city contracts, as a rule, are awarded by influential members of the corporation to their own family members or to others for cash payoffs. Moreover, observers also agreed that though there had always been corruption within the MMC, it had increased considerably under MGR.

In fairness to the political authorities in Madurai, it should be noted that whereas the city government is deeply corrupt, the city's political scene is

---

49 Much of this descriptive information was provided by the city commissioner, M. Devraj (see footnote 40).
50 Interview with M. Devraj (see footnote 40).
51 Interview with Nedumaran (see footnote 24).

not marked by violence and the use of *goondas*. Numerous observers noted that that aspect of the "northern culture" still had not penetrated to Madurai. The reasons for that, however, have less to do with effective government and more to do with the local political culture, in which violence has not yet become the norm. If the contending political parties ever decide to begin fighting their political battles on the street, however, the local authorities will have had no tradition of providing mechanisms for non-coercive resolution of conflicts. Such institutional mechanisms simply do not exist. Moreover, MGR's open call for members of his party to carry knives for self-protection in 1987 suggested that the "Sanjay culture" might intrude into Tamil Nadu. Finally, the violent mayhem within the Legislative Assembly that led to the proclamation of presidential rule in Tamil Nadu in 1988 was not a promising sign. In the future, Madurai may not remain insulated from a qualitatively different order of breakdown.

CONCLUSION

An attempt has been made in this chapter to analyze political change in a setting somewhere between India's rural districts and the major metropolitan Indian cities. The main themes revealed by this analysis can now be summarized.

One theme is the increasing significance of state-level political trends for local politics. Developments in Madurai politics are complex composites of local, state, and national political trends. However, the significance of both local and national political parties has declined. Thus, we have seen the decline of parties like the Forward Bloc, and the simultaneous transfer of the political loyalty of a city community, the Thevars, to competing regional parties. The decline in Congress's significance locally similarly highlights the degree of insulation from national politics that local politics in a city in Tamil Nadu experienced for nearly two decades. Whereas the impact that national politics will have on local politics probably will fluctuate in the future, it is not likely that local factors in Madurai will reemerge as the most important determinants of local political trends. Cities like Madurai are increasingly integrated into and thus deeply influenced by state-level politics.

A second important theme that emerges from this discussion concerns the growing fragmentation in authority structures and in the political loyalties of socioeconomic groups. The ruling national party was deposed in the 1960s by a regional nationalist party that made promises to the little man, even before Indira Gandhi discovered India's poor. The deradicalization of that party and its concomitant failure to deliver on its anti-Center, anti-Brahman, and other pro-poor goals slowly brought to the fore a ruler elected primarily by virtue of his personal appeal. His ill health and eventual death left his popular mistress struggling to fill the vacuum within the

ADMK. Thus, the political scene in Madurai has come to be characterized by numerous competing minority parties. The DMK is better organized than most local parties and thus is likely to remain politically significant. More generally, however, political fragmentation continues to inhibit the formation of an authoritative local government.

There is a general lesson implicit in this pattern of political change. In Tamil Nadu, India's main nationalist party was deposed by a party championing regional nationalism at the state level. That provided a legitimate and popular government for a while. If such a government is not effective, however, or does not deliver on its promises, that quickly leads to a power vacuum. Who would fill the vacuum left by the failure of regional nationalism? Tamil Nadu found a temporary solution in MGR, but by the very definition of personalistic rule, that was a temporary solution. Repeated failures to build institutional roots and to deliver on the promises that won elections tend to undermine, slowly but surely, the possibility of good government. Political gimmicks do not provide infinite resources with which to build authority and orderly rule.

The other aspect of political fragmentation in Madurai resides within the local civil society. Identities based on caste and ethnicity no longer readily define political behavior. As we learn from studies of other places, this is not a linear process of change; given changed political circumstances, it is reversible. Nevertheless, the fact is that the traditional identities do not predict political preference in contemporary Madurai. Likewise, class identities are not strong, and most economic groups have diverse political preferences.

Diversity of political preferences along identifiable social and economic traits is in itself neither good nor bad. When combined with a deeply fractionalized party system, however, it greatly hinders the formation of stable coalitions and a working government. Fragmentations at the levels of political institutions and socioeconomic groups create a condition that attracts rule that often is arbitrary and by fiat. As we have seen in the case of Madurai, under conditions of fiat, even the rich must shell out exorbitant payoffs to buy influence. The only people who clearly gain under these circumstances are those who control power. The rest of the local society suffers.

Conclusion: the districts

In this Part II (Chapters 3–7), an attempt has been made to describe and to explain political changes in five districts in India over the past 25 years. It is now time to pull together some of the common themes running through the changes in these districts so as to reach a few tentative conclusions concerning the kinds of political trends that have replaced the "Congress system" at India's political periphery and to identify the forces that have influenced the rates and patterns of political change.

Before addressing these core issues, an important caveat should be noted concerning the issue of how well these five districts represent India's political periphery. Given India's diversity, it is clear that no five districts, and therefore no microcosm, can capture all nuances and regional variations. Nevertheless, Weiner selected these five districts in the early 1960s in consultation with the leaders of the Congress party. At that time, these districts were deemed to represent areas of Congress strength and to give a good cross section of India's diversity. Thus, they were well suited for examining the issue of how and why Congress had succeeded in India. Some 25 years later, it is not unreasonable to hold that a study of the same five districts should have something to contribute to our understanding of the changing nature of the Congress party and the changing patterns of India's local politics.[1]

---

1 One factor having to do with the adequacy of the representativeness, however, has changed since the early 1960s. This has to do with the fact that Congress during the 1980s tended to be much more successful in elections in the Hindi heartland than in non-Hindi areas. None of the districts discussed earlier is located in these core states of Uttar Pradesh, Bihar, and Madhya Pradesh. Does that tend to bias this analysis toward highlighting the weaknesses of the Congress party? My answer to that question is no, for the following reasons: First, the focus of the preceding analysis has been as much on issues of political organization and governability as on electoral success. What is distinctive about Congress in the Hindi heartland is its electoral popularity, not its local organizational and governing capacities. This will become clear in the discussion of Bihar in Chapter 8. Second, I *did* investigate political change in the Deoria district in Uttar Pradesh for this study, but I decided not to include a chapter on Deoria, in order to maintain continuity with Weiner's earlier study and to limit this study's length.

The main themes that would have emerged from a chapter on Deoria can be summarized

Weiner sought to determine why and how Congress had succeeded, mainly as a political party but also as a force that imparted a degree of coherence and good government to a diverse subcontinental polity.[2] Among the many factors that helped him generate a full explanation of that success, three were central: (1) party organization, (2) Congress's adaptive quality, and (3) the positive role that access to patronage resources played in building electoral support.

Congress's party organization in the early 1960s was uneven. It certainly had little to do with ideological homogeneity or a disciplined hierarchy of cadres. Those things Congress never possessed. Yet Weiner found evidence

briefly. Congress has little formal organization in Deoria. Any significant local political affairs are as likely to be controlled by New Delhi as by state leaders. What is distinctive about the local Deoria Congress is the nature of its electoral dynamics. First, there is cultural continuity between New Delhi and Uttar Pradesh. Uttar Pradesh is not a distinct cultural region, and thus there are no deep political boundaries between its national and regional politics. Trends in national politics have direct reverberations in the politics of Uttar Pradesh. Second, in terms of local support, Congress enjoys the loyalty of the higher castes, Brahmans and Thakurs, and of a significant majority of the scheduled castes. Congress's local leadership is deeply factionalized, both along caste lines (i.e., Brahmans versus Thakurs) and along personality lines. The dominant castes nevertheless continue to control the local Congress as in the past.

What has changed significantly in local politics over the past few decades in Deoria is the political behavior of the backward castes. Such backward castes as the Yadavs, Koiris, and Sainthwals tend to support the old Lok Dal or one of its splinter groups. However, caste loyalties to parties are far from certain. In broad terms, however, one could do a lot worse than accept Paul Brass's contention that in districts like Deoria, Congress is the party of the highest and lowest social strata; the middle peasant strata tend to form the opposition.

The conduct of local politics still is not marred by violence and breakdown to the same degree as in neighboring Bihar. Nevertheless, 4 of the 13 MLAs from the district were described to me as having had "hooligan" backgrounds. Finally, none of the following local trends in this Congress-dominated district will surprise any reader who has followed the analysis of the five other districts: (1) Dissension over who will get tickets to stand for election often leads to "anti-party activities" by members of both Congress and Lok Dal. (2) "Booth capturing" and violence during elections do not raise eyebrows. (3) Violence of Thakurs against "uppity" Harijans, though not the norm, is on the increase. The local government is deeply marred by corruption and is quite ineffective.

For detailed analysis of district-level politics in Uttar Pradesh, Paul Brass's work remains indispensable. His first major work describing and explaining politics in several districts in Uttar Pradesh up until the 1960s is *Factional Politics in an India State: The Congress Party in Uttar Pradesh* (Berkeley: University of California Press, 1965). He revisited those districts in the late 1970s and produced a series of valuable articles that capture aspects of political change, especially the changing electoral behaviors of various socioeconomic groups: "Congress, the Lok Dal and the Middle Peasant Castes: An Analysis of the 1977 and 1980 Parliamentary Elections in Uttar Pradesh," *Pacific Affairs,* Spring 1981, pp. 5–41; "The Politicization of the Peasantry in a North Indian State," *Journal of Peasant Studies,* July 1980, pp. 395–426, September 1980, pp. 3–36.

2 See Myron Weiner, *Party Building in a New Nation: The Indian National Congress* (University of Chicago Press, 1967), part 7.

to suggest that Congress leaders were attentive to organizational concerns. Modest success in that sphere facilitated, on an ongoing basis, the social-ization of new leaders, regular internal communication within the party, peaceful local settlements of many local disputes, and a degree of party cohesion. Regular elections within the party further contributed to the perceived legitimacy of local leaders as genuine party leaders.

Congress's adaptive quality was manifest in the fact that Congress tended to build its support by incorporating those who were locally influential: the landed, the wealthy, the representatives of the dominant castes, community leaders, and the "big men" who were respected and whose opinions carried weight in their communities. For the purposes of later comparisons, it is extremely important to note that the strategy of adapting to local power structures can work only if the "big men" have considerable influence over villages, towns, or castes or over religious communities across villages and towns. The quid pro quo that Congress struck with these "big men" is well known to students of Indian politics. Such individuals received political offices or access to governmental resources in return for using their local influence to mobilize electoral support for Congress. That chain of im-portant individuals stretching from village to state and eventually to the national capital, welded by bonds of patronage, was one central feature of Congress's success until the 1960s.

Finally, what helped Congress to settle conflicts among contending in-fluentials and to sustain its patronage network was the steady growth in available resources. The state's growing economic role brought more and more resources within the sphere of the government. The establishment of *panchayati raj* made those resources available at the various levels of the government, including the village level. Because Congress controlled much of that sprawling governmental structure, the Congress elite could readily channel those economic resources to build and sustain political support. The economic developmental implications of using scarce eco-nomic resources for political ends, or, for that matter, of adapting to local power structures and thus forgoing any reforms that might adversely affect the influential "big men," probably were negative. Nevertheless, those strategies were political in motivation and, when judged by political cri-teria, were quite successful. They helped Congress build and sustain a sprawling network of supporters across India.

A functioning party organization, the tendency to build support with, rather than against, the local influentials, and access to growing re-sources that could be used for patronage were the major ingredients emphasized by Weiner in the success of Congress as India's ruling party. Other scholars of pre–1967 Indian politics may disagree with cer-tain details of that account, but overall, the independently researched macroaccounts provided by such scholars as Rajni Kothari and W. H.

Morris-Jones are not inconsistent with the conclusions reached by Weiner in his study of the five districts.[3]

This study of the same five districts some 25 years later helps trace some of the major changes in India's local politics. A summary discussion of how the local party organization, the structure of community power, and the role of patronage have changed in these five districts follows, paving the way for some general conclusions.

PARTY ORGANIZATION

Congress's party organization declined in all of the districts analyzed. That decline was most dramatic in Gujarat. The local Congress in Kheda, once vibrant and well organized, is now virtually defunct. Though Congress may still win elections there because of its appeal to the numerically significant local castes, no organizational structure has replaced the old Congress. Decline in the other four districts has been less dramatic, mainly because the local Congress party was not all that well organized to begin with. Even in those districts, however, significant organizational decline has occurred. The Belgaun local unit was moderately effective in the early 1960s. Now Belgaun's local Congress has no existence apart from those who have been elected to office on a Congress ticket. In Calcutta, Congress went from machine politics headed by a "big man" to total organizational shambles. The "Sanjay culture" dominates the factionalized and squabbling Calcutta Congress. The local organization in both Guntur and Madurai in the early 1960s was already quite faction-ridden. In Guntur, that situation continues, with the added nuance that all the local leaders are appointed and thus are not considered to be legitimate within the local environment. Finally, in Madurai, Congress has lost even its electoral significance. Local leaders are appointed from New Delhi, and there is little Congress presence or organizational structure left in the city.

Non-Congress parties also have not generated much local organizational infrastructure. The only clear exceptions are the CPM in Calcutta and, to some degree, the DMK in Madurai; such exceptions will be considered later. Other than those two, all "centrist" parties have failed to put down organizational roots. The most dramatic example was the 10-year rule of MGR in Madurai. A whole decade of relatively secure rule left no organizational legacy. NTR's experiment in Andhra was similar. Finally, even

3 See, for example, Rajni Kothari, "The Congress 'System' in India," *Asian Survey*, December 1964, pp. 1161–73; W. H. Morris-Jones, *Politics Mainly Indian* (Madras: Orient Longman, 1978), especially pp. 196–232. For a good summary discussion of these views, see James Manor, "Parties and the Party System," in Atul Kohli, ed., *India's Democracy: An Analysis of Changing State–Society Relations* (Princeton University Press, 1988), especially pp. 63–6.

the Janata party in Belgaun, which emerged victorious on its own, came to depend on Hegde for its survival. Very little effort was evident in Belgaun to strengthen the local party organization.

What were the causes and the consequences of that growing organizational vacuum at the periphery? To begin with the consequences, a number of India's growing problems of governability can be traced back to that organizational vacuum. Consider, for example, some of the "input functions" that must be performed in any setting before systematic authority can emerge. Socialization of new leaders is one such function. It has become a crucial problem in India's local politics. Because systematic mechanisms for recruiting the competent and the committed, and filtering out those who cannot serve the organization's purposes, simply do not exist, the quality of local leadership has declined. The clearest example of this is in Calcutta, where the factionalized local Congressites have themselves become a major cause of political disorder. In other words, the entry of ruffians and thugs into the body politic is, in part, traceable back to the deterioration of party organizations. Over time, the increasing significance and power of such individuals further contribute to political breakdown.

Another crucial input function that well-organized parties can perform is to help settle local political disputes, especially disputes internal to the party. Such disputes can be resolved either by finding a compromise acceptable to all or by acquiescing to the decisions of those who are perceived to have legitimate authority. Without party elections, such local conflict resolution becomes impossible. In nearly all the districts discussed, we saw how dissensions internal to the parties quickly spilled outside the party boundaries and often were fought to a decision on the streets. Again, the Calcutta Congress was a dramatic example. The consequences of dissensions within Congress in Belgaun and Kheda were only a little less dramatic. The squabbling within MGR's party illustrated that failure to develop mechanisms for internal conflict resolution is not a problem limited to the Congress party.

Well-organized parties can also help put together systematic coalitions and thus help build relatively stable social support. So far, the electoral costs of organizational weakness are not sharply evident in India's periphery. On the contrary, as in the case of Madurai, the better-organized DMK lost out to the partyless but popular matinee idol, MGR. Over the short run, therefore, it is clear that one does not have to have a well-organized party to win elections in contemporary India. As will be seen later, this is one important reason that so little effort goes into building party organizations. In the longer run, however, it is not clear that personal appeal and other electoral gimmicks will be sufficient to win elections. If the case of Calcutta is any indication, local Congresses that are parties in name only now face a formidable challenge from the better-organized CPM.

The negative consequences of the organizational vacuum for governability are further evident in the "output functions" that need to be performed, especially those tasks that may require the support of a well-organized party. For example, we noted in the case of Kheda that as the Congress-led Gujarat government sought to implement some reservation policies, the Patidars launched widespread opposition in the form of agitations, demonstrations, and riots. The implementation of such highly controversial reservation policies would have required the political capacity to confront the nongovernmental opposition launched by powerful local groups. Congress's organizational weakness made it impossible for the rulers to mobilize any sustained support for their policies; thus, Congress eventually had to cave in to the opposition. In other words, it is one thing to win elections, but quite another to translate titular power into concrete accomplishments. Without an organizational base, it is unlikely that an electoral mandate can be carried out, with centralization and powerlessness becoming simultaneous tendencies.

Finally, in this discussion of the consequences of organizational vacuum, a case can be made that well-organized parties can play important roles in making local government more effective in India. Unfortunately, local government was found to be corrupt and quite ineffective in most of the cases discussed here. Calcutta has been a partial exception to that trend. Although the city government under the CPM has not been notably effective in initiating solutions to Calcutta's numerous local problems, it is not considered to be highly corrupt. The minimum of corruption in the contemporary Calcutta city government is, in turn, not unrelated to the organizational discipline of the CPM. Elsewhere, I have argued that the CPM's organizational capacities have helped it to run more effective local rural governments and to implement modest redistributive policies in rural West Bengal. (See also Chapter 10 below.)[4] Thus, the widespread corruption and ineffectiveness in local governments noted earlier can be seen to be related, in part, to the lack of organization and discipline in most of the local ruling parties.

If an organizational vacuum has contributed to the growing problems of governability at the periphery, an important question remains: Why the organizational decline? This question really has two parts: (1) Why did some leaders destroy existing party institutions? (2) Why did the same leaders, or others, fail to rebuild new organizations that might, over time, put down institutional roots?

The 1969 split in the Congress party at the national level was at the heart of the subsequent organizational decline in the local units of the Congress party. There is widespread agreement among observers of Indian politics that Congress's split was a result of severe power conflicts among the

4 See Atul Kohli, *The State and Poverty in India: The Politics of Reform* (Cambridge University Press, 1987), chapter 3.

contending party elite. Later, Indira Gandhi's decision not to allow internal elections in the Congress party resulted in local political officers being appointed from above and losing their local legitimacy.

Elections within the Congress party might have produced leaders who would not have supported Indira Gandhi, and in order to avoid such power challenges, Indira Gandhi let Congress's organization decline. Strong institutions could only have imposed constraints on the personal power of one who had usurped power at the top. Given the circumstances, Indira Gandhi's decisions, which contributed heavily to the destruction of the Congress party as an organization, are understandable in terms of the logic of how best to preserve and enhance her personal power.

A qualifier must be added concerning Indira Gandhi's crucial role in the destruction of India's democratic institutions. Many scholars who study Indian politics hold Indira personally responsible for destroying the Congress party and other institutions. That position leaves two related questions unanswered: Would any other leader have behaved differently? What was it about the political context that gave Indira Gandhi so much power?

We shall never know what would have happened if someone other than Indira Gandhi had been at the helm in India for the past two decades. What we do know is that numerous other regional leaders did not do much better than Indira Gandhi in building up party organizations. As noted earlier, NTR, MGR, and to some extent even Hegde were all guilty of building up their personal power at the expense of institutions. Although one should never underestimate the crucial role of the individual leader, there clearly are contextual forces at work in contemporary India that tend to produce leaders who come to office by virtue of their personal appeal and then rule by fiat rather than by means of rules and established procedures. Indira Gandhi cannot be held responsible for the deinstitutionalization that occurred under the rule of other parties, and in some cases that process began around the same time that Indira came to power.

These contextual factors, as discussed later, have to do with the breakdown of established patterns of authority in the civil society. The older, pre–1967 patterns of Congress rule rested on, among other factors, the efforts of influential people who could mobilize sizable communities for electoral purposes, and over time, their influence declined. Numerous groups emerged as free-floating political forces. As that happened, the prospect of winning elections by co-opting significant members of a dominant caste or other prominent people simply declined.

The growing fragmentation of the political society left only two realistic options for winning majorities in India's very poor society. Leaders could have chosen to put together new majority coalitions in a systematic way. That would have necessitated building parties and incorporating the newly liberated lower middle class and the lower classes by offering them some concrete reward, such as land. Most centrist parties in India either chose not to pursue or simply were not capable of realistically pursuing such a reformist alternative. Thus, only one path was left for those parties: Promise something to everyone, and hope they elect you. Leaders who enjoy tremendous personal popularity are more likely to succeed at such populist strategies than are managers or organization builders. It is not surprising that over the past two decades there has been a growing tendency within the Indian political system to elect populist leaders with great personal appeal.

The growing tendency toward populism can be understood as a function of two factors: (1) the decline of the prepolitical authority patterns in the traditional society and (2) an unwillingness, or incapacity, or both, to recruit and organize the newly liberated political forces. Once in power, populist leaders have neither the capacity nor the incentive to build party organizations. They rule by theatrics rather than by the painstaking, mundane tasks of building party cells. Thus, populism tends to be inherently deinstitutionalizing. In India, it both reflects the breakdown of traditional authority in the civil society and further contributes to the spiral of growing disorder.

Well-organized parties tend to emerge from grass-roots concerns. They often develop as vehicles for capturing power. Those who have already achieved power are not likely to impose or create such parties from above. Parties as institutions constrain individual discretion and power. It is not surprising, therefore, that not only Indira Gandhi but also other rulers we have encountered in this discussion (NTR, MGR, and Hegde) tended to concentrate power in their own hands at the expense of institutional rule.

THE STRUCTURE OF COMMUNITY POWER

The pre–1967 Congress was quite good at accommodating the concerns of influential local challengers. That was in part a function of Congress's organizational capacities and in part a result of Congress's control over the growing resources available for patronage. Its success at accommodation, however, was also related to the nature of power relations in such local units as the village, groups of villages understood as a political community, castes spread over a few villages or entire regions, and districts as a whole.

In the past, a few "big men" of the dominant community often were in a position to sway the political behavior of other communities. That prepolitical structure of community power – based on a combination of control over economic resources, traditional high status, and the hierarchical nature of the traditional caste society – provided an essential building block for the early Congress. When Congress was successful in dealing with local conflicts during the 1950s and 1960s, therefore, more often than not those conflicts involved contending "big men" rather than contending socioeconomic groups. Once those influential men and communities had been accommodated within Congress, they used their local influence to sway electoral support toward Congress. That is why Congress was successful in the past.

A recurring theme in most of the preceding chapters was the growing challenge to the domination of the established elite in local communities. In Kheda, for example, the Kshatriyas have for quite some time refused to be led by the Patidars. Even among the Kshatriyas there is increasing caste conflict involving the elite Thakur leaders and the emerging leaders of the backward Bariyas. The power challenges posed by the upwardly mobile Harijans have invoked the wrath of both the Patidar and Thakur elite. Similarly, in the case of Guntur, the earlier conflict involving the two dominant castes, the Kammas and the Reddis, has now broadened. The capacity of a local Kamma or Reddi leader to sway the political behavior of backward and scheduled castes has diminished considerably. Backward castes have emerged as a significant political force in their own right. The backward castes of Guntur, however, are themselves extremely heterogeneous. They are not, as a caste community, easily swayed by symbolic rewards, such as giving visible positions to a select few caste leaders.

That pattern of growing power challenges and fragmentation of the political community was less dramatically evident in the urban districts, mainly because it had already occurred in most of those areas. Thus, for example, the influence of Brahmans in the affairs of Madurai had diminished much earlier than the mid–1960s; in some respects that had begun even before independence. Thus, a fragmented political community has been an important feature of contemporary politics in Madurai for many years.

In addition to the declining influence of traditionally powerful castes and the related proliferation of caste conflicts of various types, some new patterns of class conflict are also worth noting. Among the Saurashtras of Madurai, for example, we noted a political split along class lines within an ethnic community. In the case of Guntur, the same issue was highlighted by the tendency of both the Kamma and Reddi elite to downplay their traditional caste animosities so as to confront jointly what were perceived to be challenges along class lines. Finally, the most dramatic example of class conflict was the violence of the politicized labor unions that was unleashed in Calcutta during 1967–77. Ironically, that conflict has now been contained, probably only temporarily, by a ruling communist party.

Before analyzing the causes and consequences of the growing caste and class discord, it is important to state a normative caveat. This study is concerned with the conditions for effective government in India and thus has a bias in favor of orderly government. It will soon become clear, if it has not already, that growing caste and class conflicts have contributed to the difficulties of governing. Does that suggest that there is a normative disapproval of the increasing caste and class disputes implicit in this study? The answer is a strong no. Growing caste and class disputes reflect challenges to established patterns of domination and privilege. Judged from a liberal standpoint, such disputes reflect democratization of community power and thus must be deemed essential and desirable elements of a developing political situation in a highly inegalitarian, rigid society. M. N. Srinivas has rightly conceived of these growing conflicts as aspects of India's "democratic revolution."[5] The analytical and practical questions posed by these growing power challenges are how they can be accommodated without closing off democratic spaces, on the one hand, and without sacrificing effective government, on the other hand.

Group conflicts can have many direct and indirect consequences for anyone attempting to establish governmental authority. At the most general level of indirect consequences, power challenges within the various communities destroyed the building blocks of the old Congress party. Of course, some of the old patterns still continue, as illustrated by the case of Belgaun in Karnataka. For the most part, however, the former mode of establishing authority has vanished.

Many contemporary political trends can be understood as attempts to discover new strategies for mobilizing electoral support. Populism and its deinstitutionalizing consequences have already been discussed. Some aspects of the reassertion of religious, ethnic, and communal politics, as well as themes of regional nationalism, can also be understood as attempts to find votes in the context of a fragmented political society. Within Belgaun, for example, we noticed how the continuing reassertion of the linguistic conflict helps keep an ethnic community together as a political bloc, facilitating the electoral victories of a handful of community leaders. The themes of Bengali nationalism helped the CPM put together an unlikely coalition of conflicting classes. The BJP's continuing but reinvigorated interest and Congress's newfound interest in pro-Hindu themes serve similar political functions. The early success of the DMK as a regional nationalist party was not unrelated to the fact that in Madurai and in other parts of Tamil Nadu, the pattern of Congress's success (i.e., influential men mobilizing the many as electoral blocs) was not easy to reproduce; the Brahmans lost their hegemony rather early in that part of India, and there were no second-tier dominant castes of statewide significance.

The widespread reassertion of these "affective" themes in political competition has, in turn, contributed significantly to the growing difficulties of governing India's periphery. Thus, as noted earlier, the linguistic conflict in Belgaun easily degenerated into riots that resulted in deaths. Such other ethnic conflicts as the Gurkha conflict in West Bengal, though not discussed here (see Chapter 10), have followed fairly similar patterns. Conflict resulting from the reassertion of Hindu chauvinism was barely kept within limits in Calcutta. However, the Hindu–Moslem riots in parts of Uttar

---

5 M. N. Srinivas, "Living In and Through a Democratic Revolution," mimeograph, 1986.

Pradesh, Gujarat, and Bombay in the second half of the 1980s were dramatically more serious. Reassertion of regional nationalism has also added to the political difficulties. The DMK and the ADMK may appear relatively tame today, but they definitely were not in the past. And if the DMK continues to push its pro–Sri Lanka Tamil agitation, matters may deteriorate again in the future. The most dramatic example of this issue of reassertion of ethnic and regional nationalism in the 1980s, of course, was that to be discussed in Chapter 12: the Sikh crisis in Punjab.

In addition to these indirect consequences of power challenges in the civil society, there have been many situations in which such challenges have directly resulted in violence. The violence of the upper castes against Harijans that I reported for both Kheda and Guntur provide examples of that. It is important to note that these conflicts still tend to be local. One seldom hears of cases in which murders of members of scheduled castes in Kheda led the scheduled castes in another part of Gujarat to seek revenge. Even if such disputes get out of control in one state, as they do, for example, in Bihar, they seldom spill over from one state to another. The noncumulative nature of direct caste or class conflict remains anathema to the "grass-roots groups" or parties trying to link up the "movements of the oppressed." By the same token, but from a different normative standpoint, the localized nature of such disputes is an important part of the explanation for the modicum of political and social order that remains in India.

Finally, in this discussion of the increasing discord within communities, one must raise the difficult question of what forces are precipitating these group conflicts. Three different answers are possible: (1) Such conflict is driven by economic development, because changes in economic roles reduce the legitimizing significance of old values, thus creating a value disequilibrium that in turn gives rise to anomic behavior. (2) Such conflict is an inevitable product of the spread of capitalism, because capitalist development, while creating new wealth, accentuates material inequities and creates the conditions for more widespread awareness of these class inequities. (3) Such conflict is really political, in two senses: It is motivated by concerns of power and by the desire to gain access to the state's resources; it involves groups that are neither marginal nor class-based, but are essentially political. The empirical materials discussed earlier were not organized in a fashion that could readily enable one to assess the relative merits of these competing claims. The next part of this study is much better organized for that analytical task, and so later we shall return to a fuller discussion of this issue. For now, some general comments can be made on the basis of the empirical materials considered thus far.

The two socioeconomic hypotheses suggesting that the increase in group disputes may reflect the activities of anomic or class grouping find only limited support in the materials discussed thus far. Unless we are willing to characterize all conflict as lawlessness and thus anomic, it must be ad-

Conclusion: the districts

mitted that many of the conflicts we have discussed were purposeful and were undertaken by groups that had fairly definite positions in the society's division of labor. A few instances of conflict analyzed earlier could be classified as anomic conflict. For example, the means–ends rationality of the Naxalite frenzy in the late 1960s in Calcutta would be difficult to trace. Even in that case, however, the appropriate explanation for that behavior is less likely to be anomie in Durkheim's sense and more likely to be the local cultural traditions that romanticize terrorism as heroism. Communal mayhem involving Hindus and Moslems is also susceptible to an anomie-type analysis. Again, however, such conflict is more profitably conceived of as the result of acquired cultural suspicions (which in turn arc intensified by the political elite for their political goals) and thus as a product of acquired values, rather than of their absence.

As far as the Marxist hypothesis is concerned, clearly we have considered some instances of conflict that were beginning to resemble class conflict. If we take a fairly broad view of this hypothesis to include all conflicts over distribution of economic resources, then caste conflicts in Kheda and Guntur over land can also be viewed as instances of a class-type conflict. Even with this broadened definition, however, many of the power challenges and conflicts we considered earlier cannot really be characterized as class conflict.

Many of these growing power challenges are instead best conceived of as political conflicts, the roots of which are located in the rapid politicization of a previously rigid and hierarchical society. Let us quickly review some of the evidence. The challenge to the position of the Patidars in Kheda was launched by the Thakur elite. The Thakurs mobilized the backward castes so as to capture state power by taking advantage of the numerical preponderance of the backward castes under conditions of adult suffrage in a competitive polity. The political conflict between the Patidars and the Kshatriyas over state power is, in turn, one of the most significant conflicts in contemporary Kheda.

The conflict in Guntur between the Kammas and the Reddis has always been over political offices and the access to resources that such offices entail. When one discusses the "emergence" of the backward castes in Guntur, that emergence is political in the sense that the backward castes will vote for leaders who promise to incorporate as many of them as possible into the party and the state bureaucracy and to use the resources controlled by the state, such as access to education, to provide direct benefits.

The linguistic conflict in Belgaun, as well as the conflict involving the Lingayats versus the other backward and lower castes, is similarly deeply political. It is aimed at securing access to state power and is organized by political leaders and political parties. Moreover, for anyone looking for dramatically negative results from bitter political competition, Calcutta during 1967–77 would be a prime example. Contemporary Calcutta is relatively peaceful, but it remains deeply polarized along party lines. Finally, the significant cleavages in Madurai are nearly all political. Labor unions are divided along party lines; caste groups like the Thevars are divided along party lines; ethnic groups like the Saurashtras are also divided along party lines.

Evidence of this nature leads one to propose that a major force driving group conflicts at India's periphery is the possibility of gaining access to state resources via competitive politics. Thus, many of the political conflicts in India are not reducible to more fundamental socioeconomic conflicts. Political conflicts are about politics. They often are instigated by leaders who seek power and position in the state apparatus. The followers also often hope for symbolic or material rewards that the state controls. Finally, conflict in India often is precipitated along political party lines.

Although the motives of the leaders and of the followers involved in these power challenges are political, as are the lines of group conflict, it is important to keep in mind that these processes do not reflect some innate, overpoliticized cultural proclivities of Indians. The rapid and nearly uncontrolled politicization of traditional Indian society has been a product of the political structure of India. The most significant aspect of that political structure obviously is India's democracy. Electoral competition has unleashed many efforts at political mobilization, efforts that ironically may end up threatening that competitive system. It was probably inevitable that introduction of political equality and competitive dem-ocracy into an agrarian society that formerly was highly segmented, rigid, and hierarchical would lead to some rather disquieting consequences. This study is not leading up to an argument against democracy, but it must be noted that political matters have been made considerably more difficult to manage in India because of two specific features of India's democracy: a highly interventionist state and a system of weak parties. How the weakness of the political parties exacerbates the problem of political management has already been discussed. The implications of the extensive state intervention for the politicization of conflict are numerous and will emerge periodically throughout this study. One consequence of an interventionist state, however, has to do with the growing struggle in society over the state's resources.

THE ROLE OF THE STATE'S RESOURCES AND PATRONAGE

Control over India's increasing state resources helped the pre–1967 Congress build and sustain a sprawling patronage network across India. Many people think of that early Congress as little more than a structure of patronage links spreading out from the center of power to the periphery. Although that early Congress clearly was more, the patronage link was one central feature of Congress's success. Twenty-five years later, the strug gles over the resources controlled by the state, and thus over political patronage, have become major bones of contention in the periphery. The state's resources, therefore, no longer constitute the functional resource that at one time helped grease the Congress machine. Competition over state-controlled resources increasingly is what many contemporary political struggles are all about.

One of the major conflicts in Kheda, for example, a conflict that led to rioting and deaths, involved struggles over reservation policies and thus access to educational institutions and jobs that were controlled by the government. Similarly, in Guntur, control over *panchayats* was a central focus of the struggle and recurring conflicts between Congress and the TDP. The Janata government in Belgaun was using the refurbished local governments to build patronage networks and thus to consolidate its hold on power. Not to be outdone, the local Congress began using resources controlled by the national government (such as the "loan *melas*," using the resources of nationalized banks) to buy its own supporters. In urban districts, moreover, fear of losing control over city resources and patronage led to cancellations of local elections for prolonged periods. Although elections were held in Calcutta after a hiatus of more than a decade, MGR maintained his direct control over Madurai's resources until his death in 1987.

Leaving aside the issue of the negative economic consequences of such political uses of public funds, the political causes and consequences of these growing struggles over the state's resources are worth discussing. As to the causes of these growing struggles, the underlying dynamics are not complex. There are finite limits to the resources that any state, even the highly interventionist Indian state, can control. As long as that control was growing, over the first two decades after independence, and those contending for the resources were limited in number, patronage played a positive role in helping Congress build support and authority. Once the *panchayats* had been established, however, and financial allocations to them stipulated, the availability of governmental resources for buying support at the periphery reached a limit. Of course, the resources grew as the budgets grew, but not dramatically. The control of the regional and local governments over access to jobs and educational institutions was considerable, but hardly a match for the growing demands. The growing imbalance between the availability of state-controlled resources and the demands for those resources was at the heart of the growing struggles over patronage resources.

It is important to note in this context that the struggle over scarce resources is qualitatively different when it occurs in the public realm rather than in the private sector. Public resources are viewed as "public goods." Private or partisan use of public resources always tends to provoke hostility from those left out. No one, for example, is likely to be deeply upset by the fact that India's major business houses such as the Tatas or the Birlas do not hire enough workers from the backward castes. The failure of the Gujarat government, by contrast, to employ significant numbers of Kshatriyas in visible positions can quickly become a contentious public issue.

Following this logic, the more control a government has over its people's access to life-chances in a society, especially a society in which alternative routes to a satisfactory livelihood are scarce, the more the everyday struggles of livelihood will take on a political character. Getting one's children admitted to a school, getting a loan to buy an irrigation pump, getting a job on a new public-works project, helping a relative get a job in the municipal government – all of these require the influence of someone in power. Because those in power have been elected and can be voted out, access to government resources quickly becomes a contentious issue of democratic politics. If control over those resources falls into the hands of the "wrong" individuals, groups, or parties, those left out will tend to resent the situation and view those in power as illegitimate. It is small wonder, therefore, that Rajiv Gandhi put the issue of control over local government resources at the heart of the 1989 election campaign and that corruption remains a volatile political issue in contemporary India. Everyone in India now fully understands that those who control the government control public resources and often use them for personal or partisan ends.

Several consequences of this growing contentiousness over the state's resources are noteworthy. The first and most obvious is that many of the everyday struggles for resources are quickly politicized and add to the turmoil in the body politic. A second important consequence is the impact that patronage has on the structure of political parties. When in power, parties can quickly build a network of supporters, creating an illusion for both the rulers and the observers that there exists in the society a systematic base of support. As soon as a party's hold on power, and thus on resources, is threatened, the fragility of its support base quickly becomes evident. When out of power, India's parties have a very difficult time maintaining party structures.

Lastly, the increasing disputes over the state's patronage have indirect but profoundly disturbing long-term effects. Insofar as the state is viewed as little more than a grab bag of resources in the hands of one or another set of partisan politicians, the state tends to become part and parcel of the petty conflicts of everyday life. Thus, the state's capacity to stand above societal conflicts declines. The more frequently the state is exposed as a tool in the hands of one group or another, Kshatriyas or Patidars, Kammas or Reddis, the less likely it is to be thought of as a "rational" agent, capable of guiding socioeconomic development. In sum, whereas Weiner in the 1960s found that patronage helped explain Congress's successes, struggles over patronage now contribute one more ingredient to India's growing authority crisis.

To conclude this part of the study, we are now in a position to answer the two questions with which we began: What has replaced the "Congress system" at the periphery? How do we explain the underlying process of political change? As to the first question, it was clear in all the cases discussed earlier that nothing coherent has replaced the Congress system. As the old system has vanished, India's periphery has come to be characterized by an authority vacuum. Without doubt, there are important regional differences, but if we are looking for one simple answer, it will have to be that nothing has replaced the old system. That organizational and authority vacuum, in turn, explains why India's periphery has become difficult to govern.

What factors help explain India's erosion of authority and the accompanying difficulties of governing its political hinterland? Leaving aside the many necessary qualifications, the growing problem of governability is best understood as a product of uncontrolled politicization within both the state and the civil society. The political institutions that might have been expected to impart some degree of governmental coherence have been weakened. Power struggles at the level of the community have multiplied. The result of those twin processes of change should not come as a surprise to any political observer. Political thinkers as diverse as Lenin and Samuel Huntington have fully understood that mobilization without organization is an invitation to disorder and anarchy. What this discussion of the Indian empirical findings reveals, therefore, is not unique at this level. India's problems of governability can indeed be described in terms of the underlying weakening of institutions and the increase in power struggles. We must, however, go to the next-deeper level of causation to find a fuller explanation. Two questions remain: Why have the institutions been weakened? What has propelled the growing power struggles?

Continuing at a high level of generality, the empirical findings analyzed earlier suggest that neither the weakening of institutions nor the increasing power disputes are primarily products of socioeconomic change. It would be difficult, on the basis of the cases discussed here, to argue that either anomie (and the related irrationality released by economic development) or class conflict (unleashed by spreading capitalism) is the primary motor force behind the growing disorder. Although those factors have made contributions, they have not been decisive. The main forces propelling the disorder are political. Institutions have been weakened by leaders seeking to preserve their power and position in the context of a heterogeneous political society. Community power struggles are similarly aimed at gaining access to the state's resources. The presence of a weak-party democracy has allowed these power struggles to multiply without control. As leaders and communities struggle for shares of the state's power and limited resources, local communities have become difficult to govern.

PART III

Order and breakdown in the states

Introduction: the states

The decline of the Congress party as an organized political force and increasing challenges to the established patterns of caste, class, and ethnic domination are two general trends in Indian politics that made India's democracy much more turbulent in the 1980s than in the 1950s. This broad picture of political change, however, masks considerable regional diversity within India. Some of that diversity was noticeable in the five districts analyzed earlier. The purpose of Part III of this study is to compare selected Indian states, with the aim of answering the following questions: Why do the patterns of breakdown of order differ? What does comparative analysis of these differences tell us about the causes of breakdown?

Three states will be analyzed. Bihar and Gujarat have both experienced considerable violence and instability over the past two decades. Bihar is one of India's poorest states. Gujarat, by contrast, is one of the country's richest. Comparative analysis of Bihar and Gujarat will enable us not only to distinguish between patterns of breakdown but also to delineate the common factors that lie behind those patterns. Both Bihar and Gujarat will then be juxtaposed against West Bengal, a state that appears to have been relatively free of caste, class, and communal violence, major riots, and government instability during the 1980s. The issue of how and why political order has been restored in West Bengal after a decade of chaos (1967–77) is important in its own right. When analyzed comparatively, however, it may also shed light on this study's central questions: What factors have contributed to India's growing problems of governability?

It is important to note at the outset that what follows is not a detailed study of politics in three of India's states. Each of these states is a large and complex political unit. The largest of them, Bihar, with a population of some 85 million, is the second largest state in India, and it is larger than most of the world's countries. A detailed political analysis of these states would have to cover many more themes than are discussed here. What follows is primarily a comparative interpretation of state-level observations and evidence around a single theme, namely, the factors that help explain the relative degrees of order and breakdown.

As in Part II, on the districts, this analysis of governability focuses on the interplay between political parties and on power conflicts among contending social groups. Unlike the study of changing local politics over time, however, a comparison of varying political patterns across states should help refine the causal analysis. Two main themes that will emerge can be stated baldly at the outset. First, the fact that both Bihar and Gujarat have experienced considerable political turmoil helps make a case that economic growth is not the major corrosive force in contemporary Indian politics; rather, the main underlying force is the spread of egalitarian and democratic politics. Second, what emerges clearly when West Bengal is compared with Bihar and Gujarat is that a well-organized, reformist party in power is an important ingredient for reestablishing political order.

8

Breakdown in a "backward" state: Bihar

Bihar is India's poorest state and one of its most violent. Political killings have become so common in Bihar over the past decade that, according to *India Today,* they no longer make news.[1] India's leading newspaper, the *Times of India,* estimated that between 1980 and 1986 there had been more politically motivated murders in Bihar than in Punjab.[2]

Some of that violence has been directed at influencing electoral outcomes. Such violence occurs in bursts and is concentrated in the urban areas. An ongoing, more widespread form of violence is seen in the villages. The primary victims are members of the poor scheduled castes and tribes who may have dared to challenge the age-old patterns of domination. The killers often are members of the landowning castes or their hired thugs, or the police, or some combination of these groups.

As the killings have continued, private caste armies have proliferated. The rise of "warlordism" has generated new types of violence that do not follow the established patterns. Examples of the "forward" castes killing the "backward" or middle castes, of the backward castes killing the forward castes, and of politicized scheduled castes and tribals occasionally killing members of both the forward and the backward castes can all be found. In addition, ordinary criminals, the *dacoits,* have entered the fray, further confusing the picture of who is killing whom and why.

To the extent that patterns are discernible and systematic analysis is possible, the increase in political violence reflects two trends: the decreasing effectiveness of government and the erosion of established patterns of domination in Bihar's predominantly agrarian society. Power conflicts have multiplied, and the state simply does not have the capacity to deal with them. Periodic violence has become a pattern. Several issues are raised by this disintegration of order in one of India's important states: Why did the state become so ineffective? Why did local structures of domination erode

I should like to acknowledge the helpful comments of Harry Blair on an earlier draft of this chapter.
1 June 15, 1985, p. 28.
2 Patna edition, May 30, 1986.

so rapidly? How is the disintegration of the state and social order related to the specific patterns of violence?

It is argued in this chapter that the turmoil in Bihar is best seen as a product of two related but independent struggles: a political struggle for control of the state pitting the forward castes against the backward castes, and a socioeconomic struggle of the landless lower castes against the land-owning forward and backward castes.

The political struggle has been fought with unusual intensity because the forward castes of Bihar, and the Congress party that represented them, had long enjoyed unchallenged supremacy, but the minimal commercial impulse that existed in the state's agriculture had been generated by the backward castes. The backward castes were eventually mobilized politically; they combined their numerical and growing economic strength under the umbrella of the Janata party. That enabled them to challenge the political hold of both the forward groups and the Congress party. The resulting hostility between Congress and Janata has contributed directly to political violence. It has also had an important indirect impact. Intense political struggle has undermined the state's cohesiveness.

The political elite of Bihar were always factionalized, even within the Congress party, and even though they all belonged to forward castes. Growing power conflicts along both caste and party lines added to the political fragmentation. Many elements in the state's bureaucracy, including the police, were dragged into these growing intraelite power conflicts. Politicization of the bureaucrats, in turn, undermined their professionalism. The civil and police bureaucracies in Bihar are now among India's least effective. In sum, the more the state's cohesiveness, legitimacy, and effectiveness have disintegrated, the less the political leaders have been in a position to deal with political and socioeconomic conflicts.

Bihar's growing socioeconomic conflicts are best understood as products of Bihar's relative underdevelopment. Although most segments of Bihar's economy have failed to grow, the numbers of its people have not. The people's levels of consciousness and political organization likewise have not remained stagnant. Political mobilization under conditions of terrible economic scarcity has had perverse effects. Attempts by new power groups to challenge any aspect of the status quo have been perceived as zero-sum games and thus as major challenges to the old order. They have been met by force. The landowning castes, especially the middle castes, have sought to maintain their exactions by attempting to impose something like a "second serfdom," infuriating the lower castes. The state's incapacity to mediate such conflict has further encouraged the formation of private armies. The result has been periodic violence and the vicious cycle of retaliation.

SOCIAL AND POLITICAL BACKGROUND

Bihar is India's poorest state and one of its most densely populated.[3] Nearly 90 percent of the state's people continue to live in villages, making Bihar one of the most rural of India's major states. Agricultural production between 1969 and 1984 grew at an annual compound rate of around 0.5 percent. Because the population continued to grow at nearly 2.0 percent, overall rural incomes declined.[4] That context of severe poverty, population congestion, and rural economic decline must be kept in mind as we attempt to understand the growing political violence in the state.

Bihar is known throughout India for its rigid caste structure. Caste identities are deeply embedded and influence much of Bihar's social, economic, and political life. Table 8.1 gives a rough estimate of the distribution of various castes within Bihar. The sizable minority of "twice-born" castes is noteworthy, in contrast with the situations in many other non-Hindi states in the south, east (e.g., West Bengal), and west (e.g., Gujarat), where the upper castes tend to account for smaller proportions of the whole. The political significance of that fact will be discussed shortly. Although for some purposes the twice-born castes may act cohesively, the cleavages among them are also significant. The Brahmans of Bihar are further subdivided into the Maithali Brahmans, concentrated in the north of the state, and the Kanyakubji Brahmans, concentrated south of the Ganges River. The Bihari Brahmans tend not to marry across these subcastes, let alone across caste boundaries. Although they own considerable amounts of land, given their priestly traditions, they are seldom agriculturalists; in local parlance, "they do not pick up the plow."

The Kayasthas are a very small minority within Bihar and, in strict caste terms, really are not twice-borns. Over a prolonged period, however, they have become the educated elite of the state and have acquired the status of an elite caste. The Bhumihars claim to be Brahmans, of sorts, but are not always recognized as such by other Brahmans. As their name indicates (*bhumi* means "land"), they are closer to land and agriculture. They tend to own fair amounts of land and are definitely an elite caste. Unlike the pure Brahmans, however, Bhumihars cultivate the lands they own and, as a local observer put it, "even make their own cow dung."

The Rajputs are distinguished from other elite castes by virtue of their

---

3 Bihar's per capita income, for example, was under 1,000 rupees in the early 1980s. That contrasts with more than 3,000 rupees for Punjab and nearly 1,800 rupees for India as a whole. According to the 1981 census, only Kerala and West Bengal were more densely populated than Bihar. Bihar's figure of 402 people per square kilometer contrasts with the all-India average of 216. See Government of India, Ministry of Planning, *Statistical Pocket Book, India, 1983* (Delhi: Government of India Press, 1983).

4 For a discussion, see Pradhan H. Prasad, "Agrarian Violence in Bihar," *Economic and Political Weekly,* May 30, 1987, especially p. 851.

Table 8.1. *Estimated distribution of castes in Bihar*

Caste	Percentage	
Twice-born castes:		
Brahmans and Kayasthas	8.5	⎫
Bhumihars and Rajputs	6.5	⎬ 15
Backward castes:		
Yadavs	7	⎫
Koiris	7	⎪
Kurmis	4	⎬ 48
Other backwards	30	⎭
Scheduled castes		14
Scheduled tribes		8
Moslems		15

Source: The figures for scheduled castes, tribes, and Moslems are 1981 census figures and are taken from Government of Bihar, Directorate of Statistics and Evaluation, *Bihar Through Figures, 1981* (Patna: Secretariat Press, 1985), table 18. The aggregate figures for twice-born castes are local estimates derived from interviews, and the aggregate figures for the backward castes are the residuals. Assuming these aggregate estimates to be valid, the further breakdown of both the twice-born castes and the backward castes into specific *jatis* is calculated from a sample of 2,531 households (including 564 twice-born households and 955 backward-caste households) conducted for different purposes. The results of that survey are presented in an unpublished report: P. H. Prasad and G. B. Rodgers, "Class, Caste and Landholding in the Analysis of the Rural Economy," Population and Labour Policies Programme, Working Paper No. 140, World Employment Programme Research (Working Papers), International Labor Office, Geneva, 1983, table 1, p. 12.

martial history. Both the Rajputs and the Bhumihars are considered in local cultural stereotypes to be "tougher" than the "gentle" Brahmans, and thus quicker to resort to force and aggression. The Rajputs also own a lot of land, but they do not "pick up the plow" as often as do, say, the Bhumihars.

The backward castes, taken together, compose the largest group within Bihar. It is, however, an extremely heterogeneous group. The Yadavs, Koiris, and Kurmis are the most significant of the backward castes. Their significance derives in part from their numbers, in part from their control over small and medium landholdings, and in part from their relative standing in the caste hierarchy. Though distinctly below the twice-born castes, the Yadavs, Koiris, and Kurmis are generally the elite among the backward castes. The Yadavs are herdsmen and agriculturalists by tradition. They are followers of Krishna, and on that basis they have often tried without much success, to raise their status in the hierarchy by organized activity.[5]

5 See, for example, M. S. A. Rao, *Social Movements and Social Transformation: A Study of Two Backward Class Movements* (Delhi: Macmillan, 1978), chapter 4.

Table 8.2. *Patterns of landownership in Bihar*

Size of holding (acres)	Number of holdings (%)	Area (%)
0–2.5	72.6	23.2
2.5–10	21.4	36.9
10–25	5.2	26.6
25 and above	0.8	13.2

Source: The data are, more accurately, for holdings operated or cultivated, rather than legally owned, by a family unit and are based on the agricultural census of Bihar (1976–7), as calculated from Government of Bihar, Directorate of Statistics and Evaluation, *Bihar Through Figures, 1981* (Patna: Secretariat Press, 1985), p. 70.

Among the backwards, the Yadavs are politically the most significant. Kurmis have a reputation of being hardworking agriculturalists. Many of them own sizable pieces of land. The Koiris, by contrast, tend to be poorer than either the Yadavs or the Kurmis.

The twice-born castes of Bihar were in the past also the area's main wealthy landowners. Given their numerical significance and their control over land in an agrarian society, they were politically dominant. Francine Frankel has suggested that in the past in Bihar there was a strong correlation among the factors of high status, landownership, and political power.[6] Over the years, that monopoly of privilege has come under considerable challenge. Although the perceived legitimacy of that monopoly probably has been permanently damaged, the twice-born castes continue to control considerable land and power in contemporary Bihar.

Tables 8.2 and 8.3 provide data that help chart the interaction between caste and landownership in contemporary agrarian Bihar. The pattern of ownership according to caste (Table 8.3) is not surprising, especially at the top and bottom ends of the social hierarchy. Most big landowners are members of twice-born castes, and most of the scheduled castes are poor, landless laborers. However, a number of historical trends have made the picture in the middle a lot less neat.

There is evidence to suggest that the *zamindari* abolition (the abolition of large landholdings) of the 1950s may have led to some land transfers from the twice-born castes to their tenants, many of whom were from the

6 See Francine Frankel, "Middle Classes and Castes in Indian Politics: Prospects for Political Accommodation," in Atul Kohli, ed., *India's Democracy* (Princeton University Press, 1988), especially pp. 236–43. The argument in that essay is a summary of a major piece of research that I have heard Frankel present orally, but to which I unfortunately did not have access when this chapter was being written. That work has now been published. See F. Frankel, "Caste, Land and Dominance in Bihar," in F. Frankel and M. S. A. Rao, eds., *Dominance and State Power in Modern India: Decline of a Social Order,* 2 vols. (Oxford University Press, 1989–90).

Table 8.3. *Landownership by caste in Bihar*

	Big landowners (over 10 acres)	Midsize landowners (2.5–10 acres)	Small landowners (0–2.5 acres)	Landless laborers
Twice-born castes	80	231	217	32
Backward castes	18	89	457	392
Scheduled castes	0	7	203	477

Source: Based on a survey of 2,531 households in Bihar conducted in the early 1980s under the auspices of the World Employment Program of the ILO (see the source note to Table 8.1 for details).

backward castes.[7] Two other historical facts increased that tendency. The flight of Moslem *zamindars* from central Bihar to Pakistan at the time of the partition resulted in some backward-caste tenants becoming de facto landowners.[8] After independence, "ceiling legislation" was passed and led to pressure on traditional landowners to sell their excess lands to new groups who could afford to buy, many of whom, especially in central Bihar, belonged to backward castes.[9] One seasoned observer of Bihar estimated that as much as 10 percent of the state's agricultural land may have been transferred from the twice-born *zamindars* to backward castes.[10]

Although some members of the backward castes have gained access to land, many more have not. Growth in population and division of holdings through inheritance have created a trend whereby a large proportion of the backward castes are not middle peasants, but rather small landowners and landless laborers (Table 8.3). Similar pressures have made many among the twice-born castes middle and small landowners rather than big landowners. The common tendency to think of the twice-born castes as big landowners, the backward castes as middle peasants, and the scheduled castes as poor laborers is an oversimplification.

The pace of economic change in Bihar has been very slow. Leaving to the economists the question why that is so, the fact of Bihar's considerable degree of economic stagnation provides important topics for political analysis. Pradhan Prasad probably has done more than anyone else to document

7 See, for example, Thomasson F. Januzzi, *Agrarian Crisis in India: The Case of Bihar* (Austin: University of Texas Press, 1973), passim; Arvind N. Das, *Agrarian Unrest and Socioeconomic Change in Bihar, 1900–1980* (New Delhi: Manohar, 1983), especially chapter 8.
8 Das, *Agrarian Unrest in Bihar,* chapter 8.
9 Pradhan H. Prasad, "Caste and Class in Bihar," *Economic and Political Weekly,* February 1979 (annual number), p. 483.
10 Ibid.

the nature of Bihar's agrarian structure within that context of stagnation.[11] His detailed surveys have highlighted the continuing prevalence of share-cropping, usury, and bonded labor in Bihar's agriculture. In conjunction with the data examined earlier, that points to a central line of cleavage in Bihar's villages: Many of the landless poor from the scheduled castes and other lower castes remain tied to landowning members of the higher castes in a complex web of precommercial relationships. Those relationships probably have their harshest impact on members of the scheduled castes, who suffer from both economic and social deprivation. As will be discussed later, attempts during the 1980s to alter that severe pattern of subjugation repeatedly led to violence that came to be called caste wars.

The dominant position of the twice-born castes in Bihar's politics went largely unchallenged until the mid–1960s. The educated Kayasthas provided Bihar's earliest leaders in India's nationalist movement. Rajendra Prasad, India's first president, typified that group. Kayasthas were soon joined by other members of the twice-born castes. For example, the two Congress leaders who dominated Bihar politics from 1950 to the early 1960s, S. K. Sinha and A. N. Sinha, were a Bhumihar and a Rajput, respectively. The old established upper stratum, even though fairly narrow, was deeply factionalized.[12] In the words of one observer, that intraelite conflict occurred mainly in the form of demands for "circulation of elites."[13]

The effectiveness of caste domination in Bihar is illustrated by the repeated failure of all manner of reform. For example, in spite of the considerable activism of the "middle peasantry" and the Kisan Sabha, the preindependence Congress in Bihar managed to evade carrying out its own "no-rent campaign."[14] After independence, the failure of *zamindari* abolition similarly highlighted the dominant role of the twice-born castes.[15] Finally, even reservation policies did not reach Bihar's political agenda until the 1970s.[16] It is that pattern of fairly effective domination by the twice-born castes over both the Congress party and Bihar politics that provides an essential background to political changes over the past two decades.

11 Among his extensive writings on the subject, see his "Agrarian Violence in Bihar" and the numerous references to his earlier work therein.
12 See, for example, Ramashray Roy, "Politics of Fragmentation: The Case of the Congress Party in Bihar," in Iqbal Narain, ed., *State Politics in India* (Meerut: Meenakshi Prakashan, 1968), pp. 415–30.
13 See Harry Blair, "Structural Change, the Agricultural Sector, and Politics in Bihar," in John Wood., ed., *State Politics in Contemporary India: Continuity or Crisis?* (Boulder, Colo.: Westview Press, 1984), p. 63.
14 See, for example, Arvind N. Das, "Peasants and Peasant Organizations: The Kisan Sabha in Bihar," in Arvind Das, ed., *Agrarian Movements in India* (London: Frank Cass, 1982), especially pp. 71–2.
15 See Januzzi, *Agrarian Crisis in India*, passim.
16 See Frankel, "Middle Classes and Castes in Indian Politics," especially pp. 256–8.

Several important political forces have been eroding that system of domination. When suffrage was introduced at the time of independence, the elite castes were forced to accommodate select members of the numerically significant backward castes.[17] Continuing factionalism among the twice-born elite had a similar consequence. Competing elites sought to incorporate members of the backward castes so as to strengthen their power positions. Thus, in 1957 and 1962 in the Bihar Legislative Assembly, more than 22 percent of the legislators belonged to the backward castes.[18] Although those legislators clearly were co-opted members of the elite, the perceived need to incorporate them at that time foreshadowed their later emergence as an autonomous political force.

INCREASING GOVERNMENTAL INEFFECTIVENESS, 1967–87

The first-generation nationalist leaders like S. K. Sinha and A. N. Sinha passed from the political scene in the early 1960s. That marked the beginning of a new phase in Bihar politics. Whereas factionalism had been rampant within the Bihar Congress even before 1960, some of its more debilitating consequences had been kept within limits by "tall" leaders. The deaths of those leaders left behind a highly factionalized and squabbling Congress elite. The growing presence of backward castes among the state's leaders added another element to the factional struggles, and the issue of forward castes versus backward castes began to heat up.

The 1967 elections reduced Congress's majority in many parts of India, and Bihar was no exception. As Table 8.4 shows, Congress emerged as a minority party. Several opposition parties that claimed to represent the backward castes gained in significance. None of those parties was in a position to form a government by itself; only a coalition government was possible. Bihar thus entered a period of governmental instability. Presidential rule was imposed three times. There were 13 changes in governments in Bihar between 1967 and 1972. The longest that any government lasted was around 300 days, and the shortest was 4 days.[19]

The simple explanation of that governmental instability lies in the inability of the leaders to form a stable coalition. Closer examination reveals two factors that were at work: the disarray within the Congress party, and the growing power conflict between the forward and backward castes.

The organization of the Congress party in Bihar was particularly weak, and the passing of the first-generation leaders exacerbated the problem. The organizational vacuum, combined with the fact that the forward-caste

17 Ibid., pp. 249–50.
18 See Chetkar Jha, "Caste in Bihar Congress Politics", in Narain, ed., *State Politics in India,* p. 583.
19 See R. C. Prasad, "Bihar: Social Polarization and Political Instability," in Narain, ed., *State Politics in India,* especially pp. 62–3.

Table 8.4. *Results of Legislative Assembly elections in Bihar, 1952–85*

Party	1952		1957		1962		1967		1969		1972		1977		1980		1985	
	S[a]	V	S	V	S	V	S	V	S	V	S	V	S	V	S	V	S	V
Congress	240	41.4	210	42.1	185	41.4	128	33.1	118	30.5	168	33.1	57	23.6	169	34.2	196	39.3
Congress (O)[b]	—	—	—	—	—	—	—	—	—	—	30	14.8	—	—	—	1.6	—	—
Socialists[c]	23	18.1	31	16.0	36	19.3	86	24.6	70	19.3	33	16.4	—	—	—	—	—	—
CPI	0	1.1	7	5.2	12	6.2	24	6.9	25	10.1	35	6.9	21	7.0	23	9.1	12	8.9
Jan Sangh[d]	0	1.2	0	1.2	3	2.8	26	10.4	34	15.6	25	11.7	—	—	21	8.4	16	7.5
Swatantra	—	—	—	—	50	17.3	3	2.3	3	0.9	1	0.7	—	—	—	—	—	—
Janata[e]	—	—	—	—	—	—	—	—	—	—	—	—	214	42.7	13	7.4	13	7.2
Lok Dal[f]	—	—	—	—	—	—	—	—	—	—	—	—	—	—	42	15.5	46	14.7
Independents	13	19.6	17	20.8	12	8.4	33	17.9	24	8.3	16	10.8	24	23.7	23	12.0	30	17.9
Others	54	18.6	53	14.7	20	4.6	18	4.7	44	15.3	10	5.6	8	3.0	32	11.8	11	4.6

[a] S, seats won; V, percentage of the total vote.
[b] Formed in 1969 and merged into the Janata party in 1977.
[c] Includes both the Samukyta Socialist Party (SSP) and the Praja Socialist Party (PSP).
[d] Renamed Bhartiya Janata party (BJP) in 1980.
[e] Formed in 1977 by a merger of Jan Sangh, Congress (O), Swatantra, and others; broke apart into a number of parties after 1980.
[f] Formed in 1980 as the Janata party (Socialist), and became the Lok Dal party in 1985.
Source: Computed from the reports of the Election Commission.

elite came from divergent backgrounds and did not readily cooperate, contributed to political fragmentation. The rising significance of the intermediate castes was clearly manifest in the fact that seven of the nine chief ministers during 1967–72 did not belong to the twice-born castes. The emergence of those new elites made it even more difficult to achieve any degree of governmental cohesiveness.

Fierce competitiveness among minority parties added to the political turmoil. Figure 8.1 shows that political activism and riots in Bihar reached a peak in 1967, a year of crucial elections in which Congress declined and opposition parties gained. As coalition governments faltered, midterm elections were called in 1969, and the conduct of politics took on a new ugliness. Most observers of Bihar politics agree that the trend toward the "criminalization of politics," that is, the use of thugs to intimidate and sway political support, can be traced to the 1967–9 period. One analyst close to the situation commented as follows:

> The distinctiveness of the mid-term poll of 1969 [was that] ballot and bullet would now go together; to win the election the ballot must be backed by the bullet. [Fraudulent voting] became a common device to win the poll, acquiesced in by the gun-shy polling officers, and openly resorted to by the local group having superiority in fire arms...it came to be called the device of booth-control: it consists in frightening, through the display and, when necessary, through the actual use of fire-arms, all unfavorable voters and thus succeed in preventing them from coming to the polling station at all for casting their vote. Under the umbrella of superior arms the favorable voters are then encouraged to cast as many votes as they desire.[20]

Unfettered and undisciplined political competition brought criminals into the political system. Not only has that trend continued over time, but many party leaders since the 1970s have received their political education in that milieu of "democracy" by gun.

In 1969, the national split in the Congress party produced some confusing caste and party alignments within Bihar. Indira's Congress was supported by Brahmans and Harijans. Many of the Yadavs, however, sensing new openings within the Congress party, also supported Congress, if only temporarily. The Rajputs, Bhumihars, and Kayasthas, by contrast, moved closer to Congress (O) and later to the Janata coalition.[21] There is a tendency among some analysts to view the early 1970s as a period when the backward castes were rising slowly to challenge the power of the forward castes, culminating in the 1977 victory of the backward castes under the leadership of Karpoori Thakur. Such an analysis is somewhat misleading, because it attempts to reduce what was primarily a political conflict to a socioeconomic conflict. The caste underpinnings of the rival political

20 Ibid., p. 57.
21 Ibid., especially p. 63.

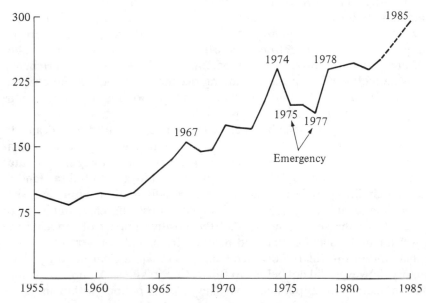

Figure 8.1. Riots in Bihar, 1955–85 (number of riots per million population). *Source:* Data for 1955–82 are from an annual publication: Government of India, Ministry of Home Affairs, *Crime in India* (New Delhi: Government Press). No data for 1983 and 1984 are available. The 1985 figures are rough estimates provided by state officials. For a discussion of what all the government data on "riots" include and why they can be used as indicators of public protest and political violence, see Baldev Raj Nayar, *Violence and Crime in India: A Quantitative Study* (Delhi: Macmillan, 1975), especially p. 17.

forces were quite confusing throughout the 1970s. By contrast, it was easy to identify those who supported Indira Gandhi and those who were against her.

The anti-Indira rebellion reached a crescendo in 1974 under the leadership of Jaiprakash Narain. Figure 8.1 shows the new peak of rioting reached in Bihar in 1974, just before the Emergency. Given the political nature of the anti-Indira rebellion and of the Emergency, a fair amount of Bihar's activism during that period must be understood more as political conflict than as socioeconomic struggle. That the rioting declined sharply during the brief Emergency was not surprising. Because opposition leaders were imprisoned, and open political activity was banned, a decline in activism was to be expected, at least for the moment.

The Emergency brought Jagannath Mishra to power in Bihar. Mishra was a "Sanjay man." Most observers of Bihar would not disagree with the claim that the Mishra period, especially during the Emergency years, turned out to be "a dark period in state administration [when] corruption, favoritism and nepotism reached [their] zenith."[22] Prior to the Emergency, rampant factionalism, governmental instability, politically motivated rioting, and escalating criminalization of politics were the major characteristics of political decay. The trend toward criminalization intensified under Mishra. Moreover, two new developments contributed to the government's growing ineffectiveness: the continuing decline of the police and civil bureaucracies as professional institutions, and the arming of private groups to cope with the increasing agrarian violence.

It is important to remember that by the time Jagannath Mishra came to power in Bihar, the Indian political system had undergone important changes. The most significant for our purposes was that power within states like Bihar had become increasingly a function of loyalty to Indira Gandhi. Indira Gandhi's popularity had soared nationally in 1971; after that, she, or her lieutenant, Sanjay, could pick and choose the chief ministers of states. Over the short run that had the positive impact of reducing the governmental instability that had resulted from coalition governments in Bihar. Indira's popularity enabled Congress to win a clear majority. That victory, however, did not belong to Bihari Congressites. As more and more officeholders were appointed from New Delhi, politics within the state took on a qualitatively new top-down characteristic.

The authority of appointed chief ministers like Mishra within Bihar was, at least initially, fairly shallow. Below Mishra was a highly fragmented political elite and a bureaucracy that did not readily respond to an appointed leader. One of the strategies adopted by Mishra and by nearly all subsequent state leaders was to consolidate control by appointing ministers, civil servants, and police officers who were loyal. Thus, the competence of the ruling elite declined further. Although that was not a new trend, the depth and scope of such political interference, especially in the bureaucracy, increased sharply in the mid–1970s. The long-term consequences of that in Bihar were growing deprofessionalization and ineffectiveness in the state's bureaucratic arm.

I interviewed a number of police officers in Bihar in 1986 in an effort to understand why the force was so ineffective in the face of growing urban and rural political violence. How that occurred and with what consequences are best brought out by some excerpts from those off-the-record interviews:[23]

There is no question that the police are corrupt and demoralized and that they often side with the vested interests. But one has to understand the reasons for this. The professionalism of the police has been totally snuffed out by political interference. At each step, politicians interfere – postings, transfers, execution of duties,

---

22 See the analysis in *Hindusthan Times,* August 15, 1986, p. 12.
23 The excerpts quoted here are from interviews with police officers of the rank of superintendent of police or higher. These interviews were conducted in Patna in August 1986.

arrests and releases.... Moreover, most of us have lost respect for politicians. Come election, they will often ask for police support for booth capturing or for this and that. We thus know that many of them are not genuinely elected. This undermines the legitimacy of power. The arrangement between the police and the politicians thus becomes one of mutual convenience. Professionalism is snuffed out. Personalism pervades.

The issue of caste had also become central to police appointments. In the words of one officer:

For example, take the area of Jehanabad [a troubled agrarian area]. Every appointment in that area has to be cleared with politicians. Those appointed have to be more or less the men accepted by the Bhumihars [the local dominant caste]. Officers have to be "their men." That is the only way things are workable in that area.

As to when that type of political interference really became the norm:

This probably happened in the 1970s – around the Emergency. Mrs. Gandhi had initially found that people would stand up to her. But since then loyalty has been at premium. Jagannath Mishra introduced this culture to Bihar. You had to be loyal to him. This was the basic criteria. Those who did not fall in line were made to or lost out.

The information in such interviews suggests that appointed chief ministers like Jagannath Mishra and his successors had repeatedly interfered in the police service to consolidate their personal control. That undermined the professionalism of the force. What started out as a strategy to enhance political control had unanticipated and unfortunate consequences: When leaders now need to call on the police arm of the state, that arm is relatively limp.

A similar process undermined the efficacy of the state civil service. As one senior IAS officer explained:

Turnover of personnel is everywhere. This is especially true in the districts and in the politically sensitive ministries. Sensitive ministries are those that either control a lot of resources or employment [e.g., departments of personnel, home, finance, agriculture, irrigation, power, and construction]. I used to be transferred every six to eight months.... In the last ten years even the IAS in Bihar is not beyond suspicion for corruption. This is because integrity and competence does not count. What matters is who you are close to. If you are close to powerful ministers [you can get choice positions]. The threat of transfers is very serious.... The politico-administrative culture is such that honest and competent people find it hard to survive.

As to how that deprofessionalization had affected the functioning of the government and the pursuit of policies:

Well, is there any policy? I still do not understand what the 20 point programme is. Now they have again changed it. It does not make any difference. What goes on is, get into power, amass wealth, keep talking about welfare of the poor, and figure out how to win the next election. No one thinks of policy.[24]

Such cynicism at the highest levels of the government only confirms what casual observers of Bihar politics already understand. Politics in Bihar means mainly a concern with winning elections and office as a source of personal aggrandizement. The concept of politics as a constructive programmatic use of power is simply missing.

The criminalization of politics intensified during Mishra's reign. As one local politician commented, "the quality of elections has deteriorated terribly since 1977. . . . There is never an election anymore without murders. [Before 1977] criminal elements used to help politicians. Sooner or later they realized, why not run ourselves."[25] Individuals like Mishra, coming from a background in the infamous Dhanbad "mafia," and with links to Sanjay's "militant" Youth Congress, typified that new genre of politicians. No precise information is available on how many criminals-turned-politicians actually entered the political arena. There is little doubt, however, that their numbers are by now considerable. The *Times of India* reported that "many MLAs strike terror in the hearts of their constituencies." That story went on to report what "most responsible politicians admit in private," namely, "that the thought that criminal politicians may actually come to control a majority in the assembly can no longer be dismissed."[26]

Finally, it is important to note that the arming of private groups began at some time in the mid–1970s, probably with government approval. The issues of why and how peasant rebellions have intensified over the past decade will be discussed in the next section. Suffice it to note here that as such rebellions grew, the government found its ability to enforce law and order quite limited. That limitation was a function of two factors. First, as has been noted, the police were becoming increasingly ineffective. In addition, one of the results of the state's low level of economic development was underdevelopment of transportation and communication networks. Police seldom could reach the scenes of disturbances quickly, even when they occurred close to the state capital.

In order to cope with peasant rebellions, therefore, the government apparently encouraged the arming of private groups. The evidence on that point is sketchy, but persuasive. For example, the following announcement made by a senior police officer in 1975 was reported in a local paper:

The Bihar government has decided to arm all able-bodied persons in Bhojpur and Patna districts for self-defense to face the extremist menace, who have recently

24 Interview with Arun Prasad, member of the Bihar Board of Revenue, Patna, August 23, 1986.
25 Interview with Ram Avtar Shastry, member of the Bihar Legislative Assembly (member of the CPI and a former member of Parliament), Patna, August 24, 1986.
26 Patna edition, July 14, 1986.

launched an armed struggle. . . . District magistrates of both the districts have been asked to visit the affected villages and issue licences for firearms on the spot to those who were able to possess them. . . . The decision was taken following a spurt in the armed attacks on landowners by the extremists in these villages. The trouble was mostly of agrarian nature.[27]

A civil-rights group conducting an investigation of agrarian violence independently reported the following:

One of the most striking aspects of central Bihar is the brazenness with which the police and the administration give support to illegal and violent activities of the *senas* [private armies]. In fact this is a continuation of the policy adopted during the seventies in the counter-insurgency operations against the Naxalites in Bhojpur and other areas, when a large number of firearms were issued to landlords and even centers for training them were set up.[28]

Unable to deal effectively with peasant insurgency, in the mid-1970s the Bihar government abandoned a quintessential task of any state: to maintain a monopoly over the use of coercion. Instead, the Bihar government definitely looked the other way as private armed groups were formed, and it may even have encouraged that practice.

The end of the national Emergency brought the Janata party to power in Bihar. Karpoori Thakur, an associate of Charan Singh, and popularly identified as a leader of the backward castes in Bihar, emerged as the state's chief minister. Both politically and socially, Karpoori Thakur symbolized a new phase in Bihar's politics: the simultaneous consolidation of an alternative to Congress and the political rise of the backward castes. The Janata reign in Bihar in the 1970s proved to be short-lived; Congress and the representatives of the forward castes came back to power in 1980. The next question is how we should interpret the brief Janata interregnum in Bihar.

The basic facts of that period are well known and require only brief reiteration.[29] Karpoori Thakur headed a coalition of forces that first sought to capture power in the late 1960s. That same coalition then backed Jaiprakash Narain's "total revolution" against Indira Gandhi in 1974. That group finally came together politically under an umbrella party that was hurriedly formed after the Emergency: the Janata party. Once in power, Karpoori Thakur sought to consolidate his power base among the backward castes by promising them reservations (quotas) in both government jobs and educational institutions. Attempts to implement that policy shift in

27 Reported in the *Indian Nation,* May 28, 1975, and cited in Kalyan Mukerjee and R. S. Yadav, "For Reasons of State: Oppression and Resistance, a Study of Bhojpur Peasantry," in Das, ed., *Agrarian Movements in India,* p. 128.
28 People's Union for Democratic Rights, *Behind the Killings in Bihar* (New Delhi: PUDR, 1986), p. 29.
29 For details, see Harry Blair, "Rising Kulaks and Backward Classes in Bihar: Social Change in the late 1970s," *Economic and Political Weekly,* January 12, 1980, pp. 64–74.

1978 led to a considerable outburst of opposition from the forward castes. Bihar during that period again experienced prolonged agitations and riots against the government. Figure 8.1 shows that rioting in 1978 climbed back to the same high level as in 1974, the year before the Emergency was proclaimed. As a result, Karpoori Thakur's government was forced to resign under pressure. A Janata government under a new leader continued to rule until 1980, but it did not pursue the policy of reservations for backward castes. Eventually, shifts in the national political situation led to an electoral defeat of the Janata party and to the reemergence of Congress in 1980.

It is tempting to see in that series of events the makings of a major socioeconomic struggle. Analysts with Marxist sympathies have indeed tended to describe a growing struggle between the "new capitalist *kulaks*" of the backward castes and the old "feudal order," dominated by the twice-borns.[30] Prominent non-Marxist scholars like Francine Frankel also have seen the "backward classes movement" led by Karpoori Thakur as "the organization of the poor in a double assault on the caste system and the class structure."[31] That approach overemphasizes socioeconomic variables at the expense of political factors.

A number of pieces of evidence indeed support a socially generated explanation of the late-1970s political conflict in Bihar. First, there can be little doubt that patterns of social ascendancy and political dominance have tended to coincide in modern Bihar. Second, the minimal economic dynamism that exists in Bihar's agriculture has been generated primarily by middle peasants concentrated in central Bihar.[32] Many in the old ruling classes, the landowning forward castes, are thus being left behind. The proposition that these middle peasants, the so-called *kulaks,* have sought a political role commensurate with their improved economic standing is not unreasonable. Finally, because of conditions of relative economic stagnation, the forward castes consider it imperative that they continue to have access to the state's patronage resources. State-controlled jobs and educational opportunities provide limited but crucial economic outlets for the progeny of an economically lethargic ruling class. As access to such opportunities was threatened by the proposed reservation policies, the new ruling groups came to be perceived as direct economic threats, and that led to the rage and violence that toppled the Thakur government.

Several other pieces of evidence, however, tend to contradict the interpretation of the political discord of the late 1970s as a conflict between the forward and backward castes. First, Table 8.3 shows that as many as 80 percent of the forward castes were not big landowners, but rather middle

30 See, for example, Prasad, "Caste and Class in Bihar."
31 See Frankel, "Middle Classes and Castes in Indian Politics," p. 257.
32 See Prasad, "Caste and Class in Bihar."

and small landowners. There is little evidence to indicate that the "objective" economic interests of those forward-caste members were sharply distinguishable from the interests of the backward-caste peasants in the middle and small ranks. Second, caste and party alignments during the late 1970s were not clear-cut. Frankel noted that some of the twice-born castes, the Bhumihars and the Rajputs, tended to support not Congress but rather the Janata party in the post-1977 period.[33] A Yadav leader I interviewed insisted that a significant minority of Yadavs had always supported Congress, even after the Emergency.[34] Thus, the caste, class, and party cleavages were far from being neat and easily identifiable during the political conflict of the late 1970s.

The way in which the political process unfolded during those years also raises doubt that the Janata interregnum should be seen as an example of emerging caste-class conflict. The rise to power of Karpoori Thakur had little to do with his mobilization of people around a pro–backward caste political agenda. On the contrary, in the words of another astute student of Bihar politics:

It is important to note that Thakur did not win the 1977 poll solely or even mostly on the basis of his Backward leadership; rather it was the same anti-Congress sentiment that swept the Indira Gandhi government out of New Delhi. But the fact of getting elected largely on the basis of one issue did not prevent him from interpreting his victory as a mandate to pursue an entirely unrelated policy initiative.[35]

That initiative involved a subsequent attempt to consolidate his power base among the backward castes. The fact that Karpoori Thakur loaded his ministry with members of the backward castes and sought to implement a new reservation policy must be viewed as a political ploy to create a power bloc where none had existed. Power came to Thakur first, and the attempt to mobilize and unify the backward castes followed. Although it might be argued that that is somewhat of an exaggeration, the situation definitely was not the other way around.

The opposition that emerged also had a highly political quality. As Thakur himself explained, "the agitations were definitely politically organized. Newspapers helped them [the agitation leaders] with publicity. There was a whispering campaign...including lies. The crowds were mainly students. Political trouble was mainly all urban....Rural masses were not involved."[36] It was that urban concentration of the opposition that gave away the fact that the cleavages in the conflict were created

33 Frankel, "Middle Classes and Castes in Indian Politics," p. 256.
34 Interview with Ram Lakhan Singh Yadav, Patna, August 26, 1986.
35 See Harry Blair, "Structural Change, the Agricultural Sector, and Politics in Bihar," note 51, p. 77.
36 Interview with Karpoori Thakur, Patna, August 23, 1986. The original interview was in Hindi. The translation is my own.

mainly by leaders and parties, rather than by mobilized socioeconomic groups. With 90 percent of the state's population living in villages, a set of civil disorders limited to the cities could hardly be seen as a major struggle between the contending caste groups in the state.

Finally, the 1980 elections, the elections that followed the turmoil over reservation policies in the 1970s, confirmed that the political support of the backward castes was quite fragmented. In spite of the fact that the backward castes constituted nearly 50 percent of Bihar's population, Karpoori Thakur's Lok Dal party received no more than 16 percent of the popular vote (Table 8.4). The rise and decline of the electoral fortunes of Congress's opposition in Bihar were largely functions of party alignments and realignments and had little to do with a supposed polarization between the forward and backward castes.

Faced with such evidence, one might be tempted to fall back on a modified position, namely, that the conflict of the late 1970s in Bihar was symptomatic of a challenge not to all the forward castes but specifically to the hegemony of the Brahman ideology and the social order created and sustained by the Brahman elite. Even that, however, will not do. We shall see in the next chapter that in Gujarat, as in Bihar, a major struggle over reservation policies broke out in the 1980s. The conflict, however, did not involve the Brahmans; the struggle pitted a somewhat lower but prosperous caste, the Patidars, against the backward Kshatriyas.

The late-1970s civil disorder in Bihar was a quintessential political conflict. Although it had certain important socioeconomic underpinnings, the evidence suggests that the lines of cleavage involved contending political groups with fairly diverse social support. The rhetoric of the conflict, backwards versus forwards, was aimed at creating caste-based political blocs out of a heterogeneous social base. Even the main political ploy, the reservation policies, would not have hurt or benefited more than a few thousand individuals in a state of some 80 million people. That was hardly the stuff of which major social struggles are made.

The contending political forces throughout the period were pro- or anti-Congress. That was the main line of cleavage in the pre-Emergency mobilization. It continued to be so in the post-1977 battle between the Janata party and Congress, and it probably was so in the late-1989 elections to the Lok Sabha. In a candid moment, Karpoori Thakur admitted that although he differed with Charan Singh on many issues, "we both believe in wanting to defeat the Congress."[37] The main enemy was not the forward castes but the Congress party.

Both Congress and the Janata party in Bihar were deeply fragmented political parties. Going into the 1977 elections, one analyst described the Bihar Congress as in organizational "shambles," and the Janata party as

37 Ibid.

incapable of working "as one cohesive unit."[38] Short-run political gains defined the horizons of both those parties. By late 1977, moreover, rioting as a way of accomplishing political ends was already becoming the norm in Bihar. Congress leaders like Jagannath Mishra had had considerable experience in unleashing semiorganized militancy against their political opponents. The prospect that Karpoori Thakur could utilize his power position to create a political bloc of the backward castes must have seemed quite threatening to the Bihari Congress elite. Students from upper-caste backgrounds were likely to be the main losers in the new policy shift. Thus, the threatened Congress elite allied themselves with the city-based forward castes, especially students, to mount an opposition movement that simultaneously put an end to reservation policies and toppled Thakur from power.

The return of Indira Gandhi to power in 1980 brought Jagannath Mishra back to power in Bihar. One senior civil servant commented during an interview that "every new government in Bihar makes its predecessor look like angels."[39] That was mainly because governmental ineffectiveness and agrarian violence were continuing to grow in Bihar. There was no major policy initiative undertaken by Mishra during his three-year rule, or undertaken by Bindeshwari Dubey between 1985 and 1988, that could have reversed the growing trend toward governmental ineffectiveness. As Figure 8.1 shows, political violence in the 1980s continued to escalate. Some examples of recent political developments will further document the continuing decay of political and governmental institutions in Bihar.

Both the Lok Sabha elections in 1984 and the Legislative Assembly elections in early 1985 were considerably more violent than those in 1977. For example, violent incidents (including assaults, bomb explosions, booth capturing, civilian shootings, and police shootings) increased from some 260 in 1977 to 617 in 1984. Moreover, nearly 100 people were killed in the 1985 election, compared with 34 in 1977, including four candidates running for office.[40] The root cause of that violence was the increasing involvement of criminals and thugs in the political process. As a senior civil servant noted, "elections have become very violent. Musclemen are central [to this process]. They are not marginal anymore."[41] The issue of the linkage between crime and politics has already been discussed. It is both a cause and an effect of the growing deinstitutionalization of political parties.

Many other indicators could be cited to illustrate the growing crisis of governability. Factional strife within the ruling party continued to make headlines.[42] Between 1988 and 1989, Bihar had four new chief ministers,

38 See Ramashray Roy, *Battle Before Ballot* (Delhi: Ritu Publishers, 1983), pp. 22, 25.
39 Interview with R. Srinivasan, Patna, August 28, 1986.
40 See *Times of India* (Patna), July 14, 1986.
41 Interview with Arun Prasad (see footnote 24).
42 See, for example, the discussion of the takeover of the L. N. Mishra Institute in the *Times*

with Jagannath Mishra reemerging in late 1989 when Congress (I) finally suffered a humiliating defeat in the Lok Sabha elections. Throughout the 1980s, the Congress government was unable to act with even a modest degree of cohesiveness. Much of the leadership's attention was focused on political intrigue. Solving the state's pressing economic and political problems was far from anyone's mind. Within the first 15 months of his rule, Dubey transferred nearly 300 IAS officers within the state. That level of turnover of personnel was unprecedented even for Bihar.[43] The traditional mechanisms for expressing and accommodating political discontent had ceased to function. For example, the government's poor handling of the Arawal massacre in 1986 led to considerable controversy, and civil-rights groups organized a large protest demonstration. Scared of even a peaceful demonstration, the government unleashed a police assault on the demonstrators and ended up arresting 30,000 people in one day.[44]

Finally, the most troublesome political development throughout the 1980s was the proliferation of private armies. As the government's effectiveness had declined, various socioeconomic groups had taken law and order into their own hands. Four to six private armies have been operating in Bihar's countryside at various times over a period of several years. Those armies, or *senas,* generally are identified with specific castes. The Lorik Sena belongs to the Yadavs, the Bhoomi Sena to the Kurmis, the Brahmrishi Sena to the Bhumihars, the Kunwar Sena to the Rajputs, and the Lal Sena (or Red Army) to the landless laborers.[45]

Details concerning the operation of the *senas* are not easily available. Senior police officers in Patna repeatedly warned that the districts of central Bihar, where these armies mainly operate, are not safe. The government's writ simply does not extend to those areas. Any one nosing around, I was warned, could easily get hurt. From the information that I could gather during interviews, these *senas* are not all alike. The Lal Sena is reputed to be the most disciplined. A government report in 1982 suggested that nearly 200 villages in central Bihar, about 10 percent of the state's administrative blocs, were under the influence of one "Naxalite" group or another and that in those areas, various armed leftist political groups were running a "parallel government."[46]

of India (Patna), April 24, 1986, and the discussion of the continuing caste-based factionalism within Congress in *India Today,* July 15, 1987.

43 See *Times of India* (Patna), August 23, 1986.

44 See *Times of India* (Patna), August 22, 1986, for a report, and see August 23, 1986, for a biting editorial on "police terror."

45 For a discussion of these armies, see *Sunday,* December 15–21, 1985, especially p. 14; *Times of India* (Patna), May 9, 1986; People's Union for Democratic Rights, *Killings in Bihar,* pp. 45–6.

46 Government of Bihar, "Notes on Extremist Activities – Affected Areas," mimeograph, May 1982.

The armies of the landowning castes that have been organized to deal with this "Naxalite menace" vary from ad hoc gangs of hired thugs to uniformed private armies of 1,000–1,500 men. As one knowledgeable local observer explained, "these [*senas*] roam around openly in armed gangs in the villages. They are mainly informal organizations. Money is provided by the rich [landowning groups]. Arms are bought. Toughs are hired, more or less permanently. In some places they even have uniforms."[47] In other places, the private armies have become closely linked with ordinary criminals, the local *dacoits*. The toughs who are hired for these armies often are mercenaries who double as part-time criminals.[48]

The dynamics of these private armies are best understood within the context of the escalating agrarian conflict in Bihar. For this analysis, the existence of these armies dramatically highlights a government that does not work. If Bihar were an independent country, such conditions of breakdown would by now have precipitated a military coup or external intervention, or some combination of the two.

There is widespread evidence that both the political elite and the police quietly condone the operation of these private armies.[49] Why, one may ask, has the state turned a blind eye to such a development? The need of the haves to protect their threatened socioeconomic interests is a fairly obvious point. What is also important to note here is that leaders are worried about their electoral prospects. They are hesitant to unleash systematic state repression against the vast majority, the rural poor. As challenges by the poor have mounted in the countryside, many in the state apparatus have chosen simply to let a decentralized pattern of private responses deal with the problem. It is doubtful that a great deal of thought went into that response. It is more likely that it emerged by trial and error as the easiest way out.

In sum, the growing ineffectiveness of political institutions in Bihar has contributed both directly and indirectly to the increase in political violence. The direct contribution is dramatically highlighted by the fact that the years of peak political violence, 1967, 1974, and 1978 (Figure 8.1), all were years of virulent political conflict between Congress and a motley opposition. The intensity of that conflict in Bihar was unusual for a number of reasons: (1) long traditions of elite factionalism, (2) unusually weak political parties, (3) agitations and mass mobilization as established modes of conducting the business of politics, (4) extreme economic backwardness that made

47 Interview with Ram Avtar Shastry (see footnote 25).
48 See People's Union for Democratic Rights, *Killings in Bihar*, pp. 21–31.
49 See, for example, *Times of India* (Patna), August 24, 1986. Also see the discussion in Prasad, "Agrarian Violence in Bihar," especially p. 852; Praveen K. Chaudhry, "Agrarian Unrest in Bihar: A Case Study of Patna District, 1960–84," *Economic and Political Weekly,* January 2, 1988, p. 54; People's Union for Democratic Rights, *Killings in Bihar,* pp. 45–6.

continued access to the state's resources a highly valued good, and (5) the long, unchallenged pattern of caste domination that made the possibility of mobilizing around caste appeals both attractive and dangerous.

Governmental ineffectiveness has also contributed indirectly to the growing violence. Policy ineffectiveness, for example, is at the root of agrarian stagnation. Prolonged political interference with the police forces and tacit political support for the growth of private armies have made the government marginal in regard to agrarian conflicts. These conditions of economic stagnation and disintegration of the government's coercive arm, in turn, provide the broad context within which new patterns of class and caste conflict are emerging.

AGRARIAN STRUGGLES

Agrarian struggles have a long history in Bihar. The conflicts in the first half of this century were qualitatively different from the more recent ones. Those earlier movements often involved "tenants," with access to considerable land, against the *zamindari* system.[50] For nearly a quarter of a century after independence, however, there was a lull. The new movements that have emerged since the mid-1970s often have featured the landless scheduled castes against various landowning castes. At stake in these conflicts are mainly economic issues of land and wages. Such noneconomic issues as violation of lower-caste women by the higher castes have also been significant.

The dimensions of the agrarian conflict are difficult to judge precisely. Most local observers tend to agree on the following: These struggles represent a major new trend in the countryside. They are not marginal phenomena, and, most important, they are likely to escalate. The *New York Times*, for example, estimated that some 3,300 people were killed in 1986 in these and related conflicts in Bihar and that this number was "certainly an understimate."[51] A well-known agricultural economist in Bihar reported another incredible figure: Nearly a quarter of the available land in Bihar was not cultivated in 1985–6 because of agrarian conflicts.[52] It is no wonder, therefore, that even casual observers of Indian politics have come to associate Bihar with periodic murders of members of the scheduled castes.

An analysis of these caste wars, as they are called, is best developed inductively. A study of some of the better-known incidents that have been reported and investigated has revealed four basic patterns of conflict.[53] The

50 See Das, *Agrarian Unrest in Bihar,* passim.
51 April 27, 1987, p. A6.
52 See Prasad, "Agrarian Violence in Bihar," p. 852.
53 In addition to local interviews and news reports, especially from the *Economic and Political Weekly,* I consulted the following sources: People's Union for Democratic Rights, *Killings in Bihar;* a survey of "caste violence" in Bihar in *India Today,* December 31, 1986, pp. 40–

first and most important pattern involves direct fighting between the land-owning castes and the landless scheduled castes over socioeconomic issues. This frequently results in the deaths of members of the lower castes, and occasionally a member of the higher caste will be killed. Let us label these as incidents of *caste-class conflict.* A second, related pattern is characterized by murders of members of the lower castes by the police. These are often called incidents of *police brutality.* A third and less frequent pattern involves almost random violence and killings between two or more castes. These are cases of *anarchic conflict.* Finally, there is a fourth pattern of increasing conflict that does not concern us directly in this study: looting and plundering by *dacoits,* the plain *criminal violence* that always increases when law and order disintegrate. Specific examples of the first three types of conflict will help set the stage for development of an adequate explanation of these new agrarian trends in Bihar.

Examples of caste-class conflict

Incidents following the end of the Emergency in 1977:

In Buxara village in Kargahar block of Rohtas district, where the labourers had organised an indefinite strike to secure the revised minimum wages, the landlords ransacked the harijan ghetto on 27 March, shot three labourers and burnt them alive in a haystack. In Gopalpur, where also strikes had been called by the labourers, the landlords on 11 June attacked the harijan ghetto with 50 armed men and wounded some half a dozen workers, humiliated their women, and looted a shop. On 19 June in Pathadda in Bhaglapur district, 36 men and women from the la-bourers' houses were taken by the landlords and incarcerated in the village school building and brutally assaulted. The cause of feudal anger was the resistance of the labourers to working on old wages and their refusal to pay debts that had been redeemed under the 20-point programme. In Dharampura, four share-croppers were massacred by the landlords for demanding occupancy rights on 20 October.

All these outrages . . . were committed by big landlords, who hold near-absolute economic, social and political power in their respective areas. In Belchhi it was Mahavir Mahato, in Gopalpur it was Birendra Singh; the landlords of Dharampura and Chhaundadano were led by mahanths who were the biggest landlords of their respective areas. In each case the big landlord concerned is virtually the "raja" of his area. He possesses one-fourth or more of the total land of his village. He lives like an aristocrat in a large brick house. He employs the largest number of both slave and free labourers for domestic and farm work. He maintains a small private army equipped with guns, spears, lathis and other weapons and himself owns a licensed gun. Often his slave labourers serve as his soldiers but he may also keep, as he does in Chhaundadano, Belchhi and Dharampura, a permanent contingent of regulars, giving them land for livelihood and cash for liquor. . . . The big landlord-raja in all the instances belonged to the caste of the dominant section of landlords in the village. To the social, economic and military power of the raja, "democracy"

3; another survey in *Sunday,* December 15–21, 1985, pp. 10–15; and a "report" by Arun Sinha, "Class War, Not 'Atrocities Against Harijans'," in Das, ed., *Agrarian Movements in India,* pp. 148–52.

had added political power. He has captured the instruments of local government. He now commands the panchayat and thus the various executive bodies at the block level. He has the services of an obsequious police force in the local thana. Mahavir Mahato of Belchhi had nothing to fear from the police. The mahanth of Chhaundadano had the police at his beck and call. When the labourers agitated for minimum wages, the police daroga would report to his bosses that "Naxalites" had sneaked into the village.[54]

Recent incidents:

[Bihar] has notched up one deadly milestone after another with sickening regularity. Among the major [recent] massacres have been Parasbigha [February 2, 1980; 11 killed], Pipra [February 25, 1980; 14 killed], Gaini [June 26, 1982; 6 killed], Kaithibigha [May 1, 1985; 10 killed], Arwal [April 19, 1986; 23 killed], Kansara [July 8, 1986; 11 killed], and Darmia [October 10, 1986; 11 killed]. Roughly one caste-cum-class carnage has been perpetrated here every four months over the last nine years. [Much] of the tension in the area can be directly traced to the juxtaposition of . . . caste-based senas [and the various left organizations]. [Much horror] has accompanied every killing. In Belchi, the Kurmi raiders prepared a funeral pyre, lined up the Harijans, shot them and tossed the bodies in, one by one. In Pipra, raiders surrounded the Harijan hamlet, set fire to their houses and when men, women and children fled outside, it was only to be tossed right back into the inferno. Parasbigha was virtually a repeat. . . . In Jaitipur village [Nalanda district], men of the Lorik Sena had captured three extremists, brutally hacked their bodies into pieces and thrown them into a nearby river. . . . Mere killings have never been enough in Bihar . . . power [of the killers] must be demonstrated. . . . The root cause of almost all rural conflicts of course is land.[55]

Conflict over violations of individual and community rights:

1. The "Naxalite" movement took root in the Sahar block of the old Shahabad district (divided into Bhojpur and Rhotas districts in 1973–4) in the early 1970s. Among the numerous causes of local anger was the local practice that "poor Harijan women who slept with Bhumihar scions got an extra bundle of grain to carry home. One of the reasons for growing unrest was the fact that the Bhumihar landlords of Chauri [a village in which considerable violence followed] were coercing the lower-caste female labourers to do harvesting work at nights for obvious sexual benefits."[56]

2. In May 1981, the wife of Ram Pravesh Thakur (a barber) was raped by Tuntun Singh and co-villagers of Raj Kishori Singh of Masaurhi block (Patna district). The landlords managed to hush up the matter, and police also refused to record the case. In retaliation, the landless peasants (mostly of scheduled-caste backgrounds) decided not to work at the farm plot of Tuntun Singh, which remained barren throughout the year.[57]

3. It was a common local practice in Bihar that if one owed money to a landlord, the landlord in exchange would ask for one's "clean daughter" at nights. That sort

54 From Sinha, "Class War, Not 'Atrocities Against Harijans,'" pp. 150–1.
55 Excerpts from a report in *India Today*, December 31, 1986, pp. 40–1.
56 Reported in Mukerjee and Yadav, "For Reasons of State," pp. 121–3.
57 Reported in Chaudhry, "Agrarian Unrest in Bihar," p. 52.

of thing is now "being resisted." Thus, the issues of agrarian conflict are "status, dignity and economic."[58]

Examples of police brutality

Early in the morning of 21 November, 1985, the police, tipped off by a landlord from Kacharia village, Sravan Pandit, attacked the *beldars* [Harijans working as manual laborers] of Ganga Bigha, killing three. About 35 armed policemen looted and destroyed almost everything in their way, beat the men and children with sticks and *khantias* [iron rods sharpened at one end] and raped the women. The villagers' crimes: one of them had the courage to quarrel with Pandit over his agricultural wage; the landlord had earlier lodged a police complaint against some of the villagers for allegedly threatening him; and a number of *beldars* had wanted to cut the crop on a 3.75 bigha government plot across the road near their village, which another landlord of the area was claiming as his own. The police, of course, settled the matter in its own way: 40 persons were rounded up and, as the villagers have alleged, made to pose with rifles and booked under several sections of the Arms Act and the IPC [Indian Police Code].[59]

In another case, 23 people were killed on April 19, 1986, when police fired on a group of some 500 people in the small town of Arwal, Jehanabad subdivision, Gaya district. The group had gathered for a political meeting organized by the Mazdoor Kisan Sangram Samiti (MKSS), an organization of poor and landless peasants in the area. The meeting was a product of a prolonged conflict over a small piece of land – about a quarter of an acre. Over the years, the conflict over that land had pitted some nine poor, backward-caste families against an engineer in the Irrigation Department who was himself a Harijan, but was quite well-off and owned this piece of land. This simmering conflict eventually led to the arrest of members of two of the nine families who decided to lay claim to the land. At that point, the MKSS got involved. Meetings were held demanding lawful transfer of the land to the nine families and the release of those arrested. The meeting of April 19 was a product of that prolonged conflict. A civil-rights group that investigated the police firings on that meeting concluded that "the massacre at Arwal was a barbarous and unprovoked firing at a peaceful meeting." To understand why the Arwal incident happened, the report went on to note that "we have to understand why people here are organizing themselves on questions of economic justice and human dignity and the response to this by the local elites and the state." The civil-rights group also gathered evidence to suggest that the attack may have been a "preplanned mass murder" as a way of thwarting the organizational efforts of local left groups.[60]

58 Excerpts from a discussion with P. K. Krupakaran, special correspondent, *Indian Express,* Patna, August 21, 1986.
59 Reported in *Sunday,* December 15–21, 1985, p. 10.
60 See People's Union for Democratic Rights, *Killings in Bihar,* pp. 32–49. The Arwal incident was reported and discussed widely elsewhere. See, for example, *Times of India* (Patna), April 20–7, 1986, and the editorial on July 12, 1986; *Decan Herald,* April 25, 1986; *India Today,* May 31, 1986; *Economic and Political Weekly,* May 31, 1986.

Example of anarchic conflict

Caste rivalry between Yadavs and Rajputs led to the brutal murder of 42 Rajputs in May 1987 in Aurangabad district (Baghaura and Dalelchak villages). Seven families, including women and children, were killed. The brutality of the murders was evident from on-the-scene reports: "frightened womenfolk [were forced] to place their necks on the improvised chopping block and beheaded with country-made axes."[61] The causes of the killings remain unclear, except for the fact that they were part of an ongoing feud between the two caste communities. Issues of land and members of the left parties may have been involved, but none of that was decisive. Both parties to the conflict were mainly middle or small peasants.[62] A telling piece of evidence, however, was the ineffectiveness of the local police. The growing tensions between the two communities had been evident for more than a month, and some outbreak of violence was expected. The state police proved to be totally ineffective, even though the violence was perpetrated openly by a mob of some 700 people. A company of the Central Reserve Police Force that had been posted in the area to prevent violence had to be withdrawn two months before the killings for "more urgent duties in Punjab."[63]

Many more examples of the increasing conflict and violence of this nature in Bihar could be cited. The purpose of these specific examples is to illustrate the variety of agrarian conflicts that plague contemporary Bihar. The next problem is how to explain such egregious atrocities. Why has such savagery flourished in Bihar and not in, say, the neighboring states of Uttar Pradesh and Orissa? And why have these conflicts intensified sharply over the past decade? Leaving the unique features of specific conflicts aside, even a general explanation for these struggles must be multicausal. This is best developed with reference to three factors: (1) Bihar's relative underdevelopment, (2) the delegitimization of established patterns of domination in the countryside, and (3) the slow but steady disintegration of the state.

The fact of Bihar's relative underdevelopment within India is well established. A number of important indicators of this have already been cited. The most important of these is worth reiterating: the steady decline in per capita rural income since the late 1960s. Economic failure in the agricultural sector has had a number of perverse consequences.

As noted earlier Bihar's countryside continues to be dominated by such precapitalist economic relationships as usury, sharecropping, and bonded labor. Faced with the prospect of declining incomes in such a context, those who own land and dominate the social structure have sought to improve their incomes primarily by squeezing those below them. The natural instinct

---

61 See *India Today,* June 30, 1987, p. 46.
62 See *Economic and Political Weekly,* June 13, 1987, pp. 912–13.
63 See *India Today,* June 30, 1987, p. 51.

to want to maintain or improve one's standard of living has led not to increased investment and to growth in productivity but rather to a labor-repressive strategy:

In order to maintain their earlier level of prosperity the rural oligarchy resorted to intensification of exploitation. One feature frequently noted in this context was the forceful ejection of sub-tenants and settling the land with others for salami [a modified form of sharecropping]. In quite a few cases landlords attempted to reduce the area of land which was on customary lease to the agricultural labourers for their services.[64]

An increasing use of force to maintain the subservience of labor has been evident throughout this discussion. It indicates a surplus-appropriating strategy that in other historical circumstances has been labeled the "second serfdom."

The growing activism of Bihar's rural poor must be understood, in part, as an attempt to resist the imposition of even harsher patterns of domination. Absolute poverty may be politically debilitating, but even absolute poverty has limits. The steady pressure generated by nearly stagnant rural incomes and the simultaneous increase in agrarian militancy appear to be logically connected. Pradhan Prasad's argument on this point is quite persuasive. Those who hold that agrarian capitalism, or the "green revolution," is the primary motive force behind the agrarian conflicts in rural India should study Bihar carefully. Probably the best thing that could happen to Bihar's poverty-stricken countryside would be the emergence of more owner-producer farms and an increase in irrigation, leading up to a little more of the green revolution and agrarian capitalism of the kind seen in western Uttar Pradesh.

The absence of economic dynamism provides the broad context for the increasing agrarian hostilities. However, it is not a sufficient explanation. It may explain the caste-class conflicts noted earlier, but it certainly will not do as an explanation for the growing police brutality. Even in regard to the former, an important fact must be noted: The agrarian struggles have been concentrated in the area that is "backward" Bihar's least stagnant region, namely, the districts of the Patna division in central Bihar. If declining income were the sole causal variable, one would expect agrarian unrest to be concentrated in the most stagnant parts of Bihar, the north and the south. Clearly, other factors are at work. Barrington Moore, Jr., one may recall, had forcefully argued that levels of objective exploitation seldom can fully explain peasant proclivities to rebel. What also must be understood is the nature of the linkages, the subjective relationships between the dominant and the subjugated castes.[65]

64 Prasad, "Agrarian Violence in Bihar," p. 851.
65 Barrington Moore, Jr., *Social Origins of Dictatorship and Democracy: Lord and Peasant in the Making of the Modern World* (Boston: Beacon Press, 1966), chapter 9.

The worst of the caste carnage over the past decade has been concentrated in the following seven districts: rural Patna, Nalanda, Gaya, Aurangabad, Nawadah, Bhojpur, and Rhotas. These districts are all located within a 150-mile radius of the state capital of Patna. For administrative purposes, Bihar often is divided into six divisions (Table 8.5). The seven violence-prone districts compose one of these six divisions, namely, the Patna division. This is not to suggest that agrarian conflict does not occur elsewhere in Bihar. Tribal movements for regional autonomy, for example, are fairly strong in the Chotanagpur division. Elsewhere in Bihar, agrarian conflicts are far from unknown. It is important to remember that after Punjab, Bihar probably is India's most violent state today. Within this violent milieu, the worst of the caste killings have been in the Patna division. That naturally raises a question: Is there something distinctive about this part of Bihar?

Table 8.5 lists three agrarian indicators for the six divisions of Bihar. The Patna division stands out on two of the three measures. It has the highest proportion of the scheduled-caste population in Bihar, and it has the highest concentration of tube wells within Bihar. Patna, however, scores somewhere in the middle on the measure of concentration of landless laborers. A discussion of these and related indicators may provide some clues as to why Patna has such a high degree of agrarian activism.

The greater use of tube wells for irrigation in Patna confirms that agrarian commercialization and efforts to improve agricultural productivity within Bihar have proceeded furthest in the Patna division. (Perspective is important here. The tube-well concentration in Bihar, standardized for population, is about one-tenth of that in Punjab and nearly half of that in Uttar Pradesh. Even the most advanced division in Bihar, therefore, is not all that well developed agriculturally by all-India standards.) It is this distinctive quality of the central districts that has sometimes led some Marxist scholars to see the emergence of *kulaks* within Bihar and to relate agrarian conflicts to agrarian capitalism. The absurdity of that proposition should be emphasized. If this minimum level of agrarian commercialization were at the root of the escalating caste carnage, then much of western Uttar Pradesh and Haryana should by now be in the throes of a full-blown agrarian revolution. Because such is not the case, we need to look for other types of specific links between conditions of modest agricultural dynamism and agrarian conflict.

Some of the peculiarities of the pattern of agrarian commercialization in this part of Bihar should be noted. Even though the efforts to improve productivity have proceeded furthest here, there is no markedly greater concentration of landless laborers in this area (Table 8.5). It is a peculiar kind of "agrarian capitalism" indeed in which "proletarianization" does not keep pace. Two detailed studies of the area have further suggested that much of the labor really is not "free labor." One of those studies of the

Table 8.5. *Some agrarian indicators in Bihar according to divisions*

Division	Population of scheduled castes (as percentage of total population)	Tube-well concentration index[a]	Agricultural laborers (as percentage of rural population)
Patna	19.6	2.4	12.4
Tirhut	13.7	1.7	11.5
Darbhanga	14.8	1.4	13.3
Bhagalpur	11.6	.05	11.3
Kosi	13.1	.08	18.4
Chotanagpur	10.8	.01	7.6

[a]This index measures the area irrigated by tube wells and is standardized per hundred thousand population.
Source: All the figures are computed from data in Government of Bihar, Directorate of Statistics and Evaluation, *Bihar Through Figures, 1981* (Patna: Secretariat Press, 1985).

Patna district noted that "payment of wages to agrarian labourers [is] in kind [and] very low wages, forced labour, [and] usury" are all common.[66] A more general survey reported the following:

Though the old forms of bondage and servitude have practically disappeared, new forms have emerged in response to protective legislations in favor of the poor. Hence, though formally "free," the majority are virtually dependent on the landowners for subsistence, and given the caste-hierarchy, also victims of caste oppression.[67]

Thus, the agrarian picture is quite complex. Old patterns of domination have been eroding. Given the relatively low levels of agrarian dynamism, however, there have been renewed attempts to impose new patterns of bondage. It is in the resulting economic and social deprivation that one finds an important clue to the higher levels of agrarian unrest.

The modicum of agrarian dynamism that exists in the Patna division is primarily a product of the actions of backward-caste landowners. Because of a number of processes mentioned earlier – *zamindari* abolition, abandonment of lands by some Moslem landowners at the time of partition, and the sale of agricultural land necessitated by ceiling legislation – the patterns of landownership by castes in these areas are more mixed than are those in the north of Bihar, for example. The following description of the Patna district probably applies to many of the neighboring districts as well:

66 Chaudhry, "Agrarian Unrest in Bihar," p. 52.
67 See People's Union for Democratic Rights, *Killings in Bihar,* p. 2.

In the western part of the Patna district . . . the landlords and nonpeasants belonging to upper castes dominate, while in the eastern part . . . the backward castes, especially Kurmi landlords and rich peasants, dominate. . . . Brahmins, Bhumihars, Rajputs and Kayasthas form the upper caste. They command strong influence in various political organizations. . . . A section of the backward castes are rich peasants who were ryots cultivators before 1952. After the Zamindari Abolition Act, they became owners of big holdings. Through cultivation, employment and other sources their incomes have gone up. They purchased land from ex-landlords at very cheap rates and through various means, they continued to enlarge their holdings. With their developing economic and social position, their political ambition too has grown. These new-style landowners are fiercely aggressive and despotic. They ruthlessly exploit the landless poor and middle peasants in numerous ways.[68]

It is this ruthlessness of a new agrarian class that is behind both the modest agrarian dynamism and the increasing agrarian conflict.

The backward castes as the new overlords enjoy less legitimacy in the social structure than do the traditional upper castes. The old relationships between the twice-born castes and the scheduled castes were relatively fixed and legitimized by well-established traditions, and they also had some built-in elements of reciprocity. Although much of the old system has been fundamentally damaged, some of it survives. It is no accident, therefore, that the only major caste in the area that does not have its own private army is the Brahman. That is probably because the Brahman landlords still are accorded some degree of deference by others and manage to accumulate their agricultural surpluses through established and accepted mechanisms.

By contrast, the newly emergent classes of backward-caste origin have a difficult time legitimizing their access to surpluses and their new positions of domination. Had the "mode of surplus appropriation" shifted sharply to a market-oriented mode, as it did in the green-revolution states, the problem of creating a new perception of legitimacy would have been qualitatively different. Thus, it would appear that when new actors on the scene who did not enjoy traditional high status attempted to enforce the traditional patterns of domination – bonded labor, very low wages, usury, and master–servant relationships – that effort provoked hostility among the landless lower castes.

It is important at this point to remember the other distinguishing characteristic of the Patna division mentioned earlier – the very high concentration of scheduled castes, the majority of whom are landless laborers. They not only are the poorest of the poor but also are socially ostracized, deemed to be the most inferior in matters of social standing. That double economic and social degradation has traditionally made these groups extremely subservient.

It is mainly on these scheduled castes that the newly emergent backward-

68 Chaudhry, "Agrarian Unrest in Bihar," p. 53.

caste landowners have sought to impose their domination. Although the scheduled castes may have been habitually subservient in the old elaborate system of traditional caste domination, they fail to see any legitimacy in this new domination. A growing population and slow economic growth have, in any case, made the problems of eking out a satisfactory livelihood quite difficult. Under these conditions of severe economic vulnerability and decreasing legitimacy of domination, the spread of new political values and organizations has finally taken root. I shall return to this issue of political mobilization later. For now, suffice it to note that challenges from the scheduled castes have increased and are being met with sharp hostility. The private caste armies are products of that hostility.

Challenges from the scheduled castes are seen by the landowning castes as threats to both their economic security and their social status. There has been a characteristic response from the landowning castes: "How dare they challenge our authority?" Much of the agrarian conflict is about teaching the scheduled castes and their organizers a lesson in subservience, about keeping them "in their place." In sum, a social structure that is characterized by minimum economic dynamism, but within which established patterns of domination have lost their legitimacy, provides the context for growing agrarian conflicts in Bihar.

One final set of issues remains to be discussed: the political context. An intriguing aspect of the pattern of agarian conflict in Bihar is that it is concentrated around the seat of power, the state capital of Patna. This has to be somewhat of a novel trend for students of agrarian radicalism. Peasant rebellions more often than not occur in the political periphery, where the reach of the state is weak, and where political spaces exist to mobilize the peasantry.[69] The explanation for this anomaly in Bihar, however, is not complex: The state has become so ineffective that even in its own backyard its grip is relatively weak.

Once the vitality of the established parties and the effectiveness of the police were seen to be declining, the urban-based counterelite sensed the opening of new political spaces. As Bihar's infamous but recurring chief minister, Jagannath Mishra, admitted in an interview:

The poor are being neglected by all parties. My own party, Congress, is losing support among the scheduled castes and the scheduled tribes. The old left has also lost the initiative. Politics, however, does not like a vacuum. Someone will move in. That is why the new left parties are being successful. This is all quite new.[70]

Because these new oppositional elite are concentrated in and around the state capital, the existing agrarian tensions in the adjacent areas have

---

69 See, for example, Eric Wolf, *Peasant Wars of the Twentieth Century* (New York: Harper & Row, 1969), especially the conclusion.
70 Interview with Jagannath Mishra, former chief minister of Bihar, Patna, August 22, 1986. Most of the interview was in Hindi. The translation is my own.

provided them fertile ground for their organizing efforts. Every successful mobilization of these groups, however, is labeled "Naxalite activity." The activities of the private caste armies grow in proportion to the mobilization of the scheduled castes and landless laborers. Some of this conflict is beginning to look like full-fledged class warfare. A fair amount of the conflict, however, is quite anarchic – an uncontrolled police force venting its frustration on one group or another, armed private groups fighting personal vendettas, and, of course, ordinary criminals gathering their booty wherever they can.

Finally, a broader point should also be noted. A clear demonstration of the governmental ineffectiveness in Bihar has been the recurring failure of its policies. Here one does not think primarily of the failure of redistributive policies. Clearly, some degree of land reform would ease agrarian tensions, but failure on that front is common to much of India, and certainly not unique to Bihar. The policy ineffectiveness in Bihar is part and parcel of the overall absence of development in the state. To be fair, it is difficult to disentangle cause and consequence in this syndrome of underdevelopment. However, government policy remains a crucial variable that could, if properly directed, begin to correct Bihar's underdevelopment. The recurring failure on that front has contributed to numerous problems in Bihar: a failing infrastructure, a low-caliber work force turned out by ineffective educational institutions, and failure to distribute agricultural inputs in a manner that would stimulate agricultural productivity. The causes of all of these failures are, without doubt, complex. Behind each of them, however, we discover squabbling politicians, massive leakages of public funds through corruption, and, generally, a government that does not work. To the extent that Bihar's underdevelopment sets the context for its increasing agrarian conflicts, Bihar's ineffective government is very much a part of the overall causal framework.

CONCLUSION

I have attempted to document and explain the process of breakdown of political and social order in Bihar. There has been no implicit assumption here that the old order was desirable and the growing turmoil is not. The old caste order in the countryside was inequitable and oppressive. The seemingly stable political rule in the 1950s and 1960s was also rule by the few, a narrow elitist political order. Challenges to the power of the few have grown in both the civil society and the state, resulting in considerable turmoil. Unless one believes that broadening the power base necessarily entails violence, or that good things come out of turmoil, the breakdown of order in contemporary Bihar is a matter of great concern.

This analysis of breakdown has focused on two simultaneous but independent processes: the declining effectiveness of the state, and the increase in agrarian conflict in the civil society. Each of these processes has been caused by a number of forces. In my discussion of governmental ineffectiveness, I have stressed the undisciplined power struggles among the competing political elite as an important causal force. The absence of economic development and the growing delegitimization of traditional caste domination, due to the spread of democratic politics, have similarly been proposed as significant forces generating agrarian conflict. In addition, it is clear that governmental ineffectiveness and agrarian conflict exacerbate one another. Agrarian conflict has given rise to private armies that have further undermined the government's capacity to rule. Governmental ineffectiveness has opened up political spaces within which agrarian struggles are growing.

As one moves from Bihar to other states and toward a comparative analysis, two broad conclusions should be kept in mind: First, the absence of economic development, when combined with a growing population and with political mobilization, can have as corrosive an impact on the social and political order as can high rates of economic development. Those who continue to believe that political disorder in India is a function of economic development should look carefully at Bihar. Second, the disintegration of the state and the growing socioeconomic conflict are partially independent processes that have combined to produce a crisis of governability in Bihar. How the parallel but independent forces in the state and civil society mold the overall pattern of political order will be the theme in the cases discussed in subsequent chapters.

9

Growing turmoil in an "advanced" state: Gujarat

Gujarat is one of India's more prosperous states. Both governmental and political processes in Gujarat used to be relatively stable, but that stability became tenuous in the early 1970s. Violence as a tool to effect political change was rare in the 1970s, but that changed in the 1980s. In 1981, and again in 1985, politics in Gujarat came to be characterized by riots, arson, and other kinds of planned violence, and there was a growing sense that the state's capacity to govern had declined sharply. Whereas the dominant image of Gujarat politics in the 1960s was one of gentility, growing conflict and turmoil characterized the 1980s.

What happened? An answer is developed in this chapter by focusing on the political events of the 1980s. The answer has several components. The main issue, introduced in Chapter 3, and widely recognized in the literature, has to do with the growing caste conflict between the two major communities in Gujarat: the Patidars and the Kshatriyas. As the socioeconomic elite in the area, the Patidars traditionally have commanded both political power and relatively high status in the caste hierarchy. By contrast, most of the Kshatriyas are lower in the socioeconomic hierarchy, but they are a significant numerical force. Over time, Kshatriyas leaders forged an alliance with other disadvantaged groups, won elections, and gradually pushed the Patidars out of government. As the new leaders sought to use state power to alter the old patterns of socioeconomic privilege, the Patidars countered with strong resistance, unleashing violence in the state. That planned violence was successful in the sense that the Patidars achieved their main goals. First, they were able to change the government leadership in 1986. More important, they were able to define the boundaries within which future governments would have to work if they did not wish to invite further violence.

An analysis of political conflict in Gujarat as a conflict involving a privileged minority and an underprivileged majority, though essentially correct, would underemphasize two important issues. First, an important reason why the privileged minority was able to bring down a majority government in 1986 was the organizational weakness of the ruling party. It will be argued that the inability of the Congress government to mobilize political support for its own program and stave off the Patidar opposition reflected the virtual absence in Gujarat of Congress as an organized political force. This argument will be more convincing when the findings for Gujarat are juxtaposed against the case of West Bengal in the next chapter. The privileged minorities were excluded from governmental power in West Bengal, but with very different political results: A well-organized party was able to consolidate relatively coherent majority rule in that state.

Another important issue for this chapter is why much of the violence in both 1981 and 1985 was unleashed not against the "backward" Kshatriyas but rather against the scheduled castes, and eventually against the Moslems. The exploration of that issue in this chapter will highlight the way in which violence was targeted against vulnerable groups, both to vent frustration and, more strategically, to undermine governmental legitimacy and destroy the electoral alliance on which Congress's power rested.

The findings reported here regarding the significance of party organization and the need to create and maintain winning electoral coalitions suggest that political variables are as important for understanding the growing turmoil in Gujarat as is the conflict between privileged and underprivileged groups. The crisis of governability in Gujarat clearly is not as serious as that in Bihar. The sporadic periods of intense turmoil, however, are indicative of changing political conditions. Both political factors and variables having to do with the social structure were found to be important in our analysis of the crisis in Bihar, albeit in a setting of nearly stagnant development. The presence of similar causal variables in the context of a growing economy in Gujarat strengthens the case for the "autonomy of the political."

An important caveat must be noted: This chapter, more than others, depends heavily on secondary materials. I conducted many interviews in Gujarat in 1986[1] and have reviewed some other primary materials, but the published studies of Gujarat are quite good. Although the interpretation developed here varies in subtle but important ways from the interpretation

---

1 I interviewed the following at some length in March and April of 1986: Babubhai Jasbhai Patel (former chief minister of Gujarat), Gandhinagar; Jinabhai Darjee [veteran Congress (I) leader in Gujarat], Ahmedabad (the original interview was in Hindi; the translation is my own); Amarsinhji Vaghela (minister of cooperation, government of Gujarat), Gandhinagar; Govindbhai J. Patel (MLA from the Kheda district), Gandhinagar; Madhevsinh Solanki (former chief minister of Gujarat), Gandhinagar; Hasmukh Patel [minister of education, government of Gujarat, and secretary, Gujarat Paradesh Committee, Congress (I)], Ahmedabad; Shivubhai Dave [correspondent for *Indian Express* (Ahmedabad)], Nadiad; Satyam Patel [secretary, Gujarat Pradesh Committee, Congress (R)], Ahmedabad. In addition, I held discussions with correspondents and editors of both the *Times of India* and *Indian Express* in Ahmedabad and with the following academics and observers of Gujarati politics: Sujata Patel, Praveen Sheth, Anil Bhatt, and Achyut Yagnik.

in previously published accounts, I have depended on those sources for basic information.[2]

SOME RELEVANT BACKGROUND

Along with Punjab and Maharashtra, Gujarat is one of India's more prosperous states, third in per capita income and second in per capita energy consumption. That prosperity is based in part on relatively high levels of industrialization. Until recently, textiles constituted the mainstay of Gujarati industry. During the 1980s, the industrial base was diversified, especially into oil-related industries. However, the state's prosperity also has a significant agricultural component. The proportions of land and manpower involved in cash-crop production are relatively high. The main cash crops of the area, tobacco, cotton, and oilseed, have fetched relatively high prices in the recent past, adding to the region's relatively high incomes.

Gujarat's overall prosperity should not be allowed to mask the inequalities and poverty that also exist within the state. Scheduled castes and scheduled tribes constitute more than 20 percent of the state's population (Table 9.1). Living conditions for the many tribal groups, concentrated in the eastern belt of the state, are especially miserable. However, the scheduled castes in Gujarat probably are more advanced (certainly so in terms of their level of awareness concerning their rights, but also educationally

---

2 Works by four scholars have been especially relevant: John R. Wood, Ghanshyam Shah, Sujata Patel, and Asghar Ali Engineer. See, for example, John Wood, "Extra-Parliamentary Opposition in India," *Pacific Affairs,* 48:3(Fall 1975), pp. 313–34; John Wood, "Congress Restored? The KHAM Strategy and Congress (I) Recruitment in Gujarat," in John Wood, ed., *State Politics in Contemporary India: Crisis or Continuity?* (Boulder, Colo.: Westview Press, 1984), pp. 197–227; John Wood, "Gujarat's Anti-Reservation Riots, 1985," mimeograph, 1986, presented at the annual meeting of the Canadian Asian Studies Association, Winnipeg, June 5, 1986; Ghanshyam Shah, *Caste Association and Political Process in Gujarat: A Study of the Kshatriya Sabha* (Bombay: Popular Prakashan, 1975); Ghanshyam Shah, "Caste Sentiments, Class Formation and Dominance in Gujarat," mimeograph, 1983, revised version to appear in Francine Frankel and M. S. A. Rao, eds., *Dominance and State Power in Modern India: Decline of a Social Order,* 2 vols. (Oxford University Press, 1989–90); Sujata Patel, "Debacle of Populist Politics," *Economic and Political Weekly* (hereafter referred to as *EPW*), April 20, 1985, pp. 681–2; Sujata Patel, "Collapse of Government," *EPW,* April 27, 1987, pp. 749–50; Sujata Patel, "The Ahmedabad Riots, 1985: An Analysis," unpublished, undated manuscript; Asghar Ali Engineer, "From Caste to Communal Violence," *EPW,* April 13, 1985, pp. 628–30; Asghar Ali Engineer, "Communal Fires Engulf Ahmedabad Once Again," *EPW,* July 6, 1985, pp. 1116–20. The following sources were also helpful: Praveen Sheth, "Caste, Class and Political Development," in D. T. Lakdwala, ed., *Development in Gujarat: Problems and Prospects* (New Delhi: Allied Publishers, 1982), pp. 193–207; Subrata Mitra, "The Perils of Promoting Equality: The Latent Significance of the Anti-Reservation Movement in India," *Journal of Commonwealth and Comparative Politics,* November 1987, pp. 292–317; Howard Spodek, "From Gandhi to Violence: Ahmedabad's 1985 Riots in Historical Perspective," mimeograph, Department of History, Temple University, 1987.

Table 9.1. *Caste distribution in Gujarat*

High castes	
Brahman	4.1
Bania	3.0
Rajput	4.9
Other highs	1.1
	13.1
Middle castes	
Patidar	12.2
Kunbi	0.1
	12.3
Lower castes	
"Lower Kshatriya"	24.2
Artisan castes	6.1
Other backwards	13.4
	43.7
Scheduled castes	7.2 (7)[a]
Scheduled tribes	14.2 (14)[a]
	21.4
Non-Hindus	
Moslems	8.5 (8)[a]
Other non-Hindus	1.0
	9.5
Total	100.0

[a]The figures in parentheses are from the 1971 census, when the scheduled castes, scheduled tribes, and Moslems were counted, but not the Hindu castes.
Source: Figures adapted from 1931 census, as cited in the following: Ghanshyam Shah, *Caste Association and Political Process in Gujarat: A Study of the Kshatriya Sabha* (Bombay: Popular Prakashan, 1978), p. 9; John Wood, "Congress Restored?: The KHAM Strategy and Congress (I) Recruitment in Gujarat," in J. Wood, ed., *State Politics in Contemporary India: Crisis or Continuity?* (Boulder, Colo.: Westview Press, 1984), p. 203.

and to some extent economically) than their counterparts in other states. The roots of such advancement go back to the relatively progressive educational policies of the former maharaja of Baroda, as well as to the influence of Mohandas Gandhi, who was a native of Gujarat. It will be argued later that the relative upward mobility of select segments of the scheduled castes has provoked considerable hostility from the upper castes.

Tables 9.1 and 9.2 show data on caste and land distributions within the state. Brahmans and Banias are among the important upper castes and tend to be concentrated in the cities. Many of the first-generation nationalist leaders in the region and the state's earlier chief ministers, such as Morarji Desai (Brahman), Jivraj Mehta (Bania), Balwantrai Mehta (Bania), and

Table 9.2. *Occupations and landholding by caste in rural Gujarat*

Caste	Occupation (%)			Landholding (%)		
	Cultivators	Laborers	Others	1–5 acres	5–15 acres	16 acres or more
Brahman	52	4	44	41	32	27
Bania	30	5	65	55	24	21
Rajput	72	15	13	42	35	23
Patidar	81	7	12	25	42	33
Koli ("lower Kshatriya")	62	24	14	66	23	11
Artisan castes	48	36	16	42	33	25
Other lower castes	45	33	22	43	41	10
Scheduled castes	43	39	18	69	26	5
Scheduled tribes	67	21	12	77	21	2
Moslems	44	35	21	36	45	19

Source: Adapted from a survey of 15,680 households conducted by the Centre for Social Studies, Surat, Gujarat, and presented in Ghanshyam Shah, "Caste, Class and Reservation," *Economic and Political Weekly*, January 19, 1985, p. 133.

Hitendra Desai (Brahman), belonged to these groups.[3] Until recently, the Banias were the dominant group in urban commerce and industry. When one talks about the "gentler" age of Gujarati politics, therefore, it is important to remember the narrow political base on which the earlier arrangement rested. It was dominated by a few wealthy upper-caste men in Gujarat.

The Patidars are the dominant rural community.[4] Their numbers across the state are substantial, and as Table 9.2 shows, 75 percent of them own and cultivate landholdings of 5 acres or more. Although a significant amount of the state's land is in very large holdings, this distribution can be somewhat misleading, because many of the very large holdings are concentrated in the arid north, where the quality of land is poor. The popular image of Gujarati agriculture as dominated by medium (5–15 acres) and large (16–50 acres) landholdings, owned mainly by the Patidars, is essentially correct. That is especially true of the central parts of mainland Gujarat. But even in peninsular Gujarat, which historically was dominated by the Rajputs, the Kunbis (historically a low-caste group, but now a *jati* or subcaste of the Patidars) emerged as a landowning group after the postindependence tenancy reforms.[5]

The Patidars of Gujarat were mobilized into the nationalist movement in the early part of this century. Their main leader, Sardar Vallabbhai Patel, rose to be one of independent India's two most important Congressites, second only to Nehru. That gave the Gujarati Patels a powerful role within the Gujarat Congress. Although the top positions within the state were occupied by Brahman or Bania leaders, many districts were controlled by the Patidars. After independence, as the significance of electoral politics increased, the Patidars came to play an even more important role.[6] It probably is only a small exaggeration to say that the Patidars, in alliance with Brahmans and Banias, dominated the regional Congress party and thus Gujarati politics well into the 1970s.

The main challenge to the power of the Patidars in recent years has come from the Kshatriyas. The designation "Kshatriyas" was essentially

---

3 For a discussion of politics in Gujarat in the 1960s, see Devarat N. Pathak, "State Politics in Gujarat: Some Determinants," in Iqbal Narain, ed., *State Politics in India* (Meerut: Meenaskshi Prakashan, 1968), pp. 122–33; Praveen Sheth, "Gujarat: The Case of Small Majority Politics," in Narain, ed., *State Politics in India,* 2nd ed. (Meerut: Meenakshi Prakashan, 1974), pp. 68–87.
4 For a study of the Patidars of Gujarat, see David F. Pocock, *Kanbi and Patidar: A Study of the Patidar Community of Gujarat* (Oxford: Clarendon Press, 1972); Anil Bhatt, "Caste and Political Mobilization in a Gujarat District," in Rajni Kothari, ed., *Caste in Indian Politics* (New Delhi: Orient Longman, 1973), pp. 299–339.
5 For a discussion of the land reform and its consequences, see Ghanshyam Shah, "Caste Sentiments, Class Formation and Dominance in Gujarat."
6 See Myron Weiner, *Party Building in a New Nation: The Indian National Congress* (University of Chicago Press, 1967).

political in origin, but has now taken on caste connotations.[7] As seen in Table 9.1, Rajputs are another important high caste in the area. Many Rajputs in preindependence India belonged to princely families, and most of them cherished their cultural traditions that glorified martial pursuits. Many of the Rajputs formerly owned large tracts of land, parts of which were lost in the postindependence land reforms. The Rajputs never became an integral part of the nationalist movement; as local princes, they were often allied with the British, and some of Congress's programs, such as land reforms, conflicted with their interests.

Outside of the Congress mainstream, the Rajputs sought to mobilize their own political force. As independence approached, it was clear that voter numbers were going to be crucial for winning elections and thus for state power and patronage. In one of the earliest examples of a "caste federation," the Rajput leaders mobilized several lower-caste groups, especially Kolis and Bariyas, as a "vote bank" of fellow Kshatriyas. Tables 9.1 and 9.2 show that these lower castes were numerically significant and that they were mainly small farmers. Many of them were actually sharecroppers on Patidar lands. The mobilization of Kshatriyas brought together groups with widely disparate socioeconomic positions, but shared cultural traditions and a common antipathy to the Patidars and their organization, the Congress party. As will be discussed later, that Kshatriya unity fell apart for about a decade (1965–75), but was reestablished, though with important differences, in the 1980s.

The current state of Gujarat was part of the larger state of Bombay until 1960, when Bombay was divided into two states: Gujarat for Gujarati speakers and Maharashtra for Marathi speakers.[8] Until well into the 1960s, the narrow alliance that ruled Gujarat – Brahmans and Banias, mainly in the major cities, and Patidars, mainly in the districts – had been cemented by a well-organized Congress party. Because the levels of mobilization among the lower strata were relatively low, and intraelite harmony was high, the area's politics had an aura of gentility.[9] As Figure 9.1 shows, there clearly was more than an aura; there was a degree of political stability, with depth. Gujarat experienced very low levels of political violence throughout the 1950s and 1960s, not only in comparison with Gujarat in

7 For a discussion of the rise of the Kshatriya movement, see Ghanshyam Shah, *Caste Association and Political Process in Gujarat.*
8 For a historical discussion of the creation of Gujarat, see John R. Wood, "The Political Integration of British and Princely Gujarat," unpublished Ph.D. thesis, Columbia University, 1972.
9 Writing in the early 1970s, Praveen Sheth observed that "modest and moderate, Gujarat politics has on the whole been gentle and peaceful in tradition and commercial in style and technique. Its predominant feature is moderation, and its keynote, its secular character. It has been devoid of anti-Brahminism or rabid caste and communal rivalries." See Sheth, "Gujarat: The Case of Small Majority Politics," p. 68.

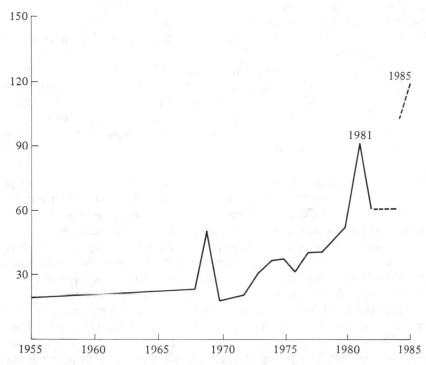

Figure 9.1. Political violence in Gujarat, 1955–85 (number of riots per million population). The pre-1968 figures are based on average figures for the preceding decade. The figure for 1985 is provisional. No official data are available beyond 1982. For the sources of these data, see the caption for Figure 8.1. *Source:* See the note for Figure 1.1.

the 1980s but also compared with many other Indian states during that earlier time period.

The gentlemen elite of Gujarat ruled relatively peacefully because they tended to agree with each other on significant issues and because they enjoyed unquestioned dominance in the social structure. Democracy, however, especially when significant socioeconomic spoils are available from the state, has a way of quickly bringing excluded groups into the political arena. That is precisely what happened in Gujarat.

The changing caste composition of the Gujarat Legislative Assembly between 1960 and 1980 provides a good indicator of the changing power positions of various Gujarati communities.[10] Three trends are especially noteworthy. First, the higher castes of Brahmans and Banias slowly began to lose political influence. Second, although the middle landowning castes

10 These figures are derived from Sheth, "Caste, Class and Political Development," Table 1, p. 198.

246   *Order and breakdown in the states*

of Patidars managed to maintain their dominance well into the 1970s, their legislative seats declined from 24 to 18 between 1975 and 1980. By contrast, Kshatriyas and other backward castes steadily improved their access to positions of power.

For the Kshatriyas, 1967 was the big year. Between 1962 and 1967, their legislative seats nearly doubled, from 9 to 17. As discussed earlier, the national position of Congress deteriorated throughout the middle 1960s, leading up to the watershed elections of 1967, when Congress lost control of several Indian states. Gujarat was not one of those states; Congress retained its control over the Gujarat Legislative Assembly. As Table 9.3 shows, however, the strength of the Congress party declined between 1962 and 1967, and a right-of-center party, the Swatantra, improved its position significantly. Politically mobilized Kshatriyas, unable to penetrate the Patidar-dominated Congress, threw in their lot with some dissenting Patidars and the Swatantra party. Although issues of ideology were not of great significance in determining which groups became aligned with which parties, the fact that Kshatriyas joined a right-leaning party reflected that the Kshatriya leadership, though increasingly challenged by lower-caste representatives, still was in the hands of former princely Rajputs.

Whereas the 1967 elections in Gujarat clarified the growing power of previously excluded groups like the Kshatriyas and of non-Congress parties, the 1969 split in the national Congress party had a decisive impact on Gujarati politics. The power struggle at the national level pitted Indira Gandhi against the Congress old guard, including Morarji Desai. Gujarat was part of Morarji's regional power base. When the national Congress party split, therefore, most of the Congress legislators elected in 1967, as well as senior party leaders, joined Desai in shunning Indira's new Congress and chose to ally themselves with Congress (O).[11] The politics of the state entered a confusing stage of shifting coalitions and alignments that would not be clarified for nearly a decade, until the 1980 elections.

The details of that decade of confusion are not important for our purposes.[12] What is important is to remember that it was a decade of major power realignments within Gujarat. Whereas prior to 1969 Gujarat had been ruled by the old undivided Congress and the upper castes, such as the Brahmans, Banias, and Patidars, Indira Gandhi's new Congress emerged after 1980 at the helm of the state, aligned with many of the state's previously disadvantaged groups, especially the lower-caste Kshatriyas. Something else was also replaced during that period: a relatively well organized Congress party. Its place was taken by a force more akin to an

---

11 Interview with Babubhai Jasbhai Patel (former chief minister of Gujarat), Gandhinagar, March 8, 1986.
12 See, for example, Praveen Sheth, *Patterns of Political Behaviour in Gujarat* (Ahmedabad: Sahitya Mudranalaya, 1976).

Table 9.3. *Electoral performances of major parties in Gujarat Legislative Assembly elections, 1962–85*

Party	1962		1967		1972		1975[b]		1980		1985	
	Seats	Vote (%)	Seats	Vote (%)	Seats	Vote (%)	Seats	Vote (%)	Seats	Vote (%)	Seats	Vote (%)
Congress	113	51	93	46	140	51	75	41	141	50	149	55.5
Congress (O)[a]	—	24	—	—	16	24	56	24	21	22	14	19.3
Swatantra	26	24	64	38	0	—	2	2	0	—	—	—
Jan Sangh[c]	0	1	1	2	3	9	18	9	9	13	11	15.0
Independents	7	10	4	10	8	12	15	12	10	10	8	9.3
Others	8	14	5	4	1	4	15	12	0	5	0	0.9
Total	154	100	168	100	168	100	181	100	181	100	182	100

[a]Formed in 1969 after the split in the Indian national Congress. Congress (O) was part of the Janata Morcha in 1973 and the Janata party in 1980 and 1985. The figures reported for Congress (O) in 1980 and 1985 are more accurately figures for the Janata party.
[b]The opposition to Congress in 1975 fought as a coalition called the Janata Morcha. The main partners in that coalition were Congress (O), Jan Sangh, and several independent legislators.
[c]The Jan Sangh merged into the Janata party in 1977, broke away in 1980, and was returned as the Bhartiya Janata party in 1984.
Source: Compiled from various sources, including the report of the Electoral Commission.

unorganized populist movement. Those two changes in regard to who ruled and how power was organized, in turn, set the stage for the eruption of the major conflicts and violence of the 1980s.

After the Congress party split in 1969, the major contenders for power within Gujarat became Congress (O), Swatantra, and Indira's Congress, Congress (R). In order to further destabilize the weakened Congress (O) government, Swatantra, with its significant minority within the legislature, intensified its attempts to lure defectors from Congress (O). Congress (R), in control in New Delhi, but fairly weak in the Gujarat legislature, attempted its own defection game, trying to draw people away from both Congress (O) and Swatantra. The ruling Congress (O), in turn, took the political battle to the streets and tried to mobilize public opinion against the "defection game." As rival parties competed for the support of legislators and for public opinion, the political situation became turbulent. For a complex set of reasons that have been analyzed elsewhere,[13] hostilities broke out between Hindus and Moslems, leading to the deaths of some 1,500 people. As Figure 9.1 shows, that was the first significant increase in the level of rioting and violence in Gujarat politics. That the first outbreak of violence coincided with growing intraelite political conflict suggests that the civil disorder was more a product of political conditions than of growing socioeconomic conflict.

As Indira Gandhi consolidated her power nationally, both Congress (O) and Swatantra legislators in Gujarat began looking at Congress (R) as a potential winner. The first significant change came in 1970, when a group of Swatantra legislators, many of lower Kshatriya background, defected to the new Congress (R). The legislators involved in that defection were too few to create any major political upset. The significance of the transition lay elsewhere: That defection revealed the growing political fragmentation among the Kshatriyas and marked the beginning of a move by lower Kshatriyas toward Indira Gandhi's Congress.[14] Some people within Congress (O), especially those who had been excluded from the perks of power, also began flirting with Congress (R). Indira's Congress began taking on the look of a party made up of previously excluded groups. As Congress (O), Swatantra, and Jan Sangh moved closer together politically at the national level, Indira Gandhi and her supporters, both nationally and in Gujarat, gave the political conflict a sharper ideological twist, suggesting that it was a battle of the right versus the left. Indira's adoption of the slogan *garibi hatao* ("alleviate poverty") for the 1971 national elections

---

13 See Ghanshyam Shab, "Communal Riots in Gujarat," *EPW,* annual number, 1970.
14 For a good discussion of how the old Kshatriya Sabha fragmented, essentially between the more privileged Rajputs and the less privileged Bariyas, and how a direct patronage-based identification with Indira's Congress reemerged, see A. H. Somjee, "Social Cohesion and Political Clientelism Among the Kshatriyas of Gujarat," *Asian Survey,* 21:9(September 1981), pp. 1000–10.

finally confirmed that the new Congress had taken a stand decisively to the left of the old Congress.

The widespread electoral appeal of Indira Gandhi's left-leaning populism is well known. Her national victory transformed the trickle of defections to her party in Gujarat into a flood. It was around that time that up-and-coming Gujarati leaders like Madhevsinh Solanki joined Indira Gandhi's Congress.[15] Congress (O) put up a last-minute fight to keep Gujarat under its control, but to no avail. After several short governments and a brief period of presidential rule, Indira's Congress came to power with a huge majority – 140 seats in a house of 168 (Table 9.3).

It is important to note that the coalition between the old Congress and Jan Sangh was defeated, but by no means obliterated. As is clear from Table 9.3, the combined popular vote of those two parties still was over 30 percent of the total. More important, many of the most significant socioeconomic groups in Gujarat, such as the Patidars, Banias, and Brahmans, though quite fragmented among themselves, were, on balance, closer in spirit to those old, well-established parties. The political support of the Kshatriyas was similarly divided, though lower Kshatriyas were increasingly attracted to Indira's Congress, both because of the opportunities available within it and because of Indira's anti-Morarji, antiestablishment populism. Although the community's battle lines were still quite fuzzy, an outline was beginning to emerge: The disadvantaged majority aligned themselves with Indira Gandhi, and the privileged minority remained with the Congress (O)–Swatantra–Jan Sangh combine.

The pattern of the political battle was much more clearly drawn. Indira's Congress stood in opposition to the old forces loyal to Morarji. Although the old guard lost a battle, it was not ready to concede the war. It took the opposition only a short time to realize that the rise of Indira Gandhi had changed the rules of electoral politics. The old game of manipulating "vote banks" was gone; the name of the new game was competitive populism. The capacity of the old established elite to command the support of the lower strata had been diminishing throughout the 1960s. Indira Gandhi was a product of that change, but she also hastened the trend. The Banias, Brahmans, and Patidars of Gujarat could no longer readily mobilize electoral majorities, certainly not through the old methods, and especially not when confronted with Indira Gandhi's widespread appeal to the disadvantaged majority. As the old guard contemplated a political comeback, two things must have been clear to them: They would have to do it quickly, before Indira's new coalition took root, and they would have to do it with their own form of populism.

It is against that background that we must interpret the two months of

15 Interview with Madhevsinh Solanki (former chief minister of Gujarat), Gandhinagar, March 11, 1986.

civil disorder in 1974, the Navnirman ("reconstruction" or "social regeneration") movement that succeeded in dislodging the majority Congress (R) government in 1974. The details of that movement and the civil disorder are available elsewhere.[16] What is important for us to note is that it was a quintessential political conflict, aimed at simultaneously influencing public opinion and toppling the Congress (R) government; it was led mainly by students and other youths, but it was encouraged and supported by the parties out of power, Congress (O) and Jan Sangh, and by those Congress (R) factions that had lost out in the division of spoils. John R. Wood captured the purposive, political quality of those disorders:

Seventy-three days of agitation had left 103 people dead, mostly by police firing, 310 injured, and 8,237 under arrest in Gujarat. And yet, within a week, colleges reopened, students became busy with examinations, and normality returned. The Gujarat agitation, having achieved the two goals of removing the Patel ministry and dissolving the Gujarat assembly, ended as quickly as it had began.[17]

It was as if the tap of violence could be turned on and off for achieving specific political goals. Those who hold the view that the growing political conflict in India reflects irrational, anomic behavior, or more fundamental socioeconomic conflicts, should ponder such examples. The violence was purposeful, and its goal was explicitly political, namely, to remove a government from power.

Indira's Congress lost considerable support in the state election that followed in 1975. Although the new Congress won more seats than any other party (Table 9.3), it was the Janata Morcha, a loose coalition among Congress (O), Jan Sangh, and others, that was able to form a government. Not only had the democratically elected government of 1972 been pushed out of power by street violence, but in the process the opposition had gained enough public support to win the next election. That mode of political change helps illustrate two important points.

First, the success of the Navnirman movement revealed the political weakness of the populist coalition Indira Gandhi had hurriedly put together. The new Congress party in Gujarat had no organization. Praveen Sheth has argued that Congress (R) during that period had "no party apparatus, no cadre of active members [and] no party offices in sight in districts."[18] The new Congress (R) could win elections because of Indira

---

16 See, for example, D. E. and R. W. Jones, "Urban Upheaval in India: The 1974 Navnirman Riots in Gujarat," *Asian Survey,* November 1976, pp. 1012–33; Ghanshyam Shah, *Protest Movements in Two Indian States* (Delhi: Ajanta Publications, 1977); Wood, "Extra-Parliamentary Opposition in India."

17 Wood, "Extra-Parliamentary Opposition in India," p. 319.

18 Sheth, *Patterns of Political Behaviour in Gujarat,* p. 135. Congress's internal weakness, caused by intraelite factionalism, was also revealed in a number of interviews. For example, Jinabhai Darjee told me in an interview in Ahmedabad, March 10, 1986, that though he was a Congressite, he had supported the Navnirman movement.

Gandhi's personal, populist appeal, but could do little in the way of systematic mobilization to confront a militant opposition. That capacity would change over time, especially after the Emergency, when Sanjay's goons were incorporated within Congress, but in the early 1970s Indira's Congress found itself quite vulnerable to a powerful, mobilized minority.

A second point had long-range significance. An antidemocratic method of turning governments out of power was in the making. That pattern would be repeated in the future. A powerful minority within Gujarat had never acknowledged the legitimacy of Indira's new Congress. Instead of serving as a loyal opposition and accepting electoral verdicts, the opposition took to the streets. Some of that opposition was spontaneous. However, it could not have begun and ended with such precision if it had not been supported by powerful groups, namely, opposition parties with backing from resourceful upper-caste men in Gujarat. Although Indira Gandhi often is held responsible for weakening India's democracy, a nonpartisan observer must note the similar proclivities of those in opposition to Indira. Instead of assigning the primary blame to one party or another, it seems fairer to argue that in addition to the increasing power conflicts, antidemocratic tendencies had begun to spread in the polity as a whole.

It is well known that the defeat of Congress (R) in the Gujarat elections in 1975 contributed significantly to Indira's decision to proclaim a national Emergency later that same year. That does not concern us for the moment. What does concern us are the political changes that took place within Gujarat politics between 1975 and 1980, that is, during and immediately following the Emergency. Leaving aside the details once again, the process of political realignment that had begun in 1969 quickened during that period, leading up to the crystallization of an alliance between Indira Gandhi and the disadvantaged groups in Gujarat.

Paralleling the political instability at the national level, four different governments were formed in Gujarat between 1975 and 1980. Interesting patterns of alignments between parties and communities were revealed in an important body of data collected by John Wood. The two Janata governments formed in that period had 14 and 16 ministers from the privileged castes (Banias, Brahmans, and Patidars) and 5 and 7 ministers from the less privileged groups (Kshatriyas, other backward castes, Moslems, and scheduled castes and tribes). The numbers in the two Congress ministries between 1975 and 1980 were nearly the reverse: 15 and 11 from the less privileged groups, and 7 each from the upper castes.[19]

Although "polarization" would be too strong a term, it is clear that a two-party system of sorts had emerged, one party aligned with the more privileged socioeconomic groups, and the other with the less privileged. The Janata coalition came to be associated with the old established groups,

19 Calculated from Wood, "Congress Restored?" Table 8.3, p. 209.

whose influence was steadily declining; Indira's Congress, increasingly as-
cendant, was increasingly identified as a party of the underprivileged.

THE RIOTS OF 1981

In the summer of 1980, the Legislative Assembly elections marked another
important transition in Gujarat politics. As is shown in Table 9.3, Indira's
Congress reemerged as the state's dominant party. The only thing the new
Congress in Gujarat shared with the pre-1967 Congress was the name. The
new Congress party had virtually no organization, and its social base was
sharply different from that of the Brahman-Bania-Patel-dominated pre-
1967 Congress.

The issue of the decline of Congress's organization has been documented
in several chapters (especially Chapter 3). As far as the issue of the changing
social base of Congress is concerned, only a few more facts need to be
added.[20] Whereas the upper castes provided nearly 60 percent of the Congress legislators in 1967, by 1980 the number was under 30 percent. The
flip side of that change was just as dramatic. The lower castes, tribes, and
Moslems held nearly 40 percent of the seats in the 1967 Legislative Assembly, but by 1980 they held more than two-thirds of the seats. There
were parallel shifts in the allocations of the powerful ministerships, as noted
earlier. The fact that the number of Kshatriya legislators tripled between
1967 and 1980, and that the new chief minister, Madhevsinh Solanki, was
a lower-caste Kshatriya, could not have escaped anyone's attention. Finally, as discussed in Chapter 3, those changing patterns reached into the
lower ranks of the government; most of the local government positions at
the level of the district had also been appropriated by the Kshatriyas.

It would be only a small exaggeration to suggest that the Kshatriyas had
finally begun to push the Patels out of the sprawling state apparatus of
Gujarat. The Patels, however, continued to control much of Gujarat's
agriculture, numerous cooperatives, such as dairies, educational institutions, some trade and commerce, and the press. The lines of conflict were
drawn. Those who controlled most of Gujarat's socioeconomic resources
had lost control over the government to the less privileged but numerically
significant groups.

Both the 1981 and 1985 riots must be understood within this broad
context. It is important to stress that the focus on the Congress-Kshatriya
combine against the Patels provides no more than a framework for the
political violence that followed. Not surprisingly, the specific patterns of
violence, in terms of who attacked whom and with what motive, were
extremely varied. Once the government's legitimacy and capacity to maintain order declined, violence broke out in many areas.

20 Derived from Wood, "Congress Restored?" Table 8.6, p. 215.

to organize grass-roots support. He was heading a party without cadres or even committed, active members. Congress could secure votes because of a combination of Indira's mass appeal, caste sentiments, and promises of patronage. However, that basis of support was quite tenuous compared with the power resource that would have derived from committed members in a well-organized party. Without the latter, Solanki could not mobilize his supporters to confront the opposition politically. His support was relatively shallow and unorganized. His opposition understood that vulnerability and took advantage of it.

Finally, a consideration of a somewhat different sort must be noted. If Solanki could not confront a militant opposition politically, why could he not deal with the rioting as a law-and-order problem? Eventually, of course, the rioting died down. But that was only after Solanki had made significant concessions and police from outside of Gujarat had been brought in to control the riots. That highlights another important variable at work: the relative ineffectiveness of Gujarati police in dealing with the riots.

The CPDR report on the 1981 riots documented many instances in which the police either stood by as the powerful Patels wreaked havoc on the scheduled castes or, worse, assisted the Patels in the violence. Instances of police violence were especially common in Ahmedabad. The lack of discipline demonstrated by the police reflected both an ongoing deprofessionalization of the service and the caste sympathies of the policeman. For example, a union of police inspectors in Ahmedabad voted to support the antireservation demands of Patel students. Could such a force act as a neutral agent of law and order?

The political arm of the government was organizationally weak, and the law-and-order arm was less than reliable. When confronted with militant opposition, the Solanki government had little choice but to yield to demands. A similar but more widespread drama would be repeated in 1985. The basic dimensions of the conflict, however, were already clear in 1981: A powerful minority had refused to accept its loss of power in a democracy, and a majority government was institutionally too weak to confront its minority opposition.

THE RIOTS OF 1985

Solanki completed his 1980–5 term as chief minister. That was an achievement, in view of the fact that no other chief minister had completed a term in nearly two decades. Solanki ruled with a comfortable majority. The opposition could create trouble for him in the streets, but could not legally throw Congress (I) out of power. Solanki could, of course, have lost out to other rivals within Congress (I), as he eventually did, but over 1980–5 he managed to avoid that mainly because of his personal rapport with Indira Gandhi. Given the top-down political system then, so long as she had not lost confidence in him, his position was secure. Solanki suggested in an interview that in spite of the pro–lower strata image of his government, he had gone out of his way to avoid radical policies and had done nothing special in the way of socioeconomic reforms.[26] As far as real policies were concerned, the message of the Patel-led demonstrations in 1981 had hit home. Solanki would not again provoke the wrath of any of the state's powerful groups.

Solanki's compromises with the powerful and his reluctance to do anything special for his own supporters would appear to have been growing electoral liabilities as the 1985 elections approached. Indira Gandhi was assassinated in late 1984. Rajiv won the "sympathy elections" that followed, including a comfortable majority from Gujarat, and that must have strengthened Solanki's hand within Gujarat. As a shrewd politician, however, Solanki must have realized that such sympathy waves were likely to be short-lived and that he would need new state-level issues to reinvigorate his campaign. With state assembly elections scheduled for March 1985, Solanki initiated an electoral ploy in January, announcing that reservations for "backward classes" in government jobs and in educational institutions were being increased from 10 to 28 percent.

There is little doubt among observers of Gujarati politics that those new reservations were aimed at securing the electoral support of the various intermediate and lower castes, especially the numerically significant Kshatriyas. The timing of the decision is the most important piece of evidence in support of the argument. If there is any remaining doubt, one need only recall that a report recommending increases in reservations, the Rane Commission report, was ready as early as 1983. It recommended the use of economic criteria rather than caste criteria for determining "backwardness." Solanki had chosen not to make the report public until just before the elections. More important, he ignored the recommendation to adopt economic criteria for reservations and instead stuck to caste-based definitions. That is readily understandable if one keeps his electoral considerations in mind. The idiom of regional politics was mainly caste-oriented, not class-oriented. Also, Solanki was no socialist. He simply wanted to win elections, and that could best be done by casting electoral appeals in a familiar idiom.

Within a month of the announcement of Solanki's new reservation policies, upper-caste students again initiated an antireservation agitation in Ahmedabad. The rioting that followed, though significant, was nothing like what was to follow a few months later. The riots did not get out of hand at that early stage for two main reasons: First, Solanki quickly reacted to the threat of agitations and closed down all the schools until after the elections on March 5. The second reason was more important: Because of

26 Interview with Solanki (see footnote 15).

the upcoming elections, all the major opposition parties were hesitant to support the agitation. The reservations, including those for scheduled castes, tribes, and backward classes, were scheduled to affect nearly half of Gujarat's population. Thus, an antireservation stance would be likely to cost a political party support. The opposition parties stayed out of the fray, and the preelection agitation remained limited.

Congress (I) won a spectacular victory in the relatively peaceful elections held in March 1985 (Table 9.3). Solanki was returned to power with an increased majority, going from 141 to 149 seats in a house of 182. Considering that Congress's share of the vote had declined in other states between the January Lok Sabha elections and the March Legislative Assembly elections, an increase in support in Gujarat demonstrated the rationality of Solanki's electoral ploy to consolidate his position among the various disadvantaged KHAM communities (the Kshatriyas, Harijans, Adivasis, and Moslems), which produced 125 of the 149 Congress (I) legislators. Within the KHAM communities, the Kshatriyas clearly were the dominant group. That was obvious when the new cabinet was announced on March 18: Fourteen of the 20 ministers, including all the important ones, were from Kshatriya backgrounds.

The rioting that commenced the next day, March 19, would last for six months. Prior to an analysis of the riots, however, an important question must be asked: Why did Solanki concentrate so much governmental power in the hands of men from his own caste? Given the background of the 1981 riots, and given that everyone in the state was aware of the socioeconomic power of the Patels, why did he choose to exclude them from the government? Was that a deliberate challenge, or a stupid miscalculation? Or was there a ruling strategy that made some sense initially but eventually failed?

Solanki was a shrewd politician. One must assume, therefore, that he had some strategy. However, the strategy simply did not work. What was that strategy? Solanki had made it clear all along that in terms of real policies, he was not radical. He had put the government's resources behind production and growth, pursuing policies that would benefit the Patels, Banias, and Brahmans disproportionately. He must have hoped that that policy would appease the most powerful vested interests within the state. In order to win elections, however, he had to create a winning coalition, and one way to do that was to pull together the middle and lower strata. He offered the leaders of those groups direct access to the state's patronage: control over ministries and seats in the assembly, government-controlled jobs, admissions to colleges, and positions in local governments and cooperatives. Thereby he also offered to the unkempt masses the symbolic satisfaction of group political achievements. In addition, Solanki must have known that opposition parties and Patel youth in the cities were likely to create some trouble. By 1985, however, Congress was a different type of party, quite capable of dealing with street violence; it had incorporated many of Sanjay's goons, even in Gujarat.[27] Thus, implementing economic policies favoring the highest groups, holding control over the state and politics in the name of the disadvantaged groups, and using goons to control the opposition's street violence must have been Solanki's ruling strategy.

That strategy did not work. The opposition turned out to be stronger than Solanki must have anticipated, and instead of neutralizing each other, the clashing goons created anarchy. As the state lost control and order disintegrated, hostilities broke out along a number of social cleavages. In general, those who could muster force did, and the vulnerable groups suffered the consequences. During the rioting, which lasted six months, approximately 275 people died,[28] thousands were injured, and scores of thousands were left homeless. According to an estimate by the Gujarat Chamber of Commerce, the cost of property damage was 22 billion rupees.[29]

The details of the six months of turmoil are readily available.[30] Most of the facts concerning what happened are well known. However, it is far from clear why events happened as they did and where the responsibility for the anarchy really lay. Therefore, I shall focus on the question why the riots occurred and, more important, what the specific incidents tell us about the larger issue of concern here, namely, the conditions that lead to crises of governability in India.

The Gujarat riots of 1985 were concentrated mainly in the cities, particularly Ahmedabad. The rioting went through four identifiable phases. After some preelection rioting subsided in February, the students resumed their antireservation agitation the day after the new government was formed in mid-March. Fairly quickly, the caste riots turned into a Hindu–Moslem riot in which Moslems in Ahmedabad city became the main victims. While both antireservation and anti-Moslem rioting continued, the police went on a rampage. Even the army had a difficult time controlling the marauding groups, which included some antireservation rioters, politically supported religious zealots, and the police. Finally, as social order totally disintegrated, criminals joined in, ranging from common thugs to

27 Solanki suggested in an interview that "we can tackle street violence; we have done it before" (see footnote 15).
28 See *India Today,* August 15, 1985, p. 32.
29 See Patel "The Ahmedabad Riots, 1985," p. 9.
30 The blow-by-blow details of the riots are available in most Gujarati newspapers between March and August 1985. I consulted the clippings from the *Times of India* (Ahmedabad edition). For a more predigested coverage, see *India Today* for the same period, but especially the following issues of 1985: April 15, pp. 34–9; April 30, pp. 20–2; May 15, pp. 24–34; May 31, pp. 38–9; July 15, pp. 18–21; July 31, pp. 30–5; August 31, pp. 11. For more interpretive accounts by firsthand observers, see the articles by Sujata Patel and Asghar Ali Engineer in *EPW* (see footnote 2). Finally, for scholarly interpretations, see Spodek, "From Gandhi to Violence"; Patel, "The Ahmedabad Riots, 1985"; Mitra, "The Perils of Promoting Equality."

well-organized groups of smugglers and bootleggers. All had a heyday looting and settling old scores.

The rioting finally subsided in mid-August, when a political solution was found. Solanki resigned, and a new chief minister agreed to meet all the demands of the antireservation students. Some Patels were incorporated into the cabinet. The law-and-order machinery was revamped by creating a totally new chain of command.

The antireservation agitations that recommenced in mid-March had a fair amount of continuity from the similar earlier agitations. The stated goal of the new agitation, in 1985 as in 1981, was to force the government to withdraw its recently announced reservation policy. As in 1981, the main participants were upper-caste students in the professional schools of Ahmedabad. Moreover, many of the leaders of the new agitation were the same people who had participated actively or even led the 1981 agitation.[31] The political parties that entered the conflict were also the same. The Bhartiya Janata party (BJP) was actively involved, and the Janata party lent quiet support, mainly via "Associations of Guardians," who were directly supporting the agitation. Thus, the main sociopolitical cleavage was similar to that in the Navnirman movement in 1974 and nearly identical with that in the 1981 riots. The powerful minorities of Gujarat simply were not willing to accept their seemingly permanent exclusion from the state apparatus.

Although the elements of continuity were critical, some differences also were striking. By 1985, both sides were better prepared to pursue street violence. Although the ruling party was not better organized than before, Solanki had employed his own cadre of street toughs. That was the major new development in the Gujarat Congress in the early 1980s. The opposition was also battle-toughened. Therefore, when the agitations began, both in February and in March, instead of attacking vulnerable groups like the Harijans, the students went straight for government property, particularly by burning public buses.

The antireservation students organized large, angry meetings in mid-March. They decided to press their demands by calling a *bandh* (i.e., by closing down the city). The *bandh* was successful, and the government immediately reacted with the proverbial carrot and stick: It retracted its reservation policy, while simultaneously unleashing the police on those still bent on agitating. It is important to note that had the main motive behind the agitations been the reservation policy, the government's immediate retraction should have led to political calm. But it did not. As in 1981, the students took the government's concessions as a sign of weakness; they regrouped and increased their demands.

Alongside the antireservation agitation, a perplexing new trend arose.

31 See *India Today,* April 15, 1985, p. 30.

Intercommunity riots involving the Moslem and Hindu communities broke out in the crowded inner city. A significant number of Moslems were killed, and a much larger number suffered injury. That pattern of anti-Moslem violence would be repeated periodically over the next six months of rioting. In spite of numerous investigations, however, it remains unclear who orchestrated the violence and why. Thus, the following comments on that aspect of the riots should be treated as informed speculation.

Two aspects of the anti-Moslem violence are clear. First, whereas Ahmedabad periodically experiences intercommunity violence, there was virtual unanimity among firsthand observers that in that instance the violence against the Moslems did not result from prior tensions between the Hindu and Moslem communities.[32] Thus, the violence appears to have been deliberately fomented. Second, the direct perpetrators of violence often were hired goons. As one observer noted: "In the hospitals, doctors describing stab wounds noted that the attackers were striking the liver and other vital organs with an accuracy suggesting professional, and presumably, hired assassins rather than simple retaliation among local communities."[33] If so, the next question follows naturally: Who was hiring the goons, and why?

The two main parties to the conflict blamed each other for unleashing the violence. Babubhai Jasbhai patel, a leader of the Patel community, suggested in an interview that Solanki had unleashed intercommunity violence to distract attention from caste riots.[34] By contrast, Solanki suggested that Patels and the opposition parties were behind the intercommunity violence; such insurrections, he reasoned, would be designed to weaken his KHAM alliance and would make him "look bad in the eyes of Rajivji."[35] As I weigh the evidence, the overall picture turns out to be more complex than either side is willing to admit, but somewhat closer to the one painted by Solanki.

Solanki had won a huge majority. His government's interests would best be served by rapidly bringing the situation of civil disorder under control, rather than by turning the violence in another direction. Thus, the argument that Solanki himself instigated the conflict between the religious communities seems farfetched. Solanki was perfectly capable of doing that, but that he actually did so seems doubtful. This in no way exonerates Congress (I) as a whole. Factions within Congress (I), especially those who had failed to get cabinet posts, had an interest in weakening the new Solanki government and thus in encouraging turmoil. It is also important to remember that Congress's national victory in January 1985 was in part a

32 See the articles covering the riots by both Patel and Engineer (see footnote 2). Also see *India Today,* May 15, 1985, p. 33.
33 See Spodek, "From Gandhi to Violence," p. 7.
34 Interview (see footnote 11).
35 Interview (see footnote 15).

function of the Hindu backlash against minorities. Even before that, since 1980, Indira Gandhi had been counting the pro-Hindu vote. In 1985, therefore, Congress was perfectly capable of committing mayhem against one minority or another. That may have contributed to Solanki's ambivalence concerning how to react to a Hindu-versus-Moslem clash and thus may have exacerbated the problem.

The main force behind the violence, however, appears to have come from militant Hindu groups, many of whom were allied with the RSS and thus with the BJP (formerly the Jan Sangh). The areas in which the initial violence broke out were BJP strongholds.[36] The inflammatory religious pamphlets that were circulated had the tone of right-wing Hindu groups.[37] However community-oriented Congress (I) had become, the religious extremism and bigotry evident in those pamphlets was not the handiwork of Congress. Although Congress was not above using religion for its own purposes, those pamphlets appeared to be the work of "true believers." Most important, a message stressing Hindu militancy against Moslems clearly would have worked against the electoral interests of the Gujarati Congress; it would have tended to split the KHAM alliance and unite caste Hindus, presumably within a caste hierarchy, with traditional high castes at the top. That was hardly Congress's political game. It was, however, the BJP's game, and it was a strategy that both the BJP and the Janata pursued throughout the second half of the 1980s, leading up to the electoral defeat of Congress (I) in late-1989 Lok Sabha elections.

The most likely explanation for the intercommunity violence in 1985 is that a number of Gujarati groups who opposed Solanki had an interest in promoting political turmoil. Once Solanki retracted the reservation policies, the antireservation caste-oriented agitations had to be sustained on the basis of other issues. Moslems and other vulnerable minorities have increasingly been seen as easy targets for such hostility in India. Whenever turmoil has seemed likely to be politically advantageous for one opposition faction or another, these groups have been attacked. In 1985, all those with an interest in seeing Solanki's government weakened – Patel youth, opposition parties, especially the BJP, and Congress (I) dissidents – had an interest in promoting the insurrections. Given the meager evidence, the group most likely to have been behind the communalization of the caste riots was the BJP.

Regardless of who was behind the communalization of the caste riots, a larger analytical point is clear: The violence was deliberately generated as part of a strategy for accomplishing political goals. As far as the chronology of the conflict is concerned, once violence against Moslems broke

36 See Patel, "The Ahmedabad Riots, 1985," passim.
37 Patel, "The Ahmedabad Riots, 1985," appendixes.

out, Solanki requested help from the national government. The government had no paramilitary reserves available[38] – most of them were already maintaining order in Punjab and in the northeast – suggesting that India's growing crisis of governability involves far more than an isolated incident in a state here or there. Instead, the army intervened, and order was restored, but only temporarily.

As the army withdrew, the students resumed their agitations. Their demand was that all the students imprisoned during earlier riots be released. The details concerning who was doing what to whom in those riots increasingly become less important for our purposes. It is clear by now that the agitation was politically motivated. Those in the opposition basically did not want the Solanki government to survive. Each concession from the government only emboldened the students and opposition parties. As long as the police force was intact, there was a feeling that order could be restored. In late April, however, even that changed. When the police themselves went on a rampage, people feared that political order in Gujarat had fallen apart completely.

The army was called back in, but it was operating in a "civil situation," with only minimum powers at its disposal. It was not easy to restore order. An orgy of violence followed. As often happens in such situations, those who could muster force did, and often they used it against those who were easily victimized. Moslem and scheduled-caste areas were hit the hardest; they were the ones who lost lives and property.

A discussion of what happened over the next few months would yield only variations on the themes already discussed. The main target of the agitation was Solanki himself. Most groups, including Congress (I), were running out of control. The state had come apart. Rioting had spread to other cities beyond Ahmedabad, and even to some rural areas. Criminals had entered the fray, fully exposing the links among politicians, criminals, and the police.

Leaving aside many of the details, the story ended when New Delhi forced Solanki to resign in mid-July. The new chief minister who replaced Solanki basically reaffirmed the concessions Solanki had already made, and political calm was restored. It is clear in retrospect that the main issue at stake in the six months of rioting was the government itself; the state was the object of contention. Solanki's removal was the main victory for the opposition. The new government went a little further, giving the opposition higher visibility by replacing some of the Kshatriya ministers with Patels. Thus, the victory for the Patels was sweetened because they again had some of their community representatives in power, and they no longer saw the state as being totally in "hostile" hands. The Patels had again won, and in doing so had once again made a mockery of democratic procedures.

38 See *India Today,* April 5, 1985, p. 35.

They also reaffirmed the significance of socioeconomic resources and militancy in struggles for power.

CONCLUSION

Mahatma Gandhi's home state, Gujarat, had once been a model of effective Congress rule in India. A well-organized Congress party had been an important ingredient in that effectiveness. Equally important, however, was a fact that is not always stressed by those who tend to glorify the past: The power competition in the past had been limited to the region's socioeconomic elite. The dominance of the upper castes in the social structure had been unquestioned. Competing members of the upper castes had been able to influence those below them for their own political purposes. Over time, those conditions changed. The Congress party was still the ruling party in the late 1980s, but it was no longer a well-organized party. Equally important was the fact that upper-caste leaders had lost their capacity to mold the political behavior of those below them. The intermediate and lower strata had emerged as significant political forces in their own right. When an alliance of the lower middle strata and the lower strata captured power through a populist party, the displaced elite sought vengeance. The refusal of a powerful minority to accept the democratic verdict of the ballot box, in turn, became an ongoing source of turmoil in Gujarat. That was true during the Navnirman movement in 1974 that contributed to the proclamation of the Emergency. It was true of the 1981 riots. It was again true in 1985 when Solanki was finally ousted from power. Whether or not the deliberate turn to religious conflict in the late 1980s will fundamentally alter the nature of the caste conflict is a question to which satisfactory answers will emerge only in the 1990s.

The failure of the Congress government to confront the privileged minority politically was a more obscure but also important variable in the political breakdown of the 1980s. Since the rise of Indira Gandhi, Congress has repeatedly won majorities by popular appeal. Just below the appointed leaders, therefore, there exists only a fragmented elite. Little connects these competing elite groups to the mildly supportive masses. This mode of organizing power turns out to be effective for winning elections, but for little else. When confronted with any real obstacle, a government established through populism tends to disintegrate like a house of cards. The opposition in Gujarat understands this vulnerability of Congress governments. As a result, they have periodically resorted to organized street violence to secure what they cannot get through the ballot box.

It should be clear from the discussion in this chapter that the nuances of the specific conflicts vary widely and tend to be quite complex. Some of them have been discussed here; many have not. The purpose of the chapter has been to delineate the major causes of increasing political turmoil in one of India's more developed states. The answer seems to be clear: The major target of the insurrections is the state itself. It is important to emphasize that the importance of the state for opposing groups is not primarily the policies the state pursues but rather the symbolism of power and, more important, the economic resources the state controls. As an articulate participant in Gujarati politics put it: "If you are not with the ruling party today, chances are life will be difficult. The state is everywhere. Life chances are influenced by the state. If you don't have access to the state, life is difficult."[39] It is the pervasive presence of the state throughout society, and the related capacity of the state to influence the life-chances of individuals and groups, that has made the state the object of such intense competition. As democracy has evolved, representatives of poorly organized but numerically significant underprivileged groups have gained control of governments in some parts of India, and the socioeconomically privileged groups have reacted violently.

39 Interview with Satyam Patel [secretary, Gujarat Pradesh Committee, Congress (R)], Ahmedabad, March 17, 1986.

10

From breakdown to order: West Bengal

West Bengal is something of an exception in India's contemporary political landscape. Whereas many states have experienced political instability over the past two decades, West Bengal has been relatively well governed since 1977. That stability has been remarkable because it has not been the result of low levels of political mobilization; West Bengal probably was India's most politically mobilized and chaotic state in the late 1960s. West Bengal's restoration and maintenance of political order naturally direct our attention to the issue of how growing crises of governability can be reversed.

This chapter traces the roots of West Bengal's recent stability to the fact that a well-organized reformist party has remained in power. The Communist Party of India, Marxist (CPM), has repeatedly been elected to office in West Bengal since 1977. The party is communist in name only and is essentially social-democratic in its ideology, social program, and policies. The party's disciplined, effective organization has minimized the debilitating elite factionalism and the related elite-led mobilization and countermobilization so common in some other states. The CPM has also consolidated a coalition of the middle and lower strata by implementing some modest redistributive programs. That systematic incorporation of the poor has reduced the attractiveness of populism and its emphasis on deinstitutionalization. And finally, the CPM has adopted a nonthreatening approach toward property-owning groups, whose roles in production and economic growth remain essential for the long-term welfare of the state.

The CPM's rule in West Bengal has not been without its share of problems. The CPM may be well organized, but its relations with other parties, especially other leftist parties, have occasionally led to political discord. Two years of ethnic strife in one of West Bengal's sixteen districts – the "Gurkhaland" troubles in Darjeeling – cast doubt on the CPM's capacity to accommodate non-class types of conflicts. The CPM's attempts to maintain an alliance of the middle and lower groups have generated serious problems for its ongoing program of redistribution. Moreover, like other ruling communist parties elsewhere, the CPM is beginning to give rise to a "new class" of privileged members who are resented by those excluded from the perks of power.

The CPM type of rule in West Bengal does not offer a model for the rest of India. Even if it did, there are historical and cultural reasons because of which it would not be likely to be replicated. Thus, a discussion of the West Bengal experience serves not a prescriptive purpose but an important analytical function. In spite of its many problems, West Bengal under the CPM probably is India's best-governed state: The coalition that supports the CPM is relatively stable; the gap between the government's commitments and its capacities is modest; and political violence along caste, class, or religious lines has been minimal. An understanding of how the CPM has achieved such effective government tends to reenforce my earlier emphasis on the political causes of the governability crisis in India.

THE BACKGROUND

West Bengal is relatively industrialized, but it also has more rural poverty than many other states in India.[1] The roots of its industry are traceable back to the colonial period, as are the origins of its agrarian structure, which supports a large population on little land. The agrarian structure has undergone some important changes since the *zamindari* abolition. Toward the bottom of the landownership hierarchy, nearly half the population own no land or have access to less than one acre of land.[2] These are the rural poor. In the recent past, a substantial rural minority used to be tenant farmers. That, however, has changed over the past decade. Legislative and political changes introduced by the CPM government have modified the old forms of tenancy; new arrangements have emerged under which tenants enjoy almost permanent leases on land.

The pattern of landholding in the middle range (1–10 acres) has changed only minimally over the past three decades. The big changes have come at the top of the pyramid. Both the area under cultivation and the number of farmers cultivating large landholdings (above 10 acres) have declined. That reflects both the pressure of land-reform legislation and, more important, the division of property at inheritance. The agrarian structure of contemporary West Bengal is characterized by numerous cultivators with

1 This discussion builds on my earlier work on West Bengal politics: Atul Kohli, "From Elite Activism to Democratic Consolidation: Political Change in West Bengal," in Francine Frankel and M. S. A. Rao, eds., *Dominance and State Power in Modern India: Decline of a Social Order,* 2 vols. (Oxford University Press, 1989–90), volume 2; idem, *The State and Poverty in India: The Politics of Reform* (Cambridge University Press, 1987), chapter 3; idem, "Communist Reformers in West Bengal: Origins, Features and Relations with New Delhi," in John R. Wood, ed., *State Politics in Contemporary India: Crisis or Continuity?* (Boulder, Colo.: Westview Press, 1984), pp. 81–102; idem, "Parliamentary Communism and Agrarian Reform: The Evidence from India's Bengal," *Asian Survey,* July 1983, pp. 783–809.

2 For land data, see Kohli, *The State and Poverty in India,* Table 3.4 on p. 118, and for more detailed discussion of the changing agrarian structure, see chapter 3.

access to middle- and small-size landholdings and a very substantial population of landless laborers.

Certain peculiarities of the caste and community makeup of West Bengal are also important. Nearly half the population of the state are not "mainstream" Hindus. They are rather scheduled castes and tribes (27.5 percent) and Moslems (20 percent). Among the Hindus, moreover, the caste divisions do not follow the "normal" fourfold division.[3] There are no indigenous Kshatriyas or Vaishyas in Bengal. The numbers of the twice-born castes are also relatively small (about 7 percent), certainly in comparison with the neighboring state of Bihar. The line of demarcation between Brahmans and such "clean Sudras" as Vaidyas and Kayasthas is not sharp. The Brahmans will "take water" from these clean Sudras, though intermarriage remains rare.

The patterns of landownership according to caste in West Bengal have important political consequences. Many Brahmans in West Bengal, as in other states, own sizable pieces of land. However, landownership by caste in West Bengal is extremely heterogeneous. There are no castes that can be considered dominant statewide. In addition to the Brahmans, other clean Sudras like the Kayasthas are concentrated in certain districts and own considerable amounts of land there. In other districts, landownership is in the hands of "lower Sudras" who farm, such as the Sadgops, Namasudras, Aguris, and Kaivartas.[4] Unlike the situation in many other Indian states, therefore, political concerns in West Bengal do not readily crystallize along statewide caste cleavages. Although caste remains politically significant at the local level, the absence of dominant castes at the state level opens up possibilities for political parties to forge coalitions along lines other than caste.

There are other noteworthy aspects of the relatively unusual political past of Bengal. The political history of Bengal and related issues have been discussed in detail elsewhere.[5] However, a brief overview of the historical inheritance is necessary in order to understand why political patterns in contemporary West Bengal tend to be distinctive.

The Congress party never put down deep roots in Bengal, but non-Congress groups, including leftist groups, have long enjoyed prominence in Bengali politics. That historical pattern reflects both the nature of the Bengali political elite and the socioeconomic divisions within Bengali society. Unlike many other parts of India, Bengal developed a regional in-

3 Studies of caste in Bengal: Jyotirmoyee Sarma, *Caste Dynamics Among the Bengali Hindus* (Calcutta: Firma KLM Private Ltd., 1980); Hitesranjan Sanyal, *Social Mobility in Bengal* (Calcutta: Papyrus, 1981).
4 For an excellent historical study that traces how that pattern of control over land evolved, see Ratnalekha Ray, *Change in Bengal Agrarian Society, 1760–1850* (New Delhi: Manohar, 1979).
5 See Kohli, "From Elite Activism to Democratic Consolidation."

telligentsia prior to the rise of Gandhi and the Congress party. That regional intelligentsia – the Bengali *bhadralok* – helped mobilize Bengali nationalism, which was never fully incorporated into the larger Indian nationalist movement.[6]

Those Bengali leaders who did join Gandhi and Congress faced significant obstacles. The preindependence Congress in Bengal remained largely Calcutta-oriented. The *bhadralok* leadership of Congress was primarily Hindu; it had difficulty in forging alliances with the Moslems concentrated in eastern Bengal.[7] Even within Hindu-dominated areas, the social interests of Calcutta-based leaders limited their political reach into the districts. Most of those leaders belonged to the upper castes, such as Brahmans, Vaidyas, and Kayasthas, and had their roots in *zamindari* wealth. Control over village life, by contrast, often was in the hands of intermediate-caste *jotedars,* the legal "tenants" of the revenue-collecting *zamindars.* The relationships between the Hindu *jotedars* of intermediate caste and the upper-caste *zamindars* often were conflictual. The former even forged a political alliance with a Moslem leadership (the Moslem party led by Fazlul Haq) that promised them "tenancy reforms."[8] It was not Congress, therefore, but the Krishak Praja party of Fazlul Haq that formed a regional government in undivided Bengal. Bengal was one of the few states in preindependence India where Congress never held power.

A significant proportion of the Bengali *bhadralok* shunned Congress. They experimented instead with radical nationalism and militant politics, both rightist and leftist.[9] A minority of them were eventually attracted to communism.[10] As long as those communists remained under Moscow's tutelage, looking for a revolutionary proletariat in a land of peasants, their political significance remained limited. Over time, however, a faction of the local communist leadership broke away from Moscow's counsel, utilized

6 The best study of the Bengali *bhadralok* remains that by John Broomfield, *Elite Conflict in a Plural Society* (Berkeley: University of California Press, 1968).
7 For example, see John Gallagher, "Congress in Decline: Bengal, 1930 to 1939," *Modern Asian Studies,* July 1973, pp. 589–645.
8 Ibid.
9 For an excellent study of the complicated divisions among the Bengali political elite in the early part of this century, see Sumit Sarkar, *The Swadeshi Movement in Bengal, 1903–1908* (New Delhi: People's Publishing House, 1973).
10 There has been no good study of the origins of communism in Bengal. Some helpful insights can be derived from the following: Gautam Chattopadhyay, *Communism and Bengal's Freedom Movement* (New Delhi: People's Publishing House, 1970); Muyaffar Ahmed, *The Communist Party of India and Its Formation Abroad* (Calcutta: National Book Agency, 1961); David N. Druhe, *Soviet Russia and Indian Communism* (New York: Bookman Associates, 1959); V. B. Karnik, *M. N. Roy: A Political Biography* (Bombay: New Jagriti Samay Publisher, 1978); Gene Overstreet and Marshall Windmiller, *Communism in India* (Berkeley: University of California Press, 1959); M. N. Roy, *Memoirs* (Bombay: Allied Publishers, 1964); Bhabani Sen Gupta, *Communism in Indian Politics* (New York: Columbia University Press, 1972).

Bengali nationalism and reformism as mobilizing themes, and made significant inroads in the Bengali countryside.[11] It was those reform-oriented communists who eventually filled the power vacuum created by Congress's weakness, and they have now ruled West Bengal for more than a decade.

The peculiarities of Bengali caste and class structure have also worked to the advantage of non-Congress political forces. The absence of a statewide dominant caste has already been noted. That hurt Congress, because its main political strategy after independence was to build electoral support through such influential groups. Additionally, as I have argued elsewhere, caste identities simply were not as deeply embedded in Bengal and did not mold the political behavior of Bengalis to the same extent as, say, those of Biharis.[12] That, in turn, has had a major political consequence. The lower-caste positions within the hierarchical structure have not always been deemed to be legitimate, and that has encouraged militancy in the lower strata and has hurt Congress's capacity to mobilize mass support.

Those tendencies were further reenforced by the *zamindari* system of land tenure introduced by the British.[13] As a result of the *zamindari* system, landowners became far removed from concerns of the land; they did not live on their lands, and many came to disdain manual labor and agricultural work. An elite social stratum arose within Bengal – the *bhadralok* – whose life-styles were devoted not to agriculture and production but to music, poetry, literature, art, philosophical concerns, social criticism, and even radical politics. Not being an integral part of the agricultural scene, and yet deriving their wealth primarily from agriculture, those owners found it difficult to mask their economic privileges with ideological cloaks. The more radical of the *bhadralok* would later exploit that situation to undermine the economic privileges of their more fortunate brethren, while enhancing their own power positions in the society.

As the elite stratum stayed away from production and commerce, urban economic activities in Bengal came to be dominated more and more by non-Bengalis: first by the British, and then, slowly but surely, by the Parsis and the Marwaris from western India.[14] Those non-Bengali entrepreneurs never became an integral part of the Bengali social structure. They chose to deal directly with New Delhi to further their economic interests. That

11 See Bhabani Sengupta, *CPI-M: Promises, Prospects, Problems* (New Delhi: Young Asia Publications, 1979); Kohli, *The State and Poverty in India,* chapter 3.
12 See Kohli, "From Elite Activism to Democratic Consolidation." For historical details of those changes, see R. C. Majumdar, *History of Bengal,* 4 vols. (Calcutta: G. Bhardwaj, 1971–8).
13 Among many good studies of the *zamindari* system in Bengal, see the "standard" work of S. Gopal, *The Permanent Settlement in Bengal and Its Results* (London: Allen & Unwin, 1948). For a "revisionist" view, see Ray, *Change in Bengal Agrarian Society.*
14 For a discussion of the non-Bengali character of capitalists in Bengal, see Nirmal Chaudhry, "West Bengal: Vortex of Ideological Politics," in Iqbal Narain, ed., *State Politics in India* (Meerut: Meenakshi Prakashan, 1968).

pattern had important political consequences: Radical Bengali leaders could mobilize against "capitalism" as an anti-Bengali alliance between Congress and the Marwaris. Themes of regional nationalism came to be combined with class themes, further working to the political advantage of the left.

Both in the cities and in the countryside of Bengal, the domination of the privileged over their subordinates was not as consolidated as in many other parts of India. Thus, the Bengali lower castes and classes provided radicalizable political material.[15] Although we should not overestimate the lower-class radicalism in contemporary West Bengal, the fact is that mere elite radicalism, without peasant and worker support for the CPM, could not have led to a democratically elected communist government.

Another important factor in the success of the left in West Bengal has been an effective, centralized political party. I have argued elsewhere that the origins of that can be traced to the terrorist backgrounds of many communist leaders.[16] Thus, a significant minority of Bengali political activists already understood the significance of disciplined organizations before they were introduced to communism.[17] Such recent communist leaders as Pramode Das Gupta, Hare Krishna Konar, and Binoy Chowdhry were all former terrorist revolutionaries who later converted to communism. Having embraced the new ideology, the organizational principles of democratic centralism must have come easily to that group. Discipline, hierarchy, and party before all else were the values integral to the political terrorist subculture. In all probability, those political-cultural traditions have facilitated the growth of relatively cohesive parties in contemporary West Bengal. Of course, this is not to ignore the legendary factionalism and sectarianism of the Indian left.[18] Nevertheless, the CPM in West Bengal stands out today as a cohesive political force in India, and the long tradition of disciplined organization is at least partly responsible for this political characteristic.

By the time of independence, radical politics had already established strong roots in Bengal. A small but significant number of the political elite had embraced communism, and the lower classes – workers and peasants – had shown ample susceptibility to radical appeals. The political traditions

15 For discussion of labor activism in the first half of this century, see Majumdar, *History of Bengal,* vol. 4. For an analysis of one of the major peasant rebellions, the Tebhagha movement, see Hamza Alavi, "Peasants and Revolutions," *Socialist Register,* 1965.
16 See Kohli, "From Elite Activism to Democratic Consolidation." For historical details of Bengal's terrorist past, see Majumdar, *History of Bengal,* vol. 4, chapter 5.
17 For interviews that establish links between "old terrorists" and the "new communists," see Chattopadhyay, *Communism and Bengal's Freedom Movement.*
18 The theme of factionalism was emphasized by Marcus Franda, *Radical Politics in West Bengal* (Cambridge, Mass.: M.I.T. Press, 1972).

of the area further enabled the radical elite to organize a small but disciplined party, which would in time grow into the ruling party.

None of this should lead to a view that Congress was an insignificant force in postindependence West Bengal. On the contrary, Congress in West Bengal, as elsewhere in India, emerged as the most popular party. The Congress party was India's nationalist party, and West Bengal, though somewhat on the periphery, was still very much a part of India. Thus, the euphoria of nationalism carried West Bengal along and led to Congress's electoral victory in West Bengal. Bengali leaders like Atulya Ghosh and B. C. Roy, who were close to Nehru, were able to ride the wave of first-generation nationalism; they formed popular governments that ruled West Bengal for nearly 15 years.[19]

The historical factors that contributed to Congress's weakness have already been mentioned. A few additional changes following independence further reinforced those tendencies. First, many among the Bengali elite held Congress responsible for the partition and loss of nearly half of Bengal to Pakistan. Thus, independence had been a mixed blessing for the Bengalis: As part of India, they had gained sovereignty; as a region with a strong "subnational" identity, however, they had suffered considerable loss. The historical ambiguity of the Bengalis toward Congress was only reinforced.

Second, *zamindari* abolition in the 1950s eliminated the intermediaries between the government and the *jotedars*. It was the latter who controlled land and exercised influence at the village level. Unlike the situation in other parts of India, the emergence of *jotedars* as local influentials did not always bode well for Congress. Although those groups had benefited from Congress's actions, and thus quite a few were attracted to the national party, there were many such village-level influentials who had opposed Congress in the preindependence period. Thus, their loyalty to Congress was tenuous. Bengali *jotedars* were also heterogeneous in terms of their caste composition. They could not easily be assembled to form a cohesive caste base for the Congress party, as were, for example, the Vokkaligas and the Lingayats in Karnataka, or the Kammas and the Reddis in Andhra Pradesh. Finally, the already precarious political hold of the landowning castes over their subordinates was further weakened as adult suffrage spread and new attempts at mass political mobilization were undertaken.

Thus, Congress in West Bengal never put down deep roots. Prior to independence, Congress had never led a government in the British-controlled legislatures. Following independence, Congress inherited nationalist legitimacy and thus managed to rule West Bengal for nearly 15 years. Both before and after that 15-year interregnum, West Bengal was

19 Ibid.

Table 10.1. *Seats won by major political parties in West Bengal assembly elections, 1952–87*

Party[a]	1952	1957	1962	1967	1969	1971	1972	1977[b]	1982	1987[c]
Congress	150	152	157	127	55	105	216	20	49	40
CPM	28	46	50	43	80	113	14	177	174	187
CPI	—	—	—	16	30	13	35	2	7	11
Forward Bloc	14	8	13	13	21	3	0	25	28	26

[a]The other significant parties that have come and gone and are not listed here include the Bangla Congress, the Praja Socialist Party, and the Revolutionary Socialist Party. The latter continues to be significant; it won 20, 19, and 18 seats in the 1977, 1982, and 1987 assembly elections, respectively.
[b]The newly formed Janata party won 29 seats in 1977, only to vanish completely in the 1982 elections.
[c]Data from *India Today*, April 15, 1987.
Source: Computed from the reports of the Election Commission.

controlled by a non-Congress political force. Therefore, those 15 years appear in retrospect to have been exceptional. As Table 10.1 shows, Congress in West Bengal has steadily lost its electoral base since 1962. What has captured the Bengali political imagination is a party that has emphasized the themes of regional nationalism and the antirich solidarity of the middle and lower classes.

THE DECADE OF CHAOS, 1967–77

The story of the changing patterns of politics in West Bengal is illustrated in Figure 10.1. The data support a commonly held impression: There was a significant increase in political violence and rioting in the late 1960s and early 1970s in West Bengal. The fairly sharp decline shown in 1972 appears more significant than it was, because in the aftermath of the Bangladesh war, Indira Gandhi virtually obliterated democratic politics in West Bengal and utilized state terror to eliminate many of the revolutionary groups. A "normal" political process resumed only in 1977, and under the CPM government the level of political violence has actually declined.

The main burden of analysis here is to explain those changing patterns of political violence and, by implication, explain the changing capacity of the government to rule within West Bengal. First, however, a caveat should be noted: Bengal has been characterized by relatively high levels of political violence for much of the twentieth century. The reason for such civil unrest over a prolonged period, say in comparison with Gujarat between 1900 and 1970, is an interesting issue, but it is not the topic of discussion here. The focus here is a more recent period, particularly some fairly sharp fluctuations in political violence over the past two decades.

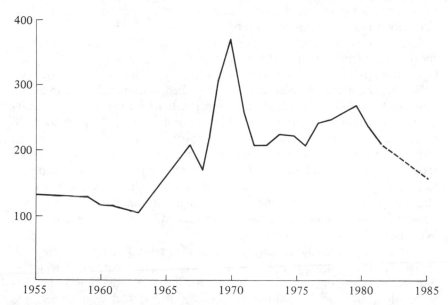

Figure 10.1. Political violence in West Bengal, 1955–85 (number of riots per million population). The data for 1955–82 are from an annual publication: Government of India, Ministry of Home Affairs, *Crime in India* (New Delhi: Government Press). Data for 1983 and 1984 are not available. The figure for 1985 is an estimate provided by government officials.

The main analytical components of the West Bengal story are fairly straightforward, as cited in the earlier chapter on Calcutta. The decline of Congress in the mid–1960s created a power vacuum within West Bengal that was not filled until 1977, when the CPM emerged as the new ruling party. The intervening period was a period of turmoil. Coalitional instability and the related ineffectiveness of the government combined with socioeconomic conflict to yield civil disorder and political instability.

The electoral decline of Congress in the mid-1960s was a nationwide phenomenon. In that limited sense West Bengal was part of a national trend. But a number of factors exacerbated the impact of Congress's decline in West Bengal: The first-generation nationalist leaders had passed away, and no one arose to take charge of the West Bengal Congress. More than in many other states, Congress in West Bengal had remained a personalistic force. "Tall leaders" like Atulya Ghosh and B. C. Roy had managed to create a party machine that kept factionalism within limits and helped transform nationalist aspirations into electoral victories. After the death of B. C. Roy in 1962, however, Congress's factionalism became more obvious. Even before the national Congress party experienced its major electoral setback in 1967, Congress in West Bengal had split; the formation of the offshoot party, the Bangla Congress, further weakened the centrist alternative that Congress had offered within West Bengal.

Second, two consecutive droughts in the mid-1960s had led to food shortages, inflationary pressures, and political difficulties for Congress throughout India. The situation was especially difficult in West Bengal. Following the partition, West Bengal had taken in more refugees than any other state in India. That had increased the demand for food, especially grain. The partition had created another disequilibrium: A large proportion of the state's arable land had come to be devoted to the production of cash crops. Prior to partition, East Bengal had produced many of the raw materials necessary for industrial production. As those sources of supply began to be cut off, the scarcity of raw materials led to high prices; the "rational peasant" began producing cash crops. An unfortunate side effect was a decline in food production. Thus, the impact of the mid-1960s drought in West Bengal was fairly serious.

A third important factor that was at work in West Bengal in the mid-1960s was the significant political presence of leftist parties. The leftist parties, including the undivided Communist Party of India (CPI), the Forward Bloc, and the Revolutionary Socialist Party, had won respectable numbers of seats in both the 1957 and 1962 elections (Table 10.1). Their collective share of the vote in each election was more than one-third of the total. They had taken advantage of a faction-ridden Congress confronting a worsening food situation and declining popularity. Food shortages, especially, provided a significant issue for political mobilization. Strikes and demonstrations against the Congress government became common. As Figure 10.1 shows, rioting and violence continued to increase throughout 1965 and 1966, leading up to the crucial elections in 1967. It was at those elections that Congress was finally defeated. Congress remained the largest single party within West Bengal; it won 127 of the 280 assembly seats (Table 10.1). A number of other parties, however, including the two main communist parties (the CPI had split into the CPM and CPI in 1964) and the Bangla Congress, succeeded in forming a United Front (UF) coalition government.

The formation of the UF government in 1967 led to a decade of chaos in West Bengal. The first UF government lasted less than a year. It was replaced, for two months, by a Congress-led coalition. When that also came apart, presidential rule was imposed. A second UF government was formed in 1969; it was also replaced by presidential rule in 1970. A coalition government with Congress as the leading force again came to power in 1971; that also did not last long. After the Bangladesh war in 1971, Congress finally swept to power with a huge majority, but under a considerable cloud of suspicion of electoral fraud. That Congress government was eventually superseded by the national Emergency in 1975. The democratic process in West Bengal was resumed only after the 1977 elections.

Figure 10.1 shows the sharp increase in political violence that accompanied governmental instability between 1967 and 1971. The data indicating that increase were collected by the police and did not include figures on the state terror unleashed against various political groups during 1972–7. The independent group Amnesty International has documented the extent of the violence.[20] A descriptive conclusion is inescapable: The decade of 1967–77 in West Bengal politics was characterized by a severe governability crisis.

What were the roots of that crisis? The casual dynamics clearly were quite complex. Both socioeconomic conflict and anomic unrest played their parts. The decisive variables, however, were political. It is clear in retrospect that coalitional instability during that period made the government relatively ineffective as an agent of law and order, and that opened the door for a variety of conflicts. Moreover, competing factions among the political elite mobilized their forces, over which they soon lost control, thus adding to the chaos. And finally, Indira Gandhi used the cloak of the Bangladesh war to impose presidential rule and eliminate many of her armed political enemies. The crisis subsided only after resumption of the democratic process in the 1977 elections and the electoral victory of a relatively cohesive political party.

Both the cities and the countryside of West Bengal were engulfed in political violence during that period. A fair amount of what happened in the cities, especially in Calcutta, was discussed in Chapter 6. Although some additional discussion of the role of factory workers and students will be provided, the emphasis here is on the dynamics of the agrarian conflicts. They were mainly of two types: seemingly "revolutionary class violence," typified by the rebellion in Naxalbari, and the land-grab movements encouraged by the UF government, especially by the CPM.

Before analyzing those factors, it is important to recall some of the traits of the UF government that were discussed in Chapter 6. The ideologically divergent parties within the UF were nearly as wary of each other as they were of Congress. They spent considerable energy devising political strategies that could help transform their temporary hold on government into an expanded political base. The CPM was the major force in that coalition government, especially after 1969. The CPM adhered to a more revolutionary line during that period. It defined its main task in government as "expanding and strengthening worker and peasant alliance." In practice, that led to a two-prolonged political strategy: neutralizing the tendency of the state to be an agent of "class repression" from above, and using its party organization to mobilize the lower classes from below.

The CPM repeatedly sought and eventually gained control over the

20 The report was discussed by Marcus Franda, "Rural Development, Bengali Marxist Style," American Universities Field Staff Reports, Asia, No. 15, 1978, p. 4.

ministries of labor, land and land revenue, and home (which controlled the police). An important aspect of the CPM's ruling strategy – an aspect that eventually would contribute heavily to the fall of the UF government – was to order the police not to interfere in "class struggles." The CPM thus neutralized the regional state apparatus as an agent of political order. Whatever the merits of such a strategy for fomenting revolution in nation-states in general, as a regional strategy its effectiveness was highly doubtful. The CPM had only neutralized the "near state" and thus invited the wrath of the more "distant state" (i.e., invited federal intervention). It took the CPM some time to internalize one of the hard lessons of realpolitik: Its powers were limited. Meanwhile, the neutralization of the police provided encouragement for many of the subsequent conflicts within West Bengal.

The best-known peasant rebellion of the period clearly was the conflict in Naxalbari in the north of West Bengal. There have been thorough studies of that rebellion.[21] For our purposes, its details are not important. What is important is to find the main causes of the rebellion. General explanations in terms of "exploitation" of the peasantry, though clearly part of the overall equation, will not suffice, because peasant exploitation in India is widespread, but rebellions are not. The Naxalbari rebellion, moreover, was not really a peasant rebellion; its protagonists were mainly semino-madic tribals, the Santhals. Not being socialized in the rigid and hierarchical Hindu caste structure, the Santhals of the area often had rebelled in the past. The border location of Naxalbari facilitated revolutionary organiza-tion. In addition, tea plantations dominated the local agriculture in Nax-albari, and they provided better conditions for political organization than would the atomistic family-owned small farms common in many other areas.

Given those contributing "ecological" conditions, the decisive causes of the rebellion were political. The local Santhals had been organized by a militant subgroup of the CPM. After the CPM came to power in 1967, the local party officers decided to take advantage of their new power. They undertook a militant land-grab movement. Local tribals, armed with prim-itive bows and arrows and spears, provided the main force for the move-ment. The tribals claimed "above-ceiling" land to be legally theirs. (There was legislation on the books stipulating a ceiling on the amount of land that one could own.) They forcibly occupied such land, and, if necessary, they killed the landlords, thus establishing "liberated" areas.

That land-grab movement spread to some 60 villages and lasted nearly

21 See, for example, Shankar Ghosh, *The Naxalite Movement* (Calcutta: K. L. Mukhopa-dhyay, 1974), especially pp. 24–35; Biplab Dasgupta, *The Naxalite Movement* (Bombay: Allied Publishers, 1975), especially pp. 1–14; Franda, *Radical Politics in West Bengal*, chapter 6.

two months. It is clear in retrospect that the movement would not have gained strength but for the fact that the UF government, especially the CPM, decided to keep the police out of the conflict. A militant peasant rebellion led by the CPM's own cadres had put the CPM leaders in a dilemma: The CPM in government was responsible for protecting basic constitutional rights, including the rights to private property and life; however, the CPM was reluctant to use state repression against its own revolutionary cadres. The CPM sought to resolve that dilemma by pursuing a two-pronged strategy: keeping the police out of the conflict, and simultaneously trying to impose the party line on its own cadres. The CPM's strategy failed. The local cadres continued to undertake militant mobilization, including the killing of landowners in the name of "revolutionary justice." Because the scope of the "revolution" was limited to one corner of one region in a giant-size nation-state, the results were predictable.

Eventually the CPM had to dismiss the leaders of Naxalbari from the party, and the UF government ordered the police back into Naxalbari to restore order. The "revolutionary movement" collapsed within weeks. Most of the leaders were imprisoned. The ease with which the entire movement was crushed strongly supports the argument that the temporary withdrawal of state power had been the most important factor in the short-term success of the Naxalbari uprising. To the extent that such deliberate abstention from the use of state power is a somewhat unusual occurrence in functioning states, the Naxalbari uprising can be viewed as an aberration. More generally, a broader insight of comparative politics also gains support from that experience: Disintegration of state power may well be an important precondition for transformation of latent socioeconomic hostilities into overt conflict.[22]

Before analyzing other types of agrarian conflicts during that period, especially those led by the CPM itself, it is important to note that both the temporary success of the Naxalbari uprising and the subsequent state repression had significant political consequences. The uprising led to the creation of a third communist party, a Marxist-Leninist party that did not believe in parliamentary democracy, but instead was committed to fomenting a revolution by following a "Maoist" strategy of "armed struggle." The temporary success of the uprising created an overinflated sense of efficacy among the Naxalites; they began acting as if a Chinese-style peasant revolution was possible in India. The participation of the CPM in the government that repressed the Naxalbari uprising alienated the more militant Bengalis from the CPM's "reformism." Thus, the stage was set for

---

22 For a broader statement of this hypothesis with reference to comparative and historical materials, see Theda Skocpol, *States and Social Revolutions* (Cambridge University Press, 1979).

battle: an alienated militant minority whose members had recently renewed their sense of political efficacy versus a fragmented state that, in spite of its strong leftist orientation, stood delegitimized in the eyes of the militants.

The Naxalites and the various governments in West Bengal had many a confrontation during 1967–77, adding to an already substantial surge in violence. Rural rebellions in the style of Naxalbari were attempted in several areas. A case in point was the attempt to establish "liberated areas" in the late 1960s in such *taluks* of Midnapore district as Debra and Gopiballabhpur. During my fieldwork in the area some 10 years later, I heard the story of the rise and decline of the insurrection from several close observers and even some participants. Although the details differ, the main contours of the story were similar to those in the Naxalbari uprising. Local militant leaders led an insurrection that resulted in the killing of some landlords and the redistribution of their land to poor peasants, with the beneficiaries being organized into armed groups to protect the gains. The CPM-dominated UF government remained hesitant to use the police to put down the rebellion and thus created de facto political spaces for the growth of a revolutionary movement. Eventually, however, after the UF government had lost power, state repression was used against the rebels, and the movement died a relatively quick death.

There were additional semirural, semiurban confrontations between the Naxalites and others, including the police and members of the CPM, that had similar qualities. An incident in Durgapur in 1969, for example, pitched student Naxalites against the "arch class enemy," the police.[23] The CPM again tried to rein in the police so as to avoid appearing counterrevolutionary. That encouraged student attacks on the police and almost led to a police mutiny. The crisis was eventually resolved when the CPM restored the powers of the police, but not before several deaths and hundreds of injuries had occurred. Similarly, the Birbhum uprising lasted some four months and resulted in more than 200 murders of "class enemies" by Naxalites, followed by elimination of the local Naxalites by the government.[24] The rebels were mainly "students, school-dropouts and antisocials of the urban areas," and the "class enemies" who were killed included not only a few big landowners and policemen but also many "small and middle peasants and petty businessmen."[25] Once the state decided to put down the rebels, the movement petered out fairly rapidly.

An important common theme ran through those recurring conflicts between the Naxalites and the various governments in West Bengal in the late 1960s. Coalitional instability within the government had created such

---

23 For details, see Franda, *Radical Politics in West Bengal*, pp. 176–81; Shankar Ghosh, *The Disinherited State: A Study of West Bengal, 1967–70* (Bombay: Orient Longman, 1971), pp. 204–8.

24 For details, see Dasgupta, *The Naxalite Movement*, pp. 113–15.

25 Ibid., pp. 113 and 115 respectively.

insecurity among the partners in the coalition that they tended to weigh any proposed governmental action primarily in terms of whether or not it would expand their respective power bases. That, in turn, led the CPM to keep the forces of law and order on a tight leash, and thus many political spaces were opened up for the hatching of petty rebellions. West Bengal had always had its share of "true believers" who were ready to use those openings to carry out the various revolutionary experiments. Such experiments added to the existing political chaos that had resulted from an unstable government. Later, the government's widespread repression of those petty revolutionaries only continued the spiral of political violence.

That same theme of the role of an ineffective state, or, more precisely, a state deliberately made ineffective, ran through the other major agrarian conflict of the period, namely, the land-grab movements initiated by the CPM. For reasons of both ideological commitment and power, the CPM leadership was committed to expanding its peasant base. The brief pockets of Naxalite success had shown how strongly the peasants felt about the "land question." Not wanting to be left behind, the CPM began pursuing its own limited version of land-grab movements.

Hare Krishna Konar was the CPM's radical land minister. He sought to identify and to redistribute all *benami* lands (above-ceiling lands registered under false names) and to ensure the occupancy rights of sharecroppers. Because the CPM was not fully in control of the government, it could not use the state machinery to attain those goals. Instead, its strategy was, again, to keep the state – especially the police, but also local administrators and, if possible, the courts – out of land conflicts and to use party-led mobilization to implement land reforms.[26] Because of the short durations of the two UF governments, major redistribution did not occur. The important aspect of that experiment, therefore, was not any concrete realization of the redistribution program but rather the political dynamics set in motion.

The CPM sought to limit the reach of the state from above and to mobilize from below. Two important consequences followed. First, even limited gains by the CPM were politically threatening to the other partners in the coalition government. Every redistributive success meant new supporters and more loyal supporters for the CPM. The membership of the CPM-affiliated Kisan Sabha (the peasant organization) rose during that period from approximately a quarter of a million to more than half a million. The other coalition partners did not want to be left out of the game of political competition. They sought to enter the fray, attempting their own versions of land redistribution, sometimes even competing with the CPM over the same piece of land. As one analyst pointed out, "there were innumerable physical clashes between the major political parties in

26 For details, see Franda, *Radical Politics in West Bengal,* especially pp. 182–90.

the United Front between 1969–70 in which two or more parties attempted to seize the same plot of land."[27] Clearly, political competition within the ruling coalition became a source of socioeconomic conflict and violence.

A second consequence was that the CPM leadership often failed to control its own "enthusiastic" local cadres, which led to "excesses" in land-grabbing and to numerous physical clashes. During my fieldwork in the early 1980s, for example, a number of local observers reported that the party line on the land question under Hare Krishna Konar was quite confusing. Konar, on the one hand, would trumpet revolutionary rhetoric, suggesting that militant confiscation of land was integral to the party's program. On the other hand, the real party line was to act with restraint on the issue, that is, to use the land program differentially according to local circumstances and mainly to enhance the party's electoral and organizational position. The need to make adjustments for local variations necessitated a decentralized strategy. Not all local cadres, however, were totally clear on how far and how fast the land program should move. The more militant cadres chose to take Konar's highly rhetorical speeches as representative of the party line, and they moved fairly rapidly and decisively during 1969–70. That was certainly true, for example, in parts of Midnapore and 24 Parganas where I did fieldwork. The results were increasing numbers of physical clashes between landowners and CPM cadres and a simultaneous rush of newspaper stories proclaiming the breakdown of law and order in West Bengal.

The UF experiments in West Bengal created peculiar conditions under which those who were in power, or, more precisely, exercised partial power, came to have a vested interest in fomenting radical mobilization. Political fragmentation within the state and deliberate, elite-led mobilization in the civil society thus combined to generate considerable violence in the agrarian sector. A similar analysis of urban developments was provided in Chapter 6. To recall briefly, statewide figures on labor problems tell the dramatic story that unfolded in the cities: Labor–management disputes increased from some 6,000 to more than 10,000 between 1964 and 1967, union membership in the same period climbed from 42,000 to 128,000, and the number of man-days lost in labor disputes went up from 1.5 million to more than 6 million. The increasing rural and urban violence set the stage for the imposition of presidential rule and state repression.

The nature of the violence in West Bengal changed midway through the decade of chaos unleashed by the UF experiments. The second five years of the chaotic decade, especially the periods 1971–2 and 1975–7, were characterized by increasing state repression. Because the violence in that period was unleashed by the government, official statistics do not reflect

27 Ibid., p. 184.

it well. The exact numbers of "revolutionaries" and other political enemies who were killed or imprisoned will never be known. There is no doubt, however, that the extent of such repression was significant. During my field visits to West Bengal in 1979–80, 1982, 1984, and 1986, nearly everyone I interviewed, including Congress leaders who were in a position to know,[28] admitted that the government had committed atrocities during 1971–7. Scattered evidence gathered from those who were close to the situation during that continuing crisis of governability provides a picture of wide-ranging, brutal repression by the Congress government.

After each of the two UF governments was dismissed, New Delhi established direct control over West Bengal. Two important "administrative" changes created a framework in which governmental repression would be relatively free of constitutional constraints. First, it was decided that a police shooting would not require a "compulsory executive inquiry." That protection gave the police a free hand in their dealings with "extremists," especially Naxalites. The second crucial change was that "Naxalite problems" came to be assigned to the same detective department that was responsible for common criminals. Having thus abolished the distinction between political extremists and criminals, and having freed the police from virtually all political oversight, the government had set the stage for state-sponsored terrorism.

Two scholars, Sajal Basu, who is now an observer for Amnesty International in Calcutta, and Shankar Ghosh, who was a correspondent at that time for the *Times of India,* independently recorded what they witnessed firsthand during the early 1970s.[29] Their accounts help fill out the picture of what went on in those years. For example, Sajal Basu reported that Congress's electoral victory in 1972 was accompanied by "widespread rigging and fraud." During the period leading up to the election and immediately thereafter, the police and the *mastans* (hired hoodlums) unleashed what was known as "white terror." He described the aftermath of the UF experiment in the following terms: "Pseudo-revolutionary violence of the later sixties has been replaced by the counter-terrorism of the establishment that culminated in the violent election of 1972."[30]

Shankar Ghosh provided further details. For example, he reported that after the Birbhum Naxalite rebellion fizzled out, as discussed earlier, the consequences of "police action" were "not that there [were] no more

28 Especially relevant here was an interview with Subrato Mukerjee (Calcutta, May 3, 1986), who was West Bengal's home minister between 1972 and 1977. For other recent interviews that I conducted, see the footnotes in Chapter 6. For references to pre-1984 interviews, see Kohli, *The State and Poverty in India,* chapter 3.
29 See Sajal Basu, *West Bengal: The Violent Years* (Calcutta: Prachi Publications, 1979); Ghosh, *The Naxalite Movement.*
30 Basu, *West Bengal,* pp. 80–3.

killings; in fact the daily average was three to four, which was higher than the average during the peak period of the Naxalite movement."[31] As another example, the most brutal of the police massacres of Naxalites clearly was the Cossipore-Baranagar incident in the summer of 1971, six weeks after the establishment of presidential rule in June 1971. More than 150 young men with Naxalite sympathies were murdered within days. Ghosh, who covered the story for the *Hindusthan Standard,* reported that "dead bodies were everywhere – bodies with heads cut off, limbs lost, eyes gouged out, entrails ripped open. They were there in the streets in broad daylight. Later they were carried in rickshaws and handcarts and thrown into the Hooghly [the Ganges]."[32] Ghosh also captured well the general mood within West Bengal as Indira Gandhi turned the police loose to do the "dirty work": "Panic and terror among the people at that time was so high that no one could stay at home at night, no young man could think of not being implicated in cases of arson and murder to be instituted by the police, no middle-aged man could avoid severe beating up in course of interrogation in a police lock-up."[33] And finally, Ghosh's conclusion concerning the scope of the state repression is noteworthy: "Even in the absence of published figures it may be safely assumed that the number of Naxals killed exceeds the number of those killed by Naxals. There should be no doubt that the Naxalite movement in India [the largest concentration of which was in West Bengal] has taken a toll of several thousand lives."[34]

One prong of the government's strategy was to kill Naxalites and anyone suspected of being associated with them. The other was simply to imprison anyone suspected of being a threat to "law and order." Again, firm evidence on the extent of such imprisonments is not available. We know little about those who were imprisoned for political reasons and under what circumstances. The imprisonments went on during the first half of the 1970s and increased considerably during 1975–7, the period of the national Emergency, when even the minimum constitutional niceties could be set aside. Amnesty International estimated that around that time nearly 25,000 people, mostly members of the CPM and Naxalites, were imprisoned for political reasons.[35]

The exact numbers of people killed and imprisoned for political reasons in West Bengal during the 1970s will never be known. Nevertheless, the important point for this study is that for much of that period the democratic rights of many citizens were violently ripped away, and repression of the left, especially the revolutionary left, virtually became the norm. The socioeconomic situation of the state also suffered adverse consequences.

31 Ghosh, *The Naxalite Movement,* p. 155.
32 The author quotes his own newspaper story in his book. Ibid., p. 167.
33 Ibid., pp. 155–6.
34 Ibid., pp. 178–9.
35 Reported in Franda, "Rural Development, Bengali Marxist Style," p. 4.

Much of the significant decline in industrial production in West Bengal was due to capital flight during the first half of the crisis, that is, during the two UF experiments, when labor militancy rose sharply. The second half of the chaotic decade brought many reverses in the land-redistribution programs. For example, whatever modest gains the CPM and other leftist parties had made in securing tenancy rights came undone, as did their progress in the redistribution of disputed lands. Again, exact figures will never be known. It was clear during my fieldwork in 1979, however, that eviction of tenants during 1971–7 had been a crucial factor behind the CPM government's decision in 1977 to give the highest priority to policies that would ensure the rights of sharecroppers.[36]

In an earlier chapter, crises of governability were defined with reference to three criteria: coalitional instability, policy ineffectiveness, and, most important, escalating violence in politics. It is clear from the discussion in this chapter that West Bengal indeed experienced a severe crisis of governability during 1967–77: It proved nearly impossible to form a ruling coalition; much of the government's energy was devoted not to dealing with issues of socioeconomic development but rather to managing political conflicts, and violence became the norm for settling political disputes. Although many factors contributed to the increase in political violence, two related political variables must be emphasized in this analysis of the origins of the crisis: a fragmented and ineffective state apparatus, and an elite-led, deliberate mobilization for short-term political gains. As the focus of this study now shifts to the political changes since 1977, the contrast between developments in the two periods will further substantiate this analysis: The emergence of cohesive party rule has led to the development of a more consolidated state and has focused the attention of the ruling elite on long-term developmental goals, thus ameliorating West Bengal's crisis of governability.

THE DECADE OF THE CPM: A GOVERNMENT THAT WORKS

The CPM emerged as West Bengal's ruling party in 1977 and has won all subsequent elections. The past decade in West Bengal has been relatively free of political violence. Prior to an analysis of what the CPM has done to provide a moderately effective government, another question must be addressed: How did the CPM manage to become the state's ruling party?

The answer is not complicated. Table 10.2 shows the shares of the popular vote received by the major parties in West Bengal between 1967 and 1982. This table reveals three important facts, each of which requires some explanation: The crucial year in which the CPM enlarged its power base was not 1977, but 1971; the 1972 elections were aberrational from the point

---

36 For discussion, see Kohli, *The State and Poverty in India*, chapter 3.

Table 10.2. *Percentages of vote won by major parties in West Bengal assembly elections, 1967–82*

Party	1967	1969	1971	1972	1977	1982
CPM	18.1	19.6	33.8	27.5	35.8	38.5
Other Left Front parties	7.5	10.7	8.5	6.6	10.5	9.9
Janata	—	—	—	—	20.5	0.8
Congress (I)	41.1	40.4	29.8	49.1	23.4	35.7
CPI	6.5	6.8	8.6	8.4	2.7	1.8
Others	26.8	22.5	19.3	8.4	7.1	13.3
Total	100	100	100	100	100	100

Source: Compiled from the reports of the Election Commission.

of view of the CPM; and the CPM emerged victorious in 1977 when the two centrist parties, Congress (I) and the newly formed Janata, split the noncommunist vote.

In 1971 the CPM emerged from the two UF experiments as a major contender for power. Because the CPM already had a strong base in the urban working class, the significant increase in its share of the popular vote in 1971 must be attributed to a successful mobilization drive in the countryside. As discussed earlier, the CPM during that period chose to keep the police out of agrarian conflicts and simultaneously mobilize both the middle and the lower rural strata. The resulting increase in the membership of the Kisan Sabha – an organization of peasants with small landholdings – has already been noted. The Krishak Mazdoor Sabha (an agricultural laborers' organization) also made significant membership gains during that period.[37] And finally, the CPM's concerted efforts to secure tenancy rights for sharecroppers, as well as its periodic efforts at land redistribution, must have established a significant degree of political affinity between the CPM and the Bengali peasantry.

Why, then, did the CPM do poorly in the 1972 elections? As a comparison of Tables 10.1 and 10.2 will show, the CPM's share of the popular vote did not drop nearly as dramatically (from 33.8 to 27.5 percent) between the 1971 and 1972 elections as did the number of seats it won (instead of 113 seats in a house of 280 in 1971, it won only 14 seats in 1972). The dramatic decline in its legislative representation was primarily a function of the nature of the first-past-the-post electoral system. The CPM's share of the vote in 1972 was, in spite of the significant decline since 1971, still substantially higher than it had ever been in the 1960s.

What requires explanation, therefore, is why Congress's popularity went up fairly sharply and why the CPM's share of the vote declined by some

37 For details, see Sengupta, *CPI-M*.

six percentage points. In the absence of detailed public-opinion surveys, only the major issues that may have influenced public "moods" can be noted. Congress's popularity was in all likelihood improved because of Indira Gandhi's decision to intervene in the civil war in East Pakistan that led to the "liberation" of Bangladesh. Given a sense of shared cultural identity with Bengalis across the border, that action by Indira Gandhi must have attenuated the normal hostility of Bengalis toward New Delhi and may even have inclined them temporarily to view Indira as a leader on their side. The decline in the CPM's share of the vote, in turn, was in part simply the flip side of Congress's gain, but in part it must also be attributed to some combination of the following: the pervasive, intimidating presence of the army during the elections; the imprisonment of thousands of CPM members; and, of course, the electoral fraud and rigging that many independent observers have noted, if not documented.

The third set of factors requiring explanation in the CPM's rise to power included some post-Emergency developments. The CPM clearly had expanded its power base significantly during the two UF experiments. A number of changed circumstances finally helped the CPM transform that popular base into a decisive electoral victory. First, the Congress party in West Bengal, as elsewhere throughout India, had lost considerable popularity because of the Emergency. The newly formed Janata party was the main beneficiary of that decline. Because the CPM was already a well-established force within West Bengal, it appears that what happened was that the nonleft vote was split between Congress and the Janata party (Table 10.2). Additionally, the CPI, because of its close association with Indira Gandhi throughout the Emergency, lost a significant share of its popular support. It is probably fair to assume that much of that decline benefited the other leftist parties of West Bengal, including the CPM.

The CPM thus emerged from the 1977 elections as the party with the largest share (35.8 percent) of the popular vote (Table 10.2). If one includes the other leftist parties that were in alliance with the CPM in the Left Front, their total share of the vote approached 50 percent. In India's first-past-the-post electoral system, especially under the circumstances of a split in the centrist vote, it is not surprising that the Left Front won nearly 80 percent of the total seats (Table 10.1). It is also important to note, however, that the CPM alone won 177 seats in a house of 280, more than sufficient to form a comfortable majority government, all on its own.

Part of the explanation for the CPM's effective ruling strategy since 1977 is its changed ideology. By the time the CPM came to power in 1977, it had moved away from a revolutionary inclination to a reformist orientation. I have discussed this in detail elsewhere,[38] but it is important to repeat the main points: First, the political experience under the Emergency gave

38 See Kohli, *The State and Poverty in India,* chapter 3.

the CPM a clearer understanding of the value of democratic institutions; the CPM's capacity to mobilize support and increase power was found to be heavily dependent on the openness of the political process. The CPM thus increasingly diminished its rhetoric of "a dictatorship of the proletariat" and committed itself to preserving India's democratic institutions. Second, the government's inability to control mobilized forces during the UF experiments led to a clarification of the "types of struggles" that the party would encourage. As a result, labor militancy and *gheraoes* in the factories, and land-grab movements in the countryside, came to be replaced by "legal" and "constitutional struggles." And finally, related to both of those changes, the CPM began defining who the "enemy" was and who its allies were according to political standards rather than class criteria; members of nearly all social classes – except for big industrialists and wealthy landowners, especially "nonproductive" absentee landowners – were welcomed into the party.

That new commitment to reformism made the CPM more a social-democratic party and less a traditional communist party. Two important features of the CPM, however, continued to distinguish it from other Indian parties. First and foremost, the CPM retained the democratic centralist pattern of internal party organization, and that made the CPM a much more cohesive party. Second, in spite of attempts to broaden its membership, the CPM has remained primarily a party of the middle and the lower strata, with an explicit commitment to reforming the social structure along class lines. The post-1977 CPM in West Bengal is best understood as a well-organized, class-oriented reformist party.

The CPM's slow but steady evolution toward a reformist party increasingly made it a viable alternative in a democratic capitalist setting. The experience of finally coming to power with a significant majority further accentuated the CPM's reformist tendencies. Once it formed a majority government, two dramatic changes followed. First, the CPM's political horizons shifted from the short-term concerns of mobilizing and expanding its power base to the longer-term concerns of consolidating its newly acquired power. Related to that was a second important change: The CPM's political prospects for the future increasingly became a function of its capacity to provide effective government. That further shifted the party's political attention away from mobilizational activities. The search was on for strategies to create political stability, facilitate economic growth, and, within those constraints, back up its rhetoric with some genuine land redistribution.

Now, it should be clear that nearly all ruling parties in the various states in India would like to facilitate political stability, economic growth, and some redistribution. Two traits distinguish the CPM: It was slower than other parties to accept those "ordinary goals" as governmental goals; more important, having accepted that ideological shift, its political capacity to pursue those goals has turned out to be greater than that of numerous other Indian parties. The differences in political capacities, in turn, are traceable back to the organizational cohesiveness of the CPM.

A well-developed party organization has enabled the CPM to devise and implement a fairly well designed ruling strategy that is periodically updated. The strategy has three main components: imposition of the party's reformist ideology on disciplined cadres, thus making the more "normal" debilitating factional conflicts and personal ambitions of the political elite subservient to larger organizational goals; implementation of modest but genuine redistributive programs, thus solidifying the coalitional base with something more than rhetoric and symbolic gains; implementation of "pragmatic" policies to placate the propertied groups and encourage production based on the principle of profit.

In the 12 years that the CPM has been in power, it has achieved some success in all of these areas. Immediately after coming to power, the CPM had the difficult task of limiting the expectations of the economically disadvantaged. Instead of making empty promises that could not be kept – a recurring recipe for short-term political gain and long-term disaster – the CPM from the beginning set a cautious ruling tone:

The aim of our programmes is to alleviate the sufferings of the rural and urban people and to improve their conditions to a certain extent. We do not claim anything more, as we are aware that without structural changes in the socioeconomic order it is hardly possible to bring about any basic change in the conditions of the people.[39]

Because "structrual changes" cannot be expected to be implemented in a single region of a large country, the CPM has been able simultaneously to point out the factors that it cannot control (thus shifting the blame to New Delhi) and to minimize what people can expect from the state government it does control.

One reason that the CPM has succeeded in minimizing deinstitutionalizing populism since 1977 is that it is a well-disciplined ruling party. Empty populist promises often are made by leaders attempting to hold together unstable coalitions. By contrast, at both the elite and mass levels, the CPM's support structure has been relatively stable. Party discipline has forced competing factions to work within politically feasible boundaries. Modest but concrete rewards have, in turn, strengthened the CPM's coalitional base among the middle and lower strata. The gap between promises and results, therefore, has been narrower in the CPM's West Bengal than in many other parts of India.

It is important to elaborate on this last statement: Though the CPM has promised less, it has done more, especially for the lower strata, than most

---

39 Government of West Bengal, *Left Front Government in West Bengal: Eight Years* (Calcutta: Department of Information and Cultural Affairs, 1985), from the Foreword by Jyoti Basu, chief minister of West Bengal, pp. i–ii.

other ruling parties in Indian states. The most successful of the CPM's programs has been one aimed at enhancing the security of tenants in the countryside. This program, called "Operation Barga," has ensured tenurial rights and improved incomes for as many as one-quarter of all the rural households in West Bengal. As discussed elsewhere, the role of a disciplined, cadre-based party has been central in the implementation of this reform program.[40] Keeping in mind that the security of these tenants often had been threatened in the past, especially under Congress governments, the political bond that has now been established between the sharecroppers of West Bengal and the CPM becomes readily understandable.

The CPM has not come up with anything as successful as Operation Barga for the landless laborers. The labor-abundant agrarian economy, with its high levels of underemployment, has proved a formidable obstacle. The CPM has put its energy into strengthening the political organization of landless laborers. Although the results have been less than spectacular, West Bengal has little of the open brutal repression of the kind seen in Bihar. This is in part a function of a less oppressive caste structure, but it is also related to the organizational presence of the CPM in the Bengali countryside.

Families with small landholdings provide the CPM's main political base. Many of the party's ideologically loyal cadres are from this social background. Additionally, the CPM has sought to build its own version of "machine politics" to incorporate this social stratum. The revamped *panchayats* (local governments), for example, provide one crucial component in this design.[41] The CPM's popularity has enabled it to win the largest number of local-government positions. The CPM also has "decentralized" power in the special and limited sense of giving *panchayats* substantial resources for local development. These activities have been closely supervised through the party hierarchy and have been aimed at minimizing corruption and waste of public resources. Although this has not eliminated charges of corruption, especially because the CPM is no less partisan than other parties in selecting its own supporters for positions of authority, it has nevertheless had two important consequences. First, many of the local development programs sponsored by New Delhi – especially such programs as the Food for Work Program (later renamed the Employment Guarantee Scheme) – have been better implemented in West Bengal than in other states. Second, systematic governmental penetration into the countryside has enabled the CPM to sustain a powerful network of supporters.

Landless laborers, sharecroppers, and small landowners constitute the majority of the rural population in West Bengal. These are also the groups that have become the CPM's main supporters, enabling the CPM to win

40 For documentation and details, see Kohli, *The State and Poverty in India,* chapter 3.
41 For a detailed discussion, see ibid., chapter 3.

three consecutive state elections. As one would expect in the case of a leftist party, larger landowners, businessmen, and industrialists tend to oppose the CPM. It is important to note, however, that the CPM has gone out of its way to make itself acceptable to such groups. For example, the CPM has argued that subsidized agricultural inputs and "fair prices" for agricultural products are necessary to ensure agricultural production. It has also offered numerous incentives to industrialists so as to increase investment. Although these policy initiatives clearly are not sufficient to turn property owners into CPM supporters, they do go some distance toward creating a workable relationship between the leftist government and the society's producers of wealth.

An additional point concerning the relationship between the CPM government and property-owning groups is worth noting. The memory of the chaotic UF experiments is still fresh in the minds of Bengali businessmen. They also know that the CPM has a strong organizational network among workers and peasants. Whereas in principle the business community definitely would prefer Congress to the CPM in power, the practical issue is more complex: It is not at all clear to property-owning groups that they would be better off with another party in government and the CPM as the opposition. Since coming to power, the CPM has restrained both labor militancy in factories and land-grab movements in the countryside. During my visits to West Bengal, I heard numerous landowners and representatives of Chambers of Commerce acknowledge this restraining role of the CPM. If forcibly removed from power, the CPM could make West Bengal ungovernable. That possibility has restrained Bengali property owners from inviting New Delhi's intervention in West Bengal politics.

This emphasis on the CPM's effectiveness in government is not meant to draw attention away from the serious problems that remain unsolved in West Bengal; some of these are intrinsically difficult problems, and others are of the CPM's making. First, the CPM's simultaneous attempts to sustain an alliance of the middle and lower strata and to avoid any further alienation of property-owning groups have placed serious constraints on any further redistribution of wealth. The problem of severe bottom-level poverty is not likely to be solved by political intervention alone. Second, business groups and industrialists have not received guarantees sufficient to encourage them to bring substantial new investments into West Bengal. That is readily understandable: If the CPM should lose an election, the party leadership could again unleash labor militancy. Third, the CPM's sustained rule is giving rise to a powerful "new class," and that naturally evokes hostility among all those left out of the power game.

The presence of entrenched cadres in an atmosphere of limited industrial dynamism and minimal new redistribution has begun to create a sense of political stagnation in West Bengal. If the CPM fails to correct these tendencies, they could lead to the CPM's undoing. Such possibilities raise an important question: Was the price that the CPM paid to restore order too high, that price being political stalemate and the related problem of economic sluggishness?

Whatever its future, the CPM has two other important problems over which it does not have full control. First, one of West Bengal's 16 districts, Darjeeling, experienced considerable political strife between 1986 and 1988. That turmoil pitted one of West Bengal's ethnic minorities, the Gurkhas, against the Bengali-dominated CPM government. The Gurkha demands varied from greater political autonomy within West Bengal to a separate Gurkha state – Gurkhaland – in India. The issue was eventually settled in mid-1988, when the CPM made some concessions and Gurkha leaders accepted an arrangement that would leave Darjeeling a part of West Bengal but also would give Gurkha leaders considerable financial and administrative control within their district.

Prior to the final settlement, however, the Gurkhaland agitations during 1986–8 caused considerable loss of life and property in Darjeeling. The dynamics of that conflict are not difficult to understand. Darjeeling is a small district in the mountainous north of Bengal. Of West Bengal's nearly 50 million people, only 1 million live in that remote district. The district is nevertheless quite important; it has strategic importance because of its proximity to China, and it has economic importance because of tea plantations and tourism. More than 80 percent of the district's people are non-Bengali Gurkhas. The Gurkhas are both racially and linguistically distinct from the Bengalis. The Bengalis tend to view the Gurkhas as "backward" people who are relatively innocent in the ways of the world and who make good domestics and hardworking laborers.

The Gurkhas of Darjeeling were never politically integrated into either Congress or the CPM. In the past, a Gurkha League usually won the political support of many Gurkhas and then often formed a coalition with the ruling party in Calcutta. The increasing identification of the CPM in West Bengal as a Bengali party and the growing political awareness among a new generation of Gurkha leaders altered that pattern in the 1980s. During the past decade the Gurkhas have demanded greater political control over their own affairs. The CPM had itself argued for such rights for the Gurkhas in the 1970s, when Congress was in power in West Bengal.

Once in power, the CPM dragged its feet on Gurkha demands. That was mainly because any major concessions to Gurkhas could have hurt the CPM politically with its major constituency, the Bengalis. What complicated that fairly normal give-and-take of politics was that the leaders of the Congress party saw in the conflict an opportunity to weaken the CPM. Following the Punjab pattern of a few years earlier – when Indira Gandhi had decided to support Bhindranwale as a vehicle for weakening the Akali Dal (see Chapter 12) – the Congress leadership decided to promote the

Gurkha leader, Subhas Ghising. Thus encouraged, the Gurkha movement became increasingly strident in its demands against the CPM government.

The Congress leadership, however, was clearly of two minds on the issue of Gurkhaland. Given Rajiv's reconciliatory position on Punjab and Assam in 1985, one faction within the ruling circles appears to have argued that national interests should come before Congress's political interests. That line of thinking would have suggested that the Gurkhaland agitation should not be encouraged, lest it become one more major ethnic strife. Conversely, the difficulties that Gurkha agitations would create for the CPM must have been far too tempting a political opportunity for the Congress to resist. That both of those arguments were operating is evidenced in the confusing policy position of Congress: Between 1986 and 1988, Congress went back and forth several times in encouraging and discouraging Ghising and the Gurkha movement.[42]

The conflict was eventually settled when Congress leaders decided that the creation of a new state for Gurkhas was out of the question. That had always been the CPM's position. The Gurkha movement was far too insignificant a political force to win out against both the national government and the West Bengal government. It was able to flourish only because of the political space created by a conflict between New Delhi and Calcutta. Once New Delhi had clarified its position, and the CPM had offered some concessions that clearly fell short of a separate state but were nevertheless significant, Gurkha leadership had little choice but to accept the deal.

The Gurkhaland crisis demonstrated that whereas the CPM was quite adept at dealing with class conflict, its capacity to manage ethnic conflict was questionable. Conversely, it was also the case that the CPM's organizational cohesiveness enabled it to devise a consistent policy position. Unlike Congress's conflicting positions and mixed signals – probably reflecting factional divisions or, worse, changing leadership whims – that encouraged the conflict, the CPM's consistent and compromising position eventually facilitated conflict resolution.

The second major political problem in West Bengal over which the CPM government has little control is the organizational decline of the Congress party. The roots and consequences of that were analyzed in Chapter 6. Of course, its organizational disintegration does not negate Congress's continuing capacity to attract popular support (Table 10.2). Congress remains India's major national party and therefore attracts considerable support in all of India's states. Within West Bengal, Congress's main support comes from several groups: non-Bengalis, especially in Calcutta; those who are

42 To get a quick sense of the confusion in Congress's policy toward Gurkhaland, see the following news coverage in *India Today:* January 15, 1987, pp. 32–3; February 28, 1987, pp. 26–7; May 15, 1987, pp. 32–3; January 15, 1988, pp. 32–4.

ideologically antileft; many of the rich peasants and most of the very large landowners; many of those in business, trades, industry, and commerce; a significant minority of the numerically significant Moslems; and those generally deprived of governmental patronage and benefits.

The main significance of Congress's organizational decline is not in its reduced capacity to attract popular support. The main significance lies elsewhere. Nearly all observers of West Bengal politics are agreed – even those who do not assess the CPM favorably – that an electoral victory by Congress would mean less effective government for West Bengal. The Congress party of West Bengal is deeply factionalized, and its leadership is of very low quality, composed mainly of former Youth Congress rowdies who moved in to fill the vacuum created by the disintegration of the old Congress. Thus, electoral support for Congress in West Bengal mainly reflects anti-CPM sentiments and support for the national leadership of Congress. For the time being, almost no one expects that the West Bengal Congress could offer effective government.

Related to that, factional squabbles within Congress continue to be sources of civil unrest in West Bengal. Much of that conflict is concentrated in urban areas, as discussed in Chapter 6. Given the CPM's organizational cohesiveness and control over the government, Congress in West Bengal has shied away from aggressive mobilizational strategies. Congress would likely be a loser in any such direct conflict. Given Congress's internal makeup, however, if the CPM's hold on power were to weaken, Congress's resurgence undoubtedly would generate considerable political turmoil in West Bengal.

In sum, West Bengal is not without its share of serious political problems, some of which are inherent to the region, whereas others reflect poorly on the CPM, and yet others are of Congress's making. In spite of these, West Bengal under the CPM remains a relatively well governed state. This assessment is especially significant if one keeps the points of comparison in mind: the chaotic decade of 1967–77 in West Bengal, and the growing turbulence in such neighboring states as Bihar.

When assessed relatively, the coalition underlying the CPM rule in West Bengal is stable. The CPM's record on economic policy is not spectacular, but not without merit: Its growth record is no worse than those of many other Indian states, and its redistribution record is distinctively superior. The most impressive achievement of the CPM, however, has been restoration of political order – and that without repression. The dramatic decline in industrial unrest was documented in Chapter 6. Agrarian conflicts over shares of crops and over land have also declined sharply. Moreover, West Bengal remains relatively free of communal conflicts of various types, including caste and religious conflicts. This is especially impressive in view of the fact that nearly 20 percent of the Bengalis in West Bengal are Moslems. The cumulative results are clearly evident in Figure 10.1. What is mainly responsible for this moderately effective ruling pattern is a well-organized ruling party that has put together a coalition of middle and lower groups, has not made extravagant promises but has delivered more redistribution than most other Indian parties, and has contained the usual debilitating intraelite conflicts and the related attempts to politicize existing socioeconomic cleavages.

CONCLUSION

After having been one of India's most chaotic states in the late 1960s, West Bengal has emerged in the 1980s as one of India's better-governed states. Surely there are lessons in this turnaround for any study of India's growing crisis of governability. For purposes of this concluding discussion, these lessons can be broadly divided into prescriptive and analytical.

The prescriptive lessons are limited. What has worked in West Bengal may not work in other states in India – and is even less likely to provide an all-India model. The emergence of the CPM as a disciplined ruling party in West Bengal is a product of an unusual sociopolitical configuration – its long regional traditions of elite radicalism and centralized organizations, the weakness of caste as a principle for political organization, and the historical weakness of the Congress party. A different set of conditions could facilitate the emergence of left-of-center parties as ruling parties in some other Indian states (e.g., Kerala). Given the absence of strong leftist traditions in most states, however, and given the widespread presence of caste and communal cleavages, the CPM type of rule is not likely to emerge in much of India. Even if it did, the outcome under different circumstances might not be as favorable.

In spite of the limited utility of the West Bengal case for generating any direct prescriptions, the analytical implications (and therefore some indirect prescriptions to be discussed in Chapter 13) are very important. The West Bengal case highlights the significance of a well-organized reformist party for generating political order. The roots of the political chaos between 1967 and 1977, though complex, were mainly two related political conditions: the fragmentation of the state itself, and virulent elite-led mobilization.

The emergence of the CPM as a ruling party tamed many of the conflicts within West Bengal. As a well-organized party with a clear electoral majority, the CPM was able to create a cohesive government and fill the existing power vacuum. Organizational discipline also enabled the CPM to limit elite factionalism and the debilitating elite-initiated political conflicts that often follow. Thus, organizational cohesion at the heart of the state was crucial for taming political chaos.

It is important to reiterate in this conclusion that organizational cohesion is a necessary but not sufficient variable in the explanation. If cohesive party rule is also to be democratic, the ruling party must put together a sustainable majority coalition. This is where the significance of implementable reforms and thus the party's reformist ideology comes into the picture. If the ruling party is not willing to reform or not capable of implementing reforms, one of two outcomes is likely: Either the party will rapidly lose power or it will be attracted to deinstitutionalizing populism, thus exacerbating the long-term problem of establishing legitimate order.

The CPM's reformist orientation has enabled it to pursue some redistributive programs without fundamentally alienating property-owning productive groups. The CPM's performance in West Bengal has by no means been spectacular; it has left quite a few problems unresolved, and it has created some new problems. At the same time, however, it is undeniable that a reform-oriented, disciplined party has generated moderately effective government in West Bengal.

Conclusion: the states

The study of political changes in five districts presented in Part II helped delineate some broad themes concerning the causes and consequences of deinstitutionalization in Indian politics. The comparative analysis of three states in this Part III helps further refine the causal argument. Of the three states analyzed, clearly the crisis is most severe in the state of Bihar. There is a qualitatively different type of sporadic turmoil in Gujarat. By contrast, political order has been restored in West Bengal after a period of considerable turmoil. How does one explain this regional diversity?

The negative conclusions that emerge from this comparative analysis are as important as the positive ones. It is clear, for example, that problems of governability do not correlate in any simple way with levels of economic development: Bihar is the poorest and most troubled state in India. But if one were tempted to conclude that prosperity produces political stability, the turmoil in the relatively prosperous Gujarat would provide a quick check. Clearly, small variations in levels of development do not provide any ready insights into the process of exercising authority in India.

The political changes analyzed here occurred over a period of nearly two decades. Given India's slow economic growth, the economic changes in that time period have been relatively small. Comparative findings for the different states suggest that such small economic shifts are not decisive in explaining political change. This does not mean that economic variables are inconsequential. That would be an absurd claim. What it suggests instead is that in India thus far, economic development has not been the major corrosive force, although the issue of whether it has the potential to be more detrimental in the future remains open.

Another negative conclusion emerges from these materials: It is best not to think of the problems of political order in India as northern problems rather than southern problems. Important scholars like Francine Frankel have contrasted Bihar with Karnataka and Tamil Nadu and concluded that the early success of the anti-Brahmanical movement in the south may provide one part of the explanation why politics in some southern states appear to be more accommodative.[1] There is some merit to this proposition. The findings reported here, however, cast doubt on the generalizability of the argument. For example, it was evident in the first part of the study that violence is quite pervasive in the politics of southern states such as Andhra Pradesh. Several "northern" states, such as Orissa and Madhya Pradesh, moreover, are not all that violent. The north–south contrast, therefore, can easily be overdrawn. More important is the underlying explanatory issue, which suggests that failure to accommodate challenges to power from below is at the root of political turmoil. This proposition also requires qualifications, which will be discussed later.

The variables that seem to explain best the relative order and disorder in certain Indian states are the nature of party organization and the patterns of power distribution. The variable of party organization is relatively easy to understand. A well-organized party can fill the authority vacuum created by competitive political mobilization. Such a ruling party can minimize factional conflicts, clarify lines of authority, define policy priorities, and impart a degree of cohesiveness and effectiveness to a government. The CPM in West Bengal is such a party, and it is not surprising that it has helped restore some order to that once violence-prone state. Powerful and competent leaders can also provide a temporary functional equivalent to a strong party. By contrast, the highly factionalized and organizationally weak Congress party has been a major factor in the increasing civil turmoil, especially in Bihar, but also in Gujarat.

The issue of how patterns of power distribution are related to problems of governability is more complex. Political power in Bihar, for example, is in the hands of the landowning high castes. We noticed earlier in our discussion of Belgaun that a somewhat similar situation is to be found in contemporary Karnataka. The political consequences of the patterns in those two states, however, have been quite different. Power challenges in Bihar are major sources of political turmoil. The reconsolidation of power by the dominant castes in Karnataka probably has forestalled instability. In contrast to the situation in both of those states, control over the state apparatus in both West Bengal and Gujarat has been wrenched out of the hands of the dominant socioeconomic groups. Again, however, the political consequences have been quite different. Gujarat has become the scene of periodic turmoil, whereas order has been restored in West Bengal. Clearly, any simple hypothesis that would trace the roots of stable and effective government back either to elite rule or to more egalitarian distribution of power will not suffice.

There are, however, two alternative hypotheses relating power distri-

---

1 See Francine Frankel, "Middle Classes and Castes in India's Politics: Prospects for Political Accommodation," in Atul Kohli, ed., *India's Democracy* (Princeton University Press, 1988), pp. 225–62.

bution to governability that are consistent with these comparative findings for various Indian states. First, as long as the dominant position of the landowning high-status groups remains more or less unchallenged in the rural social structure, state control by these dominant groups is likely to yield stable government. Lest that hypothesis appear to be a tautology, it is important to point out that it is the traditional authority in the civil society, not rational legal authority in a separate political arena, that is the source of political stability in such instances. Those who are readily accepted as leaders of communities can in such cases double up as political leaders, imparting a degree of legitimacy and stability to governments.

Karnataka, the southern state discussed in Chapter 5, exhibits these "premodern" qualities. The pattern should remind us that a component of the seemingly orderly government in the past was the unchallenged domination of the socioeconomic elite in Indian civil society. Until recently, India's modern democracy rested on and gained stability from a very traditional Indian society, characterized by widespread acceptance of caste hierarchies and the associated patterns of socioeconomic domination and subordination.

A number of forces have begun to undermine the traditional patterns of domination. Challenges to the power of the established elite have inevitably followed. The repeated exercise of the rights of democratic citizenship has been an especially important catalyst for such challenges. Thus, the power of numbers has increasingly come to be pitted against the power derived from wealth and high social status. The elite-versus-mass power conflicts, with many variations in terms of the actors involved, the strategies used, and the outcomes, have been important in the political life of each of the three states analyzed.

In both Bihar and Gujarat, the elite–mass conflicts have not been resolved, and that failure has led to severe problems for those attempting to maintain effective government. For example, the power of the landowning castes in Bihar is deeply entrenched. The mobilization of the lower castes has been a product of desperation born of scarcity. It has also been poorly organized. Such mobilization efforts threaten the existing power structure, but only weakly. Sensing the weakness of the challengers, and utilizing both public and private power, the dominant groups in Bihar have unleashed brutal violence aimed at maintaining their privileged position in both the state and society.

The pattern of conflict in Gujarat has been somewhat different. Members of a numerically sizable intermediate caste have displaced the region's dominant caste from state offices. However, the attempts of the new rulers to utilize state power to improve socioeconomic conditions for the intermediate and lower castes have met severe resistance. Periodic riots and violence incited by the dominant caste have clearly defined the limits within which the new rulers must act. Given the organizational weakness of the ruling Congress party, there is little the rulers can do but accept the boundaries defined by the socially powerful.

Elite–mass conflicts have thus contributed to political turmoil and governmental ineffectiveness in both Bihar and Gujarat. West Bengal provides a somewhat different case. Although classlike mobilization generated considerable turmoil in Bengal during 1967–77, over the past decade the power structure within the state has been broadened. The combined numbers of the mobilized middle and lower classes have enabled a left-of-center party, the CPM, to seize political power. Unlike the case of Gujarat, the CPM's disciplined party organization has made it difficult for powerful socioeconomic groups to reduce the rulers to token status. The CPM has respected the rights of the property-owning groups to pursue production and profit within a democratic capitalist system, but it also has channeled some resources to the less privileged in society. This well-organized, reform-oriented ruling party has created a moderately effective democratic government in one region of India.

A second important hypothesis emerges from these state-level observations. As the traditional domination patterns in the social structure erode, and various types of elite–mass conflicts emerge, stable democratic outcomes will increasingly require political incorporation of the newly mobilized lower strata. A well-organized reformist party is one mechanism for incorporating the poor. There are other political arrangements that could be used to facilitate such incorporation. Irrespective of the specifics, the leaders and the institutions that can help reestablish stable, effective democracy will have some things in common. Simultaneously, they will have to respect the rights of propertied groups and avoid "inefficient egalitarianism," on the one hand, and generate both symbolic and real gains for the bottom half of Indian society, on the other.

PART IV

Centralization and powerlessness at the Center

Introduction: the Center

The purpose of this part of the study is to analyze the changing nature of the Indian state at its summit. The foregoing analyses of selected districts and states will help delineate the broad political context within which India's central government (the Center) operates. This context is characterized by weakening political institutions and increasing power struggles. Several questions must now be addressed: How is central authority formed in such a context? Once it has been formed, what strategies do leaders characteristically adopt to cope with the growing problems of governability? How efficacious are the leaders and the state they control in dealing with the pressing problems of the day?

Instead of attacking these complex issues head-on, I have chosen an indirect research strategy. What follows is an analysis of how Rajiv Gandhi sought to deal with what he defined as the priority problems of India during his term in power (1984–9). First, the attempts of the Rajiv government to liberalize India's economy are analyzed. There follows an examination of how Rajiv dealt with a troubled Congress party and with a turbulent Center–state issue, the issue of Punjab.

These foci are clearly selective. They do not show all the nuances that would be revealed by a step-by-step account of how Rajiv came to power and how he used his power over the next five years. Nevertheless, we may note that his attempts to liberalize the economy were aimed at boosting India's economic growth. Similarly, Rajiv's political policies were aimed at strengthening some of India's important but troubled institutions. Judged by any criteria, slow economic growth and the breakdown of institutions would be high on the list of contemporary India's pressing problems. More important, those were the areas in which Rajiv chose to concentrate his political efforts. Therefore, it can be argued that observing the government in action in these two important policy areas will provide a microcosm of the workings of power at the highest level of the Indian government. I use the study of these two policy areas, that is, a study of government goals and performance in these areas, as a basis for generalizing about the changing nature of power relations at the national level until the new government headed by V. P. Singh came to power in late 1989.

To anticipate the argument, the central theme that runs through the two following chapters concerns the simultaneous tendencies in India toward increases in centralization and in powerlessness. Decision making under Rajiv Gandhi continued to be highly centralized in the person and office of the prime minister, but that did little to enhance the government's ability to define and pursue clear policy goals. Personalization of power is closely connected with the issue of institutional weakness, which in turn necessitates a populist orientation in order to earn legitimacy and sustain popular support. The pressure to retain the support of as many major groups as possible has made it difficult for the government to solve the problems it defines as important. Hence, the real meaning of the governability crisis emerges: Political turmoil not only threatens the prospect for establishing legitimate and coherent authority but also undermines the government's ability to facilitate socioeconomic development.

11

Managing the economy: halfhearted liberalization

Over the past decade, India's leaders have sought to liberalize their country's relatively controlled and closed economy. The initial steps in that direction were taken by the Janata government during 1977–80 and by Indira Gandhi during 1980–4. From the time he came to power in late 1984, Rajiv Gandhi made liberalization of the economy a priority. Significant changes in the domestic economy, and some changes that would alter India's links with the world economy, were introduced during 1984–8. They included an easing of state control over many of the activities of national firms (such as entry into production, production decisions, and expansion in size), a lowering of corporate and personal income taxes, a long-term fiscal policy that would substitute tariffs for import restrictions and would reassure business groups regarding future patterns of taxation, some currency devaluation, and a lowering of import barriers against selected items.

Those changes taken together did not add up to a dramatic transition in India's development strategy. A liberal model of development has not replaced the mixed-economy model premised on state controls and import substitution. The legal and bureaucratic framework of a highly interventionist state remains intact, as do the state's many public-sector activities and government restrictions on private economic activity. Nevertheless, the policy reforms have been aimed at enhancing competitiveness and broadening the scope of individual and corporate initiatives within the old framework.

The purpose of this chapter is not to assess the economic merits of those policy reforms. Serious debate on the issue of whether liberalization is the way for India to go has been under way for some time;[1] such discussions

---

1 Academic works that broadly support the liberalization-policy prescription include Jagdish Bhagwati and T. N. Srinivasan, *Foreign Trade Regimes and Economic Development: India* (New York: Columbia University Press, 1975), and I. J. Ahluwalia, *Industrial Growth in India: Stagnation Since the Mid-Sixties* (Oxford University Press, 1985). For a brief but succinct statement on the need for liberalization by a policymaker, see L. K. Jha, "In Search of a New Economic Order," *Illustrated Weekly of India,* April 6, 1986, pp. 20–3. For a sampling of the critical views, see Bhabatosh Datta, "The Central Budget and the New Economic Policy," *Economic and Political Weekly* (hereafter referred to as *EPW*), April 20, 1985, pp. 693–8; H. K. Paranjape, "New Lamps for Old!: A Critique of the 'New

are best carried out by policy-oriented economists. Rather, the purpose of this chapter is to analyze the political underpinnings of those economic policy changes. What political changes within India created the preconditions for a shift in the development strategy? Were those changes solely in the ideological realm, or did they also reflect a shifting balance of power among contending political actors? Why has the pace of reform been slow, piecemeal, even hesitant? What forces are preventing a decisive shift in development strategy? In an attempt to answer these questions, the recent roles of the political elite and of various interest groups in India's macroeconomic policy making are analyzed here. The analysis has obvious implications for an understanding of India's economic liberalization. And it should also shed some light on the changing nature of power distribution within India at the national level, especially in the area of economic policy, in addition to illuminating the central issue of the decreasing ability of the Indian government to deal with the pressing problems of the day.

I argue that the push for liberalization came from members of the bureaucratic-technocratic elite who increasingly came to control the levers of India's economic policy making in the late 1980s. The members of that elite group owed their power primarily to Rajiv Gandhi; they did not rise to power via democratic means, nor were they responsible to the electorate in any direct sense. Business groups have, on balance, supported the government's attempts to liberalize the domestic economy. However, they have been lukewarm in public, and in private they probably have opposed any serious attempt at an international opening. The policies being pursued closely follow such priorities. The professional and bureaucratic middle classes have also welcomed the economic changes, which have reduced taxes and ameliorated shortages of consumer products.

Direct, concerted opposition to the reforms came mainly from three quarters: The first group of opponents, somewhat surprisingly, included the rank and file of the Congress party. Significant sections of the ruling Congress party opposed certain aspects of liberalization, fearing they would lead the party to abandon the pro-poor populist orientation that had won it so many votes among India's numerous poor. Leftist intellectuals became another source of direct, vocal opposition. Third, the organized working class in the public sector openly opposed the liberalizing thrust of the new economic policies. More diffuse opposition began emerging from the numerically significant rural groups. The middle peasants sensed that the new

Economic Policy,'" *EPW*, September 7, 1985, pp. 1513–22; Prabhat Patnaik, "New Turn in Economic Policy: Context and Prospects," *EPW*, June 7, 1986, pp. 1014–19: K. N. Raj, "New Economic Policy," *Mainstream*, December 14, 1985 (part 1), and December 21, 1985 (part 2), pp. 15–19. There are two essays that, like this chapter, focus on political issues: Stanley A. Kochanek, "Regulation and Liberalization Theology in India," *Asian Survey*, 26:12 (December 1986), pp. 1284–308; Barnett R. Rubin, "Economic Liberalization and the Indian State," *Third World Quarterly*, 7:4 (October 1985), pp. 942–57.

economic policies, especially the tax concessions that mainly would benefit the more prosperous urban population, carried the hint of a direct antirural bias, and certainly offered very little for the peasantry. The rural poor do not react directly to such macroeconomic policy changes; however, they do react when they suspect that antipoverty concerns are being abandoned.

That diffuse opposition did not succeed in reversing the liberalizing thrust of Rajiv Gandhi's government. It did, however, contribute to the government's declining popularity. That decline, even though it was caused by many different factors, had by 1986 or 1987 forced Rajiv Gandhi to abandon the rhetoric of liberalization and readopt that of socialism or, more accurately, populism, thus reducing both the pace and the scope of the intended policy changes.

An analysis of the attempts in India to move away from a mixed-economy model and closer to a market-oriented economy has an important implication for this study. The popular sectors of India have opposed such policy changes. That is unfortunate, because India's economy, especially its industrial sector, is in desperate need of some type of policy reform. Many Indians simply are not convinced that abandoning the old model of development is the way to go, or that what is said to be good for the "economy as a whole" is necessarily good for them. The degree to which that has resulted from political mismanagement, as distinct from a reaction to the distributional implications of new policies, is difficult to ascertain. As the analysis here will demonstrate, both factors played roles. What that halfhearted pursuit of a major policy revealed, however, was that in spite of enormous electoral support, the ability of the Rajiv government to initiate major policy changes remained quite limited. The reason for that will emerge later. Suffice it for now to note that economic rationality, as defined by the ruling elite, collided with the rationality of building political support in a weak-party democracy. The new rulers of India may be able to sustain the liberalizing policy thrust if the country's economic performance improves markedly. Short of that, the liberalizing direction of economic change is likely to remain a hotly contested issue, and without a cohesive, well-organized support base the government's capacity to undertake difficult decisions will remain limited.

THE BACKGROUND

Although India's economy continued to grow at its steady but sluggish pace of 3–4 percent per year between 1950 and 1980, India's industry did not do well between 1965 and 1980. Specialists have noted that whereas India's industry grew at about 7–8 percent per year prior to the middle 1960s, its annual growth rate slowed down to around 5 percent during 1965–80.[2] In

2 Ahluwalia, *Industrial Growth in India*.

some years, such as 1979, industry virtually came to a standstill. That deceleration was concentrated mainly in capital-goods and basic-goods industries.[3]

There is disagreement among economists in India regarding the choice of the mid-1960s as a dividing point. Some have argued that the use of that cutoff point creates an artificial picture of overall deceleration.[4] However, no one claims that India's industry since that date has performed impressively, although it definitely improved during the 1980s. Nevertheless, international comparison with countries such as South Korea or even Turkey or Brazil shows what should be attainable but is not being achieved. Thus, there is widespread agreement that India's industrial growth is relatively slow and needs to be accelerated.

The issue of why India's industrial growth has been slow has puzzled both academic economists and policymakers. The issue has been especially troubling because over the past few decades India's savings rate has continued to improve, going up from under 10 percent of gross national product (GNP) in the early 1950s to over 20 percent in the early 1980s. Why, in spite of the availability of more and more savings for investment, has India's industrial growth rate not been more impressive?

As one might expect, students of the Indian economy have vigorously debated this issue. There are three basic hypotheses: (1) The root cause of the slow growth has been the inefficiency inherent in the state-controlled economy.[5] (2) The sluggishness has reflected low aggregate demand.[6] (3) The deceleration has been associated with declining public investments and the related infrastructural bottlenecks.[7] These hypotheses, and especially the policy implications that flow from them, are not necessarily mutually exclusive. Nevertheless, the arguments are distinct, and they lead to different policy emphases.

3 Ibid.
4 There is a good review of this and other debates surrounding India's slow industrial growth: Ashutosh Varshney, "Political Economy of Slow Industrial Growth in India," *EPW,* September 1, 1984, pp. 1511–17.
5 There are two analyses that broadly support this position: Bhagwati and Srinivasan, *Foreign Trade Regimes;* Ahluwalia, *Industrial Growth in India.*
6 For a statement linking limited aggregate demand to slow industrial growth, see Sukhamoy Chakravarty, "India's Development Strategy for the 1980s," *EPW,* May 26, 1984. This thesis also crops up in several criticisms of the new economic policy, as cited in footnote 1. Moreover, a statement by 29 economists criticizing the government's emphasis on liberalization suggested that one important component of any new development strategy should be "expansion of home market." That statement is further discussed later. It was published in *Mainstream,* October 26, 1985, pp. 24–5, and was discussed in many newspapers and magazines, including *EPW,* October 26, 1985, pp. 1813–16.
7 This thesis was first put forward by T. N. Srinivasan and N. S. S. Narayana, "Economic Performance since the Third Plan and Its Implications for Policy," *EPW,* annual number, February 1977. Since then it has been argued by quite a few observers, but especially by Pranab Bardhan, *The Political Economy of Development in India* (Oxford: Basil Blackwell, 1984).

The purpose of this chapter is not to take sides in this debate or, by implication, to argue for or against the Indian government's attempts to liberalize the economy. (The view of the new government of Rajiv Gandhi clearly was closest to the first of these three hypotheses.) The purpose served by pointing to the existence of these economic debates is twofold. First, they highlight the widespread agreement among economists and policymakers that all is not well in the realm of India's industrial policy. The need for a change in the industrial policy is not in question. The second and more important point is that there is no consensus on the appropriate direction for such change.

This assertion is crucial for the development of the following argument. The policy changes that the Indian government has undertaken over the past several years have not been objective responses to an objective situation. That an objective situation exists, namely, an economy whose industrial sector could perform better, is clear; the need for change, therefore, may be said to be rooted in the economic situation. The possible responses to that situation, however, will involve political choices. The specialists who study the "objective economic situation" simply are not in agreement that there is one best way to solve the problem. Given that contentiousness, the issue of why a given set of responses should be adopted by the Indian government is a political question. Does any group have the power to push through its preferred policies? Who would benefit from those policies?

LIBERALIZATION UNDER INDIRA GANDHI

The trend toward liberalization of the economy was initiated not by Rajiv Gandhi but by his mother, Indira Gandhi. That fact has not received as much attention as it deserves. An understanding of why Indira Gandhi initiated those policies after returning to power in 1980 should give a better perspective on what is really new under Rajiv Gandhi. Such background is also important for understanding why Rajiv's attempts to liberalize the economy evoked considerable reaction, including negative political reaction, whereas Indira Gandhi's attempts went relatively unnoticed.

The Indira Gandhi who returned to power in 1980, after the brief Janata interlude of about three years, was not the firebrand Indira Gandhi of *garibi hatao* vintage. Her antipoverty rhetoric, which seldom had been translated into real policy before or during the Emergency (1975–7), had been altered. Critical observers have suggested that after 1980, Indira Gandhi moved "rightwards,"[8] and her former advisors have noted that during that phase she was more "pragmatic"[9] or, by

8 See James Manor, "Parties and the Party System," in Atul Kohli, ed., *India's Democracy: An Analysis of Changing State–Society Relations* (Princeton University Press, 1988), pp. 62–98.

9 Interview with Arjun K. Sengupta, Washington, D.C., June 28, 1985.

implication, less "ideological." Whether labeled "rightward" or "pragmatic," it is clear that Indira Gandhi's political and policy orientation during that phase, as compared with her pre-Emergency orientation, was different.

That changing political orientation was evident in a number of policy areas. Communal themes, for example, especially themes of Hindu hegemony that would appeal to India's Hindi heartland, gained currency in Indira's political speeches.[10] Under the influence of her son Sanjay, militant thugs were inducted into the ruling party to serve as tools of mobilization for both mass rallies and elections. Although the rhetoric of both socialism and nationalism was maintained, antipoverty programs were put on the back burner. There was also a change in attitude toward such international institutions as the International Monetary Fund (IMF). Negotiations for the largest loan ever granted by the IMF were completed during that phase. Finally, many of the economic policies adopted tended to move India in the liberalizing direction.

After completing the loan agreement for 5 billion of the Special Drawing Rights (SDR) with the IMF, Indira Gandhi made some important economic policy decisions during 1981–2. Steel and cement prices were decontrolled, restrictions on manufactured imports were liberalized, and controls on both entry and expansion by national firms were relaxed. During 1981, the government approved four times as many applications for expansion and new undertakings as in any of the five preceding years.[11] Over the next two years, as the perspective on India's seventh economic plan developed, it became clear that the new emphasis would be on "efficiency of investment," to be accompanied by a general move "away from administrative to financial controls."[12] Soon thereafter, following the recommendations of the L. K. Jha commission on economic and administrative reforms, the government placed 20 important industries under "automatic licensing."[13] In practice, that meant that the government virtually decontrolled expansion and new production in those industries.

By the time of Indira Gandhi's death in late 1984, economic liberalization was very much the new policy trend. An editorial in the left-leaning *Economic and Political Weekly,* written around the time of her assassination, summed up the changing situation: "Liberalization of industrial licensing, easing of access to imports coupled with lowering of import duties and promotion of foreign technical collaboration have become the key aspects

---

10 See Manor, "Parties and the Party System."
11 See Prem Shankar Jha, "The End of the Tunnel: Return to Sanity in Economic Policy," *Times of India,* April 19, 1982.
12 For example, see Prem Shankar Jha, "Seventh Plan Perspectives: A New Direction for Industry," *Times of India,* August 13, 1984.
13 See *Economic Times,* September 1, 1984.

of the government's industrial policies."[14] More centrist observers of India's economic policies agreed.[15]

Why did Indira Gandhi adopt those policy changes, and what were the political consequences? Regarding the reasons for the policy shift, the new economic direction must be seen as part and parcel of Indira Gandhi's overall political shift, which involved a move away from the populist or socialist orientation that had become her political trademark. That move was dictated by urgent political needs.

When Indira Gandhi returned to power in 1980, several things must have been clear to her. Congress had been routed by the Janata party in the 1977 elections in the entire Hindi heartland. Even though she had won the 1980 election, primarily because of factionalism and incompetence within the Janata party, her support base in the Hindi heartland was, at best, soft. She had to build up that support, quickly.[16] The tremendous support that the business communities had given Morarji Desai's government must have left Mrs. Gandhi feeling peculiarly vulnerable, especially in regard to future electoral financing. After 1980, Mrs. Gandhi sought to build her support in the Hindi heartland and among the business communities by shifting away from the earlier themes of "secularism and socialism." The new political posture had two ingredients: (1) an emphasis on "Hindu chauvinism" and "communalism" that had great appeal in the Hindi heartland and (2) a more pragmatic, pro-business attitude to accelerate economic growth and to build up her support with industrial and commercial groups.

It must have been clear to Mrs. Gandhi by then that her "socialism" was not working. The antipoverty programs had not been notably successful.[17] Thus, her continuing electoral support among the poor was not due to concrete rewards but rather to her ideological and rhetorical appeal. She believed that she could maintain the rhetoric even while watering down the overall "socialist program." More socialist rhetoric would not have brought her much more political capital in any case; the limits of rhetorical socialism had been reached. She must have calculated that a movement toward liberalizing the economy, while maintaining some rhetoric of socialism, would be likely to strengthen her political base.

Besides such overtly political considerations, other factors played roles in pushing India toward economic liberalization. The extent to which the conditions on the IMF loan influenced policy changes is difficult to judge.

14 See the editorial in *EPW*, December 1, 1984.

15 Discussions with T. N. Ninan, former senior editor (now executive editor), *India Today*, New Delhi, December 11, 1985, and N. S. Jagannathan, editor, *Financial Express*, New Delhi, December 14, 1985.

16 James Manor emphasizes this as a cause of the more "communal" Indira Gandhi of the 1980s. See his "Parties and the Party System."

17 See Atul Kohli, *The State and Poverty in India: The Politics of Reform* (Cambridge University Press, 1987), especially chapter 2.

Also, the World Bank has periodically pressured the Indian government to decontrol and open up the economy. However, in a large and relatively well established polity like India ("well established" in the sense of being staffed by competent bureaucrats), it would seem that organizations such as the IMF or the World Bank can never be the decisive factors. The decision to enter into that agreement with the IMF, with all that it entailed in terms of policy changes, must be seen in the light of a prior political decision by the Indian government. But once the government chose to enter that arrangement with the IMF, clearly it must have created pressure to "get the prices right" in the economy.

Within the government, report after report put together by bureaucrats and specialists had, since the 1970s, been recommending liberalization of one or another aspect of the economy.[18] The influence of those recommendations on real policy changes can easily be overestimated. If one were not cautious, one could easily conclude that policy momentum in India has been driven by such expert knowledge periodically brought to bear on pressing national problems. Such a conclusion would be misleading. The decision to set up a commission is a political decision. Commission members are appointed by leaders, and the policy preferences of such members generally are well known beforehand. Most important, whether or not the government chooses to act on a report is a political decision. For every report that recommended liberalization of the Indian economy, there were dozens of others that were gathering dust, waiting for some action on their recommendations as to how to improve the conditions of small farmers or scheduled tribes or how to desilt India's rivers.

Another factor that is worth considering here is the changing economic situation itself. As noted earlier, industrial growth had been sluggish for quite some time, and 1979 was a particularly bad year. The Janata government had taken some economic measures around that time that could be interpreted as "liberalizing measures."[19] Industrial growth had crawled back to over 8 percent in 1980. The extent to which that "success" created momentum for further liberalization is difficult to judge; however, the timing of the adoption of the new political program seems to have been more than just mere coincidence.

The issue of India's sluggish industrial performance was, in any case, foremost. New policies were needed. The various proposals for new policy measures summarized earlier were "in the air." Whatever their economic merits, some of the alternatives clearly suited Indira Gandhi's political

18 Because most of these reports are not public documents, complete citations cannot be provided. The contents of these reports generally are made known via newspapers. Four of the important relevant documents of the past decade were the reports of the Alexander commission, the Dagli commission, the Arjun Sengupta commission, and the L. K. Jha commission.
19 See Jha, "The End of the Tunnel."

design better than others. To attack "demand constraints" would have meant, among other things, shifting resources toward agriculture, thus alienating urban industrialists and the middle classes; it would also have meant attempting what had not worked before, such as land reform and other income-generating projects for the poor. Likewise, encouraging increased public investments was not easy. If Bardhan's analysis is right, that would have meant "rationalizing" the patronage network that holds India's dominant groups in a delicate alliance with one another.[20] Given Indira Gandhi's preoccupation with her political vulnerability, she was not likely to undertake major surgery on established state–society relations on that scale.

None of this is supposed to lead to the conclusion that the liberalizing alternative is without political pitfalls. On the contrary, as we shall see later, of Rajiv Gandhi's many political difficulties, those that have resulted from his attempts to liberalize the economy are not insignificant. Indira Gandhi, however, seems to have made a different political calculation, and apparently a correct one. Her credentials with the poor were well established, and because they were based primarily on ideological appeals, she was in no danger of losing that support over the short run. Given her political difficulties elsewhere, she opted to pursue the communal appeal to the dominant Hindu community and economic measures that would please business and industrial groups.

It was not at all self-evident that the so-called liberalization measures would be welcomed by the business groups. Import liberalization seemed likely to provoke controversy and indeed was seriously resisted by India's well-established indigenous business groups. In order to put the political decision to woo business support into practice, Mrs. Gandhi and her senior advisors had to determine what was wrong with India's industry and what sorts of changes the business community wanted.

Advisors such as L. K. Jha had considerable experience in working with both the business community and the government. He had never favored a rapid opening of the economy to external forces. He had, however, argued for removing restrictions on both entry and expansion of firms, and he favored reductions in direct and indirect taxes.[21] Those were the measures supported by most business groups, and certainly all business groups favored tax reductions. Big business lobbied for removal of constraints on the right of businesses to expand their capacity. Although many small businesses feared the removal of constraints, increased freedom of entry would allow them to compete in some previously unexplored areas. Therefore, as advisors like L. K. Jha were given prominent policy-making roles,

20 The reference is to the analysis presented in Bardhan, *Political Economy of Development*.
    An interesting essay discusses these issues in detail: Rubin, "Economic Liberalization."
21 Interview with L. K. Jha, New Delhi, December 16, 1985.

and as policies favored by Jha and others like him were put into effect, the message to the business community must have been clear: Socialism was being put on the back burner, and a new policy agenda that might work to their benefit was being initiated.

The shift in economic policy under Indira Gandhi is best understood as an integral part of her overall political strategy, which was aimed at strengthening her support in "soft" areas. The question that remains to be answered in this section is why those policy changes went relatively un- noticed. Given her socialist commitments, why did a policy trend toward liberalization of the economy never become a political liability for Indira Gandhi? An important part of the answer is fairly simple: The changes were not so drastic as to raise many political eyebrows. And yet, this explanation alone will not do; in fact, it raises a thorny question of political management: What distinguished between changes that could be made to look marginal and changes that inevitably appeared significant, and thus deserving of political responses from all those who were opposed to them?

Indira Gandhi was a masterful politician. As noted earlier, she well understood that her popular image was that of a leader on the left. She built up those credentials not by careful implementation of socialist policies but by undertaking highly visible measures such as nationalization of the banks, pursuit of antimonopoly legislation, and espousal of poverty alle- viation as the central plank in the platform of her party and government. It is a well-established political adage that leaders on the left can get away with taking certain rightist steps without invoking the wrath of the left, and vice versa. When leaders are judged by their citizens, what they claim to stand for turns out to be as important over the short run as the substance of the policies they pursue. Indira Gandhi benefited from the general political trust with which she had been invested by groups ranking low on the socioeconomic scale.

Indira Gandhi further benefited from India's politicoeconomic circum- stances and the effective stage management she provided to accompany her policy changes. India's political attention was increasingly devoted to issues like Assam and Punjab, rather than economic policies. Indira down- played the significance of the economy and economic achievements as evidence of legitimacy. When attention did turn to the economy, the picture presented for popular consumption was one more of continuity than of change. The rhetoric of socialism, though toned down, was maintained. Left-of-center economic advisors like K. N. Raj and Sukhamoy Chakro- varty were kept on in visible but largely ceremonial positions in the Eco- nomic Advisory Council, but the policy changes were being implemented by advisors behind the scenes, such as K. C. Alexander, L. K. Jha, and Arjun Sengupta. The changes themselves appeared largely technical – the lowering of a limit here, an expansion of a restriction there, and so forth. It seems that the aim was to depoliticize economic decisions as much as possible. A number of advisors noted that during interviews; the focus they suggested was on "results," not "ideology."[22]

That Indira Gandhi's attempts to liberalize the economy did not draw sharp political reaction was the result of a number of factors: the scale of the change, the deliberate attempt to maintain an image of continuity as well as to depoliticize economic decisions, and, of course, other pressing political circumstances that drew attention away from the economy. The tension between the pursuit of "economic rationality" and the "rationality of democracy" was kept within manageable bounds during Indira Gandhi's last few years. It is impossible to know how far she intended to push liberalization and to what extent she would have succeeded. Her assassination rendered such questions moot. What we do know is what her son tried to do: He pushed liberalization harder than did his mother and also provoked considerably more political opposition.

LIBERALIZATION UNDER RAJIV

During Rajiv Gandhi's term in power, India's economic policy went through three phases. During the first six months of his rule there was a genuine attempt at a new beginning, an attempt to make a decisive shift from the state-controlled, import-substitution model to a liberal model of development. As that attempt ran into political obstacles, the pace of change slowed down. The next two years are best characterized as two steps forward and one step back in relation to the defined agenda. With Rajiv's political popularity continuing to decline, the loss of the state elections in Haryana in May 1987 marked the beginning of the third phase, which lasted until he lost the election in 1989. That third phase involved a return to India's muddle-through model of economic policy making, wherein the policymakers remained committed to economic liberalization, but actual policy changes were few. Thus, the sense that there was to be a new economic beginning in India was quickly lost.

Those three phases of economic policy making were intimately linked to the national political situation in the second half of the 1980s, both as cause and as consequence. Instead of analyzing the overall political situation in detail, the next three sections focus primarily on those political factors that affected and help explain the economic-policy fluctuations.

Rajiv's rise to power was largely circumstantial. There is no doubt that before Indira Gandhi's assassination, Rajiv was being groomed as heir apparent. His tutelage, however, had been in process no more than two or three years when Indira Gandhi's assassination suddenly brought him to power. He was a natural heir in the sense that he had been put into that role by Indira Gandhi and was generally accepted as such by her loyal

22 Interviews with Arjun Sengupta (see footnote 9) and L. K. Jha (see footnote 21).

second tier. The political minions in the second tier did not command any independent political support. They must have calculated that the best chance for Congress and themselves to retain power was to select Indira's son; he was likely to inherit a fair amount of Indira's popularity and to gain sympathy because of her assassination.[23] Thus, Rajiv's initial power and legitimacy were based on a series of factors that had little to do with Rajiv's preferred economic policies. As Rajiv was thrust into the vacancy left by Indira's assassination, only a handful of Indians must have known, and the rest probably did not care to know amid the postassassination trauma and crisis, what types of economic policies the new government would pursue.

During the brief period of his rise and consolidation of control, Rajiv Gandhi and his advisors must have made a crucial decision: The new regime was going to stress "a new beginning" rather than continuity with the past. That emphasis on change became clear, relatively quickly, in both the rhetoric and action pertaining to political and economic matters. In the political arena, for example, the new emphasis was revealed by a shift away from Indira's recalcitrance (as in her dealings with Punjab and Assam) to a more accommodating and compromising set of policies, which are discussed in the next chapter. Similarly, with regard to issues of primary interest in this chapter, the government promised new economic policies. Shortly after winning the election by a large margin, Rajiv summed up his government's economic approach as involving a "judicious combination of deregulation, import liberalization and easier access to foreign technology."[24] That his approach involved a fairly sharp break from Nehru and Indira Gandhi's rhetorical emphasis on "socialism, planning and self-reliance" is self-evident.

As if to underline his break with the past, Rajiv Gandhi surrounded himself with a new breed of politicians and advisors. Consider some of those who appeared influential, at least in 1985–6: Confidants like Arun Nehru and Arun Singh had backgrounds as executives of multinational corporations. His economic advisors included Montek Ahluwalia, Abid Hussain, Bimal Jalan, and Manmohan Singh. Individuals like L. K. Jha were considered to have direct access to the prime minister. Though clearly a competent group of managers, economists, and bureaucrats, they were all marked by a technocratic rather than political image. Some of them had World Bank backgrounds; most of them were known for their decontrol and pro-liberalization proclivities. If one contrasts Rajiv and his group of India's new elite with Nehru and his band of seasoned, left-leaning

---

23 For a detailed discussion of the issue of how leaders in India get into power, see Henry Hart, "Political Leadership in India: Dimensions and Limits," in Kohli, ed., *India's Democracy,* especially pp. 50–61.
24 Quoted in *Times of India,* January 6, 1986.

nationalist leaders and advisors, then the sharp break with the past is unmistakable.

It is important to note here that this issue of a new breed of economic policymakers is as much an issue of image as of substance. For example, if we focus primarily on the economic advisors of an earlier generation – Pitambar Pant, I. G. Patel, Vishnu Sahay, Tarlok Singh, Ashok Mehta, V. T. Krishnamachari – we see probably more continuity than change between that group and Rajiv's advisors in terms of both technical skills and preferred policies.[25] There have been changes, however, in both the nature of the political leadership and the sense of who (the leader or the advisors) is really in charge of economic policy making. Because Rajiv and his political cronies like Arun Singh and Arun Nehru projected a managerial, technocratic image, there was a sense that political leaders and their technical advisors were cut from the same cloth. In addition, Rajiv's relative inexperience contributed to the popular belief that policy making was increasingly in the hands of bureaucrats and putative experts. Such considerations combined to give the impression of an abrupt change in the nature of India's economic policy making.

Rajiv's attempt, part real and part imagined, to make a sharp break with the past, though probably responsible for his early popularity, may well have been his undoing. What can explain the government's emphasis on change and neglect of continuity? The question is especially salient because the economic changes that Indira Gandhi had already introduced, and those that Rajiv's government actually pursued, could easily have been accommodated within an image of continuity. Why, then, did he feel the need to emphasize a sharp break?

An important part of the answer must be that Rajiv and his advisors initially intended the changes to go much further than they actually went. That must have seemed feasible because of the circumstances of Rajiv's rise to power. His massive electoral victory was based on sympathy and on fear. That victory appeared to free Rajiv Gandhi, if only momentarily and artificially, from coalitional entanglements and interest-group pressures. That freedom from "politics as usual" must have heightened the illusion that a new beginning was possible, even in a polity like India. The politically inexperienced cronies and advisors who surrounded Rajiv, as we shall see later, did not help to dispel such illusions.

Their sudden rise to positions of considerable power must have created a sense among the new rulers that they had hijacked the state. The state suddenly stood quite autonomous, seemingly free of societal constraints, ready to be used as a tool for imposing economic rationality on the society. Such situations of state autonomy always encourage the powerful to pursue their ideological whims. It was reported that a senior World Bank official

---

25 I am indebted to John P. Lewis for bringing this point to my attention.

flew into India at that time and advised the new government to dismantle the structures of economic control "all at once."[26] The reaction of the Indian government to such suggestions is not known; at least one senior advisor reported that he reacted "very negatively."[27] That kind of economic advice, he further suggested, fails to consider the serious political consequences of sudden shifts in policy.[28]

The illusion of autonomy and the euphoria of a new beginning lasted about six months. The new government's first major product was the 1985–6 budget, presented in March 1985, less than three months after coming to power. That proposed budget created many ripples. The word "socialism" was not mentioned even once in the budget speech.[29] Substantial tax concessions were proposed for corporations and for the urban upper middle classes. Imports were to be liberalized in certain sectors, especially electronics, a sector in which Rajiv Gandhi took personal interest. Most important, licensing regulations for domestic industries were to be relaxed drastically, and the limit on the size that a firm could attain without being defined as a monopoly was to be raised substantially.

The reaction in the business community and among the upper middle classes was euphoric, as will be discussed later. India's leading news magazine, *India Today,* ran such cover captions as "The Economy: Buoyant Mood" and "We Are Gearing for Take-Off."[30] Other commentators hailed it as "the most important budget in 30 years."[31] Because Parliament was totally dominated by individuals beholden to Rajiv Gandhi for their positions, there was no question at that early date of any substantial opposition from that group. The leftists and other opposition parties reacted sharply, characterizing the budget and the government as "pro-rich." In the middle of 1985, however, those were voices in the wilderness. They were drowned out, at least momentarily, in the euphoria of the new beginning.

However, opposition had begun to appear among the grass roots, and it did not take long to become organized. It was first expressed on a

26 Interview with Raja Chelliah, member of the Planning Commission, New Delhi, December 13, 1985. I have deliberately not mentioned the name of the official in question.
27 Interview with L. K. Jha (see footnote 21).
28 Some economists who, on balance, tended to favor liberalization of the Indian economy openly worried about the capacity of Rajiv Gandhi and his advisors to appreciate the serious political obstacles that such an effort would create. For an extremely well balanced and sensible essay along these lines, see Mrinal Datta Chaudhry, "The New Policy," *Seminar,* December 1985, pp. 18–22. Other economists like Jagdish Bhagwati have also, in a more general context, recognized these obstacles. See his "Rethinking Trade Strategy," in John Lewis and Valeriana Kallab, eds., *Development Strategies Reconsidered* (Washington, D.C.: Overseas Development Council, 1986), especially pp. 100–1.
29 For a summary and a discussion of the 1985–6 budget, see *Times of India,* March 21, 1985.
30 These cover captions were for the issues of March 15 and April 15, 1985, respectively.
31 Nani Palkhiwala, in *Times of India,* April 2, 1985.

significant scale, much to the surprise of the new leadership, within the ruling party. The occasion was an attempt by Rajiv Gandhi and his cronies to have the Congress party ratify an economic resolution, but they ran into considerable unexpected opposition from the rank and file. The resolution he wanted ratified represented an attempt to get his party formally behind the "new economic beginning" that he had begun with the budget. The resolution that was eventually ratified, however, recommitted Rajiv and the Congress party to socialism.[32]

The significance of that dramatic event must not be overlooked. Many in India are so tired of hearing about Congress's socialism that further talk of it deadens their sensibilities; such polemics evoke no reaction or, worse, cynical responses. Even the head of India's leading Chamber of Commerce dismissed that recommitment to socialism on Congress's part as "mere rhetoric."[33] Rhetoric it well may have been, but its significance was considerable. Congress's recommitment to socialism starkly emphasized that the government's economic policies would retain continuity with the past, that socialism would define the limits within which new policies would have to fit. It is clear now that those limits would prove quite flexible; the economic resolution, while reaffirming socialism, accepted all the policy changes that Rajiv's government had introduced thus far.[34] Nevertheless, Congress's tolerance for what most observers would consider gross inconsistencies yields a political picture very different from what one would see if the party had wholeheartedly supported liberalization of the economy. Rajiv's first major disagreement with his own party immediately set limits on how far he could carry economic policy changes. It cannot be doubted that the dispute over the issue of socialism slowed the pace of change that Rajiv and his advisors would have achieved had the Congress party supported them fully.

That confrontation with his own party marked the beginning of the second phase in Rajiv's economic policy making. From that point until about mid-1987, the government continued to push piecemeal liberalizing reforms, most of which were carried out while reemphasizing the government's commitment to socialism. We probably will never know the entire program that was planned, but we do know that in spite of such constraints, the government managed to push through some important reforms. Other proposals, however, had to be modified or withdrawn in order to keep to the "socialist" commitment.

32 These events received considerable attention in the press. For example, see *Times of India,* May 7, 1985; *Statesman,* May 7, 1985; *Statesman,* May 9, 1985; and *Telegraph,* May 14, 1985.
33 Interview with D. H. Pi Panandiker, secretary general, Federation of Indian Chambers of Commerce and Industry, New Delhi, December 12, 1985.
34 See *Times of India,* May 7, 1985. Also see All India Congress (I) Committee, "Economic Resolution," adopted by the All India Congress (I) Committee, New Delhi, May 6, 1985.

The rhetoric on economic policy became increasingly confused. During the celebration of Congress's centenary, on the day after the confrontation with the working committee over the economic resolution, Rajiv reaffirmed that Congress's goal had always been and would continue to be socialism.[35] Over the next few months, the economic policy changes included several liberalizing measures. When presenting India's seventh economic plan to the National Development Council in November, however, Rajiv Gandhi once again stated that the "industrial policy remains unchanged."[36]

Shortly thereafter, Rajiv argued that where "import substitutes are not cost-effective," India should opt for "imports, especially of technology."[37] That was followed by the release of a report by Abid Hussain emphasizing the need to increase exports and follow an "outward-looking" industrialization strategy.[38] Two days later, government spokesmen reiterated that whatever liberalization might take place, the public sector would continue to maintain the "commanding heights" of the economy.[39] The prime minister himself went on to argue for top priority to the public sector and to reemphasize that there was "no shift from socialism."[40] The main thrust of the seventh plan, it was further suggested, would be "eradication of poverty, self-reliance and growth with social justice."[41] Finally, several months later, the government let it be known that "privatization" of the public sector was not on the agenda, that the mixed-economy model would stay.[42]

If the rhetoric was confusing, probably deliberately so, a clearer pattern was discernible in the actual policy changes. Shortly after the Congress party forced Rajiv to recommit himself to continuity with the past, a new textile policy was quietly passed. Without too much discussion or debate, that policy removed the restrictions on the capacity of the mill sector.[43] Though seemingly a minor technical change, it struck at the heart of some of the old Congress's nationalist values. The removal of restrictions, it was argued, would force both the power-loom and hand-loom sectors into long-term decline, because of increasing efficiency in the mill sector. Though clearly "rational," such a change would have been abhorrent to the first-

35 See *Deccan Herald,* May 7, 1985.
36 See the *Statesman,* November 19, 1985.
37 Ibid., November 14, 1985.
38 The report was released in mid-November. For an abbreviated discussion, see *Economic Times,* November 18, 1985. The report itself is now a public document. See Government of India, *Report of the Committee on Trade Policy* (New Delhi: Ministry of Commerce, December 1984).
39 See *Indian Express,* November 20, 1985.
40 See *Hindusthan Times,* December 6, 1985.
41 See *Indian Express,* December 19, 1985.
42 See *Economic Times,* September 14, 1986.
43 For a critical review of the new textile policy, see L. C. Jain, in *Economic Times,* September 26, 1985.

generation nationalists. The "dumping" of the more efficient textiles by the British had been understood by the nationalists to have caused the destruction of the Indian textile industry in the nineteenth century, thus crushing nascent Indian capitalism; yet only a few generations later, Indian leaders were themselves promulgating similar policies. Old nationalist themes in economic policies clearly were on the decline.

Other important policy changes followed. The role of the Planning Commission was diminished, again without any pronouncements, by the creation of a new Ministry of Programme Implementation. A significant "New Fiscal Policy" was announced in November 1985. It replaced import quotas with tariffs and laid out long-term patterns for taxation, assuring the corporate sector that no negative surprises were looming below the horizon.[44] In spite of its worsening balance of payments, the government did not reverse its liberalized import policy, even in the capital-goods sector, which had been hurt quite badly. Moreover, companies restricted under the monopoly act were given further concessions,[45] and the budget for 1986–7 proposed further excise and customs relief for national firms.[46]

All those policy changes clearly were parts of a pattern. They were aimed at restricting the scope and relaxing the degree of state control over the private economy. Curiously, there was little immediate political response to those changes. A number of factors help explain that minimal opposition. Each of the new policies tended to affect only one segment of the society, as in the case of textile policy, and the values that were violated were held less dear in the 1980s than earlier. Because neither the values nor the interests of the larger society were hurt, political opposition was minimal. Other policy changes that went unopposed, at least during the short run, shared another trait: More often than not they were supportive of powerful business interests. They were brought about quietly, without fanfare, as seemingly technical changes in a piecemeal fashion. Few political groups in India would be able to muster the resources that would be required to monitor economic policy changes at such a minute technical level. Opposition groups, therefore, generally concentrated their political energies on policies that were highly visible and that influenced widely shared interests and values in the society.

Whereas the previously cited policies went more or less unopposed, another set of changes evoked considerable controversy, and the balance began tilting toward the mounting opposition. The proposed policies that had to be modified or withdrawn showed one of two characteristics: Either they were opposed by powerful groups, such as the business community, or they created diffuse but real disenchantment among the population in

44 See *Hindusthan Times,* December 12, 1985.
45 See *Indian Express,* January 23, 1986.
46 See the editorial in *EPW,* March 1, 1986.

general. A number of examples will support these generalizations, in addition to highlighting the policy fluctuations and reversals that were forced by the growing opposition.

The seventh plan drew opposition from within the ruling party. Although the details are not known, it is clear that several groups within Congress approached Rajiv to register their protests, namely, that the plan did not assign sufficient resources to antipoverty programs. The plan was changed to accommodate that political opposition, even though the planners pointed out that resources devoted to such programs in the past had not been used effectively.[47]

A different type of policy fluctuation characterized the government's approach toward industries that imported goods and thus directly affected the balance of payments. A good example is the automobile industry. During 1985, the government let it be known that it would look kindly on expansion of automobile production, including that involving foreign collaboration, especially with Japanese manufacturers. After several efforts to undertake such expansion got under way, the government, in early February 1986, changed its mind; implementation of the new automobile policy was postponed indefinitely. Among the reasons cited were the need to conserve petroleum and the worsening balance-of-payments situation.[48] There were indications, however, that pressure had been put on the government by India's established automobile manufacturers, who feared a glut of overproduction and competition from new and probably better products.[49] What adds weight to that interpretation is the fact that the decision was never reconsidered, even though petroleum prices dropped in the world market in July 1986 and India's balance-of-payments situation improved considerably, at least over the short run. The government actually used the occasion of its withdrawal from the anticipated automobile policy to make a more general statement that marked an important policy change: "[The] pace of domestic liberalization has not been slackened . . . external liberalization [however] was not really an objective of the [overall] policy."[50]

More serious opposition among the wider population was evoked by the issue of price hikes in February of 1986. Within a few days of the announcement of price increases in petroleum and related products, such as kerosene, every opposition party in the country announced plans for strikes and the closing down of one city or another. Congress politicians themselves argued against the hike, fearing a grass-roots backlash. Before the strikes could materialize, however, the government reversed its decision.[51]

47 Interview with Raja Chelliah (see footnote 26).
48 See *Economic Times,* February 2, 1986.
49 Ibid.
50 Ibid., February 24, 1986.
51 See the editorial in the *Telegraph,* February 7, 1986.

The preceding examples revealed specific instances of opposition and associated policy reversals. However, the type of opposition that in India was the most damaging politically, and the most difficult to document, was a more diffuse disillusionment with the national leadership. Rajiv's overall political popularity declined sharply in late 1986. His party lost virtually every state election held after the assembly elections in March 1985. The loss in Haryana in May 1987 was especially devastating because it was part of Congress's traditional power base, the Hindi heartland. That defeat marked the beginning of an electoral decline that culminated in Rajiv's defeat in the 1989 elections.

The outcomes of most state elections are strongly influenced by important regional themes. Even in elections in which national themes take on particular importance, the candidates' positions on economic policies make up only one part of the voter's overall assessment. In spite of the diffuse nature of the issue of "loss of electoral popularity," the loss in Haryana in 1987 had two important implications for understanding economic policy fluctuations. First, that election confirmed that the opposition parties had succeeded in branding Rajiv and his government as pro-rich. That categorization had to do with their style of political management and with the substance of the economic policies they undertook; it also contributed to Rajiv's loss of electoral popularity. Second, irrespective of how damaging the new economic policies had been politically, one way to correct sagging political fortunes in India clearly was to adopt populist, socialistic economic policies.

It was this last set of considerations that influenced economic policy making between 1987 and 1989. It seems fair to suggest that throughout Rajiv's second economic phase, the rate of change in economic policy slowed down from what probably had been intended to be a major departure from India's mixed-economy model of development. Socialism was reestablished as the framework. In spite of that rhetorical reversal, as well as the reduced pace of the economic changes and other important setbacks, the overall thrust during the second phase was to continue to push ahead toward lifting governmental controls and restrictions on the Indian economy. Following the electoral debacle in Haryana, however, the future of economic policy became unclear; India returned to its usual pattern of muddling through.

In the aftermath of the Haryana elections there was a growing sense that a major policy reversal might be in the making, but that did not come to pass. It seems obvious that Rajiv Gandhi and his key advisors, especially those concentrated in the prime minister's Secretariat, remained committed to liberalizing India's economic policy, but the opportunities to do so were fading. As Rajiv's popularity declined, the opposition adopted a relatively populist position, criticizing Rajiv for neglect of the farmers and the poor. That challenge, led by V. P. Singh in the Hindi heartland and by others like Jyoti Basu of the CPM in West Bengal and NTR and Hegde in the south, exposed Rajiv's electoral vulnerability among the lower classes. As the challenge grew, the government's thrust toward economic liberalization slowed. The angry conclusion of a prominent Indian journalist on that score appears to be only a slight exaggeration: "While no one can doubt that Gandhi was sincere in his desire to liberalize the economy, it is equally beyond doubt that he has failed."[52] The increased allocations to pro-farmer and antipoverty programs proposed in the budget for 1988–9 revealed that electoral pressures had pushed the issues of liberalizing the economy to the sidelines. Whether or not the new government under V. P. Singh will pursue liberalization, the analytical point is clear: When pressed politically, the national leadership slowed down its attempt to change India's economic policies.

In a little less than five years, Rajiv and his bold men had dissipated the enormous political capital that they had inherited. The society had struck back, and the Congress government had once again lost much of its autonomy. The lesson of that loss of power is likely to lead politicians to pursue policies determined as much by the logic of winning elections and sustaining coalitions, the logic of democratic power, as by "economic rationality." One can only hope that it will be possible to combine these two rationalities as contemporary India continues to search for the appropriate mix.

SUPPORT FOR LIBERALIZATION

Thus far, our analysis has focused on those who directed economic policy and on the fluctuations in economic policies. The roles of other actors and groups who influenced the policy process have been mentioned only in passing, but those who supported or opposed the policies contributed significantly to the politics of economic policy making, and some understanding of the roles and the views of the more significant actors is important. Those groups that, on balance, supported the government's initiatives are discussed next, and those that opposed the policies are discussed in the next section.

Business groups

Business groups, on balance, were supportive of Rajiv's government and policies. That support, however, varied in a number of ways. At the most diffuse level, business groups felt in tune with the new government. Rajiv's emphasis on technology and efficiency, rather than on socialism, appealed

---

52 See Prem Shankar Jha, "Economic Expansion Ensnared in Red Tape," *India Abroad,*
   December 11, 1987.

to the business community's preference for results over ideology. Following the early induction of former corporate executives like Arun Nehru and Arun Singh into the ranks of the ruling coterie, moreover, business spokesmen reported that for the first time in independent India they had felt as if they were not "cheats" or "pariahs," that they were part of the "national mainstream."[53]

Beyond the most general level, the Indian business community does not interact with the state elite through any single organization or speak with a single voice,[54] but there are many points of formal and informal contact between the state and business. Business groups are formally represented by three national and many regional chambers of commerce. Of the three national chambers, only the one involving the engineering industries is organized along functional lines. The other two main chambers, the Federation of Indian Chambers of Commerce and Industry (FICCI) and the Associated Chambers of Commerce and Industry of India (ASSOCHAM), bring together a variety of industries. The ASSOCHAM started off as an association of British industries in the preindependence period and until recently had maintained its character as a representative of companies with a large component of foreign investment or foreign management or both. The FICCI, until recently the most significant voice of Indian business, has, on balance, tended to represent indigenous capital. Within the business community, the two chambers are distinguished in a somewhat lighthearted and exaggerated fashion by their cultural compositions: ASSOCHAM represents the "tie wallahs," and FICCI the "dhoti wallahs."[55]

As long as the overall policy framework was stable, the political tasks of the FICCI and the ASSOCHAM were not all that significant. Their primary role, especially that of the FICCI, was to announce periodically which policy positions represented the interests of their members. The FICCI and the ASSOCHAM seldom cooperate on the policy memoranda they present to the government, though they do cooperate on labor–management issues.[56]

The real points of contact between business and government generally have been quite decentralized. For example, it is well known that during the 1950s and 1960s, important business houses had certain "captured" members of Parliament. Because of increasing centralization, however, the business community's attention has shifted to cabinet ministers and other

53 Interview with N. D. Saxena, secretary general, Associated Chambers of Commerce and Industry of India, New Delhi, December 16, 1985.
54 There is a detailed study that is somewhat out of date by now, but it still captures important trends in this issue area: Stanley Kochanek, *Business and Politics in India* (Berkeley: University of California Press, 1974).
55 Ibid. The qualification "until recently," when discussing the FICCI and the ASSOCHAM, is added because both chambers are currently undergoing major changes in membership.
56 Interview with N. D. Saxena (see footnote 52).

leaders of the Congress party and to the bureaucracy. Members of the FICCI are generally understood to have well-established contacts with the Congress hierarchy, with bribes being passed under the table to party coffers in exchange for political favors.[57] Most business houses, moreover, maintain "liaison offices" in New Delhi that wine, dine, and probably bribe bureaucrats and senior politicians to facilitate licensing and access to other resources the government controls. Members of the ASSOCHAM claim that their points of contact with the government are not through the party. The "Congress culture," they assert, is much closer to the culture of the FICCI. "We would rather deal in a club, over a glass of whiskey, with senior administrators . . . like L. K. Jha."[58]

With major policy changes on the horizon, Indian business groups have tried to come up with a somewhat more unified agenda than their decentralized mode of operation would previously have allowed. However, that has not been easy. The interests of various segments within the business community diverge considerably. One potential divide is between those who favor and those who oppose external liberalization. It seems obvious that those in import-substitution industries will oppose liberalizing imports, whereas those who need imported technology and those who produce for external markets will favor a different set of policies.[59] Although these are important tendencies, in reality such divisions are not easy to find. Major business houses tend to do all these things: They produce for protected markets, on occasion they wish to improve their technology with imports, and many either are in or would like to enter export markets.[60] A related area of disagreement within the business community involves the more traditional business houses that fear competition versus the newer businesses with new technology and imported business-school graduates who claim to be ready to compete internationally.[61]

Another major divide, whose political significance is much less well known, is that between big business, on the one hand, and medium and small businesses, on the other. It is generally assumed by policy-makers that the freedom to enter new areas of production and to expand existing capacity will primarily benefit those who are already well established, namely, the big business houses.[62] Why should medium businesses, and

57 Interview with N. S. Jagannathan (see footnote 15).
58 Interview with N. D. Saxena (see footnote 52).
59 For an argument along these lines, see Bhabatosh Datta, "The Road to Nowhere," *Seminar,* 316(December 1985), pp. 32–5.
60 Interview with a business executive who did not wish to be identified, New Delhi, December 14, 1985.
61 Several of those interviewed suggested this as the major division within the business community vis-à-vis the new economic policies. For example, both T. N. Ninan and N. S. Jagannathan expressed this view (see footnote 15).
62 Interview with L. K. Jha (see footnote 21).

especially small businesses, support policies aimed in that direction? Are their interests not threatened by the encroaching "monopoly" houses? Because small businesses are not well organized into groups, their political opinions do not get expressed by any regular route, nor can observers easily identify those opinions.

This picture of organizational variations and divergence of interests within the business community is not intended to lead to the conclusion that the Indian business community does not have some clear and coherent policy preferences or that it is politically weak. It is intended to illustrate the mode and mechanisms by which business groups have influenced the liberalization agenda. The business community in India has tended to react to rather than to lead economic policy. Its power is closer to being one of veto than of agenda setting. The policy lead has come from the political actors. Thus, the liberalization agenda had its origin as much in the changing power structure and interests of the business community as in the changes within the state, that is, the coming to power of new leaders with new ideologies.

The nature of the division of power between state and business is clearly evident in the policy process. The FICCI had been demanding lower taxes, delicensing, and removal of restrictions on monopolies for decades, but when such changes finally came about in a big way, it was because of a new government in power. Even business representatives were taken by surprise, for example, when the government decided to revise the definition of a "monopoly company" to specify 100 crores of rupees from 20 crores, whereas the FICCI had asked for the limit to be only 60 crores.[63]

The reactions of business groups to the government's new economic policies generally were quite favorable. The initial package that the Rajiv government offered in the budget of 1985–6, which has generally been in effect ever since, was received with tremendous enthusiasm by all three of the important chambers of commerce. However, in one major area the responses of the business community were quite hesitant, or even negative: the extent to which the economy should be opened up to external goods and capital. There was widespread opinion among Indian business groups that both foreign borrowing and direct foreign investment were not desirable.[64] That coincided with the policymakers' nationalist sentiments and cautious approach to those issues.[65] The issue of trade liberalization, however, proved to be more complex. Many industries welcomed liberalized imports of technology, but liberalized imports hurt some domestic producers. Given the import-substitution bias of most industries in India, the

63 Interview with D. H. Pi Panandiker (see footnote 32).
64 Ibid.
65 Both Raja Chelliah (see footnote 26) and L. K. Jha (see footnote 21) suggested in interviews that there was no thought of altering the established national approach on these issues.

overall reluctance of business groups to support import liberalization emerged fairly clearly after a process of trial and error, which proceeded as follows: The government liberalized certain imports. It then monitored the impact of those policy changes on the balance of payments and on specific groups of industries, and business reactions were also factored in serially. What emerged was a fair amount of agreement between the political and economic elite.

Business groups have, on balance, decided that they are not ready to deal with any major international opening of the economy. In the words of the head of the FICCI, "after three decades of highly protective industrialization, liberalization cannot be taken up simultaneously on all fronts – it has to be phased. The first stage has to be to allow domestic competitiveness. Only then [after a while], we should open up to outside forces."[66] Such views from businessmen pampered by import substitution are not surprising. What is interesting, and perhaps even somewhat surprising, is that the government tends to agree. Those who seem to favor a competitive economy apparently have decided that competitiveness and the interests of business groups are mutually exclusive, and so far the latter have prevailed. Senior advisors like L. K. Jha have assured businessmen that domestic industry, "built up with so much effort and sacrifice," will not be allowed "to be killed by imports."[67] Even "outside" experts like Jagdish Bhagwati agree, because of political feasibility.[68] Finally, the prime minister stated in 1986 that import liberalization was not on the immediate agenda: "Competition within our domestic economy is being fostered. Progressively, we will open our economy to the winds of international competition."[69]

With the government's having acceded to the demand of business groups to limit trade liberalization, one would have to conclude that the Rajiv government was in agreement with business, especially big business, which was producing for the protected domestic market. Sporadic efforts under V. P. Singh, then the finance minister, to raid business houses in a search for corrupt practices only emphasized that the government badly needed some popular and visible issues in order to distance itself from the image of too close an association with business.

Middle classes

Within India's political discourse, the term "middle class" has come to refer to some 60 million to 80 million city dwellers who work mainly in

66 Interview with D. H. Pi Panandiker (see footnote 32).
67 L. K. Jha's address to the Indian Merchants Chamber, Bombay, as reported in *Economic Times,* September 16, 1986.
68 R. K. Roy's interview with Jagdish Bhagwati, as published in *Economic Times,* September 16, 1986.
69 See *Times of India,* January 6, 1986.

the professions and the civil service or are self-employed.[70] There have been no detailed studies of the socioeconomic or political characteristics of these groups. Surveys and polls conducted by journalists and impressions gathered during many discussions have led to some tentative generalizations, especially concerning middle-class support for Rajiv's new economic policies in 1985 and 1986.

The means by which the support of the middle classes for Rajiv Gandhi and his policies was expressed were quite varied. For example, such support was evidenced in popularity polls conducted by news magazines and in opinions expressed in English-language media catering primarily to those groups.[71] Through 1985 and most of 1986, the balance of such views tended to be positive. Although opinion slowly turned against Rajiv, beginning in 1987, that shift had less to do with economic policies and more to do with issues of corruption. Both the positive and negative views among the middle classes tended to have greater impact than the electoral power of those groups would indicate. Members of the middle class frequently think and write about economic and political matters. India's men and women of letters generally come from this background and tend to mold the society's opinions.

The support that the Indian middle classes provided for Rajiv and his economic program in the first two years of his rule can be understood by focusing on three different issues that linked that interest group to the government. First, there was the intangible but significant issue of a sense of identity with the leader: Urban middle-income groups felt that Rajiv was their leader. Rajiv's image was that of an urbane, westernized Indian who stood for modern technology, computers, and efficiency, who initially disclaimed the old Congress culture of corruption, sloth, nepotism, and "dhoti and kurta wallahs," and who enjoyed video cameras, hi-fi systems, jazz, and cars. Detailed studies of the values dear to the Indian middle classes are not available. If ever such a study is conducted, it will find some wide variations. Nevertheless, one gets a clear impression from the news media and from conversations that the new middle classes identified strongly with the image that Rajiv Gandhi initially projected. It would be difficult not to agree with the conclusion of a survey published in an Indian news magazine: "Over the last five years [1981–6], the Indian middle class has come into its own. It is now more assertive and confident, particularly after Rajiv Gandhi – who it sees as one of its own – became Prime Minister."[72]

Beyond shared values is the important issue of tangible economic re-

70 This figure is generally arrived at by marketing companies by assuming that the urban middle class is defined by incomes of 1,000 to 2,500 rupees. A good nonscholarly survey of the Indian middle class was published in India's news magazine *Imprint*, March 1986, pp. 14–28.
71 See, for example, the various popularity polls in *India Today* throughout 1985 and 1986.
72 See *Imprint*, p. 14 (see footnote 70).

wards. Rajiv Gandhi's early economic policies provided concrete benefits for the middle classes. Reductions in taxes and abolition of such programs as the "compulsory savings deposit scheme" were received with great enthusiasm. Moreover, the government seemed to have decided to hinge its new economic strategy on the buying power of those groups. Controls on production had been released, but exports were not going up rapidly. Who, under those circumstances, was going to buy all the new products that were suddenly appearing on the market? Clearly, the government was hoping that the middle-income groups would use their increased buying power to soak up the growing supply and thus avoid a demand constraint on growth. Whether or not that could have become the basis for a successful development strategy is not at issue here; it is a matter for the economists to debate.

From the point of view of the political inclinations of the middle-income groups, the new strategy meant not only higher incomes over the short run but also, for almost the first time in postcolonial India, an economy that was not beset by shortages of consumer goods. Growing incomes and increasing availability of products, in turn, fostered a benign view of the government, at least over the short run. That such tangible rewards were more important than any feeling of shared values with the leadership was demonstrated when those same middle-income groups threw their weight against the government's plans to raise petroleum prices in February 1987.[73]

Finally, a third issue that increasingly linked middle-income groups to government policies was more indirect, and it has not received much attention. Over the 1980s, there was a major change in how Indian industry financed itself. Significant contributions to industrial investment now come from the sale of public stocks. Although exact figures are not known, the phenomenon of middle-income groups buying stocks in a big way has been widely noted over the past decade. This is rapidly creating a "structural" link between middle-income groups and big business, and it is likely to have increasing political significance. Middle-income groups now have a stake in the economic health of industry and commerce, and policies to promote that health are receiving their support.

OPPOSITION TO LIBERALIZATION

Whereas both business and urban middle-income groups tended to support the government's new economic initiatives, a number of important actors and groups did not.

The Congress rank and file

As noted earlier, a surprising source of opposition to the new policies had been the rank and file of the ruling party. It was surprising because Con-

73 See the editorial in the *Telegraph*, February 7, 1986.

gress's party organization had been moribund for so long that observers cannot be blamed for having forgotten the party as a source of independent political initiative.

That early controversy between Rajiv and his own party provides a reasonably clear picture of the original economic intentions of Rajiv and his advisors. A summary of the main events should be revealing: Rajiv and a few of his ministers offered a carefully prepared economic resolution to a working committee of the Congress party prior to presenting it to the All India Congress Committee (AICC) for ratification. That resolution was reported to have been the handiwork of Rajiv's "whiz kids," or the "World Bank wallahs,"[74] a group of technocratic economic advisors to Rajiv, especially those in the prime minister's Secretariat. The resolution was presented to the working committee by the finance minister, V. P. Singh. His opening statement, according to the press, included such remarks as "bread, cloth and shelter were not everything of the economy."[75] The resolution itself did not stress socialism, but used language that seemed to suggest that a shift in strategy that was both necessary and justified had already been adopted over the past few months:

The strengthening of the growth impulses of the economy, through absorption of modern technology and through appropriate fiscal and legislative changes, was imperative to sustain the tempo of industrial development. In the process of continued development, the policy instruments relevant to one stage cannot be treated as permanently sacrosanct. Nor are they ends in themselves.[76]

Many Congressites read in that resolution an attempt to move away from the old development strategy of "self-reliance and socialism." The details of the internal debates that took place are not known, but it is known that many senior party members and elected officials opposed the economic resolution.[77] As was discussed earlier, the resolution that was eventually approved had been radically revised: It reaffirmed continuity with the past by emphasizing socialism as Congress's central goal.

How should we interpret those events? First, they revealed a considerable lack of political judgment on the part of Rajiv Gandhi and his economic advisors. The intended plan seems to have been nothing less than a major shift in India's overall development strategy. Even in an imperfect democracy like India, that would require a considerable amount of prior discussion and what some would euphemistically call "consensus building." Leaving aside for the moment the various contending interest

---

74 See Nikhil Chakravarty, "AICC Resists Rajiv's Kitchen Cabinet Policy," *Telegraph*, May 15, 1985. Nikhil Chakravarty also brought up these issues, including the fact that he had personally seen the original economic resolution, in a one-on-one discussion in New Delhi, December 17, 1985.
75 See the *Statesman*, May 7, 1985.
76 Reported by Nikhil Chakravarty (see footnote 74).
77 See, for example, the reports in the *Statesman*, May 7, 1985, and *Times of India*, May 7, 1985.

groups and political forces in the society, the small group of India's technocratic rulers did not even have a clear sense that they could carry their own ruling party with them. The explanation for such political behavior would have to stress some combination of extreme centralization of initiative, isolation of the rulers, lack of communication between the elite and the party ranks, and the arrogance of power that comes from absolute belief in the wisdom of one's own opinions.

Why Congressites opposed the original economic resolution and stressed the need to emphasize socialism is also something of an enigma. Press accounts and discussions have suggested that three different sets of motives were at work. According to the most common interpretation, many Congressites feared the electoral and political ramifications of abandoning socialism. Many members apparently conveyed to the leadership the following view: "Liberalization of the economy, import of technology and also opening the door to multinationals was not going down very well with the party's ground-level workers, who had to constantly meet people worried by their problems of hunger, shelter and clothing."[78] Nothing brings home that gap between the leadership and the rank and file more sharply than to sit in a district- or state-level Congress office, with an electric fan intermittently going on and off because of an electricity shortage, and ask for opinions on Rajiv's "march into the twenty-first century with computers." Those who responded honestly gave a common answer that in retrospect seems to have been prophetic: "This talk is fine in Delhi, but here it will only make you lose elections."[79]

A second set of considerations that led some Congressites to oppose the resolution had more to do with ideology than with electoral considerations. Old Congressites, such as the former president of the party, Brahmananda Reddy, apparently made strong and open pleas during the meeting, criticizing the resolution for neglecting what Congress had always stood for, namely, the "common man."[80] Although cynicism regarding such statements often is an appropriate response, it would be unwise to ignore the fact that certain ideas still had a powerful hold on older Congressites. The number of such Congressites is diminishing, but they have not all vanished. Notions of national self-reliance are very dear among that group, as is the idea that even if one cannot do much to help the poor, the rich should not be pampered. State controls on capitalism had satisfied those ideological urges. The proposed liberalization, by contrast, provoked a knee-jerk reaction because it would involve abandonment of hard-won national sov-

78 See the *Statesman*, May 7, 1985.
79 Although remarks like this were often made, this specific quotation is from an interview with Jinabhai Darjee, a veteran Congress (I) leader in Gujarat, conducted in Ahmedabad on March 10, 1986. The original interview was in Hindi. The translation is my own.
80 See the *Statesman*, May 7, 1985.

ereignty and would give the rich a green light to get away with anything they could.

Finally, and probably most important, another group of Congressites seem to have opposed the resolution not because they had any serious concerns over the substance of the economic policy but because they were generally disgruntled with Rajiv Gandhi and were in search of an issue they could use against him. That group generally consisted of individuals who had been well placed under Indira Gandhi, but had lost out in the shuffle. As many as a hundred of them, led by Dinesh Singh, met at his house the night before the meeting to chart out an opposing strategy.[81]

Various sets of factors thus motivated Congressites to oppose the economic resolution presented by Rajiv and his ministers. The event was significant because it demonstrated that the Congress party was not totally dead, at least not at the top and in the second tier, and not when issues of personal power and electoral success were involved. That same impression emerged when the party opposed the leadership's decision to hike petroleum prices. What is equally significant for the purpose of this chapter, however, is that by failing to carry his own party, Rajiv was put on the defensive concerning his economic program, which probably put important limits on both the pace and scope of the intended changes.

Moderate left opposition

Had Rajiv Gandhi carried his own party, he probably could have ignored the opposition from the left without significant political cost. The opposition within Congress, however, jelled around what can be considered a leftist position, and that increased the significance of similar opposition generated by non-Congress groups, especially leftist intellectuals and parts of the working class. What made that opposition even more credible was its moderation. The government's new economic policies were opposed not from a position demanding massive structural changes but from one that claimed to be more "broad-based" and "politically feasible."

A development of some political significance was the joint statement put out by 29 respected economists in October 1985.[82] As discussed earlier, that statement was sharply critical of the government's new economic policies. The meeting of the economists was sponsored by the CPM and was held in Calcutta, but the economists involved were not all Marxists. Although opinions within the group varied, they arrived at a joint position that not only was very critical of the liberalizing thrust of the new policies but also offered an alternative economic strategy.

The economists criticized the government's proposed strategy because

---

81 Discussion with the journalist and political observer Nikhil Chakravarty (see footnote 74).
82 See *EPW,* October 26, 1985, pp. 1813–16.

it would undermine cherished national goals of self-reliance and socialism. They argued that the new strategy would not even succeed in its growth objectives because the underlying analysis was wrong: The real constraints on growth were limited demand and declining public-sector investment. The way to boost growth, therefore, while preserving national sovereignty and facilitating some redistribution, was to increase public investments (especially for irrigation), improve public-sector performance, implement land reforms, and facilitate broad-based agriculture-led economic development.

That event had a number of political implications. First, India's economists are now more divided than in the past on the issue of the economic direction India should adopt for the future. From the time of the second five-year plan in the late 1950s onward, India has adopted a development strategy that has been considered by most Indian economists to be an appropriate strategy. There were always those who thought India should be more export-oriented and competitive, and there were always those who thought that the "feudal-capitalist" alliance was holding back India's economic dynamism. Toward the middle, however, there were many disagreements, but not over the crucial values that economic development should strengthen. Even today, one should not exaggerate the divisions, especially on one broad issue: Many government controls on the private economy have outlived their utility. And yet it is important to note that specialists are now quite divided on the issue of what values economic development should satisfy. The consensus of the specialists, which can be a powerful political glue, has come undone.

Related to this general point is a more specific issue. The divisions among the specialists have highlighted the political nature of economic decision making. The new economic policies can no longer easily be sold as technical solutions to complex technical problems. This has no bearing on which of the various specialist viewpoints is really "right." The political point is simply that the technocratic element that could help legitimize economic policies has been weakened. Increasingly the battle over economic policies will have to be fought more openly on political grounds.

No suggestion is intended here that mere opposition from specialists can provide the basis for mass political opposition. The significance of such opposition is that viable alternative economic plans are now available to be chosen by the political actors. Opposition parties like the CPM and the Lok Dal have come together under the leadership of V. P. Singh around an economic program that emphasizes "broad-based, agriculture-led development." Even in 1987, as Rajiv's popularity declined further, he continued to distance himself from the liberalization alternative and moved closer to a more populist program.

Another event that demonstrated opposition to the new policies was a one-day national strike organized by the workers in the public sector in

January 1986. The strike was organized mainly around political demands: halting the policy of privatization, stopping the flow of foreign and national private capital into public-sector activities, protecting domestic goods against imports, and ensuring the right of trade unions to have a voice in deciding technological changes, especially computerization. The strike was coordinated by an all-India committee and by all accounts was successful.[83]

The strike focused on policy issues that public-sector workers feared that the government might pursue in the future. It is difficult, therefore, to assess the political significance of the strike. Nothing concrete was up for bargaining; there were no identifiable winners or losers. What strikes like that make clear, however, is the type of opposition the government can expect if it ever really begins to privatize the public sector.

Rural groups

The political attitudes and activities of India's rural groups are the most difficult to ascertain and document. Any description of how they reacted, if they reacted at all, to changing economic policies must be largely guess-work. This is important, nevertheless, because it is in the countryside that India's elections are won or lost. What sways the rural voters remains somewhat of a mystery and a subject of considerable importance.

What is known for sure is that after the new economic policies were initiated, Rajiv Gandhi and his Congress party lost eight successive state elections and eventually were defeated at the national level. It would, of course, be stretching the evidence beyond recognition to claim that those electoral losses could be attributed to the government's new economic policies. The losses in Punjab and Assam in the mid-1980s clearly had much more to do with regional issues than national issues. Regional losses elsewhere, such as those in West Bengal, Kerala, and Haryana in 1987, had resulted from complex regional and national concerns, including the multicausal variable of Rajiv's generally declining popularity.

In spite of the foregoing caveat, there is reason to believe that the new economic policies hurt Congress politically among two numerically significant rural groups: the "middle peasants" and the scheduled castes. When trying to understand the political effects of national economic policies on these rural groups, it is important to bear in mind that the political preferences of such largely illiterate citizens are molded by a variety of factors and expressed in diffuse, general terms. Their generality, however, does not necessarily reduce the rationality of these preferences. Nehru and Indira Gandhi, for example, were never favored by the middle peasants of the backward castes, because such leaders were seen as Brahmans who lived in a city and were concerned primarily with city folk. By contrast,

83 See, for example, "Public Sector," *EPW,* January 24, 1987.

Indira Gandhi was much loved by the scheduled castes because she supposedly stood for the poor, certainly more than did other prominent national politicians. As far as Rajiv Gandhi is concerned, in the words of *India Today,* the "pro-rich image has stuck."[84]

The extent to which that image was created by bad political management, as distinct from the policies pursued, will never be known for sure, but it appears that the image had its inception in Rajiv's first major economic step: the 1985–6 budget. As mentioned earlier, that budget proposed tax concessions for corporations and middle-income groups, as well as other concessions that appeared to benefit primarily the prosperous city dwellers. Despite making policy changes at the margins, Rajiv Gandhi was never able to shed his pro-city, pro-rich image.

The political reaction of the middle peasants to that image was quite negative. That was clearest, for example, in a state that generally was dominated by Congress: Gujarat. As discussed in Chapter 9, the backward castes, the Kshatriyas, many of whom were middle-income peasants, were actually aligned with Congress. In spite of that, between 1984 and 1987, peasant agitations against the Congress state government had become a regular feature. During March 1987, for example, nearly a million peasants, generally owner-farmers, threatened *gheraoes* before the state assembly to press their demands for higher output prices and lower input prices. When the government sought to block their actions, massive violence resulted. Seventy-three government vehicles were set on fire, traffic was blocked, railway lines were damaged, 2,000 people were arrested, 10 people died, and the former chief minister of the state was beaten up.[85]

Another important example supports this thesis: the Haryana elections. Congress had never enjoyed much support from the main peasant caste in Haryana: the Jats. The popular feeling that Haryana was losing out to Punjab over various regional issues also raised the odds against a Congress victory. However, the massive electoral loss in a state that Congress had formerly controlled (Congress won only 5 of 86 announced results) revealed a further erosion of its peasant base in that largely agrarian state.

The opposition in Haryana emphasized themes that high-lighted the vast distance between the needs of the "humble peasants" and the rulers in New Delhi. It was reported that Devi Lal, the new state leader, went from village to village arguing in his down-to-earth style that the Delhi rulers were busy with their "foreign wives, foreign banks and foreign money."[86] A news weekly editorialized that

in Devi Lal's campaigning there came to be increasing emphasis on the Rajiv Gandhi government's modernization policies. The attacks on these policies were

84 See *India Today,* July 15, 1987, p. 22.
85 Reported in *India Today,* April 15, 1987, pp. 22–3.
86 See *India Today,* July 15, 1987, pp. 8–10.

rough and ready, couched sometimes in urban-versus-rural terms of the familiar Sharad Joshi variety and at other times in terms of a western-oriented upper class minority versus the mass of people. Clearly, the raising of these issues and their undoubted impact on the electorate gives the outcome of Haryana election a greater significance than if the election had been more or less exclusively focused on the Haryana-versus-Punjab issue.[87]

The message that the opposition attempted to spread, which apparently was accepted, was simple but powerful: Delhi rulers do not have peasant interests at heart.

Some have predicted that there will be a related political development that will have far-reaching consequences: loss of support among the rural poor in general, and the scheduled castes in particular, support that Congress could bank on under Indira Gandhi. That had been the major political gain that Indira had secured with her emphasis on *garibi hatao*. Rajiv's failure to shed the image of a pro-rich leader must have eroded that support base. Although hard evidence on this point is not available, there were indications as early as 1986 that such a trend had begun. As discussed previously, interviews revealed widespread concern among Congressites at the district level and below regarding how they were going to maintain the support of the scheduled castes when Congress's talk was all about computers and the twenty-first century.[88]

None of the foregoing should be read as implying that there was a groundswell of opposition to Rajiv's Congress in the countryside and that the main cause of that was the government's economic policies. Both factually and analytically, such a claim would be incorrect. Public-opinion polls continued to reflect that as late as 1988, Rajiv remained by far the most popular leader in India, especially in rural areas.[89] The reasons for that continued popularity were complex and are not the main subject of this discussion. Nor is it the purpose here to examine why Rajiv's popularity eventually slipped in 1989 and why the opposition became unified. The point argued here is more modest. Congress under Rajiv, especially in 1986 and 1987, steadily lost political support. A major indication of that was Congress's electoral losses, especially in many state elections. It was also evidenced in agrarian agitations and concerns voiced by those who had grass-roots contacts. It is not unreasonable to deduce that part of that loss of support was caused by the government's economic approach, an approach that came to be interpreted as both pro-city and pro-rich. Whatever the causes, there is an even more important point: His attempts to recapture his former popularity pushed Rajiv back in a populist direction, and the agenda for economic change was put on the back burner.

87 See *EPW*, June 20, 1987, editorial on "Haryana Elections."
88 Many of these interviews are cited in Part II.
89 See, for example, *India Today*, February 29, 1988, pp. 17–23.

CONCLUSION

This chapter has presented an analysis of the politics of economic liberalization in India. The forces that supported or opposed government initiatives, as well as how the political infighting influenced the policy process, have been discussed. Rajiv Gandhi had attempted to push economic liberalization. Major policy initiatives had been taken in that direction during 1985 and 1986. The pace of change, however, had slowed down by 1988. Whereas a technocratic leadership in alliance with businessmen and well-off urban groups had provided the main push for liberalization policies, others in that poor, agrarian society had reacted negatively. Their opposition was not based on economic issues alone, and although it was not always expressed in a coherent, direct fashion, it was nevertheless real.

It is with only slight exaggeration, therefore, that one is led to conclude that attempts within India to implement what the leaders considered to be economically rational came into conflict with the rationality of building popular support. That created difficult problems in political management for Rajiv Gandhi. The political capacity to pursue an important goal was lacking. It appears that Rajiv Gandhi, like his current successors, had little choice but to continue to push for economic liberalization. Because that is likely to continue to be politically costly, leaders will increasingly feel pressured to use noneconomic issues such as regionalism, communalism, and nationalism to build electoral majorities.

12

Managing the troubled political institutions: the Congress party and relations with Punjab

After coming to power in late 1984, Rajiv Gandhi identified the new government's policy priorities: to reform the economy, to rehabilitate the Congress party, and to repair New Delhi's relations with such troubled states as Punjab and Assam. In each of those crucial problem areas Rajiv's government committed itself to a new approach. The extent of its success in economic-policy reform was discussed in the preceding chapter. In this chapter, the focus shifts to an evaluation of Rajiv's attempts to reinvigorate the Congress party and to find a solution to the vexing problem of Punjab.[1] The primary purpose of this discussion is not to assess Rajiv's leadership qualities. Although the quality of leadership is an important variable in any government's ability to rule, a focus on the political process of problem-solving allows one to identify broader issues: the changing nature of the Indian state at its summit, and the changing ability of the state to solve political problems by action from above.

It is argued here that after a promising start, Rajiv's efforts to strengthen the Congress party and to impose political order in Punjab began to falter under familiar political pressures. That Rajiv's policies in those areas were not very successful is known to even casual observers of contemporary India. The main task in this chapter, therefore, is not to document those failures but, rather, to explain them. What we seek to understand is why electoral popularity in contemporary India, even massive electoral popularity, does not confer on the victor greater power to solve society's problems. Elections have come to be influenced more and more by "mood swings" in the body politic. In the absence of enduring coalitions and coherent programs, leaders who win elections come away with only vague mandates. Attempts to translate such general mandates into specific policies quickly bring forward many competing and diverging responses from all those who stand to be affected by the proposed policies, and leaders

---

1 This chapter is based largely on what has been reported in the Indian press. Items from the following publications were consulted: *Times of India, Indian Express, India Today,* and *Economic and Political Weekly.* Direct references to these sources are provided only when the issue is somewhat controversial or when a specific piece of information was pulled out of them. References to other sources that were consulted are in the footnotes.

find it difficult to accommodate such diverse demands. Neither the institutions that could facilitate compromise nor those that could be used to isolate the more militant opposition within the constitutional framework function well. Institutional weakness and a fragmented polity are at the heart of the growing tendencies toward centralization and powerlessness.

DEALING WITH THE CONGRESS PARTY

Rajiv Gandhi inherited a Congress party that was an organizational disaster.[2] Because he had been in charge of the party for two to three years before coming to power, Congress was one national political institution with which Rajiv had some familiarity, but that familiarity had not inspired confidence in such a motley institution. On the contrary, Rajiv quickly made known his considerable dissatisfaction with the state of party affairs. Within a year of winning the elections of January 1985, Rajiv had identified, through his speeches and actions, three important problem areas within the party that needed reform: Congress needed (1) organizational *elections;* (2) *discipline,* to control dissent, corruption, rampant factionalism, ruffians, and power brokers; and (3) a new commitment to the party's values and *ideology* on the part of all members.

During his term of nearly five years in power, Rajiv's attempts to reform the Congress party in those areas went through three phases, and those phases paralleled the changes in Rajiv's overall popularity and his sense of political security. During the first phase, which lasted some 12–15 months, observers noticed a fairly clear commitment, as well as some actions aimed at reforming the Congress party. That was followed by a second phase in which the clarity of purpose vanished. What was evident instead was a leader in search of an institutional strategy – sometimes groping, sometimes combative, sometimes reconciliatory, and often reacting in an ad hoc manner.

Between late 1987 and late 1989, when Rajiv lost power, a different, more belligerent Congress had emerged. It appeared that the plan to reform the Congress party had been postponed. Rajiv had decided to sidestep much of the organizational disorder in the Congress party. He had instead adopted a strategy similar to that practiced by his mother and brother in the post-Emergency period: to ignore the main party and to use peripheral Congress organizations, such as the Youth Congress, for belligerent mass mobilization, aimed mainly at the opposition but also at Congress dissenters. In the following chronological account of Rajiv's changing approach

2 This issue has been discussed intermittently in earlier parts of this study. For a good account of the national-level Congress party that Rajiv inherited, see James Manor, "Parties and the Party System," in Atul Kohli, ed., *India's Democracy: An Analysis of Changing State–Society Relations* (Princeton University Press, 1988), pp. 62–98.

to Congress, I analyze the reasons for those changes, as well as why it has proved so difficult to hold internal party elections and to infuse a measure of discipline and ideology into Congress.

The first phase

Rajiv's actions during his first year in office are readily understandable if we keep in mind the circumstances of his rise to power. It was his mother's assassination rather than any achievement of his own that catapulted him into the position of India's leadership, and there is no doubt that he was already being groomed for that position by his mother. Indira Gandhi's assassination, however, created an unusual political situation. The second tier of leaders – the cabinet ministers, Congress leaders, the powerful Congress chief ministers, and certain powerful aides – apparently decided, implicitly or explicitly, that Rajiv was the "natural" successor.

That calculation, in turn, must have rested on a number of political facts concerning contemporary India: None of the second-tier leaders had any significant independent political following; Rajiv was likely to inherit considerable legitimacy in the "semimodern" Indian polity and was likely to benefit more than anyone else from the sympathy evoked by his mother's death. Rajiv's massive electoral victory in late 1984 proved those calculations to be correct. For our purposes, however, it is important to note a different point. As pointed out earlier, having been given the position of leadership almost accidentally, and having gained considerable electoral support to legitimize that inheritance, Rajiv must have had a strong sense that he was in a position to initiate important political changes.

Rajiv's actions within the first few months revealed that reform of the Congress party was high on his agenda. During the 1984 Lok Sabha elections, nearly one-third of the old Congress members of Parliament (MPs) were not given tickets (i.e., were not renominated by Congress). Similarly, two of every five sitting members of Legislative Assemblies (MLAs) were denied Congress tickets in the assembly elections held in March 1985. The popular impression was that many of the "unsavory" and "corrupt" Congressites were to be replaced by a new "clean" generation of "younger people, fresh graduates, amateur party supporters and Seva Dal [a Congress-affiliated social-service organization] volunteers."[3] In that early period, Rajiv also passed an antidefection law that made it nearly impossible for elected representatives to cross party lines on the parliamentary floor for political convenience. State-level chief ministers, moreover, were encouraged to abandon the custom of frequent visits to New Delhi to pay homage to the prime minister. To break the patterns created by his mother,

---

3 See *India Today*, March 31, 1985, p. 20.

Rajiv even encouraged the chief ministers to appoint their own state-level party officers.

What heightened the feeling that sweeping reforms were in the offing were certain changes Rajiv made at the top of the decision-making pyramid. In that early period he seemed to have little use for the old Congress dhoti wallahs or for the power brokers and ruffians of the "Sanjay culture." Having worked with the Congress party for a few years as a westernized Indian, Rajiv must have developed a personal disdain for these rustic folk, who previously had been considered the backbone of the Congress party. Rajiv gathered his own team to run both the government and the party. As noted earlier, many in the new ruling circle were Rajiv's old friends and associates who, like him, had had little to do with politics in the past. The new urbane rulers were characterized by a technocratic image of "efficiency" and past records of "task accomplishment."

All of those early actions can be seen as parts in the effort to create a "clean," more disciplined, less top-heavy Congress. Careful scrutiny, however, readily reveals inconsistencies even during that early stage. First, most of the changes were in personnel, rather than in the rules or in the organizational patterns of the party. That early tendency revealed something important about Rajiv Gandhi: Whenever a problem remained unsolved, Rajiv seemed to believe that a change in top-level personnel was the solution. That is part of the explanation for the rapid turnover among high government officials under Rajiv Gandhi. Second, whereas supposedly only "clean" politicians were to be given positions of power, many of the powerful members of the old Sanjay crowd, such as Bansi Lal and Jagdish Tytler, were brought into the new power structure. A thoughtful observer of those developments was led to conclude that "many people with unsavory reputations" were retained.[4]

The attempts at reforms were opposed from the beginning, especially as Rajiv began to show political vulnerability. For example, the assembly elections in March 1985 revealed that for a host of reasons, Congress had lost considerable electoral ground since the 1984 Lok Sabha elections. Whereas states like Karnataka and Andhra Pradesh were totally lost to the opposition, even in a Hindi-heartland state like Uttar Pradesh Congress experienced a decline of some 10 percent in popular vote. That created a sense within the party that Rajiv's coattails might not be all that long. Thus encouraged, the party functionaries who had been left out of important positions began to express their dissatisfaction. We encountered two such expressions of discontent in the last chapter: The first was the opposition many Congressites expressed toward Rajiv's new economic policy in April–May 1985. The second was the opposition within the Congress party when

4 See Manor, "Parties and the Party System," pp. 95–7.

the government announced its policy to increase the prices of petroleum and kerosene.

Rajiv's attempts to accommodate such intraparty opposition revealed something important fairly early during his rule: His major power resource was, and would remain, his ability to attract the popular vote. That derived in part from his political inheritance and in part from his personal leadership qualities. However, as soon as there were indications that his ability to attract that vote was weakening, opposition began to arise from all those Congressites left out of the power structure. The attempt to load the top of the government and the party with his "clean" and "efficient" cronies provoked considerable displeasure among the Congress old guard, especially in the aftermath of the assembly elections of March 1985. Such events revealed that there would be significant obstacles ahead for the reformation of the Congress party under the conditions of Rajiv's declining popularity.

In 1985, however, Rajiv still was quite popular, and he pressed on with his reform agenda. In mid-August, Rajiv announced that Congress's organizational elections would be held in early 1986.[5] From the standpoint of reinvigorating a dormant party, especially at the district level and below, that was probably the most significant aspect of Rajiv's intended reform program. Shortly thereafter, in early September, it was announced that Congress had decided to train its party workers "from the top to the bottom." Schools that could turn out party cadres would be established. The goal was to prepare "a brigade of party spokesmen at the grassroots level, who can understand and communicate the Congress (I) ideology to rural people, [so as] to ensure that party programmes are implemented . . . and to counter the propaganda of the opposition."[6]

During that first phase, Rajiv had created a clear impression that he intended to strengthen the Congress party by initiating internal elections, imposing a measure of organizational discipline, and infusing some measure of ideology into Congressites. It is difficult to assess how seriously Rajiv intended to pursue those goals. To most people who knew the Congress party, much of that must have seemed quixotic. In order to demonstrate that he was serious, Rajiv appointed several new general secretaries to head Congress, but local observers remained skeptical. Those changes in personnel were primarily the results of an overall shuffle of the cabinet. Judging by who was assigned where, a leading news weekly concluded that Rajiv gave the "impression of treating the party rather frivolously, appointing [ministerial] rejects as its general secretaries."[7]

Whatever the seriousness of his early intent, the political situation

5 See, for example, *Telegraph,* August 14, 1985.
6 See the *Telegraph,* September 7, 1985.
7 See *India Today,* October 15, 1985, p. 47.

changed after Congress lost the Assam elections in December 1985. That again strengthened Rajiv's opposition, both within and outside of the Congress party. After losing elections in Punjab, Rajiv claimed that Congress's loss was the nation's gain. After having lost yet another state, many Congressites openly wondered about Rajiv's commitment to the electoral welfare of the Congress party and about his capacity to win elections. The pro-Congress *Times of India* editorialized that it was a serious mistake for Rajiv to think that the interests of the Congress party and of the nation were easily separable.[8] The implication was clear: Rajiv could ignore the electoral fortunes of the Congress party only at considerable political cost.

For a while, however, Rajiv still believed that he possessed considerable power. He did not feel any need for a political compromise with the Congress old guard or with the old "Congress culture" that featured patronage, corruption, and determination to win elections, no matter what was required. That stance was absolutely clear in the broadside attack that Rajiv launched against the old Congress party during his centenary speech. The message in this speech was clear: The Congress party was in crisis, and the elements responsible for that crisis, according to Rajiv, were the Congress old guard, who acted as corrupt power brokers, converting "a mass movement into a feudal oligarchy."

In retrospect, Rajiv's centenary speech must be understood more as an attack on the Congress old guard and less as a prelude to a full-blown reorganization of the party. We have already noted how that power conflict had been building throughout 1985. Rajiv's personal dislike for the old Congress culture must have added to the intensity of his vitriolic criticism of the party. Another fact strengthens the view that the power conflict, and the related desire to force the Congress old guard to the sideline, was an important reason for the attack: Rajiv offered very little in terms of how the party's problems could be resolved. The question "What is to be done?" was, as so often before, answered with meaningless generalities: "build contact with the masses" and "build a movement of epic proportions."[9]

If Rajiv's speech was meant to shake Congressites out of their slumber, it certainly did not have that effect. As the Congress centenary celebrations continued that week, it became clear that Rajiv's highly critical introductory speech had evoked either no reaction or a negative reaction from most Congressites. His concluding speech, meant to be a "call to action," was received by a "half empty stadium . . . amidst a total lack of enthusiasm and a plethora of assurances."[10] That last speech saw Rajiv already retreating from his attack, suggesting that he was only raising questions

8 December 20, 1985.
9 See, for example, *Deccan Herald,* January 5, 1986.
10 See *Times of India* (Bombay), December 30, 1985.

"which are in all our minds" and thus bridging the "I versus you" gap. Unfortunately for Rajiv, only 5,000 of the 50,000 delegates were present at the concluding session. The rest, according to a caustic comment in the local press, "found the red light areas [of Bombay] more attractive than the plenary session."[11]

The lack of enthusiasm within the party was not surprising. Rajiv had attacked virtually the entire party. He could hardly expect the party members to be enthusiastic about a program aimed at reforming them all. Rajiv, however, pressed on with his agenda.

First, there was the continuing issue of organizational elections. Sensing that party elections might be forthcoming, lower-level party officers – most of whom were appointed rather than elected – had begun enrolling new party members at the grass roots. Soon it became clear that many of the newly enrolled members were bogus: Fraudulent lists of party members were being prepared in the hope of controlling the outcomes of the organizational elections. Appointed party officers did not want to be turned out of their posts by elections. Between January 2 and 9 of 1986, therefore, the party leaders in New Delhi issued three circulars warning factional leaders across the country against enrolling bogus members. The circulars proclaimed "stern warnings" and suggested that "party discipline" would be applied with "all force."[12] As we shall see later, such warnings fell on deaf ears.

Rajiv next followed up on his centenary speech: It was proposed that a Congress working committee meet soon to come up with concrete steps for dealing with "power brokers," a code word for many of the dissenting old guard who had been in power under Indira, but had been sidelined by Rajiv. Furthermore, another plan was announced for 30,000 Congress workers to attend camps to learn about party ideals and policies. Every party worker under age 40 would undergo training in the Seva Dal. The status of Seva Dal was to be enhanced by dangling a carrot: Service in that organization would be an important route to securing party tickets for election.[13]

Finally, Rajiv announced in mid-January that the Congress party was to be given new importance. The idea was "to make government subordinate to the party."[14] As usual, such promises to "galvanize the party" were followed up by yet another round of personnel changes: Three of Congress's general secretaries, who had been appointed only four months earlier, were replaced. Local observers wondered if there was any logic in

11 See the *Telegraph*, December 30, 1985.
12 See *Indian Express* (New Delhi), January 8, 1986.
13 For a discussion of the enhanced role of the Seva Dal, see the *Statesman*, December 1, 1985; the other plans to revamp Congress were reported in the *Statesman*, January 12, 1986.
14 See *Indian Express*, editorial, January 21, 1986.

such personnel shifts.[15] One crucial personnel change, however, could not be ignored: the appointment of Arjun Singh, who had become one of Rajiv's more trusted aides, as de facto head of the Congress party. That, more than any other piece of evidence, indicates that Rajiv may well have been serious about reforming the Congress party.

The second phase

If the evidence from the first phase suggests that, on balance, Rajiv indeed intended to reform the Congress party during his first year in power, the story of the second phase concerns how and why much of that reform agenda was abandoned over the next 18 months. This analysis of that period traces Rajiv's failure in part to lack of leadership skills. More important was the increasing imbalance between the type of power resources Rajiv possessed and what would have been required to reform the party from above.

At the heart of the intended reform program were organizational elections, which would have served several functions: First, elected rank-and-file party officers would have been seen as having greater legitimacy than appointed officers. As the elected lower-level officials in turn would have elected their higher representatives, the process would have endowed district- and state-level Congress party officers with a degree of real authority. Elected, authoritative officials, would have been better able than appointed officers to deal with factionalism and dissidence. Because within small communities everyone knows who is up to what, elections would have put the corrupt and the unsavory elements within the party on the defensive. Finally, elections would have forced the contending factions to prove their strength and popularity in a legitimate arena.

Because there have not been elections in the party for nearly 20 years, it would be an exaggeration to suggest that one set of elections could have reinvigorated the Congress party. However, if they had been initiated and repeated, there seems little doubt that, over time, open elections within the party would have had far-reaching consequences.

Why were party elections never held? The answer has two related parts. First, the mere prospect of internal elections had begun to give rise to power conflicts within the party. Those conflicts pitted the appointed officials of the party against numerous challengers, who wanted to make sure that the appointed officials could not fix the elections to stay in power. Party elections definitely would have exacerbated those internal conflicts. Second, from the incumbents' viewpoint, there was no way to ensure the outcome of the elections; conducting elections always means taking risks. There was always the possibility that the Congress party could be captured

15 See *Deccan Herald,* January 20, 1986.

by those who did not support Rajiv. As long as Rajiv felt confident of his national popularity with the masses, he thought he could use that power to reorganize the Congress party. However, as his overall popularity began to decline, the idea of encouraging an additional threat from within the party must have appeared to be political suicide.

Throughout the first half of 1986, the voices of dissent grew within Congress. Most of the dissenters were individuals who had occupied powerful positions under Indira Gandhi, but had been shunted aside by Rajiv. That group included politicians like Madhevsinh Solanki, Pranab Mukerjee and Gundu Rao. There was a growing sense that they and other similarly placed individuals were looking for an opportunity to gang up on Rajiv. All such dissenters found a well-placed spokesman in Kamlapati Tripathi, who resented the fact that his position as nominal head of the Congress party had been usurped by Rajiv's favorite, Arjun Singh.

Tripathi wrote an angry and well-publicized letter to Rajiv in late April suggesting that "Indira haters were all in power" and that all those who had served Indira loyally were being pushed aside.[16] Rajiv correctly understood the meaning of that open letter: All those who had been left out of power positions had finally decided to bring the power struggle into the open. Rajiv canceled his travel plans and immediately sought an accommodation with Tripathi. For our purposes, the timing of the letter is of interest. Organizational elections were anticipated for July, and there was a growing sense among all those left out that the elections would permanently legitimize their exclusion. That followed from the widespread belief that internal elections would not be fair and would be won by the appointed officials who currently controlled the Congress party and who were busy enrolling bogus members across the country.[17] Thus, the issues of dissatisfaction among those who had failed to get plum positions, of organizational elections, and of bogus membership became intimately linked.

Toward the end of May, the outline for a major power conflict within the party had emerged. The Indira loyalists, led by Tripathi, faced off against Rajiv and his band of new Congressites. Rajiv's approach to the struggle involved the proverbial carrot and stick. Some individuals, such as Pranab Mukerjee, who enjoyed only a small independent following, were expelled from the party. Other, more powerful individuals like Solanki were given warnings, but were also extended gestures of reconciliation and eventually were brought back into positions of power. The most important carrot, however, was the promise to Tripathi that party rolls would be examined and verified before any organizational elections were held.

An examination of party rolls indeed revealed massive enrollment of

16 See *Hindu*, April 26, 1986.
17 See, for example, an analysis of the growing dissidence as the organizational elections approached in *India Today*, May 15, 1986, pp. 46–8.

bogus members. It was found that "over 60 percent of the enrolled members were either non-existent or were not eligible for membership." Moreover, some "90 percent of the new members were signed up on the last day," just before the deadline for membership enrollment. In states like Uttar Pradesh, faction leaders ended up posting armed guards at party offices to prevent rivals from enrolling their own members.[18] Clearly, such a party was not ready for open and democratic elections.

The other matter that Rajiv must have studied quite seriously at that point was how to ensure his control over the Congress party. The elections could easily backfire. For that reason, Rajiv assigned his trusted aide Arjun Singh the task of ensuring that "clean" candidates gained control of Congress, "clean" being a code word for those loyal to Rajiv. Other loyal aides were also sent to head Congress organizations in various states and to oversee organizational elections. Arjun Singh kept the crucial states of Uttar Pradesh and Madhya Pradesh under his own control, and therein lay another potential problem for Rajiv: Arjun Singh had indeed ensured that groups inimical to Rajiv's political interests could not gain control of the party organizations in those populous states, but what he had also ensured was that many members of his caste, Thakurs, and many people personally loyal to him would dominate Congress in those two states.

Arjun Singh appeared to be laying a foundation for a long-term political career of his own. Rajiv must have found that quite threatening. If elections had been called, Rajiv probably would have won in both states, but in the process he would have become crucially dependent on Arjun Singh. As long as no elections had been held, it would be fairly simple for Rajiv to remove Arjun Singh from his important position as head of the Congress party, which he eventually did. However, if the elections had been held before Singh's removal, Rajiv's leverage would have been reduced. Arjun Singh and others, who were busy ensuring that Rajiv loyalists would win in most states, would have emerged as powerful individuals. Over the long run, nothing could have prevented that second tier from dictating political terms to Rajiv.

The proposed organizational elections had come to pose a threat to nearly everyone connected with the Congress party. Those who held appointed positions naturally favored the status quo. Those excluded from positions of power knew that they were not likely to be elected if the appointed officials were going to be in charge of the elections. Most important, Rajiv must have come to view the approaching elections with considerable apprehension. The proposed party elections thus posed a classic collective-action dilemma: What might be good for the whole is not always perceived as such by its various parts. Thus, in September or Oc-

18 For details, see *India Today,* June 15, 1986, pp. 34–5.

tober of 1986, Rajiv must have decided that organizational elections really were not feasible, certainly not in the near term.

Another development during that period was that one heard less and less about attempts to infuse a measure of ideology into Congressites. For those who knew the Congress party, that was to be expected, and yet Rajiv's repeated statements during the first phase of his rule had made that seem a serious possibility.

It is clear, in retrospect, that such basic reform remains a virtual impossibility for Congress, not least because party leaders have reason to fear public exposure of what really goes on inside the party. Any attempt to define what the party stands for would risk clarifying the class, regional, and caste bases of Congress and likely would cost it electoral support, certainly over the short run. As discussed earlier, the adverse political reaction to the attempted economic liberalization had quickly forced Congress back to its populist posturing. The social bases of Congress in different parts of India are also quite diverse. The party rests on coalitions drawn from the top and the bottom of the social hierarchy in the Hindi heartland, on alliances of the middle and the bottom groups in states like Gujarat and Karnataka, and on associations of specific ethnic groups in states like Punjab and West Bengal. How could such a party clarify what it really stands for? A party whose original raison d'être was "the nation" now tries to occupy that core political space by being a little bit of something to everyone. Populism is thus a political necessity. In the absence of party ideology, therefore, any program to infuse Congressites with party ideology is a nonstarter.

Having abandoned the intention to reform the Congress party, Rajiv undertook actions in late October and November that amounted to a purge of the top party hierarchy. Tripathi was asked to resign, Arjun Singh was demoted to an inconsequential cabinet position, and all eight general secretaries of the party were nudged out of their positions. The logic behind those actions was not clear. For the next three months, all those positions remained unfilled, and state-level Congress units also came to a standstill. During that brief period, the Congress party simply ceased functioning as a party.

How should those developments be interpreted? A benign view would suggest that Rajiv may have held the top party officers responsible for the failure to translate his reform agenda into reality; therefore, having had to abandon the reforms, he got rid of the entire staff. He then needed a few months to formulate a new strategy for dealing with the Congress party. Such an interpretation would be supported by the fact that over the next few months, Rajiv consulted a series of leaders about what to do next. Rajiv even brought back 86-year-old Uma Shankar Dixit for advice on what to do with the Congress party. Those actions could be read as indicative of a leader disappointed by the performances of those in the party's opportunistic second tier and looking for "rational" advice from various sources, but especially from a man who would have little to gain from any plan of action he might recommend to Rajiv.

A less benign interpretation would stress the fact that Rajiv felt deeply threatened by those in his second tier who appeared to be laying the foundation for their own careers, especially aides like Arjun Singh. If organizational elections had been held, much of the Congress hierarchy would have been legitimized. As long as elections were not held, one strategy that Rajiv could always use was to purge the second tier of his party. After all, they had all been appointed by him. Having done that, Rajiv simply did not know what to do next; therefore, he did nothing, at least not for a few months. Attempts to seek advice from individuals like Dixit, in this interpretation, would simply be ad hoc responses of a threatened and incompetent leader.

Whichever interpretation one chooses regarding the developments of early 1987, it was abundantly clear by then that attempts to reform the Congress party had been abandoned. There was no more talk of dealing with power brokers, of organizational elections, or of infusing discipline and new values into Congressites. At a long press conference in February, Rajiv brazenly suggested that all that needed to be done to the Congress party had already been done and that he had never intended to go any farther.[19]

The third phase

During much of 1987, Rajiv faced a political nightmare. He lost some fairly crucial elections – West Bengal and Kerala in April and Haryana in June. Corruption scandals broke out. As his leadership position was weakened, opposition grew, both within and outside the Congress party. Rajiv ended up ousting other potentially threatening leaders, such as Arun Nehru and V. P. Singh. Those leaders, in conjunction with numerous opposition parties, undertook mass mobilization aimed at influencing the next round of elections. It is that background of growing mobilization by the opposition that helps us understand the reemergence of a belligerent Congress party, once again under the direction of men of the Sanjay culture.

V. P. Singh's considerable success at mobilization in the Hindi heartland must have convinced Rajiv that he could not govern without a Congress party. The pattern of V. P. Singh's mobilization was fairly straightforward: He would organize large public meetings at the level of a district's towns and below, so as to influence opinion and build an opposition movement

19 See the transcript of a long 110-minute press conference reported in most major Indian newspapers. The press conference was held February 8, 1987.

against Rajiv. (The size of such meetings often is considered in India to be an indicator of whether a movement is gaining or losing steam.) As the turnout at opposition rallies grew, Rajiv needed to counter the growing threat. The political resources at his disposal, however, were quite limited: He could use the administrative machinery to make life difficult for the opposition. That was tried, but with only limited success. What was really needed was a political program and political machinery.

The Congress party that was at Rajiv's disposal simply was not up to the political challenge. Rajiv hurriedly reappointed new general secretaries, the kind of men he tended to favor – nonpolitical, urbane individuals with a history of "getting things done." Administering a party and achieving tangible results, however, were quite different matters than organizing large public meetings in India's towns. Rajiv's newly appointed Congress officers, without political bases or experience, repeatedly failed to counter the opposition's growing success. Rajiv had similarly remodeled the Youth Congress in his own image during 1986. Led by "Indian yuppies," the youthful new party officers were not equipped to disrupt the meetings of the opposition, to protect Congress's meetings from disruption by the opposition's thugs, or generally to undertake political work in the dusty, hot, uncomfortable Indian countryside.

As a result, Rajiv seems to have decided in late 1987 to allow Congress a tougher approach toward achieving political efficacy. The idea of a reformed, democratic Congress party had been totally abandoned. The primary issue became how Congress could generate muscle power. As in the past (i.e., under Indira and Sanjay), a restructured Youth Congress was to be a major tool in the mobilizational program. Individuals like Gurudas Kamath, who had the reputation of being a "militant organizer" in a city as politically tough as Bombay, were put in charge of the Youth Congress. Kamath's mandate was to put a stop to the political rise of V. P. Singh. Other leaders, such as Ghulam Nabi Azad, a Kashmiri Sanjay protégé from the Emergency days, were put in charge of sensitive states like Uttar Pradesh and Punjab.

The political education of Rajiv Gandhi, who began as "Mr. Clean," pointed him in the opposite direction from which he started. At the time of this writing, in early 1988, Congress's return to militancy had already been demonstrated in the Tripura elections and in the municipal-government elections in Kerala. Congress's success in those elections may have confirmed for Rajiv a political lesson that his mother and brother had come to understand well: In the absence of established "vote banks," and lacking constructive programs and effective parties, aggressive militancy has become the most important ingredient for successful electoral mobilization in contemporary India. Rajiv had abandoned the attempt to rebuild the Congress party for reasons very similar to those of his mother, namely, considerations of personal power. Through trial and error, Rajiv was forced to admit the political necessity for a belligerent, militant Congress party. In contemplative moments, Rajiv must now understand why his mother and brother did what they did.

The inability of leaders to translate their stated goals into concrete outcomes has become a major theme in contemporary Indian politics. Rajiv's attempt to reorder some aspects of Center–state relations was another aspect of that theme. The discussion that follows is limited to the Center's dealings with one deeply troubled and critical Indian state: Punjab. Two caveats concerning what follows should be noted. First, the fratricidal conflict within Punjab has many elements, only some of which are discussed here. Following a summary of some well-known background information, the focus is on Rajiv's relatively unsuccessful attempt to bring political calm to the troubled state of Punjab. Such an approach directs our attention primarily to New Delhi's relations with Punjab and only secondarily to Punjab's internal politics. Second, this interpretation is based mainly on press accounts. Because research access to Punjab was denied to most "outsiders" during 1985 and 1986, I have had no independent means of confirming the information cited.

The background

The clearest illustration and most tragic manifestation of the ongoing eight-year turmoil in Punjab is the number of people who have been killed periodically in politically motivated violence. Between 1982 and 1987, some 20–50 people died each month in terrorist attacks. The figure for the number of "terrorists" killed by state repression is not known, but must be sizable. There are other clear indicators of the breakdown. The state's police expenditures increased fivefold between 1980 and 1985. For much of the past eight years, moreover, Punjab has not had a stable, elected government. The elected governments have all disintegrated, partly as a result of internal factionalism and partly because of pressure arising from growing militancy and pressure from New Delhi. Even when presidential rule has not officially been imposed in Punjab, there has been a tendency since 1980 to rule it directly from New Delhi as a "troubled state." These cumulative conditions of governmental instability and continuing militancy and political murders naturally direct our attention to two related questions: Why so much turmoil? Why has the central government repeatedly failed to find a solution to the problem?

The issue of the root causes of the turmoil is, as one would expect, an intensely emotional matter in India, and it is mired in considerable controversy.[20] If the primary purpose of this analysis, however, is not to name the heroes and the villains of the conflict, then it is not all that difficult to fit the facts into a coherent and multicausal interpretation. The interpretation proposed here is not new; it follows others that have suggested that the Punjab conflict is best understood as a political conflict that has been transformed into a fratricidal and ethnic war. Prior to developing this argument, however, three somewhat differing interpretations need to be set aside.

First, there has been a tendency in some of the literature to hold Indira Gandhi personally responsible for Punjab's political turmoil. There have been several variations on that theme: (1) Indira Gandhi was an indecisive leader who repeatedly failed to negotiate a settlement with the Akali leadership during 1980–4.[21] (2) Indira was a Machiavellian leader who created a crisis because she wanted to "save" India and thus win the next national election.[22] (3) Indira Gandhi was a power-hungry leader who repeatedly overcentralized the Indian polity and thus gave rise to numerous perverse Center–state conflicts, including the one involving Punjab.[23] The last of these three, I suggest, is the most persuasive, because it best fits the evidence. However, an important objection can be raised to all of the explanations that blame Indira Gandhi. Whatever Indira Gandhi did, she did to many states, not only to Punjab. Why, then, should Punjab have experienced more turmoil than most other Indian states? Clearly, an adequate explanation must attribute due importance to certain conditions that are unique to Punjab.

A second line of thinking on Punjab tends to put the blame on the Sikhs.[24] Again, there have been several variations on the theme: (1) The marriage of religion and politics in Sikhism has created real problems for democratic accommodation of a "nationalist" conflict. (2) Factionalism within the Akali party has made it difficult to find significant Sikh leaders with whom to negotiate. (3) The Sikh community is bent on imposing its will on the Hindus. Elements of these themes, especially those concerning

20 For a sensible review of the growing literature on Punjab, see Gurharpal Singh, "Understanding the 'Punjab Problem,'" *Asian Survey,* December 1987, pp. 1268–77.
21 See, for example, Mark Tully and Satish Jacob, *Amritsar: Mrs. Gandhi's Last Battle* (London: Pan Books, 1985).
22 For example, see the following: Rajni Kothari and Giri Deshingkar, "Punjab: The Longer View," *Illustrated Weekly of India,* July 15, 1984, pp. 20–3; D. L. Sheth and A. S. Narang, "The Electoral Angle," in Amrik Singh, ed., *Punjab in Indian Politics: Issues and Trends* (Delhi: Ajanta Publications, 1985), pp. 123–35.
23 See Paul Brass, "The Punjab Crisis and the Unity of India," in Kohli, ed., *India's Democracy,* pp. 169–213.
24 Scholarly accounts generally shy away from assigning direct blame to the Sikhs. This theme, however, is central to India's political discourse, as revealed in editorials in mainstream newspapers and political speeches by such right-wing Hindu party leaders as Bal Thackeray of the Shiv Sena.

factionalism within the Akali party, will be incorporated into a fuller explanation. What needs to be pointed out here is that none of these prop-
ositions is capable of explaining why the crisis in Punjab took on such
intensity in the 1980s. The marriage of religion and politics, factionalism
among the Akalis, and the power urge of the Sikhs as a community have
all been around for quite some time, but the violence and the governmental
breakdown have been serious only during the past decade. Thus the crucial
issue: What factors have changed over time?

A third line of thought that appears to be more sensitive to the issue of
socioeconomic changes seeks to isolate the economic origins of the conflict.
That argument points to the growing economic differentiation among the
Sikhs, especially in the aftermath of the Green Revolution. Given these
new economic differences, and the resulting antipathies, it is difficult for
the Akali leadership to mobilize all the Sikhs to press even relatively
innocuous community demands. The escalation of militancy and the mounting separatist demands should thus be seen from the standpoint of an
attempt to create political unity in a class-divided ethnic community.[25]
Again, I propose that many socioeconomic issues, including those of
mounting economic disparities, must be taken into account to reach an
understanding of what is happening in Punjab. The reason that these economic variables cannot be considered decisive is quite simple: The patterns
of economic differentiation in neighboring states like Haryana are not all
that different from those in Punjab. If class conflicts deriving from the
Green Revolution are indeed giving rise to significant political divisions,
why are similar consequences not evident in Haryana? One suspects that
the political consequences of economic differentiation are not as significant
as some observers make them out to be.

The origins of Punjab's complex and tragic civil disorder can be traced
to the political conflict between Indira Gandhi and the Akali Dal.[26] In
many respects, Indira Gandhi's attempts to keep the Akalis out of power
after 1980, and the Akalis' repeated attempts to win back Punjab, constituted a "normal" political conflict. In its main outline, that power struggle
involving the Center and a regional party was not all that unusual. During

25 See, for example, Gopal Singh, "Socio-economic Bases of Punjab Crisis," *Economic and
Political Weekly,* January 7, 1984, pp. 42–6; and H. K. Puri, "Akali Agitation: An Analysis
of the Socio-economic Basis of Protest," *Economic and Political Weekly,* January 22,
1983, pp. 113–18.
26 In constructing this background account, I have consulted numerous sources, but have
relied heavily on four useful essays: I. K. Gujaral, "The Sequence," *Seminar,* February
1984, pp. 14–17; Gian Singh Sandhu, "The Roots of the Problem," in Singh, ed., *Punjab
in Indian Politics,* pp. 61–70; Sucha Singh Gill and K. C. Singhal, "The Punjab Problem:
Its Historical Roots," *Economic and Political Weekly,* April 7, 1984, pp. 603–8; Paul
Brass, "The Punjab Crisis."

1980–4, Indira Gandhi tried to maneuver several regional parties out of power in states such as West Bengal and Andhra Pradesh.

A number of factors, however, made the political struggle in Punjab especially explosive. Two of those were givens, and they ought to be considered necessary but not sufficient conditions for the overall explanation. The first was that Punjab was relatively evenly divided between the Sikhs and the Hindus, a situation virtually unique among India's states. Second, the close linkage of religion and politics in Sikhism made it difficult for the Akalis to search for political support outside the Sikh community. Four other variables contributed to the growing turmoil: (1) the weakness of the Akali Dal as a party; (2) some egregious political errors by Indira Gandhi, such as her support of the militant religious preacher Bhindranwale and the military assault on the Golden Temple; (3) a number of socioeconomic conditions, such as the economic differentiations among the Sikhs, and their greater political impact because of their increasing wealth; and (4) the presence of large numbers of educated but unemployed Sikh youths. How those various factors combined to transform a fairly normal political struggle into an explosive situation will be outlined before we examine the main issue of concern in this subsection: why Rajiv, like Indira, found it difficult to deal with the vexing problem of Punjab.

For those not familiar with modern Punjab, a few basic facts may be useful prior to developing an interpretation. The Sikhs constitute about 55 percent of Punjab's population; the remaining 45 percent are Hindus. As many as 70 percent of the Sikhs live in the countryside, whereas nearly 65 percent of the Hindus live in the cities. The Hindus of Punjab, like Hindus elsewhere, are a heterogeneous community, divided along caste, rural–urban, and income lines. What is not always appreciated, however, is that the Sikhs are divided along similar lines.[27] A sizable majority of the Sikhs, nearly 65 percent, are Jats, and most of the prosperous, landowning, Green Revolution farmers in Punjab are Jats. The non-Jats are divided into the Bhapas or Khatris, the Majhabis, and the artisans or Tarkhans. The Bhapas generally are the well-off urban traders and entrepreneurs, constituting a little under 10 percent of the Sikh population. Many of them are former refugees who migrated from what is now Pakistan. About 20 percent of the Sikhs are Majhabis, the Sikh equivalent of the scheduled castes, of whom many are poor, landless laborers. The remaining Sikhs, another 7–8 percent, are artisans who excel in various crafts, especially carpentry. Caste divisions among the Sikhs are sufficiently pronounced that they generally do not marry across caste boundaries. It is interesting to note, how-

27 The following figures for the breakdown of communities among the Sikhs are taken from Amrik Singh, "An Approach to the Problem," in Singh, ed., *Punjab in Indian Politics,* p. 2.

ever, that until quite recently, Bhapa Sikhs often married across religious lines into Hindu Khatri families, with whom they shared caste and income status.

Prior to the political turmoil that arose in the 1980s, caste and community divisions in Punjab had given rise to easily identifiable political divisions. In the past, the Hindus generally had supported the Congress party, though a significant minority had been loyal to the Jan Sangh. The Akali Dal, by contrast, had consistently counted on the Sikh vote, but seldom had succeeded in mobilizing all the Sikhs as an ethnic political bloc. The Jats, especially in the southern districts (the Malwa region), had provided the main power base for the Akalis in recent years. The Majhabis, however, had seldom voted for the Akalis. Motivated by both caste and class animosities toward their employers, the Jat farmers, the Majhabis had tended to support either Congress or the leftist parties. The Bhapa Sikhs had also been politically divided. Many of them had resented their loss of the Akali leadership in the 1960s to the up-and-coming Green Revolution Jats. Some of the urban Sikhs had formerly supported Congress, and others the Akali Dal.

Given all those basic divisions, Congress, during the 1960s and 1970s, often had been in a position to form a government in Punjab with the help of Hindus, Majhabi Sikhs, and urban Khatri Sikhs. The Akalis, by contrast, could form only a coalition government, and that only with a seemingly unlikely partner: the pro-Hindu Jan Sangh. Those basic political and community divisions provide the background essential for understanding the intensified political activities of the Akalis over the past decade. That militancy was aimed at mobilizing as many Sikhs as possible around a platform of "Sikh nationalism." The analytical issue is why those fairly normal political ambitions generated so much chaos and turmoil.

The Akali Dal as a political party has always exhibited a mixture of religious fervor and hard-nosed political realism aimed at capturing power.[28] The party originated in the 1920s as the product of an anti-British movement for control of the *gurdwaras,* the Sikh temples. During that early phase the Akalis were hailed as a nationalist force and were treated by Mohandas Gandhi as anti-British political allies.

The early success of the Akalis in gaining control over the *gurdwaras* had a result that continues to be of political significance – the creation of

28 For general historical background on Sikh politics and the early rise of the Akali party, see Khushwant Singh, *A History of the Sikhs, Vol. II: 1839–1964* (Princeton University Press, 1966), parts IV and V; Rajiv A. Kapur, *Sikh Separatism: The Politics of Faith* (London: Allen & Unwin, 1986), especially chapters 4–7. For a good study of Punjab politics up until the mid–1960s, see Baldev Raj Nayar, *Minority Politics in the Punjab* (Princeton University Press, 1966). Also useful for background on Akali politics are A. S. Narang, *Storm over the Sutlej: Akali Politics* (New Delhi: Gitanjali Publishing House, 1983); Mohinder Singh, *The Akali Movement* (Delhi: Macmillan, 1978).

the Shiromani Gurdwara Parbandhak Committee (SGPC) to manage some of the most important Sikh temples. Over time, and through several sets of organizational changes, that body has become enormously powerful. Often compared to the Vatican and described as a "state within a state," the SGPC now controls a vast financial empire and a religious administration that runs into tens of thousands of personnel. The SGPC can also have a profound influence on Sikh opinion. It is that marriage of religion and politics, through an organization of temples and temple leaders, the *jathedars,* that is at the heart of Sikh power in Punjab. None of this is to suggest that the SGPC is a unified body or that the Akalis can always control the SGPC. On the contrary, there has always been considerable factionalism within the SGPC and between the SGPC and the political leaders of the Akali party. Also, Congress has repeatedly attempted to weaken, divide, or even control the SGPC. In spite of such conflicting tendencies, the identity of the Akalis with the SGPC has enabled the former to maintain a considerable power base among the Sikhs. That identity has also made it difficult for the Akalis to find additional non-Sikh political support.

There have been certain critical turning points in the politics of modern Punjab that have become permanently etched into the state's collective political memory. Because that memory continues to influence contemporary behavior, it is important to recall briefly some of those events. During the linguistic reorganization of the Indian states in the 1950s, the Akali Dal argued for a "Punjabi *suba.*" The Punjabi-speaking Hindus of Punjab, however, fearing Sikh domination, threw their political support to the Hindi speakers of the undivided Punjab. Under the influence of Arya Samaj, a Hindu reform organization, they declared their language to be Hindi. As a result, the Punjabis – Sikhs and Hindus – were one of the few major linguistic groups in India who did not get their own state. That anomaly was corrected in 1966 when the former Punjab was carved into a number of units, including a state for the speakers of the Punjabi language – the contemporary Punjab. The creation of a Punjab of Punjabi speakers, however, came about only after prolonged agitations, led mainly by the Sikhs and the Akali Dal. One of the lasting consequences of those early developments was the creation of political distrust among Sikh leaders. Punjabi Hindus were more likely to ally themselves with other non-Punjabi Hindus than with the Sikhs.

During the 1950s and early 1960s, the Akali Dal was controlled by urban Khatri Sikhs, typified by Master Tara Singh. Over time, however, especially with the rising economic and political significance of the Jat farmers, the leadership passed into the hands of rural landowning groups. Sant Fateh Singh represented that stratum. It was under his leadership, and because of the repeated agitations that he organized, that New Delhi finally agreed to the creation of a Punjabi *suba* in 1966. That victory raised the political popularity of the Akalis within Punjab. In any case, Congress was by then weakened. Its important first-generation leaders like Pratap Singh Kairon had passed away and left behind a deeply factionalized party. As Congress's overall popularity suffered in India during 1966 and 1967, the Akalis finally emerged victorious. They formed a coalition government in Punjab, with the Jan Sangh as junior partner.

The experience of the Akalis in and out of government during 1967–71 had some important political consequences. The fact that the Akalis were in alliance with the Jan Sangh tended to soften both the pro-Sikh communal edge of the Akalis and the pro-Hindu stance of the Jan Sangh. Thus, the more extreme communal elements among both the Hindus and the Sikhs became available for political mobilization. Congress sought to incorporate both of those extreme groups. The more Congress strengthened its alliances with pro-Hindu groups, the more Congress in Punjab came to take on a communal hue similar to that of the Jan Sangh.[29] However, in a peculiar twist that revealed electoral opportunism run amok, Congress also encouraged the more extreme Sikh factions within the Akali Dal to break away from their party. Congress's temporary success on that front (e.g., the Lakshmi Singh Gill incident) succeeded in toppling the Akali government in the late 1960s. When that did not last, and the Akalis again formed a ruling coalition, the game of overthrowing the government continued, leading up to the imposition of presidential rule in 1972.

That series of machinations by Congress must have made it clear to the Akalis that Congress leaders would go to great lengths to secure power in Punjab: If the Akalis could mobilize Sikh support around pro-Sikh issues, Congress was just as capable of playing the communal game to achieve political ends. Unfortunately for Punjab, those themes have continued into the present, contributing to the growing political conflict.

Congress came back to power in 1972. The Sikh hopes of being able to dominate the state of Punjabi speakers proved to be short-lived. The communal arithmetic was such that the Akalis could control Punjab only if all the Sikhs voted for them. Understanding that issue well, Congress sought to split the Sikh vote; the Akalis, in turn, tried to unite their power base. During 1973, therefore, with Zail Singh as the state's chief minister, Congress sought to portray itself as a champion of Sikh causes and to mobilize Sikhs along religious lines. The Akalis felt compelled to countermobilize. The first version of the Anandpur Sahib resolution, a resolution that sought to consolidate the support of all Sikhs, but especially Jat Sikhs, by demanding greater control for the Sikhs over their own political affairs, was, not surprisingly, a product of that competitive mobilizational effort by the Akalis.

29 For further discussion of this theme, see Gill and Singhal, "The Punjab Problem," especially pp. 606–7.

During the Emergency, the Akalis vigorously protested Indira's authoritarianism, partially as a matter of principle, but mainly because the issue offered an opportunity to mobilize public opinion. Many of the Akali leaders went to prison. When the embittered Akalis returned to power in 1980, again in alliance with the old Jan Sangh which by then had become the Janata party, they came down hard on the Punjabi Congressites. Congress fought back. There is evidence to suggest that Congress's support for Bhindranwale originated from that period.[30] Bhindranwale was a popular militant preacher. Zail Singh, who had become the federal home minister, and Sanjay Gandhi apparently concocted the strategy of supporting Bhindranwale in order to weaken the Akalis. It is an open secret that Congress supported Bhindranwale and his candidates in the SGPC elections of 1979. The militants' loss highlighted the Akali moderates' overwhelming dominance in Sikh politics as late as 1979.

While Congress and the Akalis continued to mobilize and countermobilize, using any means at their disposal, including instigation of religious warfare, Punjabi society had been undergoing important changes.[31] Because of the increasing wealth of the Jat farmers, their donations to the *gurdwaras,* and thus to the financial empire of the SGPC, rose enormously. That increased the ability of the Sikhs to launch and sustain political movements. Increasing personal wealth also led to rapid changes in life-styles. Growing consumerism, for example, threatened the cherished Sikh religious values of simplicity and asceticism. That opened the way for the more orthodox religious leaders to spread their message: The Sikh religion was in danger and had to be defended aggressively.[32] Increasing incomes and expenditures on consumer products had brought communications technology, such as tape recorders, to many Punjabi villages, and the recorded teachings of militant preachers like Bhindranwale spread fairly rapidly.

Finally, there were the growing numbers of unemployed youth.[33] That was not unusual in Punjab; it was a product of the high birth rate and low industrial growth common to much of India. One can speculate, however, that given the high growth rates in the agricultural sector, the sense of relative deprivation among the educated urban youth of Punjab may have been felt more sharply than elsewhere in India. Whatever the explanation

---

30 See, for example, Tully and Jacob, *Amritsar,* chapters 4 and 5; Brass, "Punjab and the Unity of India," especially pp. 192–5.

31 One study that dwells at length on the changing nature of Punjabi society – especially in terms of values and the impact of "modernization" – is by Robin Jeffery, *What's Happening to India?: Punjab, Ethnic Conflict, Mrs. Gandhi's Death and the Test for Federalism* (Basingstoke: Macmillan, 1986).

32 For a good study of the teachings of Bhindranwale, see Joyce Pettigrew, "In Search of a New Kingdom of Lahore," *Pacific Affairs,* Spring 1987, pp. 1–25.

33 For a discussion of this and other economic issues, see I. K. Gujaral, "The Economic Dimension," in Singh, ed., *Punjab in Indian Politics,* pp. 42–53.

for their relative militancy and sense of frustration, the availability of that volatile political group in an environment of growing religious and political conflict added fuel to the fire.

None of those political and social changes had to lead to the political breakdown of the 1980s. Only in retrospect can one conceive of the various developments as contributing factors, all pointing in the same direction. What finally precipitated conflict were political changes that came after 1980. It was in that year that the Janata party disintegrated nationally, and Indira Gandhi returned to power with a sizable majority. She went on to dismiss many of the state governments controlled by the opposition and to call for new state elections. The Akalis lost power in that national shuffle for the third time in a little over a decade. That must have left them with a bitter sense of having repeatedly been wronged by Indira Gandhi and Congress. In the 1980 state elections, however, the Akalis won only 27 percent of the popular vote. That must have confirmed for Indira Gandhi that she indeed had a right to dismiss an elected government and to call new elections; in her mind, the Akalis had lost popular support.

The battle lines were drawn. Indira Gandhi had the popular support. She decided to use her position of advantage to launch a political offensive and consolidate her position vis-à-vis the Akalis. If she could use Bhindranwale to split the ranks of the Akalis still further between the moderates and the extremists, victory would be hers. Her support for Bhindranwale in 1981 and 1982 – those were the years when she enjoyed considerable political advantage over the Akalis in terms of popular support – makes sense only when analyzed as an offensive posture.

The Akali Dal, in contrast, had to fight for its life. It clearly had lost considerable popular support, but it continued to possess another set of political resources, whose efficacy Indira Gandhi apparently underestimated. The Akalis still could organize around the issue of Sikh nationalism like no other party in Punjab. The chain of *gurdwaras,* moreover, provided a ready organizational network with money, personnel, and the proven ability to sway opinion. A populist national leader, Indira Gandhi, thus came to be pitted against a regional party, the Akali Dal, that had considerable potential to mobilize the forces of religious nationalism.

Both Indira Gandhi and the Akalis assembled militant forces for political ends. In retrospect, it is clear that over the next several years, the militancy led to civil disorder that took on a political life of its own, increasingly out of the control of both the Akalis and the national government. Whether that simply was not foreseen or was brazenly ignored under the short-term pressure to seize political advantage may never be known. An early sign of things to come, however, was that Bhindranwale turned against Congress, which had encouraged him and helped him to become something of a cult hero. As a result, Bhindranwale began to cultivate his own following. During 1981 and 1982, Bhindranwale increasingly took advantage of his popularity to sever his links with Congress and to enlarge his political base. The repeated failure of the Akalis to wrest power from Congress had left open a political space for those who argued that increased militancy was the only means for protecting Sikh interests. Bhindranwale stepped into that space. His appeal combined the themes of religious revivalism and the need for greater political control over the destiny of the Sikhs. Those themes found a ready audience among a significant minority who had come to distrust the maneuverings of both Congress and the Akalis.

As Bhindranwale's popularity soared, the Akalis must have worried about losing further political support to him or to other militant religious Sikh leaders. Not wanting to be left behind, therefore, they launched their own *dharm yudh* or holy war in 1982. That movement was aimed at mobilizing Sikhs to force the national government to accede to a series of demands, many of which had been spelled out in the Anandpur Sahib resolution of 1973. The demands included such items as the transfer of Chandigarh to Punjab, readjustment of irrigation allocations for some river waters, and an extension of the SGPC's control to the *gurdwaras* outside of Punjab.

The Akalis managed to launch a significant mobilizational effort. They combined economic demands, such as that for more irrigation water, with religious and political issues of greater autonomy for the Sikhs within India. That enabled them to strengthen their hold on the party's core supporters, the Jat farmers, as well as broaden their base among other Sikhs. The Akali effort also had the backing of sizable financial resources and manpower through the *gurdwaras*. Within a few months of the movement's inception, its political impact was considerable. Some 80,000 Sikhs courted arrest. The Congress governments, in Punjab as well as in New Delhi, found themselves under considerable pressure to negotiate with the Akali leaders of the civil disorder.

The failure of the negotiations between Indira Gandhi and the Akalis during 1982–4 marked an important turning point in the development of the Punjab conflict. It was during those two crucial years that the repeated inability to reach an agreement weakened the hold of the more moderate Sikh leaders over the regional nationalist movement.

The Akalis had never been a united lot to begin with. Their three prominent leaders, Badal, Tohra, and Longowal, came together during that period to bargain with Indira Gandhi, but they also fought with each other, jockeying for position within the party. Militancy, however, increasingly came to have its own dynamic. Bhindranwale continued to be the tacit leader of those willing to employ open violence to achieve the goal of greater autonomy for the Sikhs, including a more specific goal of some elements: the creation of a sovereign state of Khalistan. The militants naturally were met with repression, which, combined with the charged appeals to religious nationalism, gave rise to further conflict. The frightened

Hindus flocked to Congress, strengthening its political base. The Akalis thus found themselves being squeezed out of the political process, by the militant Sikhs on one side and by Indira's Congress on the other.

This highly condensed account of those complex events makes two things clear: First, the driving force behind the conflict was a power struggle between Indira's Congress and the Akali Dal. Both Sikh nationalism and the increasing militancy are better understood as products rather than as sources of the power struggle. Second, because of the failure to achieve a negotiated settlement during 1982–4, the leadership of the movement began to pass out of the hands of those who basically wanted to win election and into the hands of "true believers." The question that remains open, however, is why a negotiated settlement was so difficult to achieve.

Most thoughtful observers of Punjab agree that Indira's failure to accommodate Akali demands had less to do with the specifics of the negotiations than with the anticipated political consequences. Clearly, the issues of Chandigarh, allocation of river waters, and control of the *gurdwaras* were all significant and controversial issues, but not important enough to justify the loss of thousands of lives in the anarchy that followed. We now know that during 1982–4 the two sides were close to agreement on two occasions, but at the last minute Indira Gandhi and her advisors detected some hitches and recanted.[34] The most persuasive explanation for her actions is not indecisiveness, which would have been quite unlike her, but rather her typical fear of losing power. A settlement would have meant a political victory for the Akalis and would have had adverse electoral consequences for Indira's Congress. That certainly was true within Punjab, but possibly elsewhere in north India as well, especially in states like Haryana, which stood to lose Chandigarh and irrigation waters in any negotiated settlement.[35]

It is thus clear that Indira Gandhi's narrow partisan concerns were important causal ingredients in Punjab's tragic turmoil. Many innocent lives would have been saved if Indira had put the larger concern for the public good ahead of concern for her own and Congress's electoral fortunes. In retrospect, therefore, there is little doubt that a more self-assured or more enlightened leader could have put the evolving conflict in Punjab on a different track.

To jump from such an understanding of Indira Gandhi's role to a normative conclusion that she was the main villain in the conflict and, by implication, that the Akalis were heroes of sorts simply is not sustainable against the available facts. First, the Akalis in the 1980 Punjab elections

---

34 See, for example, Tully and Jacob, *Amritsar,* especially chapter 10.
35 Another author, addressing the same issue, concluded that "the most widely accepted explanation is that to evade a decision was what suited the ruling party." See Singh, "An Approach to the Problem," p. 20.

had won only 27 percent of the popular vote. Not satisfied with that electoral verdict, they decided to utilize other power resources to bolster their
political position. One such step was to launch a holy war that involved a
variety of actions: stopping all traffic coming in and out of Punjab, courting
arrest on the part of thousands of Akali politicians, and promoting a condition of civil disorder within which terrorism began to flourish. That is
hardly the stuff of which heroes are made in a democratic polity. The
Akalis, moreover, were deeply factionalized, and their leadership repeatedly demonstrated the same trait as Indira Gandhi: unprincipled electoral
opportunism.

Finally, the Akalis and the more militant Sikh leaders pursued many of
the same goals, though they differed in regard to the intensity of commitment and the means to be used to achieve those goals. The Akalis attempted to legitimize a series of goals that they proposed mainly as
mobilizational tools, but their failure to achieve those goals put the Akalis'
sincerity in doubt among their own supporters. The "true believers" thus
gained the upper hand; their more militant strategies gained respectability
in comparison with the repeated failure of the Akalis. As a result, the
Akalis have been on the defensive vis-à-vis the militants ever since the
early 1980s. Having somewhat legitimized the goals that many militants
now pursue, and having repeatedly failed to condemn or control the terrorism unleashed in the name of those goals, the Akalis can hardly be seen
sympathetically as victims of the conflict, let alone as heroes in Punjab's
civil unrest.

The unfortunate fact is that the Punjab drama is a tragedy without visible
heroes. Instead, repeated sins of omission and commission have created
numerous villains. If there are any heroes, they are the common Sikh and
Hindu folk who have helped each other survive the growing fratricide; the
main political actors have all contributed to the tragedy. The continuing
role of the militants and the factor of state repression are too obvious to
require comment. The role of the Akalis has been discussed. Indira's repeated failure to accommodate Akali demands reflected her own narrow
political considerations; as a national leader, the final responsibility for
resolving the conflict was hers. The failure to do so will continue to be a
significant debit in her leadership account. As I shall argue later, leaders
without parties and programs tend to have narrow political horizons. They
also have few institutional constraints on their ambition. The main political
actors in Punjab all have tended to act on their short-term ambitions,
without much regard for the public good. Such an unrestrained power
struggle, in turn, has been a crucial driving force behind the descent toward
anarchy.

To conclude this account, the repeated failure of negotiations between
Indira and the Akali leaders continued to swell the ranks of the militants
throughout 1983 and 1984. Under Bhindranwale's tacit leadership, many

of them began using *gurdwaras* as sanctuaries. The prominent leaders eventually made the Golden Temple, the most important of the Sikh *gurdwaras,* their base of operations. Thus, the movement for Sikh autonomy increasingly came to resemble a theocratic fundamentalist movement, complete with its own "ayatollahs" and zealous armed followers. Planned murders, as well as indiscriminate killings, continued to multiply. Hindus were killed by the militants so as to put pressure on the Congress government. Sikhs were killed so as to minimize dissent within the community. It was that atmosphere that led to the imposition of presidential rule and later to a military assault on the Golden Temple itself, the infamous Operation Bluestar. The subsequent events, including the assassination of Indira Gandhi by her own Sikh bodyguards, and the politically directed massacre of large numbers of Sikhs in New Delhi, are events too well known to require elaboration.

Punjab under Rajiv[36]

By the time Rajiv Gandhi had won his massive electoral victory in late 1984 and formed a new government in early 1985, Punjab clearly had become India's most important political issue. Rajiv attempted to take advantage of his popular victory to initiate a reconciliatory approach to the Punjab problem. Over his last five years in office, however, the civil disorder continued unabated, and Rajiv's approach toward Punjab changed at least three times.

During the early phase, when the Punjab accord was signed, an essentially political approach was adopted. That was followed by failure to implement the agreements reached in the accord. As terrorism increased and Rajiv found himself pressed on various fronts, the political approach slowly gave way to a law-and-order approach. When that failed to bring the terrorism under control, the mounting death toll and the continuing political chaos led to the approach that continues today. At the time of this writing, the government seems to have decided to return to a more political approach, but with a major difference: New Delhi's negotiating partners tend to be not the Akalis but the more militant leaders of Punjab. The main purpose of the following analysis is to explain Rajiv's changing approaches to the Punjab problem and thus to shed light on why it has become so difficult in contemporary India for even a popular prime minister to solve the pressing problems of the day.

Within six months after coming to power, Rajiv signed a negotiated accord with the Akalis. In that accord, Rajiv gave in to virtually all the demands that Indira Gandhi had rejected during 1982–4, but he went even

---

36 To reiterate, the account that follows is based mainly on press reports. For details, see footnote 1 in this chapter. Few direct citations are provided.

further: He agreed to additional demands, such as an investigation to find the guilty parties in the violence perpetrated against the Sikhs in Delhi. The signing of that accord dramatically highlighted the capacity of leaders to make the social scientist's "structural constraints" vanish with the flick of a pen. Unfortunately for both Punjab and Rajiv, many of those structural constraints remained, but either were temporarily dormant or simply were not perceived. They reappeared, and fairly quickly. Before analyzing the nature and consequences of those constraints, it is important to discuss both why the accord was signed and the processes leading up to it.

How do we explain the fact that Rajiv suddenly offered major concessions to the Akalis in 1985 after his mother had consistently refused to do so? Many observers have mistakenly attributed that change to the different political personalities of the mother and son. However, if that were the main explanation, one could not readily explain Rajiv's continually changing approach that, over time, has come more and more to resemble that of his mother. The underlying variables are not only leadership style and personality but also the contrasting political situations in which the two leaders operated.

During 1984–5, after a massive electoral victory, Rajiv was far more secure politically than his mother had been. Concessions from a position of political strength can add to a leader's popularity by presenting the face of magnanimity. That was Rajiv's situation. In contrast, Indira's contemplated concessions to the Akalis would only have dramatized the dilemma of a beleaguered leader. Rajiv's temporary sense of absolute political security enabled him to put partisan political considerations aside for the larger public good. Over time, as that sense of security diminished, so did Rajiv's largesse.

The first sign that Rajiv's government had made some important decisions on Punjab emerged in late March of 1985. That was when some Akali leaders, such as Longowal and Barnala, were released from prison. An examination of the series of steps over the next three months, that is, before the signing of the accord in July, suggests two conclusions: First, the government indeed had a new "game plan." Second, that plan had important flaws from the beginning.

The plan of action that unfolded between March and July revealed a relatively coherent strategy. Akali leaders were released from prison in stages so that there would be someone with whom to negotiate. New Delhi tolerated the "hawkish" statements of Longowal vis-à-vis Delhi, which suggests that Rajiv and his aides understood the internal political dynamics within Punjab. Step by step, then, New Delhi made several concessions: An inquiry into the killings in Delhi was ordered, some young Sikhs were released from prison, and the ban on a militant student organization, the All India Sikh Student Federation (AISSF), was lifted. All of those were clearly reconciliatory gestures aimed at generating goodwill and thus paving the way toward a major agreement. Behind the scenes, moreover, Rajiv's personal emissary, Arjun Singh, quietly held dozens of meetings with such Akali leaders as Longowal. Secretiveness was essential for the Akalis to maintain the image of independent actors. All of those actions were indicative of Rajiv's decision to compromise with the Akalis and his readiness to concede political power to the Akalis in Punjab.

In retrospect, it is clear that events did not unfold as Rajiv and the Akalis hoped. There were unsettling signs from the beginning. For example, there is evidence to indicate that Rajiv's critical decisions leading up to the accord were made in haste, without full consideration of the enormous complexity of the issues involved. The government's main advisors on Punjab at that early stage were all new: Chavan, Narasimha Rao, and Arjun Singh. Though competent politicians, none of them had a thorough knowledge of Punjab. In his role as a member of the cabinet's committee on Punjab, Chavan revealed during a press interview that he did not know of the existence of two versions of the Anandpur Sahib resolution.[37] One wonders, therefore, how serious Rajiv and his aides were from the beginning regarding the details of the agreements to be reached and whether or not they could be implemented.

As an example, Arjun Singh was also one of the three members of the cabinet committee on Punjab in the first few months of 1985. He was then sent off by Rajiv to be governor of his home state, Madhya Pradesh. One day after being sworn in as governor, as a part of the new Punjab plan he was suddenly transferred back to Punjab to be its new governor.

Other issues also highlight the haphazard thinking that seems to have informed the making of the Punjab accord. Why, for example, was Longowal released first, and other leaders such as Tohra and Badal only a month or two later? Was New Delhi expressing its preference to deal with the "moderate" Longowal over the more extreme Tohra and Badal? If so, New Delhi still was trying to manipulate the choice of Akali leadership, rather than letting it emerge on its own. Because such a manipulative attitude had been part of the original problem, one is again left wondering about the seriousness of the commitment to a "new beginning." Moreover, there is clear evidence to indicate that the government's overall strategy was not coordinated. On one hand, the government was initiating a series of seemingly reconciliatory gestures toward the Sikhs. At the same time, however, the government was decorating soldiers for their bravery during Operation Bluestar, the military assault on the Sikhs' holiest place of worship.

To be fair, the political situation in Punjab was chaotic by the time Rajiv came to power. Dealing with it would not have been an easy task for any government. Rajiv's approach, however, suggested that he and his advisors

37 See *India Today,* March 15, 1985, p. 29.

were always one step behind events in their understanding of the rapidly changing situation. The game plan leading up to the accord suggests that the government's analysis of the turmoil in Punjab was something like the following: The main cause of the conflict was the frustrated power urge of the Akalis. The best course of action would be to release the Akali leaders and let the more moderate ones consolidate their leadership. Then Rajiv could follow with substantial concessions so as to create the impression of a major Akali victory. Finally, it would be hoped that those actions would enable Akali leadership to win the elections, control the militants, and rule Punjab. As suggested by the foregoing discussion, that would have reflected a fairly accurate understanding of the root causes of the conflict. During 1984 and 1985, however, Operation Bluestar and the massacre of Sikhs in New Delhi had added some new dimensions to the overall issue.

A widespread source of dissatisfaction in Punjab was the new issue of injured Sikh pride. Analysis of that issue is difficult because it requires assessment of changing moods in a community, and under the best of circumstances, even with public-opinion surveys, variations in a community's moods are difficult to assess. For a community that lives in an area closed to researchers, analysis of changing moods can quickly become guesswork. Nevertheless, fragmentary evidence available from press reports suggests that the battle for the "hearts and minds" of the Sikhs was a significant new issue that the Rajiv government had not fully comprehended.

After being released from prison, Longowal flew into Punjab, but he was met by no more than a few hundred supporters. For someone being groomed by New Delhi to be a new leader in Punjab, that was not a good beginning. Press reports suggested that many Sikhs were disillusioned with Longowal, for it was assumed that he had escaped the attack on the Golden Temple because he had been given advance notice by the central government. Other leaders like Talwandi and Tohra sensed that mood; as soon as they were released, they began taking political postures that were quite uncompromising vis-à-vis New Delhi. Clearly, the mood within the Sikh community had hardened to a point that compromise with the Rajiv government was increasingly a political liability for Sikh leaders.

The demands of Akali leaders continued to center around issues from the past. Journalists reporting from the area suggested that many Sikhs wanted Rajiv to come to Punjab and apologize for the entry of troops into the Golden Temple. Increasing demands that the guilty in the Delhi massacre be punished also reflected the changing community mood. Besides the political issue of who would control Punjab, there was a new problem for Delhi: A community's sense of justice had been brutally violated. Thus, it should have been clear to the leaders that any long-term program to restore normal, democratic relations between New Delhi and Punjab would have to address the elusive but quite real issue of the Sikhs' injured pride.

Rajiv's game plan for Punjab had certain problems to begin with. It had been put together in haste, without enough attention to detail. It did not address the issue of how to assuage the Sikhs' sense of having been treated unjustly. This is not to suggest that the original Rajiv–Longowal accord of July 1985 was not a major step in the direction of discovering a democratic solution to Punjab's problems. It is rather to point to some of the flaws in the original accord. Those flaws, and other problems that developed later, contribute to an understanding of why the accord, which was basically a sound plan, proved to be so difficult to implement.

It was agreed in the accord to transfer Chandigarh to Punjab, to readjust some river irrigation waters in favor of Punjab, and to widen the scope of the inquiry into the killings of Sikhs in New Delhi. With those major demands of the Akalis met, the way was clear to resume a more normal political process. It was obvious to most observers that after years of turmoil, normalcy would not easily return to Punjab. And yet simultaneously it was clear that holding elections and handing power over to the Akalis was the best way, if not the only way, to begin a long-term restoration of orderly government. That was certainly the new government's understanding. Thus, even Longowal's assassination by terrorists did not lead to postponement of state elections, which were held under difficult conditions: For every 10 voters in Punjab, one policeman was posted there during the election. In spite of the obstacles, the elections went off peacefully, and, as expected, the Akalis emerged victorious.

Three pieces of evidence strongly suggest that if the long-term goal in Punjab was restoration of normal and peaceful democratic government, then the decisions of the Rajiv government to make concessions to the Akalis and to renew the electoral process were the right decisions. First, militants across Punjab opposed the Rajiv–Longowal accord. That was only a minority view, however, as indicated by a public-opinion survey conducted by *India Today.* The accord was broadly supported in various sections of the more educated Sikh community, as well as in the Hindu community.[38]

Related to this point is an even more convincing piece of evidence: The militants called for a boycott of the elections, but it did not materialize. There could be no clearer evidence of the minimal support for the Sikh militants than the results of the voting. The turnout for the elections was extremely high, nearly 70 percent of the Punjab electorate, which was higher than that in either of the preceding state elections (1977 and 1980). Considering the difficult conditions within Punjab, that participation rate must be viewed as a rejection of the more extreme demands (e.g., for Khalistan) and of the extraconstitutional political strategies adopted by the militants.

38 August 15, 1985, pp. 10–11.

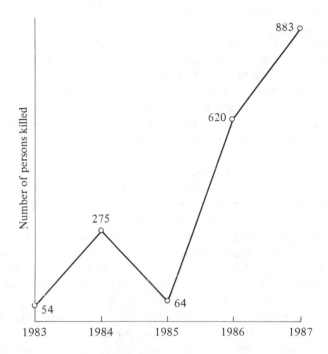

Figure 12.1. Terrorist killings in Punjab, 1983–7. *Source:* Based on data collected from *India Today*, July 31, 1987, p. 10, and February 15, 1988, p. 17.

Finally, the resumption of the political process led to a remarkable decline in deaths due to terrorism. As Figure 12.1 shows, terrorism subsided to a relatively low point in 1985. Moreover, most of the deaths in 1985 occurred in the first half of the year, before the accord was signed.

We now know that those early attempts by the Rajiv government to restore democratic political order in Punjab were not sustained. The next question for analysis is why. As in the discussion of the Indira period, there were several interrelated factors that help explain that failure. Factionalism among the Akalis and the climbing spiral of terrorism, repression, and more terrorism are independent and important contributing factors. Those factors will be discussed in passing, but the focus here is on the failure of the Rajiv government to implement the signed accord. It is proposed that that failure undermined the position of the Akali government, encouraged terrorism, and paved the way for the militants to assume positions of political prominence.

The Akalis formed a government in Punjab under Barnala's leadership in October 1985. Within the first three months of his rule, Barnala found himself politically pressed on several sides. His most immediate problem was the factionalized leadership of his own party. As suggested earlier, except for the organizational network provided by the SGPC, the Akali Dal has never been much of a political party. Other ambitious leaders in the party, such as Badal and Tohra, continued to withhold their full support from the Barnala government; they waited for a moment of political weakness in which they could extract the maximum rewards in exchange for their political support. Although that was a normal state of affairs for the Akali party, what made the situation especially precarious for Barnala were two other contextual variables: a renewal of terrorism, and failure of the Rajiv government to implement the accord.

The date announced for the transfer of Chandigarh to Punjab was January 26, 1986. It was not clear until the last minute that that crucial clause of the accord would not be implemented. The Barnala government even issued invitations to celebrate the transfer. On the evening of January 25, however, word reached Chandigarh that the date of transfer had been postponed to March. In retrospect, it is obvious that the postponement was not in good faith. When the March date came and went without the transfer of Chandigarh, it was clear that the Rajiv government had reneged on its agreement. The obvious question is why. Why did the Rajiv government bungle so badly after its promising start?

The answer is partly leadership incompetence, but mainly the changing political pressures on Rajiv. First, we have already noted that the accord was negotiated and signed in haste, before many of the details had been resolved. In retrospect, it is clear that those obstacles should have been removed in the early phase, when the political commitment to find a solution was strong.

Related to that is a second issue: the limited attention Rajiv gave to the Punjab problem. Decision making under Rajiv remained highly centralized, and under those conditions the implementation of a crucial decision like the transfer of Chandigarh would have required sustained attention and pressure from Rajiv. However, the months following the signing of the accord in July 1985 had been extremely hectic for Rajiv. For example, after the Punjab accord, the Assam accord was signed, and elections were then held in both states. There were two major cabinet shuffles in the second half of 1985. Massive reorganization of the Congress party was being discussed. The government was also attempting to liberalize the economy. And, of course, there were many foreign visits by Rajiv and other officials.

Under conditions of highly personalized decision making, such a hectic agenda would strain the capacities of the best world leaders. As a political novice, Rajiv must have acted on many issues relatively mechanically, listening to the advice of whomever he trusted at the moment. Part of the failure to implement the signed accord, therefore, and especially the tendency to leave the decision on a major issue like the transfer of Chandigarh to the last minute, must be attributed to governmental incompetence that resulted from an overcentralized, overburdened, and personalized pattern of decision making.

More important than the issue of competence was Rajiv's changing political situation. When the accord was signed in July 1985, Rajiv was still wrapped in the euphoria of a massive electoral victory. Several subsequent political changes limited his ability to implement the reforms. Important among those was the Congress party's growing dissatisfaction with Rajiv. We have already considered the consequences of that change for Rajiv's attempts to liberalize the economy and reform the Congress party. With respect to the Punjab issue, an important turning point was the loss of the Assam elections in December 1985. That fueled widespread dissension, both within and outside the Congress party. The common charge hurled at Rajiv during that period was that he did not care enough about the Congress party's electoral fortunes. As Rajiv was increasingly put on the defensive, he must have decided to give higher priority to electoral concerns.

Once that decision was made, much of the Punjab accord was doomed. The two crucial issues of the accord concerned Chandigarh and the river waters. Implementation of both those clauses would have affected Haryana adversely; Punjab's gain would have been Haryana's loss. In the second half of 1985, when Rajiv's position was strong, it is conceivable that he could have pressed the Congress chief minister of Haryana, Bhajan Lal, to go along with the accord; press statements from that period reveal a conciliatory Bhajan Lal. As Rajiv's position weakened, however, Bhajan Lal's stand hardened. State elections for Haryana were scheduled for June 1986. Having lost both the Punjab and Assam elections, Rajiv was not in a position to take additional blame for a loss in Haryana. Thus, implementation of the Punjab accord fell victim to Congress's electoral interests.

The more it became clear that crucial clauses of the accord were not going to be implemented, the more pressed Barnala felt politically within Punjab. Barnala's approval rating depended heavily on his continuing capacity to elicit benefits for Punjab from New Delhi. New Delhi's failure to implement the accord weakened Barnala. As a result, both factionalism among the Akali leaders and terrorism intensified. So distrustful was Barnala of his own party rivals that he refused to assign them to any important positions. In early 1986, therefore, Barnala simultaneously headed the SGPC, the Akali party, and the Punjab government. Such centralization was an attempt to ward off power challenges from within the party, but it also revealed that the power base of the Barnala regime was narrowing.

As Figure 12.1 shows, terrorism increased sharply during 1986. At the time, observers of Punjab had a tendency to blame the Barnala government for being "too soft" on the Sikh militants. Although that charge may have been appropriate, it would not be appropriate to link it to the increase in terrorism. A tougher, law-and-order approach adopted later in 1987 likewise did not succeed in curtailing terrorism.

The dynamics of terrorism in Punjab are poorly understood, and it would take a study quite different from this one to analyze the forces that give rise to terrorism. Such a study of Punjab probably would point to a number of causal variables: (1) the conditions of economic deprivation facing the educated youth, (2) the prevailing religious beliefs, which placed high value on sacrifice for one's cause, even martyrdom, (3) the ready availability of sophisticated arms, and (4) the spiral of terrorism, state repression, and more terrorism.

In addition to those complex contributing factors, it is clear from the limited evidence presented here that the overall political context had an impact on terrorism. The only decline in terrorism in the past several years came during 1985, the year the accord was signed and elections were held. The political mood that year probably was characterized by a belief that the Sikh community could achieve its goals through the constitutional electoral process. It was that mood that strengthened the hand of the moderate leadership and isolated the militants. Piece-by-piece implementation of the accord might or might not have eliminated terrorism totally, but it is not unfair to assume that such a process would have continued to delegitimize the militants and their terrorist political strategies.

Because the accord was not implemented, and terrorist violence increased, Rajiv increasingly came to refer to Punjab as a "police problem." Sidhartha Shankar Ray, who had been in charge of West Bengal in the late 1960s during the Naxalite terror, was sent to Punjab as the new governor. Ribero, with a reputation of being a "tough and honest" police officer, was put in charge of the Punjab police. The Ray–Ribero team began a new approach to Punjab. The reconciliatory, political period was over; henceforth, Punjab would be dealt with as a law-and-order problem.

The Barnala government remained in power for another year, but only with the help of Congress legislators. For all practical purposes, it had stopped functioning as a potentially unifying force among the Sikhs. On the contrary, the close ties between the Barnala government and New Delhi proved the militants' charges: The Akalis in power were acting as stooges for New Delhi and were doing so mainly for selfish reasons of power.

As the law-and-order approach failed to bring terrorism under control, many competing groups with unclear goals began to crop up. Some of those groups proclaimed their goal to be the creation of a sovereign state of Khalistan, and to that end they were willing to kill as many Hindus as necessary to drive all Hindus out of Punjab. Other groups were less clear about their eventual goals; they sought to avenge what they perceived to be the insults visited on the Sikhs by New Delhi. Militant groups of both types were willing to kill not only Hindus but also other Sikhs, such as those who were suspected of being informers, or dissenters with knowledge of the terrorist organizations. Throughout 1987, therefore, terrorism-related deaths continued to rise. They climbed to a record high in 1988; nearly 3,000 people, including women and children, were killed by terrorists and by state repression in that one year. Many of those killed were Sikhs suspected of betraying the militants.

As suggested earlier, the dynamics of terrorism are complex and not the focus of attention here. One ingredient, however, that sheds light on the issue of the Center's continuing failure to deal with the Punjab problem is worth mentioning: the relative ineffectiveness of the police in dealing with the terrorists.[39] Neither the Punjab police (the police force normally controlled by the Punjab state government) nor the numerous other paramilitary forces (controlled by New Delhi) were able to translate the government's law-and-order approach into an effective repressive strategy. The reasons for that were complex, and certainly included the following: First, the police were never trained to be an antiterrorist force. Second, there probably were many Sikh police officers within the force who sympathized with the militants, and that repeatedly compromised the intelligence capacity of the local police. Finally, the police themselves were afraid of the terrorists. Between 1981 and 1986, some 69 policemen, who had either vigorously pursued terrorists or tortured terrorists in custody, were put on a "hit list" and were murdered. Thus far the government has not succeeded in getting a single conviction for the death of a policeman. A force that cannot even protect its own is not likely to be able to implement a repressive strategy for controlling terrorism.

Continuing terrorism and rampant factionalism among the Akalis further weakened the Barnala government. Many of the Akali leaders were afraid of the terrorists and simply refused to speak out against them. As the militants recongregated in the Golden Temple, Barnala also was forced to send in the police, thus further alienating many in the Sikh community. Barnala's position was becoming increasingly precarious. He did not even consult his senior cabinet ministers about the assault on the Golden Temple, fearing that they might leak the information before the action.

---

39 I had initially planned to include a much longer treatment of the Indian police as another example of an ineffective institution. For reasons of space, however, I have decided not to include that discussion. For background information, see David H. Bayley, *The Police and Political Development in India* (Princeton University Press, 1969). For an excellent update, see David H. Bayley, "The Police and Political Order in India," *Asian Survey*, April 1983, pp. 484–96. An excellent analysis of all that is wrong with the Indian police is contained in Government of India, *Report of the National Police Commission* (New Delhi: Ministry of Home Affairs, 8 volumes published between February 1979 and May 1981). With specific reference to Punjab, the problem of how to deal with "civil disturbances" and "communal rioting" are discussed in volumes 3 and 6, respectively.

Barnala's more militant rival, Tohra, won the elections to head the SGPC, thus demonstrating the growing political significance of the militants. The newly appointed militant priests even sought to dislodge Barnala from his position. Barnala's government survived, but only with the support of Congress legislators. The rift was then complete: Barnala had been reduced to a token leader in Punjab, kept on in power by New Delhi. By contrast, the religious organizations that underpinned the power of the Akali party increasingly came under the control of the militants.

Throughout the many changes in the Punjab situation in 1986 and 1987, Rajiv's government did not come up with any new political initiative. The focus was on the law-and-order approach. The release of the Mishra report in March 1987 further confirmed that the government had totally given up on its reconciliatory approach. The Mishra Commission had been a one-member commission set up to investigate the killings of the Sikhs in New Delhi. Independent observers had already documented that high-level Congress functionaries had been behind those riots and killings.[40] The Sikh community obviously hoped that the government would punish the guilty and restore justice. The failure of the Mishra report to implicate any senior Congress party officials confirmed the cover-up and indicated to the Sikhs that the government was not interested in any apologies having to do with the Sikhs' injured pride.

The interests of the Congress party had once again posed an obstacle to the pursuit of a reconciliatory political approach to the Punjab problem. In that specific instance, the interests were not directly electoral; at stake were the reputations of guilty, but very senior, Congressites who had to be protected from prosecution. It would have taken an extremely forceful and principled prime minister to have allowed indictments of his senior party colleagues, including a member or two of his cabinet, for inciting communal riots and killings. As discussed earlier, Rajiv had virtually given up on reforming the Congress party, and rebellion was building within the party by early 1987. Rajiv was not willing to weaken his position further by alienating another group of senior Congressites, even if they had been partially responsible for the 1984 communal mayhem in Delhi.

A similar theme involving the interests of the Congress party was at the forefront when Rajiv finally dismissed the Barnala government and imposed presidential rule on Punjab in May 1987. Haryana elections were scheduled for June 1987, and there was growing apprehension within the Congress party that they might lose those elections. In an effort to repair relations with the Hindus in Haryana, therefore, Rajiv Gandhi made a last-minute effort to appear tough on the Sikhs. That his ploy failed totally

---

40 See a joint report of the People's Union for Democratic Rights and the People's Union for Civil Liberties, *Who Are the Guilty?* (Delhi: Summa Graphica, 1984).

and that Congress was trounced in the Haryana elections do not in any way reduce the significance of the politically motivated dismissal of the Barnala government.

The imposition of presidential rule did not make much difference for the everyday processes of government in Punjab. The Ray–Ribero team continued to exercise power, just as they had in the last years of Barnala's nominal rule. Terrorism continued, and many of the militants were again operating out of the Golden Temple. The situation in mid-1988 increasingly came to resemble that prevailing before Operation Bluestar in 1984, when presidential rule had been in effect and the terrorists had been in control of the Golden Temple. That resemblance, however, was superficial. From the standpoint of restoring democratic political order, the situation in 1988 was much more precarious than that in 1984. The Akalis had lost virtually all credibility by 1988. The militants, by contrast, were the only force with whom the government could deal. The militants, however, were a divided lot. Some factions did not want a negotiated settlement within the constitutional framework; they wanted their own sovereign state. The Rajiv government continued to face a fragmented group of gun-toting religious militants as its main adversary in Punjab, and as long as the negotiations involved Congress versus fragmented and angry Sikhs, it was difficult to foresee how democratic order was likely to be re-created in the near future.

In summary, the failure of the Rajiv government to find a solution to the Punjab problem can be traced back to the many political pressures on Rajiv, especially the pressure to protect the electoral and other interests of the Congress party. To be fair, the Punjab problem is quite complex, and its beginning and evolution involved multiple factors. Yet no national government in India can escape the responsibility of attempting to find some solution to the tragic turmoil. The rising graph of killings by terrorists in Punjab is testimony to India's growing problems of governability.

After coming to power in 1985, Rajiv Gandhi took advantage of his popularity to promise major concessions to the Sikhs and to initiate a reconciliatory political approach to the Punjab problem. As long as that approach was sustained, it produced remarkable results. Both the Sikhs and the Hindus in Punjab supported the accord. There was a large turnout at the state elections, and terrorism-related violence decreased sharply. Unfortunately for Punjab, Rajiv was not able to sustain that approach. Under pressure from his own party not to make too many concessions to Punjab, Rajiv decided not to implement the accord further. That failure encouraged factional conflicts within the Akali party, further legitimized the militants, and weakened the elected government. The continued recalcitrance of Rajiv's government contributed to the growing ineffectiveness of the elected government in Punjab and paved the way for presidential rule. The partisan political interests of Rajiv Gandhi and of his political party thus made it difficult for India's central government to pursue a political solution to the breakdown of order in one of that country's important states.

CONCLUSION

In this chapter, I have analyzed Rajiv Gandhi's attempts to reform some of India's troubled political institutions. The reform of the Congress party and the Center's efforts to bring calm to the troubled state of Punjab have been discussed in some detail. The attempts of the Rajiv government were not notably successful in either policy area. The concluding issue is why those efforts failed.

To rebuild Congress as an organized party and to restore democratic stability to Punjab clearly were complex and fairly intractable political problems. Most leaders would not have found them easy to solve, and Rajiv's incompetence did not help. In spite of those considerations, however, it has been evident throughout this analysis that there was also something "systemic" or "structural" about those policy failures. They followed a pattern: Goals that could have benefited the polity as a whole were difficult to pursue because of partisan political considerations.

After coming to power, Rajiv Gandhi, with considerable fanfare, announced his plans to reform the Congress party. The intentions to hold organizational elections and to inject a degree of ideology and discipline into the party were publicly announced as important goals. As long as Rajiv's mass popularity and related political security were intact, those efforts were considered to be serious. Over time, however, political necessities made continued reform impossible.

Internal elections could not be held, both because they threatened to precipitate a major power conflict within the party and because they eventually would have threatened Rajiv's personal power position. Congressites could not be made more "ideological," or, more precisely, sensitive to what Congress really stood for, mainly because the Congress leaders were not prepared to clarify that stand. Congress's centrist and populist orientation was part and parcel of its continuing ambition to be India's main political party. Congress thus remained a little bit of everything to its supporters. Finally, as the opposition to Rajiv grew, he came to need the rowdies of the Youth Congress and other Congressites in the Sanjay-culture mold. The resurrection of ruffians-as-politicians further diluted any attempt to create a more disciplined Congress party. With attempts to reinvigorate the Congress party abandoned, the condition of the party continued as it had been under Indira and Sanjay Gandhi.

The policy process aimed at calming tensions in Punjab followed a similar trajectory. His initial sense of political security enabled Rajiv to make major concessions to the Akalis. The resumption of the open political process that followed received broad support; militancy and terrorism declined. Fairly soon, however, it became clear that agreements reached on paper were difficult to implement. The transfer of Chandigarh and the settlement of disputes over river waters were sacrificed to protect the electoral interests of the Congress party, especially in Haryana, but also more generally. The need to protect certain Congressites was also behind Rajiv's incapacity to reveal who was behind the anti-Sikh rioting and the massacre that followed Indira's assassination. The failure to implement the accord delegitimized the Akalis and encouraged terrorism. None of this is to deny that the Punjab issue was quite complex in origin and quite difficult to solve. The fact remains, however, that the partisan political interests of India's national leaders continued to be important factors in the ongoing turmoil.

Rajiv's failure to reform the Congress party and reorder relations in the troubled state of Punjab highlights the growing incapacity in India to translate personalistic power into a problem-solving resource. India's political problems have followed a vicious cycle. Because parties are weak, the power gained by leaders does not have an institutional basis (i.e., electoral victories are not based on parties and programs). Electoral victories of that type, however, turn out to be Pyrrhic victories. They may enable incumbents to enjoy the perks of position, but they do not readily translate into a capacity to solve pressing problems. Exceptional leaders or better-organized parties could break that stalemate, but those are not on the horizon, and the major problems continue unresolved.

Conclusion: the Center

The attempts of the Indian government to implement certain important policies have been analyzed in this part of the study, and this analysis can be used to develop a concluding statement on the ability of the national state apparatus to solve pressing problems. The record reported here, though not impressive, involved selected topics and incomplete data. Before generalizing from such limited data, therefore, several important qualifications are in order.

First, the problem of "collective action" in democracies is widely recognized. One can, therefore, anticipate some of the difficulties in India of pursuing policies that bring forth competing and divergent responses. Although that is not an alibi for ineffectiveness, it should raise one's tolerance for what can and cannot be expected from elected governments.

Second, there are many policy areas in which the Indian government continues to function effectively. For example, most observers are likely to judge India's management of foreign policy, the military, or even the many daily decisions on the economy as reasonably satisfactory. What distinguishes the competence in those areas from the policy failures examined here is the scale of the decisions involved, and hence the issue of who is in charge of problem-solving. Once the basic framework of a policy is set, India's bureaucracy is quite competent at piecemeal implementation. The issues analyzed earlier, by contrast, involve important decisions and major political initiatives. It is the growing incapacity to make and implement those difficult political decisions that is of primary interest here.

Finally, in these qualifications it is important to note the issue of leadership competence. It is possible that a more able leader might have been more successful in attempting to liberalize the economy, reform the Congress party, and find a solution to the Punjab problem. Though not decisive, the issue of leadership competence clearly is one variable in the policy process. A leader with greater political acumen might well have sensed the need to build a consensus on economic policy changes, or might have insisted on Congress party elections and concessions to Punjab, while still in a relatively secure political position.

In spite of these qualifications, the foregoing analysis has some important implications. When in 1984 the new Indian leadership defined its priorities, among them were reform of the economy and the Congress party, and settlement of the Punjab dispute. Its attempts to implement all of those policies ran into similar obstacles. The push for economic liberalization slowed down as it ran into interest-group pressures and began costing the government electoral support. The reform of the Congress party proved difficult because it would have precipitated a major power struggle between the incumbents and the challengers, and because eventually it would have threatened Rajiv's personal hold on power. Finally, the proposed concessions to Punjab were not implemented because they would have undermined Congress's electoral position in important north Indian states and thus Rajiv's position within the Congress party. In all of those cases, therefore, the desire of those in power to maintain their electoral support was in conflict with their intentions to implement solutions to pressing problems, and the former always won out.

What does this disjuncture between electoral needs and the capacity to solve problems tell us about the nature of the Indian state at its summit? It suggests that the process by which power is won at the highest level increasingly has little bearing on how power is used. The personal popularity of any leader cannot easily be translated into the ability to solve problems. What is missing here are parties and programs. Without parties and programs, only leaders with great personal appeal of one sort or another are capable of winning majorities in contemporary India. Such majorities provide a modicum of coherence in what is otherwise an extremely heterogeneous polity, but they seldom are acquired while mobilizing support for a specific program. Because winning an election does not mean that the winner stands for anything specific, general mandates quickly dissipate. It is impossible to be something to everyone, especially when important national decisions need to be made. Thus, attempts to implement specific programs quickly give rise to opposition. Even those who support a given program are difficult to mobilize, because of the absence of party organizations. As opposition mounts and ready supporters are few, leaders tend not to take decisive action, but rather to muddle through.

If the role of the Indian state in India's development were minimal, if many of the country's pressing problems could be dealt with by social actors without the help of the state, then the state's relative ineffectiveness would not pose such a crisis. The Indian state, however, is highly interventionist. It controls major portions of India's resources and potential sources of initiative. Under those circumstances, the state's diminishing effectiveness is a matter of considerable concern. India's problems appear likely to increase, but the state's capacity to deal with them may not. That could be a long-term recipe for accumulating crises of governability.

PART V

Final inferences

13

Political change in a democratic developing country

In this study I have sought to describe and to explain India's growing crisis of governability. Important political institutions in India have been weakened, and power conflicts have multiplied. The result is that national leaders find it increasingly difficult to put together durable coalitions, to undertake major policy initiatives, and to settle political conflicts without violence. Although the explanation developed here for India's growing turmoil is multicausal, political variables are emphasized. Empirical materials suggest that India's political structures and the choices made by its national leaders have played central roles in molding political changes in India. With that as a general theme, this concluding discussion summarizes the empirical materials, reviews the analytical argument, and attempts to tease out some comparative implications of this study.

THE EMPIRICAL STUDY

It is important to begin this summary by restating the sense in which the terms "crisis" and "governability" are used in this study. The topic of Indian government tends to attract doomsayers. Therefore, it is especially important to reiterate that this characterization of contemporary Indian politics as being in crisis does not predict imminent breakdown of the democratic political order. Rather, the word "crisis" is used to draw attention to certain tendencies toward steady deterioration within the Indian polity. The analysis developed here suggests that the "system" in India can continue to function but that if it does so without major changes, its level of performance will remain quite low and will probably decline even further.

The concept of governability draws attention to the tasks a government can be expected to perform. For a democratic developing country like India, governability has been defined here as the capacity of the rulers to do three things: maintain coalitional support, initiate solutions to problems perceived to be important, and resolve political conflicts without force and violence. Thus, a democratic developing country is well governed if its government can simultaneously sustain legitimacy, promote socioeconomic development, and maintain order without coercion. The growing incapacity in India to perform these tasks is what has been conceptualized in this study as a manifestation of a crisis of governability.

Problems of governability are common to much of the developing world. India once was considered an exception. Scholars of Indian politics had long recognized the exceptional nature of India's stable and effective democracy within the developing world. Because specialists can easily be guilty of admiring too much the subjects they study, it is important to recall that those concerned with broader issues of comparative development also used to describe Indian politics as uniquely "modern" and well "developed."[1] Unfortunately for India, its problems of governability have grown considerably more acute over the past two decades; India is fast catching up with the rest of the Third World. Instead of a strengthening of India's democratic base, we see a steadily widening gap between institutional capacities and socioeconomic problems. This pattern of political change raises crucial questions for analysis: What happened? Was this outcome inevitable? If so, why? If not, who or what should be held responsible? More generally, what forces can help explain India's growing crisis of governability?

The empirical materials already presented help provide some answers to these complex questions. Because those materials were summarized at the end of each part of the study, only a few themes need to be reiterated. The foregoing study of five districts, four states, and economic and political decision making at the national level serves several purposes. First, it generates what can loosely be called a "thick description" of Indian politics. Second, it helps explain patterns of political change at various levels of the polity. Taken together, these three parts of the study also help address a single theme of Indian politics: the causes and the consequences of the growing gap between institutional capacities and problems requiring political solutions.

A detailed study of the same five districts conducted by Myron Weiner 25 years ago is helpful in describing and explaining broad changes in the governing of India's vast political periphery. The picture that emerges is that of an increasing authority vacuum. The organizational ability of the Congress party has declined, and popular new parties have failed to fill the organizational vacuum. In addition, traditional authority patterns in the social structure have been weakened; the capacity of the dominant castes and of other "big men" to influence the political behavior of those

---

1 See, for example, Samuel Huntington, *Political Order in Changing Societies* (New Haven: Yale University Press, 1968), pp. 84–5; Barrington Moore, Jr., *Social Origins of Dictatorship and Democracy: Lord and Peasant in the Making of the Modern World* (Boston: Beacon Press, 1966), p. 314.

below them in the social hierarchy has diminished. These two trends – the growing democratization of traditional power relations in the civil society, and the failure to create a rational basis for generating new leadership through formal political institutions – are at the heart of the increasing authority vacuum in Indian politics. That vacuum, in turn, contributes to many of the problems of governability: coalitional instability, the emergence of low-quality leaders with demagogic rather than programmatic appeal, the growing significance of toughs and hoodlums as de facto brokers of local power, ineffective and corrupt local governments, and the increasing tendency to resort to violence to "settle" political conflicts.

A complex array of forces has produced the authority vacuum in the periphery. The socioeconomic forces at work are well understood by development scholars and require only brief reiteration. Economic development has generated new patterns of division of labor that have undermined traditional caste authority. The spread of commerce has similarly replaced seemingly reciprocal patterns of exchange with the impersonal medium of money, again undermining the traditional bonds of "solidarity" between social "superiors" and "inferiors." Unequal economic gains have also generated new types of tensions that increasingly resemble class conflict.

What looms even larger than these socioeconomic forces is a series of political variables. The spread of democratic values and practices has hastened the decline of traditional authority. The deinstitutionalizing role of national leaders has thwarted the possibility of developing a new and stable set of political norms. Finally, weak political institutions have encouraged undisciplined political competition, and that has politicized all types of social divisions, including caste, class, and ethnic cleavages. Numerous strategies, including the use of violence, have been used to gain access to the state's resources, thus adding to the growing political chaos.

A comparative analysis of three states can help refine the themes concerning the causes and the consequences of deinstitutionalization. Clearly, the crisis conditions are most severe in the state of Bihar. There is a qualitatively different, sporadic pattern of turmoil in Gujarat. In contrast to both of those cases, political order has been restored in West Bengal after a period of considerable turmoil. How does one explain this regional diversity?

Our comparative analysis suggests that these regional political variations are not products of economic changes. Both Gujarat and Bihar, which respectively are better developed and less well developed economically, have experienced considerable political turmoil. Although unique conditions are operative in each state, the common issues appear to be political. Governments across Indian regions control large blocks of resources. The spread of democracy has mobilized a diversity of new groups. As a result,

power conflicts aimed at gaining access to the state's resources have proliferated. That is the common theme running through the discussion of
Bihar, Gujarat, and West Bengal.

In addition, the cohesiveness of any regional government is itself a major
variable that is best understood as a product of the nature of the ruling
party. Fragmented ruling parties in both Bihar and Gujarat not only have
made it difficult for governments to act effectively but also have encouraged
intraelite conflicts and thus elite-led movements and countermovements.
By contrast, a cohesive party in power in West Bengal has generated
moderately effective government. It has accommodated new power challenges by a combination of reformism and organizational cohesion.

Finally, an analysis of national policy making in the third part of this
study has helped focus attention on the implications of deinstitutionalization at the center of the Indian polity. Organizational weakness in the
Congress party, in conjunction with failure to provide for systematic incorporation of the bottom half of the population into the political process,
has put a high premium on personal appeal, populism, and mobilization
of "primordial" loyalties as strategies for gaining and maintaining power.
Those strategies enabled India's ruling dynasty to legitimize its hold on
power through democratic means until the end of 1989. That personalistic
and populist ruling style, however, has become a major impediment to the
use of state power to solve the nation's problems.

An analysis of the attempts by Rajiv Gandhi to liberalize India's economy, rebuild the Congress party, and resolve the fratricidal conflict within
Punjab provides support for this broad contention. Policy failures in each
of those areas can be traced back to the desire of Rajiv Gandhi to maintain
both personal power vis-à-vis other elites and a broad base of mass support.
The national political situation in India has thus begun a vicious cycle. It
is increasingly difficult to translate personalistic and populist support into
the political ability to accomplish policy goals. Policy failures, in turn, tend
to undermine popular support. The strategies for winning power thus come
to be even further removed from developmental problems. At the heart
of this growing rift between the state's representative and developmental
functions in Indian politics lies the absence of coherent parties and
programs.

This political analysis of select local, state, and national materials helps
chart out the dimensions of India's growing crisis of governability. It is
important to restate that this study does not anticipate an immediate disintegration of India's democratic political order. There are many positive
attributes in India's political economy that have not been stressed in this
study. Indians continue to enjoy more civil liberties than most populations
in the Third World. The caliber of Indian civil servants as problem-solvers
remains relatively high. India's macroeconomic performance in the 1980s
was respectable by international standards. India, therefore, is not about

to "fall apart." Nevertheless, it is also the case that India's political problems are increasing, and the causes of that have been the subjects of analysis in this study: Power challenges are multiplying, and the institutional capacity for systematic accommodation of such challenges is not keeping pace. If these trends continue, they are likely to chip away at India's democracy. No problem in contemporary India is likely to prove more serious than the disintegration of its major problem-solving institution: the democratic state.

THE ANALYTICAL ARGUMENT

This analysis of India's governability crisis has focused attention on the growing disjuncture between weakening institutions and multiplying demands. That manner of conceptualizing the problem tends mainly to identify the components of the larger problem. Clearly, that is not unimportant. The real explanatory issues, however, have to do with why institutions have weakened and how and why various groups have been mobilized at the rate and in the manner that they have. The explanation developed earlier for those processes was multicausal. Several independent variables have been identified, and it is important to distinguish the argument presented here from other arguments in the literature and to delineate some of the distinctive implications of this study.

The foregoing empirical analysis has suggested that four major factors have influenced the nature of political change in India: (1) the deinstitutionalizing role of national and regional leaders; (2) the impact of weak political parties; (3) the undisciplined political mobilization of various caste, ethnic, religious, and other types of groups; and (4) the increasing conflicts between the haves and have-nots in the civil society.

It is important to understand the sense in which these four variables are considered in this study to be independent variables. First, they are independent only insofar as they are not fully reducible to one another. For example, whereas the actions of national leaders may be important factors contributing to the weakness of political parties, that weakness is not solely a function of leadership actions. Low levels of economic development and cultural diversity are other important variables that have made it difficult to create well-organized, cohesive national parties in India. Similarly, the patterns of political mobilization may in part reflect the weakness of parties, but they also reflect the highly fragmented nature of India's premodern society.

A second caveat concerning the independent variables is that they are treated as independent only by analytical choice. If the object of this study were different, they could be considered dependent variables and thus objects for detailed analysis. The chain of causation in social life can be pushed ever further, until sometimes it even comes back to the phenom-

enon under investigation, thus completing a circle. The definitions of dependent and independent variables in any analysis, therefore, reflect
choices concerning what is being studied and why.

These four significant independent variables can be readily collapsed
into larger analytical categories. Three of the four variables – the role
of leaders, the impact of weak parties, and the phenomenon of undisciplined political mobilization – are all political variables in the sense
that they concern issues of power distribution and conflicts over access
to the state's resources. Only one of the four variables, the increasing
dissension between the haves and the have-nots, primarily reflects
changing values and the distribution of economic resources in the civil
society. I have attempted to be consistent in resisting the tendency toward a priori exclusion of significant explanatory variables, and the empirical findings have clarified that not only socioeconomic variables but
also political variables are important for an analysis of political change
in contemporary India.

Before discussing why that is so and the implications of this argument,
it may be useful to distinguish briefly the political explanation developed
here from its alternatives. The major alternative to the state-oriented argument presented here would be an explanation stressing socioeconomic
or market variables. A developmental explanation, for example, would
analyze India's growing governability crisis as an inevitable by-product of
modernization in general and economic development in particular. A related neo-Marxist argument could stress the growing conflicts over economic distribution as the root cause of India's political problems. Neither
of those explanations would be "wrong." It is rather a matter of sifting
through numerous causes and assigning them weights. The foregoing study
has found the market-related economic forces to be far from insignificant.
On their own, however, they have not proved to be the most important
factors. While taking them into account, the empirical materials that were
analyzed moved the focus away from the market and toward the state.

The state and the market compete for space in all societies. Industrial
transformation and the related developmental changes in nineteenth-
century Europe were, on balance, propelled by market forces. It is not
surprising, therefore, that major theories of development, modernization
and Marxist alike, tend to focus on market processes – division of labor or class relation – as determinants of politicoeconomic change. Those
nineteenth-century ideas have continued to influence (and, one is tempted to add, distort) how we think about contemporary developmental
experiments.

The relative roles and significance of the state and the market in economic
change have been altered in the twentieth century. For the most part,
major developmental transformations in this century, communist and capitalist alike, have been state-propelled. Our inductive social theories – and

most development theories are inductive – are only slowly beginning to comprehend the distinctiveness of state-led development. The analysis of political change in one important state-led capitalist experiment of the late twentieth century forms a small part of this large intellectual puzzle.[2]

Many of the reasons that political variables have played such important roles in molding patterns of political change in India can be traced back to the state's crucial role in India's political economy. The state is not only an agent of political order in India; it is also responsible for promoting socioeconomic development. Those dual responsibilities have led to a highly interventionist Indian state. Because that interventionist state is organized as a democracy, politics and political competition tend to permeate much of social life. Thus, the nature of India's political structure and the roles played by India's political leaders have been major determinants of political and social changes in India.

What aspects of India's political structure have made that country increasingly difficult to govern? The answer to this important question has been sometimes explicit and sometimes implicit in the preceding analysis. The "deeper structures" are often in the background in a process-oriented analysis. Without reference to them, however, important questions remain unanswered. Why should the Indian state attract so much attention from social groups? What enables a leader to play such a profound role in the Indian polity? Why should political mobilization result not in new organized political initiatives but in chaos? It is now important to move one level of causation deeper and focus sharply on the political structures that have conditioned political change in India.

The Indian state is highly interventionist, and whether one approves of this or deplores it, it is an important organizational feature in contemporary India that is not likely to change soon. An interventionist state at low levels of economic development, moreover, is a feature that India shares with many Third World countries, but it contrasts with past experiments in capitalist economic development, especially those in the Anglo-American context. Two important political implications of that state–society macro-characteristic have been evident throughout this analysis, but have not always been recognized in the literature.

First, an interventionist state in the early stages of development has difficulty establishing a separation between the public and private spheres in social life. That has many consequences. The most important from the standpoint of a study of governability is that an interventionist state cannot claim that distributive problems are social and not political problems. The coexistence of political equality with considerable economic inequality fa-

---

2 A broader research agenda of this type was laid out by a group of distinguished scholars: Peter Evans, Dietrich Rueschemeyer, and Theda Skocpol, eds., *Bringing the State Back In* (Cambridge University Press, 1985), passim, but especially chapters 1 and 11.

cilitated the establishment of proto-democracies in parts of nineteenth-century Europe. The interventionist welfare state developed only under resource-abundant, mature capitalism. In an Indian type of situation, however, a highly interventionist state is inherent to the overall design of state-led development. That tends to politicize all forms of societal cleavages – old versus new, social, and economic. Thus, the accumulating distributive claims on the state partly reflect the state's attempt to penetrate and re-organize socioeconomic life.

Second, an interventionist developing state typically controls a substantial proportion of a poor economy. Thus, many of the society's free-floating economic resources are controlled by politicians and bureaucrats. Who should have access to those resources? Unlike situations involving the products of private endeavor, the legitimacy of claims on public resources is not easy to establish. Given the scarcities in a poor economy, moreover, the competitive energies of the many individuals and groups seeking economic improvements tend to get focused on the state. Thus, competition over the state's resources often results in intense conflict, contributing to the problems of governability.

Another major characteristic of India's political structure is India's democracy. On balance, periodic elections and the existence of basic civil liberties are among India's most prized political possessions. Certain specific features of Indian democracy, however, have also contributed to India's growing problems of governability. India's democracy has been democracy from above: For most of its existence, it has been more of a gift from the elite to the masses than something the masses have secured for themselves. There is no doubt that the longer democracy is practiced, the more difficult it becomes for the elite to take away basic democratic rights. Nevertheless, a tremendous concentration of power in the hands of a few leaders is an undeniable feature of India's democracy. Leaders may not be able to turn democracy on and off, but Indira Gandhi came close.

That concentration of power cannot simply be wished away. It is part of the overall design by which the leaders have made democracy a gift to the society. One recurring consequence of that design is that whenever the ruling elite are threatened, further centralization of power is a readily available alternative. Because centralization of power in individuals nearly always emasculates fragile institutions – strong institutions do constrain the power of individuals – there is a built-in incentive in India for leaders to undertake periodic deinstitutionalization. As long as a democracy remains more a gift that a society's leaders give to its people and less an established framework that dwarfs the leaders, only exceptional leaders are likely to resist the tendency to maintain personal power at the expense of institutional development.

An elite-dominated democracy has also structured the patterns of political mobilization. Leaders have mobilized socioeconomic groups more as power resources in intraelite struggles and less to satisfy group aspirations. That pattern of elite-led mobilization is distinguishable from the more conventional concept of social mobilization that supposedly accompanies industrialization, urbanization, literacy, and so forth. Whereas social mobilization is generally produced by economic development and "modernization," elite-led mobilization often reflects patterns of intraelite conflict. Thus, Indira Gandhi discovered India's poor when she was pressed politically by other members of the Congress elite. Devraj Urs and Karpoori Thakur similarly discovered the backward castes when they desperately needed to establish new ruling coalitions. The Akalis began stressing issues of Sikh nationalism only when thrown out of power. The suggestion here is not that such patterns of mobilization are bad or wrong; they are the stuff of democracy. What is wrong here is the disregard for the consequences of such mobilizations.

The primary goal of elite-led mobilization in India has been power for the elite. The issue of whether or not the aspirations of the mobilized groups can be satisfied has always been secondary in the minds of the mobilizers. Indira Gandhi basically ignored the poor. Both Devraj Urs and Karpoori Thakur offered little more than tokens to the backward castes. The Akalis have been willing periodically to sell their nationalistic claims for state power. That is "normal" politics, but what has not always been appreciated is that mobilized but unorganized groups that are ignored by politicians once they have served their political purposes add considerable volatility to the polity. When "real groups" with "real interests," such as labor, are mobilized, there is a realistic chance that the mobilization will be accompanied by organization and that group demands can be accommodated after negotiations. By contrast, mobilization from above often attracts demagogues. Because it remains unorganized and really does not have concrete, even if incremental, gains for the mobilized groups as its priority, such mobilization periodically tends to generate political turmoil.

This focus on elite-led mobilization should not detract attention from the fact of real distributional conflicts. The developmental model that India has pursued has exacerbated existing inequalities along regional, rural-versus-urban, ethnic, class, and caste lines. The resulting dissatisfaction provides the raw material for elite-led movements. The point, however, is that dissatisfied groups have only rarely produced their own leaders and sustained oppositional movements on their own. The pattern, instead, has been one in which professional but opportunistic politicians have sensed some dissatisfaction and have mobilized it almost to the point of frenzy. Such mobilization, in turn, brings short-term partisan benefits at the expense of the political health of the whole.

Finally, the last important characteristic of India's political structure that needs to be noted is the weakness of India's political parties. The organizational viability of Congress has declined. Most other parties have failed to fill the organizational vacuum. Because party organization has been treated as an intermediate variable in this study, both the causes and the consequences of organizational weakness need to be spelled out briefly in general terms.

The diversity of India's social structure naturally militates against the development of cohesive national parties. Because regional parties have not done much better, however, one suspects that factors other than cultural diversity are also at work. One hypothesis that fits the Indian materials is that strong parties – parties with well-developed political identification, programmatic goals, and organization – develop mainly as vehicles for gaining power. Conversely, leaders who acquire power because of personal appeal have little incentive to encourage the development of parties from above; on the contrary, parties as institutions often constrain the individual discretion and personalistic power of charismatic leaders. Thus, well-developed parties often emerge from below rather than from above.

That hypothesis fits broadly the development of the preindependence Congress party, as well as the later growth of the Jan Sangh (now the Bhartiya Janata party), the Communist Party of India, and the DMK in Tamil Nadu. Conversely, we also know that many of India's popular leaders not only have not helped the development of parties, but have even sought to destroy the existing institutional constraints. That was as true of national leaders like Indira and Rajiv Gandhi as it was of non-Congress regional leaders like M. G. Ramachandran in Tamil Nadu and N. T. Rama Rao in Andhra Pradesh.

As to the consequences of party organization, well-organized parties can perform several important political tasks. To repeat, they can help train and socialize new leaders, minimize factional conflict among existing leaders, and clarify lines of authority. Mobilization undertaken by parties, rather than by individuals, is also more likely to be accompanied by organization: Not only are new participants brought into the political arena, but their political energies are simultaneously harnessed to accomplish specific goals. Most important, well-organized parties tend to have long-term programs and a stable core of membership to support those programs. When such parties come to power, they help narrow the gap between the state's representative and developmental goals. The coalition that such a party brings to power is likely to favor the policies that the new government wishes to pursue.

The logic of why weak parties are major sources of governability problems in a democratic developing country is not difficult to explicate. Ample empirical evidence supporting this claim has been provided. Not only has the presence of weak parties been systematically related to governability problems, but the opposite, namely, the positive contributions of well-organized parties, has also been demonstrated. Thus, it is not unreasonable to conclude that the organizational vacuum in Indian politics is a root cause of the growing gap in that country between how power is won and how power is used, or between personalization of power, on the one hand, and the inability to use that power to solve pressing problems, on the other.

To sum up, this study has developed a multicausal explanation of India's growing crisis of governability. The attempt to distinguish the more important causes from the less important has led to an emphasis on variables that can best be described collectively as political variables. It has been proposed further that the reason political factors play such an important role in India is traceable back to the relative balance between the state and the market in India's political economy. Given the state's pervasive presence, specific aspects of India's political structure have considerable bearing on patterns of political change. A highly interventionist state, the peculiarities of democracy bestowed from above, and the weakness of political parties have encouraged a number of trends: rapid political mobilization of diverse groups, a deinstitutionalizing role of leaders, and, more broadly, a situation in which institutions fail to keep pace with growing demands. The result has been a growing crisis of governability that has manifested itself in unstable political coalitions, governmental policy ineffectiveness, and, most important, the increasing use of force and violence in politics.

Finally, then, what are the implications of this argument for India? Three issues can be addressed: Was this pattern of political change inevitable? What is the appropriate frame of reference for the study of political change in India? What, if anything, can be done to reverse the growing crisis?

As for the complex issue of inevitability, this study leads to the unhappy conclusion that, on balance, a fair amount of what happened had to happen. Although the specific rates and patterns of changes obviously could have been different, given the emphasis on the political structures in the argument it is difficult to imagine a scenario in which India's political institutions would not have been weakened and power conflicts would not have multiplied.

India was much easier to govern when the nationalist legacy was alive, when the ruling elite were a relatively narrow and cohesive group, and when most of India's masses remained prepolitical and deeply entrenched in a traditional caste hierarchy. Over time, many of those traits had to change. Nationalism had to decline. Given a highly interventionist state and electoral competition, both intraelite struggles for power and struggles involving groups contending for access to the state's resources were bound to grow. Furthermore, the spread of commerce and egalitarian values had to undermine traditional patterns of domination, leading to growing conflicts within the civil society. Given the intraelite struggles and conflicts among competing groups, it is also difficult to imagine how a "consensual"

party like Congress could have continued as before. Such patterns of decline of major institutions and increasing power conflicts spell political
trouble in most polities. How could India have been any different?

This emphasis on inevitability needs two important qualifications. First,
at some deep level of causation, as long as human beings make decisions,
nothing in political change is ever inevitable. At some point, all paths
involve choices. However, over time, the choices that are made become
structures that mold future patterns of change. India's state, therefore, did
not have to be as highly interventionist as it was. Once the decisions on
patterns of state intervention were made, however, they were not easy to
reverse. Numerous unanticipated consequences, some beneficial and some
not so beneficial, followed. Similarly, there clearly was room for choice
on distributive issues. Land reforms could have been implemented. A more
benign pattern of stratification might well have created fewer problems of
political accommodation. Once distributive issues were ignored, however,
numerous "inevitabilities" followed. For example, populism as a leadership
strategy became one of the few alternatives for winning support among
the lower strata. Populism, in turn, is inherently deinstitutionalizing.

The foregoing emphasis on inevitability, therefore, assumes many of the
important structural decisions as given. Those decisions reflected many
constraints that were operating when they were taken. Of course, if those
major decisions had been different, the nature of political change in India
could also have been different.

A second qualification concerns choices made by leaders that were distinctly less "structural" in nature, but still had important and harmful
consequences for the quality of government in India. Indira Gandhi, for
example, came to preside over a Congress party in the 1960s that was
already deeply factionalized at the top and rapidly losing its old coalitional
base at the bottom. There is no reason to assume that the only way to
reverse that situation was to split the Congress party, let the old Congress
organization die, fail to rebuild any new organization, and revert to a highly
deinstitutionalizing form of populism. It is possible to imagine the same
rhetoric of populism that Indira adopted, combined with the old Congress
organization, leading to a marginally different political outcome. Other
examples can be presented to make the same point. Sanjay's goons and
Rajiv's incompetence were hardly sociological necessities. At numerous
points, therefore, different decisions could have led to a somewhat different
outcome. The balanced conclusion on the issue of inevitability is that
whereas the general trend of political change in India over the past two
decades had to be toward a more turbulent polity, the specific rate and
pattern could have been somewhat different.

This study also has an analytical message for those investigating political
change in India, easily derived from the foregoing discussion. There are
many schools of thought among observers of Indian politics. This study

speaks directly to two of the more popular ones. One approach to Indian politics tends to focus on the role of leaders. For example, an inordinate amount of intellectual energy has been devoted to denouncing the deinstitutionalizing role of Indira Gandhi in Indian politics. Similarly, scholars often attribute great promise to preferred new leaders as soon as they appear on the political horizon. A second school of thought continues to view politics in terms of its underlying socioeconomic determinants. Whereas there are fewer and fewer scholars who view Indian politics through the old "modernization" eyeglasses, there are many who still opt for the Marxist lens.

Those who emphasize the roles of leaders are not necessarily wrong. They do, however, tend to underestimate the deeper determinants of Indian politics. The findings in this study suggest that even without Indira Gandhi, many features of Indian politics would still be the same.[3] This is not to deny that Indira Gandhi made some of the most important decisions involved in producing the political change one sees in India today. However, the most important question remains: Would a different leader have done things very differently? Indira Gandhi operated under constraints. Different leaders might have made some different decisions, but they also would have had to cope with the broader political pressures. In general, leaders always make a difference, sometimes even a very important difference, but there are always important structural forces at work that mold patterns of political change.

Marxist scholars are more acutely sensitive to this issue of choice versus structure, but as far as India is concerned, they often are too focused on the wrong set of structures. It has been evident in this analysis that issues of class relations, conceived narrowly, or of economic distribution, conceived more broadly, are far from inconsequential for an analysis of Indian politics.[4] Given the disproportionately large role of the state in molding market relations in India, however, the roles of political structures loom larger than those of social classes. If this contention seems a bit exaggerated, a modified position might be acceptable even to some Marxist scholars. No analysis of political change in India can be complete without taking into account the significance of such political variables as electoral competition, the weakness of political parties, the roles of leaders, and the virulent competition over state-controlled economic resources.

3 For an intelligent argument that stresses the role of leadership, see Paul R. Brass, *The Politics of India Since Independence. The New Cambridge History of India*, IV.1 (Cambridge University Press, 1990).

4 One important collection (mostly non-Marxist) traces the roots of political disorder in contemporary India to issues of both class and caste distributions: Francine Frankel and M. S. A. Rao, eds., *Dominance and State Power in Modern India: Decline of a Social Order*, 2 vols. (Oxford University Press, 1989–90); see especially the contributions by Frankel.

A third implication concerns the future: This study suggests that if current trends continue unchecked, India's political crisis is likely to get worse. Given the emphasis on the structural origins of the crisis, the kinds of leadership actions that could halt or reverse India's erosion of authority would have to involve major changes. Such changes would not be easy to initiate or to implement. Although this study is primarily analytical, two policy prescriptions emerge from the discussion: the need to strengthen the organizations of the major parties, and the need to narrow the gap between the state's commitments and capacities.

The need for better-organized parties has been emphasized, as have the many obstacles that stand in the way of such a development. The agents most likely to be able to initiate such major changes would be India's prominent leaders. Given the current circumstances, however, such leaders have little incentive to strengthen party organizations, for that would tend to check their personal power. What conceivable kinds of developments, if any, could help break that vicious circle?

A party with a clear program is more likely to develop a stable membership, a core of active workers, and clear lines of authority and functions. The development of such programmatic national parties would be more likely in India if Congress were to cease being the centrist, populist majority party; all major parties compete for the central political space that Congress occupies. The most likely way for that to happen, at present, would be through the rise of an alternative leader with personal appeal who could outdo Congress's populism. That mode of political competition clearly is not helpful for organizational development. If, by chance or necessity, Congress should move to the left or the right, that could encourage the emergence of other programmatic national parties. Such a move probably would be destabilizing over the short run, as a vacuum of sorts would be created in the middle. Over the longer run, however, such a development could strengthen both Congress and the competing national parties, especially in the organizational dimension, thus adding a measure of coherence to India's turbulent polity. The debate between a democratic left and right, in turn, could help introduce real issues into what at present is largely mere populist posturing that scorns political problems. Such a debate could also cut across the caste, religious, and ethnic divisions that have become major sources of political turmoil. The findings in this study indicate that India has little to fear from the emergence of class politics; rather, centrism and populism are the primary sources of the problems in Indian politics.[5]

A prescription of this type is not the same as a prediction. Over the short run, neither Congressites nor the motley opposition groups are likely

---

5 There is a study that conceives of continued "centrism" as a source of stability in Indian politics: Lloyd and Susanne Rudolph, *In Pursuit of Lakshmi: The Political Economy of the Indian State* (University of Chicago Press, 1987).

to abandon their centrist and populist postures. If one had to predict, it would seem that the most likely outcome over the next decade would be more of the same: policy ineffectiveness and continuing turmoil, encouraging further centralization and the use of force, punctuated by occasional bursts of hope created by elections and electoral gimmicks. How long such a process can go on within the framework of a democracy is difficult to predict. One of the prescriptions that emerges from this analysis is that if one were to set out to alter the current political trends, then strengthening the party organizations would be an important area for action.

There is a related area in which this analysis suggests the need for major action: narrowing the gap between the Indian state's commitments and its capacities. That could be done by reducing its commitments, by increasing its capacities, or more likely by some combination of the two. Nonpartisan scholarship cannot suggest which alternative would be better. Those are major political issues that should be debated and settled by compromise among the contending political actors themselves. What scholarship can emphasize, however, is that the ongoing populist posturing of India's political parties, without the capacity to deliver on promises, has become a serious political problem. That pattern of rule raises aspirations without satisfying or harnessing them, thus continually contributing to the growing problems of governability.

COMPARATIVE IMPLICATIONS OF INDIAN MATERIALS

Theoretically, self-conscious case studies can have the additional function of drawing attention to novel hypotheses that may be of broader relevance, and they can also help confirm, question, or modify existing general claims in light of any new empirical findings. Finally, therefore, some comparative implications of this study of India can be suggested, although discerning readers no doubt will draw their own varied conclusions. Three issues, however, two substantial and one methodological, appear to be especially relevant. The substantial issues concern how and why centralization in developing countries creates powerlessness, and why attempts to institutionalize democracy in such settings will remain an uphill battle. The methodological issue concerns how best to study the problems of political disorder in developing countries.

Centralization and powerlessness

The findings in this study suggest that two types of power resources should be distinguished analytically: the power of leaders to control the state's decisions and exercise negative sanctions, especially coercion – let us label it "centralizing power" – and "real power," that is, power to bring about socioeconomic development, however development is defined – let us label it "developmental power." This study of India has suggested that there is no necessary link between centralizing power and developmental power. On the contrary, whereas attempts at further centralization may have helped leaders preserve their personal power, they also have enfeebled the state in terms of accomplishing socioeconomic goals. Thus, in India, centralization and powerlessness have turned out to be simultaneous tendencies.

The distinction between centralizing power and developmental power, and the related attempts to understand the conditions under which growing centralization may facilitate or undermine a state's developmental efficacy, opens up a range of comparative questions for future research. For example, we do not completely understand why authoritarianism in many African countries has failed to create developmental dynamism, whereas the results of authoritarianism in East Asian countries like South Korea have been nearly the opposite. Why are some centralized and authoritarian regimes efficacious in terms of accomplishing developmental goals, whereas others are not? This line of questioning suggests that a state's capacity to foster development is not likely to vary in a simple, linear way along the one-dimensional continuum from democracy to authoritarianism. The paramount question has to do with the the conditions under which a democratic or an authoritarian government can facilitate socioeconomic change from above – an issue that is as important as it is poorly understood.[6]

Although the findings in this study of India can help focus attention on such puzzles, they, of course, cannot come close to resolving them; that must be the function of multicountry research endeavors. One broad line of thinking, however, that emerges from the foregoing analysis may be of some utility. A state's capacity to facilitate development is primarily a function of how the state and the society relate to each other, and only secondarily a function of the characteristics of the state or the society alone.[7] More specifically, institutionalized patterns of authority that link (or do not link) the state and society are likely to be major determinants of the state's developmental efficacy. For example, leaders who preside over states that tend to exclude most social groups from both political participation and systematic economic benefits are likely to be deemed devoid of legitimacy, so that – barring extreme uses of coercion – they will

6 A wide-ranging study that addresses this question is by Joel S. Migdal, *Strong Societies and Weak States: State–Society Relations and State Capabilities in the Third World* (Princeton University Press, 1988). My major quarrel with that insightful book is its tendency to view power distribution as a zero-sum game between the state and society.

7 Peter Evans, for example, emphasizes bureaucratic competence and the presence or absence of landed oligarchies as important determinants of a state's capacity to facilitate industrialization. See his "Predatory, Developmental and Other Apparatuses: A Comparative Political Economy Perspective on the Third World State," *Sociological Forum*, 4:4, Fall 1989, pp. 561–87.

be incapable of pursuing state-led development. Conversely, states that attempt to satisfy many social groups simultaneously may be deemed more legitimate over the short run, but again may not be all that efficacious, because of the problems inherent in attempting too many things at once. That is why the most efficacious states are likely to be those that selectively and systematically incorporate some social groups in a ruling alliance while using coercion to deal with the excluded groups. Both communist experiments and successful state-led capitalist experiments in the Third World have authority organized along these principles – at least over the medium term, beyond which the solution of new or neglected problems forces reform. The implication for effective democratic governance is the utility of well-organized competing parties that can incorporate selected social groups and yet create a coherent center of national power.

Representation versus development

A second general implication of the preceding empirical analysis concerns a possible explanation of why attempts to institutionalize democracy will remain uphill battles in the developing world. Democracy in the Third World has had many false starts, a pattern that is not likely to change soon. Many countries have attempted to "democratize," but it has been a rare developing country in which stable and effective democratic government has taken root. Why is that so? A detailed study of political change in India suggests that democracy's fragility may reflect a persistent tension between the state's representative and developmental functions in the Third World.

The state in much of the developing world is not only an agent of political order; it is also responsible for socioeconomic development. The findings in India emphasize that the attempts of leaders to promote democratic political order often conflict with efforts to steer development from above. For example, if national leaders choose to build a popular base of support, that often inclines them to appeal to as many groups as possible. There are, however, few established traditions of intergroup collaboration in such settings. Therefore, a systematic ruling coalition often is difficult to sustain. The more the state internalizes the socioeconomic conflicts of the civil society, the more difficult it becomes to establish a coherent political center. Because a state without a coherent political center is really no state, there is a recurring tendency in democratic Third World states to resort to leaders with personal and populist appeal as a short-term solution to the problem of political order.

Personalistic and populist leaders are, in turn, seldom effective at building institutions or at promoting economic development. Unless leaders are exceptionally committed to the public good, the logic of their political positions militates against stimulating the development of new ruling institutions. Such institutions can develop only if rules are put above personal discretion and if authority is systematically delegated to second, third, and even lower strata in the political hierarchy. Such a policy often means putting limits on personal power. Few leaders deliberately undertake actions that will eventually undermine their own power.

Populist leaders also find it difficult to promote economic efficiency. Nationalistic and redistributive themes often are central to a populist discourse; nationalistic and redistributive economic rhetoric helps legitimize fragile democratic rule. This does not mean that redistribution is effective. Rather, it means that leaders presiding over such arrangements often are reluctant to make the difficult economic decisions. Moreover, there is a recurring tendency to use the state's resources not to promote economic development but to buy political support. That tendency exists in a wide variety of regimes, but it is especially difficult to counter in the interventionist Third World democracies.

Democracy in a Third World context has a tendency to evolve toward a populist ruling arrangement, and populism as a ruling strategy has not been notably effective either for building institutions or for promoting economic development. It is that tendency that introduces into Third World democracies the recurring tension between their representative and developmental functions. Lest one conclude that this is an argument for authoritarianism, I must reiterate a theme discussed earlier, namely, that only some types of authoritarian regimes are effective at promoting economic development, and even they do not offer long-term political alternatives. Their failure to represent diverse interests leads periodically to power challenges, again creating considerable tension that is likely to be resolved only by movement toward a more open and legitimate polity.

The Indian materials analyzed in this book point to a way out of the ubiquitous tension between the state's representative and developmental functions in Third World democracies. Well-organized political parties can help narrow that gap. Such parties can build stable coalitions around coherent programs. Coalitions and policy priorities that have been tested in electoral competition, in turn, can help reduce the tension between the state's needs to represent diverse interests and simultaneously to promote socioeconomic change from above. If democracy is an important goal in the Third World, then the development of well-organized parties will be a crucial factor in reaching that long-term goal.

The study of political disorder

The last general theme that this empirical study can help to address is how best to study political disorder in developing countries. It must be clear to theoretically inclined readers that the approach informing this study is built on some prevailing ideas and departs from others. To reiterate a general theme stated earlier, this study, while taking both developmental and class variables into account, emphasizes the political origins of political disorder. If labels are called for, the approach adopted here can best be described as a state–society approach.

This book shares with the works of Samuel Huntington, among others, the notion that the study of political order in developing countries is important. The virtual ideological disdain in some quarters concerning issues of order is short-sighted. The problem of political disorder ought to be of analytical and normative concern to diverse groups of scholars, whether they be on the left, on the right, or somewhere in between. The real debate should be about how best to explain the conditions that lead to order and disorder, and about the prescriptions that may flow from such analyses.

This study, further, shares the commonly held view that issues of order and disorder are best viewed in terms of a balance between institutional capacities to absorb societal demands and the nature and quantity of the demands themselves. As discussed in Chapter 2, this basic formulation of "institutions versus demands," "integration versus differentiation," or "hegemony versus class conflict" is common to both developmental and Marxist lines of analysis, the convergence being most evident in the works of such "political development" scholars as Samuel Huntington and Guillermo O'Donnell. The main debate, once again, should be about the forces that propel group demands and, even more important, the conditions under which adequately institutionalized, noncoercive polities become established.

There are several important points, however, on which this study departs from "developmental" formulations. First, it is evident throughout this analysis that the study of political order in a specific developmental setting is inseparable from the study of a state's ability to facilitate socioeconomic development. This view emerges from an understanding of the Third World state as an agent not only of order but also of development. Thus, a "crisis of governability" is understood in this study to be manifest not only in growing political violence but also in the state's developmental incapacity. This modified focus, in turn, leads to a view in which order is not always to be preferred to disorder; an orderly state that fails to facilitate balanced development is hardly an effective and desirable state.

On more analytical grounds as well, this examination of how demands are mobilized and how institutions become weakened (or fail to develop) departs from some of the prevailing ideas. To reiterate, India's growing demands are not mainly a function of rapid socioeconomic modernization. Instead, the spread of competitive politics in a setting in which the state has disproportionate control over societal resources provides the broad context for overpoliticization. This modified perspective aids our understanding of the high degrees of politicization in low-income settings. More important, when state-controlled resources become objects of virulent com-

petition, some of the conventional distinctions concerning whether conflict
is over politics, status, or economic resources get blurred. For example,
old group identities based on caste, language, or religion, or new identities
based on occupation or class, can be used as a foundation for mobilization
by competing groups of the political elite seeking a greater share of state-
controlled economic resources. Is modal conflict of this nature ethnic,
economic, or political? Because it is a bit of each, the dynamics and the
consequences of such group mobilizations in state-dominated contexts require wider attention in comparative studies.[8]

This analysis of Indian materials also generates an insight concerning
the dynamics of institutional development that may be of some general
interest. Powerful leaders in India often have proved to be enemies of
institutions such as political parties. Because institutions tend to constrain
personal power, those who attain positions of power because of personalistic traits usually show little interest in institutional development or,
worse, actively seek to weaken existing institutions. A similar deinstitutionalizing tendency on the part of personalistic leaders has been widely
noted in the African context.[9] It is arguable that even in a somewhat
different, nonpersonalistic context, like that of Brazil, the legacy of highly
bureaucratized authoritarian rule has hardly been strong democratic par-

8 Some analysts, working in contexts other than India, have already noted the significance
  of this link between extensive state intervention and rapid politicization. For example,
  Claude Ake has this to say about Nigeria: "The crux of the problem of Nigeria today is
  the over politicization of social life. . . . We are intoxicated with politics; the premium on
  political power is so high that we are prone to take the most extreme measures to win and
  to maintain political power. . . . As things stand now, the Nigerian state appears to intervene
  everywhere and to own virtually everything including access to status and wealth. Inevitably
  a desperate struggle to win control of state power ensues." From Claude Ake, "Presidential
  Address to the Nigerian Political Science Association," *West Africa*, May 25, 1981,
  pp. 1162–3. Other analysts of Nigeria have adopted a similar standpoint to explain why
  political breakdown is less a "tribal" and more a state-generated phenomenon in that
  country. See Larry Diamond, *Class, Ethnicity and Democracy in Nigeria: The Failure of
  the First Republic* (Syracuse, N.Y.: Syracuse University Press, 1988), especially pp. 297–
  300. In the Latin American context, where class ideologies often dominate the political
  discourse, discerning analysts have pointed out that the pattern of recurring shifts in regime
  types are rooted less in class conflict and more in the nature of the "politicized state," in
  which institutions are weak and "everything is possible." The process of politicization is,
  moreover, "reinforced" by a "central role of the state in Latin American society. . . . The
  control and manipulation of the state apparatus are therefore a major element in the political
  struggle." See Douglas A. Chalmers, "The Politicized State in Latin America," in James
  M. Malloy, ed., *Authoritarianism and Corporatism in Latin America* (University of Pittsburgh Press, 1977), pp. 26, 30, 31.
9 See, for example, Robert H. Jackson and Carl G. Rosberg, *Personal Rule in Black Africa:
  Prince, Autocrat, Prophet, Tyrant* (Berkeley: University of California Press, 1982); Richard
  Sandbrook, *The Politics of Africa's Economic Stagnation* (Cambridge University Press,
  1985).

ties.[10] Such recurring failures of rulers to initiate the rebuilding and maintenance of institutions clearly have general relevance.

One is led to conclude that political disorder results not only from the demands of newly mobilized groups but also from the institution-destroying proclivities of a powerful state elite. That, in turn, suggests that it is misleading to assume that highly mobilized social groups are the main enemies of public order and that the state is the most likely guarantor of public good. Earlier, we encountered case after case in which the state elite had proved to be a crucial part of the problem of political disorder. Clearly, in our analyses of political disorder in developing countries, the conservative bias that often is suspicious of mobilization from below while tolerant of power abuses by authorities, in the belief that the state is the ultimate provider of the public good, needs to be rethought, if not expunged.

The main prescriptive implication of this analysis is that there are no shortcuts to the establishment of noncoercive political order. Heavyhanded rule cannot be justified on the ground that it can help generate consensus-building institutions such as parties; neither logic nor evidence supports that contention. Instead, power conflicts must be negotiated and worked out. The development of integrative institutions at the interstices of the state and society, especially parties, will remain crucial for moderating these conflicts. Such developments, however, are more likely in cases in which power conflicts are worked out from below; they are less likely to result from social engineering from above.

10 See the detailed account in Thomas E. Skidmore, *The Politics of Military Rule in Brazil, 1964–85* (Oxford University Press, 1988).

Bibliography

Abdi, S. N. M. "At Loggerheads." *Illustrated Weekly of India* (April 27, 1986), pp. 20–3.

Ahluwalia, Isher J. *Industrial Growth in India: Stagnation Since the Mid-Sixties.* Oxford University Press, 1985.

Ahmed, Bashiruddin. "Emerging Indian Political System." *The Administrator* (India), 31:1(January–March 1986), pp. 27–42.

Ahmed, Bashiruddin, and Samuel J. Eldersveld. *Citizens and Politics: Mass Political Behavior in India.* University of Chicago Press, 1978.

Ahmed, Muyaffar. *The Communist Party of India and Its Formation Abroad.* Calcutta: National Book Agency, 1961.

Ake, Claude. "Presidential Address to the Nigerian Political Science Association." *West Africa* (May 25, 1981), pp. 1162–3.

Alavi, Hamza. "Peasants and Revolutions," in *Socialist Register,* in R. Miliband and J. Saville, pp. 241–77. New York: Monthly Review Press, 1965.

All Indian Congress (I) Committee. "Economic resolution." Delhi: 1985.

Bardhan, Pranab. "Poverty and Employment Characteristics of Urban Households in West Bengal." *Economic and Political Weekly,* 22:35(August 29, 1987), pp. 1496–502.

Bardhan, Pranab. *The Political Economy of Development in India.* Oxford: Basil Blackwell, 1984.

Barnett, Margurite Ross. *The Politics of Cultural Nationalism in South India.* Princeton, N.J.: Princeton University Press, 1976.

Basu, Sajal. *Politics of Violence: A Case Study of West Bengal.* Calcutta: Minerva Associates, 1982.

Basu, Sajal. *West Bengal: The Violent Years.* Calcutta: Prachi Publications, 1979.

Bates, Robert H. *Markets and States in Tropical Africa.* Berkeley: University of California Press, 1982.

Bayley, David H. *The Police and Political Development in India.* Princeton, N.J.: Princeton University Press, 1969.

Bayley, David H. "The Police and Political Order in India." *Asian Survey,* 23:4(April 1983), pp. 484–96.

Bhagwati, Jagdish. "Rethinking Trade Strategy," in *Development Strategies Reconsidered,* edited by J. Lewis and V. Kallab, pp. 91–104. Washington, D.C.: Overseas Development Council, 1986.

Bhagwati, Jagdish, and T. N. Srinivasan. *Foreign Trade Regimes and Economic Development: India.* New York: Columbia University Press, 1975.

Bhandare, Vasant R. *Maharashtra–Karnataka Border Dispute: Politics of Manipulation.* Bombay: Kirti Prakashan, 1985.

Bhatt, Anil. "Caste and Political Mobilization in a Gujarat District," in *Caste in*

Indian Politics, edited by R. Kothari, pp. 299–339. New Delhi: Orient Longman, 1973.

Blair, Harry. "Rising Kulaks and Backward Classes in Bihar: Social Change in the late 1970s." *Economic and Political Weekly,* 15:2(January 12, 1980), pp. 64–74.

Blair, Harry. "Structural Change, the Agricultural Sector, and Politics in Bihar," in *State Politics in Contemporary India: Crisis or Continuity?* edited by J. Wood, pp. 53–79. Boulder, Colo.: Westview Press, 1984.

Brass, Paul. "Congress, the Lok Dal and the Middle Peasant Castes: An Analysis of the 1977 and 1980 Parliamentary Elections in Uttar Pradesh." *Pacific Affairs,* 54:1(Spring 1981), pp. 5–41.

Brass, Paul. *Factional Politics in an Indian State: The Congress Party in Uttar Pradesh.* Berkeley: University of California Press, 1965.

Brass, Paul. "The Politicization of the Peasantry in a North Indian State – I." *Journal of Peasant Studies,* 7:4(July 1980), pp. 395–426.

Brass, Paul. "The Politicization of the Peasantry in a North Indian State – II." *Journal of Peasant Studies,* 8:1(September 1980), pp. 3–36.

Brass, Paul R. *The Politics of India Since Independence. The New Cambridge History of India,* IV.1. Cambridge University Press, 1990.

Brass, Paul. "The Punjab Crisis and the Unity of India," in *India's Democracy: An Analysis of Changing State–Society Relations,* edited by A. Kohli, pp. 169–213. Princeton, N.J.: Princeton University Press, 1988.

Broomfield, John. *Elite Conflict in a Plural Society.* Berkeley: University of California Press, 1968.

Carras, Mary C. *Indira Gandhi: In the Crucible of Leadership.* Boston: Beacon Press, 1979.

Chakravarty, Nikhil. "AICC Resists Rajiv's Kitchen Cabinet Policy." *The Telegraph* (May 15, 1985).

Chakravarty, Sukhamoy. "India's Development Strategy for the 1980s." *Economic and Political Weekly,* 19:20–1(May 26, 1984), pp. 845–52.

Chalmers, Douglas A. "The Politicized State in Latin America," in James M. Malloy, ed., *Authoritarianism and Corporatism in Latin America.* University of Pittsburgh Press, 1977.

Chattopadhyay, Gautam. *Communism and Bengal's Freedom Movement.* New Delhi: People's Publishing House, 1970.

Chaudhry, Mrinal Datta. "The New Policy." *Seminar* (December 1985), pp. 18–22.

Chaudhry, Nirmal. "West Bengal: Vortex of Ideological Politics," in *State Politics in India,* edited by I. Narain, pp. 370–404. Meerut: Meenakshi Prakashan, 1968.

Chaudry, Praveen K. "Agrarian Unrest in Bihar: A Case Study of Patna District, 1960–84." *Economic and Political Weekly,* 23:1–2(January 2, 1988), pp. 51–6.

Collier, David, ed. *The New Authoritarianism in Latin America.* Princeton, N.J.: Princeton University Press, 1979.

Committee for the Protection of Democratic Rights. *The Gujarat Agitations and Reservations.* Bombay: Super Book House, 1981.

Das, Arvind N. *Agrarian Unrest and Socioeconomic Change in Bihar, 1900–1980.* New Delhi: Manohar, 1983.

Das, Arvind N. "Peasants and Peasant Organizations: The Kisan Sabha in Bihar," in *Agrarian Movements in India,* edited by Arvind N. Das, pp. 40–87. London: Frank Cass, 1982.

Dasgupta, Biplab. *The Naxalite Movement.* Bombay: Allied Publishers, 1975.

Dasgupta, Jyotirindra. "India: Democratic Becoming and Combined Development," in *Democracy in Developing Countries: Asia*, edited by L. Diamond et al., pp. 53–104. Boulder, Colo.: Lynne Rienner, 1989.

Dasgupta, Sugata, Ronen Bhattacharjee, and Surendra Singh. *The Great Gherao of 1969: A Case Study of Campus Violence and Protest Methods.* Bombay: Orient Longman, 1974.

Datta, Bhabatosh. "The Central Budget and the New Economic Policy." *Economic and Political Weekly*, 20:16(April 20, 1985), pp. 693–8.

Datta, Bhabatosh. "The Road to Nowhere," *Seminar*, 316(December 1985), pp. 32–5.

Deshingkar, G., and R. Kothari. "Punjab: The Longer View." *Illustrated Weekly of India* (July 15, 1984), pp. 20–3.

Desai, I. P. "Anti-Reservation Agitation and Structure of Gujarat Society," *Economic and Political Weekly*, 16:18(May 2, 1981), pp. 819–23.

Diamond, Larry. *Class, Ethnicity and Democracy in Nigeria: The Failure of the First Republic.* Syracuse, N.Y.: Syracuse University Press, 1988.

Druhe, David N. *Soviet Russia and Indian Communism.* New York: Bookman Associates, 1959.

Elliot, Carolyn M. "Caste and Faction Amongst Dominant Castes: The Reddys and Kammas of Andhra," in *Caste in Indian Politics*, edited by R. Kothari, pp. 129–71. New Delhi: Orient Longman, 1970.

Engineer, Asghar Ali. "Communal Fires Engulf Ahmedabad Once Again." *Economic and Political Weekly*, 20:27(July 6, 1985), pp. 1116–20.

Engineer, Asghar Ali. "From Caste to Communal Violence." *Economic and Political Weekly*, 20:15(April 13, 1985), pp. 628–30.

Evans, Peter. "Predatory, Developmental and Other Apparatuses: A Comparative Political Economy Perspective on the Third World State." *Sociological Forum*, 4:4(Fall 1989), pp. 561–87.

Evans, Peter, Dietrich Rueschemeyer, and Theda Skocpol, eds. *Bringing the State Back In.* Cambridge University Press, 1985.

Forrester, Duncan. "Factions and Film Stars: Tamil Nadu Politics Since 1971." *Asian Survey*, 16:3(March 1976), pp. 283–96.

Franda, Marcus. *Radical Politics in West Bengal.* Cambridge, Mass.: M.I.T. Press, 1972.

Franda, Marcus. "Rural Development, Bengali Marxist Style." American Universities Field Staff Reports, Asia, No. 15, 1978.

Frankel, Francine. "Caste, Land and Dominance in Bihar," in *Dominance and State Power in Modern India: Decline of a Social Order*, 2 vols., edited by F. Frankel and M. S. A. Rao, volume 1, pp. 46–132. Oxford University Press, 1989–90.

Frankel, Francine. *India's Political Economy, 1947–77: The Gradual Revolution.* Princeton, N.J.: Princeton University Press, 1978.

Frankel, Francine. "Middle Classes and Castes in India's Politics: Prospects for Political Accommodation," in *India's Democracy: An Analysis of Changing State–Society Relations*, edited by A. Kohli, pp. 225–62. Princeton, N.J.: Princeton University Press, 1988.

Gallagher, John. "Congress in Decline: Bengal, 1930 to 1939." *Modern Asian Studies*, 7:3(July 1973), pp. 589–645.

Ghosh, Shankar. *The Disinherited State: A Study of West Bengal, 1967–70.* Bombay: Orient Longman, 1971.

Ghosh, Shankar. *The Naxalite Movement.* Calcutta: K. L. Mukhopadhyay, 1974.

Gill, S. S., and K. C. Singhal. "The Punjab Problem: Its Historical Roots." *Economic and Political Weekly*, 19:14(April 7, 1984), pp. 603–8.

Gopal, S. *The Permanent Settlement in Bengal and Its Results*. London: Allen & Unwin, 1948.

Government of Andhra Pradesh, Bureau of Economics and Statistics. *Statistical Abstract 1981*. Hyderabad: Government Secretariat Press, 1983.

Government of Andhra Pradesh, Ministry of Home and Legislative Affairs, *Police Administration, 1985–86*. Hyderabad: Government Secretariat Press, 1985.

Government of Andhra Pradesh, Panchayat Raj Department. *Report of the State Committee on Panchayati Raj Institutions*. Hyderabad: Government Secretariat Press, 1981.

Government of Bihar. "Notes on Extremist Activities – Affected Areas," May 1982.

Government of Gujarat, Bureau of Economics and Statistics, *Handbook of Basic Statistics: Gujarat State, 1977–8*. Gandhinagar: Government Press, 1977–8.

Government of India. *Report of the Committee on Trade Policy*. New Delhi: Ministry of Commerce, December 1984.

Government of India. *Report of the National Police Commission*. New Delhi: Ministry of Home Affairs, 1979–81.

Government of India, Ministry of Planning. *Statistical Pocket Book, India, 1983*. Delhi: Government of India Press.

Government of Karnataka. *Draft Five Year Plan, 1978–83*. Bangalore: Government Press, 1982.

Government of Karnataka, State Agriculture Census Commissioner. *Agricultural Census, 1976–77*. Bangalore: Government Press, 1978.

Government of West Bengal. *Labour in West Bengal*. Calcutta: Director of Information, Government of West Bengal, 1972.

Government of West Bengal. *Left Front Government in West Bengal: Eight Years*. Calcutta: Department of Information and Cultural Affairs, 1985.

Government of West Bengal, Bureau of Applied Economics and Statistics. *Statistical Handbook, 1982*. Calcutta: Sree Saraswaty Press, 1983.

Gramsci, Antonio. *Selections from the Prison Notebooks*. New York: International Publishers, 1971.

Gujaral, I. K. "The Economic Dimension," in *Punjab in Indian Politics: Issues and Trends,* edited by Amrik Singh, pp. 42–53. Delhi: Ajanta Publications, 1985.

Gujaral, I. K. "The Sequence." *Seminar* (February 1984), pp. 14–17.

Hamilton, Nora. *The Limits of State Autonomy: Post-Revolutionary Mexico*. Princeton, N.J.: Princeton University Press, 1983.

Hanumantha Rao, V. *Party Politics in Andhra Pradesh, 1956–83*. Hyderabad: ABA Publications, 1983.

Hardgrave, Robert. *India Under Pressure: Prospects for Political Stability*. Boulder, Colo.: Westview Press, 1984.

Hardgrave, Robert. "Politics and the Film in Tamil Nadu: The Stars and the DMK." *Asian Survey*, 13:3(March 1973), pp. 288–305.

Harrison, Selig. *India: The Most Dangerous Decades*. Princeton, N.J.: Princeton University Press, 1960.

Hart, Henry, ed. *Indira Gandhi's India*. Boulder, Colo.: Westview Press, 1980.

Hart, Henry. "Political Leadership in India: Dimensions and Limits," in *India's Democracy: An Analysis of Changing State–Society Relations,* edited by A. Kohli, pp. 18–62. Princeton, N.J.: Princeton University Press, 1988.

Hebsur, R. K. "Karnataka." *Seminar,* 278(August 1978), pp. 21–6.

Higgott, Richard. *Political Development Theory*. New York: St. Martin's Press, 1983.

Huntington, Samuel P. *Political Order in Changing Societies*. New Haven: Yale University Press, 1968.

Innaiah, N. *Saffron Star over Andhra Pradesh*. Hyderabad: Book Links Corporation, 1984.

Irani, C. R. *Bengal: The Communist Challenge*. Bombay: Lalvani Publishing House, 1968.

Jackson, Robert H., and Carl G. Rosberg. *Personal Rule in Black Africa: Prince, Autocrat, Prophet, Tyrant*. Berkeley: University of California Press, 1982.

Januzzi, Thomasson F. *Agrarian Crisis in India: The Case of Bihar*. Austin: University of Texas Press, 1973.

Jeffery, Robin. *What's Happening to India?: Punjab, Ethnic Conflict, Mrs. Gandhi's Death and the Test for Federalism*. Basingstoke: Macmillan, 1986.

Jha, Chetkar. "Caste in Bihar Congress Politics," in *State Politics in India*, edited by I. Narain, pp. 575–83. Meerut: Meenakshi Prakashan, 1968.

Jha, L. K. "In Search of a New Economic Order." *Illustrated Weekly of India* (April 6, 1986), pp. 20–3.

Jha, Prem Shankar. "Seventh Plan Perspectives: A New Direction for Industry." *Times of India* (August 13, 1984).

Jha, Prem Shankar. "The End of the Tunnel: Return to Sanity in Economic Policy." *Times of India* (April 19, 1982).

Jones, D. E., and R. W. Jones. "Urban Upheaval in India: The 1974 Navnirman Riots in Gujrat." *Asian Survey*, 16:11(November 1976), pp. 1012–33.

Kapur, Rajiv. *Sikh Separatism: The Politics of Faith*. London: Allen & Unwin, 1986.

Karnik, V. B. *M. N. Roy: A Political Biography*. Bombay: New Jagriti Samay Publisher, 1978.

Kasfir, Nelson. "Explaining Ethnic Political Participation," in *The State and Development in the Third World*, edited by A. Kohli, pp. 88–111. Princeton, N.J.: Princeton University Press, 1986.

Katzenstein, Mary F. *Ethnicity and Equality: The Shiv Sena Party and Preferential Policies in Bombay*. Ithaca, N.Y.: Cornell University Press, 1979.

Kochanek, Stanley. *Business and Politics in India*. Berkeley: University of California Press, 1974.

Kochanek, Stanley A. "Regulation and Liberalization Theology in India." *Asian Survey*, 26:12(December 1986), pp. 1284–308.

Kohli, Atul. "Communist Reformers in West Bengal: Origins, Features and Relations with New Delhi," in *State Politics in Contemporary India: Crisis or Continuity?* edited by John R. Wood, pp. 81–102. Boulder, Colo.: Westview Press, 1984.

Kohli, Atul. "Democracy and Development," in *Development Strategies Reconsidered*, edited by John Lewis and Valerianna Kallab, pp. 153–82. Washington, D.C.: Overseas Development Council, 1986.

Kohli, Atul. "From Elite Activism to Democratic Consolidation: Political Change in West Bengal," in *Dominance and State Power in Modern India: Decline of a Social Order*, 2 vols., edited by F. Frankel and M. S. A. Rao. Oxford University Press, 1989–90.

Kohli, Atul. "Parliamentary Communism and Agrarian Reform: The Evidence from India's Bengal." *Asian Survey*, 23:7(July 1983), pp. 783–809.

Kohli, Atul. "The NTR Phenomenon in Andhra Pradesh: Political Change in a South Indian State." *Asian Survey*, 28:10(October 1988), pp. 991–1002.

Kohli, Atul, ed. *The State and Development in the Third World*. Princeton, N.J.: Princeton University Press, 1986.

Kohli, Atul. *The State and Poverty in India: The Politics of Reform.* Cambridge University Press, 1987.

Kothari, Rajni. "The Congress 'System' in India." *Asian Survey,* 4:12(December 1964), pp. 1161–73.

Kothari, Rajni. "The Crisis of the Moderate State and the Decline of Democracy," in *Transfer and Transformation: Political Institutions in the New Commonwealth,* edited by P. Lyon and J. Manor, pp. 29–46. Leicester, U.K.: Leicester University Press, 1983.

Kothari, Rajni. *Politics in India.* Boston: Little, Brown, 1970.

Kothari, Rajni. *State Against Democracy: In Search of Humane Governance.* Delhi: Ajanta Publications, 1988.

Kothari, Rajni, and Deshingkar, Giri. "Punjab: The Longer View," *Illustrated Weekly of India* (July 15, 1984), pp. 20–3.

Linz, Juan. *The Breakdown of Democratic Regimes.* Baltimore: Johns Hopkins University Press, 1978.

Madurai Municipal Corporation. *Madurai Master Plan.* Madurai: Madurai Planning Authority, 1981.

Majumdar, R. C. *History of Bengal,* 4 vols. Calcutta: G. Bhardwaj, 1971–8.

Manor, James. "Blurring the Lines Between Parties and Social Bases: Gundu Rao and the Emergence of a Janta Government in Karnataka," in *State Politics in Contemporary India: Crisis or Continuity?* edited by John Wood, pp. 139–68. Boulder, Colo.: Westview Press, 1984.

Manor, James. "Karnataka: Caste, Class, Dominance and Politics in a Cohesive Society," mimeograph, 1983.

Manor, James. "Parties and the Party System," in *India's Democracy: An Analysis of Changing State–Society Relations,* edited by A. Kohli, pp. 62–99. Princeton, N.J.: Princeton University Press, 1988.

Manor, James. *Political Change in an Indian State, Mysore, 1915–55,* Australian National University Monographs on South Asia, No. 2. Columbia, Missouri: South Asia Books, 1978.

Manor, James. "Pragmatic Progressives in Regional Politics: The Case of Devraj Urs." *Economic and Political Weekly,* 15:5–6(annual number, 1980), pp. 201–13.

Manor, James. "Structural Changes in Karnataka Politics." *Economic and Political Weekly,* 12:44(1977), pp. 1865–9.

Migdal, Joel. *Strong Societies and Weak States: State–Society Relations and State Capabilities in the Third World.* Princeton, N.J.: Princeton University Press, 1989.

Mitra, Subrata. "The Perils of Promoting Equality: The Latent Significance of the Anti-Reservation Movement in India." *Journal of Commonwealth and Comparative Politics,* 25:3(November 1987), pp. 292–317.

Moore, Barrington, Jr. *Social Origins of Dictatorship and Democracy: Lord and Peasant in the Making of the Modern World.* Boston: Beacon Press, 1966.

Moorhouse, Geoffrey. *Calcutta: The City Revealed.* New York: Penguin Books, 1984.

Morris-Jones, W. H. "India – More Questions than Answers." *Asian Survey,* 24:8(August 1984), pp. 809–16.

Morris-Jones, W. H. *Politics Mainly Indian.* Madras: Orient Longman, 1978.

Mukerjee, Kalyan, and R. S. Yadav. "For Reasons of State: Oppression and Resistance, a Study of Bhojpur Peasantry," in *Agrarian Movements in India,* edited by Arvind Das, pp. 119–47. London: Frank Cass, 1982.

Naidu, Ratna. "Symbolic Imagery Used by the Telugu Desam in Andhra Elections

(1983)," in *Shift in Indian Politics: 1983 Elections in Andhra Pradesh and Karnataka,* edited by G. Mathew, pp. 128–40. New Delhi: Concept Publishing, 1984.

Narang, A. S. *Storm over the Sutlej: Akali Politics.* New Delhi: Gitanjali Publishing House, 1983.

Natraj, V. K., and Lalitha Natraj. "Backward Classes, Minorities and the Karnatka Elections," in *Shift in Indian Politics: 1983 Elections in Karnataka and Andhra Pradesh,* edited by G. Mathew, pp. 35–60. New Delhi: Concept Publishing, 1984.

Nayak, Pandava. "Tamil Nadu: Politics of Pragmatism," in *State Politics in India,* edited by I. Narain, pp. 404–36. Meerut: Meenakshi Prakashan, 1976.

Nayar, Baldev Raj. *Minority Politics in the Punjab.* Princeton, N.J.: Princeton University Press, 1966.

Nayar, Baldev Raj. *Violence and Crime in India: A Quantitative Study* (Delhi: Macmillan, 1975).

O'Donnell, Guillermo. *Modernization and Bureaucratic Authoritarianism: Studies in South American Politics.* Berkeley: Institute of International Studies, University of California, 1973.

Overstreet, Gene, and M. Windmiller. *Communism in India.* Berkeley: University of California Press, 1959.

Paranjape, H. K. "New Lamps for Old!: A Critique of the 'New Economic Policy.'" *Economic and Political Weekly,* 20:36 (September 7, 1985), pp. 1513–22.

Patel, Sujata. "Collapse of Government." *Economic and Political Weekly,* 20:17(April 27, 1985), pp. 749–50.

Patel, Sujata. "Debacle of Populist Politics." *Economic and Political Weekly,* 20:16(April 20, 1985), pp. 681–2.

Patel, Sujata. "The Ahmedabad Riots, 1985: An Analysis," unpublished manuscript.

Patel, Sujata. "The Anand Pattern: A Socio-historical Analysis of Its Origin and Growth," mimeograph, 1986.

Pathak, Devarat N. "State Politics in Gujarat: Some Determinants," in *State Politics in India,* edited by I. Narain, pp. 122–33. Meerut: Meenakshi Prakashan, 1968.

Patil-Okaly, B. B. "Karnataka: Politics of One Party Dominance," in *State Politics in India,* edited by I. Narain, pp. 129–41. Meerut: Meenakshi Prakashan, 1976.

Patnaik, Prabhat. "New Turn in Economic Policy: Context and Prospects." *Economic and Political Weekly,* 21:23(June 7, 1986), pp. 1014–19.

People's Union for Civil Liberties. *Who Are the Guilty?* Delhi: Summa Graphica, 1984.

People's Union for Democratic Rights. *Behind the Killings in Bihar.* New Delhi: PUDR, 1986.

Pettigrew, Joyce. "In Search of a New Kingdom of Lahore." *Pacific Affairs,* 60:1(Spring 1987), pp. 1–25.

Pocock, David F. *Kanbi and Patidar: A Study of the Patidar Community of Gujarat.* Oxford: Clarendon Press, 1972.

Prasad, Pradhan N. "Agrarian Violence in Bihar." *Economic and Political Weekly,* 22:22(May 30, 1987), pp. 847–52.

Prasad, Pradhan H. "Caste and Class in Bihar." *Economic and Political Weekly* (annual number, February 1979).

Prasad, R. C. "Bihar: Social Polarization and Political Instability," in *State Politics in India,* edited by I. Narain, pp. 51–67. Meerut: Meenakshi Prakashan, 1976.

Puri, H. K. "Akali Agitation: An Analysis of the Socio-economic Basis of Protest." *Economic and Political Weekly,* 18:3(January 22, 1983), pp. 113–18.

Raj, K. N. "New Economic Policy." *Mainstream,* 24:15(December 14, 1985), part 1, and 24:16(December 21, 1985), part 2, pp. 15–19.

Ram Reddy, G. "Andhra Pradesh: The Citadel of Congress," in *State Politics in India,* edited by I. Narain, pp. 1–29. Meerut: Meenakshi Prakashan, 1976.

Ram Reddy, G. "Politics of Accommodation: The Case of Andhra Pradesh," mimeograph, 1983, Indira Gandhi National Open University; a revised version of this paper appears in *Dominance and State Power in Modern India: Decline of a Social Order,* 2 vols., edited by Francine Frankel and M. S. A. Rao, volume 1, pp. 272–323. Oxford University Press, 1989–90.

Rao, M. S. A. *Social Movements and Social Transformation: A Study of Two Backward Class Movements.* Delhi: Macmillan, 1978.

Ray, Ratnalekha. *Change in Bengal Agrarian Society, 1760–1850.* New Delhi: Manohar, 1979.

Roy, M. N. *Memoirs.* Bombay: Allied Publishers, 1964.

Roy, Ramashray. *Battle Before Ballot.* Delhi: Ritu Publishers, 1983.

Roy, Ramashray. "Politics of Fragmentation: The Case of the Congress Party in Bihar," in *State Politics in India,* edited by I. Narain, pp. 415–30. Meerut: Meenakshi Prakashan, 1968.

Rubin, Barnett R. "Economic Liberalization and the Indian State." *Third World Quarterly,* 7:4(October 1985), pp. 942–57.

Rudolph, L. I., and S. H. Rudolph. *In Pursuit of Lakshmi: The Political Economy of the Indian State.* University of Chicago Press, 1987.

Sandbrook, Richard (with Judith Barker). *The Politics of Africa's Economic Stagnation.* Cambridge University Press, 1985.

Sandhu, G. S. "The Roots of the Problem," in *Punjab in Indian Politics,* edited by A. Singh, pp. 61–70. Delhi: Ajanta Publications, 1985.

Sanyal, Hitesranjan. *Social Mobility in Bengal.* Calcutta: Papyrus, 1981.

Sarkar, Sumit. *The Swadeshi Movement in Bengal, 1903–1908.* New Delhi: People's Publishing House, 1973.

Sarma, Jyotirmoyee. *Caste Dynamics Among the Bengali Hindus.* Calcutta: Firma KLM Private Ltd., 1980.

Sen, Mohit. "Showdown in Andhra." *Economic and Political Weekly,* 7:52(December 23, 1972), pp. 2487–9.

Sengupta, Bhabani. *Communism in Indian Politics.* New York: Columbia University Press, 1972.

Sengupta, Bhabani. *CPI-M: Promises, Prospects, Problems.* New Delhi: Young Asia Publications, 1979.

Shah, Ghanshyam. "Caste, Class and Reservation." *Economic and Political Weekly,* 20:13(January 19, 1985), pp. 132–6.

Shah, Ghanshyam. "Caste, Sentiments, Class Formation and Dominance in Gujarat," mimeograph, 1983, Centre for Social Studies, Surat, Gujarat; a revised version of this paper appears in *Dominance and State Power in Modern India: Decline of a Social Order,* 2 vols., edited by Francine Frankel and M. S. A. Rao. Oxford University Press, 1989–90, volume 2.

Shah, Ghanshyam. *Caste Association and Political Process in Gujarat: A Study of the Kshatriya Sabha.* Bombay: Popular Prakashan, 1975.

Shah, Ghanshyam. *Protest Movements in Two Indian States.* Delhi: Ajanta Publications, 1977.

Shatrugna, M. "Emergence of Regional Parties in India: Case of Telugu Desam," in *Shift in Indian Politics,* edited by G. Mathew, pp. 95–103. New Delhi: Concept Publishing, 1984.

Sheth, D. L., and A. S. Narang. "The Electoral Angle," in *Punjab in Indian*

Politics: Issues and Trends, edited by A. Singh, pp. 123–35. Delhi: Ajanta Publications, 1985.

Sheth, Praveen. "Caste, Class and Political Development," in *Development in Gujarat: Problems and Prospects,* edited by D. Lakdwala, pp. 193–207. New Delhi: Allied Publishers, 1982.

Sheth, Praveen. "Gujarat: The Case of Small Majority Politics," in *State Politics in India,* edited by I. Narain, pp. 66–87. Meerut: Meenakshi Prakashan, 1968.

Sheth, Praveen. *Patterns of Political Behaviour in Gujrat.* Ahmedabad: Sahitya Mudranalaya, 1976.

Shue, Vivienne. *The Reach of the State: Sketches of the Chinese Body Politic.* Stanford, Calif.: Stanford University Press, 1988.

Singh, Amrik. "An Approach to the Problem," in *Punjab in Indian Politics,* edited by A. Singh, pp. 1–32. Delhi: Ajanta Publications, 1985.

Singh, Gopal. "Socio-economic Bases of Punjab Crisis." *Economic and Political Weekly,* 19:1(January 7, 1984), pp. 42–6.

Singh, Gurharpal. "Understanding the 'Punjab Problem'." *Asian Survey,* 27:12(December 1987), pp. 1268–77.

Singh, Khushwant. *A History of the Sikhs, Vol. II: 1839–1964.* Princeton, N.J.: Princeton University Press, 1966.

Singh, Mohinder. *The Akali Movement.* Delhi: Macmillan, 1978.

Singh, V. B., and Shankar Bose. *Elections in India: Data Handbook on Lok Sabha Elections, 1952–80.* New Delhi: Sage Publications, 1984.

Sinha, Arun. "Class War, Not 'Atrocities Against Harijans'," in *Agrarian Movements in India,* edited by A. N. Das, pp. 148–52. London: Frank Cass, 1982.

Skidmore, Thomas E. *The Politics of Military Rule in Brazil, 1964–85.* Oxford University Press, 1988.

Skocpol, Theda. *States and Social Revolutions.* Cambridge University Press, 1979.

Smelser, Neil. "Mechanisms of Change and Adjustments to Change," in *Political Development and Social Change,* edited by J. Finkle and R. Gable, pp. 27–43. New York: Wiley, 1971.

Somjee, A. H. "Social Cohesion and Political Clientilism Among the Kshatriyas of Gujarat." *Asian Survey,* 21:9(September 1981), pp. 1000–10.

Spodek, Howard. "From Gandhi to Violence: Ahmedabad's 1985 Riots in Historical Perspective," mimeograph, Department of History, Temple University, 1987.

Srinivas, G., M. Shatrugna, and G. Naravana. "Social Background of Telugu Desam Legislators," in *Shift in Indian Politics,* edited by G. Mathew, pp. 104–24. New Delhi: Concept Publishing, 1984.

Srinivas, M. N. "Living in and Through a Democratic Revolution," mimeograph, 1986, a revised version of this paper is available in *India 2000: The Next Fifteen Years,* edited by James R. Roach, pp. 3–26. Maryland: Riverdale Co., 1986.

Srinivas, M. N., and M. N. Panini. "Politics and Society in Karnataka." *Economic and Political Weekly,* 19:2(1984), pp. 69–75.

Srinivasan, T. N., and N. S. S. Narayana. "Economic Performance since the Third Plan and Its Implications for Policy." *Economic and Political Weekly,* 12:6–8(annual number, February 1977), pp. 225–40.

Stepan, Alfred. *The State and Society: Peru in Comparative Perspective.* Princeton, N.J.: Princeton University Press, 1978.

Trimberger, Ellen Kay. *Revolution from Above: Military Bureaucrats and Development in Japan, Turkey, Egypt and Peru.* New Brunswick, N.J.: Transactions Books, 1978.

Tully, Mark, and Satish Jacob. *Amritsar: Mrs. Gandhi's Last Battle.* London: Pan Books, 1985.

Vakil, F. D. "Congress Party in Andhra Pradesh: A Review," in *Shift in Indian*

Politics, edited by G. Mathew, pp. 61–93. New Delhi: Concept Publishing, 1984.

Varshney, Ashutosh. "Political Economy of Slow Industrial Growth in India." *Economic and Political Weekly,* 19:34(September 1, 1984), pp. 1511–17.

Washbrook, David. "Tamil Nationalism, Dravidianism and Non-Brahminism," mimeograph, 1983, Department of History, Warwick University, U. K.; a revised version of this paper appears in *Dominance and State Power in Modern India: Decline of a Social Order,* 2 vols., edited by Francine Frankel and M. S. A. Rao, volume 1, pp. 204–64. Oxford University Press, 1989–90.

Waterbury, John. *The Egypt of Nasser and Sadat: The Political Economy of Two Regimes.* Princeton, N.J.: Princeton University Press, 1983.

Weiner, Myron. "Congress Restored: Continuities and Discontinuities in Indian Politics." *Asian Survey,* 12:4(April 1983), pp. 339–55.

Weiner, Myron. *Party Building in a New Nation: The Indian National Congress.* University of Chicago Press, 1967.

Wolf, Eric. *Peasant Wars of the Twentieth Century.* New York: Harper & Row, 1969.

Wood, John R. "Congress Restored?: The KHAM Strategy and Congress (I) Recruitment in Gujarat," in *State Politics in Contemporary India: Crisis or Continuity?* edited by John Wood, pp. 197–227. Boulder, Colo.: Westview Press, 1984.

Wood, John R. "Extra-Parliamentary Opposition in India." *Pacific Affairs,* 48:3(Fall 1975), pp. 313–34.

Wood, John R. "Gujarat's Anti-Reservation Riots, 1985," mimeograph, 1986, Department of Political Science, University of British Columbia, Vancouver, Canada.

Wood, John R. "The Political Integration of British and Princely Gujarat," unpublished Ph.D. dissertation, Columbia University, 1972.

Index

dira Gandhi in, 353–64; and Sikh crisis, 352–76; terrorism in, 372–3
Punjab accord, 364–73
Purohit, Shankar Lal, 42n

Raj, K. N., 314
Rajputs, 207–8, 244, 246
Rama Rao, N. T. (NTR), 17, 62–3, 65, 67, 75–9, 81–2, 86, 91, 118, 187, 190, 191, 324, 392; leadership style of, 69–72, 88–90
Ramachandran, Janaki, 164
Ramachandran, M. G. (MGR), 17, 157, 159, 187, 188, 190, 191, 197, 392; in Madurai, 172–9, 180–3; in Tamil Nadu, 161–6
Ramaswamy, M. A. M., 163
Rane Commission report, 258
Rao, Gundu, 96, 111, 347
Rao, Narasimha, 82, 366
Ratnaiah, Makineni Peda, 77
Ray, Sidhartha Shankar, 372
Reddis: in Andhra Pradesh, 66–7; in Guntur, 61–2, 75–80
Reddy, Brahmananda, 68, 79, 84, 88, 332
Reddy, G. Ram, 75
Reddy, Sanjiva, 79
regional nationalism, 193–4; in Andhra politics, 69–70; in Tamil Nadu politics, 157–65
religious conflict, 193–6; Hindu vs. Moslem, 54, 142–3, 195, 239, 248, 260–5; Sikh crisis in Punjab as, 352–76
reservations, conflict over, 18, 219–23, 252–65; *see also* caste conflict
Revolutionary Socialist Party, 274, 276
Ribero, 372
riots, *see* political violence
Rodgers, G. B., 208
Roy, B. C., 126, 128, 273, 275
RSS, 263
Rudolph, Lloyd I., 7n, 396n
Rudolph, Susanne Hoeber, 7n, 396n
rural poor: national economic role of, 307, 336–7; *see also* Harijans

Sahay, Vishnu, 317
Sain, Dhiraj, 135
Sainik, B. B., 105
Sanjay culture, definition of, 57n
Sankranand, 113, 114, 116
Santhals, 278
Sanyal, Mani, 137, 138
Sarada, Jagdish, 104
Saurashtras, 154–5, 173–6
scheduled castes, *see* Harijans
Sen, P. C., 126, 128
Sengupta, Arjun K, 314

Seva Dal, 341, 345
Sheth, Praveen, 244n, 250
Shiromani Gurdwara Parbandhak Committee (SGPC), 357, 359, 361, 370, 371, 374
Shiv Sena, 99, 100, 107, 118, 353n
Sidnal, S. B., 113, 114
Sikhs: and Indira Gandhi, 357–64; and Punjab politics, 352–76; and Rajiv Gandhi, 364–76; and relations with Hindus, 355–6, 357, 363, 372–3; separatist demands of, 357, 361–2; subgroups of, 354–6
Singh, Amrik, 362n
Singh, Arjun, 347–50, 366
Singh, Arun, 316, 317, 325, 346
Singh, Birendra, 227
Singh, Charan, 219, 222
Singh, Dinesh, 333
Singh, Manmohan, 316
Singh, Master Tara, 357
Singh, Raj Kishori, 228
Singh, Sant Fateh, 357
Singh, Tarlok, 317
Singh, Tuntun, 228
Singh, V. P., 6, 17, 303, 323, 324, 328, 331, 334, 350, 351
Singh, Zail, 353, 359
Sinha, A. N., 211, 212
Sinha, S. K., 211, 212
slum dwellers, political behavior of: in Calcutta, 123–4, 140–1; in Madurai, 177
Smelser, Neil, 25
Solanki, Madhevsinh, 44n, 49, 50, 55, 56, 249, 260n, 347; role of, in Gujarat, 40–2, 242–3, 256–65
Solanki, Natwar Singh, 41, 45
South Korea, 308, 398
Soviet Union, 127, 138
Sri Lanka, 172, 179, 194
Srinivas, M. N., 193
state repression: in Punjab, 364, 372–5; in West Bengal, 282–5
students' role in DMK, 159–61, 170–1, 178–9
Swatantra party, 246–52

Talwandi, 367
Tamil Nadu, 297, 392; political overview of, 156–60
Tarun Bharat, 99, 100
Tatas, 197
technocrats: in Congress party, 342; role of, in economic policy making, 306, 316–17, 331–2
Teluga Desam Party (TDP): in Andhra Pradesh, 70–2; in Guntur, 75–80, 86
Thackeray, Bal, 353n